THE LIFE OF RUDYARD KIPLING

THE LIFE OF
RUDYARD KIPLING

BY

C. E. Carrington

*The Curse of all Art is that the devotee or disciple
is always more certain than the Priest*

RUDYARD KIPLING

Garden City, New York

DOUBLEDAY & COMPANY, INC.

1955

Library of Congress Catalog Card Number: 55-11329

PREFACE

MY qualifications for writing this book are not unique, but are shared with thousands of my contemporaries.

I learned to read in the year when *Just So Stories* was the children's book of the season, and when I asked for more the *Jungle Books* were waiting for me. In a manner of speaking, I went to school with *Stalky & Co.* I discovered English History with 'Dan' and 'Una' and, as I remember, *Plain Tales from the Hills* was the first 'grown-up' book that I found out for myself. In 1914, as a very young soldier, I formed my notions of the grandeur and misery of army life upon the *Barrack-room Ballads,* and knew from the story of the 'Brushwood Boy' that a hard conventional exterior might conceal a strange and sensitive inner life. It was my good fortune, when young, to travel a great deal about the world, always with the rhythms of *The Seven Seas* singing themselves in my ears. Every later publication of Kipling's was an event in my life, though I could not, in maturity, give him the uncritical support I had given in youth; and when he died I judged — rightly — that an epoch had ended.

At times I have been infuriated by some facets of Kipling's sparkling talent; but, looking back on my life, I find no other writer who has seen through the eyes of my generation with such a sharpness of observation. I owe far more to Kipling than to some of the great classic figures of literature, who inspire my reverence but do not draw me with them into their higher sphere. There is no other writer, great or small, whose work I know so well, and I have been often astonished to find how many others, of all ages, knew him as well as I did, even when the critics told us he was clean out of fashion.

I never set eyes upon the man! He shunned publicity and begged his critics not to question other than the work he left behind; but such a desire was too much to expect of a generation which had watched the progress of his work with such attention. Even before his death, Mrs. Kipling had been putting some materials together for the use, as it seems, of a biographer. This was the exception she made to the rules that every in-letter was destroyed as soon as it was answered, that no unauthorized scrap of her husband's handwriting should be taken out of their house.

To draw out the elusive, retiring figure of Rudyard Kipling from behind the screen of his published works required the willing co-operation of those few who knew him well. When his surviving daughter, Mrs. George Bambridge, authorized me to begin my work upon the family papers, I knew little of his personality and doubted whether a stranger could break through his rule of privacy. The frankness with which I was received soon dispersed my fears and — far more than that — Mrs. Bambridge has given me so much good advice, has corrected so many errors I had fallen into, has contributed so many comments, anecdotes, side-lights, and episodes, in addition to providing me with several long descriptive passages, that her name should properly appear with mine as part-author, on the title-page. I hasten, however, to assert that the final responsibility for what appears in this book is mine, and that I must accept the blame for any errors which Mrs. Bambridge has not eliminated.

At the end of our long and pleasant co-operation I can express my gratitude only by dedicating the book to the lady who is already known to thousands of readers as 'Una'.

C. E. CARRINGTON

LONDON,
March 1955

ACKNOWLEDGMENTS

HER Majesty the Queen has graciously approved the publication of those paragraphs which describe Rudyard Kipling's relations with the Royal Family.

My obligation to Mrs. George Bambridge, without whose constant help this book could not have been written, is recorded elsewhere. I next mention Miss Cecily Nicholson, Secretary, successively, to Rudyard Kipling, to Mrs. Kipling, and to Mrs. Bambridge. The Kipling Papers have been arranged and indexed by her with such skill and judgment that my task has been much lightened. Her transcripts are models of accuracy. I am also obliged to Miss R. D. Groom for secretarial assistance, to Mr. P. G. Burbidge for making the index, and to Dr. C. P. Snow for editorial advice.

It is a privilege to mention the owners or curators of the larger collections which have been thrown open to me: Mrs. W. M. Carpenter, Mrs. Nelson Doubleday, Mr. and Mrs. F. Cabot Holbrook, Mr. John Connell, Mr. Howard C. Rice, Jun., Mr. W. A. Jackson (the Houghton Library, Harvard), Mr. John Gordan (the New York Public Library), Mr. Frederick R. Goff (Library of Congress, Washington), the Librarians of Rhodes House and of New College, Oxford, of the Toronto Public Library, and of the Yale Library.

For personal information about Kipling I am obliged to several of his relatives: Mrs. G. L. Thirkell, Miss Florence Macdonald, Sir Hugh Poynter, Bart.; and to the Viscountess Milner, Mrs. H. Babcock, Mrs. B. Lee-Booker, Mrs. A. Ogilvie, Lord Beaverbrook, Lord Dunsany, The Rt. Hon. L. S. Amery, Mr. F. H. Andrews, Sir S. C. Cockerell, Dr. Philip Gosse, Mr. T. E. Elwell, Mr. Edwin Haward, Mr. E. C. Kyte, Mr. E. Price, and Mr. W. P. Watt. I must specially mention a group of friends in Vermont: Mr. Howard Rice, Sen.; Mrs. H. Gale, Mrs. W. S. Grey, Mrs. Holbrook, Mrs. Knapp, Miss Ruth Knapp, and Miss Manly.

I am obliged to the following ladies and gentlemen who have helped me on particular points: Mr. E. E. Allen (of the P. & O. Company), Mr. B. M. Bazley, Lady Violet Bonham Carter, Mr. J. H. C. Brooking, Sir F. Brown, Lieut.-General Sir F. M. Browning, Mr. T. S. Eliot, Mr. T. E. Elwell, Mr. R. E. Harbord, Mr. I. Kaplan, Sir George Malcolm of Poltalloch, Mr. E. C. Matthews, Sir Owen Morshead, Mr. Carl

Naumburg, Mr. F. C. Pritchard (of Woodhouse Grove School), Mr. E. E. Reynolds, Mr. R. H. Rogers (of Rochester, New York), Dr. T. G. P. Spear, Mr. E. J. Storer (of the Macmillan Co., Bombay).

My general thanks are due to Mr. Archibald Lyall with whom I planned the first draft of this book many years ago, to Mr. and Mrs. Christopher Morris for their kindly but penetrating criticism, and to my brother the Archbishop of Quebec who may usually be held responsible for any bright ideas that find their way into my work.

I have also received countless suggestions and hints from others who are too numerous to distinguish here, and I beg them to accept my general thanks.

For permission to quote copyright passages I am obliged to the *Atlantic Monthly,* to the Clarendon Press, and Mr. George Cumberlege, to Miss Dorothy Ponton, to Mr. R. Hart-Davis, to Mr. John Murray, to *The Times Publishing Co.,* to Messrs. John Farquharson on behalf of the estate of the late Henry James, to the estate of the late Theodore Roosevelt, and to the estate of the late H. G. Wells.

CONTENTS

ILLUSTRATIONS

CHRONOLOGY OF KIPLING'S LIFE AND WORK

1865   R. K. born at Bombay

1871–7   At Southsea

1878–82   At the United Services College, Westward Ho!

1881   *Schoolboy Lyrics* privately printed in India

1882–7   On the Staff of the *Civil and Military Gazette,* Lahore

1886   *Departmental Ditties*

1887–9   On the Staff of the *Pioneer,* Allahabad

1888   *Plain Tales from the Hills,* and stories for the Indian Railway Library (collected, 1890, in *Soldiers Three* and *Wee Willie Winkie*)

1889   To London via Japan and U.S.A.   *From Sea to Sea*

1890   Literary success in London.   *The Light that Failed*

1891   *Life's Handicap.* Voyage to South Africa, Australia, New Zealand.   Last visit to India

1892   Marriage. *The Naulahka. Barrack-room Ballads.* Voyage to Japan.   To Brattleboro, Vermont

1893   *Many Inventions*

1894   *The Jungle Book*

1895   *The Second Jungle Book*

1896   *The Seven Seas.* Return to England.   Torquay

1897   *Captains Courageous.* Removal to Rottingdean. ' Recessional '

1898   *The Day's Work*

1899   *Stalky & Co., The White Man's Burden.* Last visit to U.S.A. Death of R. K.'s elder daughter

1900–8   In South Africa every year from January to March

1901   *Kim*

1902   *Just So Stories.* Removed to ' Bateman's ', Burwash, Sussex

1903   *The Five Nations*

1904   *Traffics and Discoveries*

xiii

1906   *Puck of Pook's Hill*

1907   Nobel prize for literature. Voyage to Canada

1909   *Actions and Reactions*

1910   *Rewards and Fairies*

1912   *Songs from Books*

1913   Voyage to Egypt. *Letters of Travel*

1915   R. K.'s son missing, believed killed, in France

1917   *A Diversity of Creatures*

1919   *The Years Between*

1923   *Land and Sea Tales, The Irish Guards in the Great War*

1924   R. K.'s younger daughter married.

1926   *Debits and Credits*

1927   Voyage to Brazil. *Brazilian Sketches*

1928   *A Book of Words*

1930   *Thy Servant a Dog.* Voyage to the West Indies

1932   *Limits and Renewals*

1936   Death of R. K.

1937   *Something of Myself* posthumously published.

1937–9 Sussex Edition, complete edition of R. K.'s acknowledged works

1939   Death of Mrs. Rudyard Kipling

A FRAGMENT

Written before Kipling's sixteenth birthday

Lo! as a little child
Looks from its window on a mighty town,
And sees the roofs as far as eye can reach,
But thinks not, knows not — nay, will not believe —
That there are Fathers, Mothers, Sisters, Homes
All like his own, a thousand homely talks,
Manners, and customs — so I saw the world
With millions of my brethren. Then I wrote;
And all my verse sprang fire-new from a brain
That loved it and believed it. But the world
Coldly, in silence, passed my numbers by.
Therefor I sang in fury! When the years
Brought with them coolness, all too late I found
There were ten thousand thousand thoughts like mine!

PROLOGUE

THE Queen's first Jubilee in 1887 came at the height of the Victorian achievement. For thirty years the English had enjoyed peace at home while all the other great nations had in turn been racked by war. Not Spain in the sixteenth century, nor France in the eighteenth, had so demonstrably led the world as did Victorian England with its utilitarian outlook, liberal policy, maritime power, and exuberant vitality; and now there were signs, visible at least to some shrewd observers, that the best days were over. English supremacy, unchallenged in the eighteen-sixties, the Age of Palmerston, had been asserted a little too self-consciously in the eighteen-seventies, the Age of Disraeli, and was openly challenged in the eighteen-eighties, the Age of Gladstone. The United States had surpassed Great Britain in population and was increasing its production at a higher rate of acceleration; the new German Empire had appeared as an industrial and colonial competitor; the Russians, now masters of Central Asia, seemed to threaten the North-West Frontier of India. Gladstone's second administration ended in a torrent of troubles; his mission to pacify Ireland had led to the entanglement over Home Rule; the death of Gordon had lowered British prestige in the East; the memory of defeat at Majuba rankled. Meanwhile strange stirrings in the working-class at home betokened the rise of a revolutionary movement which had been dormant since the days of the Chartists. The Trafalgar Square Riots, when the West End of London was in the hands of a mob, were a portent, something that had not happened within living memory.

'Society', which, in the era of prosperous agriculture, had been almost frozen into an exclusive caste by the country gentry, was cracking up, under pressure of new money from outside and agrarian distress from within. Forty years of Free Trade had established the victory of the shippers, bankers, and merchants over the squires and farmers, by filling London with new men. A general sense that the times were changing, that the continuous progress of the Victorian age was taking some new turn, was expressed in the fashionable phrase, *fin de siècle*.

While the old Queen lingered on the stage, through the 'eighties and the 'nineties, the statesmen of her mature middle period had gone, except Gladstone, who still survived and, in old age, still towered over

the younger men of both parties. As with the statesmen, so with the
thinkers and writers to whom the Victorians looked for guidance; they
were dead before the Jubilee year or, like Newman and Ruskin,
they were exhausted. Thackeray and Dickens had long since departed;
Browning died in 1889 and Tennyson, though he lived till 1892, had
finished his work; Swinburne published nothing of note after 1889.
With the deaths of George Eliot in 1880, Trollope in 1882, Charles
Reade in 1884, Wilkie Collins in 1889, the great age of the Victorian
novel drew to a close. Then came a pause in English literature,
Thomas Hardy completed his series of Wessex romances in 1887 and
did not begin to shock society with his tragedies until *Tess* was
published at the end of 1891; all Meredith's best work was written
before 1885; George Moore and Henry James were hesitating between
their earlier and their later manner. Gissing, though much of his
work appeared in this interval, attracted small attention. The novelists
of the next generation, Wells, Conrad, Bennett, Galsworthy, all
appeared some years later than Kipling, their precocious contemporary;
nor did the revival of the theatre belong to these years; neither Wilde
nor Shaw nor Barrie nor Synge had yet produced a play. Between
1887 and 1890 the only publishing 'sensation' was Mrs. Humphry
Ward's *Robert Elsmere* (1888), no more than a competent piece of
fiction and an interesting social document. It was Kipling who wrote
the epitaph upon the 'three-deckers', the serious portly novels in three
volumes which had formed the provender of the educated reader for
a hundred years. After *Robert Elsmere,* no worthy successor appeared.
   There were no giants in literary London in those days, not even
giants of the decadence. Hitherto, the 'aesthetic movement' had
been more concerned with the decorative arts than with literature,
taking the form of a revolt against the prevailing ugliness of life in
the new machine age, and often advocating a return to the supposed
virtues of the Middle Ages. If Morris and Burne Jones have a lesson
for posterity it is respect for technical accomplishment; not Art for
Art's sake but artistry for honour's sake. Their characteristic weakness was escapism, turning away their eyes lest they should behold
ugliness. At the same time, in the world of letters, light romances,
and tales of fantastic or comical adventure written for boys and
enjoyed by adults, cut to such length that they could be read in one
long evening and could even be printed in one number of a monthly
magazine, were capturing the public taste. *Treasure Island* in 1883,
King Solomon's Mines in 1885, *Three Men in a Boat* in 1889 were the
new rivals to the traditional three-volume novel. To be sure, when so
great a master as R. L. Stevenson told so good a yarn as *Treasure
Island,* there was justice in receiving it as a masterpiece in its kind.

He wrote like a gentleman, like an artist, like an angel as some would say; but he failed to find subject-matter in the working world around him.

In 1889, the year of the London Dock Strike and the Parnell Commission, the year when *The Gondoliers* filled the stalls of the Savoy, no novel remembered today was published except Stevenson's *Master of Ballantrae,* a sombre tragedy which has never been a favourite among his works. At the end of the year, a young man arrived unnoticed in London with a sheaf of ballads and stories to sell, and with two or three introductions to editors. The December number of *Macmillan's Magazine* contained one of his ballads which set the town on fire, with words which are not likely to be forgotten:

> Oh, East is East, and West is West, and never the twain shall meet,
> Till Earth and Sky stand presently at God's great Judgment Seat.

Eighteen-ninety was Rudyard Kipling's year. There had been nothing like his sudden rise to fame and fortune since Byron awoke one morning to find that the publication of *Childe Harold* had made him famous. Whereas the public knew nothing of Kipling, several discerning critics had heard rumours of a new literary star arising in the East, and were on the watch for him. He had no difficulty in disposing of his wares. Eighteen-ninety saw the publication or re-publication, in England and America, of more than eighty short stories from his pen, many ballads, and, at the end of the year, a novel. The market was flooded with his work in verse and prose, with his juvenile and his more mature writing, with much that has outlasted its critics, and with much that would have been better forgotten. A chorus of praise, not unmixed with astonishment, was the first reaction of the reviewers, and a judicious leading article in *The Times* assured Kipling's position as a star of the first magnitude. Enthusiastic as these eulogies were, the shrewdest of critics made some reservation. Mr. Kipling was very young and very confident, but had he staying-power? The literary world waited agog for his novel and hastily reconsidered its verdict when the novel appeared, for *The Light that Failed* revealed many weaknesses of taste, of construction, and of style. It was in some respects an unpleasant book and, with its publication, the inevitable reaction set in against an author who had enjoyed, so easily and so early in life, a literary success for which master-craftsmen had toiled half a lifetime in vain. Voices arose decrying Kipling, sometimes for his faults of style, but more commonly out of dislike for his subject-matter. The unqualified praise of his wonder-year, 1890, was succeeded by a period of violent controversy about Kipling, in no wise mollified by the author's studied contempt for the critics.

Little was known of him but that he loved privacy, a characteristic that always attracts publicity.

The paradox of Kipling's career is that his popularity with the reading public grew in inverse proportion to his reputation with the critics. The cult of Art for Art's sake made its devotees less able and less anxious to observe objectively, or to record their impressions faithfully. They hated Kipling because he told them truths they did not wish to hear, among others the simple fact that England's greatness lay in her dominions overseas. Kipling used golden words to demonstrate that words were worth little in the presence of deeds. This literary man seemed to betray his order by asserting that literary men were not the most important people in the world, or not until they practised their Art for Duty's sake. But what were the sources and the sanctions of Duty? That, the reading public seemed to understand rather better than the critics. The quirks and twists of literary fashion, the loves and hates of the professional men of letters, meant little to Kipling, as they meant little to the mass of his fellow-countrymen. To the masses, the writers of the decadence were a topic for sly jokes and for no other consideration. The progress of English Society in the 'nineties moved another way, towards the acceptance of new burdens, new responsibilities, new rewards. Its prophets were not Wilde and Beardsley, but Kipling and Wells and Shaw, and for the moment, for the year 1890 at least, Kipling alone.

The body of poetry and prose which he issued in authorized editions in his lifetime, includes four or five complete romances, two hundred and fifty short stories, a thousand pages of verse, and several miscellaneous volumes. The first book produced under his own authority in London and New York appeared in 1890; the last in 1932, by which time there had been violent and repeated changes in literary fashion. According to the verdict of the critics, Kipling's literary credit reached its zenith in the early eighteen-nineties, declined and was almost extinguished before his death, to be revived by some connoisseurs in the nineteen-forties. By another criterion, his reputation moved through quite different phases. Not only his most approved writings but all his authorized work, year after year, and decade after decade, remained in the class that the book trade calls 'best-sellers', and were still in that class twenty years after his death, although these books were never issued in cheap editions. What other contemporary writer has enjoyed this longevity?

Successful writers, in general, fall into two classes. Either they are the sensation of a season and soon forgotten for ever, or they are raised by the critics into a higher grade and regarded as classics. Kipling, like Dickens and like Defoe, was a popular writer whose work had a

'sensational' success that did not die with the season, that did not
need puffing by the reviewers. From 1890 to 1932, and even to 1955,
there was no lack of buyers for this line of goods even though the
publicists no longer urged the public to acquire it. When his politics
were most out of fashion, he still had no lack of readers, and many an
anti-imperialist of the left wing read him on the sly.

The coldness of the critics, after their first incautious enthusiasm, is
not so remarkable as the downright hostility of some of the best of
them. It was not perversity that made men so different as Frank
Harris and Arnold Bennett, William Sharp and Max Beerbohm, Oscar
Wilde and George Sampson, attack him so bitterly. To this day he
makes men lose their tempers, a sure proof of his importance. The
student of literature cannot neglect or ignore him. So good a critic as
Mr. Edmund Wilson displays most clearly a characteristic that many
readers of Kipling have shown; he loves and hates, he abuses Kipling
and cannot abstain from reading on. A writer of the younger generation has described himself as one of those to whom 'No single syllable
of Kipling's has ever given a moment's pleasure'.* Is not this an
extraordinary observation? The power and the style of Kipling, it
implies, are so effective that those who dislike the matter will not
allow themselves to admit any merit in the manner. No Protestant
critic writes of Newman in that way; no Tory man of letters reacts
like that against Bernard Shaw.

Rudyard Kipling's power lies in his ability to evoke love or hate, or
love and hate together, in almost every reader; his lovers are still
innumerable, and often as blinded by emotion as the haters. What
was the message that struck so deeply into the hearts of those who
first heard it in 1890? What sort of man was it who did so much to
form the characters of all that generation which is now elderly or
middle-aged? What was the secret of his strength?

* *The Modern Short Story*, by H. E. Bates.

Table 1

KIPLINGS AND MACDONALDS

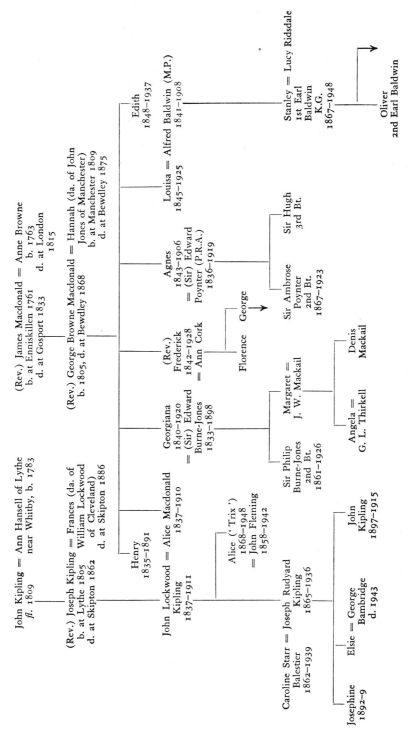

CHAPTER I

KIPLINGS AND MACDONALDS

THE PUZZLER (1909)

The Celt in all his variants from Builth to Bally-hoo,
His mental processes are plain — one knows what he will do,
And can logically predicate his finish by his start;
But the English — ah, the English! — they are quite a race apart.

Their psychology is bovine, their outlook crude and raw.
They abandon vital matters to be tickled with a straw;
But the straw that they were tickled with — the chaff that they were fed with —
They convert into a weaver's beam to break their foeman's head with.

For undemocratic reasons and for motives not of State,
They arrive at their conclusions — largely inarticulate.
Being void of self-expression they confide their views to none;
But sometimes in a smoking-room, one learns why things were done.

Yes, sometimes in a smoking-room, through clouds of 'Ers' and 'Ums',
Obliquely and by inference, illumination comes,
On some step that they have taken, or some action they approve —
Embellished with the *argot* of the Upper Fourth Remove.

In telegraphic sentences, half nodded to their friends,
They hint a matter's inwardness — and there the matter ends.
And while the Celt is talking from Valencia to Kirkwall,
The English — ah, the English! — don't say anything at all.

ON more than one occasion Rudyard Kipling described himself as a Yorkshireman, although he never lived in Yorkshire and rarely visited the North Country. Towards the end of his life he was engaged in desultory correspondence with a Mr. Sunderland, a Yorkshire acquaintance who had made a hobby of investigating the origins of the Kipling family. Kipling's replies to Sunderland's observations and inquiries were courteous but cool. 'I am sorry', he wrote, 'not to be able to respond to your interest — as a matter of fact, I do not; and as I have no son to whom this information would later possibly be of interest, I cannot trouble you to proceed any further in this matter.' He had, however, supplied Sunderland with some scraps of family lore, and these may be worth preserving as Kipling's own belief about his ancestry. 'Yes, the family is certainly Yorkshire, and I believe some of it came from Snaith way and thereabouts. . . . I don't think a genealogical hunt would be of much use. . . . I abandoned the search long ago . . . my knowledge of my family is of the sketchiest. They seem to have included small farmers, bell-founders, clock-makers, and the like, scattered all over the Ridings, and, I suppose, originally with some far-off connexion with the hamlet [Kipling] that carries their name. . . . I believe the sons were christened Joseph and John in alternate generations.' * 1

We may begin with the Rev. Joseph Kipling, son of John Kipling a farmer, a respected Methodist minister who, according to the rules of his Church, occupied a succession of pulpits in Yorkshire. He married Frances Lockwood, † the daughter of an architect, and the family tradition ran that her father thought she might have made a better match. While the Rev. Joseph held the circuit at Pickering, his eldest son was born on 6th July 1837,² and was christened John Lockwood. Ministers' families were accustomed to frequent removals, and little John Kipling went with his parents to Horncastle, Howden, and Bridlington. They sent him to school at Woodhouse Grove, the well-known Methodist boarding-school near Leeds. In 1851, when no more than thirteen years old, John went up to London by excursion train to see the Great Exhibition in Hyde Park, an experience that directed the course of his life. Ten years later, in 1861, he was employed as a sculptor during the building of the Victoria and Albert Museum at South Kensington, where his portrait is to be seen in a mural for which he stood as a model. Of his early manhood little is known except that he eked out his earnings in London by giving French lessons until, at about the age of twenty-two, he settled at Burslem to get practical experience of pottery-designing in the firm of Pinder, Bourne & Co. His father died at Skipton, in the West Riding, in 1862; his mother lived on at Skipton until 1886, the grandparent whom young Rudyard Kipling knew best, and his only link with his Yorkshire forbears. ‡

* The numbers used after some of the passages quoted in the text are intended to refer the reader to the sources given in the Notes at the end of the book.

† Her maternal grandfather, Mr. W. Merry, was agent to Lord Mulgrave. He appears as the seated figure in Wilkie's well-known picture, 'Rent-day', and closely resembles his great-grandson, Lockwood Kipling.

‡ Lockwood Kipling had a younger brother, Joseph, and two sisters, one of whom, Rudyard's Aunt Hannah, lived to a great age. Rudyard helped to support her in the nineteen-thirties, when she was past ninety years old.

John Lockwood Kipling at Burslem was a notable young man, who would be better remembered today if he had not been overshadowed by his more celebrated son. His schooling at Woodhouse Grove, where he had been unhappy, had been thorough, and much more liberal than it was likely to have been at a Public School in those unreformed days. He was a man of wide reading and close observation. In the Arts-and-Crafts movement which derived from the Great Exhibition his was a strictly practical contribution. He had a never-failing zest for technical processes, an almost feminine sensibility to textures and tones and scents, an artisan's skill with tools and implements; above all, he was himself an artist, expressing his sense of form and colour and touch, with pen, brush, and modelling-clay. His son always admitted that the father had the surer prose style. He was a little man, remarkably solid and immovable, and always good-humoured. No one ever said a hard word about John Lockwood Kipling.

A scholar and artist, primed with the newest principles from South Kensington, must have been a rarity in Staffordshire ninety years ago, and so it was inevitable that he should fall into the company of other people in the Midlands with literary tastes and advanced views. It was through the young Methodist minister at Burslem, the Rev. Frederick Macdonald, that John Kipling found himself admitted to such a society. 'He brought intellectual and artistic qualities into our midst,' wrote Frederick Macdonald, 'as from another and different realm. Companionship with him was a continual refreshing.' Frederick Macdonald was one of a large family, two sons and five daughters, all lively, handsome, and intelligent, and his sisters occasionally came over to Burslem to visit him. According to the most reliable of several reminiscences, it was at a picnic party at Lake Rudyard, given by the Miss Pinders, the daughters of his employer, that John Kipling met his future wife in the spring of 1863. Among the guests were Frederick Macdonald and his sister Alice, whom, two years later, John Kipling married in London.[3]

The Macdonalds were a truly remarkable circle of relatives, one of those affectionate family groups that maintain an intimate sense of union when their members are physically separated, that absorb into the group the wives and husbands of their members. The Kiplings of Yorkshire parted, went their own ways, and disappear from the story; the Macdonalds clung together, generation after generation.

Their blood was exclusively Scottish, Irish, and Welsh. In the dispersion that followed the '45, a family of Macdonalds had emigrated to Ulster and there, at Enniskillen, James Macdonald was born in

1761. Brought up a loyal episcopalian, he came under the direct
influence of John Wesley, who persuaded him to join the Methodists.
James Macdonald educated himself, entered the ministry in 1785, and
was appointed to an English circuit. He died in 1833, by which time
his son, George Browne Macdonald born in 1805, had also entered the
ministry. George Macdonald had an advantage which had been denied
to his father; he was given a good education at Woodhouse Grove,
the school at which his future son-in-law was also to be a pupil a few
years later. The simplicity of those days may be judged by the fact
that James Macdonald brought up his family in comfort, and educated
them, on a salary of £80 a year; George Macdonald, a generation
later, on £160 a year.

The vagaries of life as a Methodist minister took the Rev. George
Macdonald to Birmingham in the eighteen-fifties. There his eldest
son, Henry, was one of a conspicuous group of scholars at King
Edward's School, whose leader was Edward Burne Jones. Some years
later when Burne Jones set himself up as a painter, sharing a studio in
London with William Morris, Henry Macdonald was a frequent
visitor. So was the younger brother Frederick and his sister Georgiana.
She married Burne Jones in 1860 and, four years later, they settled in a
large old-fashioned house, The Grange, North End Road, Fulham,
which had once been the home of the novelist, Richardson. The
Grange was the gathering-place of the Macdonalds and all their set
for more than thirty years.

Georgiana was already married and assuming the position of head
of the family when Frederick introduced their sister Alice to John
Kipling at Lake Rudyard. Since their parents were old and ailing it
was Georgiana who managed her sister's wedding, from North End
Road, and it was Frederick who gave his sister away. John Lockwood
Kipling and Alice Macdonald were married at St. Mary Abbotts'
Church on 18th March 1865, a bitterly cold day. There was a lavish
reception where they should have met all the lions of literary and
artistic London. Swinburne was there, the two Rossettis were there,
but not the bride or the bridegroom, who had made the bold decision
to go to India, and whose ship unexpectedly sailed on the day of the
party. In their absence, Ford Madox Brown made merriment by
stumbling over the bridegroom's unusual name, referring to him as
'John Gilpin'.

Lockwood Kipling cared little for the blandishments of society; his
head was never turned by fashionable cults in art. Serene, smiling,
and indifferent, he went his own way. His wife, a handsome, sharp-
featured little woman with auburn hair, blue eyes, and a very lively
tongue would have been a match for any wit the Burne Joneses could

have entertained. 'My sister had the nimblest mind I have ever known', wrote Frederick Macdonald. 'She saw things in a moment and did not so much reason as pounce on her conclusions. Accuracy in detail was not so much her forte as swift insight, and the kind of vision that is afforded by flashes of lightning. Her power of speech was unsurpassed — her chief difficulty being that she found language a slow-moving medium of expression that failed to keep up with her thought. She tumbled over her words, because they could not come out fast enough.'

But the Kiplings were off, with no more than a stock of self-confidence and self-reliance to support their marriage. John Kipling, popular though he was with all who met him, was socially no great match for the witty Miss Macdonald. He was lucky to have got a minor appointment as principal of a new school of art at Bombay, supposedly through his brother-in-law's influence. But India was far away, an unknown land, with which neither his nor her family had any previous association, unless it was Henry Macdonald's abortive bid for a post in the Civil Service. To India they went, in spite of the anxiety of her parents, determined to stand on their own feet and make their own way.

Their first child, born at Bombay before the end of the year on 30th December 1865, was given two names, Joseph after his Kipling grandfather, and Rudyard, at the suggestion of his aunt, Louisa Macdonald, after the place where his parents had first met. At Bewdley, where the Macdonald grandparents lived in retirement, Louisa met and married the wealthy iron-master, Alfred Baldwin (who, later, was to be Chairman of the Great Western Railway and father of a Prime Minister). He was something better as a match than the unknown penniless art-teacher who had carried Alice off to India. Louisa's was a double wedding for, on the same day, her sister Agnes married one of Edward Burne Jones's friends, a young artist named Poynter who had already made a name at the Royal Academy.

Four of the five Macdonald sisters were now married, and it may be noticed that all had been wedded according to the rites of the Church of England. Macdonald Methodism had never been a narrow sectarianism. The original James Macdonald seems to have been one of those early Methodists who regarded themselves rather as a party within the national Church than a sect outside it. His son George, though a Methodist minister, was married in Manchester Cathedral. George's son Frederick, who had brought John Kipling into their circle, was a well-read, widely travelled man of the world. His sisters regarded him as the intellectual member of the family. Though he lived to become President of the Methodist Conference, he expressed deep sympathy and respect for orthodox churchmen. The drift back from 'chapel' to 'church' began with Georgiana when she married Edward Burne Jones. Alice conformed to what was becoming the family tradition, though neither she nor her husband became regular communicant Church members. The little Rudyard was never a Methodist; he was baptized in Bombay Cathedral, his sponsors being John Griffiths, his father's assistant, and his Aunt Louisa, by proxy.

CHAPTER II

CHILDHOOD: BOMBAY AND SOUTHSEA (1865-77)

THE CITY OF SLEEP (1894)

Over the edge of the purple down,
  Ere the tender dreams begin,
Look — we may look — at the Merciful Town,
  But we may not enter in!
Outcasts all, from her guarded wall
  Back to our watch we creep:
We — pity us! ah, pity us!
  We wakeful; oh, pity us! —
We that go back with Policeman Day —
  Back from the City of Sleep!

B OMBAY, when John and Alice Kipling arrived there, at the beginning of the hot weather of 1865, was a new commercial city at the crest of a wave of prosperity. The Indian Empire itself was not yet seven years old, and the memories of the Mutiny, which darkened its origins for dwellers in the old Bengal Presidency, did little to disturb the western seaboard. Under the enlightened rule of Sir Bartle Frere, Bombay, which had been a backwater, was rapidly becoming the most progressive of Asiatic cities, the most European in appearance, with its broad streets of solid masonry, behind which were hidden the slums that housed the new proletariat of workers in the cotton-mills. Even the setback, when American cotton reappeared in the market at the end of the Civil War, not long after the Kiplings' arrival, was less disastrous than at first it appeared to be. During the boom years, the main railway lines had been linked into an Indian system which established Bombay as the western outlet for all Indian trade; and the opening of the Suez Canal in 1869 made Bombay, in fact, the Gateway of India. Much of the wealth and enterprise belonged to the Parsee community, then as now, remarkable for their public spirit; and no citizen of Bombay was more rightly respected than Sir Jamsetjee Jeejeebhoy, who endowed the school of art where Lockwood * Kipling was appointed 'Professor of Architectural Sculp-

---

* His wife and family usually called him John. To the rest of his acquaintances he was known as Mr. Lockwood Kipling and by that name he will be called in this book.

It was Lockwood Kipling's task to foster the decaying arts and crafts of India, and to oppose the tendency of Indian craftsmen to copy all that was worst in Victorian commercial art. He was to induce them to adapt their own craft traditions to the needs of the industrial age; in short, to conduct a crusade in India like that which William Morris had undertaken in England. His restless curiosity, his friendly manner, his minute observation, his manual dexterity, his skill with pen and pencil, soon made him the repository of information, on the costumes, devices, ornaments, tools, utensils, materials, and techniques of almost every trade and caste in India, an indispensable adviser to anyone who was getting up an exhibition, founding a technical school, or investigating an industrial process. He began with sculpture, an art that needed reviving, not founding, in India, and it is remembered that he carved one, at least, of the public monuments of Bombay with his own hands.

In this new bustling city with its fluctuating prosperity, Rudyard Kipling spent his infancy, ignorant both of the new wealth and the old poverty around him. His world was the garden of a bungalow in the compound of the school of art. Across a strip of watered grass, wide as a prairie to a little boy in the burning sun, was his father's studio where fascinating games were played with modelling-clay and chips of sculptor's-work. It was inhabited by his father's friends, men who wore the strangest clothes and answered to the oddest names. One of them, a Parsee named Pestonjee Bomonjee, wearing the shining, cylindrical hat that was the mark of his people, lived to record, sixty years afterwards, that Rudyard, at five years old, never forgot a face or a name. [1]

More familiar than these persons in the studio was Meeta, the Hindu bearer, with whom Rudyard talked so constantly in the vernacular that it was necessary to remind him to speak English, when he joined his parents in the drawing-room. The *ayah,* who belonged more properly to his baby sister, was a Goanese Roman Catholic, and on their early morning walks sometimes took him into the chapel of her faith; as Meeta, when he was in charge, did not scruple to take the little boy to Shiva's temple. He did not much distinguish between these alternate devotions.

A break came in this course of life, when Rudyard, at no more than two years and six months old, was taken home to England by his parents and, so precocious was he in his development, so retentive of visual memories, that he was able to recall one scene, at least, of this journey, forty years later when next he passed that way again. His recollection went back to a time before the Suez Canal was cut through the Isthmus, when passengers from India went overland from Suez to

Alexandria. 'There was a train across a desert, and a halt in it, and a small girl wrapped in a shawl on the seat opposite me whose face stands out still.' He was lifted down from the train because, he was told, it was on fire, a problem that did not alarm him as, no doubt, it alarmed his parents. 'What stuck in his sleepy mind was the absurd name of the place and his father's prophecy that when he grew up he would "come that way in a big steamer". So, all his life, the word "Zagazig" carried memories of a brick shed, the flicker of an oil-lamp's floating wick, a sky full of eyes, and an engine coughing in a desert at the world's end.'[2]

It was March 1868 when the Kiplings returned to England and the house of the Macdonald grandparents at Bewdley: 'a dark land', thought little Rudyard, 'and a darker room full of cold, in one wall of which a white woman made a naked fire'. He cried out with dread, not having seen such a thing before; nor had he ever seen a staircase. His old and ailing grandparents noted him down as a talkative, inquisitive child, more forward and self-assertive than Victorian children were expected to be. The Kiplings did not stay long at Bewdley, and did not see Grandfather Macdonald again; he died that autumn murmuring on his death-bed, 'Lord, what things I lie here and remember'.

Again it was to the Burne Joneses' house that Alice Kipling turned for hospitality. Her second child, Alice, always known as 'Trix', was born there on 11th June 1868, the event for which, we may suppose, they had come to England.

For four more cool seasons and three more hot seasons, Rudyard, his sister, and their parents lived a happy uneventful life in Bombay, broken only by visits to the hill-station at Nassick. A land filled with wonders, and a westward sea, were crystallized in his infantine memories by drives to the coconut groves of Mahim in the sunset. Seaward, 'there were far-going Arab dhows on the pearly waters, and gaily dressed Parsees wading out to worship the sun'; landward, the palm-groves swaying in the sunset breeze. 'I have always felt', wrote Kipling in old age, 'the menacing darkness of tropical eventide, as I have loved the voices of night-winds through palm or banana leaves, and the song of the tree-frogs.'[3] It was in this afterglow that he pictured the family circle of indulgent parents and kindly, obsequious, native servants; this was the background of his age of innocence, the heaven that lay about him in his infancy.

All Anglo-Indian * families were haunted by a spectre, the dreaded day of separation when the children must be sent home for their

---

* In this book the word 'Anglo-Indian' is used, as Kipling and his contemporaries always used it, to signify an Englishman residing in India.

education. It came early, by customary standards, to the Kipling family, when Rudyard was five and a half years old and Trix not yet three, perhaps because of their mother's uncertain health. Her eldest son's birth had cost her a long and dangerous labour (relieved, the servants said, only when one of them hastened to ransom the child's life by sacrificing a kid to Kali); her daughter's birth in London had been even more difficult; a third child was born, and died, in the hot weather of 1870. Probably she was determined to be in England with her two children before the hot weather returned again. Whatever the reason, the decision was taken and the four left Bombay, on 15th April 1871, for a six-month furlough. Again a sea voyage marked an epoch in Rudyard's infant mind, or rather, the two voyages blended together in his hazy recollection to form a single image, ' a time in a ship with an immense semi-circle blocking all vision on each side of her '.

In December the parents deposited their children in lodgings at Southsea before returning to India. Perhaps unwisely, they made no effort to forewarn little Rudyard of this calamity, but slipped away without stirring the children's emotion by any passionate display of affection. Rudyard, just before his sixth birthday, was left to discover for himself the meaning of separation from his father and mother; Trix was still too young to know what was the nature of her misfortune. The two children had been left as paying guests in the house of a retired naval officer [4] whose name had been obtained from an advertisement in a newspaper. According to Anglo-Indian custom their new guardians were given honorary rank as relatives, becoming ' Uncle Harry ' and ' Aunty Rosa '. Rudyard lived with them for five years and three months, from his sixth to his eleventh year; Trix remained some years longer.

Since this period of deepening misery was to leave unhealed scars upon the spirit of Rudyard Kipling, it is necessary to ask why this child of loving and intelligent parents was compelled to suffer so long, unpitied and unnoticed. Why were the children entrusted to the naval captain's wife, and not to either of their grandmothers or to one of their married aunts? Trix used to say, in later life, that her Kipling grandmother at Skipton ought to have been chosen as her guardian, but old Mrs. Kiplings name does not appear in such few letters as survive from this period. Aunt Louie (Baldwin), Aunt Aggie (Poynter), above all Aunt Georgie (Burne Jones) — Rudyard's beloved Aunt Georgie to whom he afterwards paid such tributes of affection — all three were making their way in the world and had young children of an age with the young Kiplings. Was it, in fact, necessary to board the Kiplings out with strangers? The talented Macdonald sisters met as frequently as they could, visited one another's houses, spoke in the most affectionate terms of one another, not least of Alice exiled among the unfamiliar perils of life in India. They were good-natured, they were hospitable, they were amusing; but they were not forthcoming, nor were they motherly. Even Aunt Georgie, who spent her life in managing and protecting her unworldly genius of a husband, was found a little formidable by strangers until a breach was made in the reserve with which she surrounded herself. She did not give her confidence, or open her heart, easily. Her nephew and niece adored her; they seemed well-fed and well cared for; why should she doubt that her highly competent sister Alice had done what was best for them. Alice Kipling, for her part, agreed with her husband that self-reliance was the master-virtue. She was not well off. Who can say what economies and restraints were necessary at Bombay in order to maintain the two children at Southsea; yet the Kiplings would pay their own way and not admit dependence upon relatives who, in the 'seventies, were beginning to outstrip them in worldly success. The Macdonald grandmother with two of the aunts came down to Southsea in 1872 to visit the two children, and found them thriving in apparent comfort.

Four accounts survive of Kipling's childhood at Southsea, and differ only in emphasis. He wrote his own account in *Something of Myself,* the fragment of autobiography begun, but neither completed nor revised, in his old age; before his death, Trix gave her account of the same events, and from these two versions a reliable story can be constructed. But more significant are the two imaginative versions which Kipling issued under the guise of fiction, much earlier in his life, when the events were clearer in his memory and when the emotions of childhood were more compelling. His readers could not know, when the story called *Baa, Baa, Black Sheep* first appeared, in 1888, that it was a piece of autobiography, heightened in colour, yet following the events of his childhood in all but a few details. Nor could contemporary readers say more of the first chapter of *The Light that Failed* than that it was out of key with the rest of the book. It is another version of the same story with the material factors transposed, and, in this form, it reveals more passion, more of the unconscious working of the 'black sheep's' mind than either of his plain narratives.

At Southsea little Rudyard became the black sheep of his new family. So long as 'Uncle Harry', the old sea-captain, was alive, Rudyard got some protection. 'Uncle Harry' liked the boy, taught him old sea-songs, introduced him to *Jorrocks,* and delighted him by talking like a sailor in a book; he actually used to say, 'Shiver my timbers!'[5] But, soon, he died, leaving Rudyard to the mercies of 'Aunty Rosa' and her son. She was jealous for her own young Harry, five or six years older than Rudyard but, we may suppose, without a quarter of his vivacity and eager interest in the world. This motive of unconscious jealousy did not affect her conduct towards Trix who was a general favourite with her and with the whole family. It would be easy to dismiss 'Aunty Rosa' as a tyrant, a cruel foster-mother, and, no doubt, easy for her friends to defend her character. She must have been a good woman and a good housewife, or the sad story of 'Black Sheep' would have ended with exposure and disputation. It did not; even when the wretched Rudyard was at last released from her domination, there was no breach between the two families. Trix remained in her house several years longer, and Rudyard visited Trix at Southsea as a big boy, without, so far as we know, any awkwardness over meeting 'Aunty Rosa' again. The wretchedness of those five years lay buried in that inaccessible hiding-place, the secret heart of a child.

'Aunty Rosa' had difficulties to contend with. Rudyard was a restless, clumsy boy, very little used to genteel discipline. He sprawled over the sofas, he talked continually, he asked the most searching questions, he knew more than little boys were expected to know and paraded his knowledge in the company of his elders, he had Anglo-Indian notions of nursery etiquette, he was unresponsive to demonstrations of sentiment, and altogether unlike his sweet, affectionate little sister. It was disgraceful, 'Aunty Rosa' must have thought, that, at nearly six years old, he had not yet begun to read or write; and disconcerting that, as soon as he did learn, he talked incessantly about characters from books. If he had been spoiled by indulgent parents in Bombay, 'Aunty Rosa' was determined to do her duty by him in Southsea, to correct his manners and cure him of 'showing off'.

It was an establishment run with the full vigour of the Evangelical as revealed to the Woman. I had never heard of Hell, so I was introduced to it in all its terrors — I and whatever luckless little slavey might be in the house, whom severe rationing had led to steal food. Once I saw the Woman beat such a girl who picked up the kitchen poker and threatened retaliation. Myself I was regularly beaten. The Woman had an only son of twelve or thirteen as religious as she. I was a real joy to him, for when his mother had finished with me for the day he (we slept in the same room) took me on and roasted the other side.

If you cross-examine a child of seven or eight on his day's doings (specially when he wants to go to sleep) he will contradict himself very satisfactorily. If each contradiction be set down as a lie and retailed at breakfast, life is not easy. I have known a certain amount of bullying, but this was calculated torture — religious as well as scientific. Yet it made me give attention to the lies I soon found it necessary to tell: and this, I presume, is the foundation of literary effort.

But my ignorance was my salvation. I was made to read without explanation, under the usual fear of punishment. And on a day that I remember it came to me that 'reading' was not 'the Cat lay on the Mat', but a means to everything that would make me happy. So I read all that came within my reach. As soon as my pleasure in this was known, deprivation from reading was added to my punishments. I then read by stealth and the more earnestly.

Coming out of church once I smiled. The Devil-Boy demanded why. I said I didn't know, which was child's truth. He replied that I *must* know. People didn't laugh for nothing. Heaven knows what explanation I put forward; but it was duly reported to the Woman as a 'lie'. Result, afternoon upstairs with the Collect to learn. I learned most of the Collects that way and a great deal of the Bible. The son after three or four years went into a Bank and was generally too tired on his return to torture me, unless things had gone wrong with him. I learned to know what was coming from his step into the house.

But, for a month each year I possessed a paradise which I verily believe saved me. Each December I stayed with my aunt Georgie, my mother's sister, wife of Sir Edward Burne Jones, at The Grange, North End Road. At first I must have been escorted there, but later I went alone, and arriving at the house would reach up to the open-work iron bell-pull on the wonderful gate that let me into all felicity. When I had a house of my own, and The Grange was emptied of meaning, I begged for and was given that bell-pull for my entrance, in the hope that other children might also feel happy when they rang it.

.   .   .   .   .

Nor was my life an unsuitable preparation for my future, in that it demanded constant wariness, the habit of observation, and attendance on moods and tempers; the noting of discrepancies between speech and action; a certain reserve of demeanour; and automatic suspicion of sudden favours. Brother Lippo Lippi, in his own harder case, as a boy discovered: —

> 'Why, soul and sense of him grow sharp alike,
> He learns the look of things and none the less
> For admonition'.

So it was with me.

My troubles settled themselves in a few years. My eyes went wrong, and I could not well see to read. For which reason I read the more and in bad lights. My work at the terrible little day-school where I had been sent suffered in consequence, and my monthly reports showed it. The loss of 'reading-time' was the worst of my 'home' punishments for bad school-work. One report was so bad that I threw it away and said that I had never received it. But this is a hard world for the amateur liar. My web of deceit was swiftly exposed — the Son spared time after banking-hours to help in the auto-da-fé — and I was well beaten and sent to school through the streets of Southsea with the placard 'Liar' between my shoulders. In the long run these things, and many more of the like, drained me of any capacity for real, personal hate for the rest of my days. So close must any life-filling passion lie to its opposite. 'Who having known the Diamond will concern himself with glass?'[6]

Five long years of life at Southsea taught Rudyard some lessons that he never forgot, the stoic lessons that the mind must make its own happiness, that any troubles can be endured if the sufferer has resources of his own to sustain him. He learned, too, that family affection is the greatest good in life, and the absence of it the greatest evil. The loyalty of Trix, who repeatedly defended him against 'Aunty Rosa's' sharp tongue — it was all she could do — was the great comfort, and another was the glimpse of happier life at North End Road, where everyone was kind and trusting. Best of all pleasures at North End Road was to lean over the banisters on the top landing when Uncle Ned was entertaining his friends 'and listen to the loveliest sound in the world — deep-voiced men laughing together over dinner'. If it was 'Uncle Topsy', the name the children gave to William Morris, he might regale them with stories of the Vikings, but if it was a person called Browning his conversation would be for the grown-ups alone.

But on a certain day — one tried to fend off the thought of it — the delicious dream would end, and one would return to the House of Desolation, and for the next two or three mornings there cry on waking up. Hence more punishments and cross-examinations.

Often and often afterwards, the beloved Aunt would ask me why I had never told anyone how I was being treated. Children tell little more than animals, for what comes to them they accept as eternally established. Also, badly-treated children have a clear notion of what they are likely to get if they betray the secrets of a prison-house, before they are clear of it.[7]

The Grange, in North End Road, offered a gleam, a vision of happiness which was not his own. Far away in the East, and half-forgotten, was his real home, linked to him only by letters from his father who sent him books to read, his chief resource, if Harry and 'Aunty Rosa' would leave him in peace to read them, if his eyes did not fail him in the dark basement nursery.

There came a time when even 'Aunty Rosa' learned that her charge was not naughty but ill. A doctor soon diagnosed the trouble as a neglected defect in Rudyard's eyesight which must be corrected by the use of glasses; and, for a time, forbade him to strain his eyesight with reading. Thus, his last weeks at Southsea were spent in a boredom that was worse than punishment. Then, suddenly, without warning, his mother arrived from India. When she first came into his room to kiss her son good-night, he flung up an arm to guard off the cuff that he had been trained to expect.

The happiest year of Rudyard's young life began with his mother's arrival, in March 1877. She took him away from Southsea to a farm near Loughton in Epping Forest, where he and Trix were allowed to run wild, and ride ponies, all the summer. Their cousin, Stan Baldwin, a year or two younger than Rudyard, came to stay, and the two boys got into healthy mischief together. Return to the House of Desolation no longer threatened, and its terrors slipped out of his consciousness like the oppression of a nightmare. The shadow lifted from his mind as the material shadow lifted from his eyesight; his mother's presence (for a boy of eleven can stand a great deal of mothering) was a cure for one, as the doctor's prescription for the other. That he must wear powerful glasses for the rest of his life was no great burden if they gave him access again to his story-books. In 1877 Rudyard had no story of his own worth telling, only the carefree life of a boy in a happy home. But not altogether, 'for when young lips have drunk deep of the bitter waters of Hate, Suspicion, and Despair, all the Love in the world will not wholly take away that knowledge'.[8]

CHAPTER III

PUBLIC SCHOOL (1878–82)

A SCHOOL SONG (1899)

Western wind and open surge
  Took us from our mothers;
Flung us on a naked shore
(Twelve bleak houses by the shore!
Seven summers by the shore!)
  'Mid two hundred brothers.

.   .   .   .

There we met with famous men
  Set in office o'er us;
And they beat on us with rods —
Faithfully with many rods —
Daily beat us on with rods,
  For the love they bore us!

.   .   .   .

Each degree of Latitude
  Strung about Creation
Seeth one or more of us
(Of one muster each of us),
Diligent in that he does,
  Keen in his vocation.

.   .   .   .

This we learned from famous men,
  Knowing not its uses,
When they showed, in daily work,
Man must finish off his work —
Right or wrong, his daily work —
  And without excuses.

.   .   .   .

Wherefore praise we famous men
  From whose bays we borrow —
They that put aside To-day —
All the joys of their To-day —
And with toil of their To-day
  Bought for us To-morrow!

.   .   .   .

Bless and praise we famous men —
Men of little showing —
For their work continueth,
And their work continueth,
Broad and deep continueth,
Great beyond their knowing.

WHEN, at twelve years old, it was time for Rudyard to resume his schooling, his parents can have had little doubt about where to send him; their dear friend Cormell Price, already well known to Rudyard as 'Uncle Crom', would be his teacher.

In the days when Price and 'Ned' Jones and Henry Macdonald had been school-fellows at Birmingham, there had been little to show which of the three would go farthest in the world. At Oxford, 'Crom' had been an active, popular member of William Morris's set, and had taken a hand with 'Ned' and the others in painting the celebrated pre-Raphaelite frescoes at the Union, but, when 'Ned' and William Morris decided to throw in their lot with Rossetti, he parted from them to try his fortune as a medical student. Rossetti, who wanted all his friends to be painters, deplored 'Crom's' defection and would not let him lapse from their group. He made fun of 'Crom's' new trade, sought out his company, and took him about the town to Bohemian parties with 'Jones' and 'Hunt' and 'Brown', none of them yet distinguished by their more elegant second names.

But 'Crom' was still unsatisfied; he abandoned medicine and went off to Russia as English tutor in a noble family. In the anglophile period after the Crimean War there was a great demand in Russia for English tutors and governesses, a stream of well-educated young persons who brought back with them, and popularized, the taste for Russian literature — mostly in French translations. Burne-Jones and Morris often wished 'Crom' home again, and welcomed him when he returned in 1863 to organize the 'modern side' at Haileybury, one of the new Public Schools founded in imitation of Arnold's Rugby.

Another new Public School, the United Services College, was founded in 1874 by a group of Army officers who wanted to provide their sons with a cheap education. They were fortunate in getting 'Crom' as their first headmaster, and he was able to take away with him from Haileybury a nucleus of boys who 'migrated' for the privilege of being coached for their Army Entrance Examination under 'Crom's' skilled tuition. The rise of the new schools was closely connected with the introduction of competitive examinations as the sole means of qualifying for the public services. The Indian Civil Service had been recruited from the successful candidates in an examination since 1855, Gladstone had made competitive examination the rule in the home Civil Service in 1870, and the last great stronghold of privilege fell when he abolished the purchase of officers' commissions in the Army, in 1871. The 'Army Exam' now became a challenge to the new Public Schools, a formidable obstacle at the end of the school course for many a boy of the upper middle-classes.

In later life, Kipling's devotion to his headmaster, and through his headmaster to his old school, led him to make exaggerated claims for the United Services College, as a 'school before its time'. That is just what it was not, it was a school that precisely satisfied a need by preparing boys for the new competitive examinations; and when the Army Exam ceased to be a troublesome obstacle the school lost ground.

The system and spirit of the United Services College were largely borrowed from Haileybury, that is to say, it was Anglo-Indian in tradition. Most of the boys were soldiers' sons, and many had been born in India. But in spite of its name and its martial origins the United Services College was as unlike a 'Military Academy' as a school could be. In the first place it was cheap, the boys lived in Spartan simplicity, and the management was conducted with parsimony. There were no parades, no uniforms, no bands or flags, no school cadet corps, no patriotic propaganda, nor would it have occurred to any master or boy that such things could be regarded as anything but gross bad form. It was a training ground for youths who were assumed to be gentlemen, and who were qualifying for entrance to the public service where they would work professionally, unobtrusively, anonymously, for entrance to an army whose officers changed into plain clothes at the instant of coming off duty.

'Crom' Price was no militarist, he was russophile and francophile and disposed to be a liberal, as were his friends the Burne-Joneses, especially 'Aunt Georgie'. It was recorded that, though they cared little for party politics as a rule, Price and Burne-Jones had once appeared together on a public platform at a meeting of protest against Disraeli's foreign policy.

The respect in which the College differed from the general run of mid-Victorian Public Schools was its secular tone; there was no school chapel; Price was not in holy orders and was not a strong churchman. Rudyard Kipling passed through his hands quite untouched by the religious enthusiasms, either evangelical or high-church, that stirred the hearts of so many intelligent young men in the eighteen-eighties.

The strength of the school was its position at the little watering-place in Bideford Bay which had been fancifully named Westward Ho! as a tribute to Charles Kingsley's popular romance. The proprietors of the school had bought up a row of lodging-houses, 'twelve bleak houses by the shore', and had converted them into a school building, by running a corridor or covered way the whole length of the terrace. At one end they had added a large bare hall, known as the gymnasium, which served for assemblies, daily prayers, and indoor exercise. Other amenities there were none but those provided by nature; 'western wind and open surge'; miles of cliff and combe and headland running westward to Hartland Point; Bideford Bay with the broad estuary of the Torridge; a rough expanse of scrub and sandhills, known as the Burrows and laid out for the newly imported game of golf; and the Pebble Ridge where the Atlantic surf beat on a steep rough bar of shingle.

The school was in only the fifth year of its existence when Kipling arrived as a new boy. As yet, the traditional rules of conduct which stabilize school life and which give a sense of security, even if they are felt to be constricting, had not crystallized. Discipline, both in respect of the authorized school rules, and of the code which the boys enforced on one another, was irregular and harsh. The masters, like the senior boys, were a job lot, got together, as chance had permitted, to give the place a start. It was a rough experience and again Kipling was cut off from the family life that alone satisfied his deepest emotion, but he was not wretched as he had been at Southsea. He was bigger and stronger now, and he acquired a new comfort in masculine comradeship. From the very first day he found a friend, a sharp-featured Irish boy with a detached air and an acidulated tongue. His name was George Beresford and though, perhaps, he never meant as much to Kipling as Kipling meant to him, he broke the spell of solitary homesickness. In later years, Kipling wrote of him under the name of 'M'Turk'.

Beresford also wrote reminiscences of his 'Schooldays with Kipling' and, though they sometimes seem no less imaginative than the account which Kipling put forward as fiction, the two versions yield much authentic information when collated.

Into the small-boys' house at Westward Ho! [wrote Beresford] in the grey chill January days of 1878 there fluttered a cheery, capering, podgy, little fellow, as precocious as ever he could be. Or, rather, a broad smile appeared with a small boy behind it, carrying it about and pointing it in all directions. . . . Over the smile there was strangely enough, a pair of spectacles. The two did not seem to go together, as in those days spectacles were regarded as a mark of extreme seriousness and crabbed age. . . . When you looked more closely at this new boy, you were astonished to see what seemed to be a moustache right across the smile, and so it was — an early spring moustache just out of the ground of his upper lip. . . . Kipling was rather short for his age of just twelve years, but he took it out in extra width. He was not noticeably muscular or sinewy, and was accordingly ineffectual at fisticuffs, for which, in any case, his exceedingly short sight unfitted him.   He preferred to side-track physical violence by his tact and friendliness and by not quarrelling with any boy unless he had allies.   He was always noticeable for his caution and his habit of ' getting there ' by diplomatic means.[1]

By all accounts, Kipling's appearance was most unusual.   The golden-brown hair of his childhood was now darkening and, above the faint pencilling of moustache which so surprised his contemporaries, there already protruded the heavy black eyebrows which caricaturists enlarged upon, in later years.   The thrusting line of his profile with its protruding, deeply-cloven chin gave him a singularly aggressive appearance which was dispelled when he raised his round thick glasses, resting them on the penthouse of his eyebrows, to confront his ques-tioner with a humorous gaze from brilliant blue eyes.   In those days, he used his glasses for long sight, and read — he was always reading — with the naked eye, jerking his head backwards and forwards as he pored over the page.   He was the only boy in the school to wear spectacles, from which came his school nickname of ' Gig-lamps ' or ' Gigger '.

In Kipling's early years at Westward Ho!, which he spent in daily company with Beresford, they passed through a period of ill-treatment by a brutal assistant-master who might have strayed out of some novel by Dickens.   This was the Rev. J. C. Campbell, the school chaplain, of whom another boy wrote, ' I can never recall his face without an expres-sion of ferocity on it, nor his hand without a cane in it '.[2]   Modern readers will not be surprised to learn that Campbell was an emotional preacher.   When, in Kipling's second year, Campbell left for another appointment he preached a farewell sermon of such unctuous eloquence that the hearts of his little victims were melted.   They mutually agreed that old Campbell should be forgiven and should be offered some parting testimonial.   Not so thought ' Gigger '; he brought them all to their senses by saying emphatically: ' Two years' bullying is not paid for with half an hour's blubbering in a pulpit '.

Campbell's place was taken by the Rev. C. Willes (' Gillett ' in *Stalky & Co.*), a comfortable easy-going ' muscular Christian ', who won the friendship if not the particular respect of Beresford and Kipling.   They were prepared for confirmation under his perfunctory instruction, and were confirmed in Bideford Church by the Bishop of Exeter, an event that seems to have made no mark upon the mental development of either boy.   Nothing was added to Kipling's religious training at Westward Ho!; all that he had, he owed to ' Aunty Rosa ' who had drilled the Prayer-book collects and the Bible stories into him at Southsea.

As yet, in his first years at school, the real interest of his life was elsewhere. His father had again come home from India in 1878 to supervise the Indian exhibit at the Paris Exposition and, in the summer holidays, took young Rudyard, not yet thirteen, to Paris with him.

Lockwood gave his son a free pass to the Exposition, which was not yet open to the public, and a franc or two daily to buy his lunch at a cheap restaurant. Rudyard ran wild in Paris, playing at paper-chases in the Tuileries Gardens with an English friend, a Christ's Hospital boy in blue cassock and yellow stockings. Mostly they prowled in the back premises of the Exposition, talking to the workmen in schoolboy French, and exploring among curiosities and art treasures, all the more alluring when half-disengaged from their wrappings. How things were put together, and what they looked like in the workshop, interested Rudyard most of all. A strange interest for a boy was his notice of a subject-picture in Paris, an illustration of the death of Manon Lescaut. Why it should have haunted his imagination he could not say nor, twelve years later, when the seed bore fruit, could he yet express all that he wished to say of it. He did not learn how much France and the French way of life meant to him until, in middle age, these boyish memories of his first visit gained a new significance.[3]

At thirteen years old, Rudyard knew that he belonged to a different world from the other boys at his school, or rather that he belonged to two worlds, theirs and the world of literary London. He had a secret bond of union with the headmaster who, in the holidays, was by courtesy his ' Uncle Crom '; he and ' Crom ' were at home among people who wrote, people who painted, people who exhibited in Paris. Beresford noticed that young Kipling seemed to have read everything, all sorts of grown-up books, while the other boys were content with ' Jack Harkaway ' and ' Ned Kelly '. In ten minutes he seemed to extract the essence of a difficult book which anyone else might have taken a week to read. Though he never paraded his knowledge and certainly never alluded to his distinguished friends, he gave the impression of being the perfectly well-informed man of the world. At one time he and Beresford studied contemporary art together in the Bideford print-shops. It was plain that ' Gigger ' knew all about the rival schools, the Academy and the Aesthetes, though he never mentioned the fact that one of his aunts was married to Edward Poynter, R.A., and another to Burne-Jones, a pillar of the Grosvenor Gallery. Beresford did not know this in his schooldays.

Then came a time when Beresford and Kipling with three other boys were allowed the privilege of sharing a large study. They now began to cultivate an adolescent social life, of which one manifestation was amateur theatricals. The study produced a play, a burlesque pantomime, to the old story of Aladdin, with topical songs which 'Gigger' could turn out with easy fluency. This was an epoch in the school life of the group, but was followed by what seemed a disaster. The room was required for another purpose and the group of five friends was dispersed. 'Gigger' and Beresford looked about and found an unused closet — it was hardly more — which they got permission to convert into a study for three boys. It was then necessary to admit a worthy partner to their enterprise; they soon agreed to invite 'Stalky' Dunsterville.

Thus began, in 1880, the partnership, known in the school as 'Stalky & Co.', which has given delight to hundreds of thousands of readers, for more than fifty years, in one of the classic tales of boyhood. Books about the life of children written from their own point of view were an original invention of the nineteenth century. Stories for children and even stories about children there had always been, and children had always told stories to one another, but the cult of childhood as a mode of life with its own values and its own standards gave a new impulse to literature. By any reckoning Kipling's *Stalky & Co.* must stand high in the list of books in this *genre*. It shares a peculiar quality of fantasy with another classic of childhood, published a few years earlier, Mark Twain's *Tom Sawyer*. Each of these books is 'true' in the sense that the local colour is minutely accurate and the characters drawn from life; each is a romance in the sense that the incidents are vastly exaggerated. No schoolboys ever carried out, or could have carried out, such audacious enterprises as did 'Stalky', 'M'Turk', and 'Beetle' (the name Kipling affixed to himself), or such as are ascribed to Tom Sawyer and Huck Finn. But the fantasy, in both instances, is true to the imaginative life of many a boy. This is how they behave in their daydreams, these are the witticisms, the ingenuities, the audacities they would have produced if only the world of fact resembled the world of fancy.

This is only half the account that must be given of *Stalky & Co*. To many readers the book seemed grossly offensive. So judicious a critic as George Sampson dismissed it as 'an unpleasant book about unpleasant boys in an unpleasant school'. The realism was somewhat shocking to a generation accustomed to the evangelical sobriety of earlier school stories. The best book of this kind ever written, *Tom Brown's Schooldays,* contains horrider brutalities and wilder lawlessness than anything in *Stalky & Co.,* but it is a moral tale written upon the theme of the moulding of Tom's character into the pattern of ethics approved at Dr. Arnold's Rugby. In Kipling's story, the violence and the heartless cruelty which, as everyone knows, occur wherever boys are gathered together, are paraded with boyish gusto, and the formation of character at Westward Ho! is less explicit. Kipling put it on record that he wrote the book as a tract, and, on a closer examination, it will be found that the crudities and flippancies of this book, too, conduce to a moral purpose.

School life can be a microcosm of the greater world, and Kipling's cosmology took shape at Westward Ho! From the alternating light and darkness of his childhood he had stepped out into a wider world, a masculine world, and a world of work like manhood, not a world of play like childhood. School life was ordered, progressive, and directed to an end which all approved. A willing subordination to the fundamental rules was then right and reasonable, but this did not in the least imply a pedantic adherence to all the superficial and accidental observances and prohibitions to which prigs gave an inflated importance. The school itself was a praiseworthy, a useful institution, because of its immediate relation to the processes of adult life; its whole was greater than the sum of its parts, and a respect for the whole did not imply a respect for the parts considered separately; nor did the system require toleration of those who did not understand its real nature and direction. A man should keep the rules or take the consequences; he should finish his daily work, whole-heartedly, and without offering excuses for failure. Self-reliance meant not merely a willing acceptance of the Law, but much more than that, a readiness to exploit every opportunity to be found within its widest limits, a contempt for short views and niggardly interpretations of its purpose.

> This we learned from famous men,
> Knowing not we learned it.
> Only, as the years went by —
> Lonely, as the years went by —
> Far from help as years went by,
> Plainer we discerned it.

It may be thought difficult to reconcile this explanation with the fact that most of the incidents in *Stalky & Co.* deal with breaking school rules. But the three confederates set firm limits to their irregularities, in the book; and, in real life, were not such miscreants as they pretended to be. 'Stalky', like each of the others, wrote his reminiscences of schooldays, and his account is the least imaginative of the three. Lionel Dunsterville, though of about the same age as his two friends, had been sent to Westward Ho! two years before them. As the youngest boy in the school he had been cruelly ill-treated by the undisciplined young ruffians who made the first generation of seniors. When Beresford and Kipling arrived, in more civilized times, they listened with horrified fascination to his reminiscences of the heroic

age. He was an adventurous unaccountable boy, with an unhappy
home life, and a taste for solitary escapades. There was a type of
exploit in which he excelled, a feat or practical joke achieved without
leaving any trace by which the perpetrator could be identified. This
was the sort of conduct which, in the school slang, was described as
'stalky', the quality of a scout or stalker; and this was the meaning of
Dunsterville's nickname.[4] Beresford recorded a number of 'Stalky's'
actual feats which are of no great interest except as suggesting the
petty episodes which Kipling worked up into the epical adventures of
'Stalky & Co.' He would sit in an examination laboriously hiding a
paper on his knee until he could provoke a master into ordering him
to produce it. The paper would then prove to be blank. He would
allow himself to be seen going a little way out of bounds and, as soon
as he was sure of being pursued, would double back and establish an
alibi. He would evade the Church Service on Sunday morning by
slipping behind a buttress as the procession filed into the porch and,
an hour later, would join the emerging crowd, conspicuous with 'top
hat, gloves, and prayer book'.

The three boys in Number Five Study made 'Stalky' their leader
in most enterprises. All three cultivated an air of detachment from
the merely boyish activities of their fellows. Beresford's line was
ironical superiority, 'Stalky's' was adventurous individualism, while
Kipling, with his spectacles, his moustache, and his worldly knowledge,
seemed years older than his age. One pedant who was exposed to the
criticism of Number Five Study was their housemaster, Mr. M. H.
Pugh ('Prout' in *Stalky & Co.*). A suspicious, humourless, well-
meaning man, who could make nothing of these three boys because
they did not conform to the stock pattern of schoolboy life, he recognized no loftier conception of loyalty than observance of routine.
They obeyed his petty regulations so far as was inevitable and, otherwise, ignored him. A more sympathetic teacher was Mr. H. A. Evans
('Hartopp') to whom the boys owed a debt of gratitude for many
acts of kindness and encouragement. He was that useful sort of
schoolmaster who does more work out of class than in class at
organizing activities and stimulating hobbies. He formed a natural
history society, which Stalky & Co. frankly adopted as a justification
for long rambles along the cliffs and up the lanes of rural Devon. He
was an assiduous promoter of theatricals, with a talent for acting. A
great event at Westward Ho! was the performance of the *Rivals,* in
December 1881, with all three members of Number Five Study in the
cast.

Evans was not very handsomely treated in *Stalky & Co.,* where his
character is played down by contrast with that of 'Mr. King', Kipling's

most celebrated schoolmaster. 'King' is a composite character, chiefly built upon William Crofts who instructed Kipling in Latin and English Literature. The real Crofts is now so deeply buried beneath the fictitious 'King' that it is difficult to restore him to life. There is no doubt that their verbal duels marked a deep-seated bond of sympathy between this enthusiastic teacher and his talented pupil; and that the other boys were amazed at their dialectical exchanges. Kipling made it his business in class to draw out Mr. Crofts, and Crofts made it his to stimulate Kipling by irony and allusion. What would have been cruelty to a less mature pupil, and perhaps was cruelty to Kipling's fellows, was nourishment to Kipling's faculties. He throve on the abuse that Crofts lavished on him, picked his brain, looted his rich vocabulary, stored away his epigrams for digestion at leisure, and kept his own temper under the lash of the master's tongue, meeting the harshest strictures with a bland smile and a vacant stare from those brilliant blue eyes, which actually saw very little when his glasses were perched up on his eyebrows. Of all Kipling's teachers, Crofts taught him most, by damping down his exuberance, by forcing him to study the classical writers, by ridiculing his more pretentious experiments in verse. At no time in his adult life did Kipling much care what the critics said of him. They could hardly be ruder to him than Crofts had been, and they could not force him to attend, as could Crofts.

But 'King' in *Stalky & Co.* is not quite the same man. * He owes some features to another member of the staff, F. W. Haslam, who grounded Kipling in Latin during his first two years at school and then departed, to become a professor of classics in New Zealand. Haslam introduced Kipling to Horace, which he 'loathed for two years, forgot for twenty years, then loved with an abiding passion for the rest of his life'. The great political odes in the third Book of Horace made a substantial part of Kipling's education, which revealed itself ever more clearly in his mature verse style. Westward Ho! was a modern school, in which the old-fashioned classical training was neglected, to the great disgust of Haslam and Crofts. Apart from those Odes of Horace which he was obliged to study, Kipling had small Latin and less Greek — no Greek at all beyond a few elementary lessons on the Greek Testament.

It was Crofts who guided Kipling's taste in English Literature, largely by indirect methods. 'Gigger' was already known as the school poet when Crofts referred to him as 'Gigadibs, the literary man', and hurled a copy of Browning's *Men and Women* at his head so that he could find out for himself where the quotation came from.

* The later 'Stalky' stories: 'Regulus', 'The United Idolaters', 'The Propagation of Knowledge' present 'Mr. King' in a more favourable light.

This was the most judicious of gifts, which taught him more than whole seminars of formal instruction. He was already in a mood to imitate any new model. Poe and Swinburne began to give way to Browning, who provided him with a new wealth of matter and style. He was prepared to accept the name of 'Gigadibs' and to furnish his cabin for the voyage outward-bound into life as 'Bishop Blougram' recommended; he saw himself again as 'Fra Lippo Lippi' 'watching folks' faces'.[5]

> The shapes of things; their colours, lights and shades.

Behind Crofts, as a background to the life of Number Five Study, was the serene, unobtrusive figure of Cormell Price, the headmaster, a believer in the art of solving problems by judiciously leaving things alone. Not a classic, not a pietist, not a sportsman, not even a strong disciplinarian, Cormell Price was unusual among Victorian head-masters. It was Crofts, the second master, who embodied these tradi-tional characters, and deplored that classics, cricket, and churchmanship were not taken more seriously at Westward Ho!; it was Crofts who worked to build up the United Services College as a conventional Public School. He believed, as his contemporaries mostly did, in the virtues of corporal punishment. Not so the headmaster, a mild and kindly man. Price, who is called 'Bates' in *Stalky & Co.,* is there represented as a flogging teacher in the old tradition, a character which, said Beresford, was quite inconceivable to anyone who had known him. No such episode as that described in the story called 'A Little Prep' in which 'Bates' flogged all the senior boys, ever occurred at Westward Ho!, though similar holocausts were known at some other schools. As for the suggestion that Price could have flogged Kipling, Beresford regarded it as laughable. Rudyard and his 'Uncle Crom' conferred not only as family friends but, said Beresford, almost as social equals. Kipling's mature manner was such that he could not be treated as a child during his residence in Number Five Study.

Cormell Price never preached, and rarely addressed the assembled school. He devoted himself to managing his mixed team of assistants by tactful adjustment, and to getting his Army Class through their examinations. He was a brilliant teacher of English composition, and it was a shrewd decision on his part to put Kipling through the usual 'grind' although he was not going 'up for the Army'. He coached Kipling especially in précis-writing, a dreaded obstacle in the Army Examination, and a discipline that Kipling, the born writer, would need more than any soldier. There seems never to have been any doubt that 'Gigger' would become a literary man. His defect of sight prevented him from playing ballgames with the other boys, and gave Price the opportunity to nourish his talents, by special treatment, apart from them.

An attempt had been made to produce a school journal which had lapsed after three numbers, as such attempts often do. In 1881 Price launched it again with Kipling as editor. The *United Services College Chronicle* does not differ much from other such journals, nor are Kipling's own contributions much above the standard of what may be expected from clever schoolboys. It was, however, the first injection into his veins of the printer's ink that he never again worked out of his system. He was delighted with his school magazine, wrote three-quarters of it, sub-edited it, corrected proofs, and took the deepest interest in its production at a little printing shop at Bideford.

What were the formative influences in literature that gave direction to his thoughts, and mannerisms to his style, in this early imitative period of youth? He had pored over Defoe and Bunyan, Fielding and Smollett, Dickens and Thackeray even in his Southsea days. The first unusual book — unusual, that is to say, for a Victorian child — recorded by him as significant was Emerson's *Poems,* which he tackled in Epping Forest at the age of twelve. Contemporary American writing always attracted him. Echoes of Edgar Allan Poe recur again and again in his early verse and prose; he rated Longfellow higher as a poet than the common estimate today; then, with the easy receptiveness of youth, he was swept away with enthusiasm for Walt Whitman, to the disgust of Mr. Crofts who ridiculed this esoteric craze. Milton and Tennyson were enough for Mr. Crofts. The American humorists were much to the taste of Number Five Study, and, if the young Kipling can be said to have belonged to a 'literary school', it was to the school of Bret Harte. He was an admirer of Mark Twain too, and, when Harris's *Uncle Remus* came out in 1880, Kipling, like all the school and half the nation, was inflamed by it as by a fever. Boys and girls, if they are to be readers, should be omnivorous, and find their own way from softer to harder morsels. The boy who had found something attractive in Emerson at the age of twelve was ready for solid fare at fifteen. Beresford, like his betters in that age, was a disciple of Ruskin, and read *Fors Clavigera,* as it came out in weekly parts in the early 'eighties. This, and Carlyle's *Sartor Resartus,* no easy reading whatever else may be thought of it, were the books that the three boys talked over, in the hiding-place they made for themselves among the furze-bushes of the Burrows, and, later, in the room they hired from a cottager as a secret retreat. Emerson, Carlyle, Ruskin, Browning account for the mode of thought in which young Kipling began to form his own philosophy.

A book that taught him a technique was Landor's *Imaginary Con-*

versations, which set him to the task of writing in various styles and manners. Throughout life he easily composed parodies and imitations, and used them as an exercise in his craft of writing. More than most authors he wrote verses and tales in character, as conversation pieces in which the plot is revealed by a monologue, necessarily delivered in another style than his own; and, before he had learned the mastery of this technique, his work was coloured with derivative patches of imitation, conscious or unconscious. Especially in his early verse, characteristic though it is, the reader may remark with assurance, this stanza is after Swinburne, this after Poe, this after Browning.

It was now that Cormell Price took the decisive step in Kipling's education. He gave Kipling

the run of his brown-bound, tobacco-scented library; prohibiting nothing, recommending nothing. There Beetle [Kipling] found a fat arm-chair, a silver ink-stand and unlimited pens and paper. There were scores and scores of ancient dramatists, there were Hakluyt, his voyages; French translations of Muscovite authors called Pushkin and Lermontoff; little tales of a heady and bewildering nature, interspersed with unusual songs — Peacock was that writer's name; there were Borrow's *Lavengro;* an odd theme, purporting to be a translation of something called a ' Rubaiyat ', which the Head said was a poem not yet come to its own; there were hundreds of volumes of verse — Crashaw, Dryden; Alexander Smith; L.E.L.; Lydia Sigourney; Fletcher and a Purple Island; Donne; Marlowe's *Faust;* Ossian; *The Earthly Paradise; Atalanta in Calydon;* and Rossetti — to name only a few. Then the Head, drifting in under pretence of playing censor to the paper, would read here a verse and here another of these poets, opening up avenues. And, slow-breathing, with half-shut eyes above his cigar, would he speak of great men living, and journals, long dead, founded in their riotous youth, of years when all the planets were little new-lit stars trying to find their places in the uncaring void, and he, the Head, knew them as young men know one another.[6]

In his last year at Westward Ho! Kipling was already reaching forward to the wider world. His education had become a matter of personal relation with ' the Head ', his private life was concentrated in the happy family of Number Five Study. The three had made a compromise with the school organization and did not allow it to dominate their lives; Dunsterville and Beresford had their examinations to prepare for; Kipling was steeped in his reading and writing, and editing. Unknown to the school in general, unknown even to his study-mates, was the fact that Kipling was already the author of a book. Far away in India, his mother had collected, and persuaded his father to print for private circulation, a volume of *Schoolboy Lyrics* (1881), written by their talented son. Even the author did not know of this until much later. None of these verses have been reprinted in the standard collections of Kipling's poetry, and the volume is of interest today only as a collector's rarity. When the Kiplings left Lahore, twelve years later, heaps of unwanted copies of *Schoolboy Lyrics* were thrown away, as the collectors had not yet got wind of them. Cormell Price must, surely, have been in the secret of their publication, and must have corresponded with his old friend, Lockwood Kipling, now at Lahore, though the letters are not extant; it must have been with 'Crom's' connivance that young Rudyard's career was fostered. As early as December 1881, about the date when *Schoolboy Lyrics* appeared, Lockwood Kipling wrote to another friend that he proposed to 'bring Rudyard out to India next year, and get him some newspaper work. Oxford we can't afford. Ruddy thirsts for a man's life and a man's work'; and Ruddy developed so fast in the next six months that his promotion to manhood came even sooner. The little, chubby, laughing boy whom Beresford had befriended in 1878 was now, in 1882, a sturdy, talkative fellow of sixteen, muscular but not athletic. Swimming was the only sport permitted by his bad eyesight and swimming was his pleasure in the last year at school.

The three boys were venturesome, careless of the petty restrictions imposed by school-law, but innocent of all the grosser vices, ignorant of all the rending passions. A little poaching, a little smoking (which for some obscure reason was regulated by taboos in Victorian schools), some expeditions out of bounds, some calculated defiances of the school authorities, were not seen as grave matters by anyone except by Mr. Pugh and his kind. It was more significant that Kipling and Beresford were the arbiters of taste in the school, and Dunsterville learned how to profit from their reputation. They decorated the study with a stencilled pattern of chocolate and French grey in the best style of the aesthetic movement, bought pottery in the Bideford curiosity shops, and took pride in preserving rejected fragments of mediaeval wood-carving when Bideford church was restored. But when their taste developed and they wearied of these acquisitions, it was 'Stalky' who thought of selling them by auction to their envious school-fellows. 'Stalky', always penniless, was an adept at raising funds by selling what was superfluous, somebody's Sunday trousers to the Bideford pawnbroker, if the financial stringency was tight enough. Kipling, too, could raise money in his own way, and impressed the other two by selling an article to a London newspaper for no less than a guinea. *

The summer term of 1882 was the last in which the partnership was maintained. Kipling was to leave for India in the autumn while the other two were to sit for their examination in 1883. Kipling was

---

* We have Kipling's authority for this, in *Land and Sea Tales*. The article has not been identified.

restive, he was not sure that he wanted to go to India even though it meant rejoining his beloved parents. He was not to be a soldier like Stalky, nor a civil engineer like Beresford; he intended to be — was already — a literary man, and London, not Lahore, was the centre of the literary world. He told Beresford that he would cable to his father: ' I have married a wife and therefore I cannot come ', a remark that Beresford regarded as a mere joke, though it had a sharper point to it than he supposed. For a few weeks more, Kipling could be a boy and be amused by childish things. A lucky chance arose of scoring a last point against Mr. Crofts, when Beresford found a duplicate of the examination paper which Crofts had set, on Milton's *Lycidas*. No question of honour was involved since Beresford was not sitting for the examination and Kipling was taking it as a mere test of industry, which could bring him no prize or promotion. Kipling learned the answers to all the questions and Crofts, with the utmost reluctance, was obliged to award him full marks. Crofts bore no malice, and gave his best pupil a copy of *Aurora Leigh* as a parting gift.

Kipling's last numbers of the *College Chronicle* reflect the rapid maturing of his own character. Number ten contains the first of his early poems to display the Horatian neatness and compression which are so typical of his later verse. Confronted with Horace's Ode, *Donec gratus eram tibi,* as a task, which he had omitted to prepare and which he was punished for neglecting, he reproduced it in broad Devonshire, a version that merits preservation.[1]

> *He*—So long as 'twuz me alone
>   An' there wasn't no other chaps,
> I was praoud as a King on 'is throne —
>   Happier tu, per'aps.
>
> *She*—So long as 'twuz only I
>   An' there wasn't no other she
> Yeou cared for so much — surely
>   I was glad as glad could be.
>
> *He*—But now I'm in lovv with Jane Pritt —
>   She can play the piano, she can;
> An' if dyin' 'ud 'elp 'er a bit
>   I'd die laike a man.
>
> *She*—Yeou'm like me. I'm in lovv with Young Frye —
>   Him as lives out tu Appledore Quay;
> An' if dyin' 'ud 'elp 'im I'd die —
>   Twice ovver for he.

He—But s'posin' I threwed up Jane
  An' niver went walkin' with she —
  An' come back to yeou again —
  How 'ud that be?

She—Frye's sober. Yeou've allus done badly —
  An' yeou shifts like cut net-floats, yeou du:
  But — I'd throw that young Frye ovver gladly
  An' lovv 'ee right thru!

Number eight of the *Chronicle,* March 1882, contains the poem, ' Ave Imperatrix! ', which Mr. Eliot found worthy of a place in his selection from Kipling's Verse. It surprised Beresford, it surprised Stalky, and Beresford stated that it even surprised the author. Perhaps no critic then noticed that it was a direct imitation of a poem which Oscar Wilde had published, with the same title, a year earlier. It was a tribute, in the conventional language of patriotism and loyalty, to Queen Victoria, after her escape from death by assassination. No one then regarded ' Gigger ' as a writer of ' patriotic ' verse. He was a rebel and a progressive which is to say, in 1882 — paradoxically — that he was a decadent. His friends, his teachers, were liberals, his tastes were ' aesthetic ', the writers he most admired were the fashionable pessimists. One of his favourite poems was James Thomson's *City of Dreadful Night.* If he were to take the loyalist side in controversy, it could only be as another provocation to Crofts, the pacifist and liberal. The poem hardly seemed in character, but, before another year was out, Kipling's view of life would be revealed as something unsuspected.

There was much about Rudyard Kipling that Beresford and Dunsterville did not know. In the holidays he vanished into a world that differed profoundly from that known to the average officer's family. As he grew older and could travel alone, he paid visits to a widening circle of cousins on the Macdonald side, most of them a year or two younger than himself. His English home, in his later years at school, was with three sisters, Mrs. Winnard, and the two Miss Craiks, old family friends who lived at Warwick Gardens, South Kensington. They were immersed in literary society, proud of having known Carlyle, and intimate with the admired writers of the 'eighties. But theirs was a little house and their habits too neat and quiet to satisfy a singularly active, curious, noisy, talkative schoolboy, always prying into things to find out how they worked, a boy who never for a moment abstained from laughing and joking. There was one year (1880) when his mother came home, in time to nurse him through a bout of quinsy at Warwick Gardens and, when Trix came to join them, the little house overflowed. Ruddy was then sent to his cousins, Fred Macdonald's children, who never forgot his visit; never had they known such larks.* Not far away were the Poynters, at that date the most eminent branch of the family, since their father was a fashionable R.A. At the Poynters' or at the Burne-Joneses', as in his father's house, all the talk was of the fine arts and in the jargon of the studio. Later in life, Ruddy was to be on the closest terms of friendship with Ambrose Poynter; at this time he saw more of his Burne-Jones' cousins. Perhaps his closest friend was Margaret Burne-Jones, the cousin nearest his own age, who shared with him, and Trix, a round of private jokes and secret nicknames. The earliest writings of Rudyard Kipling to see the light were in the family magazine, *The Scribbler,* which he produced with the Burne-Jones and Morris children in 1879.

Rudyard and Trix sometimes spent holidays together. She recalled one summer at Witley in Surrey, where the nightingales kept them awake, and another occasion when he came down to Southsea to bring her away from Mrs. Holloway's. This was in 1880, when Rudyard was fourteen and a half years old, and when something occurred which may explain why he was more mature than Beresford or Dunsterville. He fell in love.

Another paying guest whose parents were abroad, a girl called Florence Garrard, had come to live with 'Aunty Rosa' at Southsea; she was a little older than Rudyard, a straight slender girl with a beautiful ivory-pale face and a cloud of dark hair, but badly brought up in continental hotels and very ill-educated. With a shrewd sophisticated manner, she was self-centred and elusive, lacking in sympathy and affection. Trix was devoted to her and pleased to supervise her reading, while Rudyard fell an easy prey. Manlike he idolized her as a Pre-Raphaelite heroine; and boylike he noticed with malicious pleasure that she kept a pet goat which always butted 'Aunty Rosa'. Calf-love is not to be despised because it shows symptoms which the immune consider ludicrous. Where and how often Flo and Rudyard met was their own secret. He was faithful to her image for five or six years at least, and hard-hit again when he met her long afterwards. When he was ordered off to India, he begged her to consent to an engagement — he was then sixteen and she seventeen or eighteen; when he sailed, he supposed himself to be engaged to her.[8] But she? Her story is lost. She reserved herself, to make a career of her own

* He came in one day tense with anger — rolled on the nursery floor in fury. 'Why, Ruddy! What's the matter?' 'The porter at the station boxed my ears.' 'But what made him box your ears?' 'Oh, I expect I cheeked him.' His manner changed; he smiled, and went towards the door with a purposeful look. 'Where are you going, Ruddy?' 'Back to the station to cheek that porter again' [Miss F. Macdonald].

with her drawings, which were not much admired by the Kiplings. A sketch-book of hers which survives in America is decorated with 'doodles' by Rudyard, on the blank pages. Her drawings are the conventional studies of Victorian art schools; his scribbles reveal a much stronger line and clearer vision.[9]

Rudyard was to leave England in September so as to arrive in India at the end of the hot weather. His last summer holiday he spent partly at Rottingdean where a colony of cousins on the Macdonald side made their holiday home, and partly at Skipton with his Kipling grandmother 'an old-fashioned Puritan saint, with a face like a chaste cameo'. On 20th September 1882 he sailed from Tilbury by the P. & O. steamer *Brindisi*, alone and seasick, in drizzling rain.

CHAPTER IV

LAHORE AND SIMLA (1882–7)

THE NEW KNIGHTHOOD (1909)

Who lays on the sword?
'I,' said the Sun,
'Before he has done,
'I'll lay on the sword.'

. . . .

Who gives him his spur?
'I,' said his Chief,
Exacting and brief,
'I'll give him the spur.'

Who'll shake his hand?
'I,' said the Fever,
'And I'm no deceiver,
'I'll shake his hand.'

Who brings him the wine?
'I,' said Quinine,
'It's a habit of mine.
'*I'll* come with his wine.'

Who'll put him to proof?
'I,' said All Earth.
'Whatever he's worth,
'I'll put to the proof.'

Who'll choose him for Knight?
'I,' said his Mother,
'Before any other,
'My very own Knight.'

And after this fashion, adventure to seek,
Was Sir Galahad made — as it might be last week!

TO a boy who was just beginning to take an interest in public
affairs, a voyage to India in the autumn of 1882 was indeed an
adventure; it took him through the middle of a battlefield. The year
1882 was the climax of a period of colonial wars, which, according to

34

your political alignment, you might describe as the bloody consequence of Disraeli's aggressive policy, or the confusion caused by Gladstone's weak handling of situations bequeathed to him in hopeful shape. The nation had muddled through the Zulu War in 1879, had accepted defeat at Majuba in 1880, had watched without comprehension the wanton invasion and the equally wanton evacuation of Afghanistan, uncertain whether to applaud Roberts's brilliant campaigns or to lament a costly reverse at Maiwand. But it was Gladstone, not Disraeli, who intervened in Egypt with operations by sea and land, which were a model of efficiency. Egypt was bankrupt, and controlled by an international commission which was obliged to act when the nationalist revolt of Arabi Pasha broke out. Massacres took place in Cairo, the British Consul was attacked and, when Arabi's men mounted batteries on the foreshore against the French and British fleets in the harbour at Alexandria, Gladstone authorized the bombardment of the forts by the British fleet alone, a naval operation that won great celebrity. This last appearance in action of the old three-decker navy occurred on 11th July 1882, during Kipling's final term at school. A few days later Sir Garnet Wolseley landed at Ismailia with an army that included the Brigade of Guards. All went like clockwork and, after a night march through the desert, Sir Garnet totally defeated Arabi Pasha at the cost of 450 British casualties, and thus began the British occupation of Egypt.

Nine days after the battle of Tel-el-Kebir, Rudyard Kipling's ship left London River for the East. The newspapers, in this golden age of the war-correspondents, were filled with telegraphed reports of the battle; the weeklies with pages of illustration worked up from sketches made by war-artists at the front. The Suez Canal was the prize of victory, the centre of attention, and it was reported that snipers had fired upon the last P. & O. mailboat as it passed through. Dunsterville, a schoolboy still at Westward Ho!, must have been consumed with envy of 'Gigger' now a man of the world, outward bound for the seat of war. On 2nd October he was at Port Said where his ship lay four days before venturing into the Canal; he reached Suez on the 7th. Not a line of direct evidence survives to show what this born journalist made of his opportunity then and there. While, fifty miles from Port Said, the battlefield lay open, strewn with unburied corpses, the exits from the town were blocked by sentries, and it is unlikely that he saw more than 'the straight line of the Canal, the blazing sands, the procession of shipping, and the white hospitals where the English soldiers lay'.[1] That he absorbed and remembered the sights and sounds of a base-camp close behind the battle, and sensed the raffish atmosphere of Port Said and Suez, is evident from the boldly

imaginative sketches he inserted into *The Light that Failed,* ten years
later.

More directly he was moved by the two-sidedness of his life. The
two halves of it were symbolized by the contrast between Europe and
Asia. 'East of Suez' he was in an old mental atmosphere as well as
in another economy. In childhood the voyage to England, from light
to darkness, had symbolized a transition from perfect happiness to
protracted misery. But now, he was not so sure. Dark Europe had
given him friendship and promised him love. What more had bright
Asia to offer? Recalling this hesitation at the edge of the East, he
wrote in later years:

> Port Said marks a certain dreadful and exact division between East and
> West. Up to that point — it is a fringe of palms against the sky — the
> impetus of home memories and the echo of home interests carry the young
> man along very comfortably on his first journey. But at Suez one must
> face things. People, generally the most sympathetic, leave the boat there;
> the older men who are going on have discovered each other and begun to
> talk shop; no newspapers come aboard, only clipped Reuter telegrams; the
> world seems cruelly large and self-absorbed. . . . Then one begins to
> wonder when one will see those palms from the other side. Then the
> black hour of home-sickness, vain regrets, foolish promises, and weak
> despair shuts down with the smell of strange earth and the cadence of
> strange tongues.

He reached Bombay, his birthplace, on 18th October 1882, and the
bright world of Asia revealed to him a new nostalgia. This, not dark
Europe, was after all his home, the place of his happy childhood. He
would warn his school-fellows to have no regrets or fears, for each of
them, Anglo-Indians by right, would make a discovery on returning
to India.

> The evening smells and the sight of the hibiscus and poinsettias will
> unlock his tongue in words and sentences that he thought he had clean
> forgotten, and he will go back to his ship as a prince entering on his
> Kingdom.[2]

Lahore, where Lockwood and Alice Kipling had been living for
seven years, was a pleasant station during the cool season, with about
seventy British residents in the civil lines. Lockwood had come from
Bombay to continue his former work as Principal of the Mayo School
of Art and Curator of the Lahore Museum. In the first days after his
arrival Rudyard helped in the Museum which his father had made a
model collection of Indian arts and archaeology, much used by students
and crowded with Indian sightseers.

The Museum stands, just as it is described in the first chapter of
Kim, near the Mall, the wide boulevard that runs from the European

quarter to the old walled city. Out beyond the canal was Mian Mir, the military cantonment that housed a British Infantry Battalion and a battery of Artillery. Nearer to the city, stood bungalows in large gardens, the Punjab Club, colleges and schools, and a row of shops and offices in European style behind a line of acacias. Among them, in two wooden sheds was placed the printing office of the *Civil and Military Gazette,* the provincial newspaper of which Rudyard was to be assistant editor. In November he commenced work and on Christmas Eve, a week before his seventeenth birthday, he found himself in temporary control, because the editor, Stephen Wheeler, was in bed after a carriage accident. Stephen Wheeler was perhaps a little piqued at being confronted, and then temporarily supplanted, by this lively subordinate, none the less because the youngster was a *protégé* of the proprietors.

The *Civil and Military Gazette* had been founded, ten years earlier, by two remarkable men, both of them sons of British soldiers, who had taken their discharge in India, had settled, and had married in the country. Rudyard's first patron, James Walker, had started a prosperous career by organizing transport between the Plains and the summer capital at Simla; the other founder, William Rattigan, was a leading member of the Lahore Bar. Together they made a success of their journal, largely because it was carried by a well-established printing house, which held the printing contract for the provincial authorities and, accordingly, their editorial policy was presumed to be a reflection of the views of the Punjab Government. Next, they had taken the bold step of buying a controlling interest in a larger concern, six hundred miles down-country, the *Pioneer,* which George Allen had established at Allahabad, then the railway centre of India. Unlike the *Civil and Military Gazette,* the *Pioneer* became an all-India newspaper with a name for being so well-informed that its pronouncements were often taken as demi-official. Howard Hensman, the *Pioneer* representative at Simla, was reputed to know all the secrets, especially to be in the confidence of Sir Frederick Roberts, the Commander-in-Chief. ('Roberts made him', it used to be whispered, 'and he made Roberts.') Down at Allahabad Allen was known as a brilliant organizer whose success was due to finding talented subordinates and riding them with a loose rein, a system that sometimes ran him and his paper into trouble. Allen, like Walker, was an old friend of Lockwood Kipling and his wife, both of whom wrote occasionally for the *Pioneer.* He watched over Rudyard, too, and found openings for him.

A paper in Lahore was worthwhile because of the key position of the Punjab in the Indian Empire. It was a new province, conquered and annexed less than thirty years before the Kiplings came to Lahore, the scene of the labours of John Lawrence and his team of assistants, the most efficient band of administrators in Indian history. The Punjab was notable for progress in irrigation, land settlement, and afforestation, for roads and railways; it was a healthy prosperous wheat-growing province with a population of sturdy peasants, a more pleasing place to English eyes than crowded fever-stricken Bengal, the land of political unrest.

In the cool weather the civil lines at Lahore were agreeable enough, but the Mall led to something more significant, the old walled city, perhaps the most picturesque of all the cities of Islam, where two hundred thousand people of all the races of Asia lived as their forefathers had lived in the days of the Arabian Nights. Lahore was predominantly a Moslem city famous for the Mosque of Wazir Khan, for the Shalimar Gardens, and for the tomb of the Emperor Jahangir, beyond the broad shingly bed of the River Ravi. It was more recently celebrated for the short-lived and memorable Sikh kingdom of Runjeet Singh, the last lord of the grim square fortress stained with much blood, haunted by many ghosts, which commanded the town, over against the great mosque. Many old men, still living in Lahore in 1882, could well remember the great king whose court was the last in India quite untainted by western progress. In Kipling's day, a company of British infantry were encamped among the faded splendours of Runjeet's Palace, to overawe Sikh and Moslem alike. Now they, too, are gone, and the Moslems have resumed their sway over a city half in ruins that hide the bodies of uncounted Sikhs killed in the massacres of 1947.

In 1883 the re-discovery of India was a complete and absorbing occupation to young Rudyard; it was sheer delight to be treated as a man, not only at home but at work and at the Punjab Club. He had his personal servant, a Moslem and the son of his father's servant, his own quarters in his parents bungalow, his horse — a temperamental bay pony named 'Joe' which he found difficult to manage — and a trap in which he drove down to the office. There, he was half the European staff, and sometimes more than that, because Stephen Wheeler was often ill with fever. Machines and type, which he thought he understood already, and one hundred and seventy Indian printing-hands were under his eye, but when Wheeler was on duty, he was kept hard at routine. Wheeler formed the notion that young Kipling was too literary a chap; and was concerned to knock the nonsense out of him. The junior's task was to read the telegrams from the news-agencies and make up copy for the edition that went to press at midnight. To that he was restricted and for that work 'Uncle Crom's' training had prepared him. Lockwood Kipling thought that routine under an exacting chief was a useful discipline for his talented exuberant son.

Ruddy is getting on well, [he wrote to a friend] having mastered the details of his work in a very short time. His chief, Mr. Wheeler, is very tetchy and irritable, and by dint of his exertions in patience and forbearance, the boy is training for heaven as well as for editorship. I am sure he is better here . . . where there are no music-hall ditties to pick up, no young persons to philander about with, and a great many other negatives of the most wholesome description. All that makes Lahore profoundly dull makes it safe for young persons.[3]

Mrs. Kipling was not so sure. Her boy was devoted to her, but his temperament caused her some little anxiety. What boy of seventeen does not arouse questionings in his mother's heart? She had regretted the reticence of his school letters, had questioned the prudence of forcing so lively a youngster on the three old ladies of Warwick Gardens, had waited avidly for his arrival, and now found him strangely moody. If 'Trix's' story may be accepted, Ruddy sulked for three days, when he found that his mother had printed his *Schoolboy Lyrics* without his permission. A man's life and a man's independence did not, at first, quite sort with domesticity. What appealed to him was a room of his own.

In June 1883, having stayed down on the Plains later than usual to see Rudyard through his first bout of Indian heat, she left her husband and her son, while setting sail for England to meet her daughter. For some weeks, when his father went on leave to the Hills, Rudyard was alone in the house with the Indian servants. Then he, too, had his thirty days at Simla, staying with James Walker, his employer. In August he was again alone at Lahore with the season at its most oppressive, much fever in the station, and the number of Europeans reduced to a dozen jaded, sickly men whose women-folk were away at the Hills. Work was more exacting in short-handed times, and must be done, fever or no fever. The *Civil and Military* must go to press. The modern reader should be reminded that this was India in the heroic age, without refrigerators, without electric fans, without D.D.T. It was hardly yet understood that cholera was a water-borne infection, not known that mosquitoes carried malaria. An English *sahib* might enjoy some rude luxuries in India, but tropical disease then struck down its victims, high- or low-caste without social discrimination. Was it more disheartening to sit alone, sweating in a darkened bungalow, or to spend the evening in chance company at the Club where prickly heat made prickly tempers? Kipling was the youngest Englishman in the station, the junior in a newspaper office, a post which did not rank high among appointments in that caste-ridden society. As yet he was only an honorary member of the Club, lucky to have the entrée, and not a popular member. Political feeling ran high that season over the Ilbert Bill which deprived Anglo-Indians of the legal privilege of trial by European judges in special courts. When the proprietors of his newspaper, * who at first had opposed the Bill, decided to withdraw from active opposition, Kipling was actually hissed in the smoking-room of the Club, and was so green that he did not know why.

During that hot weather of 1883, for the first time in his life, he knew loneliness and found it unbearable. His work was night-work, his lifelong habit to wander in the small hours. After the paper had been put to press in the sultry Indian midnight, he would find his way into the old walled city, penetrating into courts and alleys where few Europeans went, watching for the dawn which might bring a breath of cooler air. There was a theme that ran in his head, uniting loneliness, fever, and a sleeping city; it was James Thomson's *City of Dreadful Night.*

> The street-lamps burn amidst the baleful glooms
> Amidst the soundless solitudes immense
> Of ranged mansions dark and still as tombs.
> The silence which benumbs or strains the sense
> Fulfils with awe the soul's despair unweeping;
> Myriads of habitants are ever sleeping,
> Or dead or fled from nameless pestilence!

The motive of sleeplessness amid silent multitudes in the tropical darkness recurs again and again in Kipling's early verse and prose:

a stifling hot blast from the mouth of the Delhi Gate nearly ends my resolution of entering the City of Dreadful Night at this hour. It is compounded of all evil savours, animal and vegetable, that a walled city can brew in a day and a night. The temperature within the motionless groves of plantain and orange trees outside the city walls seem chilly by comparison.

Then silence follows — the silence that is full of the night noises of a great city. A stringed instrument of some kind is just, and only just, audible. High overhead some one throws open a window, and the rattle of the woodwork echoes down the empty street. On one of the roofs a hookah is in full blast: and the men are talking softly as the pipe gutters. . . . It is close upon midnight and the heat seems to be increasing. The moonlight stripes the Mosque's high front of coloured enamel work in

---

* In *Something of Myself,* R. K. hints that one of his proprietors was angling for a knighthood. Actually, Allen, Walker, and Rattigan were all knighted, but not until a much later date.

broad diagonal bands, and each separate dreaming pigeon in the niches and corners of the masonry throws a squat little shadow. Sheeted ghosts rise up wearily from their pallets, and flit into the dark depths of the building. . . .[4]

'Doré might have drawn it! Zola could describe it—' so young Kipling commented on the scene, and so, by night and alone, he formulated his own version of it. In the morning, having bathed and breakfasted and taken 'Joe' for a canter, from which horse and rider sometimes returned separately, he could put all that morbidity aside, and keep a stiff upper lip before Stephen Wheeler or the fellows at the Club. He wrote long letters to Margaret Burne-Jones, and to his Aunt Edie, the youngest of the Macdonald sisters and the only one to remain unmarried. She was at this time his confidante and, as boys do, he showed off his manliness to her.

Rudyard Kipling to Miss Edith Macdonald

LAHORE, August 14th, 1883

DEAREST AUNTIE,

Your 'expansive' note greeting me on my return from Simla where I had been spending a month with one of the proprietors to my own exceeding delight. Privilege leave, as I may have told you before gives you the pleasant duty of enjoying yourself in a cool climate for thirty days and being paid £20 for that duty. The month was a round of picnics, dances, theatricals and so on — and I flirted with the bottled up energy of a year on my lips. Don't be horrified for there were about half a dozen of 'em and I took back the lacerated fragments of my heart as I distributed my P.P.C. cards and returned the whole intact, to Flo Garrard's keeping as per usual. I was nearly eight hours a day in the saddle and at the end of the month found out that I could actually ride anywhere without turning giddy. Simla is built round the sides of a mountain 8400 feet high and the roads are just ledges. At first they turned my head a good deal but in a little I was enabled to canter anyhow and anywhere. Now of course Lahore is as level as a billiard table and Joe had had no work for a fortnight when I came back so you can imagine what a time we had. There are 9 men and 2 ladies in the station and most of these are going away. Practically I am living at the Club. I dine there every night and go home to the big house to sleep. The dullness is something hideous after all the bustle of Simla.[5]

At last, the rains broke, the cool weather came and life at Lahore was again endurable without sleepless vigils, but 1883 ended in solitary discomfort for young Kipling. Again he was left alone for two months in the bungalow while his father went down to Bengal to prepare a display for the Calcutta Exhibition. He had no resource as yet, but to write contributions for the *United Services College Chronicle* which he despatched to 'Stalky'. He started a friendly correspondence with

Mr. Crofts, sending him copies of all the verses he wrote in India, and telling him of his dull routine. Crofts preserved these letters with care and made a collection, probably the most complete collection, of Kipling's early work.* Then in the New Year came the beginning of a new life, when his mother arrived from England with his sister, Trix, not yet sixteen but as advanced for her years as Rudyard for his. It was unusual to bring out so young an English girl to India.

The next four years (January 1884 to November 1887) made a rounded, complete, and satisfying period in Rudyard Kipling's life, they formed his mental habits. At seventeen he was a clever, precocious boy, high-spirited and assertive but untidy and untrained. Only those who knew him intimately, his mother and his 'Uncle Crom', distinguished him in quality from other clever boys. At twenty-one he was astonishingly mature, already the Rudyard Kipling whose name and features and point of view were to be world-famous. It was not the glamour of the East, nor the splendour of the British *Raj,* nor the knowledge of cities and men, that formed his character, he was observant enough to have found 'copy' anywhere; it was — to use a favourite expression of his mother's — the Family Square. He surveyed the Indian scene, which happened to be his field of action, from the secure base of a family life that was not only happy but four-square and, it seemed, impregnable. Father, mother, son, and daughter, all were talented, all different in their talents, all appreciative of each other's qualities, all devoted to one another and to the family group. The father — solid, practical, genial, with a hard core of north-country granite in his composition; the mother quick, intuitive, sympathetic, witty, and sharp-tongued; the daughter slight and graceful, poetic, ethereal, 'fey'; the son — as yet the least prepossessing member of the family but abnormally receptive. His father's wide range of knowledge, wise simplicity, and manual dexterity held his respect; his mother's easy skill at managing men, her natural ascendancy in any company compelled his wonder, his sister's young charm — he spoke of her as 'the Maiden' or 'the Ice-maiden' — delighted him. At home he could be candid and happy; and at home the other three, whom he so deeply admired, who made his life so pleasant, whose criticism was welcome because kind, fostered his genius which they had not failed to recognize. The family square made the only audience he cared to please. Let the world outside approve or disapprove. The family square could resist any external pressure.

They knew he had another love and it is hard to say how deeply the separation from Flo Garrard wounded him. A favourite theme

* William Crofts died in 1911. His collections were sold in America and dispersed.

of his early stories is the fading out of a romantic attachment between a young man in India and a girl at home. In these stories he not infrequently caricatures himself in a sentence or two.

Next to a requited attachment, one of the most convenient things that a young man can carry about with him at the beginning of his career, is an unrequited attachment. It makes him feel important and business-like, and *blasé,* and cynical; and whenever he has a touch of liver, or suffers from want of exercise, he can mourn over his lost love, and be very happy in a tender, twilight fashion.[6]

Eighteen months after his departure from London, about July 1884, Flo Garrard wrote to put an end to the engagement. Perhaps the association had been wearing thin, perhaps the breach when it came was not unwelcome, even though he remained enslaved to her memory. His comment was a set of verses written before the end of the year.

> One brought Her Fire from a distant place,
> And She — what should She know of it? . . .
>
> .   .   .   .   .
>
> Sudden She crushed the embers 'neath Her heel, —
> And all light went with Her.[7]

Rudyard Kipling had no other passionate love affair in India. His work, which was always based upon his experience, reveals some study of feminine psychology, some interest in the variations of the sexual pattern, even at one time a strong attraction towards illicit unions between European men and Asiatic women, but no shred of evidence survives of any amorous experience more moving than a drawing-room flirtation, while there is much evidence that he shrank from intimacy with women, other than the two who fixed the base of the family square.

Throughout the cooler half of the year, from November to April, the four lived happily together, in a square brick-built bungalow at Lahore. It differed from twenty others only in standing isolated in a dusty compound, because the Kiplings had progressive notions that insects brought disease, and that shrubberies too near a house brought insects. The neighbours called the bungalow 'Bikanir House' because its surroundings reminded them of the Great Indian Desert. Here 'the pater' had his workroom filled with tools and patterns and materials of his many arts. Mrs. Kipling was an expert housekeeper, and noted for inducing her native servants to keep a standard of cleanliness rare in India in those days.

Rudyard's room was devoted to literature and, after Trix's arrival, to the joint study of English poetry. The two were continually read-

ing and rhyming, with some sharp but helpful criticism from their
mother who had an ear for a false rhythm or a false sentiment. She
pruned Rudyard's verses as effectively as she eliminated Trix's school-
girl clumsiness; he was trained into terseness of style, and she into
elegance of figure. In the evenings, if he could find an hour, she
taught him to dance; and in the mornings the two young people went
riding — Rudyard taught Trix to ride. Poor as was his eyesight, he
took pains with his riding and even played a little polo, in spite of his
parents' prohibition, when time permitted.

Soon his directors began to send him off as a special reporter on
public events. In March 1884 he went to Patiala State, in the train
of Lord Ripon the Viceroy, and wrote home with gusto about the
splendours of princely hospitality. Even a journalist, at such a time,
had horses and a carriage, then actually an elephant, placed at his
disposal. As a newspaperman it pleased him that he forestalled his
rivals in getting off a despatch by riding thirty miles at night, across
country, on a borrowed horse. This starlit ride was to provide him
with an incident for *The Naulahka.*

It gratified his sense of responsibility, on this expedition, to be offered
— and of course to refuse — more than one bribe from agents of Indian
princes. One such affair he described, with gusto, and perhaps with
some heightening of colour, in a letter to his Aunt Edie. He was
invited into the room of an Afghan *sirdar* at Lahore and was, he said,
baldly invited to help himself to a bundle of bank-notes as an inducement to use the influence of his newspaper on the *sirdar's* behalf.
When he indignantly replied that he was not a *bunnia* but an English
sahib, the *sirdar* changed his ground.

Finally he blurted out that the English were fools and didn't know the
value of money but that ' all *sahibs* knew how to value women and horses '.
Whereupon he sent a small boy into an inner chamber and, to my intense
amusement, there came out a Cashmiri girl that Moore might have raved
over. She was very handsome and beautifully dressed but I didn't quite
see how she was to be introduced into an English household like ours. I
rather lost my temper and abused the Khan pretty freely for this last piece
of impudence and told him to go to a half-caste native newspaper-walla for
what he wanted.

The third temptation was that Rudyard should take his pick of a
string of horses, such beauties that, he admitted, his resolution began
to waver. However, he concluded: 'I explained very gravely that I
wasn't going to help him a bit and he ought to have known better than
to "blacken an Englishman's face" in the way he had done'. The
interview ended amicably over a cup of coffee which, he was pleased
to find, contained no poison after all.[8]

In May the family moved to the Hills, leaving him to face the dismal, feverish, hot weather again. For six months there would be nothing to relish but the dwindling company at the Club. At best, he and his father would sustain one another at Bikanir House; and worse would be the long weeks when he was alone with fever, sleeplessness, and nightmares. Eighty-four was worse than eighty-three; it was a cholera year at Lahore. 'Professional nurses had not been invented, the men sat up with the men and the women with the women. The station had eleven cases in a white community of seventy, and thought it lucky that only four died.'[9] Later in the season Rudyard was laid low with gastric pains and was saved from collapse by his bearer, who dosed him with drugs compounded of opium, drugs that cured his stomach and troubled his dreams. This hot season was worse than the last because he felt his separation from the family square. The other three were at Dalhousie, a cheaper hill-station than Simla, and better suited to their slender purse. For one month he joined them, and returned to the Plains with the manuscript of *Echoes,* a volume of imitations and parodies in verse, written by himself and Trix. Most were humorous mock-heroic trifles, but one or two (among them the poem called 'Failure' which has already been quoted) were serious exercises in the style of contemporary writers. The book was printed at the *Civil and Military* office in November, and received some kindly notices from reviewers. When the first issue, a very small one, was sold out, there was even an enquiry from a Calcutta publisher about a new edition. The parodies, especially those of Robert Browning, are remarkably facile and show a neat sense of varieties in rhythm, but none of them has been thought worth preserving in the popular collections of Kipling's work. *Echoes* and the articles he wrote for his newspapers were beginning to attract a little notice in India, among the well-informed. Most of his work was still anonymous journalism, and he used several pen-names for the articles he was beginning to contribute to down-country journals.

Rudyard Kipling to Miss Edith Macdonald

LAHORE, Nov. 21st, 1884

DEAREST AUNTIE,

The beginning of your last letter cut me to the core of my somewhat leathery conscience; for, as a matter of fact, I haven't sent you a line since you acknowledged the receipt of *Echoes* and so wildly mistook the dedication thereof. No dear I did *not* write those verses for Flo, and if I had should certainly not have sent you a duplicate. Pope was the only man who ever did that and he came to a bad end. I must confess that at first I was a good deal hurt at the mistake but accidents will occur in the best regulated families and I suppose your error was one of 'em. By the way

that book has been most favourably noticed all round India and the whole
edition is sold out. *The World* too was good enough to give me a nice
little notice and I'm proportionately pleased. There was only one paper —
The *Indian Review* that cut 'em up savagely and by way of showing that
I bore no malice I cut out the slashingest parts and put 'em into the
advertisement — the consequence was all the world and his wife when they
heard that the poems were vicious sent in orders for the book and we
scored hugely.

Like you I've been writing a story in my leisure. It has only taken me
three months and is only six pages long but I've never fallen in love with
any tale of my own fashioning so much — not that it has any merit. I'm
trying to work it off on some alien paper to get myself pice thereby. Now
that I'm allowed to write to any rag I please I find that I can always get
a few odd pounds a month for myself apart from my screw and incidentally
can get myself a little bit known in our small world out here. This is an
empty headed sort of letter I'm afraid but there's really nothing to write
about except the weather and crops — and they won't interest you. My
Love to Aunt Louie and Uncle Alfred Baldwin — It's curious to think,
how little I've ever seen of the two — and my salaams to Stanley. I'd give
something to be in the Sixth at Harrow as he is, with a University Education
to follow.[10]

At the end of 1884 a new Viceroy, Lord Dufferin, arrived in India,
an event which proved to be of personal interest to the Kiplings.
Obscure hitherto, and not ranking high in the Anglo-Indian hierarchy
they soon found themselves exalted into vice-regal society. The first
event of Lord Dufferin's term of office was his ceremonial reception
of the Amir Abdurrahman in March 1885 at Rawalpindi, where
Rudyard was special correspondent for his paper. The Frontier had
been remarkably quiet since the close of the Second Afghan War in
1881 and the new Amir, a formidable autocrat, had proved a staunch
ally to the British. Nevertheless it was a diplomatic triumph to
persuade him to pay a state visit to the Viceroy, who made preparations
for his entertainment on a splendid scale. A city of marquees was
erected and lavishly furnished for the Viceroy's camp, and a long
programme of ceremonies, reviews, and festivities was arranged. All
went well except the weather, which was abominable, a constant down-
pour of drenching rain; and all was described at length by Rudyard
for the *Pioneer* and the *Civil and Military*. Kipling was among those
who went on to Peshawar and nine miles farther to Fort Jumrood at
the mouth of the Khyber Pass, to attend the formal reception of the
Amir at the frontier post. While waiting some days at Jumrood,
Kipling wandered into the Pass, turning back only when a tribesman
'took a pot-shot' at him. This was his first and last experience of the
North-West Frontier.[11]

He was by no means ignorant of the Central Asian problem, because for months past Wheeler had kept him grinding away at translating Russian newspaper reports. (In those days many Russian newspapers were issued in French.) Rudyard's articles on Afghanistan and its neighbours attracted notice and he remarked, with mixed pride and annoyance, that the London *Times* appropriated one of these articles without acknowledgment. *

At the height of the festivities at Rawalpindi, all Asia was thrown into panic by the news that the Russians had made a calculated aggression against Afghanistan, invading the Amir's territory at Penjdeh in his absence. But the Amir and Lord Dufferin faced the crisis with equanimity, and it was considered an achievement for Dufferin that he concluded the proceedings at Rawalpindi with assurances from the Amir of a firm front against Russian penetration. The tension was relaxed, Dufferin returned in triumph, and even young Rudyard won some credit as a useful, well-informed journalist.

Though he had completed his task, he suffered for it; the hard work and the bad weather wore him out. His eyes were giving him trouble and he slept badly, with nightmares of endless columns marching in the rain. The rhythm of ' Boots, boots, boots, boots, moving up and down again', to the tune of 'John Brown's Body', drummed itself into his memory and lay dormant there for years. He got his needed holiday in May when the chance came of an adventurous trip from Simla up the Himalaya–Tibet Road that loops and twists across the screes and the fertile valleys, through forest-belts of deodar, to the high mountain ranges that command the gorges of the Sutlej. The party consisted of young Kipling, a man in the Public Works Department named De Brath with his newly wedded wife, their servants from down-country, and relays of hill-coolies to carry baggage. They rode on ponies and spent the night at the wayside dâk-bungalows — mere huts — provided by the Government at the regular stages. Kipling found himself odd man out in what was almost a honeymoon party and was envious of his companions' happiness. On the journey the wife coyly admitted that she was in the family way, a felicitous event that Kipling remembered to use in *The Story of the Gadsbys.*

The two men were sadly out of condition for mountain marching. 'I feel,' wrote Kipling in his diary, 'as if hot irons were stuck down my marrow bones.' On the 1st of May they reached Mahasu, lay on the grass watching the eagles fly in the valley below them, and felt the strength flowing back into their limbs in the mountain air, where idleness was a blessed luxury. On the fourth day's march they climbed

---

* To readers of Kipling's collected works, the Rawalpindi Durbar is best remembered for the final story in the *Jungle Book* (' Soldiers of the Queen ').

from the Mutiani Pass * to Narkunda with its long view of the high ranges, then dropped three thousand feet from the forests of deodar to the poppy-fields about Kotgarh, a solitary mission-station, forty miles from the nearest relief, and here they rested two days while De Brath took photographs and Kipling studied the ways of the missionary, ' the queerest little devil you ever saw '. The chief compensation Kipling could find for such a secluded life was the beauty of the strong, un-veiled hill-women, always loaded with ornaments of uncut turquoise. ' I should like to be padre in these parts ', he wrote.

After a further march of two days and a gruelling climb to Baghi (9000 feet), Kipling rather reluctantly turned back towards Simla, the only *sahib* now in his little caravan. Near Narkunda, going on alone he was a little disconcerted to meet a family party of bears, the bad-tempered black bears of the Himalaya, ' all talking at the tops of their voices '. He ' thought of Elisha the Tishbite and bolted like blazes. Hadn't seen a bear loose before. '[12]

On this day [he wrote] my servant embroiled himself with a new quar-tette of coolies and managed to cut the eye of one of them. I was a few score miles from the nearest white man, and did not wish to be hauled before any little Hill Rajah, knowing as I did that the coolies would unitedly swear that I had directed the outrage. I therefore paid blood-money, and strategically withdrew — on foot for the most part because ' Dolly Bobs ', (his grey pony), objected to every sight and most of the smells of the land-scape. I had to keep the coolies who, like the politicians, would not stay put, in front of me on the six-foot-wide track, and, as is ever the case when one is in difficulties, it set in to rain. My urgent business was to make my first three days' march in one — a matter of thirty odd miles. My coolies wanted to shy off to their village and spend their ill-gotten silver. On me devolved the heart-breaking job of shepherding a retreat. It did me great good, and enabled me to put away bottles of strong Army beer at the wet evening's end in the resthouse. On our last day, a thunderstorm, which had been at work a few thousand feet below us, rose to the level of the ridge we were crossing and exploded in our midst. We were all flung on our faces, and when I was able to see again I observed the half of a well-grown pine, as neatly split lengthwise as a match by a pen-knife, in the act of hirpling down the steep hillside by itself. The thunder drowned everything, so that it seemed to be posturing in dumb show, and when it began to hop — horrible vertical hops — the effect was of pure D.T.[13]

Simla was again the hill-station chosen by the Kiplings for the hot season of 1885. They could afford it, since Mrs. Kipling had been earning money with her pen, and Rudyard joined them for a long visit, as special correspondent for his paper, at a respectable salary. It

---

* Now usually spelt Mathiana. Kipling spells the name Kotgarh four different ways in a few pages of diary.

was his duty to describe the annual spectacle of an Empire ruled from a remote and almost inaccessible village, seven thousand feet above the Indian Plains.

As a hill-station, the history of Simla went back to the eighteen-twenties. In the middle of the town was a building like a Swiss chalet which had been occupied by an early Governor-General, and had long since been converted by a viceregal chef into Peliti's Grand Hotel. There had been no carriage-road to Simla until the eighteen-fifties when Lord Dalhousie projected the Himalaya–Tibet Road as one of his far-reaching lines of communication. Till then there were no wheeled vehicles in Simla, but only *jampans,* or litters for the ladies, carried by relays of coolies. In Lord Lytton's time a stretch of level road, the Ladies' Mile, was constructed round the foot of the hill called Jakko which commands the town and, thereafter, 'rickshaws' began to replace the more cumbrous *jampans.* Still, the steepness of the slopes restricted road-making and building.

The Viceroy's palace was a cramped, inconvenient shooting-lodge named 'Peterhoff', where the English ladies'-maids complained at being obliged to share bedrooms, where the secretaries and A.D.C.s were parked out in neighbouring cottages, and where an extension for a ballroom meant that visitors stepped out from front-door and side-door alike on to the edge of a precipice. All the houses of the town were in imminent danger of slipping away down the *khud* in the land-slides that occurred every wet season, when thirty or forty inches of rain might be expected. Yet it was the wet season, July and August, that filled Simla with refugees from heat and fever in the Plains. Lucky were they who could spend six or seven months in the Hills, from April which was bright and cold until October when Simla had the finest climate in the world.

The Government of India, inheriting the tradition of those martial rulers, the Great Moguls, was a marching camp. The Viceroy was accustomed to carry with him his Sirdar and his Divan of Councillors, to make progresses of his realm, to receive and to answer petitions wherever he might be. In the vast spaces of India, Simla was no more remote than Calcutta. A mobile administration, not yet swathed in red tape, nor hampered by parliamentary controls, was as efficient in one place as in another. Efficient or not, it was from Simla that the Indian Government was administered, in days of strong personal rule, for six or seven months in the year. There the Viceroy exercised his mighty authority, shouldered his crushing responsibility, met his daily council, received envoys, summoned his vassals the provincial governors and ruling princes to audience, and managed all through a civil and a military secretary, a dozen A.D.C.s and a corps of messengers, the red-uniformed *chaprassies,* who were believed, by Indian gossips, to wield untold influence. The Commander-in-Chief too had his establishment, a rival military court, with its secretaries, A.D.C.s, and *chaprassies,* at 'Snowdon' on a rather distant hillside. Humbler, but by no means unimportant, was the summer establishment of the Lieutenant-Governor of the Punjab, in a converted villa which had been decorated by Lockwood Kipling and his pupils.

From a very early time there was a legend of fast life in Simla. Perhaps it was at the end of the Mutiny, when the revolt had ebbed far away into Central India and the hill-stations were full of wounded officers enjoying their convalescence, that the town won its reputation for gaiety. Other hill-stations were just as blest with climate and scenery, but they were dull, while Simla had the glamour of a court. Even more, it was described by prudish Victorians as a haunt of gilded luxury, a 'Capua in the Hills', and quite unjustly. But the presence of the Viceroy with his circle of young aides, he a nobleman of high rank and they often sprigs of the peerage, gave it some social importance, while for quite other reasons, it abounded with place-hunters and fortune-hunters. It was an old joke in India, long before the Kiplings' day, that grass-widows flocked to Simla, not altogether heart-broken at the prospect of staying there six months while their husbands must be content with thirty or sixty days' leave from the Plains. 'Simla is full of pretty girls', wrote Lockwood Kipling, 'and has a strong light-brigade of sportive matrons of all ages. I never go near a dance, but I hear the nicest possible girls sit out in rows.'

The interest of life in Simla was its dual character, as a political headquarters and a pleasure resort. Very hard slogging work was done there, especially if there was a stiff Viceroy; the gay life flourished when there was a society leader in the Viceroy's seat.

The second season that Rudyard spent at Simla, 1885, was the first year of Lord Dufferin's rule. The newcomer was a wealthy, sophisticated *grand seigneur,* equally compounded of Irish charm and worldly wisdom. A traveller, a scholar, a wit, he had governed Canada, led an embassy to the Sultan of Turkey, given Egypt a constitution, done everything, met everyone, been everywhere; and his wife, celebrated in verse by three poets, was that rarity, a Governor's wife who strengthened her husband's hand. Neverthless, she was a little taken aback at Simla. 'Peterhoff', she said, was the smallest house that she had ever lived in. She and her husband were too genuine and too courteous to stand on ceremony or to let their lives be regulated by the rules of precedence to which middle-class officials give such weight, but they had to distribute their favours. Lady Dufferin calculated that she entertained 640 guests to dinner in a season, in twelve large parties and twenty-five small parties; she invited 250 guests to each of her six evening receptions. To the large parties she must invite by seniority; at her small parties she could choose for herself, and need not be bored by high-ranking mediocrities. She soon discovered that the art-teacher and his family from Lahore were worth cultivating. One connexion was Lockwood's sketching-class, which Lady Helen, the Viceroy's daughter, attended. The Viceroy would drop in to talk art and letters with Lockwood, and would stay to enjoy Mrs. Kipling's conversation. 'Dullness and Mrs. Kipling cannot exist in the same room', he used to say. Furthermore, Trix, in her second season, was an acknowledged beauty, a breaker of hearts, and an expert dancer. She had talent for writing both verse and prose, and was an accomplished amateur actress. When she also took the fancy of Lord Clandeboye, the Viceroy's son and A.D.C., it was rather more than the Dufferins approved. One day the Viceroy called on Mrs. Kipling to discuss this dangerous development. 'Don't you think, Mrs. Kipling, your daughter should be taken to another hill-station?' 'Don't you think, your Excellency, that your son should be sent home?' It was Clandeboye who went, and Trix who remained. The Viceroy, though defeated, was no less friendly. One day he dropped in, unheralded, at 'The Tendrils', the Kiplings' Simla lodging, and was turned away by the servants because the family was out, a rebuff that this autocrat accepted meekly enough.[14]

The Kiplings had now been brought into the inner ring of Simla society, to the disgust, no doubt, of many social climbers with better official qualifications. Mrs. Kipling's wit, Mr. Kipling's range of knowledge, Miss Kipling's charm and lightness of foot, were the factors that brought about this social triumph. Young Rudyard as yet had less to offer to the social feast. It embarrassed him, a little, that he was at Simla on business, hired to write up the social functions he attended; pleased, though, to earn a good salary and to spend all July and August in the Hills. 'The boy has taken enthusiastically, all at once, to dancing,' wrote Lockwood Kipling to a friend, 'and being determined to do it well, bids fair to be a very good dancer. His proprietors told him, as he is going to Simla to represent his paper, that he must waltz well; so what we at home couldn't persuade him to like became a duty (an odd, but really very necessary sort of duty) and he has gone in for it heartily.'[15]

What a wealth of social life there was in Simla! There was Christ Church, where Lady Dufferin played the organ and trained the choir. But the Kiplings were no great church-goers, though Lockwood was so obliging as to design frescoes for the walls. There was the amateur dramatic club; Simla was always renowned for theatricals organised

for many years by Lord William Beresford, the Military Secretary. *
This was a field where talents would not lie hidden, and soon it was
discovered that the boy from the *Civil and Military* could dash off the
wittiest of prologues in verse which his sister would recite to perfection.

There was the Club: there was the public assembly-room at Ben-
more; there was polo at Annandale, the only flat green space in Simla;
there was Peliti's, almost a continental café; there was the *tonga*-
office in the Mall, with its bustling commerce of jaded faces coming
up from the Plains, and fresh full-blooded faces returning to their
duty. There were rides on sure-footed hill-ponies, every cavalier
attending a lady's rickshaw; and for Rudyard there was tea in the cool
dusk, beside a roaring log-fire, in the company of the other three.

Rudyard Kipling to Miss Edith Macdonald

NORTH BANK, SIMLA. July 30th, 1885

I'm here at Simla with the Mother and Trix as Special Correspondent
for the Civil and Military Gazette. I told you that for my work at the
Durbar they raised my screw to £420 English or £35 a month. For that
sum I try to give my paper as near to £40 a month of editorial notes;
reviews; articles and social Simla letters. That in itself is fairly lively work
and — tho' this may sound strange to you — entails as much riding, waltz-
ing, dining out and concerts in a week as I should get at home in a lifetime.
Then I have been working on Indian stories for other papers — notably the
Pioneer which has professed its willingness to take anything I might choose
to send. I've sent them a mixed assortment of verses; and some prose
stuff. All of which have taken the public's somewhat dense soul and been
largely quoted. Also the *Calcutta Review* has written very sweetly about
a poem of mine — in blank verse — which appears in the August number,
and is going to put in a long ghost story of a wholly novel type. Like the
Quarterlies the C.R. isn't much read but it gives one a certain amount of
prestige to have a foot in it.

Further I have really embarked to the tune of 237 foolscap pages on my
novel — Mother Maturin — an Anglo-Indian episode. Like Topsy ' it
growed ' while I wrote and I find myself now committed to a two volume
business at least. It's not one bit nice or proper but it carries a grim sort of
a moral with it and tries to deal with the unutterable horrors of lower class
Eursasian and native life as they exist outside reports and reports and
reports. I haven't got the Pater's verdict on what I've done. He comes
up in a couple of days and will then sit in judgement. Trixie says its
awfully horrid; Mother says its nasty but powerful and I know it to be in
large measure true. It is an unfailing delight to me and I'm just in that
pleasant stage where the characters are living with me always. The Parents
say ' publish it at home and let it have a chance '. I hold that India would

* Lockwood Kipling hinted in a letter that Beresford was the original of ' John
Wonder ' in ' A Germ-destroyer '.

be the better place and have already received one offer for the book from an Indian Paper. A few years ago one Proprietor offered My Mother Rs 1,000 for an Anglo-Indian story. If he renews the offer to the son I close at once and Mother Maturin, whatever her after fate, shall appear in weekly parts. Then maybe, I might be able to struggle home for six weeks with what I've got already. Fancy six whole weeks at home.[16]

In 1885, as in 1883, the Kiplings spent part of the season staying at North Bank with James Walker who made his home in Simla. Another friend who often entertained them was the head of the agricultural department, Edward Buck, a member of the Viceroy's council and therefore a powerful ally. Buck was a Simla resident of long standing and a repository of Simla lore. He had bought from Allen Hume, the founder of the Indian National Congress, the house in which Madame Blavatsky produced the manifestations that made her world-famous. It was in 1879, three years before Rudyard came to India, that Buck had exposed her methods and ridiculed her new cult with its miraculous messages that dropped from the ceilings written on palm-leaves, and its teacups materialized under bushes in the garden. Lockwood Kipling had attended these seances, and quietly observed that Madame Blavatsky was 'one of the most interesting and unscrupulous impostors' he had ever met.[9] Many Anglo-Indians were more credulous about the 'teacup creed', among them A. P. Sinnett, the editor of the *Pioneer,* who introduced more theosophist propaganda into its columns than his colleagues approved.

Simla always abounded in eccentrics: mystics and psychopaths and nymphomaniacs. The most celebrated courtesan of the century, Lola Montez, began her career at Simla. The older residences had their ghosts, especially the house called Alice's Bower (which also belonged to Buck), the traditional scene of the episode described in Kipling's 'Lispeth'. Even more spooky was the jeweller's shop kept by A. M. Jacob, the 'healer of sick pearls'. No one knew who he was or where he came from. Some said he was a Russian spy but, spy or no, he was a conjurer and hypnotist, who bought and sold jewels with an air of mystery that enabled him to outwit most customers. There was much buying and selling in Simla, especially of house property. Another Simla landlord was Major Goad, whose son, Horace Goad, was well known in the Kiplings' day, as the smartest police officer in the Punjab. He was 'supposed to have the gift of invisibility and executive control over many Devils'. His reputation with the natives provided Rudyard with copy for several stories.

There were thirty or forty thousand Indian natives at Simla in the season, half of them plainsmen who had come up with their masters because the hillmen were reputed bad servants. The Simla bazaars were rookeries of wooden chalets, piled high on the steepest slopes, teeming with sojourners from all the races in India, alive with intrigue and rumour. As Kipling wrote, some years later, in *Kim,*

a man who knows his way there can defy all the police of India's summer capital; so cunningly does verandah communicate with verandah, alley-way with alley-way, and bolt-hole with bolt-hole. Here live those who minister to the wants of the glad city — jhampanis who pull the pretty ladies' rick-shaws by night and gamble till the dawn; grocers, oil-sellers, curio-venders, firewood dealers, priests, pickpockets, and native employees of the Government: here are discussed by courtesans the things which are supposed to be profoundest secrets of the India Council; and here gather all the sub-sub-agents of half the native states.[17]

The season that the four Kiplings spent together led to the pro-duction of a family magazine called *Quartette,* which they persuaded their friends of the *Civil and Military Gazette* to issue as a Christmas Annual, at the end of the year. It contained the first two stories by Rudyard which he thought worthy of preserving in the collected editions of his later life, 'The Phantom Rickshaw' and 'The Strange Ride of Morrowbie Jukes', both of them tales of horror written markedly in the manner of Edgar Allan Poe. 'The Phantom Rick-shaw' has some claim to consideration as a study of hallucination, the first and not the weakest of the many tales of psychopathic states which he was to publish. His later comment on it was: 'Some of it was weak, much was bad and out of key; but it was my first serious attempt to think in another man's skin'. It is well worth reading today. 'Morrowbie Jukes' was a grotesque, an expedition into the half-world of Indian life, far away from 'Levées and Government House Lists, past Trades' Balls — far beyond everything and everybody you ever knew in your respectable life'. In September 1884, a whole year before the publication of *Quartette,* he had written one sketch of life in an opium den, 'The Gate of the Hundred Sorrows', which showed amazing precocity. Since then he had immensely widened his range of knowledge and interest. On 7th March 1885 he noted in his diary that the notion first dawned on him of the book that he meant to be his masterpiece. For years he worked at it, accumulating material, but the book never crystallized. It remained in solution in his notebooks, an unwritten masterpiece. All Kipling's friends waited anxiously for *Mother Maturin* which was the hobby of his remaining years in India.

One of the channels by which he penetrated the underworld was Freemasonry, a system which gratified both his craving for a world-religion and his devotion to the secret bond that unites the 'Sons of Martha', the men who bear the burden of the world's work. Since first he came to India, the land of caste, in which the English *sahibs* had followed Indian custom by forming themselves into a caste as restricted as any other, he had been fascinated by the limbo that lay between and beneath caste-rules. Freemasonry was a cult for adult responsible males, a cult that transcended all castes and sects. In 1885, when still below the proper age, Kipling was admitted to the Lodge, 'Hope and Perseverance, No. 782 E.C.', at Lahore, because they wanted a secretary; and, he said, they got a bad one. In caste-ridden India, Freemasonry was the only ground on which adherents of different religions could meet 'on the level'. 'I was entered', wrote Kipling, 'by a member of the Brahmo Somaj (Hindu), passed by a Mohammedan, and raised by an Englishman. Our tyler was an Indian Jew.'[18]

Rudyard Kipling to Miss Margaret Burne-Jones

[It was an old nursery joke between them that each addressed the other by the name of 'Wop'.]

Sunday. LAHORE, Sept. 26th, 1885

DEAR WOP,

Now how am I to tackle your letter properly: throwing in the 'dear me how interesting' at the proper time. I will e'en turn it upside down and work backwards. Para. two from the butt end asks me if I know *The City of Dreadful Night*. *Do* I know it? Oh Wop! Wop! What a question.

Furthermore, did I not, one month ago, spend one weary weary night on the great minar of the Mosque of Wazir Khan, looking down upon the heat tortured city of Lahore and seventy thousand men and women sleeping in the moonlight: and did I not write a description of my night's vigil and christen it 'The City of Dreadful Night'. Go to — go to Uncle Crom and ask him for a copy of that article. . . .

LAHORE. Friday, December 18th, 1885, 10 in the morning.

Still working by lamplight with a general impression that I've been doing nothing else for the past six hours. . . . 'This morning' was *Quartette* cleared away at five before the dawn had broken and when the rain was coming down hard . . . In my bedroom I remember Chalmers the Scotch foreman and his forty thieves and wondered what the end would be — wondered so much that I left the house secretly and plashed over to the press. As I thought, the men were on the verge of mutiny — saying they wouldn't work any more and C. was tearing his hair over the advertisements. Ram Dass said he was cold and hungry and eyed the brandy bottle. Now a man — any man except an assistant editor — when he works overtime is paid for his labour but there is no law which enforces his working all night — and that was just what I meant my friends to do.

And what a mad night it was — Something went wrong with the two colour title page. The type in 'Civil and Military Gazette' was worn out and wouldn't come up properly. With gum and bits of paper and paste and brown paper I 'packed the lay' with these lily fingers. Stuck bits of paper behind the piece of paper that it pressed against the type in order to bulge out the paper into the face of the worn letters. I don't know whether that's clear enough to your mind. It was a long and dirty job and I got foully mired with the droppings of candle ends and paste. Chalmers was correcting proofs of advertisements, standing over the men to see they did it — and I assure you that by the inadequate candlelight and under the hands of asinine Punjabis proofs were uncommon queer. As soon as I got the title page moderately decent — it looks pretty well but a practised eye could tell I'd been 'faking it' I placed myself under Chalmers' orders for the rest of the time. So when I wasn't correcting proofs of superior saddles and watches and medicines — not the outpourings of my mighty genius — I was going round from shift to shift and keeping 'em in a good temper and chaffing the men who were smoking and patting the children — for that's all they are in their tempers — on the back and telling 'em how such work was never before produced in India and how the Calcutta printers would think shame of themselves when they heard that Punjabis worked all night like elephants. Never have I seen Ram Dass toil as he did in the early hours of this morn and never did he handle his men so neatly.

We felt mighty proud and sleepy. I got to bed at 5.30 a.m. and was exceeding late for breakfast. 'My boy,' said the Pater, eyeing my weary eyes and dishevelled locks, 'if you would only get up in the mornings and do your work you'd be ever so much better.'

And now at the end of this awful pile of M.S. to ask you a favour, and a big one. In the course of your wanderings do you ever come to know anything about the Slade Art School and the students there — the female ones I mean of course. Circumstances over which I have not the smallest control prevent my going home and seeing the school itself. There is or was a maiden there of the name of Garrard — Flo Garrard and I want to know, *how* she is and what she is doing. So far as I know youre the only person who's likely to be able to find this out for me and if possible I want you as quietly and as unobtrusively as possible to learn all you can about the girl. It's a cool sort of request to make isn't it? And I shouldn't ha' done it, but that I am at my wits end for news in this particular instance. If I said that for *any* information you gave me you should have anything in my power to give 'even unto the half of my Kingdom' you would naturally be offended so I appeal humbly to the Wop of Albion to help me for old sakes sake. I only want to know if the girl looks well and — so far as your eyes can judge — happy. Thereafter if I can serve you in any way you know who to go to.

Yours expectantly,

THE WOP OF ASIA.[19]

His curiosity to know what had become of Flo Garrard did not prevent Rudyard from forming other attachments. About the same time when he was writing this long letter, it happened that his father also wrote, and to the same address:

We have been immensely amused by his falling in love recently, a most wholesome sign that he is growing to his proper boyhood — which sounds more topsy-turvy than it really is. The Rev. Duke is an awful military chaplain at Mian Mir, who, I am told, preaches impossible sermons but who has a lovely daughter — like the pictures of Lady Hamilton says Ruddy.

These people do not join Lahore society in dances, garden parties etc., so the boy for 2 Sundays has driven five miles to attend Mian Mir church! None of us, by the way, ever go to church.

But for the storm that has raged all day Trixie was to have gone with him, for she wishes to see the paragon.

I have not seen her, but she ought to be nice to be worth a chill drive of 5 miles, an absurd sermon and a cold church with a company of rifle-clanking soldiers and about half a dozen other people for congregation. He is vastly funny about it and I cannot make out whether there is anything in it.[20]

Among the friends Kipling made in the world of free-lance journalism was Kay Robinson, a young man not much older than himself, who had recently come out from Fleet Street to be assistant editor of the *Pioneer*. Early in 1885 Robinson wrote some dog-Latin verses for his paper, signing them ' K. R. ', which many people assumed to be an anagram for ' R. K. ', since at that time Kipling was producing ephemeral verse and prose for many Indian journals. The bibliographers have identified between twenty and thirty pseudonyms which Kipling used in early life for his miscellaneous work; he wrote under the names of ' Nickson ', ' Yussuf ', ' Esau Mull ', ' E. M.', as well as ' K.' and ' R. K.', but he did not use the anagram ' K. R.', and wrote to Robinson to apologize for the misapplication. A friendship sprang up, by correspondence, between the two young journalists. At the end of the year Kipling was asked to write a Christmas poem for the *Pioneer,* and produced the well-known ' Christmas in India ', a doleful exile's lament. It aroused the derision of Robinson who revelled in the Indian sunshine and even enjoyed the hot weather. Rather maliciously, and in some trepidation lest he should offend his ally at Lahore, Robinson wrote a parody, ' Christmas in England ', and the two sets of verses appeared in the *Pioneer,* side by side, signed respectively ' K. R.' and ' R. K.' Kipling was delighted, and asked Robinson to visit him on his next short leave.

In the spring of 1886 Robinson spent some weeks with the Kiplings at Lahore and preserved an account of his impressions which is the clearest description we possess of the family square. The two women made the most mark on him, Mrs. Kipling for her lively wit and Trix for her statuesque beauty. It was Trix who astonished him by her knowledge of English poetry, while Rudyard revealed himself as still a boy with a bad social manner, abrupt in his ways and so untidy that, at the end of the day's work his tropical suit was spotted all over with ink-stains 'like a dalmatian dog'.[21]

As well as Kay Robinson, a friend of his schooldays re-entered Kipling's life in 1886.

Rudyard Kipling to Lionel ['Stalky'] Dunsterville

LAHORE, Jan. 30th, 1886

DEAR OLD MAN —

(On second thoughts — you unmitigated old Blackguard.)

I saw your name in the trooper list, but never a hint as to your destination and I've been cursing you fluently ever since. Of course if you had rheumatic fever I don't mind forgiving you but the next time you drop into India in this casual manner just you let me know, or the consequences will be serious.

So you're at Nassik are you. Hum! There's a big house on the top of a hill there, where Proctor Sims the Engineer lives or used to live — close to the river. Make a reverent pilgrimage thither O my Son and reflect that in those walls did the Saintly Gigger spend the fourth and fifth years of his life — many ages ago. If you know P. Sims he'll tell you. A lovely spot is Nassik. You know the rhyme of course —

> There was a young lady of Nassik
> Whose attire was graceful and classic
> For all that she wore
> Both behind and before
> Was a wreath of the roses of Nassick.

Sorry to find you haven't even a medal for your manly breast. Do you know I believe, if in a weak moment Government gave you such an article, you'd go and pop it somewhere — that is to say if you haven't outgrown our old instincts in the little study. Loss of *batta* is more serious. However you may get your chance of something festive up here. The Bonerwals have killed a man — a Colonel Hutchinson — and I fancy they will be expeditioned. *Nota Bene*. Never close with an Afghan. Plug at him from a distance. There's no glory if he sticks you and precious little if you pot him. I had an experience at Jumrood which brought this home to me. I stood afar off and heaved rocks at mine adversary like David did and providentially smote him on the mouth insomuch that he lost interest in me and departed. He had a knife and seemed to object to my going on foot towards the Khaiber. Narrow-minded sort of cuss who couldn't appreciate the responsibilities of journalism. That's been all the active service I've ever seen, and I didn't like it. I tried to go to Burma for the paper but I couldn't be spared. By the way did you see that poor Durey was killed by those swine? There's £1800 worth of education gone to smash and a good fellow with it.

Thine ever

GIGGER.

P.S. Your handwriting is damnable. Take a lesson by mine.

P.S. Ain't Quartette thrilling — There's a ' Jenny say qwai' about that Phantom Rickshaw that positively haunts me. I have built up a reputation in the Punjab as a chartered libertine on the strength of it.[22]

' Stalky' Dunsterville had passed through Sandhurst into a line regiment with which he served in Malta and Egypt. He had seen much gaiety and sport, and had commanded men in the desert behind Suakin, though he had not fought in any of the fiercer battles in the Sudan campaign. But 'Stalky' could no longer lord it over ' Gigger' in the old style of Number Five Study, because 'Gigger' was an old hand while 'Stalky' was a newcomer in India. They were soon parted, when 'Stalky' was posted away to his regiment, the 20th Punjabis, at Amritsar.

Kipling, too, was sent away to Jammu, to report the installation of a new Maharajah of Kashmir. His most graphic columns dealt with the wild-beast fights staged for the public amusement, between pairs of buffaloes, fighting rams, and elephants.[23] Some squeamish critics have found these descriptions disgusting, though Kipling was chiefly concerned to point out how much sound and fury was released and how little damage done, except when a buffalo charged the spectators. After this expedition, he returned to Lahore for the worst of the hot weather.

Rudyard Kipling to Miss Margaret Burne-Jones

LAHORE, June 17th, 1886

Do you know what hemicrania means? A half headache. I've been having it for a few days and it is a lovely thing. One half of my head in a mathematical line from the top of my skull to the cleft of my jaw, throbs and hammers and sizzles and bangs and swears while the other half — calm and collected — takes note of the agonies next door. My disgusting doctor says it's over work again and I'm equally certain that it rose from my suddenly and violently discarding tobacco for three days. Anyhow it hurts awfully — feels like petrifaction in sections and makes one write abject drivel.

I slept right round the clock on Tuesday night from 9.30 to 9.30 and was so delighted at having my rest I forgot to bother about the heat which is seasonable — too seasonable. Three soldiers died in Cantonments last night of heat apoplexy and they've been having a funeral nearly every day for a fortnight. But Tommy *is* so careless. He drinks heavy beer, and sleeps at once after a full flesh meal and dies naturally. Did I tell you a rather grim story of what I saw the other night when I went round the guards in Fort Lahore with the subaltern of the day. I'd been round often before but never on a night like this. It was pitchy black, choking hot with a blinding dust storm out.   Fort Lahore is wickedly hot always as I've learnt to my cost before now.   I went into the main guard at midnight (it marked 97° in the guardroom verandah) and I saw by the lamp light every man jack of the guard stripped as near as might be *sitting up.*   They daren't lie down for the lives of 'em in heat like that.   It meant apoplexy.   However none of my men — the gunners are the ones I know most of have collapsed so far.   Personally I'm in the lap of luxury.   My bedroom even at midnight which I consider the hottest time of the twenty four hours never goes beyond 86° but that means six men are working night and day in relays to keep it cool.   They are queer fellows my coolies.   They talk to me in the evening and tell me about their crops and families.   Half the year they cultivate and the other half they come into the cities and hire out as Punkah coolies.   It's worth while petting the men who keep you cool.   They have a child's weakness for sweets (serves 'em instead of flesh meat) and 3½d give them all oceans of sticky sweet cakes.[24]

It was not until August 1886 that he joined the family, at Simla. This was the season when Lord Clandeboye paid attention to Trix, and Rudyard moved in the same circle.   Untidy he may have been, but the Viceroy now took notice of him, wondering — as everyone wondered — how he came to know so much, as if he had 'photographed the inmost councils of state'.   Among his friends that season were two of the A.D.C.s, Lord Herbrand Russell, the Duke of Bedford's heir, and Captain Ian Hamilton of the Gordons, a rising young soldier.   In his memoirs written in extreme old age, Sir Ian Hamilton related that he sent one of Kipling's early stories home to some literary friends who tried it on William Sharp, the critic and poet.   According to Hamilton, Sharp shrank from it in horror.   Old men's memories of youth are not always to be trusted, and Ian Hamilton's memory may have deceived him as to the date, but he goes on to say that when he went home, a year later in 1887, to stay with the Balfours at Whittinghame he found everyone in that intellectual stratosphere talking of the new prodigy from India.   If so, they were two years ahead of the market.

It was in the cool weather of 1886–7 that Kipling, aged just twenty-one, began to produce the stories and verses that made him famous. He returned from Simla to find with delight that Stephen Wheeler was going home, exhausted by fever and the climate.   Wheeler had kept his assistant's nose pretty well to the grindstone for the best part of four years, filling his time with routine work and discouraging his imaginative writing, but Kipling was thankful to his exacting chief and never regretted having earned his living the hard way.   Wheeler taught him, he said, 'that an order was to be obeyed at a run, not a walk, and that any notions of the fitness or unfitness of any particular kind of work for the young had better be held over till the last page was locked up for press'. In later years he and Wheeler were to meet again, and each was to do the other a service. For the present Kipling was relieved to see the last of him, and was delighted when Kay Robinson was sent up from Allahabad to be the new editor of the *Civil and Military*. Under Wheeler the paper had been dull, and Robinson was commissioned to 'put some sparkle into it'. He and his sparkling assistant drank a bottle of champagne together to inaugurate the livelier age. It was now August, the hottest of the hot weather, and they sat at work in singlet and cotton trousers, smoking perpetually, each with a fox-terrier at his feet — Kipling's 'Vic' as full of sparkle as his master. Robinson had worked for the London *Globe,* an evening paper with the special feature of a short middle-page article every day on some popular theme, that occupied the right-hand column and 'turned over' to finish on the following page. 'Turnovers' on the model of the *Globe* were to be the field for Kipling's talents in the new reign of Kay Robinson at Lahore. They must be topical, arresting, and short, restricted to 2000 words, just the discipline in letters that Kipling needed. The best of them are still in print as *Plain Tales from the Hills.*

Kay was delighted with his new assistant, astonished at his abounding energy and wit. 'He had the buoyancy of a cork, he was bubbling over with poetry', said Kay. 'If you want to find a man who will cheerfully do the work of three men, you must catch a young genius.' For a year they worked together at Lahore with happy enthusiasm and, knowing his man better, Kay discovered that he was not the hobbledehoy he seemed to be. When the cold weather came, and 'society' returned to Lahore, Kipling grew careful and correct in his costume and showed a liking for feminine company. He neither played whist (bridge was not yet invented) nor tennis, and now rarely took horse-exercise, but he was regular at the dances. Strange to say, he avoided the Club, said Kay. His conversation was so brilliant that he did not care to show it off. There was a senior member at the Club who disapproved of Kipling and persistently tried to snub him. Though Kipling's power of repartee was so striking that he always had the best of his exchanges with this curmudgeon he disliked the atmosphere of ill will, yet he was no shirker. Kay was surprised at the chances and risks he encountered to get copy in the lowest quarters of the town in the midst of communal riots; and, one night when some gay young sparks invaded Kipling's room with the intention of ragging him, Kipling leapt from his bed to confront them with a revolver. The most remarkable thing about him, as Lord Dufferin had noticed, was his mysterious faculty for assimilating local colour without apparent effort. He knew more about the low life of Lahore than the police, more about the tone of the regiments at Mian Mir than the chaplain. Kay particularly remembered one of his confidants, a Pathan called Mahbub Ali, 'indescribably filthy but with magnificent mien and features' who used to visit Kipling whenever he came to Lahore, with news of the unruly almost unknown world of Central Asia beyond the Khyber Pass. The cavalry subalterns were astonished at Kipling's knowledge of horses and steeple-chasing. 'Where does the youngster pick it all up?' asked the Veterinary Officer of Kay Robinson in the Club.[25] Part of the answer is to be found in his natural faculty, part in the fact that he was his father's son. Few Englishmen knew India better, and few were more generally loved and trusted than Lockwood Kipling, whose name opened many doors.

The time had come for Kipling to launch a volume of collected verse in a style which was popular, even traditional, in Anglo-India.

There is always an under-current of song, a little bitter for the most part, running through the Indian papers. Sometimes a man in Bangalore would be moved to song, and a man on the Bombay side would answer him, and a man in Bengal would echo back, till at last we would all be crowing together like cocks before daybreak.[26]

So Kipling described the literary background of his first acknowledged book. The verses appeared in his newspapers, some under the heading of 'Bungalow Ballads', and then were reissued with the better title of *Departmental Ditties*. The book did not look like a book; it was part of the joke that he printed and bound it in the style and shape of a Government office file, tied up with a bow of the pink tape that is called 'red tape'. The first edition was immensely popular in India, soon sold out, and is now a rarity. Though issued without an author's name, there was little doubt who, in the small world of Anglo-India, had written these verses. Before the end of the year, a second edition, more conventional in form, and bearing the name of Rudyard Kipling, was issued by the firm of Thacker & Spink at Calcutta, who bought them outright from the author for five hundred rupees. Though some copies were offered for sale in London they attracted little attention outside India, as yet. These verses were topical in character and local in their appeal. Kipling himself had no illusions about *Departmental Ditties* which he regarded as frivolity.

They were made to ease off the perpetual strife between the manager extending his advertisements and my chief fighting for his reading-matter. They were born to be sacrificed. Rukh Din the foreman would say: 'Your potery very good, sir; just coming proper length to-day. One third column, just proper.'[27]

The author was sufficiently gratified when the critics compared them with Bret Harte's poems, which was not rating them high as poetry. Like Bret Harte's verses, the *Ditties* are largely echoes from other writers; some are imitations of W. M. Praed, W. S. Gilbert, or J. E. Fitzgerald; some are no more than family jokes. One light piece describing the envy of a young girl for an older woman's popularity has given pleasure to many readers:

> The young men come, the young men go,
> Each pink and white and neat,
> She's older than their mothers, but
> They grovel at Her feet.
> They walk beside Her *rickshaw*-wheels —
> None ever walk by mine;
> And that's because I'm seventeen
> And She is forty-nine.

It can hardly be a coincidence that this verse was written when Kipling's shy sister was seventeen, and his brilliant talkative mother forty-nine years old. The book made its name for the cynical comments on patronage and promotion in the Anglo-Indian hierarchy. It was the talk of Simla, in the season of 1886, since everyone understood the allusions and recognized the caricatures. Lockwood Kipling had the satisfaction of hearing all sorts of complimentary things about his son. 'Lord Dufferin, who frequently comes into our sketching-room, professed to be greatly struck by the uncommon combination of satire with grace and delicacy, also with what he calls the boy's infallible ear for rhythm and cadence.' Another grandee, Sir Auckland Colvin, who was himself a victim of the poet's satire, wrote him a 'most enthusiastic note'. And the Walkers, his employers, now treated young Kipling as 'a spoilt child of the house' when he came up to stay with them in Simla.

Towards the end of the year he made his first dent in the protective crust of the London literary circle. Kay Robinson had sent home eight review copies to friends in the Trade and one attracted the attention of Andrew Lang, the writer of a monthly article of literary gossip for *Longman's Magazine*. He gave *Departmental Ditties* a kind but condescending column of notice beginning with regret that the modest author did not reveal his name. The book, he said, was a

quaint and amusing example of the variety of literature known as Anglo-Indian verse. . . . On the whole these are melancholy ditties. Jobs and posts and pensions, and the wives of their neighbours appear to be much coveted by Her Majesty's Civil Servants in India.

With relief, Andrew Lang turned away to Kipling's pretty verses on 'Springtime in India' with their nostalgia for springtime in England.

This was what he found most admirable in *Departmental Ditties*. The first effect of Kipling's work, here and in general, was shocking; he was regarded as a cynical young man who laid bare the seamy side of Indian life; but the first edition did not include the pieces which have best stood the test of popular approval. *

The approval of the Viceroy and the grave councillors at Simla was not a negligible start for a young man, though satire is a dangerous weapon to flourish under an autocratic Government. It is unjustified to suppose that Anglo-India was a philistinish community with low literary standards, since every prominent person in Simla had qualified for his post by examination, and the best appointments were reserved for men with high academic honours. Yet, to versify at Simla, even with a court jester's licence, was not a sufficient career.

Kay could not understand why Kipling was content to stay in India where his talents were hidden. Why did he not go to London? Kipling's reply was that he thought it his duty to serve seven years with the newspaper that had given him his chance and had taught him his trade. He was happy at heart and willing to suffer the misery of the hot weather, even to take a sort of pride in his endurance of it, for the sake of his work. The family square still made a secure background to his life; the office — since Kay Robinson had come — was a place of joyful activity not of grinding routine. At Simla he felt himself to have penetrated the arcana and to have his finger on the pulse of empire; at Lahore he was absorbed in his study of the Indian underworld. His verses had won him a little modest fame; his 'turn-over' articles for the *Civil and Military* were extending his powers, and in his own room at Bikanir House was the mounting pile of sheets that were to make the *Book of Mother Maturin*. Some day, he knew, he must leave home and return to the literary world. A novel he read in the autumn of 1886, *All in a Garden Fair,* by Sir Walter Besant, proved unsettling and pointed out his next step though he was not yet ready to take it.

This forgotten Victorian favourite had an obvious relation to the life of Rudyard Kipling. It is a pleasant tale of three young rivals, who compete for the love of a girl they have all known since a childhood spent in Epping Forest (where Rudyard too had spent his happiest hours). The young men grow up and separate. One of them goes into the City where he quickly makes, and loses, a great fortune by shady finance, thus sacrificing to mammon his chance of winning the prize of love. The second is a poet who first starves in a London garret, then compounds with the world by working as a

---

* 'The Galley-Slaves ', his valediction to India, appeared only in the third edition, published in London in 1890.

journalist. Although preyed upon and fleeced by unscrupulous editors, he wins a sufficient reputation to support his Art, and to this Art he dedicates his life. The third lover goes to Shanghai on business, remains faithful to his love, and returns, at the end of the book, to win her.

Just what lesson Kipling deduced from this simple story is not at once apparent, beyond the obvious lesson that, whether he wanted easy money, or literary fame, or his first love, he must look for them in London not Lahore. He was certainly not averse from money-making, and his conduct when he did return to London suggests that his notions of editors and publishers in Fleet Street were derived from the sharks who preyed upon the poet in Besant's novel. Beyond that, some of the novelist's remarks about the East sowed a seed of doubt about the utility of life in India.

' I have seen a great quantity of most interesting things,' says ' Will ' in the novel, as Rudyard might have said in real life. ' I am living among a most remarkable people, whose ways are not our ways. . . . Besides dancing, I have learned to ride, to talk without arguing, to smoke cigarettes, and to play whist. . . . As for adventures, there are none as yet; as for work, it is as monotonous here as in England. I am like a knight who put on all his armour and went out in search of adventures and found none. I might as well have looked for them in the Chigwell Road.'

Upon this revolutionary report, that life overseas might be as commonplace as life at home, Besant had a further comment to make in his novel, and made it with a mannerism that later critics have supposed peculiar to Kipling.

Which things are an allegory [wrote Besant]. There is a thing concerning colonial life which is little comprehended. It is that ideas change slowly out there. The things which change ideas are the new discoveries, the new theories, the new men which are continually turning up at home. We who stay at home are borne along, whether we like it or no, by the current; we change our thoughts, our faiths, our standpoint, with the change that goes on around us. What is wild Radicalism one day is mild Liberalism the next. But in the colonies it is not so. One takes out a stock of ideas and comes home again with them practically the same, and it is not till returning home again that one finds how great is the gulf which a few years have made.

We have Kipling's word for it in his autobiography, amply supported from his family letters, that this popular novel by a writer of the second rank was ' a revelation, a hope and strength ' to him, about the time of his twenty-first birthday. He read and reread it, and learned from it what he might achieve. Many a young man has got a first-rate idea out of a second-rate book. This idea was working at the back of Kipling's mind while he was writing weekly 'turnovers' for Kay Robinson at Lahore, and finding arguments for maintaining his corner of the family square a year or two longer. While the West began to pull at his heart-strings, at the string of ambition, he saw the Indian Empire in a clearer light: the gigantic bulk of native India, so complex, so rich with humanity, so remote from western understanding, so lovable, so helpless, was organized, modernized, protected, and cautiously moved forward into the path of progress by a corps of young English officials who gave to it their youth and health with no expectation of any reward beyond a bare livelihood. If India was being wickedly exploited, certainly they were not the exploiters. It could not be denied, by anyone who took the trouble to enquire, that they were giving India internal security, communications, precautions against famine, irrigation, afforestation, even the rudiment of an educational system, on a scale that no other country in continental Asia or Africa could approach. These young Englishmen had much to be proud of, and it was a matter of pride with Kipling to serve for seven years in this unselfish army.

Everyone who lent a hand to keep the machine running was a comrade. Idlers, critics, and reformers who wanted to tamper with the works, were treated with contempt. At Lahore in the hot weather one could see the engines running with the cowling stripped off; at Simla in the season one could divert oneself with satirical comment about the passengers on the top deck of the Ship of State. But these passengers could not hinder the relentless progress of the machine which was sustained by the labour of an anonymous, unthanked multitude of working officials, inspired by the public-school tradition which Kipling expressed in the phrase:

> The game is more than the player of the game,
> And the ship is more than the crew![28]

So, he thought, it might drive on its course down the centuries. Nevertheless, as a connoisseur of personalities, it gave him pleasure to see at the head of affairs the slightly bored, slightly cynical figure of Lord Dufferin, who was so brightly aware that 'ideas changed slowly' at Simla, so convinced of the necessity to make the best of the second-rate. This was the background to *Plain Tales from the Hills*.

CHAPTER V

SIMLA AND ALLAHABAD (1887-9)

JOBSON'S AMEN (1914)

'Blessèd be the English and all that they profess.
Cursèd be the Savages that prance in nakedness!'
'Amen,' quo' Jobson, 'but where I used to lie
Was neither shirt nor pantaloons to catch my brethren by:

'But a well-wheel slowly creaking, going round, going round,
By a water-channel leaking over drowned, warm ground —
Parrots very busy in the trellised pepper-vine —
And a high sun over Asia shouting: "Rise and shine!"'

　　　　•　　•　　•　　•　　•

'Blessèd be the English and all they make or do.
Cursèd be the Hereticks who doubt that this is true!'
'Amen,' quo' Jobson, 'but where I mean to die
Is neither rule nor calliper to judge the matter by:

'But Himalaya heavenward-heading, sheer and vast, sheer and vast,
In a million summits bedding on the last world's past —
A certain sacred mountain where the scented cedars climb,
And — the feet of my Belovèd hurrying back through Time!'

EIGHTEEN EIGHTY-SEVEN was the year of *Plain Tales from the Hills.* Throughout the early months of the year Rudyard was working with Kay Robinson at Lahore. In the summer he again spent his month's leave with the family at Simla and, on returning to the Plains, began a new way of life. George Allen made the decision on a point which had often been discussed before, to bring his fledgling genius to the more important office of the *Pioneer,* at Allahabad in the region now called the United Provinces, a change from Moslem to Hindu India. It was also a break with the family square, but that was not so formidable an event as it would have been three years earlier. Rudyard was twenty-two years old, and in appearance remarkably mature for his age. He was not now disposed to be desperately lonely and he prided himself on being a salted Anglo-Indian, nor was he without friends in Allahabad. His Simla patron, Sir Edward Buck, could introduce him to Professor S. A. Hill, a meteorologist in Government service, who had recently been appointed to Allahabad as professor of science at the Muir College. Aleck Hill was a quiet, burly man with a bushy dark beard. Except that he was a devoted amateur photographer (in that heroic age of dark-rooms, tripod-mountings, and patent developers) we can find little to record of him. His wife, Edmonia Hill (known as 'Ted') was to play a principal part in Rudyard Kipling's life. She was a lively young American lady from Beaver, Pennsylvania, aged about thirty, with a broad plump face, a pretty snub nose, and a shock of dark curls coming down in a widow's peak on her brow.[1]

Towards the end of the year Mrs. Hill met Rudyard, at the Allens' house, and wrote to her young sister who was still in Pennsylvania:

When we were seated at table and conversation was in full swing, my partner called my attention to a short dark-haired man of uncertain age, with a heavy moustache and wearing very thick glasses, who sat opposite, saying: 'That is Rudyard Kipling, who has just come from Lahore to be on the staff of the *Pi*. He is writing those charming sketches of the native states, *Letters of Marque,* which the *Pi*. is publishing.'

Mr. Kipling looks about forty, as he is beginning to be bald, but he is in reality just twenty-two. He was animation itself, telling his stories admirably, so that those about him were kept in gales of laughter. He fairly scintillated, but when more sober topics were discussed he was posted along all lines. After dinner, when the men joined the ladies in the drawing-room, evidently the retiring young author had marked me for an American, and, seeking copy perhaps, he came to the fireplace where I was standing and began questioning me about my homeland. I am surprised at his knowledge of people and places. He is certainly worth knowing, and we shall ask him to dinner soon.[2]

The acquaintance quickly ripened but it was not until the following June that a close and daily association grew up between Rudyard and his new friend. During the cool weather of 1887–8 he was living a bachelor life at the Allahabad Club with his own horse and trap, and his Moslem servant, Kadir Baksh. There was a much larger European resident population at Allahabad than at Lahore and a less interesting native city. No longer 'a full half' of the managing staff of a country newspaper, he was a special reporter employed by the large organization of the *Pioneer*. Since one of his tasks was to edit its magazine supplement, the *Week's News,* he immediately offered to supply fiction from his own pen, at a cheap rate, in order to save the expense of buying the serial rights of established and costly authors. What he wanted was a wider spread of canvas for his teeming compositions and, modestly, he omitted to secure his copyright in the material he now turned out in profusion. The 'turnovers' for the *Civil and Military* were discontinued, and the best of them were published as *Plain Tales from the Hills,* a few weeks after his meeting with Mrs. Hill. He sent her a copy with a dedicatory verse:[3]

> Would they were worthier. That's too late —
> Framed pictures stand no further stippling.
> Forgive the faults. March '88
>
> To Mrs. Hill
>
> From Rudyard Kipling.

Thirty-two of the *Plain Tales* had been printed in the *Civil and Military;* the remaining eight made their first appearance when the book was published, in January 1888. This time, there was no question of private distribution, and the book was released through the ordinary channels of the Trade by Thacker Spink & Co. of Calcutta. The Indian allotment was sold out rapidly, while the thousand copies despatched to London for the English market long remained on the publishers' shelves unnoticed. These stories, however, were so competent that they were bound to find their place; they were laconic, brilliant, versatile, knowing, cocksure, provoking, and sometimes scandalous. Above all, they were startling and that was a great merit in the decline of the Victorian age. Later, they were allowed by Kipling's admirers in England to fall into the second rank of popularity, but not so abroad. They translated well into French (as *Simples Contes des Collines*), perhaps because they are loaded with gallicisms, and in France they have always been rated high. They are essential to an understanding of Kipling's place in literature.

Written in haste and written to order, the stories are of uniform length, 2000 to 2500 words, that is to say, very short. The limitation of space to a column and a half in his newspaper obliged the author to compress his effects and to eliminate superfluous words. The style, to put it baldly, is that of the gossip-column. In good popular journalism today this conversational style is common, but what other popular journalism than Kipling's has never been allowed to run out of print for sixty years. Not only did he display a talent for finding 'copy' in unexpected places, he devised a way of working up the merest trifles, the tritest anecdotes, into stories, *contes,* that reminded well-read reviewers of Maupassant. Sometimes it was a court-case at Lahore, sometimes a confidence whispered by his partner at a Simla Ball; a scrap of gossip from the Punjab Club; a yarn told by a tipsy soldier to impress a civilian; a beggar's hard-luck story; or, if nothing else was to hand, an anecdote from some old-fashioned book served up *réchauffé*. The tone was always that of smoking-room conversation, beginning and breaking off abruptly, interleaved with asides and cynical comments. These diversions, having served their purpose of focusing some point, were chopped off short with the catch-phrase, 'but that's another story', a phrase which caught on like an epidemic in the nineties. From Emerson, Kipling borrowed the device of heading every tale with a relevant scrap of original verse, and these poetical fragments reveal, even more clearly than the prose stories, his facility at getting the strongest effect from slight material.

The earliest in date of the *Plain Tales,* and one of the most powerful, is 'The Gate of the Hundred Sorrows', written before the author's nineteenth birthday. It has no plot, no climax, but conveys by word-painting the drugged, drowsy atmosphere of an opium-den. 'My friend, Gabriel Misquitta the half-caste, spoke it all, between moonset and morning, six weeks before he died.' It is one of six stories that deal with Indian low life, in the Eurasian borderland where loss of caste brings unavoidable penalties. Two more stories, of Indian domesticity within caste-rules, are told with deeper sympathy. Twenty-four stories, more than half the book, relate events in Anglo-Indian society, many of them in the vice-regal circle at Simla. Four turn on the character of 'Mrs. Hauksbee', a married woman living apart from her husband and able to manipulate affairs of state by social pressure. 'She was a little, brown, thin, almost skinny woman, with big, rolling violet-blue eyes, and the sweetest manners in the world.'[4] In two other stories the hero is the police-officer, 'Strickland', who 'held the extraordinary theory that a policeman in India should try to know as much about the native as the natives themselves. But this has done him no good in the eyes of the Indian Government.'[5] Nine of the stories are about army life, and in four of them there appear the group of three common soldiers, 'Mulvaney, Learoyd, and Ortheris', who were to become Kipling's most celebrated characters. As yet they were but lightly sketched and none of these early soldiers' tales ranks high in popularity, unless perhaps 'The Madness of Private Ortheris' (1888) with its cockney litany of homesickness for London. 'I'm sick to go 'Ome — go 'Ome — go 'Ome. . . . I'm sick for London again; sick for the sounds of 'er, an' the sights of 'er, and the stinks of 'er; orange-peel and hasphalte an' gas comin' in over Vaux'all Bridge.' Five or six of the stories have an uncanny twist, reminiscent of Edgar Allan Poe, and one, 'By Word of Mouth', is a convincing ghost-story. Four or five are farcical, with intimations of Kipling's taste for rather cruel practical jokes. Two of the stories deal with child-life and one of them, 'The Story of Muhammad Din', revealed that love and understanding of little children was already a dominant in Rudyard Kipling's character.

As an example of the technique that distinguishes *Plain Tales* from other contemporary short stories, I propose to examine the tale called 'False Dawn', which first appeared in the published book. It is an anecdote about a man who accidentally proposed to the wrong woman during the darkness and confusion of an Indian dust-storm. The misunderstandings of a night are relieved only by the coming of the dawn.

No man [the tale begins] will ever know the exact truth of this story; though women may sometimes whisper it to one another after a dance, when they are putting up their hair for the night and comparing lists of victims. A man, of course, cannot assist at these functions. So the tale must be told from the outside — in the dark — all wrong.

Darkness is the prevailing tone and 'dark' the keyword of the tale. After a sentence or two about jealousy between sisters, Kipling begins to talk about a man called Saumarez — never clearly described — and about his attachment to the two Miss Copleighs.

The Station wherein all these things happened was, though not a little one, off the line of rail, and suffered through want of attention. There were no gardens, or bands or amusements worth speaking of, and . . . people were grateful for small things to interest them.

It was at the beginning of the hot weather when most people were moving away to the Hills, that 'we' — that is Kipling the narrator, and some undifferentiated others — arranged a moonlight, riding picnic, 'the great Pop Picnic', in order to provide Saumarez with a decent opportunity to pop the question to the elder sister, Maud Copleigh.

We met at the parade-ground at ten: the night was fearfully hot. The horses sweated even at walking-pace, but anything was better than sitting still in our own dark houses. When we moved off under the full moon we were four couples, one triplet, and Me. Saumarez rode with the Copleigh girls, and I loitered at the tail of the procession wondering with whom Saumarez would ride home. Every one was happy and contented; but we all felt that things were going to happen.

The tempo of the story rises as the lovers lose themselves in the darkness and Kipling remarks upon the coming of a storm.

I had felt that the air was growing hotter and hotter; but nobody seemed to notice it until the moon went out and a burning hot wind began lashing the orange-trees with a sound like the noise of the sea. Before we knew where we were the dust-storm was on us, and everything was roaring, whirling darkness.

At the height of the storm 'with the thunder clattering overhead, and the lightning spurting like water from a sluice', the younger sister, Edith Copleigh, came stumbling against Kipling, calling for her horse and to be taken home.

I felt her brush past me and go away. It was too dark to say where. Then the whole sky was split open with one tremendous flash as if the end of the world were coming, and all the women shrieked. Almost directly after this I felt a man's hand on my shoulder, and heard Saumarez bellowing in my ear. Through the rattling of the trees and howling of the wind, I did not catch his words at once, but at last I heard him say, 'I've proposed to the wrong one. What shall I do?'

Against this background of violence and noise, the vulgar conventions and the sly cynicism of the opening paragraphs take on a new complexion. The storm has broken down the reticence of the lovers, and gradually breaks down the misunderstanding of the narrator. In the darkness Saumarez has chosen the wrong woman to whisper to, and the intently prurient spectators have also deceived themselves. He has fulfilled their expectations by proposing to the elder Miss Copleigh although the younger has been his intended quarry.

Kipling now rides away in the confusion to find the right Miss Copleigh, while Saumarez is left to make the best of his explanations to the wrong one, 'to wipe the happy look out of Maud Copleigh's face'. 'I had a perfectly unnecessary notion that everything must be done decently and in order.' The storm had died away, and in the deceptive pallor that precedes the dawn the party reassembled.

As Miss Copleigh and I limped up, Saumarez came forward to meet us, and when he helped her down from her saddle, he kissed her before all the picnic. It was like a scene in a theatre, and the likeness was heightened by all the dust-white, ghostly-looking men and women under the orange-trees clapping their hands — as if they were watching a play.

The story ends with the request that Kipling should ride home with the rejected elder sister. '"Nothing would give me greater pleasure," I said. So we formed up, six couples in all, and went back two by two. Maud Copleigh did not talk to me at any length.'

A vulgar, improbable tale, revealed, as Oscar Wilde put it, by lurid flashes, but strangely moving. The desultory talk, the suburban morality, the salacious prying into this very private affair, form the monochrome background against which the lightning reveals the naked will of the lovers in reckless realism. When daylight comes the other jaded picnickers look as unreal as actors bowing before the curtain. 'I never saw anything so un-English in my life,' says the knowing narrator.

This was the method that Kipling was to elaborate in his maturer works; he would construct a frame about his picture and contrast the picture with the frame. He would intensify his effects by placing them under a spotlight at the back of the stage, as a play within the play. At one remove from the audience, the Player-king can put across melodrama that would be tearing a passion to tatters if delivered directly over the footlights by the Prince of Denmark.

Sometimes the dramatic quality is that of a tableau or set-piece. The scenery is built up, the characters are grouped, and, by the whole context, a situation is revealed with awful clarity. Kipling rarely used the device of the 'twist' by which Maupassant, for example, releases in the last few sentences the hidden key that suddenly enables the reader to see the matter in a new light. Nor is there much narrative, as a rule, in the best Kipling stories. He shows us characters in action by suggesting rather than describing their deeds. What a man does, that he is! The nearest parallel in English literature to these short, intense, concentrated dramas is to be found in verse not prose — in Browning's *Dramatic Lyrics* which so strongly influenced Kipling as a schoolboy. The *Plain Tales* are constructed on the same plan as 'My Last Duchess' or 'The Bishop Orders his Tomb'.

The immediate and astonishing success of the *Plain Tales* in India was inevitable, since the characters were recognized as typical and were often identified. Kay Robinson said that everyone in the Punjab knew who 'Mrs. Hauksbee' was, but Mrs. Hill, who lived far away from Simla and frequented another hill-station in the hot weather, was not so sure. She thought she knew, and Rudyard rallied her playfully about her guesses. Some of the other characters were plain enough, and are revealed under their true names in his letters, but 'Mrs. Hauksbee' — certainly founded upon an actual person — was disguised, as were most of Kipling's story-characters.

Rudyard Kipling at Allahabad to Mrs. Hill at Mussoorie

May 1st, 1888

You ask what did Mrs. Kipling say to it — the Sermon. She didn't say much but she wrote a good deal. Here's an extract from her letter. 'It's clever and subtle and all that and *I* see the morality in it but, O my boy, how do *you* know it? Don't tell me about " guessing in the dark ". It's an insult to your old Mother's intelligence. If Mrs. Hauksbee enlightened you I'm not sorry that she has gone home.' Mrs. H's departure to other and better climes was postponed from the 13th to the 27th and now that I have read the passenger list of the steamer of that date I see why. Well, she was very kind to me in her curiously cynical way and I owe her thanks for half a hundred ideas and some stories. A hasty pencil note from Bombay gives me her farewell and her opinions. She says: —

'Goodbye and cultivate humility. Your last is not bad — very bad — but
it lacks depth and you have made a mistake in not marking the change
between the moods, towards the end. They should slide into one another,
whatever they may do in real life. You have painted them without transition and the effect is streaky. Otherwise it is passable. I leave you to
make my peace with the infuriated amateurs who will have read " All these
men and women merely players ". My barque is on the strand and my
ship is on the shore and, please God, I shall not return.'

                                                        May 2nd, 1888
    I dined with him [Straight] on Monday and the talk turned on the ever-
lasting battle between the Law and the criminal. For one hour and a half
from the coffee to the second cheroot Straight unburdened himself of anecdote after anecdote — each one more grisly than the last. He has been
concerned in most of the more distinguished murder trials of the past
twenty years and 'what he don't know aint hardly worth the knowin''.'
I learnt how the Condemned receive their death sentences and how they
stood at the last moment; how one hair and an overlooked blood spot
supplied a chain of evidence strong enough to draw a man to the gallows
— and a score of other equally fascinating and equally horrible things till,
at last, as Hawthorne says, ' Me seemed that I should never draw a breath
of pure air again.' I am not much in love with my own mind — its a
scrubby grubby sort o' thing but my faith! 'tis cream laid, wire wove,
triple glazed, ivory bank post note paper compared to the mental condition
of one who has sat in judgment professionally upon his fellow men.[6]

Rudyard's new duties at Allahabad required him to travel to various
parts of northern India. In November 1887 he visited the Rajput
states of the Indian Desert, a memorable journey which filled his
notebooks with ' copy '. He used it then for the series of articles entitled
Letters of Marque (afterwards reissued in the volume, *From Sea to
Sea*), and drew on this journey extensively for local colour in *The
Light that Failed, The Naulakha,* and many short stories. His visit
to the abandoned city of Amber was a memorable experience which he
turned to much advantage, above all in the *Jungle Books* where it
reappeared as the ' Cold Lairs '. A rather foolhardy walk, by night
and alone, in the ruins of Chitor gave him further material to be
worked into these pictures.

But when he began to write fiction for the *Week's News,* his new
liberty allowed him to extend his scope, perhaps a little imprudently.
Henceforth no mere Plain Tales ' jammed into rigid frames, but three-
or five-thousand-word cartoons once a week. So did young Lippo
Lippi, whose child I was, look on the blank walls of his monastery
when he was bidden decorate them.'

' 'Twas ask and have, Choose for more's ready.'[7] His work appeared,
far too copiously, in the *Weekly News* and the *Pioneer Mail* through-

out the whole of 1888. Of all his life-work this is the most various in quality, since no writer could maintain his standards when writing so fast and publishing so quickly. Mrs. Hill was a kinder critic than Stephen Wheeler, kinder, too, than Kipling's sharp-tongued mother, and at this time there was no one to discourage him from printing whatever he liked for a hungry market. First issued in the *Pioneer* supplements, his stories were quickly published in groups as paper-backed books. The firm of A. H. Wheeler & Co. held the contract for Indian railway bookstalls and their Mr. E. E. Moreau hit upon the admirable plan of issuing cheap reprints, at one rupee each, for reading in the train. Six volumes of Kipling's new short stories were issued as the first six numbers of the Indian Railway Library before the end of the year 1888. These little books in grey paper covers created the first Kipling boom; they were carried by travellers and tourists, all over Asia and all over the world, getting the notice in London and New York that *Departmental Ditties* and *Plain Tales* at first failed to get. These were the stories that gave the public, outside India, its first impression of Rudyard Kipling, and the £200 he received on account of royalties gave him, for the first time, a balance in the bank.

To modern readers this section of Kipling's work is known from the two larger volumes (*Soldiers Three* and *Wee Willie Winkie*) into which the Railway books were afterwards collected. The most ambitious was *The Story of the Gadsbys,* a short sentimental novel, consisting of eight episodes told in dialogue. Sentimental though it is, *The Story of the Gadsbys* was considered 'daring' in 1888, because of its satirical reflections on *mariage à la mode*. Captain Gadsby of the Pink Hussars is represented as spoiling his career by making a love-match, and the ironical comment of his friend, Captain Mafflin, that 'a good man married is a good man marred' is presented by the author as his final word on the subject. If *The Story of the Gadsbys* had been written by an elderly *roué* in 1912 it would have been nothing much; written in 1888 by a young bachelor aged twenty-two, it was astonishing. Kipling thought it had some merit, and even his father admitted that 'it wasn't all so damned bad'. It is one of those derivative pieces of Kipling's earlier years, which we can trace back to its several tributary sources. The notion was taken from a fashionable French novel of the period, Gyp's *Autour du Mariage*. The plot, which is developed with a great parade of feminine observation and not without some revealing naïvetés, describes the courtship and early married life of a man of the world and an innocent girl.

A study of Kipling's letters reveals the whole background of the tale. The original 'Gadsby' was a Captain Beames of the 19th Bengal

Lancers who used to visit Kipling in his quarters late at night, to unburden himself about a love-affair with a girl of seventeen. Kipling quite openly exploited him as 'copy', and reported the progress of the affair in his letters to Mrs. Hill, whom he consulted about feminine niceties in the first instalment. 'The man was a fiction, was he? I've had him under the lens since 8.15 this evening.'

The fifth volume in the Railway Series includes 'The Man who would be King' which several good critics have selected as Kipling's masterpiece. The method of picture-and-frame is nowhere more effectively developed. The tale begins with a night journey in an 'intermediate' railway carriage in company of a whisky-sodden ne'er-do-well who ingratiates himself by exchanging masonic signs with Kipling, and persuades him to carry a confidential message. So far, the story is an actual experience in Kipling's life. The loafer re-appears one hot night with a companion when Kipling is sitting up late at the newspaper office, feverish and exhausted, but tense with anxiety for some scrap of news from the West which must be inserted before the morning edition can go to press. This again was his frequent and actual experience. Against the frame of observed fact, the author placed his contrasting fiction, in which the two vagabonds, regarding him as their accomplice, unfolded their crazy scheme for carving out a kingdom in Central Asia, a news item that would have eclipsed the expected telegram from Europe, if one could believe in it. To Kipling's surprise they equipped themselves with disguises, camels, and arms, and vanished over the Frontier. 'I would have prayed for them,' he wrote, 'but, that night, a real king died in Europe, and demanded an obituary notice.'

Two years passed, and again Kipling was waiting at night to send the newspaper to press.

> At three o'clock I cried 'Print off', and turned to go, when there crept to my chair what was left of a man. He was bent into a circle, his head was sunk between his shoulders, and he moved his feet one over the other like a bear. I could hardly see whether he walked or crawled — this rag-wrapped, whining cripple who addressed me by name, crying that he was come back . . . 'I've come back,' he repeated; 'and I was the King of Kafiristan — me and Dravot — crowned kings we was! In this office we settled it — you setting there . . . and you've been setting here ever since — O Lord!'

Then follows the long recital, patiently drawn from this crazy, broken creature in fragmentary phrases, of the Kingdom won and lost by the two adventurers, alone, beyond the Pamirs. It runs to 7000 words out of the 12,000 required for the whole story, and the emphasis is skilfully reversed. Hitherto all the force and drama of the tale have been concentrated upon the routine of the newspaper office which has ears only for rumour from the Western World. Now tragedy on an epic scale has started up at the door, a tale of horror like one of those decadent Jacobean dramas that Kipling studied so closely all his life long. The two vagabonds, who had formerly seemed impertinent intruders on the stage, steal the limelight, one dying and the other dead, having played out his part. As the cripple ended his tale

he fumbled in the mass of rags round his bent waist; brought out a black horsehair bag embroidered with silver thread, and shook therefrom on my table — the dried, withered head of Daniel Dravot. The morning sun that had long been paling the lamps struck the red beard and blind sunken eyes; struck, too, a heavy circlet of gold studded with raw turquoises . . . on the battered temples.

'The Man who would be King' is a long story, but not a word too long. Such high praise cannot be given to some others of Kipling's stories written at this period. Even 'The Drums of the Fore and Aft', though generally ranked among Kipling's successes, drags a little. It starts too slowly and too captiously, with 1500 words of rather petulant talk about Army Reform. Then Kipling turns to the barrack-life of the 'Fore and Aft', a regiment that has not been under fire in a generation. Their self-confidence and their innocent delight when ordered on active service, their childlike pretence of being soldiers is exemplified in the character of the two naughty drummer-boys, Lew and Jakin, whose indiscipline defies control by the bandmaster, the sergeant-major, and even by that remote demi-god, the Colonel. Drummer-boys in mid-Victorian fiction were wont to be child-heroes, and not seldom child-saints. It was with gusto that Kipling developed the theme of precocious depravity in the drums of the Fore and Aft.

Jakin was a stunted child of fourteen and Lew was about the same age. When not looked after, they smoked and drank. They swore habitually after the manner of the barrack-room, which is cold-swearing and comes from between clinched teeth; and they fought religiously once a week. Jakin had sprung from some London gutter and may or may not have passed through Dr. Barnardo's hands ere he arrived at the dignity of drummer-boy. Lew could remember nothing but the regiment and the delight of listening to the Band from his earliest years . . . he was most mistakenly furnished with the head of a cherub: insomuch that beautiful ladies who watched the Regiment in church were wont to speak of him as a 'darling'. They never heard his vitriolic comments on their manners and morals, as he walked back to barracks with the Band.

After this long introduction (another 4000 words) the tale moved swiftly to its climax — a rout. The regiment breaks, in panic flight, before a charge of Afghan fanatics. Such things have happened to many regiments, in many battles, and this episode is based upon no one disaster.* But in this instance the situation is retrieved by the two boys who rally the fugitives, with fife and drum, not moved to this action by a desire for glory but because they were a little tipsy with rum from a soldier's bottle. While pricking the bubble of mock-heroism and sham-romance, Kipling does not shirk the admission that the spark of real heroism was there too, beneath the surface. Whether brought into play by rum, necessity, or hysteria, it was indeed used, and valued.

'The Drums of the Fore and Aft' is not a nursery tale. The same volume, *Wee Willie Winkie,* contains three other stories which established Kipling's reputation as a writer on child-life. Two of them, the story which gives its title to the volume and 'His Majesty the King' are conventional tales in a *genre* which delighted our grandparents. The heroes of these two stories are angel-children whose innocent pranks reconcile quarrelling lovers and unite broken families. They are studio-pieces not much unlike Mrs. Burnett's *Little Lord Fauntleroy* (1886) the masterpiece among sentimental juveniles. Insincerity in the subject-matter produced a corresponding insincerity in the style, with the result that these stories provide the crudest examples of the young Kipling's characteristic faults.

The fourth story, 'Baa, Baa, Black Sheep' (1888), falls into a very different category. Though many incidents in Kipling's books are founded upon incidents in his life, his works include only this one fragment of candid autobiography. Kipling's unhappy childhood at Southsea is a well-attested period of his life. But candid revelations of childhood were not so popular in 1888 as they became a generation later, and at least one serious reviewer expressed a preference for angel children. He explained at length in the *Athenaeum* for December 1890 that all the tales in *Wee Willie Winkie* were commendable except 'Baa, Baa, Black Sheep' which was 'not true to life'.

One more of the stories in the Railway Library deserves mention, 'A Wayside Comedy' which appeared in the volume, *Under the Deodars.* At the end of his life, Kipling selected this story as one of the half-dozen in which his 'daemon', the intuitive sense of fitness, did not play him false. He worked hard for 'economy of implication', and struck the keynote for his tale, a rather unpleasant picture of

---

* The episode of the two drummer-boys is taken from *Military Transactions of the British Nation in India,* vol. iii, p. 486, by R. Orme (1763). But the battle is based upon the action of Ahmed Khel, 19th April 1880, in which the 59th Regiment made a good recovery after a momentary panic. The 59th, Mulvaney's 'Ould Regiment', was amalgamated with the 30th and renamed the East Lancashires. They were stationed at Mian Mir, 1880–5.

adultery and deception in an isolated group of friends, with a single phrase, the 'burdensome geniality' of the unobservant husband who, alone, did not know what all the others knew. It was the kind of story that, in those days, was described as a shade too 'French', and in France it has always been much admired.

One whole volume, the first, was devoted to stories about the 'Soldiers Three', Mulvaney, Learoyd, and Ortheris, and the other volumes also included stories of military life. What, in fact, did Kipling know of the Army in 1888?

Throughout the seven years that Kipling spent in India, the whole Indian Empire was prosperous and internally peaceful. After the conclusion of the Second Afghan War, in 1881, there was no heavy fighting on the North-West Frontier for many years though, as ever in the days of the British *Raj*, a large army was deployed on the frontier, mobilized for active service.

While never quite at peace, the tribes of the debatable area across the border did not provoke another large expedition until October 1888, a few weeks before Kipling's departure from India. Then it was necessary to march a whole division of troops into a region never before penetrated by the British, the Black Mountain at the northern extremity of the North-West Frontier. It was an arduous but not a costly campaign, and was concluded after a few skirmishes, with a loss of twenty-five British soldiers.

Kipling's early stories of frontier fighting must therefore have been derived from books, or from soldiers' yarns about their experience in earlier wars before he came to the East. His later stories, written after his return to the West, contain several clear references to the Black Mountain Campaign. But, during the 'eighties, the Indian Army was twice employed in foreign wars: in the Egyptian War of 1884-5 and in the Conquest of Burma, 1885-7. Kipling's sole experience of Egypt was his passage through the Suez Canal in 1882. We know that he had an informant in the person of 'Stalky' whose stories he would readily accept, and who came to Lahore from Egypt. Of Burma, Kipling knew nothing at first-hand, until he called in a sea-going liner at Rangoon and Moulmein for a few days in 1889. Accordingly, we find his Burmese pieces somewhat remote and romantic. Two that give graphic accounts of incidents in the war ('The Ballad of Boh da Thone', August 1888; 'A Conference of the Powers', May 1890) are carefully disposed to focus attention on the circumstances in which the tale is told afterwards, not on the local colour of the Burmese jungle. It is of the North-West Frontier that he writes with a sort of authority and, again, we know that he spent only a few days there, in 1885. What, then, are the sources of his information?

Critics of Kipling's work have tended to underestimate his debt to books. As he could glance at a scene, and pin-point and recall the touch of colour that he needed, so he could glance through a book, select an incident, and make it his own. The files and the works of reference in the *Civil and Military* office, his father's library, and his father's encyclopaedic knowledge of India, gave him many an anecdote or queer scrap of information which he did not hesitate to use where it would fit.

No one need be surprised to learn that 'Cupid's Arrows' is based upon an incident in *Daniel Deronda,* that 'The Killing of Hatim Tai' is taken from Hone's *Everyday Book,* that the story of the two drummer-boys who saved the army is to be found in Orme's *History of India,* that 'Snarleyow' is an episode from Sergeant Bancroft's history of the Bengal Horse Artillery, that 'The Ballad of East and West' is a romantic version of a tale that was in print long before Kipling's day, that 'Gunga Din' was the name he gave to Juma, the heroic water-carrier of the Guides at the siege of Delhi.

Some of the stories were historic before Kipling gave them his distinctive mark, some were the current coin of the barrack-room, the tall stories told by the old soldiers to the recruits. 'The Lost Legion' was a tradition of 1857 arising out of John Nicholson's punishment of the mutinous 55th Native Infantry. 'The Jacket' was an exploit ascribed to Captain Dalbiac, a gunner-officer in the Egyptian War. 'The Big Drunk Draf'' (not an unfamiliar episode to those who remember the old army) was claimed by Lieutenant A. A. Howell of the Northumberland Fusiliers as his own. 'The Taking of Lungtungpen' by a raiding-party of naked soldiers was reported in the *Civil and Military* as an actual achievement of the 2nd Queen's Regiment, a few weeks before Kipling wrote it up as fiction. 'Namgay Doola' was an incident of the Black Mountain Campaign.[8]

Without doubt there are many other military episodes and characters that might be identified from Kipling's soldier stories. He never pretended to invent; it was his pride to record the traditional army legends, and he took the liberty of a Walter Scott or a Robert Burns in remodelling them for a new audience. Where he differed from other writers of battle-pieces was in his extraordinary talent for getting under the skin of his characters and seeing what their eyes must have seen.

> An' now the hugly bullets come peckin' through the dust,
> An' no one wants to face 'em, but every beggar must;
> So, like a man in irons, which isn't glad to go,
> They moves 'em off by companies uncommon stiff an' slow.[9]

Let that be compared with any other account that has ever been written of soldiers going into battle! How did he know that they looked like that?

English literature had long been rich in songs and stories about the navy. Both in romantic and in realistic writing, the Jolly Tars had for centuries enjoyed the favour and the understanding of the reading public. The English tradition, rightly or wrongly, associated the sailor with the fight for freedom, with defence against foreign tyrants; while the soldier, however courageous, was the hireling of usurpers, the instrument of unpopular aggressive war-makers, and so was despised, disliked, and ignored. In literature, the attention he got was confined to the professional heroics of the military historians, while amateur opinion was mostly based on Wellington's cynical remark that his army was recruited from the scum of the earth. Socially, the private soldiers were in fact drawn from the unemployed or unemployable, so that ' going for a soldier' was, in the respectable working-class, regarded as the last degradation, analogous with ' going to the bad '. Once enlisted and marked out by a uniform, the soldiery formed a caste apart and a caste of untouchables, living under conditions in barracks that were not even healthy. Particularly, the incidence of venereal disease was appalling.

Between officers and men there was a social barrier that could rarely be surmounted. The officers, above all, were gentlemen, and it was only by showing aristocratic qualities that a ranker might, in some rare instances, qualify for an officer's commission. Among the gentry, commissioned rank was regarded as a social guarantee; but among the great mass of the Victorian English, the evangelical middle-classes, an army officer commanded scant respect. Yet, underlying the surface flow of anti-militarism there remained a hidden current of admiration, not rational and not articulate, for the red coats, with their strange insignia and pomp, whose life seemed so far removed from the workaday world of England in the nineteenth century. Who were they then, these smart neat young officers, this rough and hearty rank and file who led a double life: appearing sometimes in the police-court news as drunken, diseased reprobates; sometimes as the heroes of quite fabulous adventures in far distant lands, the thin red line of Balaclava, the storming-columns of Delhi, the defenders of Rorke's Drift, the men who advanced across the desert by night to Tel-el-Kebir, who marched through the mountain-passes in tropical heat from Kabul to Kandahar?

Search English literature and you will find no treatment of the English soldier on any adequate scale between Shakespeare and Kipling. He who wishes to know how British soldiers fight, how officers and men regard one another, how they talk the night before the battle, will seek the information in *King Henry V,* or in *Barrack-room Ballads,* for it is to be found almost nowhere else in our English classics. Cromwell's and Marlborough's and Wolfe's and Wellington's soldiers are vanished as though they had never been; they have their panegyrics but not their living records.

It does not appear that Kipling paid much attention to the army during his first two or three years in India. He tells us that he dined with the British regiment at Mian Mir (presumably the 30th East Lancashires) a few weeks after his arrival. A boy of seventeen, and a civilian, he was too shy to speak. Although he met some subalterns on leave at Simla there is no record of his striking up any close friendships with them. From the visit to RawalPindi and the frontier in 1885 we may safely derive his first original composition on a military subject with a smack about it of that penetrating realism which marked his best work.

> The flying bullet down the Pass,
> That whistles clear: 'All flesh is grass.'

These lines give the key to the poem, 'Arithmetic on the Frontier' which appeared in the first edition of *Departmental Ditties* (June 1886).

> A scrimmage in a Border Station —
> A canter down some dark defile —
> Two thousand pounds of education
> Drops to a ten-rupee *jezail* —
> The Crammer's boast, the Squadron's pride,
> Shot like a rabbit in a ride!

The two earliest of the *Plain Tales* to deal with military subjects are 'The Arrest of Lieutenant Golightly', November 1886, and 'His Wedded Wife', February 1887. 'Lieutenant Golightly', a slight anecdote, is given the local colour of Kipling's own retreat from Narkunda to Simla in the previous summer. 'His Wedded Wife' is a clever story, with a smack of 'Stalky' about it, describing a practical joke played in an officers' mess. Everything Kipling wrote about the army before 1887 deals with the officers and the life of the officers' mess. When he began to investigate the canteen and the barrack-rooms with his unobtrusive observation we do not know, but Kay Robinson said that he knew the 'tone' of the regiments at Mian Mir better than the Chaplain.

The first story in which Mulvaney, Ortheris, and Learoyd* appear

---

* Kipling liked to give his characters unusual names. In 1886 there was a Surgeon Mulvaney and a Lieutenant Learoyd at Mian Mir. The names of the characters in ' The Man who would be King ' were suggested by Mrs. Hill.

is 'The Three Musketeers', March 1887, not in its own right an important story. Kipling describes it as told to him, by the three in chorus, in the refreshment room at Umballa Station where he used to change trains for Simla. Though the characters of the soldiers, the Irishman, the Cockney, and the dalesman from the West Riding, are clearly distinguished, the author did not claim to know them well. 'Young mon, what's the notebook for?' asked Learoyd pointedly at the end of the anecdote. But since the three proved useful as a medium for 'turnover' articles, he reproduced them three times again before the year was out. The fourth of these stories, 'The Madness of Private Ortheris', October 1887, is by general consent important. Here it will be sufficient to say that by the time we reach it, the three soldiers have been provided with personal histories from which it should be possible to identify them, if indeed they are founded on fact.

Before investigating Kipling's soldier friends in India it may be well to recall the first two soldiers whom he ever knew well, Sergeant Kearney and Sergeant-major Schofield, the two veterans employed successively at Westward Ho! as 'school sergeants', that is as janitors, drill-instructors, and general assistants with the school discipline. When Kipling went to school as a little boy it was in the time of Sergeant Kearney, a huge, drunken old Irishman who delighted in talking about the Sikh Wars of the eighteen-forties. Kearney retired in 1879, giving place to Schofield, a smart brisk little cockney whose character is indicated by his school nickname of 'Weasel'.* It seems unlikely that these two, who gave Kipling his first impressions of the soldier's character, should not have contributed some features to the characters of Mulvaney and Ortheris.

We are told of the three musketeers in the four early stories that they had seen service at the battle of Ahmed Khel in the second Afghan War, and that when these stories were told, they had recently returned from the war in Burma. In a later story it is expressly stated that they fought in these two wars and in another on the northern frontier, which must be the Black Mountain campaign of 1888. No line regiment in the British Army actually served in all three of these wars. We are therefore forced to assume that Kipling took liberties with his substratum of fact (as he usually did) when writing his soldier tales. They are not to be regarded as told, like *Stalky & Co.*, within a framework of actuality. No evidence has come to light that he did in fact maintain a three-year friendship with any three soldiers, and the disposition of troops in India with their frequent changes of station makes it unlikely. It may be that a chance meeting with three

* 'Foxy' in *Stalky & Co.* He disliked the character Kipling gave him. (*Kipling Journal*, No. 23.)

soldiers at Umballa gave him a peg on which to hang all his succeeding stories of barrack-life, whatever their origin.

He grew tired of writing about them. He tried an alternative line with stories about 'Gunner Barnabas' who never became a favourite with the public.* Then, in March 1888, he discharged Mulvaney from the Army and wrote a story ('The Big Drunk Draf') about him as a civilian on the Indian Railways. By July, all three had been discharged, and 'Private Learoyd's Story' was written in a reminiscent vein about past happenings. In September, he boldly wrote a sketch called 'The Last of the Stories', in which he called up these and others of his characters to bid them farewell. It was no good; he could no more kill them than Conan Doyle, a year or two later, could kill Sherlock Holmes. Mulvaney would crop up time after time with an Irish accent that was ever more outrageous.

After his return to England, Kipling again revived the 'Three Musketeers', and then wrote the stories about them which have been most noticed by modern critics, 'The Courting of Dinah Shadd', 'On Greenhow Hill', and 'Love o' Women'. They made a deep impression on the public and won extravagant praise from some critics, bitter hostility from others. Liked or disliked, they could not be ignored.

Kipling's view of army life in India is gloomy on the whole, a life with few pleasures, no glamour, and no luxury for the rank and file.† The heat and the fever, the recurrent epidemics of cholera, the boredom that leads to hysterical outbreaks of insubordination and violence, the jealous rages that flare into fighting madness among men who have loaded weapons always to hand; such features as these compose the picture. 'Hot-weather shooting cases' were part of the routine of the law-courts, to be reported by the sweating feverish assistant editor of the *Civil and Military,* as his letters testify from 1884 onwards. Murders, courts-martial, executions bulked big in his picture of a soldier's life. The relief of tension came with the recurring campaigns on the frontier, to which the soldiers looked forward with excited pleasure, though the wars offered small prospect of plunder or promotion.

' 'Tain't so much the bloomin' fightin', though there's enough o' that.

---

* A powerful story that does not use the 'Three Musketeers' is 'In the Matter of a Private' (*Soldiers Three*).

†   'We aren't no thin red 'eroes, nor we aren't no blackguards too,
   But single men in barracks, most remarkable like you;
   An' if sometimes our conduck isn't all your fancy paints,
   Why, single men in barracks don't grow into plaster saints.'
                (*Tommy*)

It's the bloomin' food and the bloomin' climate. Frost all night except when it hails, and bilin' sun all day, and the water stinks fit to knock you down. 'Tain't no bloomin' picnic in those parts, I can tell you.'[10]

Nor were the campaigns uniformly victorious. His most successful battle-picture is of a failure in morale, the breaking of the 'Fore and Aft' under fire.

The regiment of the line that Kipling knew best was the 5th Northumberland Fusiliers, who were stationed at Mian Mir from 1886 to 1888; he calls them the 'Tyneside Tail-twisters'. They had fought in the Afghan War, though not in any action which can be identified in a Kipling story; and they fought again in the Black Mountain in 1888; they did not serve in Burma. Kipling knew the officers rather than the men, and it was of this regiment that he wrote the story, 'Only a Subaltern', which contains 'Bobby Wicks', the very young officer, whose devotion is given absolutely to the regiment, and whose virtues are circumscribed by the limits of his profession. Later, when he has made good as an officer, there will be time to explore the higher octaves of life. He has the goodness of simplicity, and his crowning merit is unflinching moral and physical courage, for which there should be a testing time, the day when he must lead his men to face fire; but for 'Bobby Wicks' the time never comes. His tragedy is that he dies young and untried, in the minor heroism of a cholera epidemic, not in the crucial test of battle to which he has devoted himself as a willing victim.

'Bobby Wicks' is the finest specimen of a type which recurs in Kipling's stories, the only typical series in the whole of his cast of characters. They have the public-school virtues of loyalty and common sense, and their absolute standard of honesty is taken for granted. If they drink a little, the habit never interferes with their duty; if they wench, the weakness is kept decently out of sight. They are the young Anglo-Indians for whom and about whom much of his early work was written.

You might suppose 'Bobby Wicks' crude, a philistine or a prig, but you would be wrong. His inarticulate unexpressiveness is a mask put up against the world to hide an emotional life which may be as strange as that of the 'Brushwood Boy', as rich as that of Holden, who married 'without benefit of clergy'. These two are revealed, in their private lives, as individuals of rare distinction, though, in their public lives, they are English types, flattened and smoothed by a conventional education.

The other characters are seen as if through the eyes of these young men. None of his women in the earlier stories quite stands alone, they are as they would appear to a very observant dancing-partner.

His private soldiers (excepting the later Mulvaney) are seen as the pride or the exasperation of their company officers, not as men on their own. His colonels and headmasters and viceroys are regarded from below with a satiric touch that reveals the underlying hero-worship. Every elderly man has a smack of his wise father, every competent middle-aged woman a hint of his mother. 'Bobby Wicks' is, as yet, the only kind of man he has fully understood, and it is through the eyes of 'Bobby Wicks' that he sometimes sees with a flash of intuitive genius into the soul of some drunken soldier, or unfortunate half-caste, or neglected child.

With 'Bobby Wicks' he was so sure, the portraiture so firm, the observation so true, the diagnosis so apposite, that he moulded a whole generation of young Englishmen into that type. They rose up in their thousands, in 1914, and sacrificed themselves, in the image that Kipling had created.

Early in 1888 he made a trip down-country for the *Pioneer,* visiting Benares where, characteristically, he was more interested in the re-actions of the other tourists than in the sights shown to them. Then at the Great Eastern Hotel in Calcutta he smelt the unforgettable sewage-smell of the Hugli and saw the dull correct commercial society of the British-Indian capital. He wrote at large on municipal politics, on harbour-control, and on the pilot-service that so cheaply, safely, and quietly mastered the shifting sand-banks of the Ganges Delta. Night in the sleeping city as ever fascinated him, drawing him on to go the rounds with the vice-squad of the Calcutta police. On its own account, dissipation in that world had no charm for him.

When Rudyard came back to Allahabad in April, it was as a guest of Professor and Mrs. Hill in a ramshackle bungalow called 'Belve-dere', which became his home for his last year in India. It stood in

a large garden, only half-cultivated, with bushes as big as summerhouses of Marshal Niel roses, lime and orange trees, clumps of bamboos, and thickets of high grass

where Darzee the tailor-bird stitched his nest of leaves and Nag the cobra hatched out eggs in the heaps of garden refuse — one of the best-known gardens in the world.[11] Soon his hosts went off to Mussoorie which was their hill-station, and then Rudyard was suddenly recalled up-country to Lahore, as deputy for Kay Robinson who was going on leave. For the last time, since he had made up his mind to quit India soon, he spent the hot season in the Punjab plains, grinding away at the routine of the *Civil and Military.*

His compensation now was to write long gossiping letters, in the form of a running journal kept almost every day, to Mrs. Hill at Mussoorie. One topic he wrote about at length was Captain Beames's confidences, which he was regurgitating as 'Captain Gadsby's'; another was a love-affair of his own. But who was the unknown 'My Lady' to whom he declared an undying though unrequited affection in his letters to Mrs. Hill? It was not, he assured her, Tillie Venner with whom he promenaded to the bandstand in the jaded dusty public garden at Lahore. It was not Ethel Edge, the Chief Justice's daughter, though he admitted his name had been coupled with Ethel's; nor was it Miss Parry-Lambert though everyone supposed Rudyard was engaged to her since he had written that story, 'Venus Annodomini', about her mother. In letter after letter, 'My Lady' appears, but not in any materialized form. The reader begins to suppose her a figment of the young writer's fancy, a projection, perhaps, of Mrs. Hill herself, to whom he must not declare his devotion.

The heat in Lahore became intolerable. He suffered from heart palpitations, and hardly held out till mid-June when, at last, he was released to join his friends at Mussoorie, for a short visit. Then driving through the Sewalik Hills and the Doon Country, he made his way to join the family. From 22nd June to 15th July 1888 was his last Simla season, when, with the added delight of writing every day to Mrs. Hill, he was happier than ever before.

Rudyard Kipling at Simla to Mrs. Hill at Allahabad

At 'Craigsville': Simla. 22.6.88

It was a pleasant home coming but what touched me more than all was the folly of my small terrier — parted with and forgotten seven months ago. She heard my step, this fat white waddler, and was the first to come to me with ecstatic wriggles and jumps and bounds and fawnings such as dogs use to fill in their lack of speech. Then she promptly foreswore her allegiance to both mother and maid who had petted her and fed her as no dog has been fed I am sure, and for the rest of the evening would have nothing of any one but me whom she nuzzled and whimpered over, thrusting her nose into my hand and demanding imperiously that I should notice her. None of us thought that she would remember and I own that I had quite forgotten; but she belied us all — dear little beast. In a moment of expansiveness I said egotistically: — 'I shall think better of myself henceforward.' 'Hear him!' said the Mother. 'Anyone but a man would have said that he would think better of the dog.' Whereby I knew in verity that I had come back to the old life and the ways thereof.

But not wholly, for it is owned that I am no longer ownable and only a visitor in the land. The Mother says that is so and the Sister too and their eyes see far — 'You belong to yourself,' says the Mother, and the Maiden says: — 'You don't belong to us at any rate,' and even in the making of this confession we come together after the wreck of the old home on a new and pleasant platform.[12]

His mother was pleased that he had made up his mind to live with his new friends at ' Belvedere ', if only he would control his temper, and watch his surly moods. ' Living alone has made you so old and uninterested,' she said. ' You'll have to be civil, Ruddy.'

Meanwhile Simla abounded as ever with pretty unattached girls. There was no escaping from Miss Parry-Lambert, until his mother produced a counter-irritant in ' Gussie ' Tweddell whom he was expected to like because she, too, wrote poetry, but Trix and Ruddy only thought her verses as funny as her name. Though a carefree time for Ruddy, it was not so for Trix who was in and out of a love-affair that would not come to a crisis. Another sign of change in his little world was the end of his old easy correspondence with Margaret Burne-Jones. She was to be married to an Oxford Don, named Mackail, a liberal in politics of whom Ruddy could not much approve. He could hardly address her again as ' Dearest Wop '.

Part of this holiday was spent by the Kiplings with a rather distinguished house-party at the ' Retreat ', Sir Edward Buck's villa a few miles away. The letters to Mussoorie, now, were full of talk about Mrs. Napier, a gossiping, over-dressed lady who believed herself to be in the Viceroy's confidence. That season, the Kiplings moved rather in the military than in the civil set. * There were amateur theatricals at the Commander-in-Chief's where Rudyard played ' Brisemouche ', in *A Scrap of Paper,* to the satisfaction of the company. To have won the confidence of England's greatest soldier was an achievement for a young press reporter. Rudyard said the proudest moment of his life was when he rode up Simla Mall, on ' Dolly Bobs ' his grey catlike pony, beside Sir Frederick Roberts, a little red-faced man on a huge fiery chestnut, who consulted him, Mr. Kipling, about what the men in barracks were really saying.

There are tales of Rudyard's last year in India implying, not improbably, that this very young man who had suddenly achieved a little fame, was sometimes too forward in the company of his seniors, too ready to assert his views. He celebrated the conclusion of Lord Dufferin's reign in India with a set of verses which their subject received with something less than good humour, an experiment in the style of Browning's ' Bishop Blougram ' called ' One Viceroy to Another '. A few weeks later he got the *Pioneer* into difficulties by a satirical ballad that accused Roberts, his hero, rather too pointedly, of favouritism in his military appointments. This episode was followed

* His colleague, Howard Hensman of the *Pioneer,* who could tell him more than any man about frontier fighting, was with him at Simla that season.

by a more serious error when the Indian National Congress, then a new young institution which Rudyard was not at all disposed to admire, held its annual convention at Allahabad. A remark about a sympathizer with the Congress, in Rudyard's report, provoked a personal assault upon the editor of the *Pioneer;* and an undignified exchange of lawsuits followed. So characteristic a writer as Rudyard had become could no longer be held to the task of routine reporting.

But now he was looking forward to his next move, since the conditions of his home life, as well as of his work, were changing. His father was in England that summer, on professional business, and Trix at last announced her engagement to John Fleming, a soldier seconded to the Survey Department. Both Rudyard and his mother had suffered much from the heat, and he was advised by his doctor not to spend another hot-weather on the Indian Plains. He had begun to save a little money, and the £200 advance which he had received for his 'Railway' books would buy him a steamer passage to England. London, the theatres, springtime in the English Home Counties called him; he made up his mind to go.

After returning to Allahabad, he had one more journey to make for the *Pioneer,* to the railway workshops and coal-fields of industrial Bengal, before settling down happily in his own room at 'Belvedere' to write his soldier stories. For some weeks he had the house to himself while the Hills went off to Jubbulpore. Almost every day he wrote to Mrs. Hill, and her replies included the professor's photographs of Central India, a district which he knew by hearsay from Sterndale's books on sport and natural history. The marble cliffs of the Nerbudda Gorge, thronged with wild bees, the bald harsh outcrops of rock on the stony plains, the line of the Satpura Hills, and the jungles and grazing-grounds along the Waingunga River, were fixed in his inward vision, though he never saw them outwardly.

For company, in October, he was thrown back upon the Club, where, as a rule, he was a shy and silent member. He struck up a communal friendship with the British regiment in the fort, the 31st East Surreys, a lively corps of cockneys. Captain Bayless of the East Surreys was just then his closest companion. It was a time for renewing his army connexion because the frontier was stood to arms. Rudyard lost a friend, killed in action with the force that marched into the Black Mountain that month, and anxiously awaited news of the Northumberland Fusiliers, who were there.

When the cool weather came, the happiness that he hoped for at Allahabad was marred by the serious illness of Mrs. Hill. Her life was in danger from meningitis, and, when she recovered, she decided to spend her convalescence at home in America. A new plan formed in his mind, he would travel east-about to England and would visit her at her home in Pennsylvania. As he so often felt at the crises of his life, fate dealt the cards. George Allen encouraged him to go by asking him to write a set of travel-sketches for the *Pioneer*. Introductions to new friends in America showered on him: Captain Bayless of the East Surreys had relatives in Montana; his mother recalled that she had an elder brother in New York whom she had not seen for near thirty years; she could recommend him, too, to the painter Edwin Abbey, who was almost an American Pre-Raphaelite. Through masonic friends Rudyard got other names, and best of all was his father's letter to an old friend, Lockwood De Forest (not a relative in spite of the coincidence of their rare Christian names). Rudyard decided to leave India at once, without waiting even for Trix's wedding. Eventually he managed to book a passage with Professor and Mrs. Hill on s.s. *Madura* of the British India line, bound from Calcutta to Rangoon. His weekly letters to the *Pioneer* would bring in something, but neither he nor his editor bothered about the further rights in these travel-sketches which were regarded by both as ephemeral journalism, a negligence that was to cause trouble to Rudyard for many years.[18]

In February 1889 he went up to Lahore to say farewell to the family. Lockwood was in India again, more busy, and more variously interested than ever. Had Ruddy never flown kites in Indian fashion? Well! they must go to the bazaar, now, buy some kites, and plunge into the crowd of Punjabi boys and men, who flew kites every evening beside the River Ravi. Everything was laid aside until they'd exhausted that game. Lahore in February has the pleasantest climate in the world. In the month of roses it was a paradise for ' globe-trotters ', that class of alien intruders which Ruddy had so despised, which he was now to join.

Rudyard Kipling at Lahore to Mrs. Hill at Allahabad

February 23rd, 1889

The quietness of our life here is extreme. I've looked all through T's negatives. I've teased Vixen, smoked baccy, written a turn-over for the C. & M., driven Trixie nearly wild with rude remarks about her cooking — she is doing something with lemon, white of egg and sugar on a stove and she says its cheese-cake; gone over to the School of Art and played havoc with everything I could find there, twisted the turnstile of the Museum until it registered more people than ever come in one day, and generally made myself a surpassing nuisance. There isn't anything more to do except eat, and try to imitate a new salad dressing that the Mother is proud of. I have filled the Mother's heart with envy by describing your short pastry — the stuff that crumbles into white flakes. ' But what's the good of you if you can only *gorge* it, and then know nothing of how it's made,' says Trixie who is prancing round the house with a spoon in one hand and a cookery book in the other. They are an awful busy couple, those two. Always sewing something or cooking something. One of the first questions the Mother asked when I told her of your illness was: '*Does* she worry herself about the servants?' So you see you have deep and genuine sympathizers up here in the Black North.

Sunday

Gott in himmel! An incursion of Austrian maniacs has just swept through the house, gutted the studio and fled, carrying the Pater with 'em to the Museum. There were two of 'em — one a Count something or other — simply wild about India and all that is therein. They had been consigned to us from Bombay and we were first aware of their presence by shrill shrieks from the drive for 'Meestare Kipleen'. Then they pranced in, one a red bearded tornado with a cracked voice, and t'other a dried up walnut looking sort o' man who couldn't speak English. They wanted to go to Peshawur. They wanted to see Graeco-Bhuddist sculptures — they wanted to encamp on the Attock; they wanted to embrace the whole blazing East and they wriggled with impatience as they explained their needs. Pater took the wildest and I tackled t'other in a wild polyglot of French and vernacular. I guess that was a fair enough approximation to Austrian. They tore through the Pater's portfolios; they seemed ready to tear down the pictures from the walls and the big one, backing the Pater into a corner, stood over him while he shouted: 'Tell me now about Alexandare. I am in him mooch interest. *Did* he now come to this place, and where is Taxila.' All this as though Alexandare was a brother globe-trotter who had just gone through. It takes a good deal to put the Pater out of countenance (He's my father you know) but he collapsed when he was called upon to give a résumé of Indian archaeology and I chuckled. The other man had got hold of T's photo studies of men and animals taken to help the Pater's drawings and between gasps of Austrian admiration was wildly appealing to me for duplicates. 'I am artist you know,' was his explanation and he spoke as who should say: — I am the Almighty.[14]

Lockwood was always being saddled with such visitors. Not long before it had been two mysterious Frenchmen who had arrived at Simla across the passes from the north, no one knew when or how. No less a man than F. H. Cook (manager of Thomas Cook & Son) had visited Lockwood at Lahore, and the personal attention of the world's leading travel-agency was given to Ruddy's globe-trotting. He set off for Calcutta with enthusiasm, like a schoolboy released for a holiday; he had liberty, money in his pocket, and a sense of pride in his seven years' apprenticeship.

CHAPTER VI

A RETURN TO LONDON (March–October 1889)

---◆►---

THE SONG OF THE BANJO (1893)

By the bitter road the Younger Son must tread,
  Ere he win to hearth and saddle of his own, —
'Mid the riot of the shearers at the shed,
  In the silence of the herder's hut alone —
In the twilight, on a bucket upside down,
  Hear me babble what the weakest won't confess —
I am Memory and Torment — I am Town!
  I am all that ever went with evening dress!

      With my '*Tunka-tunka-tunka-tunka-tunk!*'
        So the lights — the London Lights — grow near and plain!
      So I rowel 'em afresh towards the Devil and the Flesh,
        Till I bring my broken rankers home again.

In desire of many marvels over sea,
  Where the new-raised tropic city sweats and roars,
I have sailed with Young Ulysses from the quay
  Till the anchor rumbled down on stranger shores.
He is blooded to the open and the sky,
  He is taken in a snare that shall not fail,
He shall hear me singing strongly, till he die,
  Like the shouting of a backstay in a gale.

And the tunes that mean so much to you alone —
  Common tunes that make you choke and blow your nose —
Vulgar tunes that bring the laugh that brings the groan —
  I can rip your very heartstrings out with those;
With the feasting, and the folly, and the fun —
  And the lying, and the lusting, and the drink,
And the merry play that drops you, when you're done,
  To the thoughts that burn like irons if you think.

KIPLING the globe-trotter left Calcutta on 9th March 1889. On the 14th he was at Rangoon, on the 24th at Singapore, on 1st April at Hong-Kong, on 15th April at Nagasaki; on 11th May he left Yokohama for San Francisco: a month for renascent Japan and a month for the rest of the Far East. It is hardly to be expected that his comments on the politics and economics of farther Asia will have the weight of his comments on the Punjab where he lived and worked so long. The articles he wrote light-heartedly for the *Pioneer* were never meant to be perpetuated. He was on holiday, on s.s. *Madura* with 'Ted' and 'Aleck' Hill (he sometimes now ventured to use short names), as happy as a child, and with a child's enthusiasm he explored the new world of commerce and seafaring. The routine of shipboard life, so dull for a lonely traveller, so entertaining in a congenial party of friends, presented him with a range of technical topics which occupied his mind for the next ten years.

This was the moment in history when the steamship and the submarine cable had removed the uncertainty of sea travel, when voyages were still long but had become sure, so that the life of a ship's passenger had become a new social mode — safe, select, and utterly isolated from the world. For a few years only, not more than two generations, did this phase endure, until space-divisions were eliminated by the radio techniques, and time-periods minimized by swift air travel. The liner life that Kipling knew is as extinct as the stagecoach life that Dickens knew, and Kipling is the poet of the steamship as Dickens is the novelist of the stagecoach. It is Kipling's discovery of ships and harbours and seafaring men that is noteworthy from this voyage; he was quickly fascinated by the yarns that are told in liners' smoking-rooms. More than once he used his graphic, vulgar little phrase about 'men in pajamas sitting abaft the funnel and swapping lies of the purple seas'. There was the man's world of the smoking-room and the deck on the tropical night, and there was the woman's world of the saloon, where every gentleman scrupulously dressed for dinner — a world of rippling talk and laughter with 'Ted' and 'Aleck', of paper-games and rhymes scribbled on menu-cards which Ruddy threw off lightly, and which she preserved as the precious workshop chips of her young genius.

At Rangoon they went ashore together to the Shwe Dagon Pagoda where Rudyard was intoxicated with the colour. 'Give me lilac, pink, vermilion, lapis lazuli, and blistering blood-red under fierce sunlight that mellows and modifies all.' He confessed himself overcome with mixed emotion while he derided himself for being a mere tourist. But Rangoon meant more to him as the base-camp of the Burmese campaign; its streets were thronged with his beloved British 'Tommies', on the best of terms with the population here, whatever might be their relation to the dacoits in the jungle.

The three friends transferred themselves into a smaller ship which took them eastward across the Bay to Moulmein where, on a day that

Rudyard never forgot, 'Aleck' set up his tripod and photographed
first the elephants at work, and then a view of the sea from the terrace
beside an old pagoda hung with bronze bells that the worshippers
smote with stag-horns. 'I should better remember what the pagoda
was like,' wrote Rudyard, 'had I not fallen deeply and irrevocably in
love with a Burmese girl at the foot of the first flight of steps.'

When he reached Malaya, it had hardly yet begun to move into that
current of progress which made it so prosperous twenty years later.
At Penang and Singapore he first found himself face to face with the
Chinese race, to whom he took an unaccountable dislike. He tasted
the night-life of Hong-Kong with another young globe-trotter, and
hated it. Canton he described as 'a big blue sink of a city full of
tunnels, all dark and inhabited by yellow devils', which, said Professor
Hill, 'was an intemperate libel on a hard-working nation'. Rudyard
and the Professor wrangled about China.

Neither at Penang, Singapur, nor this place have I seen a single China-
man asleep while daylight lasted. Nor have I seen twenty men who were
obviously loafing.

It grieves me that I cannot account for the ideas of a few hundred million
men in a few hours. This much, however, seems certain. If we had
control over as many Chinamen as we have natives of India, and had
given them one tithe of the cosseting, the painful pushing forward, and
studious, even nervous, regard of their interests and aspirations that we
have given India, we should long ago have been expelled from, or have
reaped the reward of the richest land on the face of the earth.

They crossed to Japan in a P. & O. liner, which Rudyard found to
be as hidebound in its regulations and as deficient of comforts as any
P. & O. liner west of Suez; he was also seasick. Then came a month's
idleness in old Japan, in a country hardly yet touched by western
influence and touched — or so he thought — entirely for the worse.
The brand-new tailor-made western clothes of the bureaucrats and
soldiers were as ugly and ill-fitting as the tailor-made western political
constitution. A man who was learning to think poorly of votes and
resolutions and caucuses in the West could not be expected to admire
them when imposed, corruptly, upon an indifferent people in the East.
A parliamentary system, as he supposed, was unlikely to do much good,
anywhere; industrialism was not to be commended in the only country
in the world where arts and crafts, as William Morris commended
them, were universally practised and respected; the westernized army
did not impress him very favourably; he considered the cavalry poor
and the infantry perhaps inferior to the British Gurkha regiments. No
one thought differently in 1889.

The Japan of romance — cherry-blossom, geishas, traditional courtesy, family devotion, all set against the landscape that was so fashionable in London studios — it was here indeed; and on this score he
agreed with the Professor.

All the pretty maidens put on their loveliest crêpe sashes — fawn colour,
pink, blue, orange, and lilac, — all the little children picked up a baby each,
and went out to be happy. In a temple garden full of blossom I performed
the miracle of Deucalion with two cents' worth of sweets. The babies
swarmed on the instant, till, for fear of raising all the mothers too, I
forebore to give them any more. They smiled, and nodded prettily, and
trotted after me, forty strong.

Japan is a great people. Her masons play with stone, her carpenters
with wood, her smiths with iron, and her artists with life, death, and all
the eye can take in. Mercifully she has been denied the last touch of firmness in her character which would enable her to play with the whole round
world. We possess that — We, the nation of the glass flower-shade, the
pink worsted mat, the red and green china puppy-dog, and the poisonous
Brussels carpet. It is our compensation.

Having come to these conclusions they set sail in an American ship,
the *City of Peking,* for a twenty days' voyage across the stormy North
Pacific. If, from Rudyard's loose, slight, and gay impressions for the
readers of the *Pioneer,* we are to deduce anything about his considered
opinion of Asia, it is a sense of distaste for lazy, dirty Hindustan where
the college-trained Bengali does not ' sink his money in railway companies, or sit down and provide for the proper sanitation of his own
city, or of his own motion cultivate the graces of life '. There was
hope for Japan, where craftsmanship and cleanliness were still practised,
if only western political corruption could be held off. Japanese imperialism never entered his mind, and it was with satisfaction that he
revised his first impressions of the army; on a second inspection they
fared much better, and much, he thought, might be done with them
under European command.

Seaborne trade, financial organization, naval power were the Englishman's prerogative, solely because he alone could operate them in
1889, and for many years afterwards. Kipling began to see that British
India was not the centre of the system, not the normal pattern of
British expansion. The sailor and the merchant, not the soldier and
the Indian civilian, were the common types of British overseas. India
had one solid asset — an army, and there was no other worth a
moment's alarm in the Far East, as yet. He threw a careful glance at
the fortifications wherever he went and speculated on the range of the
British China Squadron. As far as the China Coast, British sea-power

was unchallenged. In Japan he felt himself to be in the American sphere, and approached the coast of California with his critical faculties sharpened.[1]

California, sixty-five years ago, was still the 'Wild West', 'where the blindest bluffs hold good and the wildest dreams come true'. Perhaps Kipling, fresh from the gravity of the Indian Administration, was a little too ready to accept the tales told him by bar-loafers who knew nothing of the English talent for understatement. Perhaps his love of prying into unsavoury byways of foreign towns misled him, since, in a fortnight at San Francisco, he encountered two crimes of violence. It was the lawlessness, the custom of carrying a pistol in the pocket, the contempt for legal niceties that impressed him most.

He was a young tourist, and a young politician. With a singular lack of discretion, which he bitterly lamented and never repeated, he delivered himself into the hands of the newspaper reporters who met the ship. What he said, except that he criticized a dozen cherished institutions before he had been three days in the country, will never be known. What the reporters credited him with saying was served up hot and dished up cold again and again. He never lived down his first comments on America; he 'blazed away at us', said the *New York World,* 'with a ferocity that throws Dickens and Mrs. Trollope into the shade'. The letters he wrote to the *Pioneer* were damning enough and, since they were not secured by copyright, they were reprinted with horrified gusto in America. His very first comment on San Francisco harbour was somewhat tactless:

When the *City of Peking* steamed through the Golden Gate I saw with great joy that the blockhouse which guarded the mouth of the 'finest harbour in the world, Sir', could be silenced by two gunboats from Hong Kong with safety, comfort, and despatch.

'Joy' was a hard word to digest in that context, though he meant no more than that his estimate was right. A week later, he applauded with real sincerity an appeal for a stronger American Navy made by Lieutenant Carlin, the hero of the Samoa hurricane. What he condemned in American policy was their aggressive talk and actual impotence. If they would take part in the white man's task of pacifying the world he would be the first to encourage them. While Lieutenant Carlin spoke modestly of the need for more warships he was supported by a 'coruscating Niagara of blather-skite'. 'How in the world can a white man, a Sahib of Our blood, stand up and plaster praise on his own country?'

His introduction to 'the American Eagle screaming for all it was worth' sickened him with American politics — not a difficult matter since all politics sickened him.[1]

Scores of men have told me [he said in his first week] that they would as soon concern themselves with the public affairs of the city or State as rake muck. Turn now to the august spectacle of a Government of the people, by the people, for the people. . . . This mass of persons who vote is divided into two parties — Republican and Democrat. . . . The Democrat as a party drinks more than the Republican, and when drunk may be heard to talk about a thing called the Tariff, which he does not understand, but which he conceives to be the bulwark of the country or else the surest power for its destruction. Sometimes he says one thing and sometimes another, in order to contradict the Republican, who is always contradicting himself.

These were unfortunate words for launching the career of a man of letters in America, and it was little help to know that he could write as intemperately of liberals in England.

He delivered himself of many other shallow comments:

When the hotel clerk . . . stoops to attend to your wants, he does so whistling or humming, or picking his teeth, or pauses to converse with someone he knows. These performances, I gather, are to impress upon you that he is a free man and your equal.

Most of the men wore frock-coats and top-hats — but they all spat. They spat on principle.

They delude themselves into the belief that they talk English — and I have already been pitied for speaking with 'an English accent'. The man who pitied me spoke, so far as I was concerned, the language of thieves.

There was wealth — unlimited wealth — in the streets, but not an accent that would not be dear at fifty cents. . . . These persons are harmless in the earlier stages; that is to say, a man worth three or four million dollars may be a good talker, clever, amusing, and of the world; a man with twice that amount is to be avoided; and a twenty-million man is — just twenty millions.

The American does not drink at meals as a sensible man should. Indeed he has no meals. He stuffs for ten minutes thrice a day. . . . He pours his vanity into himself at unholy hours, and indeed he can hardly help it. You have no notion of what 'treating' means on the Western slope. It is more than an institution; it is a religion.

From these angry and ill-judged comments, the reader might suppose that Rudyard hated America and the Americans, but he did not. He was amused and fascinated, made many friends, and enjoyed himself immensely in San Francisco, even though the Hills had gone off by train, leaving him there alone. He was befriended by a Mrs. Carr, a friend of his mother's, who took him about in wealthy society. Best of all he liked a picnic on the beach with her children whom he 'filled up with ice-cream soda and peanuts'. It was pleasant to talk with

Mrs. Carr about old days in North End Road. The other half of his life was spent with professional friends, journalists, who twice interviewed him for the San Francisco *Examiner*.* Many accounts of other adventures in California were afterwards put out, but all seem equally fictitious. He was pleased by his reception as a distinguished guest from overseas, as his hosts were astonished at this 'little dark man with a perfectly villainous briar-pipe', but he made no great mark. 'I never knew a foreigner who asked so many questions, and such strange ones', said one journalist.

After a few days in 'Frisco he went up the coast to Portland, Oregon, and again made friends with local newspapermen. 'We spent most of the night', wrote one of them, 'in side-splitting laughter over a line of barrack-stories in a vernacular almost unintelligible to a New Englander.' Rudyard had come to Portland for a fishing-trip up the Columbia River, when he caught his first salmon, a twelve-pounder. Fishing was the one outdoor sport at which Rudyard was not too near-sighted to excel, and it is also on record that in his fishing-kit the natives described him as the very caricature of a travelling English-man; they called him 'Johnny Bull'.

From Portland he went to Tacoma, then in the crisis of a land-boom which he described, with great vivacity, in *Letters of Travel;* and, fore-warned against speculation, he risked no investment there. It was a different matter when he crossed the border to law-abiding British Columbia and, proud to become a landowner under the British flag, he treated himself to a town lot in Vancouver City. It must be admitted that his confidence was misplaced; they out-smarted him in Vancouver, B.C., just as they would have out-smarted him in Tacoma.

Early in July he moved across the ranges into Montana, to a cow-town where the cowboys were gathering to celebrate the 'Fourth'; then spent a week in the Yellowstone Park. He did not omit to report the wonders of nature faithfully for his paper, but was more interested in making friends with a detachment of the American army. They were slovenly, they were undrilled, they were despised even more heartily by the civilians than British soldiers were despised, but they could shoot and they could ride; and their officers were serious students of their profession. Perhaps it was the discovery that many of the troopers were time-expired men from the British service that made Kipling take them seriously. He thought there was something in their mounted-infantry tactics which even Captain Gadsby of the Pink Hussars might study with advantage.[2]

* If Mrs. Hill may be believed, he wrote a signed article for the paper, though it seems to have escaped the notice of the collectors.

Kipling's accounts of Salt Lake City, or of the stockyards of Chicago, do not differ from those of other tourists, except in sharpness of observation. It was when he reached the eastern States that he became something more than a globe-trotter. For nearly two months he made his home at Beaver, a little country town on the Monongahela, in the house of Mrs. Hill's parents, leaving them occasionally to visit places of interest in the east. Mrs. Hill was living with her father, Professor R. T. Taylor, the president of a small college, and with them was her young sister, Caroline Taylor, a cheerful, plump, young girl. 'Ted' had often written to Caroline about her friendship with Rudyard, and we may imagine the mixed emotions with which she presented him. 'Ted' must have been occasionally embarrassed by her devoted admirer, though no grain of evidence survives to suggest that Rudyard ever spoke to her as a lover. Almost any happily married woman in her position would have discreetly diverted his attention to her younger sister, unattached and near to Rudyard's age. By 11th August we find him somewhat coyly asking after 'Miss Carrie' when writing his usual narrative letter to Mrs. Hill. He had gone off to Buffalo, in company with her cousin, Edgar Hill, to see the Falls, but what he most enjoyed on that journey was watching a grain-elevator at work. He made a trip to Washington, where some keen soldiers from the War Department found him out, and cross-questioned him about the North-West Frontier. At Philadelphia, too, it pleased him best to yarn with the deep-sea sailors along the waterfront.

In a hotel he had a refreshing experience:

'There are three gentlemen from India here, natives of your country,' quoth the clerk. 'Amen,' said I, and turned up the register to find the names of Allbless, Rustomjee, and Bryamjee, all Parsees — and Allbless, at least, of a family I knew something about. When I went in to supper I found 'em seated at a table and stealing behind 'em spake in the sweetest of vernaculars.

At Boston the historic associations caught his fancy — and more so at Lexington and Concord than at any other place he had visited. He had, also, a pilgrimage to make to a literary shrine, not to one of the New England sanctuaries, but to the house of Mark Twain, at Elmira, New York. Rudyard, who so resented intrusion on his own privacy, seems not to have noticed that his visit to Mark Twain was equally impertinent. Mark Twain received him with courtesy and gave him 'copy' for an interview which was reprinted in uncounted American papers.

Imagine a rolling, wooded, English landscape, under the softest of blue skies, dotted at three-mile intervals with fat little, quiet little villages, or aggressive manufacturing towns that the trees and the fold of the hills mercifully prevented from betraying their presence. The golden-rod blazed in the pastures against the green of the mulleins, and the cows picked their way home through the twisted paths between the blackberry bushes.

This sightseeing was irrelevant to his real study of American life at Beaver.

Here were Americans and no aliens — men ruling themselves by themselves and for themselves and their wives and their children — in peace, order, and decency. . . . they were Methody folk for the most part — ay, Methody as ever trod a Yorkshire Moor, or drove on a Sunday to some chapel of the Faith in the Dales. The old Methody talk was there, with the discipline whereby the souls of the Just are, sometimes to their intense vexation, made perfect on this earth in order that they may ' take out their letters and live and die in good standing'.

This unusual throw-back to the methodist morale of his father's family did not distract Rudyard's eye from present humanity. He liked

The absolutely fresh, wholesome, sweet life that paid due reverence to the things of the next world, but took good care to get enough tennis in the cool of the evening; that concerned itself as honestly and thoroughly with the daily round, the trivial task as with the salvation of the soul. I had the honour of meeting in the flesh, even as Miss Louisa Alcott drew them, Meg and Joe and Beth and Amy, whom you ought to know.

He was now in love with America and with the American girl in general, rather than with the specimen that Mrs. Hill had laid before him in particular, and through the American girl he came to a better understanding of the American man.

Pick an American of the second generation anywhere you please — from the cab-rank, the porter's room, or the plough-tail, — especially the plough-tail, — and the man will make you understand in five minutes that he understands what manner of thing his Republic is. He might laugh at a law that didn't suit his convenience, draw your eye-teeth into the bargain, and applaud 'cuteness on the outer verge of swindling, but you should hear him stand up and sing:

' My country, 'tis of thee . . .

He rhapsodized, a little recklessly, about the supposed Anglo-Saxon race.

There must be born a poet who shall . . . compose the greatest song of all — The Saga of The Anglo-Saxon all round the earth — a paean that shall combine the terrible slow swing of the *Battle of the Republic* with

Britannia needs no Bulwarks, the skirl of the *British Grenadiers* with that perfect quickstep, *Marching through Georgia,* and at the end the wail of the *Dead March.* Will any one take the contract? [3]

When he had cooled down a little, it was to be his own.

His holiday over and his money spent, he went to New York in September and seriously set himself to work. A cheerful sign was the sudden appearance of a whole crop of reviews of his Indian 'Railway' stories in the English magazines, while an American publisher had already paid him the compliment of issuing a pirated version of the *Plain Tales.*

No more promising work has recently appeared in the English tongue [said the *St. James's Gazette*] than the Anglo-Indian stories of Mr. Kipling.

A more readable or amusing book we have seldom come across [said *Vanity Fair*].

Mr. Kipling does not write with rose-water [said the *World*]. The story called 'His Majesty the King' is moreover somewhat maudlin at the best and 'Baa, Baa, Black Sheep' is too grim and unlovely to be associated with the playfulness of childhood. But 'The Drums of the Fore and Aft' is a fine tale, full of rough life and spirit and touched with just the right proportion of pathos to redeem its coarseness.

The worst of recommending these publications [said a writer in the *Saturday Review*], which we do very heartily, is that apparently they are difficult to procure. They appear in paper-covered little vols., but these vols. are not found on English railway bookstalls. Very little that is so new and so good can be discovered on these shrines of fugitive literature. Mr. K. is a new writer, new to the English as distinct from the Anglo-Indian public. He is so clever, so fresh, and so cynical, that he must be young.

The first analytical essay by a writer who knew Kipling's background, and knew India, was an article in *The Academy* by Sir William Hunter, a member of Lord Dufferin's Council, who had himself been satirized in *Departmental Ditties.*

Some day a writer will arise [he wrote], perhaps this young poet is the destined man — who will make that nobler Anglo-Indian world known as it really is. It will then be seen by what a hard discipline of endurance our countrymen and countrywomen in India are trained to do England's greatest work on the earth . . . of this realistic side of Anglo-Indian life Mr. Kipling . . . gives glimpses. His serious poems seem to me the ones most full of promise. Taken as a whole his book gives hope of a new literary star of no mean magnitude rising in the east. [4]

Though Kipling had published little or nothing in America he was thus not quite an unknown man when he arrived in New York. His first call was on his father's friend, De Forest, who gave him an introduction to Henry Harper, the head of the New York publishing profession, and this introduction was backed by Edwin Abbey the painter. He called at the office of Harper Brothers on 10th September and met with such a reception that he never forgave them. They dismissed him with a letter 'just one and a half lines long'. Tradition gives the words spoken to him as: 'Young man, this house is devoted to the production of literature'.[5] Whatever were the words, they did not damp his ardour; he was off next day in the best of spirits, with a fund of lively messages for Caroline Taylor. He never had to ask a favour of an American publisher again.

His last fortnight in the United States was given to the De Forests on Long Island, and to his uncle Henry Macdonald in New York City.

My uncle reminds me pathetically from time to time that I am the only one of his blood-kin who has come to him for thirty years; speaks of me as 'my boy' and yarns away about literature. The Aunt, who does not care for books, is different, but I am making good headway there. This evening I spent in their company and she out-thawed much. . . . Some day we will put it in a book, and laugh at it all to ourselves.[6]

It was to Mrs. Hill that he wrote these words. She was still his confidante, and again he was to have the happiness of travelling in her friendly company. Mrs. Hill was returning to India by way of Europe, and was taking Caroline Taylor with her; Edgar Taylor, their cousin, squared off the party. They arrived at Liverpool by the s.s. *City of Berlin* on 5th October 1889, and all four went on to London.

What were Rudyard's first impressions of England after seven years' absence? No record has survived. He had gone away a boy, certainly a precocious boy but not yet seventeen years old; he returned a man nearing his twenty-fourth birthday and conscious of a fund of experience that marked him out among conventional Londoners. World-travel was rarer then than it is today, and the raw physical danger of life in tropical Asia seemed far removed from the security of Victorian Kensington. Young Rudyard felt himself to have an advantage over his London acquaintances in knowing two worlds, East and West, while they knew one only. If they regarded him as an outlandish provincial, he returned their condescension with amused contempt, not unmixed with a tinge of unconscious envy.

It appears that he resumed his connexion with his childhood friends, with the 'Three Old Ladies', now very old, and with the Burne-Joneses. While looking for a lodging, he stayed at North End Road

RUDYARD KIPLING, THE LAST PHOTOGRAPH, AGED 68

and, after a short holiday in Paris, found an eyrie from which to survey London, in two rooms and a landing on the third floor of a tall house called Embankment Chambers at the foot of Villiers Street, with a view southwards across the river, and only a few doors away from the London office of the *Pioneer*. Mrs. Hill and Miss Taylor were there to see him established, to arrange his sitting-room with the Bokhariot rugs and Japanese knick-knacks he had collected on his travels, to provide company and conversation in a chilly autumnal world.

At Lahore his mother complained that she had little news of her son. The only intimate picture of Kipling's life in London is revealed in the series of letters which he wrote to his two friends after their departure for India on 25th October. This new world in which he now felt quite alone was as strange to him as a desert island; and its inhabitants offered him no comfort. Though they took notice of him, it was as a rarity, as a curiosity from overseas, not as a comrade.

Many persons of distinction, after his fame was assured, claimed to have launched Kipling in the literary world and, indeed, the rumour of his Indian reputation had preceded him. He had not been more than a few days in London before he was taken by Andrew Lang to the Savile Club, the acknowledged meeting-place of critics, editors, and novelists. Andrew Lang, ' detached as a cloud but never kinder in your behalf than when he seemed least concerned with you ', was, among other things, reader for the publishing firm of Sampson Low, and had already advised them to take over the English rights of the six volumes in the *Indian Railway Library*. Arrangements were made for their reissue in London by Kipling in person, the only occasion in his life, as he said rather defiantly, when he negotiated directly with a London publisher. He visited Sampson Low's office, at St. Dunstan's House near the bottom of Fetter Lane, in November, and struck some sort of bargain, but not a good one for himself. The first volume, *Soldiers Three,* in an edition of 7000 copies for the English market, was published early in 1890, and it was not until then that Kipling's stories first became known to the general reading public in England.[7]

Meanwhile he had to live; the £200 with which he had set out from India did not carry him far; he had sold little or nothing in America, and money for his articles in the *Pioneer* was slow to arrive. Though half the editors in London, and two or three publishers, were anxious to make his acquaintance, he was too proud to ask them for money in advance.

People who ask for money, however justifiably, have it remembered against them. The beloved Aunt, or any one of the Three Old Ladies would have given to me without question; but that seemed too like confessing failure at the outset. My rent was paid. I had my dress suit; I had nothing to pawn save a collection of unmarked shirts picked up in all the ports, so I made shift to manage on what small cash I had in pocket. My rooms were above an establishment of Harris the Sausage King, who, for tuppence, gave as much sausage and mash as would carry one from breakfast to dinner when one dined with nice people who did not eat sausage for a living. Another tuppence found me a filling supper. The excellent tobacco of those days was, unless you sank to threepenny 'shag' or soared to sixpenny 'Turkish', tuppence the half-ounce: and fourpence, which included a pewter of beer or porter was the price of admission to Gatti's Music hall.[8]

Kipling's earliest introductions in London were through two journalists to whom he was already indebted in India. One was Mowbray Morris, the editor of *Macmillan's Magazine,* who had once been Art Editor of the *Pioneer;* the other was his old senior, Stephen Wheeler, a friend in need. Wheeler was on the staff of the *St. James's Gazette,* a literary evening paper of a kind long since defunct, and introduced Kipling to the editor, Sidney Low, who thus described their meeting:

> I spent an afternoon reading *Soldiers Three* and when I went out to a dinner-party that evening I could talk of nothing but this marvellous youth who had dawned upon the eastern horizon. My host, a well-known journalist and critic of those days, laughed at my enthusiasm which he said would hardly be justified by the appearance of another Dickens. 'It may be,' I answered hotly, 'that a greater than Dickens is here.'
>
> I got Wheeler to put me in touch with Kipling on his arrival in London, and one morning there walked into my office a short, dark, young man with a bowler hat, a rather shabby tweed overcoat, an emphatic voice, a charming smile, and behind his spectacles a pair of the brightest eyes I had ever seen. He told me that he had to make his way in English literature, and intended to do it, though at the time he was young, very poor, and (in this country) quite unknown. I suggested that he might help to keep his pot boiling by writing sketches and short stories for the *St. James's,* which suggestion he willingly accepted. He also accepted my proposal to come out and lunch with me.
>
> We sat down in the grill-room of Sweeting's Restaurant in Fleet Street. I wanted to 'draw' Kipling, and I drew him to some purpose by getting him to tell me about places he had seen in India and elsewhere. He was in no wise reluctant, being exceedingly frank and communicative, and overflowing with ideas and memories which had to find vent; and he talked in those days with the same abandon and energy as he wrote. One after another of the lunchers laid down knife and fork to listen to him, and presently he had half the room for his audience. He was quite unconscious of the attention he evoked. . . . A day or two later he sent me a contribution, which I received with delight and promptly printed. This,

as far as I know, was the first piece from Kipling's pen published in England. * [9]

In the same month, November 1889, the first of two long ballads was accepted by Mowbray Morris. It was typical of Kipling that his first step in starting a new career, in a new country, should be under a new name; he would not derive adventitious support from a reputation earned elsewhere. Accordingly, the poems appeared in *Macmillan's,* under the pseudonym, 'Yussuf'. The first of these two, 'The Ballad of the King's Mercy', has never been regarded as one of his major works; the second of them, 'The Ballad of East and West', which followed in the December issue, at once raised its author into the first rank of contemporary writers. No one ever seems to have doubted that it was written by Kipling. George Saintsbury selected it as one of two examples of contemporary verse worth mentioning by name in his *History of English Prosody;* and down at Farringford the aged Tennyson growled to a friend that young Kipling was 'the only one of them with the divine fire'.

> Oh, East is East, and West is West, and never the twain shall meet,
> Till Earth and Sky stand presently at God's great Judgment Seat;
> But there is neither East nor West, Border, nor Breed, nor Birth,
> When two strong men stand face to face, though they come from
>   the ends of the earth!

No lines of Kipling's have been more freely quoted, and more often misquoted in exactly the opposite sense which Kipling gave them. The first couplet is an echo from the Psalms where the figure of speech is used to express the universality of the divine law in spite of estranging seas; the second couplet is Kipling's commentary, with the same theme as the psalmist. The divine spark in human nature also transcends all earthly distinctions. This was the lifelong message that Kipling preached, acceptance of 'the Law', revealed to strong men who recognize one another's valour.

The strength of the Ballad lies in its galloping rhythm which suggested to Saintsbury that Kipling had a 'soul for the anapaest'. Its rapid and varying pace, exactly suited to the development of the theme, showed an extraordinary ease and mastery of words. Even Swinburne could not show such vigour and flexibility. The subject, though painted with the local colour of northern India and painted with brilliant realism, was a human drama which is likely to attract readers

---

* It has not positively been identified. Kipling himself disowned 'The Comet of the Season' (*St. James's Gazette,* 21st November 1889), which is ascribed to him in Livingston: *Bibliography,* p. 72. Internal evidence of style and subject make it pretty clear that it could have been written by no one else. He could have had no imitators at that date.

as long as men admire courage and love a good horse. It is founded
upon the true story of Dilawur Khan and Colonel Lumsden of the
' Guides ', an episode of the Indian frontier in 1848; it might as well
have been told in the idiom of the Scottish Border, or of the Mexican
Border, for its theme is not that East and West differ but that men of
all races are alike at heart.[10]

   As formerly at Lahore, so in London during his first English winter,
Rudyard's letters to Mrs. Hill are in the form of an intermittent
journal. It reveals that, in spite of his immediate success with editors
and publishers, he was lonely in London and sick at heart. He longed
for sunshine and for the feminine company that had given him happiness for two years past. At that time, when the critics were astonished
at Rudyard's precocity, asserting that he seemed to have learned all
about Life before his twenty-fourth birthday, his personal letters display an engagingly boyish side to his character, and nowhere more so
than in his relation to the two women upon whom he had set his
affections. The letters to the younger sister, Caroline Taylor, whom
he had known only for a few weeks, are beyond question love-letters.
Whether, in the formal society of the eighteen-nineties, the understanding between these two young people amounted to an engagement
is not now clear, but the endearments he used, and the prospects of
marriage which he discussed with Miss Taylor, were the language of
conventional love-making. They reveal, too, that however ' knowing '
he had been about Mrs. Hauksbee and Captain Gadsby, he had not
plumbed the depths of his own heart.
   Rudyard wrote to Caroline Taylor with the mixture of dog-like
devotion and bland condescension that is perhaps characteristic of the
very young lover. These letters are not, in themselves, interesting,
they are the common form of calf-love and may, for the most part, be
left in the oblivion where their writer would wish them to lie. ' Heart
o' mine, you, as well as I, must have discovered by this time that the
writing of love-letters is no easy thing. I own that I laughed, dis-
respectfully, at the delicious one you sent off by the pilot — happy man
was he.' No more of this! There is, however, one letter to Miss
Taylor, dated 9th December 1889, from Embankment Chambers, which
should perhaps be recorded in spite of the writer's disgust at any
intrusion on privacy; it is his confession of faith.
   Miss Taylor's father was a clergyman, of stricter puritan views even
than Rudyard's Methodist grandparents, and she seems to have shared
her father's orthodoxy. In a world where *Robert Elsmere,* the novel
of the day, turned upon a partial loss of faith, Rudyard's laxity in his
religion was no small consideration. Something Professor Hill had

said gave her the impression that Rudyard was in danger of conversion to Rome. A story which he published a few months later, 'On Greenhow Hill', gives, in the stage-Irish of Mulvaney, a comment on the Churches which may reveal its author's tendency in 1890. His enthusiasm for the Methodist ways of Pennsylvania had been short-lived.

'I misdoubt you were built for the Primitive Methodians,' says Private Mulvaney to Private Learoyd. 'They're a new corps, anyways. I hold by the Ould Church, for she's the Mother of them all — ay, and the father, too. I like her, bekaze she's most remarkable regimental in her fittings. I may die in Honolulu, Nova Zambra or Cape Cayenne, but wherever I die, I go under the same orders an' the same words an' the same unction as tho' the Pope himself come down from the roof at St. Peter's to see me off. There's neither high nor low, nor broad nor deep, nor betwixt nor between wid her, an' that's what I like.'

Though some such tribute to the Roman Church may have escaped Rudyard's lips, he responded gamely to the Professor's challenge.

No. Aleck was a little wrong. Your slave was baptised in Bombay Cathedral into the Church of England, which you call Episcopalian, was brought up as you have read in that church, and confirmed by the Bishop of Exeter in Bideford Church, in '80 or '81. Does that satisfy that I am not a veiled adherent of the Church of Rome? You have got from he what no living soul has ever done before [he went on]. I believe in the existence of a personal God to whom we are personally responsible for wrong-doing — that it is our duty to follow and our peril to disobey the ten ethical laws laid down for us by Him and His prophets. I disbelieve directly in eternal punishment, for reasons that would take too long to put down on paper. On the same grounds I disbelieve in an eternal reward. As regards the mystery of the Trinity and the Doctrine of Redemption, I regard them most reverently but I cannot give them implicit belief.

The letter concludes with an affirmation which the young man seems to drag out of himself with an effort:

I believe in God the Father Almighty, maker of Heaven and Earth and in One filled with His spirit Who did voluntarily die in the belief that the human race would be spiritually bettered thereby.

It would not be proper to deduce the theological position which Rudyard eventually reached, from this emotional outburst addressed by a very young man to a very young woman. It was not, we may suppose, enough to satisfy Miss Taylor, or her father; it is likely that Rudyard's unorthodoxy was the reason why the affair came to nothing. Perhaps it is relevant that in his next letter, addressed to Mrs. Hill the elder sister, he remarks, lightly, as something unusual, that he has 'been to church — St. Clement Danes'.

Rudyard Kipling's extraordinary facility for keeping his interests in distinct compartments of his mind was never more marked than in his London period.

> I would go without shirt or shoe,
> Friend, tobacco or bread,
> Sooner than lose for a minute the two
> Separate sides of my head! [11]

So he wrote, on some later occasion, and so he always seemed to organize his thought. Those who knew him best remarked upon the intensity of his interest; in conversation with friends he threw himself so absolutely into the subject under discussion that, for the time, nothing else seemed to exist for him. He opened his mind to the persons he spoke with so fully, so candidly as to penetrate their interests, see with their eyes, and enter into their emotions. 'His mind', said one who knew him well, 'was like the leaves of a book, which could be quickly turned to suit the company he was in'. When with the Hills he was all alertness to their concerns, all sympathy for their feelings; but when they were gone, his mind was too active to rest in disconsolate loneliness.

Within twenty-four hours of the departure of his friends, he had been composing light verse for the amusement of another entirely masculine circle of acquaintance. He had been taken to the Savile Club by Andrew Lang and for his new friends there he wrote a letter in verse, a spirited parody of Bret Harte's 'Truthful James', with critical allusions to the new romance, *Cleopatra,* just published by Rider Haggard. It does not read like the work of a man with a newly broken heart. A year later, when his name came up for election to the Savile, the page in the candidates' book looked like a roll of English men of letters. He was supported by Walter Besant, James Bryce, Edward Clodd, John Collier, Sidney Colvin, Austin Dobson, Edmund Gosse, Rider Haggard, Thomas Hardy, W. E. Henley, Henry James, J. H. McCarthy, J. W. Mackail, Walter Pollock, George Saintsbury, and by others who were hardly less eminent.[12]

Very soon after Kipling's arrival in London, Edmund Gosse, with the intention of finding a friend for the newcomer, introduced him to a young American literary man named Wolcott Balestier who strongly desired his acquaintance. It did not, however, ripen into friendship until some months later. In the literary world his earliest friends were Lang, Haggard, and 'Anstey' (T. A. Guthrie, author of *Vice Versa*) and, even among these light-weights, he felt himself to be out of his element.

London is a vile place, and Anstey and Haggard and Lang and Co. are pressing on me the wisdom of identifying myself with some set, while the long-haired literati of the Savile Club are swearing that I 'invented' my soldier talk in *Soldiers Three*. Seeing that not one of these critters has been within earshot of a barrack, I am naturally wrath. But this is only the beginning of the lark. You'll see some savage criticism of my work before spring. That's what I am playing for.

Perhaps this defiance need not be taken at quite its face value, for he could be receptive of good advice. On Lord Mayor's day he fought his way through the crowds to Macmillan's office, delighted that he had finished 'The Ballad of East and West' to his satisfaction, and amenable to criticism of his other work. He even allowed Mowbray Morris to censor thirty lines of his first story written in London, the extravaganza called 'The Incarnation of Krishna Mulvaney', which was 'a little too drunken' for English middle-class taste.

Next, calling on his relatives, the Poynters, at Knightsbridge, he was in his element. There were his Aunt Aggie (Poynter), his Aunt Edie (Macdonald); his cousin Margaret, no longer his 'Dear Wop' but Mrs. J. W. Mackail, and a new young cousin in the nursery, Hugh Poynter aged eight, his favourite among them all. But the party was spoiled by the presence of a literary lion, Sidney Colvin, who wrote the Life of Keats.

The same is an all-fired prig of immense water and suffers from all the nervo-hysterical diseases of the nineteenth century. Went home with him as far as Charing Cross in a 3rd smoking (which made him sick). He recounted all his symptoms and made me sick. A queer beast with match-stick fingers and a dry unwholesome skin.

Another day it was lunch with Pollock, the editor of the *Saturday Review*,

in grisly grey chambers in the Albany met Saintsbury and Jebb [he wrote]. A vile lunch. No talk. Pollock half asleep and the forks dirty. Dined at 6 (ungodly hour) with Hooper of the *Spectator*. Met a wild socialist who told me that the working man was a god. 'Then kill him,' said I and levanted.

Worst of all was a visit to George Meredith at Box Hill, an expedition which most young men of letters would have made in a different frame of mind.

Show me no more celebrities for they disillusion me sadly. Imagine an old withered little man very deaf in one ear who, as did Dagonet in the *Morte d'Arthur*

'Skips like a withered leaf upon the floor.'

He is full to a painful overflowing of elaborated epigrammatic speech which
on the first fizz strikes one as deuced good.   Five minutes later one cannot
remember what on earth it was all about.   And neither time, tide, Heaven
nor Hell, nor the sanctities of five-o'-clock tea seem to be able to stop that
flow of talk.   The raucous voice continues; the little old man balances
himself on his toes like a Shanghai rooster to command attention, and that
attention *must* be given or he sulks like a child. *

So homesick was Kipling for India that he clung to anyone who
could remind him of it.   When opening an account at the West End
branch of his bank, the Oriental Banking Corporation, he found
pleasure in being received by the manager as an Anglo-Indian cus-
tomer, and greater pleasure in meeting an Anglo-Indian acquaintance
in the street outside.   It was Logan of the Bombay Cavalry, no doubt
as lonely in London as was Kipling, and they 'danced on the pavement'.   The letters to Mrs. Hill recount many such incidents; a man
who lives at Charing Cross and does much prowling about the streets
is sure to meet his travelling acquaintance.   His story 'A Conference
of the Powers', no very profound matter, is taken from the common
form of these entries in his journal.

Not many weeks after his arrival, he sent a set of verses in the style
of Lewis Carroll to the *Civil and Military Gazette.*

> The sky, a greasy soup-tureen,
>   Shuts down atop my brow.
> Yes, I have sighed for London Town
>   And I have got it now:
> And half of it is fog and filth,
>   And half is fog and row.
>
> But I consort with long-haired things
>   In velvet collar-rolls,
> Who talk about the Aims of Art,
>   And 'theories' and 'goals',
> And moo and coo with womenfolk
>   About their blessed souls.
>
> But what they call 'psychology'
>   Is lack of liver-pill,
> And all that blights their tender souls
>   Is eating till they're ill,
> And their chief way of winning goals
>   Consists of sitting still.

* S. S. McClure, afterwards R. K.'s friend and publisher, gives the other side of these
conversations in his *Autobiography.*   Colvin recommended R. K. to McClure as the
'coming man'.   McClure consulted Meredith, who said emphatically: 'The coming
man is James Matthew Barrie'.

It's Oh to meet an Army man,
   Set up, and trimmed and taut,
Who does not spout hashed libraries
   Or think the next man's thought,
And walks as though he owned himself,
   And hogs his bristles short.[13]

The P. & O. steamers disgorged no such companion, no subaltern or junior civilian, to share his life in London. His two most regular callers were his cousins, Ambrose Poynter and Philip Burne-Jones, both mightily impressed by his man-of-the-world airs. 'Ambo' Poynter was the nearest thing Kipling possessed to a confidant; he would come into Embankment Chambers and lay bare his soul, hour after hour, until he was turned out at one or two in the morning. His trouble, apart from mere green-sickness, was the common misfortune of a successful man's son; he had inherited his father's nervous temperament without his father's talent. What he had to exhibit was a five-act tragedy in verse, full of allusions which Kipling, with his meagre classical knowledge, found formidable. 'Ambo', of course, was grateful for advice and eager for help, but unwilling to be told the truth about his work. It was to Mrs. Hill that Rudyard wrote a candid opinion.

He estimates his poems not by the thing actually put down in black and white but by all the glorious inchoate fancies that flashed through his brain while his pen was in his hand.

Though 'Ambo' Poynter had his own career, as an architect, his poetical aspirations had their consequence in providing 'copy' for Kipling, who throughout life was haunted by the notion that buried and even inherited memories reveal themselves in dreams. Long before the Viennese scientists formulated the new psychology of the unconscious, the writers of the 'nineties focused attention on these problems, thus creating the mental climate in which the new psychology was born. The conflict between 'Ambo' Poynter's unrealized visions and inadequate expression suggested to Rudyard the plot of a story which, again, showed an advance in human sympathy and understanding. 'The Finest Story in the World' his tale of a London clerk who almost, but not quite, recalls memories inherited from a remote past, owes much to 'Ambo' Poynter.

The Poynters were 'society' people and Edward Poynter a fashionable painter of historical tableaux on the largest scale. His *Solomon and the Queen of Sheba,* which was to be his masterpiece, moved Rudyard to ribaldry in the style of Uncle Remus.

It's old Brer Solomon coming down the steps of his throne to welcome

Sis Sheby as she comes along with apes and peacocks and all that truck. I never saw such a blaze of colour or jumble of notions in my life. 'I thought it was oriental,' said Poynter, 'and no one knows any better here.' It's mighty curious to see behind an R.A.'s piccy and note the bits of things it is made up of. In my usual genial way I proffered advice and suggestions — two of which were accepted and as I ran out of the studio (it's one of a great range) I stepped into or onto the tray containing Hamo Thornycroft's modest lunch. He does his sculpture on milk and rusks. He was not pleased but they should not leave his lunch at the door.

Mrs. Poynter (Aunt Aggie) took Rudyard into Society, to a dance in Rutland Gate and to a reception in Mayfair where he was made much of. 'Lady Wentworth, Lords Pembroke and Grosvenor backed me into a corner', he wrote to Caroline, 'and stood over me pouring out melted compliments into my throat, one after the other. And through it all I kept thinking to myself, "Unless it happened that I was the fashion for the moment, you'd let me die of want on your doorstep." And so they would.'

On the whole, the Burne-Joneses were nearer to him, less fashionable and less academic. Uncle Ned, that shy genius, was a 'mine of wisdom', the best of talkers if only he could be persuaded 'to uncork himself'; and Aunt Georgie was as dear to Rudyard Kipling the man as she had been to the boy — but she was down at Rottingdean that winter. Their son Phil was a painter, making some progress in his father's profession; though not so communicative as 'Ambo' Poynter, he, too, had troubles to confide to his cousin from the wide world. He had sold an autobiographical article to a disreputable publishing syndicate, and regretted it. Rudyard had to go down to Fleet Street to get Phil out of their clutches, an episode which he worked up into a chapter for *The Light that Failed*.

On Christmas Day, he looked out to find London shrouded in fog, 'the streets nearly empty and those who were in the streets nearly full'. Never had he felt more solitary. Only Uncle Ned and Phil were at call since they too were spending a bachelor Christmas. The three went out to dine together at Solferino's, the little foreign restaurant in Rupert Street that Rudyard favoured, to find themselves the only customers, and the proprietor sitting down with the staff to a Christmas dinner, in which the three joined. Though that was a mildly pleasant experience, Rudyard went home to write at midnight to his friends in India:

there are five million people in London this night and, saving those who starve, I don't think there is one more heartsick or thoroughly wretched than that rising young author known to you as — Ruddy.

One of his observations upon London life, which recurs again and again in his writing at the period, is his disgust at the hordes of prostitutes who infested the streets about Charing Cross; he had seen nothing like it in oriental cities.[14]

> And when I take my nightly prowl,
>   'Tis passing good to meet
> The pious Briton lugging home
>   His wife and daughter sweet,
> Through four packed miles of seething vice,
>   Thrust out upon the street.

It exceeded the 'City of Dreadful Night' in horror, and offered no allurement to him.

He did not eschew humble company; there was a barber's and bird-shop in Drury Lane where he sometimes went to be shaved; there was a fishing-tackle shop which gave a meeting-place to a coarse-fishing club; there were the police of E Division who dealt with the rows of 'real ladies' outside Gatti's music-hall, and fetched the ambulance when a man cut his throat under the windows of Embankment Chambers; there was the clerk who came up to Rudyard's rooms to tell the life-history which, combined with 'Ambo' Poynter's, became the framework for 'The Finest Story in the World'; there was the comic man from Gatti's who kept on 'knocking 'em', but commented that 'life's all a blooming kick-up'; there was the elderly but upright barmaid who told Rudyard a story which he made into the poem called 'Mary, pity Women!'; there was a lascar from the Docks whom he thought of employing as a 'bearer' and who vanished after giving him the notion that became 'The Limitations of Pambé Serang'; and there was the incident of Aunt Georgie's housemaid which made a whole sub-plot in *The Light that Failed*.

My spirits were most awful low and I was beginning to weep audibly when a knock arrived at the door, and Aunt Georgie's housemaid — the cross-eyed one not the pretty one — arrived with a packet of letters from India. Then I whooped. It struck me as queer that the girl should have come across London to give the letters into my hand when she could have posted 'em. So I made enquiries. 'Where's Aunt Georgie?' 'Oh, she's gone to Rottingdean,' said the artless Anne who, I dare say, desired amusement and sought it in my chambers. So I treated her with immense distinction — the buttons are beginning to drop off my shirt-collar you must understand — and then I gravely gave her tea, and she discussed house-keeping details — coal, wrist bands, darning stockings *etc*. In the end, emboldened by much tea, which made her glisten like a newly buttered muffin, she said that it would be fit and proper for me to settle down and

marry a nice steady young woman because I 'kept my things dreadful'.
With a large smirk she left me to digest the advice.

There was no lack of 'copy' in London, and no lack of gratuitous
advice; there were, he wrote, 'proposals from "certain people of importance", insistent and unscrupulous as horse-copers, telling me "how
the ball was at my feet" and that I had only to kick it — by repeating
the notes I had already struck and trailing characters I had already
"created" through impossible scenes — to achieve all sorts of desirable
things.' Among the advisers there was one whom Rudyard followed,
Walter Besant, who would

sit behind his big frosty beard and twinkling spectacles, and deal me out
wisdom concerning this new incomprehensible world. He advised me to
'keep out of the dog-fight'. He said that if I were 'in with one lot' I
would have to be out with another; and that, at last, 'things would get
like a girls' school where they stick out their tongues at each other when
they pass'. One heard very good talk at the Savile.

Besant was one of the founders of the Authors' Society and an active
worker for an agreed system of international copyright. He introduced
Rudyard to A. P. Watt & Son, the literary agents, and in a few weeks
they had got his affairs in order. On 5th March 1890 he was able to
thank them for doubling his income in three months, and, forty years
later, declared that he could not 'recall any difference that three
minutes' talk could not clear up'. But the year 1890 was to reveal
some knotty problems for them to solve.[15]

On 7th February Rudyard wrote to Caroline Taylor:

I am just now being chased by several publishers. I reply with great
sweetness that my engagements are *complet* and that they had better go
and take a walk. Publishers are not used to being treated in this manner
and they return to the charge like Jew hawkers with proffers of ready
money down. See'st thou the drift of this? It is to make the new man
write as swiftly and as largely as possible on the novel subject. Then
when he is squeezed dry they heave him away and call the newspapers to
witness that there is no originality in the present writers.

Wherefore I have refused in a brief poem of five stanzas the *St. James's
Gazette* offer of a permanent engagement. Catch me putting my head into
that old noose again — and me hardly recovered from the constant surprises
of seven years' journalism.

The situation stands thus, I hold work on *Macmillan's Magazine* up to
£300 a year. The Lahore paper stands me for £100 (and that's four
hundred). On those two alone therefore, without turning my attention
to the *St. James's,* the *Spectator, Longman's,* and *Punch* (who all want
me), I could devote myself to building up the American connection and
going on straight with the books and poetry.

It will be recognized that his success was still on a modest scale, and his reputation still dependent on his earlier work. He wrote post-haste to his parents for the manuscript of *Mother Maturin* which he had left in India; perhaps it would work up into something for Long-man's; but new poems just then were singing themselves most urgently in his head, ballads about soldiering set to the rhythms of the London music-hall.

On his old record, he was suddenly swept into fame by *The Times* which gave, on 25th March 1890, the signal honour of a full leading article to the whole range of his work in the Calcutta editions:

India has given us an abundance of soldiers and administrators, but she has seldom given us a writer. There is no question, however, that she has done this in the person of the author of the numerous short stories and verses of which we give the titles below. Mr. Rudyard Kipling has the merit of having tapped a new vein, and of having worked it out with real originality. He is even now a very young man, in spite of his seven or eight small volumes; in fact, we believe he is not yet twenty-five.

Mr. Kipling found himself famous in Indian society as the writer of sketches which were generally accepted as representing, with a fair amount of truth and a great amount of pungency, scenes of a very diverse kind. . . . He is at home at Simla, and in the life of 'the station'. He deals also with that unfortunate result of our settlement in India, the Eurasian, and some of the most brilliant of his tales have this seldom successful growth for their topic. . . . He may be almost called the discoverer, as far as India is concerned, of 'Tommy Atkins' as a hero of realistic romance. . . . Some of the best and most penetrating of the *Plain Tales* deal with various aspects of native life, and in this department Mr. Kipling's curious and seemingly almost instinctive knowledge is not less evident than in his stories of European life. . . . That very grim story 'In the House of Suddhoo', the tragedy called 'Beyond the Pale', and one or two of the 'Black and White' series seem to be almost the best of Mr. Kipling's writings, perhaps because they appear to lift the veil from a state of society so immeasurably different from our own. . . .

In nothing is Mr. Kipling more successful than in his truly lurid descriptions and indications of what Indian heat can be, and what its effect on the minds and bodies of the Europeans who have to suffer it. . . .

Plain Tales from the Hills is the longest of the volumes, and, as its title implies, it deals mostly with Simla life. The picture that Mr. Kipling gives is not altogether a pleasant one; but then he does not pretend to be an optimist or to represent society as all varnish and veneer. . . . If it fails of being a first-rate picture, it is because Mr. Kipling, though an admirably direct writer, is comparatively wanting in style. People have compared him with Guy de Maupassant, not, let it be observed, that he shows any disposition to emulate the French writer in his choice of subjects (which would be, indeed, even now, an impossibility for an Englishman) but because of his incisive power of drawing vignette portraits and of representing in half a dozen pages a complete action. . . . Guy de Maupassant, is, however, a stylist of the first order, and this Mr. Kipling is not, yet, whatever he may come to be. . . . He may go very much further than he has yet gone. Many of the stories which he has lately published in the English magazines . . . show a distinct advance in artistic power . . . and the volume called *Departmental Ditties* is in no respect on the same level with certain verses which have appeared with and without his name during the present year. . . .

But, as yet, he has not attempted the 'long-distance race', and the question in which the rapidly-growing number of his readers are now most interested is whether he possesses staying power. . . . It is to be hoped he will not write himself out. Modern magazines and their eager editors are a dangerous snare in the way of a bright, clever, and versatile writer, who knows that he has caught the public taste.

Which of his kindly elderly patrons at the Savile Club was responsible for this good-natured admonition and qualified praise we do not know. His own letters prove that he had not been spoiled by flattery but responded somewhat ungraciously to professions of esteem. The fear that he might over-write, or, at least, over-publish seemed justified, for the reissue of his early work went on apace, far more actively in America than in England, and the weeks that followed *The Times'* review saw a new Kipling boom, in the literary circle of Henley and the *Scots Observer*.

CHAPTER VII

KIPLING IN LONDON (1890–91)

IN THE NEOLITHIC AGE (1893)

In the Neolithic Age savage warfare did I wage
  For food and fame and woolly horses' pelt.
I was singer to my clan in that dim, red Dawn of Man,
  And I sang of all we fought and feared and felt.
      .   .   .   .

Then the silence closed upon me till They put new clothing on me
  Of whiter, weaker flesh and bone more frail;
And I stepped beneath Time's finger, once again a tribal singer,
  And a minor poet certified by Traill!
      .   .   .   .

Still a cultured Christian age sees us scuffle, squeak, and rage,
  Still we pinch and slap and jabber, scratch and dirk;
Still we let our business slide — as we dropped the half-dressed hide —
  To show a fellow-savage how to work.

Still the world is wondrous large, — seven seas from marge to marge —
  And it holds a vast of various kinds of man;
And the wildest dreams of Kew are the facts of Khatmandhu,
  And the crimes of Clapham chaste in Martaban.

Here's my wisdom for your use, as I learned it when the moose
  And the reindeer roared where Paris roars to-night: —
'*There are nine and sixty ways of constructing tribal lays,*
  '*And — every — single — one — of — them — is — right!*'

WILLIAM ERNEST HENLEY, a lifelong invalid, is best
remembered today as the author of one poem, a defiant assertion of will, from what seemed likely to be a death-bed:

> In the fell clutch of circumstance
>   I have not winced nor cried aloud,
> Under the bludgeonings of chance
>   My head is bloody but unbowed:

lines which were read and stored away for reference by young Kipling
in Lahore.

Some of Henley's associates in Edinburgh set him up as editor of a weekly magazine which they intended as a contribution to the Scottish literary revival, but Henley made it much more than that. The *Scots Observer* first came out in August 1889, when Kipling was on his way to London, and within a few months it captivated the taste of the younger literary set. Henley knew everyone from Oscar Wilde to the young musical critic Bernard Shaw, and everyone liked him. He sedulously hunted for coming young men, and Yeats and Barrie, as well as Kipling, were among his early discoveries; in later years he produced Wells and Conrad. The *Scots Observer* was new in style and presentation, a landmark in typography as well as in literature, but it did not pay. The circulation never reached 7000 and was usually under 2000, in spite of the good names of the contributors, the brilliant editing, and the elegant lay-out. It remained one of those literary ventures that arise in every generation, to provide a platform for young men of talent, and to influence public opinion only at second hand.

Rudyard Kipling could hardly be said to have graduated in the world of letters, in 1889 and 1890, without coming into Henley's orbit, and Henley was one of those who awaited Kipling's return from India with attention. The first approach seems to have been made from Kipling's side. On 1st February 1890 the *Scots Observer* published a slight piece from Kipling's pen, a lyric in the style of Lyly:

> Love and Death once ceased their strife
> At the Tavern of Man's Life.
> Called for wine, and threw — alas! —
> Each his quiver on the grass.

of which we may say that it might have been written by almost any one of Henley's young men. It gave an introduction, and Henley's patron, F. Bell, was taken by Herbert Stephen, one of Kipling's Savile Club friends, to visit the new poet at Embankment Chambers.

The subject of conversation with Bell was the provision of a series of verses which Kipling called *Barrack-room Ballads*. The first of these, 'Danny Deever', appeared in the *Scots Observer* on 22nd February and astonished the critics. According to the legend, it made Henley stand up and dance on his wooden leg, while Professor Masson, the grave commentator on Milton, waved the paper before his delighted students, crying: 'Here's Literature! Here's Literature at last!'

Bell and Stephen asked Kipling at Embankment Chambers whether he had anything else on hand, whereupon he reluctantly fished out of the waste-paper basket some political verses which, he supposed, had missed their market and were out-of-date. They were seventy lines of bitter invective against the Liberal Party, denouncing its association with the Irish Nationalists, as revealed by the Parnell Commission, the sensation of the month. A panel of judges had acquitted the Irish leaders of complicity in political murders in Ireland, not so much because they repudiated the policy of violence as because the evidence in a particular instance was shown to be a malicious forgery. The weight of Kipling's attack fell, not upon Irish Nationalists but upon English Liberals, especially upon Gladstone who relied on Irish support in parliament.

> Hold up those hands of innocence — go, scare your sheep together,
> The blundering, tripping tups that bleat behind the old bellwether;
> My soul! I'd sooner lie in jail for murder plain and straight,
> Pure crime I'd done with my own hand for money, lust, or hate
> Than take a seat in Parliament by fellow-felons cheered,
> While one of those 'not provens' proved me cleared as you are cleared.

All that the Parnell Commission had demonstrated was summed up in the last line of his satire:

> We are not ruled by murderers, but only — by their friends.

Kipling's account of the publication of this explosive piece is that *The Times* considered and rejected it. They had burned their fingers so badly over the forgeries that they were unlikely to take risks again, though, after a discreet interval, they quoted the verses in full without permission. Next, Kipling had offered it to Frank Harris, the editor of the *Fortnightly,* who had just published 'One View of the Question', his virulent prose satire on the state of London as seen by an Indian Moslem visitor. Frank Harris's account of his dealings with Kipling does not quite square with Kipling's, but at least he declined to take the verses. Kipling's comment was that Frank Harris was the one human being that he 'could on no terms get on with'. After two rebuffs, Kipling preferred to put his verses in the waste-paper basket, where they would have remained but for the visitors from the *Scots Observer.* Henley published them on 8th March.

Broadminded though he was in his literary taste, Henley was a partisan in politics, a Tory of the new imperialist school, and his London representative, Charles Whibley, was still further to the right. In the successive reorganizations by which they endeavoured to keep their literary venture afloat, Henley and Whibley tended to move from *belles-lettres* to politics, from Scottish to Imperial affairs; and the attachment of Kipling to their group was a step in this direction. Yet they were too intellectual, too fastidious, to catch the ear of the mob.

The decade of the 'nineties saw the beginning of 'yellow' journalism in England, and it was Harmsworth, not Henley, who was to provide the masses with imperialist propaganda in a form they could appreciate and at a price they could pay. Henley's only appeal to a wider public was by printing *Barrack-room Ballads,* and even these did not reach that wider public until the author reissued them in book form. It was the literary world that succumbed to the spell of 'Danny Deever'. Week by week, the ballads burst upon their shocked but delighted readers; 'Tommy' on 1st March; 'Fuzzy-Wuzzy' on 15th March; 'Loot' on 29th March; 'The Widow at Windsor' on 26th April; 'Gunga Din' on 7th June; 'Mandalay', perhaps the favourite of all, on 22nd June.

Henley, too, was delighted with his new discovery, and more delighted still when he came south, in March, to meet the man. It was his custom, during his visits to London, to give bachelor dinner-parties to his literary friends, at Sherry's in Regent Street, and, for a few months, Kipling was the lion among his guests. The flavour and wit of these young men's meetings — for Henley was forty and most of his guests much younger — has vanished and is lost, unless some hint of them can be discovered in the bachelor parties described in *The Light that Failed.* Whibley, a scholarly *bon-viveur* with a well-earned liver complaint, convened the dinners, and students of Kipling will notice with relish that his private address was in Brook Green, Hammersmith. Almost did this new friend occupy the place in Henley's affections left vacant since his celebrated quarrel with R. L. Stevenson, a year earlier. Kipling was more cool, though later he defended Henley vigorously against detractors.

Henley's demerits were, of course, explained to the world by loving friends after his death. I had the fortune to know him only as kind, generous, and a jewel of an editor, with the gift of fetching the very best out of his cattle, with words that would astonish oxen.

His first letter to Henley, written from Embankment Chambers, early in 1890 shows a side to Kipling's character that is not widely known; it is largely about sea-fishing:

Since we be only islands shouting misunderstandings to each other across seas of speech or writing I am going to say nothing about Henley's *Hospital Sketches.* I take off my hat and drop my sword-point. You have been where I have yet to go so I dare not ask you why you are so tired. When you get my stuff you will see how far I've walked, and where.

Yes, men tell me I am young in this country but I have put seven years of India behind me and they do not make a man younger or more cheerful. Also, luckily, they don't lead him to believe the protestations of the disinterested publisher or the blandishments of the people to whom a new writer-man is as a new purple monkey on a yellow stick. I live very largely alone and my wants are limited to a new fly-rod and some flies. *But,* you can do me immense service by sending in a memo. of reminder if it seems to you that I am spinning out my guts too swiftly, at any time.

To a young man the temptation is strong and it is to nobody's interest to tell him to go slow. Rather they want all he has at once and then he can go to the deuce, being squeezed dry. I've treated men in the same way when I was an editor. I see now [that] I was unkind.

I am off for a month's idleness now 'cause of my head. . . . If it is written, I come to Edinburgh ere long and then I shall see you and — this is business — if you think it worth while you shall give me my riding-orders by word of mouth and we will elaborate a line of work.

At present I am divided between the broken top-joint of my rod and a reel that won't 'croon' properly. Literature is a weariness to the flesh — all books are wicked and the only real thing in the world is a four pound bass coming up with the tide at the mouth of the Torridge, my hook in the right-hand top angle of his mouth.[1]

While he gave Henley his entire confidence in literary concerns Rudyard kept his private life quite separate. His sister Trix, now Mrs. Fleming, arrived in England with her husband, on 11th February, and turned her steps at once to Embankment Chambers. It was a shock to her to find her brother, in spite of his prosperity, in deep depression of spirits and a low state of health, not altogether due to the influenza which raged like a pestilence that winter. When she spoke to him of the kindness shown to her by Mrs. Hill, at Allahabad, 'his face began to work', and, in a tangle of words, he admitted that his affection for Caroline Taylor had been mistaken. Even this was not all; something had happened in London, which struck a deeper chord in his nature, revealing a harmony that he had almost forgotten. He had met his old sweetheart, Flo Garrard, by chance in the street, and had realized in a moment that she still retained her power over him.[2]

Rudyard's prolonged ill-health and unhappiness in 1890 was the consequence of this mental conflict which, according to his custom, he shut up in his own heart, leaving no scrap of direct evidence to mark the progress of his love-affairs. He plunged himself in work with reckless energy, producing, in the spring of 1890, the greater part of the *Barrack-Room Ballads,* and half a dozen long stories.

As his estrangement from Caroline Taylor widened, he resumed his attentions to Flo but without arousing her emotions. She was, as Trix said, 'naturally cold, and she wanted to live her own life and paint her very ineffective little pictures'. Rudyard had still one re-source; his parents were coming home on leave to reunite the family square in London. In a mood of optimism, earlier in the year, he had telegraphed to them, proposing a holiday in England, sending them merely a reference to Genesis xlv. 9.

Haste ye, and go up to my father, and say unto him, Thus saith thy son Joseph, God hath made me lord of all Egypt: come down unto me; tarry not.

In May they arrived, protesting that they would be independent of his bounty, and settled for some months in Kensington, first at 29 Wynnstay Gardens and later at 101 Earl's Court Road. Rudyard retained his foothold in Embankment Chambers, but with renewed happiness since his father would spend the days there working with him. Father and son went down to Westward Ho! in June to visit Cormell Price. Averse as he was from publicity, Rudyard's one concession to flattery was to appear at his old school as a celebrity on whose account the boys were given a half-holiday.

Then came more work at Embankment Chambers and Earl's Court Road. In spite of his resolution not to write himself out, the bulk of his new work in the summer of 1890 was prodigious, and was accompanied by volume after volume of reissued Indian stories. Some time in August, Lockwood Kipling wrote to a friend to say that 'each new boom is more portentous than the last'. Meanwhile Rudyard had made himself ill with overwork, since he went at his tasks 'with a sort of fury and a bad cold'. Lockwood admitted that he collaborated in a political article that Rudyard published that month in the *Contemporary Review*, with the title of 'The Enlightments of Pagett, M.P.' Though much quoted by the reviewers and discussed by the politically-minded, this piece was, wisely, never reprinted in the standard edition of his works; it was an attack upon the Indian National Congress in the form of a series of imaginary conversations between Pagett, a globe-trotting M.P., and various characters from earlier stories.

In the same letter Lockwood mentioned another piece, just finished, in which we may also detect signs of his helping hand; this is the Yorkshire tale, 'On Greenhow Hill'. Against a background of fighting on the North-West Frontier, Private Learoyd the Yorkshireman tells of his youth near Skipton (where Rudyard as a boy had gone to visit his Kipling grandmother). It is his only Yorkshire story, the only one of the soldier yarns in which Learoyd comes to life, for elsewhere he is no more than a foil to Mulvaney and Ortheris. More than that, it is a work of great emotional power, almost worthy of Emily Brontë. The inner drama of Learoyd's hopeless passion for the dying daughter of the Methodist preacher is much heightened in effect by the contrasted picture of the godless, bloodthirsty, campaigning scene in which Learoyd tells his tale. Its climax is Learoyd's failure to satisfy his sweetheart's father as to his Methodist orthodoxy, and his consequent flight from Methodism, with the approval of Mulvaney the papist and Ortheris the infidel. The influence of Lockwood Kipling, who knew Yorkshire and Methodism so much better than his son, is an obvious factor, but Rudyard, too, had something to say from the depths of his own heart. The story can hardly be considered in any other light than Rudyard's farewell to Caroline Taylor, or, at least, that is how she and her family must have taken it. Her father, Dr. Taylor, had been in England in August, when Rudyard had shown him some courtesies. But when 'On Greenhow Hill' was published, the effect upon the old minister and his daughter must have been final. Yet a few weeks later his association with her family took a new turn, when Professor Hill died suddenly in India. Their friends must have wondered whether his young and handsome widow, to whom Rudyard had been devoted, long before he met her less attractive sister, would not resume her sway over her admirer. She did not do so. In December 1890 Mrs. Hill and Miss Taylor passed through London on their way back to America. Though they exchanged calls with Mrs. Kipling, no more came of it than the continuance of a cool and distant acquaintance.[3]

Never before had Rudyard handled the tones of a composition with so sure a touch as in the bright hard foreground and the deftly suggested background of 'On Greenhow Hill', a demonstration of the progress he had made in his art during the previous year of enriched experience. The early months of 1890 had seen the production of *Barrack-room Ballads,* a new *genre* in poetry, and of a series of stories which far surpassed the overloaded pieces of his Allahabad period, in delicacy and insight. 'The Head of the District' had appeared in January, 'Dinah Shadd' in March, 'The Man who Was' in April, 'Without Benefit of Clergy' in June, 'On Greenhow Hill' in September, and, in the summer months, two stories of horror and gloom which reflected his own mood of nervous exhaustion, 'The Mark of the Beast' and 'At the End of the Passage'. Some of these stories were the working-over of old material, but the *Ballads* were brand-new, and there is still more to be considered. According to his father's account, *The Light that Failed* was completed by August 1890, and it was this that wore him out. The novel was not a version of *Mother Maturin,* but a quite new realistic piece, based upon his own life in Embankment Chambers.

When the book was finished Rudyard was at last ready to go for a

long sea-voyage, on his doctor's advice. He had called upon Lord
Dufferin, now appointed Ambassador at Rome, characteristically announcing himself to the servant as ' Mr. Lockwood Kipling's son '.
Dufferin, who of course remembered him well enough, invited him to
pay a visit to his villa at Sorrento, and Rudyard booked his passage to
Naples in a P. & O. steamer.   Several newspapers, in announcing the
forthcoming appearance of *The Light that Failed,* the event of the
publishing season, announced also that the author was going abroad
to recruit his health.

Most of the month of October he spent at sea or in Italy.   At
Dufferin's villa he learned, for the first time as he admitted, how the
administrative machinery of government is handled from above.   Previously he had seen it only 'from beneath, all stripped and over-
heated '.   Lord Dufferin talked — 'sliding into a reverie — of his work
in India, Canada, and the world at large'.   And the sentence that
Rudyard treasured in his memory was, 'so, you see, there can be no
room' (or was it allowance) 'for good intentions in one's work '.
Nothing mattered in a career but to do one's best, merely 'to do the
work for which you draw the wage '.[4]

Two days after he sailed for Italy a storm broke in London over
American piracies.   One of the first endeavours made on Kipling's
behalf by A. P. Watt had been the sale to Harper Brothers in January
1890 of ' The Courting of Dinah Shadd ', the first of five of his stories
which they issued in their *Weekly.*   In September Harper's reissued
them in a paper-bound cheap edition with a preface by Kipling's friend
and patron, Andrew Lang.   Perhaps, so far, they were within their
rights, and acting legitimately, if not generously.   They put themselves
quite out of court with Kipling, however, by making up their book
to the required length with 'Krishna Mulvaney', a sixth piece to
which they had no right at all; and annoyed the author still more by
offering him £10 as a solatium, which he indignantly rejected.

This new annoyance threw him into a fury of indignation against
the American 'pirate' publishers who were making free with his work.
Great as the Kipling Boom was in England, it was far greater in
America and, there, nothing prevented any printer from producing
unauthorized editions unless the copyright had been secured by the
production in America of an authorized American edition.   Even
before Kipling left India, a pirated edition of *Departmental Ditties*
had appeared in the United States and, in the years of his fame, there
was a scramble to collect and reissue any of his works that were unprotected.   For many years it was a principal task of A. P. Watt, to
forestall the pirates in respect of new work, and to outwit them in

respect of the earlier work for which there was an uncertain degree of protection at law. Since most of Kipling's early work was journalism written to order for the *Civil and Military* or the *Pioneer,* there was genuine uncertainty as to the ownership of copyrights. The ' pirates' took full advantage of this uncertainty, and Kipling, in order to protect himself, reissued some of his early work in authorized editions, including some pieces which he would have preferred to let die — if only the ' pirates' would let them die, too. This is the reason why his books of the early 'nineties contain some slight and trivial pieces, which his maturer judgment would have treated as ephemeral. The copyright struggle was at its height in the summer of 1890 and raged for several years. A. P. Watt lost a round when an enterprising American bought up the files from the London office of the *Pioneer,* for £1500, and carried them off, to search them at leisure for real and fancied Kiplingiana.

All this was bad enough, but Kipling found it intolerable when a respectable firm, Harper Brothers of New York, helped themselves to one of his recent stories, thus adding injury to insult, since they had ignominiously snubbed him a year previously when he offered to write for them; and insult to insult because *Harper's Monthly,* at just the same time included a condescending allusion by W. D. Howells, the New England novelist, to ' Mr. Kipling's jaunty hat-cocked-on-one side, wink-tipping sketches '.

His frayed nerves and exhausted health can be detected in the stabbing pen-strokes with which he wrote to Henley, before leaving for Italy.

DEAR HENLEY,

I am in trouble and furious. You know that I have written within the past few months some tales for MacM. Mag. and others. Harper & Co. bought the serial rights for American and paid me. The series in MacM. I intended to be one of twelve stories into which I purposed to put as good stuff as I could do: revise extensively and eventually republish with a preface. Today I receive a note from Harpers (leading publishers) announcing that they have reprinted in book form *The Courting of Dinah Shadd, The Incarnation of Krishna Mulvaney, The man who was,* and all the others. They will give it their own title. (They have given it their own title). They have not had the decency to apprize me of their intention, and to complete the insult they fling a £10 note (the wages of one New York road scavenger for one month) at my head. They call it an *honorarium.* Now I may turn out work too quickly. They are at perfect liberty to steal when I have done my work but the grotesque Yahoodom of nipping pieces off a half-presented foetus and slamming it into the market makes me jump. It isn't literature, it isn't honour. It is simply a piece of cowardly and huckstering sharp-practice to exploit a name that, for the time being, sells.   Rather less than 12 months ago that firm in a letter one line and seven words long told me that they would not republish *Soldiers three, the Gadsbys,* and all the rest.

What do you recommend me to do? I have of course returned the money and told them that I cannot authorise the thing which they call an ' Edition '.   This month's Harpers magazine brings in an elaborate patronization of me in the Editors Receiving Shop.   Look at it.   It completes the circle.   I don't know who the man is but the whole notion of the article is intensely funny.   The American he says, lives in a ' nimbler atmosphere' or something of the kind.   When the man was writing that, his blasted owners were stealing my work.   The critic himself was criticizing stolen work with adjectives stolen from England.   I am much too wroth just now to write to the papers disclaiming the edition, but I must blow off somehow so I go to you, who can see the insult of the burglary, the savage indecency and the utter disregard of anything except the dollars on the part of the leading publishing firm in America.

Send me your notions on the matter.   As a journalist, two years ago I should have lifted the scalp of Harpers and the amiable critic who ' deplores ' for me, and my vulgarity.   It isn't the critics fault that he lives, as every man must live, under the laws of his own life and environment, when he calls my stuff lacking in appreciation of the subtler values. The thing that makes it like a Gilbert-Sullivan opera is the raw, rank theft that runs through the ' business ' of his firm.   When a burglar sits down on the front door steps to quarrel with the pattern of the silver-ware that he hath stolen he may be an authority on silver but he is first of all a thief and secondly he lacks a sense of humour.   I suppose I shall be able to laugh at the business in a little time but at present I'm too savage to do more than swear.

RUDDY.[5]

He returned from Naples to find a first-class quarrel raging in literary London over the proper reward for his labours. Norman McColl, the editor of the *Athenaeum,* had taken up his case in a leading article, and a statement from Harper Brothers had appeared in the *Athenaeum,* making the situation rather worse. Harper's admitted that they had rejected his early work and had accepted his later, and better, work with deliberation. In offering him £10 for the odd story, they had followed the custom of the trade. Kipling replied in person with a long and angry letter, relating the history of his agents' correspondence with Harper Brothers, and denouncing them as simple pirates, pirates ' like Paul Jones '. Beyond that there seemed little that he could do; there was no redress at law.

Three weeks later, 22nd November 1890, there came an intervention from an unexpected quarter. A letter appeared in the *Athenaeum* over the three signatures of Sir Walter Besant, Thomas Hardy, and William Black, perhaps the three most respected novelists of the day. While regretting the unsatisfactory state of the American copyright law, they championed Harper Brothers, not precisely in respect of their dealings with Kipling, but in respect of their general conduct. Harpers, they said, were honest folk who endeavoured to treat their English authors fairly. It was an error of tactics, and perhaps of taste, they implied, to accuse Harpers of piracy when an English author could only protect himself against disreputable publishers in America by relying upon well-meaning firms such as this one.

This appeasing pronouncement, intended, no doubt, to further the progress of negotiations for an international copyright agreement, exploded Kipling's wrath. In the *Athenaeum* of 6th December he published a satirical ballad, a puzzle to many a reader who has found it, out of context, in the Collected Works. It begins abruptly with a complaint made to 'The Three Captains' by the skipper of a trading brig.

'I had no fear but the seas were clear as far as a sail might fare
'Till I met with a lime-washed Yankee brig that rode off Finisterre.
'There were canvas blinds to his bow-gun ports to screen the weight he bore,
'And the signals ran for a merchantman from Sandy Hook to the Nore.
'He would not fly the Rovers' flag — the bloody or the black,
'But now he floated the Gridiron and now he flaunted the Jack.
'He spoke of the Law as he crimped my crew — he swore it was only a loan;
'But when I would ask for my own again, he swore it was none of my own.'

The ballad goes on with fifty lines of ferocious invective that has tingled in the ears of countless readers who may not have understood the allegory (of which the key is given in the punning words 'the bezant is hard — aye — and black'). But to the complaint of ill-treatment and the threat of reprisal that the skipper would have liked to inflict, the Three Captains reply with fair words:

'Good Sir, we ha' dealt with that merchantman or ever your teeth were cut.
'Your words be words of a lawless race, and the Law it standeth thus:
'He comes of a race that have never a Law, and he never has boarded us.
'We ha' sold him canvas and rope and spar — we know that his price is fair,
'And we know that he weeps for the lack of a Law as he rides off Finisterre.'

The skipper called to the tall taffrail: — 'And what is that to me?
'Did ever you hear of a Yankee brig that rifled a Seventy-three?
'Do I loom so large from your quarter-deck that I lift like a ship o' the Line?
'He has learned to run from a shotted gun and harry such craft as mine.

'It's mainsail haul, my bully boys all — we'll out to the seas again —
'Ere they set us to paint their pirate saint, or scrub at his grapnel-chain.
'It's fore-sheet free, with her head to the sea, and the swing of the unbought brine —
'We'll make no sport in an English court till we come as a ship o' the Line.'

This is a spirited ballad and, though rather long drawn-out, it is effective satire. There was little more worth saying on either side. Before they had an opportunity to read 'The Rhyme of the Three Captains', Harper Brothers wrote again from New York in reply to Kipling's earlier letter. They 'regretted that Mr. Kipling should assume such an ungracious attitude', protested again that they were strictly within their rights, and pointed out that he would have received much worse treatment from one of the frankly piratical firms. This was the truth, evident to Kipling, who had in fact been robbed right and left, but it was a poor line of defence which Kipling had already pierced in the ballad:

'Does he steal with tears when he bucaneers? 'Fore Gad, then, why does he steal?'

The correspondence in the *Athenaeum* merely came to an end. Harper Brothers continued to sell the disputed edition, and Kipling could assert his rights only by arranging for the publication of a rival but authorized edition of the stories with an introduction by his friend Henry James. It was published by J. W. Lovell & Co. under the title *Mine Own People*.

The episode is of importance in the development of Rudyard's character. It deepened his mistrust for publishers; it shook him free of dependence upon the literary grandees like Besant and Andrew Lang who had given him less than no help in the struggle. 'Good intentions' counted for nothing. A man must stand upon his own feet, make his own way in the world, be responsible to his own conscience for the value of his work. Very well, he would launch another venture, bring home another cargo, and watch the higgling of the market more closely next time.

Eighteen ninety-one was to be a year of new effort and of independence. The voyage, to the seas again, 'on the outward tack', might be an actual withdrawal from London — as the doctors recommended — or a symbolical voyage into new regions of endeavour. Just what did his ambition to return 'as a ship o' the Line', imply? Not only material but moral success, so great a degree of self-reliance and self-sufficiency as to be indifferent to the annoyance of Yankee pirates and the condescension of the Three Captains.

He had already taken one step forward in this new career. *The Light that Failed,* in its first form, had been published by J. W. Lovell in America on 27th November, that is a few days before the appearance in London of 'The Rhyme of the Three Captains'. The first

English appearance of the novel was in *Lippincott's Monthly Magazine* for January 1891.*

Light fiction in the late Victorian age was purveyed principally in the monthlies which enterprising publishers used for launching new authors and testing new lines of appeal to the public taste. A widening public of readers demanded something brisker and livelier than the decorous three-volume novels which the circulating libraries had distributed to a genteel public in the previous generation. Lippincott, the American publisher, interested himself in this market by issuing a monthly magazine simultaneously in New York and London with a complete new novelette by a reputed author in every number. Its length, therefore, could be no more than 50,000 or 60,000 words, whereas *Robert Elsmere,* the best-seller of the previous season, had run to 300,000. Eighteen-ninety was a good year for *Lippincott's;* it began with Conan Doyle's *Sign of Four,* went on with Oscar Wilde's *Dorian Gray,* and finished with the number containing *The Light that Failed,* which was five times reprinted in January 1891. J. W. Lovell published the Lippincott version as a book in New York, dating his edition a few days before the release of the monthly magazine; and Lovell's London agent, Wolcott Balestier, secured English copyright by issuing a few copies in London bound up in book form. These contrivances defeated the 'pirates' in both countries, while providing bibliographers with some puzzles for the future about priority of editions, but this was only a beginning of the mystery that shrouds *The Light that Failed.* The author allowed Lippincott's a good run with the magazine version before releasing the book in normal form to the English trade. In the magazine version the book had been a comfortable tale in which the hero and heroine decently got engaged to be married on the last page. When, in March 1891, Macmillan's published *The Light that Failed* as a bound volume in London, it was found to be a quite different book, one-third longer, and with a tragic ending that threw the whole of the plot and the characterization into a new light. The author added to the mystery by his preface which stated baldly: 'This is the story of *The Light that Failed* as it was originally conceived by the writer'. Why, then, had so furiously independent an author allowed his book to appear in the form in which he had not conceived it? The reviewers were astonished. The magazine edition had been 'announced' with a blaze of publicity; the public had waited eagerly for the event of the season, a novel by this prodigy among authors; the critics had received it with many

* McClure in his *Autobiography* says that Lippincott paid R. K. $800, a modest sum compared with his earnings three or four years later.

columns of judicious comment — for it was by no means all that had been expected: and their pens were hardly dry before they were called upon to review it again, converted from a pleasant piece into a bleak tragedy with four new chapters of that sort of realism which the author's detractors called brutality.

One feature of the book that contemporaries could not observe was its autobiographical quality; the incidents in the life of its hero, 'Dick Heldar', were the incidents of Rudyard's life superficially transformed. The story begins with two neglected children brought up together at the seaside by a tyrannical housekeeper. In life they had been brother and sister, in the book they are unrelated so that the author can portray their childhood friendship maturing into calf-love, until in adolescence they separate for years. 'Maisie' the heroine, like Rudyard's former sweetheart Flo Garrard, sets her heart upon a career and goes to an art-school; Dick disappears into the East for seven years of hardship and struggle, in circumstances which the stay-at-home English descry but dimly. Then the scene shifts to Egypt where Dick is a war-artist. Writer to painter is a transformation that presented Rudyard with no great difficulty. He had been brought up among painters and knew the jargon of the studios; but he had never been in the African desert, never seen a battlefield, and it was his realistic accounts of fighting in the Sudan that impressed the critics, that still impress and perhaps shock the modern reader. His uncanny skill in picking the brains of his acquaintance and making a convincing picture, replete with accurate detail, from a few hints picked up in conversation, was never more evident. The critics supposed him to be writing from personal knowledge, while he had no more than soldiers' hearsay to go upon.

When the campaign was over, so the tale ran on, Dick Heldar appeared in London and took rooms in a tall building overlooking the Thames near Charing Cross. Here, at first, he was lonely, and poor, though too proud to admit as much to the agents who pestered him for orders. Fame, won overseas, caught him up quickly, and after fame came money which he hugely appreciated. But he disliked London, found intellectual society distasteful, defied and despised the critics, treated the salesmen who handled his pictures as mere robbers. In the book, Dick Heldar triumphed over a rapacious art-dealer by threatening him with physical assault, a dream-picture of what Kipling would have liked to do to the Yankee pirate. But most surprising of all, Dick Heldar's contempt for public opinion went so far that he painted a picture in two versions, one in the 'realistic' style that his artistic conscience imposed on him, the other in a pretty Christmas Annual style that would fetch the public.

After these three disjointed episodes, in which the early life of Rudyard Kipling is presented in heightened colours as the life of Dick Heldar, the action of the novel begins to develop, and thereafter, though the book contains many studies worked up from real life, we may no longer suppose that the story is autobiographical. The author's shortness of sight can hardly be considered relevant to the realistic description of Dick Heldar's blindness. To ask who is the original of his dim little heroine, Maisie, is unreasonable. No doubt, she derives something from the author's sister, Trix, who had shared his childhood at Southsea. This alone will explain what many cirtics have noticed, that Maisie in childhood is a quite different person from Maisie in maturity, and a much firmer character. No doubt the later Maisie derives much from Flo Garrard, who had re-entered the author's life so dramatically, while he was at work upon the novel. But, if Kipling based the frustrated love-affair of Dick and Maisie upon his own, we may be sure that he disguised it, just as he disguised India as Egypt, and writing as painting, when presenting himself in the character of Dick Heldar. The frustrated love-affair with Caroline Taylor left no visible mark on the book.

Long afterwards, he described *The Light that Failed* as his ' transmogrified' version of *Manon Lescaut,* a tale that had fascinated him from boyhood. Like the Chevalier des Grieux in *Manon,* Dick is drawn back, like a moth to a candle, again and again, whatever may be the defects of his sweetheart; like Manon, Maisie retains a certain aloofness, whatever may be the concessions she makes to her lover. Beyond that it is hard to find any resemblance between the French novel and the English. In *The Light that Failed,* we are not confronted with the destroying passion that burns up the lovers in the French book. *Manon,* for all its bareness and austerity, is written with the firmest realism; thus do human beings behave. By comparison *The Light that Failed* is a romantic piece. Dick faces his fate with the illusions of a Byronic hero, and, rough as he is in his dealings with men, he is prim — Tennysonian — in the war of sex, too genteel to come to grips with Maisie, too self-centred in prosperity and in adversity to make any surrender to her, too bemused to love her or leave her. He is, at once, brutal and sentimental, a singularly unpleasant hero.

The critics have always been puzzled by Kipling's motive in writing this book. J. M. Barrie, who was Kipling's contemporary and friend, wrote a well-meaning column of warning in the *Contemporary Review*.

His chief defect is ignorance of life. This seems a startling charge to bring against one whose so-called knowledge of life has frightened the timid. But it is true. ' Dick Heldar's ' views are Kipling's views. . . .

He believes that because he has knocked about the world in shady company, he has no more to learn.'

To writers of the other school, words could hardly be found for condemning the book; Richard Le Gallienne described the final paragraphs as 'squeals of homicidal mania'.[6] More damaging was Max Beerbohm's mockery of *The Light that Failed* written some years later when a dramatized version appeared. *

Should the name of Rudyard Kipling [he asked] be put between inverted commas? Is it the veil of feminine identity? If of Mr. Kipling we knew nothing except this work, we should assuredly make that conjecture. . . . Dick Heldar doted on the military . . . strange that these heroes with their self-conscious blurting of oaths and slang, their cheap cynicism about the female sex, were not fondly created out of the inner consciousness of a female novelist.[7]

In spite of such voices as these, the book has been much read and admired, especially in France, and the author himself admitted that he preferred the French version to the English. A study of Kipling's earlier work reveals *The Light that Failed* as a *pastiche* of extracts from his notebooks, strung together with an autobiographical motive which, here and there, is emphasized so strongly that the actual reminiscences intrude upon the feigned story. Kipling confessed, in a letter to Mrs. Humphry Ward, that he was not satisfied with the composition of his book.

It will always be one of the darkest mysteries to me that any human being can make a beginning, end and middle to a really truly long story. I can think them by scores but I have not the hand to work out the full frieze. It's just the difference between the deep-sea steamer with twelve hundred people aboard, beside the poor beggars sweating and scorching in the stokehold, and the coastwise boat with a mixed cargo of notions.[8]

The strangest feature of the book is a strain of ill-nature that runs through it; the cargo includes some very angry notions, especially in those places where the book is mostly plainly autobiographical. Kipling works off his rages against precious critics and greedy publishers through the mouth of Dick Heldar, who seems to be the author in his most awkward frame of mind. By contrast Maisie is an unrealized phantom figure, not half so actual as the two minor female characters, Bessie the sluttish model, who is founded upon Aunt Georgie's parlour-maid, and the 'red-haired girl' who is not even

---

* *The Light that Failed* was dramatised at least once, and filmed at least three times. Forbes-Robertson's production (1903) was the only one of R. K.'s works to succeed on the stage. At one time Sarah Bernhardt wrote to R. K., offering to produce a version. But whether she was to take the part of Dick or of Maisie, wrote R. K. to his agent, she did not say.

given a name. These two are depicted in a few strokes with such superb economy and strength as gives them more vitality than any of the major characters. Maisie may be a composite character, but the ' red-haired girl ' is surely drawn direct from the life.

Can it be doubted that such a book, written at such a time in Kipling's career, composed of elements which can largely be traced to identifiable scenes from his own past, does not reflect, consciously or unconsciously, the emotions of his own love-affair? No clue remains to the puzzle, and the author's contempt for the prying eye of the commentator is as pungent as Dick Heldar's — no other clue, save the dedication. Dick Heldar would have no women about him at the end. Like Captain Mafflin of the Pink Hussars he still clung to the subaltern's slogan that ' a young man married is a young man marred '. His letters to Henley (who knew nothing of Caroline Taylor or Flo Garrard) repeated this hostility to the married state, in 1890. The ' family square ' was still sufficient, and the complete version of *The Light that Failed* was dedicated to his mother, the only woman Kipling had yet learned to love.

CHAPTER VIII

KIPLING AND THE BALESTIERS (1891–2)

———————◄◆►———————

THE MIRACLES (1891)

I sent a message to my dear —
  A thousand leagues and more to Her —
The dumb sea-levels thrilled to hear,
  And Lost Atlantis bore to Her!

Behind my message hard I came,
  And nigh had found a grave for me;
But that I launched of steel and flame
  Did war against the wave for me.

Uprose the deep, in gale on gale,
  To bid me change my mind again —
He broke his teeth along my rail,
  And, roaring, swung behind again.

          .   .   .   .

Earth sold her chosen men of strength
  (They lived and strove and died for me)
To drive my road a nation's length,
  And toss the miles aside for me.

          .   .   .   .

I sent the Lightnings forth to see
  Where hour by hour She waited me.
Among ten million one was She,
  And surely all men hated me!

Dawn ran to meet me at my goal —
  Ah, day no tongue shall tell again!
And little folk of little soul
  Rose up to buy and sell again!

SO large a part did the Balestiers of Beechwood, Vermont, play in
Rudyard's life that a digression into their history will be apposite.
It will be remembered that, soon after his arrival in London, he had
been introduced to a young American named Wolcott Balestier, in
Mrs. Humphry Ward's drawing-room.

RUDYARD KIPLING'S FATHER, JOHN LOCKWOOD KIPLING,
IN LATER LIFE

During the eighteenth century, a Huguenot family named Balestier had emigrated from France to America where one of them married a daughter of Paul Revere, the Huguenot patriot of Boston. They were a roving breed with interests in the East and West Indies, and it was at Martinique that Wolcott's grandfather, Joseph Balestier, was born. He went out west in the eighteen-thirties, made money as a real-estate lawyer in the first Chicago land-boom, and, at Chicago, in its wild heroic age, he met and married Caroline Starr Wolcott, a notable woman who lived till 1901. Both sides of her family, Starrs and Wolcotts, were New Englanders of five or six generations, the best blood of Connecticut. The Wolcott family had given three Governors to the State, and one of Caroline's forbears had signed the Declaration of Independence. This intelligent and well-born couple, Joseph and Caroline Balestier, settled in New York where he prospered at the law.

In 1868 the Balestiers bought a handsome old farmhouse (to which they gave the name 'Beechwood') as a summer resort near Brattleboro, a small country town in Vermont, and there they lived in somewhat grander style than was customary in rural America, dressing for dinner and drinking French wines, two practices which provided Brattleboro with gossip. Otherwise they were as American as their neighbours, who pronounced their name 'Ballis-teèr'. Joseph Balestier died in 1888, worth more than $600,000.

His widow still spent her summers at Beechwood, as the head of a large family of children and grandchildren. A very determined, handsome, opinionated old lady, she gave much time to the affairs of the Unitarian Church in Brattleboro, where she is still remembered as 'Madam Balestier'. Her children and grandchildren were as strong-minded as she was, united by a strong family feeling and yet rather disposed to disagreement over their social responsibilities and the disposition of the family fortunes. One of the sons, Henry, married Anna Smith, an episcopalian, who drew his branch of the family into that church, and so caused a division of interests in Brattleboro. It was noticed that family parties at Beechwood were strictly selective since brothers- and sisters-in-law did not always mingle easily. Henry's wife Anna usually stayed at Mrs. Kirkland's boarding-house in the town when she visited her husband's family. She was a pleasant, sensible woman, the daughter of Judge Peshine Smith, an international lawyer of world-wide repute, and she, too, was left a widow with a young family. Her four children lived with their mother at Rochester in New York State but often visited their grandmother at Brattleboro; all had a part to play in the life of Rudyard Kipling.

The eldest child, Wolcott, was the hope of the family, slight and dapper in appearance, gay and lively in manner, the idol of his classmates at Cornell and their leader in college pranks, but delicate in health. His sisters, who had unbounded confidence in his career, adored him. Wolcott had some success as a journalist in the Western States and in New York, and was regarded as a rising man when, at the end of 1888, he established himself in London, as agent for a New York publisher.

Next came Caroline, who was to be Rudyard Kipling's wife, a little active clever woman, much like her grandmother in feature and strength of character. Josephine, the younger daughter, was considered the beauty of the family; and last came Beatty, the scapegrace, the spoiled darling of his stern old grandmother. Beatty (they always called him 'Baty' at Brattleboro) had the vitality and intelligence of his sisters, and all the ease and frankness that they lacked. A sportsman and a good fellow, he was strong and handsome, free with his money when he happened to have any, and a careless borrower when he ran short. His language was rich with picturesque profanity, and he drank a great deal more than was thought proper in 'dry' Vermont. 'Baty's' exploits with horses and dogs shocked and delighted Brattleboro, where the school-children were warned to climb the bank if they heard his sleigh-bells, jingling 'as loud as cow-bells' down the narrow snow-bound roads. Uphill and downhill he always drove at a gallop. His reputation as a wild guy was his particular pride.*

When Wolcott Balestier went to London, the family and all the élite of Brattleboro watched with admiration. He was to make his fortune by persuading authors to entrust their books to his firm; he was to solve the problem of international copyright (that Anglo-American dispute which so infuriated Rudyard); and then — he was to astonish the world as a writer. In the first stage of this programme, his success was instantaneous. He set up an office in Dean's Yard, beside Westminster Abbey; imported a young friend from Brattleboro as his assistant; and worked habitually till past midnight, though not without finding time to attend literary parties where he made the contacts for which he had crossed the ocean.[1]

Edmund Gosse, who brought Rudyard and Wolcott Balestier together, rightly surmised that there were grounds for a close friendship between them, though this friendship seems not to have matured for several months. There was much, also, about Balestier against which Rudyard might have been expected to react with disgust. He had

---

* Alexander Woollcott, who knew Beatty well, collected some materials for a memoir but never completed it. Beatty, he said, was a 'violent, warm-hearted, disorderly creature . . . a charming, contentious rattlepate'. (A. Woollcott: Letters typescript in Library of Congress.)

invaded Europe as the representative of an American publisher, J. W. Lovell, to arrange for cheap reprints of any popular books that might come his way, the sort of publisher that Rudyard most detested. Like Rudyard, Balestier was a journalist by training, but unlike him in having a flair for imposing himself upon celebrities. Within a few months he had collected Mrs. Humphry Ward, the season's best-seller; he had Henry James on a string; he was on close friendly terms with Whistler; and Kipling was to be his next capture. When Balestier heard about the newcomer from India, he was all afire with interest: 'Rudyard Kipling? What is it? Is it a real name? A man or a woman?' By one account, he followed up the first meeting with a call at Embankment Chambers where, finding Rudyard out at seven o'clock, he resolutely waited till midnight for his return and then plunged into a business discussion. He had made up his mind; he wanted Rudyard to collaborate with him in writing a novel.

The progress of their friendship and the steps by which Rudyard, who distrusted publishers and was wary with intruders, was talked into this agreement are not now recoverable, but on 12th July 1890 Balestier wrote to William Dean Howells, the novelist: 'lately I have been seeing even more of Kipling with whom I am writing a story in collaboration. The scene is to be partly far Western American (W. B.) and partly Indian (R. K.).' The news reached Howells about the time he wrote the article in *Harper's Monthly* which so infuriated Kipling; and a service that Balestier was able to do was to bring his two friends into harmony. He assured Howells that Kipling had 'not a single grain of vanity or self-love' and conveyed some message from Howells which Kipling instantly accepted 'with a shout of delight'. Thereafter Kipling maintained his vendetta only against Harper Brothers and regarded Howells as a friend. In general, Kipling was slow to forget an injury, and this conciliation was a triumph for Balestier. No other man ever exercised so dominating an influence over Rudyard Kipling as did Wolcott Balestier during the eighteen months of their intimacy. It must be deduced from his behaviour, not from his words, for he liked to keep his friendships in different compartments, and there is no single allusion to his new friend in his letters to Mrs. Hill, nor more than a phrase or two in his letters to Henley. The compact with Balestier was made and, during the autumn, in spite of Rudyard's exhaustion and illness, some progress was made with the book they were to write together. By the end of the year 1890 Rudyard was taking Wolcott's advice on business questions, rather to the disgust of A. P. Watt, the literary agent, who was at last getting his affairs in order. Watt wrote rather plaintively that he could have made a better bargain for the American rights of *The Light that Failed* than Rudyard had got for himself through his new friend. It is significant that Balestier's firm, J. W. Lovell & Co., published the edition with the happy ending; and a plausible explanation of the two versions is that Wolcott Balestier persuaded him to play for the big sales in the American market at the cost of replanning his novel. Who else in Rudyard's whole life could have persuaded him to do it?

He was not alone in being fascinated by Wolcott Balestier. This American charmed literary London, as the memoirs of the day bear witness; but charm is volatile and when he died young, having accomplished very little, it evaporated, leaving nothing but allusions in old books. Justin McCarthy, Edmund Gosse, Arthur Waugh, Henry James concur in describing him as a man of quite extraordinary merit and talent. Henry James, in particular, framed and reframed his eulogies in letter after letter, though perhaps it will be fair to admit that he was disposed to think all his ducklings were swans. Wolcott Balestier's short-lived celebrity has vanished; few of his letters, and only one or two faded photographs of him, are extant; the two novels he left behind are insipid; the international publishing house he founded perished with him. Yet his conquest of literary London is undoubted and his personal conquest of Rudyard Kipling was an event in the history of literature.

All the Balestier family flocked to share Wolcott's success in London, even Beatty, who was allowed to savour the delights of the West End for a short time, until the pace he went was too hot for the family reputation, whereupon he was hurried home to Vermont by his elder brother. When Wolcott's mother came with her two daughters, she was a little discomfited to find that his literary connexion did not supply them with an entry into 'Society', though they regularly met the literary lions at Edmund Gosse's Sunday evening parties. Life in London was dull, until Caroline, the elder daughter, took Wolcott's domestic affairs in hand. She kept house for him with devotion and tireless industry; she ran the country cottage in the Isle of Wight where he spent his holidays. According to the family tradition, she first met Rudyard Kipling at Wolcott's office in Dean's Yard, where she had gone to consult him, with the housekeeping books under her arm. She was three years older than Rudyard.[2]

Marriage was far from Rudyard's thoughts in 1890. Flo Garrard had failed him and his first novel had resolved itself — in its more perfect form — as an anti-feminist tract. The abortive affair with Caroline Taylor had done nothing to alter Rudyard's views; but it must be remembered that he was still a very young man and, in spite of his reputation, not widely experienced in the ways of women. The family square which had been so happily reformed in London, was his social ideal, and the happy Christmas party of the four at Earl's Court Road just before Rudyard's twenty-fifth birthday was the last, perhaps the gayest, of their family festivals.

Rudyard's mother was much in his thoughts that winter. He was at work upon a more ambitious poem than he had yet attempted, as well as upon his novel, a poem which was to point out to the English people their destiny overseas, and the sacrifice demanded from them by that destiny. Hitherto he had been regarded as a hostile critic of Indian policy and administration. This was the first work of Rudyard Kipling which might have been described (if the hideous modern jargon had been then current) as imperialist propaganda. The poem would not frame itself in words; he fumbled for a phrase until his mother intervened with, 'Surely this is what you are trying to say . . .' And the opening lines of 'The English Flag' took shape.[3]

> Winds of the World, give answer! They are whimpering to and fro—
> And what should they know of England who only England know?—

For the second time he had astonished the world with a phrase. The poem appeared in the *St. James's Gazette* on 4th April 1891, and within a week Henley had decided to give it the place of honour in the new anthology of English Verse, *Lyra Heroica,* which he was just about to publish. For many years *Lyra Heroica* was the most popular collection of verse for boys and girls and, through this book, 'The English Flag' became, for a generation, one of the best-known of all English ballads. It contains, like so many of Kipling's writings, a line or two of contemptuous denunciation, but no arrogance about the Flag as a symbol; it asserts no moral or material superiority for Englishmen or the English way of life; it is a call to service and to sacrifice in every land and sea.

> 'Never the lotos closes, never the wild-fowl wake,
> But a soul goes out on the East Wind that died for England's sake—
> Man or woman or suckling, mother or bride or maid—
> Because on the bones of the English the English Flag is stayed.'

The sentiment is now a little out-moded, but it was new in Victorian England, when the 'street-bred' English were hardly yet aware that they had responsibilities away from home. The poem was the first of a series in which Kipling revealed these responsibilities in word-pictures of the British territories overseas.

Meanwhile, Wolcott Balestier had been at work upon the novel. He wrote to Howells, 18th February 1891: 'Kipling and I have been wading deep into our story lately, and have written rather more than two thirds of it. It begins in the West where I have a free hand for several chapters. Then we lock arms and march upon India. The process of collaboration is much easier than one could have supposed. We hit it off together most smoothly. . . . [Henry] James has been reading the first part of it, and professes himself delighted with the Western atmosphere.' *

The title of the book was to be *The Naulahka, a Novel of East and West.* 'Naulakha', as the word should properly be spelt, was the Hindu word for nine 'lakhs' of rupees (one lakh = 100,000), and the name was applied in India to a fabulous jewel. The plot of the story, mere melodrama, is concerned with an attempt by an American engineer to get possession of the jewel, as an act of bravado with which to impress a woman in his native town, a boom-town in Western America. The contrast between life in the Far West, and life in the Indian principality where the 'naulakha' lies hidden, is revealed successively, and appropriately, to the American engineer and to the missionary lady with whom he is in love. The American scenes bear a resemblance to one of Balestier's earlier stories where the same place-names occur; the Indian scenes are plainly derived from the same source as Kipling's *Letters of Marque.* It seems likely that they were written up by Balestier from Kipling's notes.

The characterization owes an evident debt to Kipling. The two principal persons are developed from the characters in *The Light that Failed.* Nicholas Tarvin, the American engineer, seems to be Dick Heldar with an American accent, and Kate Sheriff, the missionary, a more submissive, more alluring Maisie. Again the crux of the story is the heroine's dilemma, whether to renounce her career for marriage and, in *The Naulahka,* as in the American version of *The Light that Failed,* the book ends with a conventional decision to marry.

> 'I left 'em all in couples akissing on the decks.
> I left the lovers loving and the parents signing cheques.' [4]

So Kipling wrote in rather ribald mood of similar conventional endings by other novelists.

The Naulahka is readable — anything in which Kipling had a hand is readable; here and there it is enlivened by piercing observations and forcible expressions such as no one but Kipling could have penned,

---

* The following account, probably by Will Cabot, appeared in the *Vermont Phœnix,* 13th November 1891: '. . . the work was done by the two friends — Balestier, who is an accomplished typewriter, sitting at the machine and dashing off the sentences and chapters while Kipling paced the room, each composing, suggesting, or criticising in turn, and the mind of each stimulating the other to its best work.'

but it added little to his reputation as a novelist, and not much to Wolcott Balestier's. If the book is loved, it is for the sake of the Indian palace scenes, and for the pathetic picture of the Hindu child-prince. Kipling's sympathy with the child, caught up in a world of intrigue he could not understand, and his own understanding of that oriental world, were faultless. In Kipling's own mental development we can detect some progress since *The Light that Failed;* he is not so crudely opposed to marriage as a way of life.

Before *The Naulahka* began to appear in print, there was an understanding between Rudyard and Wolcott's sister, Caroline. The family square was again broken and Rudyard was disposing himself to devise a new formula. Mrs. Kipling, it is credibly recorded, no sooner set eyes on Carrie Balestier than she said: ' That woman is going to marry our Ruddy ', and showed little enthusiasm for the prospect. Lockwood Kipling, always genial and accommodating, merely remarked upon her universal competence: ' Carrie Balestier ', he said, ' was a good man spoiled '. The progress of the love-affair, as its two principals would have wished, remained their own secret, and has died with them. It did not run smoothly.[5]

Rudyard's health remained extremely bad throughout his second English winter, with continual recurrence of the malarial bouts and the dysentery that he had brought from India, aggravated by mental exhaustion after his prodigious output in 1890. His parents and his doctor repeatedly urged him to take a long sea-voyage, and it may have been more than a coincidence that Edmund Gosse, his friend and Wolcott's, gave him the same advice in a long and generous, but candid, criticism of his work which appeared in the *Century Magazine,* in May 1891. ' Go east, Mr. Kipling, go back to the Far East. Disappear! another Waring. Come back in ten years' time with another precious and admirable budget of loot out of wonderland.' For the present, Gosse warned him, he was publishing too much.

He did not quite take Gosse's advice, but slipped off to America, on a short voyage with his Uncle Fred Macdonald, the Methodist minister. By this time his celebrity was so great that he was much persecuted by press reporters for interviews. When first he came to England he had not spurned publicity and had even allowed an elaborate account of his life, conduct, appearance, possessions, and surroundings at Embankment Chambers to be released for publication in the *World*.[6] As his fame grew, he learned to hate the symptoms of it, and to shun intruders upon his privacy. This man whom everyone wanted to see found it difficult to remain unnoticed. His moustaches, eyebrows, spectacles were recognized, wherever he went. Not only were all his

movements recorded in the press, but there was also a steady stream
of quite unfounded rumours about him. Very early in his day of
fame, piratical publishers got hold of the articles about America which
he had contributed to the *Pioneer,* and reproduced them in many unauthorized editions. The pirates outsailed him, in spite of A. P. Watt's
efforts, launching version after version of his travel-sketches. Some
American critics, never noticeably thick-skinned about foreign criticism
of America, denounced him with fury. The Kipling boom, in 1890,
was vastly inflated in America by piratical publications, by the copyright struggle with Harpers, and by continual controversy in the Press
about his intentions. Had he not insulted America? There was no
doubt that another visit to New York would involve broadsides of
publicity from friends and foes and it was, perhaps, unwise of Rudyard
to attempt a visit incognito. He let it be known that ill-health obliged
him to go to Italy again, and so the New York *Herald* reported, on
the word of 'a friend from Beaver (Pa.)', on 13th June 1891. A week
later, the *Herald* found out its mistake and published a short account
of an interview with Rudyard Kipling in a New York hotel.

Fred Macdonald had set out for America to visit his brother Henry,
and Rudyard accompanied him on the ship, having registered under
the name of 'J. Macdonald'. It was a German ship, the food was
abominable and the sea 'loppy and choppy', but the two tourists
enjoyed the voyage. Someone else was so entranced by the conversation of 'J. Macdonald', and so observant of his moustache and eyebrows, as to tip the wink to the *Herald* when they reached New York.
The guileless Fred Macdonald told the truth to the first reporter who
came for news, merely protecting his nephew by saying that he was
unwell. This, too, was news, and the reporter, whether he actually
spoke to Rudyard or not, described him as almost speechless with a
diseased throat — a diplomatic dumbness, perhaps. Meanwhile the
two travellers found that a tragedy had made their voyage pointless,
since Henry Macdonald had died while they were at sea. Fred
Macdonald remained to administer his dead brother's affairs, while
Rudyard, piqued at having been unmasked, at once returned to
England. This rather absurd episode added to the mystery.[7]

In July he evaded the reporters. Wolcott Balestier was ill that
month and the two friends were together in the Isle of Wight with
Wolcott's mother and sisters. The visit provided Rudyard with his
story of the lighthouse-keeper ('A Disturber of Traffic'), but, whether
with an eye to his health or to his peace of mind, he was restive. As
the dull English summer drew to a close with the days turning sick
and cold, he set off on a voyage round the world. In August 1891

s.s. *Moor* of the Union line left London Docks for Madeira and the
Cape, carrying him on his first voyage into the southern hemisphere.

He was alone. On this ship there was no friendly Mrs. Hill to
share his jokes and applaud his rhymes and sketches. It was a second
start in life like his voyage to India in 1882, but was it the means of
felicity which he had supposed? The adventure and an unrealized
yearning shaped themselves in verses which by the complexity of their
rhythm and the depth of their feeling showed themselves the work
of a maturer man. This, among Kipling's longer poems, was thought
worthy of a place in the *Oxford Book of English Verse.*

> See the shaking funnels roar, with the Peter at the fore,
>   And the fenders grind and heave,
> And the derricks clack and grate, as the tackle hooks the crate,
>   And the fall-rope whines through the sheave;
>   It's 'Gang-plank up and in,' dear lass,
>   It's 'Hawsers warp her through!'
>   And it's 'All clear aft' on the old trail, our own trail, the
>   out trail,
>   We're backing down on the Long Trail — the trail that is
>   always new.
>
> O the mutter overside, when the port-fog holds us tied,
>   And the sirens hoot their dread,
> When foot by foot we creep o'er the hueless viewless deep
>   To the sob of the questing lead!
>   It's down by the Lower Hope, dear lass,
>   With the Gunfleet Sands in view,
>   Till the Mouse swings green on the old trail, our own trail,
>   the out trail,
>   And the Gull Light lifts on the Long Trail — the trail that
>   is always new.
>
>   .   .   .   .   .
>
> Then home, get her home, where the drunken rollers comb,
>   And the shouting seas drive by,
> And the engines stamp and ring, and the wet bows reel and swing,
>   And the Southern Cross rides high!
>   Yes, the old lost stars wheel back, dear lass,
>   That blaze in the velvet blue.
>   They're all old friends on the old trail, our own trail, the
>   out trail,
>   They're God's own guide on the Long Trail — the trail
>   that is always new.

The poem is very much more than an exulting paean of delight in
a sea-voyage to the Cape; it looks forward to a goal, twenty thousand

symbolic miles away, where felicity is to be shared, not savoured alone.

Rudyard spent the greater part of September and October in Cape Town, then a sleepy, dusty, little dorp where teams of oxen dawdled down Adderley Street, and where Boer and Briton still lived amicably together. In a city club he found himself one day at a lunch-party with Cecil Rhodes whose new colony of Rhodesia had just come into being, but Kipling was unobtrusive and Rhodes, as ever, inarticulate, and they made no mark on one another. More to his fancy at the time was the British naval station at Simonstown where he struck up a friendship with Captain Bayley, getting from him an invitation to go for a cruise. It was his first contact with the Royal Navy, and sailors were new types of men whom he now began to study with his penetrating eye. 'Judson and the Empire',* his first naval story, about a tiff with the Portuguese on the East African coast, was a by-product of this new range of interests.[8]

Among friends he made at Cape Town was Olive Schreiner the novelist, who had the hardihood to ask him about the background to *The Light that Failed*. This was his reply:

> If all the girls in the world sat quiet and still, at the right moment, by all the men in the world, when those were in trouble, we should all be perfectly happy instead of being hurt and worried. I'll show you about this time next year why Maisie was made as she was.[9]

The reader may interpret this letter as he will.

Two days after writing this letter, on 25th September 1891, Rudyard left Cape Town for the long lonely voyage to Hobart and Wellington, in the Shaw Savill liner, s.s. *Doric*. She followed the great circle far to the southward to get the advantage of the westerly winds in the roaring 'forties, the run that has been made familiar by 'McAndrew's Hymn':

> We'll tak' one stretch — three weeks an' odd by ony road ye steer —
> Fra' Cape Town east to Wellington — ye need an engineer.
> Fail there — ye've time to weld your shaft — ay, eat it, ere ye're spoke;
> Or make Kerguelen under sail — three jiggers burned wi' smoke!
> An' home again — the Rio run: it's no child's play to go
> Steamin' to bell for fourteen days o' snow an' floe an' blow.
> The bergs like kelpies overside that girn an' turn an' shift
> Whaur, grindin' like the Mills o' God, goes by the big South drift.
> (Hail, Snow and Ice that praise the Lord. I've met them at their work,
> An' wished we had anither route or they anither kirk.)

---

*It was based upon a conversation overheard in the naval mess at Simonstown. Lieutenant S. de Horsey, R.N., then commanding H.M. gunboat *Gryper,* was the original of 'Judson'. (Letter, S. de Horsey to B. M. Bazley, 23rd July 1933.)

While he studied the sea and the men who made their living by it, a slow uncertain correspondence was passing by infrequent mail steamers between two men who had interested themselves in his affairs: Henry James in London and Robert Louis Stevenson in Samoa.

James to Stevenson, 21st March 1890

We'll tell you all about Rudyard Kipling — your nascent rival. He has killed one immortal — Rider Haggard; the star of the hour, aged 24 and author of remarkable anglo-indian and extraordinarily observed barrack life — Tommy Atkins tales.

Stevenson to James, August 1890

Kipling is too clever to live.

Stevenson to James, 29th December 1890

Kipling is by far the most promising young man who has appeared since — ahem — I appeared. He amazes me by his precocity and various endowments. But he alarms me by his copiousness and haste.

James to Stevenson, 12th January 1891

The only news in literature here — such is the virtuous vacancy of our consciousness — continues to be the infant monster of a Kipling.

Stevenson to James, 28th September 1891

R. K. is planning to visit us.

James to Stevenson, 30th October 1891

That little black demon of a Kipling will perhaps have leaped upon your silver strand by the time this reaches you. He publicly left England to embrace you many weeks ago — carrying literary genius out of the country with him in his pocket.[10]

On 13th October the *Doric* reached Port Hobart in Tasmania, where some passengers trans-shipped for Melbourne; and then left without delay for Wellington, a five-day run across the cold, stormy Tasman Sea. Rudyard landed in New Zealand on 18th October, submitted gracefully to a newspaper interview, and left for the north a day or two later by horse-and-buggy through the central plains to the 'thermal district' of Rotorua where, even in 1891, some provision was made for tourists. At Auckland his fancy was so far taken that he contributed an essay to the *New Zealand Herald* — it has never been reprinted; and to Auckland he paid the tribute, in his 'Song of the Cities' that, there, one might

Wonder 'mid our fern why men depart
To seek the Happy Isles!

It must have been at Auckland that Kipling visited the aged states-man, Sir George Grey, whose knowledge of the Empire was unrivalled, whose memory of fifty years' service in Australia, Africa, and New Zealand was ripened by scholarship and by acquaintance with all the sharpest intellects of the age. Of this meeting no record has sur-vived except a wildly inaccurate sentence in *Something of Myself*, Kipling's fragment of autobiography which, on the events of this voyage, is quite unreliable.

It had been his intention to extend his tour for another three months, in order to visit Samoa, had not something now happened to make him change his plans and turn towards home.

On 30th October Rudyard took ship again at Auckland and travelled down the coast of New Zealand to Wellington, to Lyttelton the port of Christchurch, to Dunedin, and to the Bluff, the most southerly settlement of the English-speaking peoples in the world. At Christ-church he met an old friend, Professor Haslam who had excoriated him with sarcasms for his errors in elementary Latin at Westward Ho!, whose tongue was so sharp that even Mr. Croft's had been a pleasant relief. Haslam admitted that his pupils now had the best of him. He lectured to mixed classes and when he reproved the girls for false quantities they made eyes at him. Nothing else survives of Rudyard's visit to New Zealand except a memory of a boating picnic in Wellington harbour, and a phrase he heard spoken at Christchurch, which, years afterwards, he made the starting-point of a story called 'Mrs. Bathurst'.[11] Early in November he left the Bluff for Mel-bourne, travelling in company with 'General' Booth of the Salvation Army, who was making an apostolic tour of the world. An odd friendship sprang up between these two dissimilar characters, the old evangelist and the young writer, a friendship which may throw a gleam of light on both.

Rudyard's visit to Australia was briefer even than his visit to New Zealand. He spent a few days at the Melbourne Club, where the newspaper-men took him up, chaffed him because *Plain Tales* had just been banned by the public library for its impropriety, and begged him to 'report' the Melbourne Cup, the greatest horse-race in the world, for one of the papers. He would not; he wrote no revelation of Australia except — ten years later — the vivid poem called 'Lichten-berg', and that was based upon no more than a train journey to Sydney and back.[12]

After three weeks in Australia he left Adelaide in s.s. *Valetta* for Colombo, again in the company of 'General' Booth. At Colombo he left his ocean-liner, crossed to Tuticorin, and took the train through southern and central India to Lahore. For four days and nights he travelled through an India more strange to him than to the untravelled Englishman — the flat red India of palm-tree, palmyra-palm, and rice, the India of the picture-books, of *Little Henry and His Bearer* — all dead and dry in the baking heat.

A week before Christmas he reached Lahore. The 'station' was disposed to make an honoured guest of this young man who had won so much fame since he had left them thirty months previously. He appeared at the fancy bazaar organized by the Lieutenant-Governor's lady and made no objection when his portrait appeared 'among those present' in the *Civil and Military*. The proprietors, down at Allahabad, were anxious to detain him for business discussions, but he could not be held.

It must have been some message from Carrie Balestier that induced him to turn back from Auckland without visiting Samoa. Tidings of Wolcott's illness, even by cable, cannot have reached him earlier than 25th November, when he was at Adelaide. Not till he was with his parents at Lahore did he receive the decisive blow, a cable from Carrie, sent from Germany, summoning him because Wolcott was dead. Without waiting even over Christmas Day Rudyard left Lahore for Bombay, where he stopped only to visit the *ayah* who had nursed him as a baby. This was his last view of India. Travelling to Trieste and taking the overland route, he reached London in fourteen days,[13] a remarkably rapid journey.

The story of Wolcott's last days is to be read in the correspondence of Henry James. Wolcott had formed a new partnership with William Heinemann to produce an international library of cheap reprints, in competition with the *Tauchnitz* editions. Late in November, after sending the first instalment of *The Naulahka* to press, Wolcott went over to Dresden on the affairs of his new venture, and there he was taken ill with typhoid fever. It happened that Mrs. Heinemann, his partner's wife, was visiting Dresden, and she sent for Wolcott's mother, who arrived in Dresden with her two daughters to find Wolcott dying. Mrs. Balestier and her younger daughter, Josephine, were reduced to dismay and impotence, and it was Carrie, the elder daughter, who took charge of everything. She sent for Henry James, their family friend.

Henry James to William James, 13th December 1891

Europäischer Hof,
 Dresden.
 I came off hastily to this place a week ago on a miserably sad errand — a sense of obligation created by the death here, 8 days since, in a private hospital, of a most malignant and hideous typhoid (brought from London)

of poor dear Wolcott Balestier, whom you saw three or four times while you were with me. He had left England ill, three weeks previously, and I thought the change of climate and forsaking of high pressure business would work an improvement. But the poison was in him and he has gone — to my very serious loss and sorrow and that of many other people as well. I was greatly attached to him — with reason — for he had rendered me admirable services and was destined to render still more and greater. . . . He had a great spirit and great ideas, and his writing (which was his real ambition) . . . will give those who didn't know him but little idea of what those who *did* know him (and I think I did so better than anyone) found in him.

Henry James to Mrs. M. Sands, 12th December 1891

I am working through my dreary errand . . . as smoothly as three stricken women — a mother and two sisters — permit. They are, however, very temperate and discreet — and one of the sisters a little person of extraordinary capacity — who will float them all successfully home. Wolcott Balestier, the young American friend beside whose grave I stood with but three or four others here on Thursday, was a very remarkable creature . . . and I was exceedingly attached to him. And now, at 30, he dies — in a week — in a far away German hospital — his mother and sisters were in Paris — of a damnable vicious typhoid, contracted in his London office, the ' picturesqueness ' of which he loved, as it was in Dean's Yard, Westminster, just under the Abbey Towers.

Henry James to Edmund Gosse, 10th December 1891

The English chaplain read the service. The three ladies came insistently to the grave. . . . By far the most interesting is poor little concentrated Carrie, with whom I came back from the cemetery alone in one of the big black and silver coaches, with its black and silver footmen perched up behind. (She wanted to talk to me) and . . . is remarkable in her force, acuteness, capacity, and courage — and in the intense — almost manly nature of her emotion. She is a worthy sister of poor dear big-spirited, only-by-death-quenched Wolcott. . . . She can do and face . . . for all three of them, anything and everything that they will have to meet now. They are going home (to the U.S.) as soon as they can, and they are going to London first. I suppose about a week hence.[14]

The news of Wolcott's death reached Brattleboro on 7th December. Beatty, the younger brother, was established there with a pretty young wife, on a farm called ' Maplewood ' which his doting grandmother had given him. With proper feeling, Beatty was proposing to return to England to take charge of his brother's affairs, until another cable assured him that this would not be necessary. It was, in fact, Carrie who disposed of the house in the Isle of Wight and made business arrangements with Wolcott's partner, William Heinemann; but Beatty and his friends in Brattleboro rightly surmised that the three women in

London were not unsupported. It was not known in Brattleboro until 28th December that the man who had been collaborating with Wolcott was to marry Wolcott's sister. Beatty then understood why his presence in London was not required, though for several days he did not know which sister; and the same doubt was current among their friends in London. It was Carrie the dominating, clever sister, not Josephine the pretty one. In letter after letter, Henry James expressed his doubts about the wisdom of the match.

Rudyard arrived in London on 10th January 1892. It was bitterly cold and the whole town seemed to be down with influenza. Without regard to any social niceties, Rudyard and Carrie arranged to be married by special licence within eight days. There were no festivities, and only a few close friends were notified by letters from the bride and bridegroom. Even of these friends very few came to the church; the Burne-Joneses had influenza, the Poynters had influenza, Mrs. Balestier and Josephine had influenza. The wedding was at All Souls', Langham Place, on 18th January, in the presence of a congregation of five. 'Ambo' Poynter, as best man, was the only representative of Rudyard's family; Henry James gave away the bride; Edmund Gosse, with his wife and son,* and William Heinemann made up the congregation. Even with this haste and privacy the news leaked out and, as they emerged, the bridegroom was disgusted to see in the porch a newspaper poster announcing his wedding. At the church door the bridal couple parted (since Carrie was obliged to nurse her mother) to meet again at Brown's Hotel where, two days later, 'Ambo' Poynter and Stan Baldwin came to lunch, the only entertainment that accompanied the marriage.[15]

Henry James to William James, 6th February 1892

I saw the Rudyard Kiplings off by the *Teutonic* the other day. . . . She was poor Wolcott Balestier's sister and is a hard devoted capable little person whom I don't in the least understand his marrying. It's a union of which I don't forecast the future though I gave her away at the altar in a dreary little wedding with an attendance simply of four men — her mother and sister prostrate with influenza. Kipling strikes me personally as the most complete man of genius (as distinct from fine intelligence) that I have ever known.

The reason why Rudyard hurried half-way round the world to marry Wolcott's sister is bound up with his devotion to Wolcott. There is little doubt that Wolcott fostered the match, that Wolcott on his death-

---

* Dr. Philip Gosse, who attended the wedding as a child, has described it to the present writer. The bride, a little woman with tiny hands and feet, was wearing a brown woollen dress with buttons all down the front.

bed commended the care of his family to his friend Rudyard, that
Wolcott's wishes were accepted by Rudyard as obligations, yet this
does not imply that Wolcott's sister was hurried into a match. She
had been engaged, or almost engaged, to Rudyard many months
earlier;[16] and their parting then had been signalled by the verses which
have already been quoted:

> Ha' done with the Tents of Shem, dear lass,
> We've seen the seasons through,
> And it's time to turn on the old trail, our own trail, the out trail. . . .

This had been the burden of his song when he left his two friends, the
brother and sister, in August 1891. But what were the 'Tents of
Shem', and, if the 'dear lass' was not Carrie Balestier, who was she?
The obscurity is deepened by an early draft of the poem, now in an
American library, where the line runs: 'Have done with the Tents of
Shem, dear lad!' Was it originally an appeal to Wolcott? Even if
this theorizing be rejected and the 'Long Trail' taken as fictitious
writing with no subjective undertone, the fact remains that Wolcott's
death marked a crisis in Rudyard's life. During the previous year, he
had written rather cynically about the reaction of civilized Europeans
at the approach of death. In London, he said, there was a pompous
display of grief when an old man slipped comfortably away in a bed
surrounded by loving relatives. How different it had been in India
where active young men lived in expectation of being struck down by
disease in the pride of their youth, and of being buried, replaced by a
substitute, and forgotten, in twenty-four hours. Though he had seen
men die swiftly of cholera at Lahore, no death had actually intruded
into the family square, or into the circle of his friends during his
seven years in the East. It was in tame, civilized Europe, after all,
that a bereavement first struck him to the heart. He never forgot the
blow though, characteristically, he rarely referred to it. On one occasion, he forced himself to say a few words to a close friend of Wolcott's
whom he had long wanted to meet: 'He died so suddenly and so far
away; we had so much to say to each other, and now I have got to
wait so long before I can say it'.[17]

Devotion to Wolcott's memory was a habit of mind that Carrie
shared with Rudyard. She had bent all the energy of her untiring
mind to the service of her family, that is to the forwarding of Wolcott's
career. By his wish — as a trust from him — she renewed and re-
doubled her devotion to her lover. Until Rudyard's death, forty-four
years later, the two were inseparable and her services to him were
indispensable. She now had a genius to care for, not only a man

whose friends thought that he ought to prove himself a genius. Emotionally, Rudyard was satisfied with a marriage that provided him with a clear field for exploiting his talents, nor did he ever again miss the comfortable stability of the family square, which he had often missed in his London year. Carrie was the mother of his three children; she provided him with his creature comforts, shielded him from intruders, watched his health, kept his accounts, took charge of all his affairs — sometimes with an irksome particularity. The marriage, perhaps, was more satisfactory on his side than on hers. 'Poor concentrated Carrie', as Henry James described her, gave Rudyard her life's endeavour and grudged him, perhaps, his faculty for withdrawing into a world of the imagination where she could not follow him.

From the day of their marriage, Carrie Kipling began to keep a diary. After 18th January 1892 there is rarely any doubt where Rudyard was or whom he met. They had agreed to set off together on the Long Trail, a honeymoon that would take them round the world. Rudyard had about £2000 in his bank account, and as many contracts as he cared to sign with publishers; Carrie had expectations from her mother and her grandmother, both of them widows with comfortable fortunes. Though their own affairs seemed promising enough, there was much business to be concluded in the fortnight after the marriage. On his wedding-day Rudyard found time to write to Henley, about some verses which he had brought back to England with him, a ballad called 'Tomlinson', which Henley thought 'infernal strong'. Rudyard's letter about it concluded:

I have married Miss Balestier, the sister of the man with whom I wrote the yarn in the *Century* [the *Naulahka*]. I don't as a rule let men into any part of life outside the working sections, but in this case methinks you are entitled to know.

Henley took the news sadly; R. L. Stevenson's marriage to a strong-minded American had been the end of his first literary partnership, and he much feared that Rudyard Kipling's marriage would have the same effect upon his second. 'Tomlinson' was some compensation, especially as Rudyard allowed him to correct it for the press, and sent with the proof a handsome tribute to Henley's 'Song of the Sword'. Rudyard never allowed himself to be swallowed up into the group that was called the 'Henley Regatta', and when he had another poem to sell, about a tramp steamer, he let it go elsewhere. 'The Ballad of the Bolivar' had been singing itself in his head for months and he was able to sit down in the office of the *St. James's Gazette* with Sidney Low and strike off the fair copy, for payment on the nail, the modest sum of fifteen guineas.[18]

While it was Carrie's affair to wind up Wolcott's business with his partners, Heinemann in London and Lovell in New York, it was Rudyard's to complete the *Naulahka,* of which two monthly instalments had already appeared in the *Century,* and of which the last instalment had not been written when Wolcott died. The third was now published, the fourth in the press, and four or five more were to be got into print. The book had been announced with immense publicity, on both sides of the Atlantic. It went with Kipling on his honeymoon, and the last few pages were written on s.s. *Teutonic.* *

In addition to *The Naulahka,* Kipling had another book ready for publication. Now he released the volume of *Barrack-Room Ballads,* for which the trade was clamouring. Indeed, an American firm had already paid him the indirect compliment of issuing a piratical edition. With the original ballads from the *Scots Observer* he included ' The Ballad of East and West ', ' The English Flag ', ' Tomlinson ', the ' Bolivar ', and the ' Long Trail ', a collection of such richness, variety, and gusto, if we claim no other merit for it, as to inflate the Kipling boom seven times larger. The authorized English edition was published by Methuen in April; it was reprinted three times in 1892, and fifty times in the next thirty years, much the most popular book of verse in the world for more than a generation.

Not even Rudyard's most ardent admirers have found much to say in favour of the dedication, a rhetorical Swinburnian poem to the memory of Wolcott Balestier.

> Beyond the loom of the last lone star, through open darkness hurled,
> Further than rebel comet dared or hiving star-swarm swirled,
> Sits he with those that praise our God for that they served His world.

The oddest feature of this dedication is that it was not original. Several verses of it had already appeared in the *National Observer,* in another context. What it shows defiantly is his extraordinary admiration for the lost friend in whose honour he adapted these wildly adulatory verses.

---

* The misspelling of the title *The Naulahka* remains a puzzle. Balestier may have been responsible for the error while Kipling was abroad, but Kipling never corrected the title, though when he named his Vermont house after the book he spelt it correctly, ' Naulakha '. What would he have said if any other publisher than Balestier had been responsible for such an error?

CHAPTER IX

A HOME IN VERMONT (1892–6)

THE FIRES (1912)

Men make them fires on the hearth
Each under his roof-tree,
And the Four Winds that rule the earth
They blow the smoke to me.

.   .   .   .   .

Until the tears are in my eyes
   And my heart is wellnigh broke
For thinking on old memories
   That gather in the smoke.

With every shift of every wind
   The homesick memories come,
From every quarter of mankind
   Where I have made me a home.

Four times a fire against the cold
   And a roof against the rain —
Sorrow fourfold and joy fourfold
   The Four Winds bring again!

How can I answer which is best
   Of all the fires that burn?
I have been too often host or guest
   At every fire in turn.

.   .   .   .   .

Oh, you Four Winds that blow so strong
   And know that this is true,
Stoop for a little and carry my song
   To all the men I knew!

.   .   .   .   .

WHEN the Kiplings, a new-married couple, crossed the Atlantic in February 1892, they had for travelling-companion an observant critic of Anglo-American relations, who relished their society. *The Education of Henry Adams* contains the following unexpected comment:

Fate was kind on that voyage. Rudyard Kipling . . . thanks to the mediation of Henry James, dashed over the passenger his exuberant fountain of gaiety and wit — as though playing a garden hose on a thirsty and faded begonia. Kipling could hardly ever know what peace of mind he gave, for he could hardly ever need it himself so much; and yet, in the full delight of his endless fun and variety, one felt the old conundrum repeat itself. Somehow, somewhere, Kipling and the American were not one, but two, and could not be glued together. . . .

The 'old conundrum' did not force itself upon Rudyard's notice during the wedding-trip. On 17th February, with a sigh of relief at leaving New York behind them —'New York with her roar and rattle, her complex smells, her triply over-heated rooms, and much too energetic inhabitants'— the Kiplings arrived at Brattleboro.

They stepped from the train to find Beatty Balestier waiting with a sleigh.

Thirty below freezing! It was inconceivable till one stepped into it at midnight, and the first shock of that clear, still air took away the breath as does a plunge into sea-water. A walrus sitting on a woolpack was our host in his sleigh, and he wrapped us in hairy goatskin coats, caps that came down over the ears, buffalo robes and blankets, and yet more buffalo-robes till we, too looked like walruses and moved almost as gracefully. . . . But for the jingle of the sleigh-bells the ride might have taken place in a dream, for there was no sound of hoofs upon the snow. The runners sighed a little now and again as they glided over an inequality, and all the sheeted hills round about were as dumb as death. Only the Connecticut River kept up its heart and a lane of black water through the packed ice; we could hear the stream worrying round the heels of its small bergs. Elsewhere there was nothing but snow under the moon — snow drifted to the level of the stone fences or curling over their tops in a lip of frosted silver; snow banked high on either side of the road, or lying heavy on the pines and hemlocks in the woods, where the air seemed, by comparison, as warm as a conservatory.[1]

The crisp New England winter, such wintry weather as Rudyard, brought up in southern England and matured in India, had never seen before, began to work in him a current of new life and vision. It was stimulating to stand on ground, now hard with frozen snow, ground in which he felt his wife's family to be rooted deep. They left the Main Street of Brattleboro where the road ran northward over a covered bridge, and drove two miles along the river-flats to the corner by Waite's Farm. A winding steep road led off among the elms and maples, up a hill to 'Beechwood', the family house where old Madam Balestier, the matriarch, lived with her termagant Irish housekeeper. A mile farther, the road came out across a sloping pasture with a wooded hillside on the left, and on the right a broad view over the valley towards a distant semicircle of pine-covered hills. Here stood 'Maplewood', Beatty's new home on his seventy-acre farm, and here the Kiplings stayed three days with Beatty and his pretty young wife. The favourite in the party was Marjorie, their new baby — a delight to Rudyard.

On the second day they climbed the hill to admire the view and saw the cone of Mount Monadnock rising above the foothills thirty miles away to the east, 'like a giant thumbnail'. If Rudyard knew himself at home among his wife's people, he had a longer association then, for Monadnock was Emerson's favourite mountain, familiar to Rudyard from his earliest reading:

> High over the river intervals,
> Above the ploughman's highest line,
> Over the owners' farthest walls!
> Up where the airy citadel
> O'erlooks the surging landscape's swell!
> Youth, for a moment free as they,
> Teach thy feet to feel the ground,
> Ere yet arrives the wintry day
> When Time thy feet has bound.
> Taste the bounty of thy birth,
> Taste the lordship of the earth.[2]

There was no doubt of it from that day; Rudyard and Carrie must stake out a claim on the family property, and by Rudyard's choice it must be high up the hillside, in sight of Mount Monadnock. Beatty, with his easy liberality, would have given him a plot of ground as a wedding-present; Carrie, with her business-like notions, was for negotiating a deal. She offered to take over the whole farm and to finance Beatty who was always short of cash. They all went down to New York to consult the lawyers about the Balestier reversions, and the end of the matter was that Beatty conveyed about ten acres of land to the Kiplings for a nominal consideration, reserving to himself the use of the pasture and some other rights. It was a friendly agreement between two young newly married couples, conceived in generosity and good humour. The Kiplings spent another day or two at Brattleboro then, having concluded their business and paid many calls in New York, they resumed their honeymoon.

It will not be necessary to retrace Rudyard's steps throughout his wedding tour, much of it following the path he had taken with his friends the Hills, in 1889. At one stage of the journey, however, he broke new ground, turning north from Chicago to St. Paul, and so to Winnipeg and across the Canadian prairie to the Rocky Mountains and

Vancouver. The C.P.R., then the only trans-continental line in North America, made a noble impression on him as did the effective administration of law in Canada, signified by the scarlet tunics of the Mounted Police. 'Her Majesty the Queen of England and Empress of India has us in her keeping', he wrote, with a new awareness that Canada differed from the United States. Again, he paid his way by writing travel-sketches, innocent this time of the indiscretions that marred his first juvenile essays in the field, and much more lucrative. They appeared in the *Civil and Military Gazette,* for what that was worth — and simultaneously in the New York *Sun* and the London *Times.*[3] Kipling was famous. No longer did he fill in his dull evenings by chumming up with newspaper men who were then free to mis-report his words; they came, hat in hand, and were firmly kept at bay, by Carrie, his business manager.

On a second visit, even to Japan in spring, a man need not repeat the tourist's round, but might merely luxuriate in form and colour. Much of his honeymoon he spent at Yokohama where a Mrs. Hunt acted as host to him and Carrie. Each of them had friends in Japan, where the name of her grandfather, Judge Peshine Smith, was well-remembered as legal adviser to the Mikado who broke down the barriers that had closed Japan against the world. Rudyard enjoyed his visits to the Yokohama Club where he could listen to the yarns of shipping magnates, particularly about the lawless skippers who poached seal-skins in waters which the Russians claimed as their own, though

'there's never a law of God or man runs north of Fifty-Three.'[4]

Into these northern seas he never penetrated, even if he wrote of them with understanding. In Yokohama, he recalled:

an earthquake (prophetic as it turned out) overtook us one hot break of dawn, and we fled into the garden, where a tall cryptomeria waggled its insane head back and forth with an 'I told you so' expression; though not a breath was stirring. A little later I went to the Yokohama branch of my bank on a wet forenoon to draw some of my solid wealth. Said the Manager to me: 'Why not take more? It will be just as easy.' I answered that I did not care to have too much cash at one time in my careless keeping, but that when I had looked over my accounts I might come again in the afternoon. I did so, but in that little space, my Bank, the notice on its shut door explained, had suspended payment. . . . I returned with my news to my bride of three months and a child to be born.[5]

The sum he had drawn was the exchange value of ten pounds sterling; his loss when the Oriental Banking Company failed, on 9th June 1892, was nearly £2000; his immediate resources were a return ticket to Vancouver by the *Empress of China,* and $100 in a New York bank. They had intended to cruise in the Pacific as far as Samoa at least, but all plans for a longer honeymoon were cancelled and again the prospect of a visit to R. L. Stevenson was abandoned. Thomas Cook handsomely refunded them the value of their cancelled reservations and they faced the world with equanimity, even with gaiety. During their last three weeks in Japan they danced at a ball given by Mrs. Hunt, and went about as though nothing had happened. Rudyard attended a meeting of creditors and it was he who proposed that they should make a composition with the insolvent bank for preference shares to the value of 25 per cent of their lost deposits. The value of these shares was eventually paid off at even better terms, though not until the Kiplings had become too prosperous to depend upon so modest a sum.[6] On 27th June 1892 he left Yokohama.

Already he was sending his travel-sketches to *The Times* and the other papers, and he had begun to work on verse and prose fiction. He was busy with ' The Rhyme of the Three Sealers' and with ' Judson and the Empire'. Lack of ready cash was no great obstacle to a man who could always sell his wares and always command hospitality, and on the voyage, with unusual geniality, he gave readings of his work at ship's concerts. He crossed Canada as the guest of William Van Horne, the Chairman of the C.P.R. In July 1892 he bade farewell — finally — to Asia.

Never again did he take ship east of Suez.

At Montreal the Kiplings had a telegram from Carrie's mother offering them the chance of a home at Brattleboro for $10 a month. It was the hired-man's house on the Bliss Farm, quite near to ' Beechwood'. On 26th July they reached Brattleboro, billeted themselves on Beatty and ' resumed the worship of Marjorie', his little daughter. After a family council with ' Madam' Balestier, the offer of the ' Bliss Cottage' was accepted, not quite the homecoming they had foreseen. For a year they lived in the simplest style, at first with one Swedish maid at $18 a month, which Carrie thought excessive. The neighbours, who were accustomed to regard the Balestiers as swell folks with style and money, were inclined to look askance at the penniless Englishman whom Miss Carrie had brought into the family, but not for long. *The Naulahka* and *Barrack-room Ballads,* published while they were away, had begun to bring in royalties — a modest $150 in September, $260 in October, and a cheque for no less than $3888 in November from A. P. Watt; and these were but foretastes of what was coming.

Their happiness, in the ' Bliss Cottage ', is plain in Rudyard's reminiscences:

We took it. We furnished it with a simplicity that fore-ran the hire-purchase system. We bought, second or third hand, a huge, hot-air stove which we installed in the cellar. We cut generous holes in our thin floors for its eight-inch tin pipes (why we were not burned in our beds each week of the winter I never can understand) and we were extraordinarily and self-centredly content.

As the New England summer flamed into autumn I piled cut spruce boughs all round the draughty cottage sill, and helped to put up a tiny roofless verandah along one side of it for future needs. When winter shut down and sleigh-bells rang all over the white world that tucked us in, we counted ourselves secure. Sometimes we had a servant. Sometimes she would find the solitude too much for her and flee without warning, one even leaving her trunk. This troubled us not at all.

When our lead pipe froze, we would slip on our coonskin coats and thaw it out with a lighted candle. There was no space in the attic bedroom for a cradle, so we decided that a trunk-tray would be just as good. We envied no one.

My first child and daughter was born in three foot of snow on the night of December 29th 1892. Her Mother's being the 31st and mine the 30th of the same month, we congratulated her on her sense of the fitness of things, and she throve in her trunk-tray in the sunshine on the little plank verandah. Her birth brought me into contact with the best friend I made in New England — Dr. Conland.[7]

Rudyard did not produce much written work in his honeymoon year. He finished off two or three belated soldier stories from his Indian period — notably ' Love o' Women ' which he described to Carrie as a ' doleful tale ', and worked a little at verses inspired by his travels. Mostly, he was occupied with making a home for Carrie and the baby, whom they called Josephine, after Carrie's sister.

Rudyard and Carrie had never swerved from their decision to build a house of their own. Even in their penniless days they were negotiating with an old friend named H. R. Marshall, a New York architect, for a house to be built to a novel design, on the plot of land they had acquired from Beatty, and as soon as the snow melted, they contracted to bring in labourers.

The house was named ' Naulakha ' in memory of Wolcott, and the contracts for building it were handled by Beatty. The drive ran up the pasture from the road, near ' Maplewood ', to a porch on the west side between the house and the hill. All the living-rooms were on the outer slope with wide windows to south and east. Rudyard used to say it lay on the long slope like a ship mounting an ocean swell, and like a ship, it was long and narrow. At one end was the kitchen, then came the dining-room, then a lounge into which you came from the entrance hall, then Carrie's boudoir where she sat at her desk facing the door and guarding the last room in the line, Rudyard's library at the south end. To this room there was no admission except past her chair; and no tradesman or artisan, no business caller, journalist, or busybody got through her guard to intrude upon the Master. It was a house of modest size with no room more than twenty feet in length, and no accommodation for more than a few guests.

Beatty acted as general agent for all their concerns and made at first a pretty good thing of them. It was Beatty who bought a team of oxen, hired labourers, got contracts for drainage, supplied farm horses, and took the hay off the meadow. Like many Vermont farmers he was always sagging along behind his liabilities, living on a mortgage, in farming country that steadily deteriorated. But Beatty and his pretty young wife, Mai, were alive, amusing, witty, hospitable. They gave memorable parties in which the Kiplings took the greatest pleasure. With cakes on a plank table, jugs of home-brewed cider, a fiddler from the town; with all the neighbours in, they would dance in the barn till past midnight — ungodly hours for Brattleboro. All the family assembled at Beatty's house for their Thanksgiving Dinner and when Conan Doyle came to stay with the Kiplings Beatty swept him into the party. 'No one', he said, 'would want to keep Thanksgiving in an Englishman's house.' In the afternoons Rud and Beatty would drive off to town while Mai sent her little Marjorie to spend the day at 'Naulakha'. Carrie had a good nursemaid now, Susan Bishop, who could look after the little girls together. When Rud came home he always had stories for the children, animal stories about camels and whales and the cat that walked in the wet wild woods up the road from Beatty's house.

Beatty was not a man to worry overmuch, and his worst trouble was that his elder sister would treat him as a boy. Whatever the nature of their contract, she regarded it as a means of controlling his extravagance. Two or three times a week, she had him up to 'Naulakha' to talk business, handing him out his commission in irregular doles of petty cash; five dollars one day, two dollars twenty-five another day, then fifteen dollars cash and a cheque for a larger sum with it, two dollars just before the Christmas party at 'Maplewood', and five dollars more, two days later. Sometimes there was a large settlement to make, scrupulously noted in her diary, as much as $257 at a single payment when the building of 'Naulakha' was finished, but the following month she slipped back into her routine of small sums. In aggregate the amount paid to Beatty was considerable wealth in the values of those days, over four thousand dollars in three years, but when the works about the house and garden, the stable and drive, the well, the avenue and tennis-court were finished, the flow of dollars dried up.

Before the house was quite ready, Rudyard and Carrie had the supreme pleasure — as welcome to her as to him — of a visit from Lockwood Kipling who had at last retired, with a decoration, the C.I.E., as his reward for thirty years' service in India. Rudyard had used his influence with the new Viceroy, through their old friend Lord Dufferin, to get him a pension. Lockwood had before him twenty years of comfortable old age which he filled with literary, artistic, and archaeological activity, and with travel. Far more than his son, he was addicted to voyaging in remote countries. It was Lockwood rather than Rudyard who refreshed his tired soul from time to time with the 'bucking beam-sea roll of a black Bilbao tramp'. The Brattleboro people soon learned to recognize this very English figure tramping the roads with stick and pipe; and he soon fired Rudyard with the wanderlust. They went off together on a trip into Canada, just when the new house was ready. Carrie had to see to the removal from the 'Bliss Cottage', with the added trouble that both her maids gave notice on moving-day, the waitress merely because the cook was going, the cook because she disliked the caps that Carrie desired her to wear.

In August, when the two men came back, 'Naulakha' was ready for occupation. Lockwood approved of everything, especially of Rudyard's library with its spacious outlook for the day's work and its open fireplace for the evening's comfort. He inscribed a text on the massive chimney-piece: 'The Night cometh when No Man can Work', and so the title of Rudyard's next volume of stories was determined.

Lockwood, also, had been venturing into authorship. In 1891 he had published his *Beast and Man in India*. The book was dedicated to 'the other three' of the family square, and Rudyard loyally declared it to be superior to all his own works. It is a miscellany gathered from wide observation and wider reading, packed with legend, folk-lore, anecdotes from the Indian classics, descriptions of contrivances, utensils and costumes, and sketches by the author in pen-and-ink. The whimsical and the technical, the learned and the popular, the theoretical and the practical are heaped together on every page.

The book is a standing record of the mutual stimulus exerted between Lockwood and his son. The father quotes many of his son's verses, 'collected' and 'uncollected'. In countless instances the father's anecdotes and allusions reveal the son's debt to his father's omniscience. Here you may find Chil the kite and Tabaqui the jackal, the method of catching crows by a decoy, the nursery song about the wild plums in the jungle, the behaviour of snake and mongoose around the house, the habits of battery-mules, the legend of a place where the elephants dance, the story of Moti Gaj, mutineer, the story of Ganesa and the money-lender, the customs of the *bandar-log*. The range and scope and fullness of Lockwood's collections reveal a mellower, more tolerant, view of life than Rudyard's. The whole work is a comment on Indian ethics, which he regards with gentle scepticism and with no hint of western condescension. ' If we did not daily see by how slack a hold the faith of the West controls its life, we might marvel at the indifference of the East, to the suffering of animals whose bodies are believed to be tenanted by human souls.' Not cruelty but carelessness, indifference to suffering, apathy, are the tendencies he observes, predominantly, of Man towards Beast in India.

Lockwood's appearance in Vermont was fortunate for Rudyard who was again at work upon stories which called for his father's advice. ' The Bridge-Builders' [8] * was written that autumn, and Rudyard was also busy with an experiment in a new field; in November 1892 at the ' Bliss Cottage' he had written ' a wolf-story called "Mowgli's Brothers"'. We have his word for it, supported by Rider Haggard's, [9] that the impulse was derived from a scene in Haggard's Zulu romance, *Nada the Lily*, where, in a riot of supernatural fantasy, Umslopogaas is presented as running with a pack of wolves (though there are no true wolves in Zululand). This was but the beginning of a train of thought, and much more is necessary to account for the origins of the new, powerful, and lasting myth which Rudyard was to elaborate in the first and second *Jungle Books*, the best-sellers among his works. The fable of the man-child who became master of the jungle, but who could not resolve the dilemma of his ambivalent life, the apparatus of Indian animal lore, the strange ethical concept called the Law of the Jungle, are Rudyard's own and have no counterpart in Rider Haggard's work.

It would be a shallow criticism of the *Jungle Books* to call them animal stories for children, though that is the mode in which they first enthral readers. Like their great original, Aesop's Fables, or like the *Jataka* tales which the Kiplings knew so well, they impress themselves on the mind at more than one level. The fables illustrate truths which — for such is the nature of successful fable — are not made more explicit by being interpreted at second hand. Every reader may find out for himself who is Mowgli, that strong, beautiful youth belonging neither to the village nor to the jungle; what allegory is expressed by

---

* In India Rudyard had written accounts for the *C.M.G.* of new bridges over the Sutlej on the Lahore–Ferozepore line, and over the Jhelum at Chak Nizam, both in 1887. Sir A. Geddes in his *Founding of a Family* claims that his father was the original of Findlayson in ' The Bridge-Builders'.

his two kindly mentors, Bagheera the panther and Baloo the bear, by Shere Khan the bully whose great strength and ferocity fail him at every test, by the *bandarlog,* those gentry of the tree-tops whose only ambition is to be noticed, who suppose a thing has been done if it has been cleverly talked about, and what is the nature of 'the Law' which binds the Jungle world into an integrated whole while allowing and even enjoining ruthless individual action within admitted bounds — the Law which especially constitutes Mowgli's brothers as the 'Free People'.*

As the creeper that girdles the tree-trunk the Law runneth forward and back —
For the strength of the Pack is the Wolf, and the strength of the Wolf is the
    Pack.
The Jackal may follow the Tiger, but, Cub, when thy whiskers are grown,
Remember the Wolf is a hunter — go forth and get food of thine own.
Keep peace with the Lords of the Jungle — the Tiger, the Panther, the Bear;
And trouble not Hathi the Silent, and mock not the Boar in his lair.
Now these are the Laws of the Jungle, and many and mighty are they;
But the head and the hoof of the Law and the haunch and the hump is —
    Obey!

Soon after his father's return to England, there came an evening when Rudyard confided to his wife that he had received an access of power, the 'return of a feeling of great strength, such as he had when he first came to London and met the men he was pitted against'.[10] Then, in 1890, he had been inspired but unhappy, and the fruit of his labour had been the *Barrack-room Ballads, The Light that Failed,* and a set of powerful but gloomy stories. The new flow of genius produced the verses collected in *The Seven Seas,* the two *Jungle Books,* and the diverse set of stories in the volume called *The Day's Work.* At the time when he admitted Carrie to this secret, he was engaged upon 'M'Andrew's Hymn', the most elaborate and perhaps the most effective of his dramatic lyrics. It launched upon the world the new concept of the romance of machinery, a notion which he expressed succinctly, a few weeks later, in the lines:

* As for the topography, the local colour which has given two whole generations of men an understanding of the Indian Jungle, he got it mostly at second hand. The adult story, 'In the Rukh', published before 'Mowgli's Brothers' though written after it, is located in the forests of the Doon which Kipling knew pretty well. All the other Mowgli stories are precisely placed in a part of Central India which he never visited, the banks of the Waingunga river in the Seonee district. He knew this best through the description given by his friends the Hills who were there in 1888, and brought back photographs which may be seen in the Carpenter Collection at Washington. Jungle-lore and the ways of wild animals, if he did not learn of them from his father, he drew from a well-thumbed copy of Sterndale's *Mammalia of India,* which still exists. Stories of the nursing of abandoned infants by she-wolves Sterndale regards as ' not improbable '.

Confound Romance! . . . And all unseen
Romance brought up the nine-fifteen.

The stories which developed the same theme, a sort of pantheism
that felt the world-soul throbbing with life, even in railway engines
and steamships, were written a little later ('The Ship that Found
Herself' in 1895, '.007' in 1896).

The two volumes of jungle stories were polished off, pretty regularly,
the first in November 1892 and the last in March 1895, when 'The
Spring Running' brought the series to a conclusion, and the impulse
to write more was switched off as water is turned off at a tap.* The
poems mostly lay on his hands much longer. When a boy in India,
he had scribbled his light verse to pay his way while he gave sustained
attention to prose composition. Now he sold stories for a living and
so bought leisure for working at his poems.

Among the pieces published in *The Seven Seas* (October 1896),
'A Song of the English', a long sequence of lyrics in various moods
and styles was conceived at least as early as 1889. The greater part of
it, especially the 'Song of the Cities', reflected — not always discreetly
— his impressions of the seaports visited during his voyages in 1891
and 1892; the final draft was ready for the printers in March 1893.
Rather earlier were 'The Gypsy Trail', Rudyard's prothalamium, and
'The Last Chantey', a variant on a theme which always fascinated
him, the survival of simple earthly individuals in an ideal eternal
world. 'The Last Chantey' was written before Rudyard's return to
Vermont. His first winter in the 'Bliss Cottage' produced, as well as
the satire, 'In the Neolithic Age', a new group of Indian Army
ballads, 'Gentlemen-Rankers', 'Shillin'-a-day', 'The Lost Legion',
'The Widow's Party', 'Bobs', and 'Back to the Army again', all
slight and casual pieces, which neither got much notice nor brought
in much money. Rudyard was still sending occasional contributions
to the *National Observer* which kept its head just above water.
Henley, however, could not afford to pay more than fifteen guineas
for 'The Dove of Dacca', in April 1893. Not many months earlier
Rudyard had been glad to accept that sum for the 'Bolivar'; it now
seemed a poor return for an author who already commanded $100 per
thousand words for his prose and was likely to double that sum shortly.
Scribners gave him $500 for 'M'Andrew's Hymn', a record price for
a poem in America.

* 'That ends up Mowgli and there is not going to be any more of him. After that,
I expect to try my hand at a series of engineers' tales — about marine engines and
such like.' From a letter, dated 3rd November 1895, quoted in the *Kipling Journal,*
April 1946. It was written to an unknown admirer of his work.

Rudyard did what he could for Henley and corresponded with him gaily:

Rudyard Kipling to W. E. Henley (Autumn 1893?)

After many wanderings your book has come in and it is a Book. What impresses me most is naturally the *Voluntaries* which are high water mark. Over and above everything else I love the way in which the music gives back the dull boom, pause, mutter and boom again of the London Traffic as you hear it from the centre of the Parks.

My poem Song of the Sword, dedicated to Kipling please you will write it over again with rhymed endings. Swords sing, O Henley *sahib!* And yet the way in which your blade comes out of the scabbard inch by inch till it drives back again with a clang on the last line is Good Enough. . . .

My time is divided among many things — stables and sewers and furniture and the settling down of a house. Its great fun and it keeps the mind off dwelling too much on words and their texture and composition. . . .

I've brought back a deck-load of notions from beyond sea and I'm busy putting 'em in order against the time that I can write 'em out. Mostly it's a bloody flux of verse which I'm curious to see developed. The sun and the air and the light are good in this place and have made me healthy as I never was in my life. I wish you could see the place. It's three miles from anywhere and wondrous self-contained. No one can get at you and if you don't choose to call for your mail you don't get it. . . .[11]

The 'Anchor Song', finished in January 1893, was the first to take shape, of his more substantial notions in the new manner; it was followed, in March, by 'The Song of the Banjo', a more important piece than its title suggests, and in May by 'The Merchantmen'. Later in the year Rudyard was busy with the verses for the *Jungle Books,* and in December Carrie reported him as humming and strumming all over the house with rhythmical experiments. The hymn-tune, 'The Church's One Foundation', gave him a set of rhythms which he used, in part at least, for 'M'Andrew's Hymn'; he went on to 'The King' ('Farewell, Romance'). Then came the second set of *Barrack-Room Ballads* which range over a wider field of emotion than the first. No author in any literature has composed, in verse or prose, so full and varied and so relentlessly realistic a view of the soldier's life, with its alternations of boredom and terror, its deadening routine, its characteristic vices and corruptions, its rare glories and its irrational fascination, as Rudyard Kipling in the series of verses he produced in the next two years: 'The Sergeant's Wedding' and 'For to Admire' in February 1894, 'Follow me 'Ome' in April, 'Cholera Camp' in October, 'The 'Eathen' in February 1895, 'That Day', 'The Men that Fought at Minden' and the 'Birds of Prey March' before April 1895, 'Soldier and Sailor Too' in November, 'The Ladies' and 'The Shut-eye Sentry' early in 1896. If he had written nothing else, this group of ballads, from which many lines have become familiar quotations, would preserve his name as long as soldiering remains the unavoidable lot of half-willing young men.

Other compositions of this period are not less noteworthy. Early in 1894 he completed the strange ballad called 'The Last Rhyme of True Thomas', to which I shall refer again; and during his summer visit to England he concluded several half-finished pieces which had lain on his hands, among them 'The Miracles'. His amusing comment on the decline of the three-volume novel, 'The Three-decker', was written on that holiday, as was his harsher comment on the New World as revealed in the Chicago railway-strike, the Emersonian *pastiche* called 'An American'. After his return to Vermont, he wrote 'The "Mary Gloster"', a companion piece to 'M'Andrew's Hymn', the one, as Mr. Eliot has said, exposing the failure of success, while the other exalts the success of failure. These were his boldest experiments in the *genre* of Browning's *Men and Women*. Among his minor verses may be mentioned 'The Mother-Lodge', a flashlight on his attitude to racial problems, which he wrote in a single morning of November while Conan Doyle was in his house as a guest.

Then came a pause; he was silenced by bad news, the death in Samoa of Robert Louis Stevenson, whom he greatly admired but had never met though they corresponded as friends. Rudyard was so deeply moved that he wrote nothing for a month.

In the following year a new range of interests provoked a new series of prose stories while the flow of dramatic lyrics was resumed: 'The Explorer' begun in January, 'Pan in Vermont' in February,* 'The Native-Born' in September, 'The Bell Buoy' and 'The Flowers' begun in November.

Eighteen ninety-four had been a year of great content and prosperity for the Kiplings. They allowed themselves a long holiday, first an ocean cruise, and afterwards a visit to Rudyard's parents in England. On the voyage, to Bermuda, they struck up an acquaintance with a New York family, Mrs. Catlin and her two daughters, who became their lifelong friends. In Prospero's magic isle Rudyard found a key to Shakespeare's art which he often pondered over in later years. Seeing with his own eyes that the set of the beach was congruent with

---

*   It's forty in the shade to-day, the spouting eaves declare;
        The boulders nose above the drift, the southern slopes are bare;
        Hub-deep in slush Apollo's car swings north along the Zod-
        iac. Good lack, the Spring is back, and Pan is on the road!

the scenery of *The Tempest,* he conceived the notion of a shipwrecked sailor spinning a yarn from which Shakespeare visualized the island.

> For a bite and a sup, and a bed of clean straw
> We'll tell you such marvels as man never saw,
> On a Magical Island which no one did spy
> Save this Master, that Swabber, yon Bo'sun, and I.[11]

This was certainly the method by which Rudyard picked up his own notions.

At Bermuda, though he stayed in a hotel with Carrie and the Catlins, he was much invited out by the Governor, the Admiral, and the officers of the garrison. It was a pleasure to dine in the officers' mess of the Royal Berkshire Regiment and to smell again the smell of the barracks, but best of all was the friendship of a sergeant with whom he got into casual conversation. After a time they exchanged names. 'Mr. Kipling. What! the celebrated Rudyard!' and the sergeant carried him off in triumph to the sergeants' mess. He and Carrie took tea with the sergeant's wife in the married lines, and not long afterwards appeared a ballad called 'That Day', which has impressed one young soldier, at least, as the masterpiece among Rudyard's soldier-songs. It is the account of a disaster:

> It got beyond all orders an' it got beyond all 'ope;
> It got to shammin' wounded an' retirin' from the 'alt.
> 'Ole companies was lookin' for the nearest road to slope;
> It were just a bloomin' knock-out — an' our fault!

> *Now there ain't no chorus 'ere to give,*
> *Nor there ain't no band to play;*
> *An' I wish I was dead 'fore I done what I did,*
> *Or seen what I seed that day!*

Fourteen years had passed since the Royal Berkshire Regiment had made its heroic last stand at Maiwand in Afghanistan, where one wing of the regiment had fought and died beside the colonel and the regimental colour, while the other wing had made a fighting retreat to Kandahar in a broken, routed army. Whoever survived from this affair, and was still serving at Bermuda in 1894, had a sorry tale to tell, but such a tale as every soldier knows to be true to the realities of war.

After three weeks in Bermuda, the Kiplings went back to New York and Brattleboro. It was a little disconcerting to find that Beatty, who had been left in charge of the household at 'Naulakha' including Josephine and her nurse, had run into debt, so that accounts had to be settled before they could leave for the second part of their holiday. On

10th April they reached Southampton and went at once to Tisbury, a lonely village in the Wiltshire Downs, where Rudyard's parents had made their home after their return from India. His mother found another house which Rudyard and Carrie could rent for the summer, and all four lived for three months at Tisbury. Lockwood was busier than ever at drawing, carving, modelling, in a workshop behind their cottage. The most delicate passages in *The Jungle Book,* notably 'The Miracle of Purun Bhagat', were written at Tisbury under the fastidious eye of Lockwood Kipling, always his son's severest critic.

Not far away were three great country houses where old English hospitality was practised on the most lavish scale. The Arundells at Wardour Castle, the Wyndhams at 'Clouds', and the Morisons at 'Fonthill' had taken up Lockwood Kipling, as the Dufferins had taken him up at Simla, and the unchanging life of feudal Wiltshire in this social circle spurred Rudyard to write of the contrast between American and English country ways. The astonishing farce, 'My Sunday at Home ',* with its richly-tinted pictures of an English summer evening, was re-cast and completed at Tisbury; and the tartly unkind story of an anglicized American, which he called ' An Error in the Fourth Dimension', was also written that summer. So much were Rudyard and Carrie taken with the English countryside that they began to talk of employing his cousin, 'Ambo' Poynter, to build them an English holiday cottage, by the sea; but Carrie thought better of it. There were several family reasons, she thought, why they must live in America.

Rudyard often went up to London by train, sometimes taking Carrie with him, to Brown's Hotel. He saw something of Henley and Whibley, as in his bachelor days in London; and struck up an acquaintance with Aubrey Beardsley, the new boy-genius who had just burst upon the town. If Rudyard had not been a writer, he might have been a black-and-white artist. He had a singularly clean flowing line and, writing all his books — as he did — with a fine pen and the best Indian ink, he was inclined to decorate the margins of his manuscripts, while pausing for thought, with arabesques and grotesques in what is now called the Beardsley manner. It was not imitative, however, but due to sympathy of another sort, for the habit was most pronounced in his earlier days when Beardsley had not yet drawn a line.

In the London season of 1894, Rudyard allowed himself to be lionized. His portrait appeared as one of the weekly cartoons in *Vanity*

---

* R. K. to E. L. White, 17th August 1894. — ' Heaven was kind to me in England, where I was safely delivered of several poems, four new Jungle Stories and a piece of broad farce, viler than " Brugglesmith ", which made me laugh for three days. . . . I wonder if people get a tithe of the fun out of my tales that I get in doing 'em.'

Fair; he went about with 'Ambo' Poynter to social functions; he was present at the 'private view' and at the Royal Academy banquet. Nothing, perhaps, was more socially eminent than a dinner given by Lord George Hamilton for him and Lord Roberts who now appeared almost as equals.

A distinction which he valued more highly was a visit to his old school as the guest of honour on a solemn occasion. 'Uncle Crom' was retiring from the headmastership and was to be given a testimonial, to which Rudyard contributed twenty pounds. On 25th July 1894 Rudyard made one of his rare appearances on a public platform, at 'Uncle Crom's' farewell to the past and present pupils of the United Services' College. He even made a short speech on behalf of the 'Old Boys', congratulating Cormell Price on having created 'the best school in England'. It was Price's day of triumph, not Rudyard's, but Price made it clear that his pride as a teacher lay in having educated the literary man who had sprung up among his military pupils.

'You, my dear Kipling,' he said, in his reply, 'are the mouthpiece of a body dear to me beyond expression. You have rightly dwelt upon the spirit of comradeship that prevails among our Old Boys. . . . You are the arch-apostle of comradeship, and you practise what you preach, and you preach it as no other living man has done or can do.'[13]

Cormell Price lived for fifteen years in retirement, resuming his old association with the friends of his youth, the Burne-Joneses and the Lockwood Kiplings. When in England, Rudyard too was drawn into this circle with the consequence that he renewed an interest in his schooldays which had been overlaid by the experiences of his young manhood. His defiant assertion that 'Uncle Crom' was a great head-master, and the United Services College a great school, reflected his own sense of loyalty rather than a considered view of contemporary education, since the school was, in fact, declining. Deprived of Price's leadership it languished, and, after some misadventures, was removed from Westward Ho! to another part of England. 'Crom' Price, though he retained the respect and affection of all his friends, lingered pathetically on the scene as an old man who had not fulfilled the promise of his youth; and Rudyard, who now began to think of a book about his schooldays, was to write the epitaph of the school and its creator.

Rudyard Kipling to Robert Barr (Editor of The Idler)

ARUNDELL HOUSE, TISBURY. July 28, '94

A regular weather-breeder of a day today — real warmth at last, and it waked in me a lively desire to be back in Main Street, Brattleboro', Vt., U.S.A., and hear the sody-water fizzing in the drug-store and discuss the outlook for the episcopalian church with the clerk; and get a bottle of lager in the basement of the Brooks House, and hear the doctor tell fish-yarns, and have the iron-headed old farmers loaf up and jerk out: 'Bin in Yurope haint yer?' and then go home, an easy gait, through the deep white dust with the locust trees just stinking to heaven, and the fireflies playing up and down the Swamp Road, and the Katy-dids giving oratorios, free gratis and for nothing, to the whippoorwill, and everybody sitting out in the verandah after dinner, smoking Durham tobacco in a cob pipe, with our feet on the verandah railings, and the moon coming up behind Wantastiquet. There's one Britisher at least homesick for a section of your depraved old land, and he's going, Please Allah! the first week in August, by the *Kaiser Wilhelm,* and won't New York be hot — just! There's a smell of horse-piss, Italian fruit-vendor, nickel cigars, sour lager, and warm car-conductor drifting down Carmine Street at this minute from Sixth Avenue, which I can smell with the naked eye as I sit here. I shall go to Long Island, to a friend's, and eat new corn, and I wish you were coming, too.[14]

After the vacation in England, Rudyard and Carrie returned with renewed vigour to 'Naulakha' and to little Josephine. 'My daughter is growing into a beauty', he wrote to a friend, and he was right. She had the fair colouring of her Yorkshire forbears, with very beautiful, large, blue eyes. Even as a tiny child she had a remarkable and endearing personality, with a charm and quickness of mind far in advance of her years. Rudyard was entirely devoted to her and spent much time every day playing with her and telling her stories. When a friend wrote to ask Rudyard what was the proper tune for 'Danny Deever', he replied that he couldn't say. His small daughter divided his tunes into the 'howly-growly' ones and the 'tinkley-tinkey' ones. Which was it? Perhaps both![15] He used to regale her in the evenings with Hindu rhymes and folk-tales which she repeated word-perfect to her dolly the next morning. At two years old she was the equal of her cousin, Beatty's daughter Marjorie, who was twice her age; and Josephine was much better brought up, for down at 'Maplewood' the Balestiers lived a harum-scarum life, while at 'Naulakha' all the English proprieties were observed. There were two maids at 'Naulakha' as well as Miss Josephine's 'nanny', and after the return from England in 1894, an English coachman whose livery and style and indubitable cockney accent caused no little stir in Brattleboro.

The Kiplings had advertised in New York for a man and wife, without encumbrances, and had been pleased to engage the services of Matthew Howard, formerly coachman to an English peer. A little, smart man, he was just the same size as Rudyard — five feet six inches tall — but made his first mark by refusing to wear a suit of Rudyard's old clothes for rough work. He wore top-boots and cord breeches even when cleaning out the stable. Howard was a good horse-master and, before he had been many weeks at 'Naulakha', he endeared himself to the Kiplings by handling a carriage accident most skilfully. When he was driving Carrie behind their pair of horses, 'Rod' got his leg over the trace, 'Ric' bolted, the carriage overturned, 'Rod' was lamed, and Carrie was severely shaken. The general view was that Howard had been the hero of the day.

Not long afterwards, when Carrie wanted a housemaid, Howard offered to produce a likely girl, who was appointed, and then admitted that she was his daughter. Presently there was another vacancy, for which Howard promptly produced another daughter. He was now living in a comfortable cottage, halfway down the drive, and he smuggled into it child after half-grown child. Having got himself the post as a childless man, he revealed himself the father of six bonny children, all of whom settled in the neighbourhood. He was by then so useful to the Kiplings that his philo-progenitiveness was forgiven. The more he found to do, the less there was for Beatty to do about the place, and the smaller were Beatty's chances of earning the commission on which he lived. Everyone liked Howard, except Beatty, and Howard was the one person at 'Naulakha' who was never impressed by Beatty's blarney.[16]

'Rod' and 'Ric', the carriage-horses, continued to give trouble, and the climax of equestrian life at 'Naulakha' was Rudyard's gift of a new pair of thoroughbreds, 'Nip and Tuck', to Carrie after her illness in 1895. He had bought them for $650 from Beatty, a windfall which kept Beatty solvent a few months longer. This concern with horses found its way into Rudyard's work, in the allegory of American life, 'A Walking Delegate', his first task after the return from England in 1894. Though told as a horse-story, it is more remarkable for the skilful use and contrasting of several American dialects, than for horse-lore. It led to another experiment in that vein, a few months later, a story far more deeply felt and wrought out from the heart, 'The Maltese Cat', a throwback to his own attempts at polo-playing, in India ten years earlier, and to the recollection of his own grey pony 'Dolly Bobs'.

Two years had passed since Carrie Balestier had first brought her penniless English husband to Brattleboro. A quiet, unassuming young man dressed in old country clothes, he had then seemed no great addition to the town's society. 'The Kiplings were nice people to work for', said a carpenter whom they employed, 'but you could never get real close to them, not like you and I chatting together now.' They did not mix much in the social life of the place which centred on the church meetings. They rarely attended the Episcopalian church and, though Rudyard was on friendly terms with the Rev. C. O. Day, the Congregational preacher, he did not attend his Sunday services, but met him so that they could practise golf-strokes together in the horse-pasture. A strange rumour that Rudyard spent his Sunday mornings at home 'writing hymns' made his ethical status not much clearer. The one place in Brattleboro where he was a willing visitor was the village school, and the one party the Kiplings always gave was their Christmas party to the school children, with a tree and carol-singing by the choirboys from the Episcopalian church. If he had been a good guy like Beatty, whom everyone knew and made allowances for, the town would have taken his measure, but he was incalculable by Brattleboro standards, and more so when he began to make big money.

In his letters to his English friends, Rudyard harped upon the solitude of his life as its chief merit. ' It's three miles from anywhere ', he wrote to Henley; ' I have time, light and quiet, three things hard to come by in London ', he wrote to William Heinemann.

There were, however, a few families to whom the Kiplings gave their friendship, notably some farming families back in the hills. There were also Doctor Conland their physician, old ' Governor ' Holbrook who had been State Governor of Vermont through the Civil War, there were Will and Mary Cabot who had been friends of Wolcott Balestier. Mary Cabot was one of the few women with whom Rudyard made a close friendship after his marriage. She was admitted to confidences about his work, and she used to say she once heard him improvise seventy lines of rhymed verse without a pause. Several young men in Brattleboro long remembered his conversation and his encouragement. John Bliss, with whom he walked or drove about the countryside, and Merton Robbins, whom he advised on starting a career in publishing, spoke of him with affection, and a tribute of another kind came from Dave Carey, the baggage-master at the railway station. ' Kipling had the darndest mind ', he used to say. ' He wanted to know everything about everything, and he never forgot what you told him. He would sit and listen and never stir.'

The Brattleboro gossips would have been more than human if they had not shown some signs of petty jealousy when Carrie Balestier's husband, after beginning his married life in so small a way, became in eighteen months one of the richest men in town. It was his custom at the end of the year to write a note of thanks in Carrie's personal diary, and when, in December 1894, he recorded for the third time his gratitude for a fortunate year, he noted that he had earned $25,000 (£5000), a great sum in the values of those days.

As his fame grew, the pressure of sightseers hoping for a glimpse of the new celebrity, and of newspapermen in search of gossip, grew more intense, with the consequence that the Kiplings withdrew into a stricter privacy. It was the ill-mannered summer-boarders, not the self-respecting townsfolk, who annoyed him, and especially, he was so plagued by autograph-hunters that Carrie organized a scheme for selling his autographs at $2.50 each for the Fresh Air Fund, sponsored by the *New York Herald*. To her chagrin this was regarded as a publicity device and brought in several abusive letters.

Among their friends in New England, none were dearer to them than Charles Eliot Norton of Harvard, and his daughters. Many years before he became a Harvard professor, Norton had made a business trip to India, which placed him in sympathy with the Kiplings. In middle life he had been one of the Pre-Raphaelite circle in London, and Rudyard had played with Sallie Norton in childhood at North End Road. When Lockwood renewed the connexion, in New England, an instant bond was formed between the Kiplings and the Nortons. Visits were exchanged between 'Naulakha' and the Nortons' home at Ashfield in Massachusetts, where Rudyard found himself free of Boston society, and of the most austere circle of the transcendentalists. Since Henry James was a family friend of the Balestiers, his brother William, the pragmatist philosopher, received them into the intellectual society of Harvard.

They were Brahmins of Brahmins, living delightfully, but Norton himself, full of forebodings as to the future of his land's soul, felt the established earth sliding under him, as horses feel coming earth-tremors.[17]

So Kipling interpreted the decline of New England transcendentalism at the zenith of the 'Gilded Age'. His own comment on the American tendency was to deplore the 'apparent waste and ineffectiveness, in the face of the foreign inrush, of all the indigenous effort of the past generation'. Too many real Americans had been killed off in the Civil War and too many unassimilable foreigners were drifting in.

> His easy unswept hearth he lends
>   From Labrador to Guadeloupe;
> Till, elbowed out by sloven friends,
>   He camps, at sufferance, on the stoop.[18]

Meanwhile the tension of a nation expanding too fast, growing rich too easily, losing its traditions, and feeling no need of self-restraint, expressed itself in jangling nerves. The New England tradition, as he found it in the company of the Nortons, was the foundation on which he had planned his household in Vermont, and it was vanishing before his eyes, as America, under President Cleveland, moved into another phase and mood.

Rudyard Kipling to C. E. Norton

Feb. 1895

There were two days of knife-edged cold, and a cloudless sky, a sun grinning like a skull, and a wind that ripped the bones off you. Today is only blizzard and tho' I do not see when we shall be able to use the roads we are warm and of good heart. But our house has been singing like a ship brought up in the wind's eye and the old maple has been creaking and there are five or six feet of snow generally about the place and at least ten in the air.

Beatty has achieved a magnificent cold which after skirmishing all over his body has blossomed into a sharp touch of rheumatism, and he now lies in his bed too stiff and sore to do justice to the situation. . . . Did you know that Carrie burned her face opening the furnace door, about three weeks ago. It was more in the nature of a scorch than a burn but it naturally upset her very much and since then we have been living small and going softly together seeing no company. . . . We talk of going to Washington to play for a month.

The baby (glory be) keeps her rude health and becomes to us daily more charming. We are sending the Pater (he is getting fat in Florence and sends me the most contemptible stories of contessas and contadinas and all the draggly out-at-elbows messy polyglot society that camps on the continent) a small pastel study of Josephine, her head, reading a book. But what can we do with a small impudence who stops the coachman and enquires magisterially after the health of each horse by name. . . . We love her apropos.

Work has been going easily. I have a yearning upon me to tell tales of extended impropriety — not sexual or within hailing distance of it — but hard-bottomed unseemly yarns. One can't be serious always.[19]

The year 1895 began with Carrie's impetuous mishap in throwing open the furnace door. For a fortnight she lay ill and then, when recovery seemed near, a painful inflammation of the eyelids appeared, to the alarm of Dr. Conland, who ordered her away for a long rest in a milder climate. Rud and Carrie went to Washington for six weeks and lived in rooms, which they found very expensive and not very comfortable. She complained at paying no less than fifteen dollars a day for their board, and it was long before she felt well enough to enjoy her holiday. As she slowly recovered, her soft brown hair turned grey and in a few years was white.

They saw much society in the capital that season. John Hay from the State Department, Lady Paunceforte, and Mr. Spring Rice from the British Legation, Professor Langley from the Smithsonian, Mr. Bliss Carman 'a so-called poet', Mr. Theo. Roosevelt, Lady Aberdeen, and Miss Leiter the heiress who was engaged to the Hon. G. Curzon, are noted among their callers in Carrie's diary. After the Smithsonian, the Zoo was Rudyard's favourite resort; he frequented the beaver enclosure and gave serious thought to re-establishing a colony of beavers in the Connecticut River, where they were long extinct. A friend made at this time, who told him much of American wild life, of Indians and Eskimos, was W. Hallett Phillips, a Washington lawyer.

Rudyard made some progress with his work in Washington. The last of his Mowgli stories, 'The Spring Running', was no sooner finished, in March 1895, than his mind turned to a new task that again marked an extended range of observation. It was a story about 'a new sort of woman', wrote Carrie, and 'she turned out stunningly'. The subject of this story, to which he gave the rather inappropriate title of 'William the Conqueror', is the effort made by a group of administrators from the Punjab, when drafted south to deal with a famine. According to his custom, he painted in the backcloth with a Pre-Raphaelite brilliance of colour and accuracy of detail. The scene was southern India, as he had observed it on his last visit in December 1891, and the climax of the story — as of that Indian visit — was a Christmas party at Lahore. But the feature which has made some readers select this story as a masterpiece is the character of the heroine, a 'new sort of woman', a practical, lively, boyish woman with a man's nickname, a woman with a crop of dark curls growing low on her forehead in a widow's peak. In several of these respects she seems to be based upon the figure of Mrs. 'Ted' Hill, whom Carrie Kipling never met. She is presented in the round, as no earlier of Kipling's heroines had been, and the story, in some phases, is told from her point of view. The episode that no one forgets is her gleam of vision, when she sees her lover not as a commonplace civil servant organizing the distribution of goats' milk to starving children, but as a demi-god:

an accident of the sunset ordered it that, when he had taken off his helmet to get the evening breeze, the low light should fall across his forehead, and he could not see what was before him; while one waiting at the tent door beheld, with new eyes, a young man, beautiful as Paris, a god in a halo of golden dust, walking slowly at the head of his flocks, while at his knee ran small naked Cupids.

In April, just before the end of the holiday in Washington, Kipling was taken by Secretary Lamont to call on the President at the White House, and came home disgusted with the company he met there. To Carrie he confided that it was 'awful; inexpressible; incredible; a colossal agglomeration of reeking bounders; it made him very sorrowful'. No one is likely to assert that President Cleveland's circle of associates represented American public life at its highest, and the impact of this group upon a man with a lifelong distrust for politicians of any kind was shattering. He found in the White House all that he most disliked, a readiness to compromise with violence and dishonesty, a habit of talking loudly and acting meanly. These men might remind him of the *bandar-log* who 'sit in circles on the hall of the King's council chamber, and scratch for fleas and pretend to be men'.

The same day, the corrective was applied. He dined that evening at a man's party with Theodore Roosevelt who, as head of the Civil Service Commission, was engaged in introducing sounder standards into the public service. Roosevelt was not much older than his guest and, like him, had made a name before his thirtieth birthday as an uncompromising champion of manliness and efficiency, as an enemy of all pretentious shams.

I liked him from the first [said Rudyard] and largely believed in him. He would come to our hotel, and thank God in a loud voice that he had not one drop of British blood ['English' he should have said] in him; his ancestry being Dutch, and his creed conforming-Dopper, I think it is called. Naturally I told him nice tales about his Uncles and Aunts in South Africa who esteemed themselves the sole lawful Dutch under the canopy and dismissed Roosevelt's stock for 'Verdomder Hollanders'. Then he became really eloquent, and we would go off to the Zoo together, where he talked about grizzlies that he had met. It was laid on him at that time, to furnish his land with on adequate Navy; the existing collection of unrelated types and casual purchases being worn out. I asked him how he proposed to get it, for the American people did not love taxation. 'Out of *you*,' was the disarming reply. And so — to some extent — it was. The obedient and instructed Press explained how England — treacherous and jealous as ever — only waited round the corner to descend on the unprotected coasts of liberty, etc., etc. . . . The trick worked.

But those were great and spacious and friendly days in Washington which — politics apart — Allah had not altogether deprived of a sense of humour; and the food was a thing to dream of.[20]

There was a natural sympathy between Rudyard Kipling the Englishman and Theodore Roosevelt, the American of the old stock. His doctrine of the Strenuous Life was directly drawn from Emerson's essay on Self-reliance, and, consciously or unconsciously, the two young men followed the same master. During Rudyard's last few days at Washington they saw much of one another and, though they rarely met again, they corresponded intermittently, as friends, a cross-fertilization that was to have a notable effect both upon Kipling's philosophy and upon Roosevelt's political career.

The spring was well forward in Vermont when Rudyard and Carrie returned to 'Naulakha'. Each year they watched for the blood-root beside the stone wall at the foot of the home pasture. Rudyard used to say, whimsically, that he could not bear to see it picked, as he expected the frail plant to cry out like a mandrake when its fibres were torn.

When Mr. and Mrs. William James from Harvard came to stay at 'Naulakha' in June, Beatty's tennis-court was finished to admiration, but the contract displeased Carrie. She paid Beatty seventy dollars, then disagreed with him about the hay-crop, and about his further contract for draining the pasture. He had overdrawn the account for his own use, and before the end of the month all the neighbours knew that brother and sister had quarrelled. What was distress and annoyance for her was ruin for Beatty, who was deep in debt, and without resources, since he had even exhausted the patience of his stern old grandmother down at 'Beechwood'. The worse his position the more he drank, and the Kiplings, who hated drunkenness, began to regret that under his agreement he had the run of the estate. 'Naulakha' was no longer a happy place when the Balestiers were at loggerheads with one another. After an unsatisfactory settlement with Beatty, on 1st July 1895, the Kiplings set off for their usual summer tour. Luckily it was no longer necessary to leave him in charge, since there was Matthew Howard, entirely trustworthy, and much more careful with the horses. They crossed the Atlantic in a German ship, which gave Rudyard a notion for a story, 'Bread upon the Waters', and spent a month in England between Tisbury and Brown's Hotel.

It was good to be home again at 'Naulakha' at the end of August, and to find that Howard had everything in perfect order. Rudyard had come back from England with a notion about a boy who lived a dream-life. Absorbing himself in it, he completed it in a fortnight, and sold it to the *Century Magazine* for $170 per thousand words. All through September and October he was busy 'singing at his Brushwood Boy poem' and polishing off the new set of Barrack-Room Ballads, while Carrie was week by week more deeply embroiled in the unfortunate affair with Beatty, lending him money now and backing his bills.

It was peculiarly annoying that the pump was out of order again, the one domestic convenience at 'Naulakaha' that never worked right. Just at the hottest season of the year, the water-supply ran out so that they were dependent on water from 'Maplewood', at a time when the two families were no longer on speaking terms, and conducted their affairs by exchange of notes. In such times the Kiplings could no longer expect Beatty, who drove into town every day, to collect their mail, and it was no pleasure to them to go where they would be stared at by sightseers and gossips. It was a comfort when, by the influence of Hallett Phillips with the President, a new branch Post Office for their own use was opened at Waite's Corner.

November brought some unexpected consolations. Kay Robinson wrote from the Middle West to say he was visiting America with his brother. They came to stay, to Rudyard's great delight — he was busy that week with 'The Flowers'; and Kay commemorated his visit by writing a long account of Kipling for *McClure's Magazine,* on the whole, the best account of Kipling's life at Lahore. A few days after Kay's visit there arrived unexpectedly from New York a huge, cheerful, fair-haired young man named Frank N. Doubleday, whom they received coldly at first since he came on business from a publisher, but who soon broke down Carrie's defences. His business was to open negotiations for a complete edition of Rudyard's works to be published by his firm, Scribners. 'Frank', F. N. D.', 'Beloved Effendi' as he soon became, achieved what no other publisher in England or America could achieve, by putting his business on a personal footing, and so became the lifelong intimate friend of Rudyard and Carrie.

Rudyard's dislike of President Cleveland's administration was fanned into a flame in July 1895, when a long-standing dispute flared up between England and America, about the frontier between Venezuela and British Guiana. For some reason or other, President Cleveland thought the time ripe to twist the lion's tail and, on 20th July, his Secretary of State made a highly offensive reply to the British offer, roundly accusing the British of violating the Monroe Doctrine. Just then there was a change of Government in England with the consequence that the British attitude stiffened.

President Cleveland succumbed to the temptation of rallying the American people by a jingo outburst. In his message to Congress, 17th December, the last before the presidential election year, he denounced the British as aggressors against Venezuela, and asserted the right of the United States to restrain them. During the next six months, while the party organizations were preparing their election campaign, the crisis between England and America was still acute. War, on this unworthy pretext, seemed threatening, and Rudyard Kipling was not alone in thinking it inevitable. In May and June 1896, just when the party conventions were meeting in America, the Secretary of State again endeavoured to whip up the anti-British fury, while Lord Salisbury, the new Prime Minister, kept his temper. The arbitrators decided, most positively, that the British were in the right, and President Cleveland who had nothing more to gain by violence, withdrew, in his last message to Congress, from the position he had taken up a year earlier. The Venezuela incident was closed, and Cleveland's device for winning the election was unsuccessful.

This was the series of events which Rudyard Kipling found so distressing that he decided to leave America. He was convinced that there would be a purposeless and disastrous war, and the Nortons at Harvard were disposed to agree with him.[21]

At the height of the Venezuela crisis, in January 1896, another threat of war appeared in another quarter of the globe. Dr. Jameson's attempt to filibuster the Transvaal Republic into the British Empire was defeated by the Boers, and this setback to the imperialists was exploited by the German Kaiser, who sent a telegram of congratulation to the Transvaal Government, in terms as provocative to Britain as had been President Cleveland's message to Congress. It inspired Rudyard to send a solemn poem to *The Times* with the title, ' Hymn before Action '. Though not a favourite with Kipling's readers it was at least more dignified than the absurd verses in praise of Dr. Jameson, put out by Alfred Austen the new poet laureate.

Rudyard Kipling to C. E. Norton

8th, Jan. 1896

I seem to be between two barrels like a pheasant. If the American mine is sprung it means dirt and slush and ultimately death either across the Canada border or in some disembowelled gunboat off Cape Hatteras. If the German dynamite is exploded, equally it means slaughter and most probably on the high seas. In both cases I am armed with nothing more efficient than a note-book a stylographic pen, and a pair of opera-glasses. Whether or no, anyway and inevitably, C. will be confined within the next three or five weeks and till that time I am tied here by the leg.

I have arranged things so that C. ought not to starve; and she has the house and all my copyrights to boot. You see it is obviously absurd for me to sit still and go on singing from a safe place while the men I know are on the crown of it; and it may be that when I am closer to the scene of action I may be able to help with a little song or two in the intervals of special correspondence. But it is borne in upon me by the inner eye that if trouble comes I shan't live to see it out: unless I bolt and hide myself in the wilds of Patagonia or the Pole. Even in that resort I should be dead or worse than dead.

All these things fill me with a deep love for Mr. Cleveland who is responsible for the letting in of the waters. I permit myself however to cherish a hope that the row or rows may be delayed till May when I can hope to pick up C. and the children (D.V.) and take 'em to England. I shan't mind so much then; but whether it be peace or war this folly puts an end to my good wholesome life here; and to me that is the saddest part of it. We must begin again from the beginning and pretend that we are only anxious to let the house for a year or two. It's hard enough, God knows, but I should be a fool if, after full warning, I risked my own people's happiness and comfort in a hostile country.

As to the German situation I don't care a continental. It will wake up the colonies, I believe, and teach us to keep our powder dry. But the American thing makes me sick and sore and sorry to my heart's core. People can say what they please. There was a much more genuine absence of hostility on the English side than there was on the American. And I do sincerely believe that the American interior press is responsible for the cherishing of that hostile feeling.

Looking at it in other lights it seems to me that it will help the Empire enormously, will definitely shut out all notion of Canada's absorption into the States, except by force, and will teach us the beauties of an inter-colonial tariff — may even send us to ally with France and Russia to re-arrange the rest of the world, but these are long long looks ahead, and I can only say that whatever comes I and mine are always affectionately yours.

P.S. But why Alfred Austin? * Pater told me he was living in Salis-bury's pocket ever since Tennyson died; but I never expected he'd get it.[22]

Carrie's mother stayed with the Kiplings for Christmas 1895, with-out effecting a reconciliation between her son and daughter. Yet, with a certain bravado, Rudyard wrote in Carrie's diary on New Year's eve, 'So ends our fourth and best year'. When the snow came, Rudyard experimented with the Norwegian skis that Conan Doyle had sent him, probably the first pair of skis in Vermont. Another new sport was golf on the frozen snow, with golf-balls painted scarlet, not altogether a success because there were no limits to a drive; the ball might skid two miles down the long slope to the Connecticut River. Indoors he worked at 'The Tomb of his Ancestors',† the last of the great series of longer Anglo-Indian stories which he had begun, seven years back, with 'A Wayside Comedy'. Then he turned to his oft-considered plan for a picaresque novel of the Indian underworld. The manuscript of *Mother Maturin* was still among his papers, and not altogether abandoned. Three times at 'Naulakha' he put his hand to the old notes which he now thought of using as the raw material of a quite new book. The notion of *Kim* was stirring in his mind, but would not take shape; 'it must be revised by the pater', he said.

Carrie, who had spent a wretched autumn over Beatty's affairs, was

---

* On 1st January 1896 Alfred Austin, a conservative journalist, was appointed to the office of Poet Laureate which had been vacant since the death of Tennyson in October 1892.

† 'John Chinn' the elder, in this story, is based upon James Outram, 'the Bayard of India'. Philip Woodruff (*The Guardians*) has more to say on its origin.

now expecting her second child. Another daughter, Elsie, was born on the morning of 2nd February 1896. When Dr. Conland paid his regular visits to Carrie, he found time for conversation with Rudyard. Conland had been to sea as a young man, and had many yarns to spin of the fishermen on the Grand Banks. On 9th February, when all was pronounced well with mother and child, and Josephine was introduced to her new little sister, a spark was struck between Rudyard and the doctor. Rudyard would lay aside *Kim* to write a tale of the Grand Banks; for which he found the title, *Captains Courageous*, in one of his favourite old ballads, 'Mary Ambree'. 'It grows under my hand', he said a few days later.

No other of Rudyard's romances absorbed his energies so completely as *Captains Courageous*, which took his mind off threatening politics and family quarrels. It is the only one of his stories in which all the characters are typical Americans in an American setting, and its merits are due largely to the easy comradeship with Conland which he found so stimulating and satisfying.

My part was the writing; his the details. This book took us (he rejoicing to escape from the dread respectability of our little town) to the shore-front, and the old T-wharf of Boston Harbour, and to queer meals in sailors' eating-houses, where he renewed his youth among ex-shipmates or their kin. We assisted hospitable tug-masters to help haul three- and four-stick schooners all round the harbour; we boarded every craft that looked as if she might be useful, and we delighted ourselves to the limit of delight. Charts we got — old and new — and the crude implements of navigation such as they used off the Banks, and a battered boat-compass, still a treasure with me. (Also, by pure luck, I had sight of the first sickening uprush and vomit of iridescent coal-dusted water into the hold of a ship, a crippled iron hulk, sinking at her moorings). And Conland took large cod and the appropriate knives with which they are prepared for the hold, and demonstrated anatomically and surgically so that I could make no mistake about treating them in print. Old tales, too, he dug up, and the lists of dead and gone schooners whom he had loved, and I revelled in profligate abundance of detail — not necessarily for publication but for the joy of it. And he sent me — may he be forgiven! — out on a pollock-fisher, which is ten times fouler than any cod-schooner, and I was immortally sick, even though they tried to revive me with a fragment of unfresh pollock.[23]

The book is rich in technicalities, which are the more remarkable because Kipling's chances of studying deep-sea fishermen had been so scanty. He paid three visits to Gloucester, Mass., and one to Boston Harbour, the period of all four together being no more than fourteen days; and all that critics have been able to urge against his local colour is that it represents rather the fishing-fleet as it had been thirty years earlier when Conland was young, than the fleet as it was in 1896. A favourite with its author, *Captains Courageous* has been more admired by American than by English readers. It is an enlarged short story, not a novel, exploring a situation rather than tracing the development of character. The conversion of Harvey Cheyne from a spoilt boy into a serviceable young man is achieved too suddenly to be convincing, and too early in the book to provide a lasting theme. The reader is left with seascapes, at which Kipling excelled, and at studies of American types, caught and reproduced with photographic accuracy. As types, the fishing-skipper, the mate, the ship's boy, the Nova Scotia negro, the railway magnate,* and the rest, tell us what sort of men Kipling admired, while Harvey's mother, and her part in the story, provide a comment on the corrupt Americanism of the 'Gilded Age' that was driving him away. *Captains Courageous* began to appear serially, in *McClure's Magazine,* soon after the number which contained Kay Robinson's account of Kipling in India. Sam McClure was an American business man who won Kipling's heart. 'He had been everything from a pedlar to a tintype photographer along the highways, and had held intact his genius and simplicity. 'I liked and admired him', wrote Kipling, 'more than a little, for he was one of the few with whom three and a half words serve for a sentence, and as clear and straight as spring water.' The best of Kipling's earlier work in America had been sold to Richard Gilder for the *Century Magazine,* and Gilder offered $10,000 for the serial rights of *Captains Courageous.* Kipling preferred to let it go to Sam McClure for the same price.[21]

The quarrel with the Beatty Balestiers took a worse turn in 1896.

It is all most dolefully true [wrote Rudyard to Sallie Norton in January] and, having said that one feels as if there ought to be some way out of it — the consequences, I mean. I'm going to hope for the best very hard. C. is wonderfully well, considering all things, and I'm proud of her.

She had hardly recovered from the birth of Elsie when a new crisis brought the publicity they so much dreaded. On 6th March, Beatty filed a petition in bankruptcy. Opinion in Brattleboro, where everyone was now aware of the Balestier feud, was critical of both parties. Those who knew them best blamed Carrie for her tactless hectoring of her brother; it was easy to make allowances for a generous good fellow like Beatty, even if his generosity was at his sister's expense; easy to abuse Carrie who was rich and economical and anglicized.

* F. N. Finney, a real railway magnate, supplied the railway technicalities. He then beat the record claimed in the book for a trans-continental journey by running a train over the route.

With her strong sense of family responsibility, but with singular lack of tact, Carrie made some sort of proposal to the Balestiers that if Beatty would leave 'Maplewood' and take regular work, she would finance him and bring up his daughter, Marjorie.

The prying eyes of Brattleboro were, perhaps, the greatest annoyance of the whole affair, to Rudyard. It was noticed that Carrie consulted none of her Balestier relatives, that Rudyard no longer went down the road to 'Beechwood' to read his verses to her old grandmother. Though 'Madam' Balestier was growing very old and crotchety, and was unable or unwilling to arbitrate between Beatty and Carrie, it was yet thought strange that Carrie, who drove past 'Beechwood' whenever she went to town, was never seen to bring her new baby on a visit to the old lady. Newspaper reporters scented 'copy', and were repulsed from 'Naulakha' more brusquely than ever.

'I decline to be interviewed,' Rudyard is reported as saying to one of them. 'American reviewing is brutal and immoral. It is an outrage to be insulted on the public highways and asked to give the details of one's private life. . . . Your copyright laws have swindled me out of considerable money. Is it not enough to steal my books without intruding on my private life? When I have anything to say, I write it down and sell it. My brains are my own.'

Whatever the annoyance, Rudyard and Carrie were determined to live their own lives and maintain the routine unchanged at 'Naulakha', until they could conveniently return to England. Visitors came and went, among them Owen Wister, Sam McClure, Mrs. Pen Browning, the Catlin girls from New York, and Sallie Norton. New works were planned to improve the property and there was one summer day when Rudyard was so deeply interested in the erection of a pair of ornamental gate-posts that he abandoned a day's writing to watch it. In April he and Carrie, both of them rather low in health and spirits, took a few days' holiday at New York, where he met Stephen Crane and other friends. Rudyard took lessons in a New York school at the fashionable sport of bicycling, and was pretty competent when they returned to 'Naulakha'.

The spring had come and Rudyard was content to sit in the sunshine through the first days of May, amusing himself with a set of verses for a society of college boys at Yale. He had nothing much else on hand, except a scheme, never carried out, for a children's 'fairy book' about the natural history of New England.

On the afternoon of 6th May Rudyard set off alone for a spin on his wheel, along the winding, steep, and rough road that led down from

'Beechwood' to Waite's Corner. At the foot of the slope he had a spill and was ruefully picking himself up when Beatty, in a furious temper, came driving down at his usual galloping pace. 'See here! I want to talk with you!' he shouted, brandishing his whip. 'If you have anything to say, you can say it to my lawyer,' said Rudyard. Beatty broke into a torrent of oaths and accusations: Rudyard had been talking about him behind his back, had been abusing him in Brattleboro. Would he retract? Would he apologize? There was no answer. 'If you won't retract the lies you have been telling about me within a week, I'll blow out your god-damn brains!' shouted Beatty, to which Rudyard quietly replied: 'If I don't do certain things, you'll kill me?' 'By Jesus, I will,' said Beatty. 'Then,' said Rudyard, 'remember you will only have yourself to blame for the consequences!' 'Do you dare to threaten me, you little bastard?' shouted Beatty, and drove off.

These were the first words exchanged between the two brothers-in-law in six months or more, and why Beatty burst out in this way and at this time is not evident. A friend of both families has recorded that, immediately after this ludicrous scene, Beatty drove to her house in great concern, sorry that he had made an exhibition of himself. Those who knew the two men best supposed that they would have laughed off the quarrel if their wives had allowed them.

On the same authority it is said that Mai Balestier was the most vindictive of the four. It was she who resented Carrie's patronage and was deeply hurt by Carrie's proposal to bring up her child. Rudyard's action, whatever else, was remarkably imprudent; he went down to Brattleboro next morning and laid an information against his brother-in-law for threatening to murder him, and from the moment that the officers of the law took hold, his cause was lost. Publicity was what Rudyard most dreaded and, by appearing in court, he exposed himself to the full glare of the yellow press; while Beatty's point of view was just the opposite, since publicity was meat and drink to him, and might even help him to pay his debts.

On Saturday, 9th May, Beatty was arrested, and Carrie recorded in her diary that it was the most wretched and unhappy day in her life. He was arraigned before William S. Newton, Justice of the Peace, in Brattleboro for 'assault with force and arms, for using opprobrious and indecent names, and for threatening to kill' his brother-in-law. After a formal statement the proceedings were adjourned until the twelfth, that is over the week-end, and the prisoner was released on bail. As if he had not made blunders enough, Rudyard, the plaintiff, now appeared and quixotically offered to go bail for Beatty the defendant. A man as quick-witted as Beatty did not fail to see that

the game was going his way. Indignantly repudiating Rudyard's offer,
he found bail elsewhere and rushed to the telegraph office — this was
before the day of long-distance telephones — to sell his story to the
press. During the week-end, more than forty reporters from metro-
politan newspapers assembled in Brattleboro where such publicity was
never known before or since. Beatty met them at the railway station
and Rudyard had the mortification of seeing him whirl carriage-load
after carriage-load of the hated tribe, in sight of his windows, to
'Maplewood', where they were entertained with Beatty's whisky and
the company of his pretty wife.

The hearing was resumed on Tuesday, 12th May, in the Town Hall
of Brattleboro. The number of spectators who crowded into Justice
Newton's office made it necessary to transfer the proceedings to the
larger assembly hall where town meetings customarily took place. It
was a field-day for the lawyers, who played up to the press by forcing
Kipling to answer the questions he had often refused to answer, thus
making an end of his boasted privacy. The proceedings began with
the cross-examination of Kipling, the one witness, who was kept on
the stand all day. The quarrel with Beatty in the lane was told in
Kipling's words and displayed in its most ludicrous aspect. Was
Kipling afraid? Had he run away? Had he any reason to suppose
that Beatty was armed? 'He was crazy,' said Kipling, 'not in his
right senses.' Would Rudyard retract his words? 'I would not retract
a word under threat of death from any living man.'

Then the dealings of the brothers-in-law over the last four years
were relentlessly dragged into the light. Was it not true that Kipling
had made large sums of money in America? Was it not true that he
had spoken certain words to Colonel Goodhue in the Brooks' House
at Brattleboro? Had he said something about 'holding Beatty up by
the slack of his pants'? It was true, said Rudyard, that he had said
it, and that he had done it since Beatty's dead brother, Wolcott, had
asked him to look after Beatty. Rudyard had settled in America, he
said, largely so that he could help him, whereupon Beatty laughed
out loud in court.

Why had they quarrelled? It was Beatty who had dropped him,
a year ago, said Rudyard, and since then there had been nothing to
discuss between them. Rudyard had employed Beatty in the past but
found him unreliable; he began his undertakings well and then tailed
off. But did he actually owe the Kiplings money? No! Rudyard
was forced to admit that Beatty had paid back the cash that he had
borrowed. 'You had him arrested without making any effort to
correct the false impression you had given of his dependence on you?'
That was a shrewd blow. Rudyard made it clear that he had done

his best for Beatty to the end. He had made an offer — which was rejected — to take charge of Beatty's family, if Beatty would stop drinking, but nothing had come of his offer.

Nothing but publicity came of the proceedings. Upon motion of the States Attorney, Beatty was bound over for trial ' under the familiar statute of disturbing the peace '. Justice Newton placed him under bond of $400 to keep the peace and an additional bond of $400 for appearance at the next appointed session of the County Court. * Beatty left the hearing in triumph to sell his story. Rudyard, too, had something to say; with unusual frankness, he admitted to a reporter — or so the reporter said — 'that he intended to leave that part of the country as soon as possible '.

Opinion in Brattleboro was sharply divided: there was some animosity against Rudyard in the town, and the vulgar press crowed over him in triumph. At the following week-end, the Sunday papers splashed the story, the most offensive among them being a Boston journal which printed a not very clever parody of ' Danny Deever ':

> ' Who's that a-loping down the lane? ' said the copper-ready-made.
> ' It's Rudyard running for his life,' the First Select-man said.
> ' Who's pawing up the dust behind? ' said the copper-ready-made.
> ' It's Beatty seeking brother-in-law,' the First Select-man said.

The serious press, though not neglectful of the publicity value of the story, reported it fairly enough, the New York *Times* and the *Tribune* with approval of Kipling's conduct, the *Herald* with a reasoned defence of Beatty Balestier. The best-informed and the most judicious comment was that of the local paper, the *Vermont Phœnix*. After deriding the travesties published in Boston, ' the descriptions that did not describe and illustrations that did not illustrate ', the leader-writer of the *Phœnix* wrote a paragraph in praise of Kipling's genius with an expression of hope that he would continue to reside in Brattleboro. Then, in terms of courteous reproach, he deplored that Kipling ' had undertaken no social responsibilities, and made few personal friends ' in the town. Kipling, said the writer of the article, had ' won a reputation for brusqueness by what seems to us his unfortunate way of meeting the well-meant advances of newspaper men '.[25]

On the other hand, a group of leading citizens, including Governor Holbrook and the Episcopalian and Congregational ministers, let it be known that they were on Rudyard's side, and Carrie, too, was backed by her own family.

* Since the Kiplings left the country before the next session, the case never came to trial.

Mrs. Anna Balestier to Rudyard Kipling

May 15, 1896

Dear Rud,

I have your letter of 14. Thank you for writing but I am in no wise competent to formulate any ideas as to the future concerning Beatty. . . .

Whatever Beatty has done or may do, I must ever continue to keep an affectionate interest in him, being his mother, with the continual hope that it may have some spark of influence, however faint — but it will not be in the wrong direction, I promise you.

He is his own worst enemy and always has been, but he has *some* good impulses, if he would allow them to come to the surface. He has always been an enigma to me which has increased with time. . . . I do not wonder that *your* patience was exhausted, but mine must hold out — always, however tried, and I shall always be,

Your loving,

Mother.[26]

Meanwhile the Kiplings had withdrawn into their seclusion, consulting nobody but their lawyer, Dr. Conland, and an uncle of Carrie's on her father's side. What Brattleboro was saying and what the rest of the Balestier family were doing passed them by. 'These are dark days for us,' wrote Carrie, 'Rud is dull, listless, and weary', but, within a week, he had returned with interest to his work. On 16th May he was weighing the rival offers of the *Century* and *McClure's Magazine* for the serial rights in *Captains Courageous;* and on the 19th he went down to Gloucester with Conland for one last look at the fishing-fleet. This was not enough, as Carrie wrote to a friend, to restore the 'nerve and strength which was frittered away in so unworthy a cause' and, as in other times of trouble, he turned to Lockwood de Forest, his oldest friend in America. They spent a fortnight on the Gaspé coast, salmon-fishing, and it was at this time that he wrote his spirited ballad, 'The Feet of the Young Men':

Do you know the blackened timber — do you know that racing stream
  With the raw, right-angled log-jam at the end;
And the bar of sun-warmed shingle where a man may bask and dream
  To the click of shod canoe-poles round the bend?
It is there that we are going with our rods and reels and traces,
  To a silent, smoky Indian that we know —
To a couch of new-pulled hemlock, with the starlight on our faces,
  For the Red Gods call us out and we must go!

When he returned it was to resume the normal life at 'Naulakha', busy with his own work and interested in plans for the estate. His correspondence gave no hint of any interruption in his plans, other than telling his friends that he would be going to England in September for a long visit. Only in one letter, to W. D. Howells, did he make an admission:

4th June 1896

I don't think quite of quitting the land permanently. It is hard to go from where one has raised one's kids, and builded a wall and digged a well and planted a tree.

I do remember that once in your general capacity you said something about a work of Mr. Kipling which was salutary and chastening to that young man. But, as Boswell once remarked to Dr. Johnson in the stately phrase of the eighteenth century: — 'It would need a hell of a lot that I took unkindly from you, Sir.' [27]

The last two months at 'Naulakha' slipped away, as the Kiplings maintained their way of life, unchanged. One day in July Rudyard sat down and completed, in a few hours, a composition in one of the most rigorous of all verse-forms. He called it 'Sestina of the Tramp-royal'.

> Therefore, from job to job I've moved along.
> Pay couldn't 'old me when my time was done,
> For something in my 'ead upset it all,
> Till I 'ad dropped whatever 'twas for good,
> An', out at sea, be'eld the dock-lights die,
> An' met my mate — the wind that tramps the world!

It was resolute, still forward-looking, but without that youthful spirit with which he had written the 'Long Trail' in 1891. Taking stock of his life, the four happy years in Vermont and the memories of India which Vermont had allowed him to recall, he found his gaze settling most clearly upon remote childhood. *The Seven Seas* was coming into proof, and he now prefaced to it a dedication addressed to the City of Bombay, his birthplace. On 28th August, his last day at 'Naulakha', Mrs. Holbrook and Mary Cabot came to call, rather to the dismay of Carrie who was overwhelmed with her packing. They found Rudyard walking up and down the terrace. 'There are only two places in the world,' he said, 'where I want to live — Bombay and Brattleboro. And I can't live at either.'

Early on 29th August their neighbour John Bliss, from whom the Kiplings had once rented a cottage, drove them to the station. Only Conland was there to see them go and he discreetly slipped away without formally saying goodbye.

CHAPTER X

AT TORQUAY (1896–7)

THE SECOND VOYAGE (1903)

We've sent our little Cupids all ashore —
    They were frightened, they were tired, they were cold.
Our sails of silk and purple go to store,
    And we've cut away our mast of beaten gold.
             (Foul weather!)
Oh 'tis hemp and singing pine for to stand against the brine
    But Love he is our master as of old!

The sea has shorn our galleries away,
    The salt has soiled our gilding past remede;
Our paint is flaked and blistered by the spray,
    Our sides are half a fathom furred in weed.
             (Foul weather!)
And the Doves of Venus fled and the petrels came instead,
    But Love he was our master at our need!

'Was Youth would keep no vigil at the bow,
    'Was Pleasure at the helm too drunk to steer —
We've shipped three able quartermasters now.
    Men call them Custom, Reverence, and Fear.
             (Foul weather!)
They are old and scarred and plain, but we'll run no risk again
    From any Port o' Paphos mutineer!

．   ．

NEVER again was Rudyard so happy, never so sure of himself, as in the honeymoon years at 'Naulakha'. Since his wretched childhood the cards had been dealt to him by the Lords of Life — the Emersonian phrase he sometimes used — just so that he could play them to the best advantage. His understanding and mastery of his world had been adequate for his purpose.

        Ah, but a man's reach should exceed his grasp,
        Or what's a heaven for?

At the end of his rustication in Vermont his grasp had fallen short, but it was the whole world, not Beatty Balestier, that scored a point off him. The world was moving into a political crisis, the crisis of imperialism, and the decision would not be made in rural Vermont. Small-town life in a country where politics were nourished on anti-British hysteria was not a life for Rudyard Kipling, a man whose message could not be delivered from that platform. Rudyard loved Vermont, and in his letters to American friends, would often reveal his hankering for the pleasant life of 'Naulakha'. Not even to himself would he admit that he was leaving Vermont for ever and, though he never spoke of it, his letters tell how often it was in his thoughts.

The summer was ending when they reached England. From Southampton, the Kiplings went straight to a house they had arranged to rent at Maidencombe near Torquay, a house in which they never felt at home. Long afterwards, Rudyard made his irrational dislike for a place that should have been likeable, the subject of a psycho-analytical story ('The House Surgeon'), rather in the manner of Henry James. But the reason of his dislike for 'Rock House' at Maidencombe never came to light and when he revisited it, thirty years later, the place still cast its oppressive spell over him.

Rudyard Kipling to Dr. F. Conland

October 1, '96

Now imagine to yourself a big stone and stucco Naulakha, long, low with two stories, stuck on the side of a steep hill falling away almost as sharply as the lower slopes of Wantastiquet to a hundred-foot cliff of pure red soil. Below that is the sea, about two hundred yards from the window. . . . I look straight from my work table on to the decks of the fishing craft who come in to look after their lobster-pots.

They settled in amid storms of wind and rain.

The glass dropped about an inch and then began pumping up and down. The wind took about a day to get up and when it really took hold, it licked the Channel into lather. A big poplar on our lawn was the first to go. The wind lifted the top out of it. Then our back-gate was sent flying, and then a huge elm came over by the roots and nearly assassinated a hired yellow cow we keep in the meadow. About the beginning of the storm I saw a trawler blown out to sea — just a rag of brown sail in the smother; and once I heard the whistle of a steamer. But though it was clear overhead, the scud was thick over the sea; and from a sheltered angle of the kitchen garden we looked down on a bath of lather. Then it rained and then it blew some more, and then the glass went crazy.[1]

How unlike was 'Rock House' to the warm wood-scented 'Naulakha' with its familiar trappings, the bokhara rugs he had brought from India, the tiger-skin which he used as a carriage-rug to the astonishment of gossips in Brattleboro, the big water-colour of the camel-corps in the desert, the military sketches given him by Détaille, the carved figures of *Jungle Book* animals given him by Joel Chandler Harris, the beam carrying his father's inscription over the mantelshelf, and the photograph of Emerson beside his desk. Best of all had been the broad view from the library window, of woodland and meadow sloping down to the Connecticut River, the amphitheatre of hills from Sky Rocket on the left to Wantastiquet on the right, with the remote blue dome of Mount Monadnock dominating the far sky-line.

Landscapes in England were praised because they reminded him of the view from 'Naulakha'. Little Josephine often asked when they were going home and clung, as children will, to her first memories of it. Rudyard described her to a friend as altogether a little American.

Carrie Kipling to Mary Cabot

1 December, 1896

As Mr. Kipling never talks of Brattleboro or reads a letter from America or does anything which remotely reminds him of that last year of calamity and sorrow, I have not told him the piece of family news. But I have put your letter away against the time when he returns to these things, and know he will enjoy it as I did. He seems now better and stronger and I hope he may turn to his work again after a little. But all the events of the last year with the leaving of 'Naulakha' as we did have made us sore and bruised, and it takes us longer than the rest to forget. Which shows me we are wrong to feel so keenly. . . . I hope very much Mr. Kipling will want to return, and see no reason, under certain changed conditions, why he should not.[2]

Rudyard Kipling to Dr. F. Conland

October 1, 1896

Josephine, after considering things in her little head, has pronounced that 'this England is stuffy', but the moist climate agrees with her. Elsie eats and sleeps, and sleeps and eats. . . . I think the wife's health is considerably better, but, as you know, she wants to take hold of all the earth and shake it. As we have a conservatory, and a gardener and his wife and a garden, and an orchard and about forty-five acres of out-houses to look after, you can guess she has a large field to exercise her talents.

I spend my time doing nothing very hard — chiefly on a wheel. There are times when I'd give a good deal for the keen sniffs of an autumn morning up on the hillside, when the first frost has wilted things in the

garden and the leaves are dropping of themselves. They tell me our
new barn at 'Naulakha' is rather a success. Have you seen it?

I've arranged all my stories for the Scribner edition — getting 'em into
groups according to their subjects, while my father is making pictures
for them. The book of verses is all but finished and I've revised the
proofs for *Captains Courageous*.[3]

A few miles down the railway was Dartmouth where the old three-
decker *Britannia* was still used as a training ship for naval cadets.
The officers lost no time in attracting Rudyard into their society and,
during October, he spent several days visiting them. His letters to
Conland are full of nautical observations, and, with his usual facility,
he now began to master naval techniques. *The Seven Seas* was published at the beginning of November, with a subscribed figure of
22,000 copies sold before publication, no small success for a book of
verse. It was reviewed at once, and enthusiastically, in all the principal
daily papers, and the author of 'M'Andrew's Hymn' became a welcome figure in any company of seamen. The poet of the barrack-
room had enlarged his repertory and had become the poet of the
engine-room. Having changed his allegiance to the Royal Navy he
renewed an acquaintance with Captain E. H. Bayley, R.N., whom he
had met at the Cape in 1891, and joyfully accepted an invitation to
take a cruise with the Channel Fleet.

Rudyard Kipling to Dr. F. Conland

March 23–29

I have at last found a Captain of our Navy, an old friend of mine,
who offers me a berth aboard of a new 20-knot cruiser for the Naval
Manoeuvres. Can you imagine me in oilskins chasing up and down the
English Channel, playing at being a sailor? I rather look forward to the
fun which begins about the middle of June.

For the last two months we — and incidentally all Europe — have been
living on the edge of a volcano and even now the betting is about level
as to whether the damn thing will blow up after all. I've got my billet in
event of a big shindy; but it wasn't worth while going down to the
Mediterranean and hanging about on a lee shore (Crete has a *vile* coast)
to see Turks and Cretans fighting. One good result of the mess has been
to show the continent that England has rather more of a navy than the
rest of 'em put together.[4]

A succession of relatives and old friends came to visit the Kiplings
at 'Rock House'. The first was 'Ambo' Poynter, and after him came
his schoolboy brother, Hugh Poynter, to whom Rudyard gave a gun,
and with whom he went out after the rabbits. The 'pater' came from
Tisbury to set up his studio in the coach-house with a whole kit of
tools and apparatus. Soon he and Rudyard were elbow-deep in

modelling-clay and absorbed in plans for illustrating the complete edition of Rudyard's works with photographs of figures in low relief. This involved technical discussion with Scribner's office in New York. Frank Doubleday, their correspondent at Scribner's, had now become a dear friend of the family and, very cautiously, he consulted Rudyard about another plan — to set up publishing on his own. He could raise only $50,000 capital, and Rudyard advised him not to do it unless he could find five times as much. Early in 1897 Frank paid a short visit to England and, not long after, he and Sam McClure made their venture with the firm of Doubleday and McClure, which published all Kipling's new books, in America, for the rest of his life.

Rudyard Kipling to Dr. F. Conland

March 23–29, '97

I've done a yarn about a locomotive for Scribners. ['.007 ']. It may make you laugh when you see it. Doubleday, of Scribners, and his wife dropped in here to tea the other day and stayed to dinner, and we heard a whole lot of news. It was very pleasant to listen to the energetic New York accent once more, and to learn who had been doing what and why, since we left. They said that Fifth Ave is being laid down in asphalte. I'll believe that when I see it. Also I had a note from Teddy Roosevelt who, in the intervals of scrapping with the rest of the police board, finds time to remember me.[5]

Rudyard Kipling to C. E. Norton

October 30, '96

Mother and Father have been staying with us down here in our stone barrack of a house overlooking the sea. Our weather is and has been — British. ' Bloody British ' is the only word for it; and I have been studying my fellow-countrymen from the outside. Those four years in America will be blessed unto me for all my life. We are a rummy breed — and O Lord the ponderous wealthy society. Torquay is such a place as I do desire to upset by dancing through it with nothing on but my spectacles. Villas, clipped hedges and shaven lawns; fat old ladies with respirators and obese landaus. The Almighty is a discursive and frivolous trifler compared with some of 'em.

But the land is undeniably lovely and I am making friends with the farms.

They are in deep sorrow at the ' Grange ' over Morris's death which seems to have been unexpected to the last. Uncle Ned [Burne-Jones] is naturally very broken up. He felt Millais' going more than anyone thought, the father told me. Of course he won't leave London but we have hopes of getting Aunt Georgie down here. Aunt Aggie [Poynter] is coming for Christmas and we are in treaty with Henry James for a visit. But he is an evasive man, and won't leave London either. By the same token, he's seconded me for the Athenaeum and I hope to be a bishop before I die.

Carrie Kipling to C. E. Norton

December 31st, 1896

'Uncle Crom' Price, Rud's old headmaster and the beloved of the 'Grange' folk has been with us for a few days. He brings better news of Aunt Georgie, who has not been strong recently.

We are thoughtful over your admonition as to further verse-making, but it's not easy to make Rud take what you are pleased to call his genius seriously. He does not believe in it, in the very least. However we have set ourselves a more serious standard and have thrown several delightful things into the scrap-basket. At present there is a story being done, and that and the *Bell-buoy* are all the work done since we came over. Rud seems happier and better than for the past year, and feels there is a lot of work in the back of his brain.

Rudyard Kipling to C. E. Norton

December 31st, 1896. C's birthday.

We are both of us awed, and if the truth be told a little scared at your article [on Kipling's poems] in the *Atlantic Monthly*. . . .* True it is, most sadly true that I have not been true to my duties but I did not know that I had been so untrue. As you know I love the fun and the riot of writing (I am daily and nightly perplexed with my own private responsibilities before God) and there are times when it is just a comfort and a delight to let out with the pen and ink — as long as it doesn't do any one any moral harm. I don't believe very much in my genius. My own notion being rather that I am set to do Fergusson for some like-to-come along Burns whose little finger will be thicker than my loins. At least I have shown him his lead.

Then there is the danger, it seems, of a man running off into William Watson's kind of wordy rot if he, at a comparatively tender age, considers himself a poet.

But — you are the only man except my father and Uncle Ned whose disapproval or advice slays me; and I will say just as one says to one's father when one is little, 'I'll try to think and be better next time.' But, even now, the notion that *you* should have reviewed me rather makes me gasp.

I get very little American news except a line or two from Brattleboro. But among my letters I note with pain, as they say, a cutting from the *Evening Post* in which Mr. E. L. Godkin is pleased to turn up his nose at my babel of Americanisms in *Captains Courageous*. Now I would be loath to destroy and abolish Godkin for that he is a friend of yours and a man who washes his literary hands, to boot, but if he continues in this form of sin, he will presently be annihilated by an avalanche from

* See below, Chapter XIV.

quarters that he would least suspect. I did not embark upon the dialect of *Captains Courageous* to be scoffed at by a New York mugwump.[6]

To those who watched world politics with an eye to the map of the world, 1897 was an anxious year. Though the Venezuela crisis had passed away, there was a stir throughout Islam from the Sudan to Malaya. A war in the Balkans was damped down by the greater powers before the blaze got out of control, and Kipling did not find it necessary to serve as a war correspondent off the Cretan coast. On the Indian frontier, which Kipling watched with understanding, a series of tiresome campaigns had been touched off by the outbreak in Chitral in 1895, and the Indian Army was more heavily engaged in 1896 and 1897 than it had been in any of the years that he had spent in India. It was his stories that had made the people at home aware of the problem of the frontier where, decade after decade, a force of seventy thousand men was always on active service; and it was his verses that had provided the British public with a new hero in 'Bobs', Lord Roberts of Kandahar. But Kipling was no blind hero-worshipper and, at Simla, he had been known as a sharp critic of 'Bobs's' administrative weakness. In January 1897 'Bobs' published his memoirs, *Forty-one Years in India,* which was to be the year's best-seller. He sent Kipling a copy which provoked the comment that it was most remarkable for what it left out.[7]

As a rule he did not affect an admiration for the grandees of government; his interest lay in the administrators and technicians who took the personal risks. Young Frederick Roberts who won the V.C. in the Mutiny was his hero, rather than the be-medalled Commander-in-Chief at Simla, forty-one years later. And, while the English people lionized Lord Roberts, Rudyard entertained at Torquay the hero of the Siege of Chitral, Sir George Robertson, who told him tales of the heathen of those parts that made his hair stand on end.[8] Rudyard had been turning his mind to a series of stories about his schooldays, and was then writing the two episodes which he called 'Slaves of the Lamp', the first describing 'Stalky's' life at school, and the second his application — not far from Chitral — of the lessons he had learned at school.

The next visitor at 'Rock House' was Rudyard's cousin, Florence Macdonald, who was allowed to sit in the room where he was working at his 'Stalky' stories. He would write and write; then lay down his pen and roar with laughter; then read a passage aloud to her till she would roar with laughter. 'Come on, Florence,' he would say. 'What shall we make them do now?'[9]

Philip Burne-Jones, another cousin who re-entered the Kiplings' circle, had attained some success as a painter in a conventional style

very different from his father's. Phil's picture for the year 1897 made
a sensation, not least because Rudyard wrote a set of illustrative verses
which were printed in the catalogue.   Since Rudyard made a present
of them to his cousin they were never copyrighted, with the result that
unauthorized versions of the picture and the poem appeared in all
sorts of shapes, all over the world.   On the whole, they did Rudyard's
reputation little good.   He was then winning a name as a serious,
even a solemn, writer, a position that was recognized by his admission
to the Athenaeum Club, under Rule Two which provides for the
election of a small number of persons eminent in public life.   Not yet
thirty-two, Rudyard was by far the youngest member of the Club, and
gratified by his election.   On the day of his admission he dined with
Alfred Milner, Cecil Rhodes, and the editor of *The Times*.   A fortnight later, on 17th April, his verses for Phil's picture appeared in the
Daily Mail and, on the 24th, the picture itself was shown at the New
Gallery.

It was a specimen of an art-form which has since been superseded
by the techniques of cinematography — the 'problem picture'.   Slickly
and competently painted in contrasted tones of dark green, white, and
crimson, with a high finish, it was the kind of picture that told a
story, or rather gave a hint to the spectator of a story he was expected
to find out for himself, a dramatic puzzle.   The scene was a bedroom:
against dark curtains stood a bed and on it lay a figure of a young man,
dead or swooning, while over him towered with a triumphant sneer
on her lips, a tall full-blooded woman in white.   The picture was
called *The Vampire;* and the only explanation offered was Kipling's
set of verses:

> A fool there was and he made his prayer
> (Even as you and I!)
> To a rag and a bone and a hank of hair
> (We called her the woman who did not care)
> But the fool he called her his lady fair —
> (Even as you and I!)
>
> *Oh, the years we waste and the tears we waste*
> *And the work of our head and hand*
> *Belong to the woman who did not know*
> *(And now we know that she never could know)*
> *And did not understand!*

'A rag and a bone and a hank of hair' — this was strong stuff.   It
brought Rudyard's reputation back to its earliest phase; it was a piece
by the author of *Plain Tales from the Hills* grown ten years older;
and though no one rated it high as poetry, no one who had once heard

it was likely to forget it. Prick it, and the blood would spurt. Yet Rudyard seems not to have taken it seriously and never admitted it among his 'collected' works until the inclusive edition of 1919. It was an occasional piece, a compliment to cousin Phil — no more — and critics who tried to read into it Rudyard's philosophy of sex failed to recognize his faculty for putting himself into the skin of a fictitious character. Only those who knew them well commented on the fact that Phil Burne-Jones was making a fool of himself over Mrs. Patrick Campbell.[10]

When the spring came, in 1897, Rudyard and Carrie took rooms in a London hotel, where Carrie rested — she was expecting another child — while Rudyard made house-hunting expeditions in Kent and Sussex.

Rudyard Kipling to Dr. F. Conland

June 1, '97

We've been living a chaotic and disorganized life for the last few weeks. You see we gave up the house in Devon — a lovely place but eight months damp, rain, sea fog and mildew were rather more than we would stand. Then we decided to take a holiday from housekeeping while we hunted for a new house; and to London (London in Jubilee year!) we came three weeks ago and have been living in a hotel overlooking the Park: both children with us. The wife is hugely enjoying the rest from housekeeping and the demoralizing comfort of not having to think about meals. Meantime a kindly relative has placed her house near Brighton at our disposal for as long as we want; and we go down on Wednesday next; to resume the dreary game of house-hunting. I feel like a houseless gipsy; and would almost be thankful for a tent and that — and the damnable? grind of society in London — is my excuse for silence.

Life has been pretty mixed — not to say exciting for me lately. I went to the big banquet of the Royal Academy to begin with: sat next to Irving and the Poet Laureate [Alfred Austin]. Incidentally I met Hamo Thorneycroft the sculptor — brother to *the* Thorneycroft who builds the torpedoboats. Sez he to me 'Would you like to attend the steam-trials of a new thirty-knot destroyer.' 'Rather!' sez I; and about three days later I got a telegram advising me to come down to Chatham dockyard. So down I went and on the way picked up the Thorneycroft crowd who represented the contractors' interests at the trial (she had to do her 30 knots an hour for three consecutive hours before the government would take her) and a most fascinating old navy engineer who represented the admiralty.

We pulled out of the Medway into the mouth of the Thames at an easy twelve knots to get down to our course — from the Mouse Light to the Lower Hope reach — a lumpy sea and a thirty knot breeze.

They wrapped my neck up in a comforter, gave me heavy oilskins; and tied a souwester over my ears. The wind was pretty keen and now and then the top of a sea came aboard. She was steered from the bridge forward and we all huddled under the protection of the turtleback — practically the break of the foc'sle. Then we struck a twenty-two knot gait — and very nice it was. They began to rig up the indicators, to know how many revolutions we were doing and I went down into the engine room. Two engines of 3,000 h.p. apiece were making about 230 to the minute — maybe a trifle less.

It was like a nightmare. The vibration shook not only your body but your intestines and finally seemed to settle on your heart. The breeze along the deck made it difficult to walk. I staggered aft above the twin-screws and there saw a blue-jacket, vomiting like a girl; and in the ward-room which is right in the stern of her, I felt my false teeth shaking in my head! The pace was too good for her to roll. All we could do was to get under the lee of the conning tower while this devil's darning needle tore up and down the coast. We passed 17-knot passenger boats, flew ten miles past 'em, turned and came back and overtook them. By the way when she turned she slung you to one side like a bicycle.

The wake ran out behind us like white hot iron; the engine room was one lather of oil and water; the engines were running 400 to the minute; the gauges; the main-steam pipes and everything that wasn't actually built into her were quivering and jumping; there was half an inch of oil and water on the floors and — you couldn't see the cranks in the crank pit. It was more like Hell on a ten foot scale than anything you ever dreamed of and through the infernal din of it George Brown shouted in my ear 'Isn't she a darling!' Well, I climbed out of the engine-room rather thankfully and went up on the bridge by the Captain. You never saw a boat steer as she did. One grey headed old quarter-master held her at the wheel; and her two heavy drop-rudders swung her over the face of the waters. We shaved a brig coming up the Thames just to show how near we could go; and our wash threw her up and down as though we had been a liner. We skimmed past buoys with about five into that thirty knot gale and for the honour of the thing I *had* to say up yards to spare, running all along the edge of the Maplin Sands. We faced into that thirty knot gale and for the honour of the thing I *had* to stay up on the bridge. At last those awful three hours came to an end: but not before the speaking-tubes to the Captain's bridge had been smashed off by the vibration. Then we drew breath: and every one said Thank God! She'd done ninety knots in those three hours: but if it had been straightaway in deep sea, we'd have done 31. Everything was quite cool and nothing had smashed up and they all said I was the Mascotte. Every engineer aboard knew *M'Andrew's Hymn* by the way and enjoyed it. Well, then we jogged back to Sheerness at 20 knots an hour. We were all as black as sweeps; and utterly played out. It took me two days to get the 'jumps' out of my legs. But I wouldn't have missed the trip for anything.

Three days later I went down to Oxford among the four hundred year old universities and dined with the tutors and so on at Balliol College. The boys cheered me so that the Master couldn't say grace and altogether

I had a most wonderful time. Since then I've been flourishing about in a frock-coat and top-hat when I wasn't dining out. Can you imagine me as a dude! But the wife and I thought we might as well play the game now that we were in for it. We went to the Lyceum the other night: Irving put a private box at our disposal; and after the play we went round and saw him and Miss Terry in their war-paint on the stage. He's rather keen that I should write a play for him; and I should rather like it. But actors are rummy folk. Then Henry James came to dine with us and then I went out to a man's party of generals and military . . . where I met George Curzon — him that married old Leiter's daughter: and is now a flourishing political person. Also we lunched with Hay who has a lovely house here — overlooking the line of the Jubilee procession. He has all his work cut out for him to manage his share of the Jubilee. London is simply packed and double packed. There are stands and seats everywhere: and like the embassies the police are praying for the day to be over without accidents. Estimates say between 8 and 10,000,000 people will attend. There are 80,000 *extra* Americans in town; and Cook the tourist man has practically chartered all the suburb of Richmond for their accommodation.

We are going down to Brighton to be out of it all. There we have a house lent us by my aunt, Lady Burne Jones; and from there we hope to find a house for ourselves. . . .[11]

CHAPTER XI

THE WHITE MAN'S BURDEN (1897–8)

'A SONG OF THE ENGLISH' (1893)

We were dreamers, dreaming greatly, in the man-stifled town;
We yearned beyond the sky-line where the strange roads go down.
Came the Whisper, came the Vision, came the Power with the Need,
Till the Soul that is not man's soul was sent us to lead.
As the deer breaks — as the steer breaks — from the herd where they graze,
In the faith of little children we went on our ways.
Then the wood failed — then the food failed — then the last water dried —
In the faith of little children we lay down and died.
On the sand-drift — on the veldt-side — in the fern-scrub we lay,
That our sons might follow after by the bones on the way.
Follow after — follow after! We have watered the root,
And the bud has come to blossom that ripens for fruit!
Follow after — we are waiting, by the trails that we lost,
For the sounds of many footsteps, for the tread of a host.
Follow after — follow after — for the harvest is sown:
By the bones about the wayside ye shall come to your own!

I T was Derby Day in Queen Victoria's Diamond Jubilee year, 2nd
June 1897, when the Kiplings moved to Rottingdean which was to
be their home for five years. A lonely seaside village, off the railway,
and therefore out of reach of trippers from Brighton, four miles away,
it had the special merit of being a family resort, where Mr. Bleyber,
the landlord of the 'Plough', could remember Rudyard as a plump
schoolboy.[1]
Around the village green, a mile inland from the sea, stood several
houses, of which one was the summer home of the Burne-Joneses and
appropriately called 'North End House'. Across the green was the
large house of the Ridsdales who were members of the family, since
Stan Baldwin had married the daughter of the house. Other aunts
and cousins came and went, and Rudyard found himself at the centre
of a large and varying group of intimate friends, all allied by marriages:
Burne-Joneses, Mackails, Baldwins, Ridsdales, Poynters, Macdonalds,
and Kiplings. There were many young children, down for the summer, to be deposited on the beach or sent off in wagonettes to picnic

in the Downs, under convoy of aunts and governesses; there were men
of Rudyard's own age to sit up late in 'North End House' engrossed
in that shop-talk which Rudyard thought the best of all social pleasures.
At Rottingdean, in 1897, Rudyard first formed a close friendship with
Stan Baldwin — each of their wives was expecting a child; and there
would often be Phil Burne-Jones, 'Ambo', and Hugh Poynter; or
Jack Mackail — but Rudyard found him too donnish and radical for
intimacy.

'North End House' was large and rambling, furnished by William
Morris with an eye more to the principles of craftsmanship than
comfort. However, the Kiplings were comfortable enough, for the
summer season. Aunt Georgie willingly let the Kiplings use her seaside house, persuaded them to stay so that their child could be born
there, and encouraged them to rent the house called 'The Elms' which
stood like an island in the village green.

Rudyard was quietly busy at 'North End House' in June, working
at some verses on 'Destroyers' and was beginning to put together
some nursery stories about animals with which he had amused the
children at Brattleboro, three or four years back. Much as he disliked
publicity, he could not ignore the Jubilee celebrations. The 'colonies',
as they were still called, were much in the public notice, and the
author of *The Seven Seas* was expected to be on his mettle. He
attended a luncheon to the Colonial Premiers in London, on 11th
June, and met the High Commissioner for Canada, a few days after
the verses, 'Our Lady of the Snows', had appeared in *The Times*.
Rudyard's mind was turned to colonial affairs as Carrie noted in her
diary, making what is perhaps the first use of a celebrated phrase.
On 15th June, she wrote, he was at work upon a poem called 'The
White Man's Burden', which he did not complete until eighteen
months later. Not this poem but another, a poem which at first he
rejected, was to contain his Jubilee message, effacing the bad impression
he had made with 'The Vampire', and instantly raising him, in public
esteem, to the place left vacant at the death of Tennyson.

For several years Rudyard had been in a special relation with the
London *Times*. When he left England in 1892 Moberly Bell had told
him that *The Times* would publish anything that he cared to submit,
an offer that he interpreted in two ways. He had begun by sending
Bell a series of travel-sketches in the ordinary way of journalism, and
later he used *The Times* as a platform for the major poems which he
designed to carry a message to his generation.

On 14th October 1895 *The Times* had published Rudyard's poem,
'The Native-Born'.

Editor of The Times (*Moberly Bell*) *to Rudyard Kipling*

October 14th, 1895

MY DEAR KIPLING,

Let me thank you very heartily on my own behalf and on behalf of the proprietors of *The Times* for the really beautiful poem you have allowed us to publish in *The Times* this morning. It is, I think, the first time we have ever published a poem not written in relation to any one definite event and this caused us (as a good old conservative institution) to hesitate, but as we read and re-read your poem our scruples disappeared.[2]

'Here's richness for me,' wrote Kipling to Norton, 'and I should never have thought of trying the austere old *Times* but for you.'

'The Native-Born', an appeal from the colonial born overseas for a little understanding on the part of his English brother, was the first of these public poems. During the next forty years, about twenty more of them were given to *The Times,* including 'Our Lady of the Snows', 'Recessional', 'The White Man's Burden', 'The Islanders', 'The Dead King', and 'For all we have and are'. 'Given to *The Times,*' said Kipling, 'because for this kind of work I did not take payment'; and accordingly they involved him in difficulties over copyright.

It was by these rare and solemn verses that Kipling came to be accepted as the people's laureate. Since much legend has grown up about his relation with the Court, it may be useful to recall the following points. The ancient office of Poet Laureate, which had been honoured by the tenure of such men as Ben Jonson and Dryden, fell into contempt in the eighteenth century when its small emolument was used to provide a pension for some courtier with literary tastes, who was expected to produce neat complimentary odes for royal anniversaries. During the nineteenth century there was a change in policy, and the emolument had been conferred, successively, on three professional poets, Southey, Wordsworth, and Tennyson. Each had been something of a rebel in youth and each was reproached by his younger contemporaries for accepting a pension from Government in middle age.

When Tennyson died, in October 1892, he had held the office for forty years, through the whole Victorian summer and autumn. His influence had contributed largely to the revival of attachment to the monarchy and to the old Queen, and several of the state poems he had written for royal occasions had genuine poetic merit. He was one of the makers of the Victorian age and, except for the Queen herself and Mr. Gladstone, he was one of the last to survive among those makers. In August 1892 Gladstone had become Prime Minister for the fourth time and, looking around for a successor to Tennyson, could find no

one. There was, indeed, one other major poet in England — Swinburne. But Swinburne's verses had appealed to the younger generation
in the 'sixties, not least because of their defiance of the Victorian code
of morals. Though he had abandoned his paganism and repub-
licanism, it was at the cost of his poetic inspiration. The only other
comparable poet was William Morris who was regarded as a dangerous
revolutionary. Setting aside Swinburne and Morris, no candidates
were to be seen but minor poets who were mostly 'decadents or
detrimentals'. There seemed to be no one qualified for the post of
Poet Laureate, either in the eighteenth- or the nineteenth-century
manner.

In March 1892, just before Tennyson's death, a well-known critic
and historian, H. D. Traill, wrote an article for the *Nineteenth Century* on this very theme. He enumerated fifty contemporary writers
in whose work he found some merit, but not one who could rank with
the aged Tennyson. Then, in a postscript, he apologized for having
overlooked the muse of the new young man, Rudyard Kipling. For
the sake of 'The Ballad of East and West', he awarded Kipling the
fifty-first place on his list, and thus Kipling became 'a minor poet
certified by Traill'. The first collected edition of *Barrack-Room
Ballads* was published in the following month, and it was only then
that the public (and the politicians) could judge his adult work in
bulk. But the early Barrack-room ballads were rather shocking, and
some of the accompanying poems were worse. If the volume included
'The English Flag', the first of Kipling's national odes, it also included 'Cleared' which was his contemptuous attack launched against
the Liberal Party and Gladstone. 'Go, scare your sheep together,'
Kipling adjured him, 'the blundering, tripping tups that bleat behind
the old bell-wether.' Since the old bell-wether now had the appointment of a Poet Laureate within his patronage, he was not likely to
appoint Rudyard Kipling.

If there had been any likelihood — and there was none — Kipling's
claim for consideration would have been much strengthened after the
publication of 'The Song of the English', which appeared in a
popular illustrated monthly, in March 1893. In mere extent it is the
longest of his poems; in content it is the most rich and varied; its
composition most elaborate, its harmonies most surely integrated. Although the author of this work was without question a mature and
responsible interpreter of the nation's mood, he hastened to counter
any suggestion that he should be given official status, by a purer poem
with a simpler theme, 'The Last Rhyme of True Thomas', which,
by chance, was published a few days after Lord Rosebery succeeded
Gladstone as Prime Minister. Kipling had been at work upon it for
several months before Gladstone's retirement.

'The Last Rhyme' is a direct imitation of a Border ballad, written in dialect. It describes, in an allegory too plain to need interpretation, how a king offers to ennoble a poet and how the poet demonstrates his superior power to enchant the king.

> The King has called for priest and cup,
>   The King has taken spur and blade
> To dub True Thomas a belted knight,
>   And all for the sake of the songs he made.
>
> .   .   .   .
>
> 'And what should I make wi' blazon and belt,
>   'Wi' keep and tail and seizin and fee,
> 'And what should I do wi' page and squire
>   'That am a king in my own countrie?
>
> .   .   .   .
>
> 'For I make Honour wi' muckle mouth,
>   'As I make Shame wi' mincing feet,
> 'To sing wi' the priests at the market-cross,
>   'Or run wi' the dogs in the naked street.
>
> .   .   .   .
>
> 'I ha' harpit ye up to the Throne o' God,
>   'I ha' harpit your midmost soul in three.
> 'I ha' harpit ye down to the Hinges o' Hell,
>   'And — ye — would — make — a Knight o' me!'

The ballad is of great length and contains many descriptive passages in the tradition of the Border. If Lord Rosebery's advisers read it through, they could be in no doubt about the author's view of official poetry. Apparently it was unnecessary, since Rosebery had already let slip the opinion that he would as soon appoint a court jester as a Poet Laureate.

A year passed and, in August 1895, the Conservatives regained office. Lord Salisbury now became Prime Minister, and we have it on the authority of one of his private secretaries, Sir Ian Malcolm, that the appointment of a Poet Laureate was discussed with interest. The Prime Minister's nephew, Arthur Balfour, pressed for the appointment of Kipling (who was in America throughout the time of discussion). * A discreet inquiry quickly revealed his antipathy to any official recognition. Balfour's proposal was dropped and, on 1st January 1896, Lord Salisbury appointed a Tory journalist named Alfred Austin who had written some patriotic jingles, and, only ten days later, Austin made

---

* 'That ass Austin was made P.L. in 1896 — after much hesitation and no reflexion. I was a bottle-washer at Hatfield then. Lord S. certainly thought of Kipling for the job " though he blows his own trumpet rather loud sometimes ". A. J. B. more than thought of him and wanted him to take it. So he was sounded and the answer was just as you said and as might have been expected.' (Sir Ian Malcolm to Lord Baldwin, 15th July 1943.)[3]

an ass of himself by a laughable set of verses on the Jameson Raid.
The appointment was so derisory, and was greeted with such contempt
in literary society, that it was generally regarded as mere cynicism
on the part of the Prime Minister. Alfred Austin did not neglect his
duties, and his official utterances are still occasionally quoted as examples of unconscious humour. Meanwhile Kipling's deeper notes
were being heard, and the publication of *The Seven Seas,* in November
1896, revealed his full powers. As a national poet, he was everything
that Austin was not, and the great occasion of the Queen's second
Jubilee, in 1897, called his powers into play.

A persistent rumour appeared, at an early date, that Kipling's candi-
dature had been vetoed by Queen Victoria, who took offence at his
ballad on ' The Widow at Windsor '. No evidence has been adduced
for this story except a letter (which, judged by internal evidence,
cannot be authentic) in an American library.* The only connexion
that can be established between the Kiplings and the Court is through
Lockwood Kipling, who was well known at Windsor. He had struck
up a friendship in India with the Duke of Connaught who engaged
him to decorate a room in his house at Bagshot, in Indian style. This
proved so pleasing that the old Queen herself desired him to arrange
a suite of Indian rooms at Osborne. Lockwood installed a Hindu
craftsman and supervised the work, which was watched with interest
and approval by the royal family. The Widow of Windsor certainly
had no antipathy for the elder Kipling, and she certainly shared the
common contempt for Alfred Austin.

Suggestions were made to Rudyard from several quarters that he
should write a Jubilee ode and to these he reacted, as might be expected, negatively. It was never his practice or intention to write to
order. According to an account which seems reliable, though published long afterwards, Rudyard was persuaded by the editor of *The
Times* to attempt something but made no progress. '*The Times*
began sending telegrams so I shut myself in a room. . . . I found just
one line I liked — " Lest we forget " — and wrote the poem round
that, arranging it to the tune of the hymn, " Eternal Father, strong to
save ".' [4]
Kipling was not Poet Laureate, and there was little in his early
record to suggest that he would write a ceremonial ode. His comment
on the Queen's first Jubilee, in 1887, had been anything but enthusiastic:

> * 'Ave you 'eard o' the Widow at Windsor
>   With a hairy gold crown on 'er 'ead?
> She 'as ships on the foam — she 'as millions at 'ome,
>   An' she pays us poor beggars in red.

And the Ploughman settled the share
More deep in the sun-dried clod:—
'Mogul, Mahratta, and *Mlech* from the North,
'And White Queen over the Seas —
'God raiseth them up and driveth them forth
'As the dust of the ploughshare flies in the breeze;
'But the wheat and the cattle are all my care,
'And the rest is the will of God.' [5]

During the six months before the Diamond Jubilee *The Seven Seas* had passed through three large editions which had introduced the reading public to a new note in Kipling's repertory. The sense of climax which stirred the whole Empire in June 1897 called for an expression of faith, and no one who had read 'The Song of the English' with attention could doubt that, if Kipling spoke on such an occasion, it would be with solemnity.

On Jubilee Day, 22nd June, he set aside his other tasks, his draft for a set of nursery stories, and his draft for a set of verses on the White Man's Burden, in order to return to the set piece which was to carry the refrain 'Lest we forget'. After a day that was overcast and dull in Sussex, the evening brightened as he and Carrie walked out to hear the church-bells chiming, and to watch the chain of bonfires rise and sink 'on dune and headland' along the South Coast. A poem of seven stanzas began to take shape in his mind, but he was dissatisfied with it and laid it aside. The next day he went off at a tangent; he busied himself with a political dialogue for the *St. James's Gazette,* and with finishing a dramatic lyric, 'The Explorer':

Till a voice, as bad as Conscience, rang interminable changes
    On one everlasting Whisper day and night repeated — so:
'Something hidden. Go and find it. Go and look behind the Ranges —
    'Something lost behind the Ranges. Lost and waiting for you. Go!'

Again the thread was broken by a message from Captain Bayley which drew Rud and 'the Pater' off to Portsmouth on a visit to H.M.S. *Pelorus* for the Naval Review and manœuvres. They were away for a fortnight and when the fleets had sailed, far-called to their tasks at the world's end, he returned to Rottingdean where Sallie Norton, on a visit from America, had been making company for Carrie. Aunt Georgie had also come down from London, as a guest of the Kiplings in her own house.

On the morning of the 16th July, hosts and guests were sitting together in one of the rooms of the house, Kipling at his desk, where he was running through some papers and from time to time flinging one of them into a waste-paper basket close to where Miss Norton sat. Her attention

attracted, she asked if she might look at the contents of the basket. Leave
was given and she picked out a sheet of paper on which was written a
poem on the Diamond Jubilee, headed 'After'. She was at once struck
by its quality and protested at the idea of destroying it. It ought, she
declared, to be published.

Kipling demurred at this idea, but finally he yielded so far as to say
that he would refer the matter to the decision of 'Aunt Georgie'. . . .
Lady Burne-Jones fully agreed with Miss Norton's verdict. The poem
must be published; and published it was. Kipling sat down to revise it,
reducing its length from seven to five stanzas. Miss Norton suggested
the repetition of the last couplet of the first stanza,

> 'Lord God of Hosts, be with us yet,
> Lest we forget — lest we forget!'

as a refrain in the second and fourth, and this suggestion Kipling adopted,
borrowing her pen for the purpose and writing opposite the first insertion
'written with Sallie's pen — R. K.' Then, still using Sallie's pen, he
altered the last line to

> 'Thy mercy and forgiveness, Lord!'

(a change subsequently abandoned in favour of the original version),
added an 'Amen' and his signature, and then wrote beneath: —

> 'done in council at North End House, July 16
> > > > Aunt Georgie
> > > > Sallie
> > > > Carrie and me.' [6]

A fresh copy was made, taken up to London by Aunt Georgie whose
visit to Rottingdean had come to an end, and was despatched to
The Times office, that evening, by special messenger. She wrote next
day to her niece and nephew ('very dear, both of you') to tell them
with what contentment she thought of his 'splendid hymn speeding
over the world'. It appeared, 17th July, on the middle page of *The
Times* under a new title 'Recessional' and with a studied paragraph
of approval in the leading article. Again Kipling astonished the
nation by revealing its heartfelt but unrealized emotion. Humility
not pride, awe not arrogance, a sense of transience not a sense of
permanence were to be the keynotes of the imperial festival. Again
Kipling confounded the critics by revealing an aspect of his genius
which many of them grudged him.

But the poem, to which the symbolic name, 'Recessional', had been
given, had certain flaws which the anti-imperialists were quick to
work upon. The first verse — plain hymnology — with its echoes of
the psalms and its phrase borrowed from Emerson's 'Wood-notes' —
was unexceptionable, a prayer for the pervading presence of God in
our consciousness so that we should never lose our sense of obligation
to His Law; for the sober and temperate sense of duty that justifies
the will to power.

If, drunk with sight of power, we loose
   Wild tongues that have not Thee in awe,
Such boastings as the Gentiles use,
   Or lesser breeds without the Law —
Lord God of Hosts, be with us yet, . . .

'Such boastings as the Gentiles use', the couplet gave much offence, especially among those who were sufficiently instructed in politics to appreciate that the cap fitted them. But the distinction between those who are 'within' and 'without the Law' is a distinction between the men of any class or creed who are humble because they submit to the Law and those who are arrogant because they override it. By their words and deeds you might know them, not by their accents or the colour of their skins.

The poem is open to criticism on another count; it is not so neatly phrased as some others of Kipling's verses. Like many of them it has its involved and obscure lines, its complicated metonymies in the Horatian mode, and once, at least, the syntax fails from over-compression. When, in the third stanza, he varies the refrain with the phrase:

Judge of the Nations, spare us yet,

he fails to notice a contradiction. If he says, 'be with us . . . lest we forget', he should say, 'spare us . . . even though we forget'.

Admit that this celebrated poem contains a contemptuous phrase which may be counted an error in taste, admit it contains a solecism which may be counted a fault in style, and then admire its solemnity, its vision, its permanence. This was the word given at Britain's proudest moment by the great imperialist, a call to humility and a warning that the proudest empire is ephemeral as a day's pageant.

The Kiplings admitted the special value of 'Recessional' by keeping a few of the many letters of praise that Rudyard received; it even moved his literary agent to unusual eloquence.

A. S. Watt to Rudyard Kipling

Allow me to offer you congratulations on the appearance in today's *Times* of your magnificent poem. It strikes the right note with regard to the Jubilee Celebration and will recall the nation to the source of its real strength. You are the only rightful heir to the mantles of Shakespeare, Milton, and Tennyson, and the laureate *de facto!* I tried to read 'God of our fathers' aloud this morning at home but I broke down.

S. S. McClure to Rudyard Kipling

You and the Queen made the *Times* for last Saturday the greatest newspaper ever published.

John Hay (American Minister in London) to Rudyard Kipling

I thank you for the high pleasure we all had in reading your noble ' Recessional '. It has struck everybody — not merely the critical people — as the one utterance of the year worthwhile.

Sir Walter Besant to Rudyard Kipling

It was far away the finest thing in the whole Jubilee literature. If the poor old Queen — or any of them — had the least feeling for letters they would — what would they do? Write and thank you at the least. . . .

You caught the exact feeling — what all decent people with the Puritanic touch in us wanted to have said and couldn't say. That is genius.

The Rev. F. W. Macdonald to Rudyard Kipling

My DEAR RUDYARD, — I am, as you know, the sole survival of Methodism in our family and line. I should like, then, to tell you how deeply your ' Recessional ' has touched our whole community. You will not resent the fact that our people claim a certain interest in you, and that the thought occurred to many that the grandfathers had spoken in you, to which I would add that your verse would ' find ' multitudes who would fly their sermons.

You have added a quotation to the common store, and a phrase to the language.

J. W. Mackail to Rudyard Kipling

DEAR RUDDY, — In our household at least your poem in the *Times* of this morning was read with tumult of acclaim. I cannot tell you how glad I am of it, or forbear writing to say so. There are all the signs of England saving up for the most tremendous smash ever recorded in history if she does not look to her goings.

This letter from the pacifist intellectual who had married his cousin Margaret roused Rudyard to reply in terms that showed the other side of his nature, that revealed, too, some irritation at Mackail's patronage. While preaching humility and moderation to his fellow-countrymen, Rudyard did not forget that they were surrounded by armed and (in 1897) mostly hostile nations. There was a proper answer to ' such boastings as the Gentiles use '.[7]

Rudyard Kipling to J. W. Mackail

DEAR JACK, — Thank you very much: but all the same, seeing what manner of armed barbarians we are surrounded with, we're about the only power with a glimmer of civilization in us. I've been round with the Channel Fleet for a fortnight and any other breed of white man, with such a weapon to their hand, would have been exploiting the round Earth in their own interests long ago. This is no ideal world but a nest of burglars, alas; and we must protect ourselves against being burgled. All the same, we have no need to shout and yell and ramp about our strength because that is waste of power, and because other nations can do the advertising better than we can.

The big smash is coming one of these days, sure enough but I think we shall pull through not without credit. It will be common people — the 3rd class carriages — that'll save us.

Ever yours,

RUDDY.

The chorus of applause which greeted 'Recessional' far surpassed his earlier triumphs, and this public tribute was accompanied by an event in Rudyard's private life which meant a thousand times more to him. Very early in the morning of 17th August 1897 a son was born to Carrie at 'North End House'. In accordance with the family tradition he was given his grandfather's name of John.

Rudyard Kipling to W. J. Harding

Ref: t.b.d. trials. My attention is at present taken up by one small craft recently launched from my own works — weight (approx.) 8.957 lbs: h.p. (indicated) 2.0464, consumption of fuel unrecorded but fresh supplies needed every 2½ hrs. The vessel at present needs at least 15 yrs for full completion but at the end of that time may be an efficient addition to the Navy, for which service it is intended. Date of launch Aug. 17th, 1.50 a.m. No casualties. Christened John. You will understand that the new craft requires a certain amount of attention — but I trust ere long to be able to attend a t.b.d. trial.[8]

In September, when Carrie was fit to be moved, they transferred themselves across the green from 'North End House' to 'The Elms' which they rented for three guineas a week. Even this was not their ideal house and Rudyard spent much of the autumn house-hunting again, east into Kent and west as far as Dorset. On 11th September he went to Dorchester where Thomas Hardy carried him off to inspect a lonely house occupied by an elderly lady. While Kipling examined the premises high and low, Hardy was left making conversation in the parlour. 'I think you would like to know, Madam, that the gentleman I have brought to your house is no other than Mr. Rudyard Kipling.' The remark fell flat; she had never heard of Rudyard Kipling. A few minutes later, Rudyard found himself alone with the lady and, not knowing what had passed, made the complementary remark, 'My sponsor is Thomas Hardy himself'. It was no use, she had never heard of Thomas Hardy; and the two celebrities admitted their insignificance to one another on the way home.[9]

Rudyard did not find the house he wanted, and decided to stay on at 'The Elms', but to spend the winter in a warmer climate. The whole family, and the 'Pater', prepared to leave for South Africa in the New Year. Meanwhile, at Rottingdean, they were never idle or lonely. Rudyard had much correspondence: with Beerbohm Tree who wanted him to write a play, with Arthur Sullivan who wanted to set 'Recessional' to music, with several influential persons who were working to get a civil list pension for W. E. Henley, now so crippled that when he came to stay at 'The Elms' his only outings were in a bath-chair. 'Uncle Ned' came down to 'North End House' in October, bringing with him 'Crom' Price and a friend, J. M. Barrie, with whom Rudyard went for mighty walks across the Downs. He was working steadily at his schoolboy stories, and there was a day when he read some of them aloud to Price and 'Uncle Ned' and their young friend Sydney Cockerell. 'Do you remember that, sir?' he would say to 'Crom' Price, after each uproarious incident, and 'Crom' would reply, 'Yes, I remember that.' They enjoyed the stories and there was no ill-will in the remark that 'Crom' made afterwards to Cockerell. 'Yes, I remember many other things, too, that he might not wish me to remember.' [10]

Christmas at Rottingdean, with his own family around him, his mother as a guest, and a circle of relatives and friends, was happy indeed. On the last day of the year he wrote, as usual, a coda to Carrie's diary. 'The sixth year of our life together. In all ways the richest to us two personally. "She shall do him good and not evil all the days of her life."'

On 8th January 1898 the Kiplings embarked at Southampton for Madeira, Cape Town, and the sunshine, in s.s. *Dunvegan Castle*. Rudyard's earlier voyage, in 1891, had given him some acquaintance with Cape Colony but, as yet, he had no connexion in South Africa and wrote around to friends for advice about housekeeping at the Cape. They settled, uncomfortably, in a boarding-house at Newlands on the slope of Table Mountain, and stayed three months. South Africa was to provide the fourth corner-stone in the edifice of his material life. India, New England, Sussex, South Africa, east and west, north and south, were the four lands in which this world-observer struck root.

The climate — for the southern tip of Africa can be very hot in February — restored memories of his childhood.

> 'We shall go back to the boltless doors,
>   To the life unaltered our childhood knew —
> To the naked feet on the cool, dark floors,
>   And the high-ceiled rooms that the Trade blows through:

'To the trumpet-flowers and the moon beyond,
  And the tree-toad's chorus drowning all —
And the lisp of the split banana-frond
  That talked us to sleep when we were small.

'The wayside magic, the threshold spells,
  Shall soon undo what the North has done —
Because of the sights and the sounds and the smells
  That ran with our youth in the eye of the sun.' [11]

There were in Cape Town, in 1898, two others of the most eminent personalities in the English-speaking world. Within a few days of their landing, the Kiplings were invited into two social circles, that of Sir Alfred Milner and that of Cecil Rhodes. Milner had recently arrived as the Queen's High Commissioner, bearing instructions from Joseph Chamberlain, the Colonial Secretary, to bring the two Boer Republics to a settlement with the British Empire. Still a young man, and still unknown to the world, Milner was nevertheless a statesman to whom Kipling could give his approval. He was entirely straightforward and devoted to efficiency, almost unaware of emotional considerations in politics, patient, hard-working, and distrustful of rhetoric. He could never quite bring himself to believe that sensible men were swayed by sentiment. He was enlightened; and was convinced that enlightenment as understood in the most progressive circles of European society must convince even the Boers of the Transvaal back-veldt where their true interest lay. He did not much like the Boers, nor did they like him.

The other statesman at the Cape was Cecil Rhodes, also an Oxford man but as different from Milner in character, temperament, and upbringing as he could be. A comfortable, practical, easy-going man, Rhodes loved the land and the people. Milner was a man of great competence and force, a man of many talents, but what was Rhodes? While no one doubted his greatness, its secret was and is elusive. A self-made millionaire, he seemed careless of money and the toys that money can buy; a silent man, he said something memorable whenever he opened his mouth; a man's man, he was bored by sport, unmoved by women; a money-spinning man of affairs, he lived in a fantastic world of dreams.

I'd not give way for an Emperor,
I'd hold my road for a King —
To the Triple Crown I would not bow down —
But this is a different thing.
I'll not fight with the Powers of Air,
Sentry, pass him through!
Drawbridge let fall, 'tis the Lord of us all,
The Dreamer whose dreams come true! [12]

Rhodes had a habit [wrote Rudyard] of jerking out sudden questions as disconcerting as those of a child — or the Roman Emperor he so much resembled. He said to me apropos of nothing in particular: 'What's your dream?' I answered that he was part of it, and I think I told him that I had come down to look at things. He showed me some of his newly established fruit-farms in the peninsula, wonderful old Dutch houses, stalled in deep peace, and lamented the difficulty of getting sound wood for packing-cases and the shortcomings of native labour. But it was his wish and his will that there should be a fruit-growing industry in the Colony, and his chosen lieutenants made it presently come to pass.

My use to him was mainly as a purveyor of words; for he was largely inarticulate. After the idea had been presented — and one had to know his code for it — he would say: 'What am I trying to express? Say it, *say* it.' So I would say it, and if the phrase suited not, he would work it over, chin a little down, till it satisfied him.[13]

In March 1898 Rhodes sent Rudyard up-country to visit his province of Rhodesia newly pacified after the Second Matabele War and now made accessible by railway. His route was 'from Kimberley to Khama's Country and from Khama's Country east by north until he came to the great grey-green greasy Limpopo River all set about with fever-trees'.[14] Bulawayo, when Rudyard reached it, was a township of shacks scattered hopefully along the broad streets that Rhodes's visionary eye had planned for the future, where, only five years earlier, Lobengula, with the smoke-reddened eyes, had kept his savage court. So rapidly had the work of progress gone that the fashionable sport of bicycling had reached Bulawayo and, in March 1898, the proprietor of the town's cycle-shop was surprised at the appearance of a face, instantly recognizable, even in Central Africa, by the spectacles, moustache, and eyebrows. It was with a hired bicycle that Rudyard explored Bulawayo, and visited the Matoppo Hills, in the company of Sir Charles Metcalfe. At the end of the month he returned by way of Johannesburg with a bagful of Matabele curiosities for Carrie and the children, and in April they returned to England.[15]

In September Rudyard fulfilled one of his wishes, by going for a summer cruise with the Channel Squadron. They made a rendezvous in Bantry Bay where Rudyard went ashore, his first landing in Ireland. Students of Kipling's style might do well to study his original journal of the voyage (now in the New York Public Library); it is two or three times as long as the version which appeared in print as *A Fleet in Being,* and shows how he got his effects, by skilful cutting.

For Rudyard himself, as the author of 'McAndrew's Hymn', the visit to the fleet was a personal triumph ending with a party in the wardroom of the flagship, where he recited some of the *Barrack-Room Ballads* and was carried round the room shoulder-high. Rudyard was as much at ease among the ratings on the lower deck, where, on 14th September, he was talking to a seaman when the news came round the ship that Kitchener had defeated the Khalifa at Omdurman, so that Gordon's death was at last avenged. 'Well,' said the seaman, 'we've waited about long enough, 'aven't we?' and then, 'This ought to make the French a bit sickish.'

The Battle of Omdurman was followed by a clash with the French on the Upper Nile — the Fashoda Incident, which ended with a French withdrawal in Africa and renewed negotiations in Europe. By then Kitchener had made his plans for reorganizing the Sudan, his first concern being to appeal for funds with which to found a college at Khartoum. This called forth an immediate tribute from Kipling:

For Allah created the English mad — the maddest of all mankind!

They do not consider the Meaning of Things; they consult not creed nor clan.
Behold, they clap the slave on the back, and behold, he ariseth a man!
They terribly carpet the earth with dead, and before their cannon cool,
They walk unarmed by twos and threes to call the living to school.

Lord Kitchener to Rudyard Kipling

December 14, 1898

DEAR MR. RUDYARD KIPLING,
I wish to express my thanks to you for the poem on the Memorial College at Khartoum. I feel that you have greatly assisted me in the object I have in view and am very grateful. I feel sure the College will do a great deal of good throughout Northern Africa.
Yours truly,
KITCHENER OF KHARTOUM.[16]

The first crisis of imperialism became acute in 1898. 'One had a sense of "a sound of a going in the tops of the mulberry trees — of things moving into position as troops move".'[11] It was in South Africa that Rudyard felt this stir, and the personality of Rhodes revealed to him the spirit of the age.

No man had done more than Kipling to stimulate interest in the opening-up of the new worlds in the east and south. He never doubted the validity of western civilization, never lapsed into sentiment over the supposed virtues of savages; but it was the spread of law, literacy, communications, useful arts that he applauded, not the enlargement of frontiers. The Flag of England stood for service and sacrifice, not for racial superiority. The true sanction of Dominion (the phrase recalls John Wycliffe) was not national pride but 'a humble and a contrite heart'. Civilizing the world was a worthwhile task, and though likely to be thankless, a task in which all might join if they would accept the Law. Rhodes, in his chastened mood after the failure of the Jameson Raid, was fully occupied with agricultural reform at the Cape, with railway construction in Rhodesia, with land-settlement, with the Cape-to-Cairo telegraph which was to be a pilot-line for the Cape-to-Cairo Railway. Rhodes immersed in plans for material progress rather than in politics, was the leader Kipling adhered to.

The breaking-point was not in the Sudan, nor in the Transvaal, but in Cuba where, on 15th February 1898, the U.S. battleship *Maine* was destroyed by an explosion. Whoever was responsible, the Spaniards were blamed, and the Spanish-American War ensued. Spanish rule in Cuba and the Philippines seemed to the Americans, as Boer rule in the Transvaal seemed to the British, unjustified because anti-progressive and, as in the case of the Transvaal so in the case of Cuba, the sentimental popular appeal was thought, by liberal critics, to mask the schemes of the commercial men. At least the hysteric fit of imperialism produced the same phenomena in America in 1898, and in England a year later. Kipling's prayer, though unheeded, was never more apposite:

> If, drunk with sight of power, we loose
> Wild tongues that have not Thee in awe,
> Such boastings as the Gentiles use, . . .

The Kiplings had landed in England to learn that Spain and the United States were at war, and it is significant that, on the night of their arrival in London, John Hay the American Minister came to visit them at their hotel. Three days later Hay and Kipling dined at the Savoy with Rhodes who had come to England a few weeks earlier. The Spanish War drew England and America closer together and there was even talk of an alliance.

But at the same time Germany declared her policy of naval rivalry with Britain by the new Navy Law, and in Kipling's eyes it was sea-power that counted most. He had satirized the Kaiser in an early ballad ('An Imperial Rescript', 1890), and continued to regard his political vagaries with contempt. At this time Rudyard mistrusted the continental states. The well-intentioned moves of the Czar towards a general treaty of arbitration and disarmament, a few months later, provoked the fierce satire:

'Make ye no truce with Adam-zad — the Bear that walks like a Man!'[18]

And there is evidence that even the French, for whom Rudyard cultivated such strong sentiments of affection, were out of favour with him in 1898 and 1899. He would have preferred to leave the war-lords alone.

'Keep peace with the Lords of the Jungle — the Tiger, the Panther, the Bear;
And trouble not Hathi the Silent, and mock not the Boar in his lair.'

Sea-power and the White Man's Burden were the two subjects that held Kipling's attention in 1898, and both subjects led him to Anglo-American co-operation.

What did Kipling mean by the White Man's Burden? In answering this question, we must recall that, at that time, he habitually wrote verses in contemporary colloquial language, the language of the streets. In the eighteen-nineties, the phrase, 'a white man', did not only mean a man with an unpigmented skin; it had a secondary symbolic meaning: a man with the moral standards of the civilized world. Of all Kipling's ballads, the most familiar, the most quoted, the most often parodied was 'Gunga Din', a ballad so hackneyed that it is difficult to regard it now with an unprejudiced eye. It presented a cockney soldier's comment on a dark-skinned hero, 'the finest man I knew', and what the soldier says is:

> An' for all 'is dirty 'ide
> 'E was white, clear white, inside.

These words were not pretty, and were not physiologically informative, nor were they meant to be; but they were perfectly intelligible as the language of the people. The image of the 'white man' and his code of conduct appears repeatedly in Kipling's verse and prose, and always with a secondary as well as a primary connotation.

No one will assert that Rhodes and Kipling and Theodore Roosevelt believed in the political equality of all men, regardless of their social status, as it is asserted today; they would have contemptuously rejected any such notion. It is equally unjust to suppose that they believed in the absolute superiority of certain racial types. They lived in a world, in which the British and the Americans were immeasurably the most progressive of nations; in which their standards of conduct prevailed wherever civilization spread; in which they were in fact spreading those standards all over the world. The partition of Africa, of South-East Asia, and of the Pacific, the revelation by explorers of the last secrets on the earth's surface, the linking of all the world's seaports by telegraph cables and steamship routes, the crossing of all continents by railways, the bridge-building, the engineering, and the commerce: these astonishing achievements made a revolution in history unlike anything that had ever happened before, and Kipling's genius had revealed to his generation what it was that they had done.

It had been substantially a British achievement. British rule in India which Kipling, as a young man, had light-heartedly explained and exposed to the understanding of the world was the training-school where the 'white men' had learned the nature of their mission. The moment had come, in 1898, to call in the New World; the other half of the English-speaking race — 'white men' too — should join in the task.

The word that Kipling spoke in this crisis was again composed to the rhythm of a hymn-tune, and the language was again biblical. The theme was Empire and, with characteristic recklessness, he inserted a phrase or two that shocked the strait-laced:

> Take up the White Man's burden —
> Send forth the best ye breed —
> Go bind your sons to exile
> To serve your captives' need.

It was the first appearance in print of the famous phrase which was to echo round the world for fifty years, released in an appeal to the American people to join in the world-wide task of extending 'the Law' and all it implied to the remoter regions of the earth.

Their short campaign against Spain, undertaken — rightly or wrongly — in a crusading mood, to free the Spanish colonies from misgovernment, had ended after a few weeks' fighting, with the consequence that America found herself a naval and colonial power. What were the conquerors to do with Cuba and the Philippines which had fallen so suddenly into their hands? Just like the other colonial powers, the Americans found that — willy-nilly — they must face the problems of empire; they could not disengage. In the Philippine Islands (as on a huger scale in British India) there were peoples at every stage of culture, from Filipinos who had been good Catholics for ten generations to jungle tribes still in the Stone Age, and it was true enough, though tactless, of Kipling to point out that the Americans must

> . . . wait in heavy harness,
> On fluttered folk and wild —
> Your new-caught, sullen peoples,
> Half devil and half child.

These phrases, perhaps the best-remembered lines in the poem, need the corrective of what he displayed as the prize of imperialism; it is a task to be done without material reward, without thanks, without even a confident hope of success.

> Take up the White Man's burden —
> And reap his old reward:
> The blame of those ye better,
> The hate of those ye guard —

> And when your goal is nearest
> The end for others sought,
> Watch Sloth and heathen Folly
> Bring all your hope to nought.

Nor are those who take up the burden to suppose that imperial rule is anything but drudgery — 'no tawdry rule of kings'. The inducement lies only in the sense of duty; the burden comes 'to search your manhood'; and the justification will be

> edged with dear-bought wisdom,
> The judgment of your peers!

By 22nd November 'The White Man's Burden' was at last finished to Rudyard's satisfaction, and his first use of it was to send a copy to Theodore Roosevelt who had just been elected Vice-President of the United States.

T. Roosevelt to H. Cabot Lodge

January 12, 1899

I send you an advance copy of a poem by Kipling which is rather poor poetry, but good sense from the expansionist standpoint.

H. Cabot Lodge to T. Roosevelt

January 14, 1899

Thanks for the advance copy of Kipling's poem. I like it. I think it is better poetry than you say, apart from the sense of the verses.[19]

The poem appeared in the London *Times* on 4th February and on the following day in the New York *Sun* and *Tribune*. On the 6th the American Senate voted by a sufficient majority to take over the administration of the Philippines; and not too soon, because in the same week a revolt broke out in Luzon against the American military occupation.

It was Rudyard's usual practice to run some verse and prose work side by side. While he was polishing 'The White Man's Burden' in November, he also had in hand two more 'Stalky' stories. One of them which he intended as an introduction to the series, explaining how 'Stalky' won his nickname, did not satisfy the author and was rejected from the volume called *Stalky & Co*. The other story, 'The Flag of his Country', reflected, in the medium of a tale for boys, the topics that just then ruled the author's emotions; it describes a schoolboy's reactions to patriotic propaganda. No liberal pacifist has ever scarified the wordy exponents of lip-service to loyalty more ferociously than 'Stalky' and his friends; and, in this story, there is no doubt when the author is speaking with his own voice. No character in Kipling's portrait gallery is more cruelly satirized or more heartily condemned

than the 'impeccable conservative M.P.', whom 'Stalky' described as
a 'jelly-bellied flag-flapper', when he addressed the College on the
subject of patriotism.

> With a large and healthy hand he tore down . . . veils, and trampled
> them under the well-intentioned foot of eloquence. In a raucous voice
> he cried aloud little matters like the hope of Honour and the dream of
> Glory, that boys do not discuss even with their most intimate equals. . . .
> He pointed to them shining goals, with fingers which smudged out all
> radiance on all horizons. He profaned the most secret places of their
> souls with outcries and gesticulations.[20]

Strange that Kipling who, so consistently and so powerfully, derided
and condemned these goings-on, should often be accused of promoting
them! That, in fact, was his comment on the jingoism of 1898. Five
years passed before Rudyard could estimate the effect of his words upon
American policy. At the end of Roosevelt's first term as President,
he wrote to Rudyard about his attempt to take up the White Man's
Burden; it was on this record that he stood, and was elected, for a
second term.

Theodore Roosevelt to Rudyard Kipling

1 November 1904

I have done a good many things in the past three years. . . . It is natural
that some people should have been alienated by each thing I did, and the
aggregate of all that have been alienated may be more than sufficient
to overthrow me. Thus, in dealing with the Philippines I have first the
jack-fools who seriously think that any group of pirates and head-hunters
needs nothing but independence in order that it may be turned into a
dark-hued New England town-meeting, and then the entirely practical
creatures who join with these extremists because I do not intend that
the islands shall be exploited for corrupt purposes.

I have accomplished certain definite things. I would consider myself
a hundred times over repaid if I had nothing more to my credit than
Panama and the coaling-stations in Cuba. So that you see my frame
of mind is a good deal like that of your old Viceroy when he addressed
the new Viceroy.[21]

CHAPTER XII

LAST VISIT TO THE UNITED STATES (1898–99)

MERROW DOWN (1902)

I

'There runs a road by Merrow Down —
    A grassy track to-day it is —
An hour out of Guildford town,
    Above the river Wey it is.

'Here, when they heard the horse-bells ring,
    The ancient Britons dressed and rode
To watch the dark Phœnicians bring
    Their goods along the Western Road.

      .   .   .

'But long and long before that time
    (When bison used to roam on it)
Did Taffy and her Daddy climb
    That Down, and had their home on it.

      .   .   .

'The Wey, that Taffy called Wagai,
    Was more than six times bigger then;
And all the Tribe of Tegumai
    They cut a noble figure then!

II

'Of all the Tribe of Tegumai
    Who cut that figure, none remain, —
On Merrow Down the cuckoos cry —
    The silence and the sun remain.

'But as the faithful years return
    And hearts unwounded sing again,
Comes Taffy dancing through the fern
    To lead the Surrey spring again.

'Her brows are bound with bracken-fronds,
    And golden elf-locks fly above;
Her eyes are bright as diamonds
    And bluer than the sky above.

'In moccasins and deer-skin cloak,
  Unfearing, free and fair she flits,
And lights her little damp-wood smoke
  To show her Daddy where she flits.

'For far — oh, very far behind,
  So far she cannot call to him,
Comes Tegumai alone to find
  The daughter that was all to him!'

THE summer of 1898 was marred for Rudyard by a domestic blow.
Sir Edward Burne-Jones, his dear 'Uncle Ned', died suddenly in
London on 17th June, and his ashes were buried in the little church at
Rottingdean, a few yards across the green from 'The Elms'. In his
last years, Burne-Jones had achieved great fame and success, recognized
by a baronetcy, but had remained the same shy domestic man, so
difficult to draw out in conversation, so well worth drawing out. His
occasional letters, 'wild, nonsensical "lark" letters', revealed a side to
his character that the public never supposed to exist in this grave Pre-
Raphaelite. All the family assembled at Rottingdean, and Rudyard,
Stan, 'Uncle Crom', and the others in turn watched the dead man's
ashes through the night before the funeral. Rudyard wrote in great
unhappiness to C. E. Norton about his loss. Uncle Ned had been, he
said, 'more to me than any other man. He changed my life by his
visits down here.' That was now over, and Aunt Georgie, living alone
at 'North End House', drew even closer to the Kiplings whom she
consulted about writing her husband's life. Her little granddaughter,
Angela Mackail, came several times to stay with her relatives that
autumn, and from Angela's childish memories we can derive a picture
of the Kiplings at a new angle.

The three Kipling children, Josephine, Elsie, and John were about the
same age as our nursery three. Josephine very fair-haired and blue-eyed,
was my bosom friend, and though we both adored her father, the stronger
bond of patriotism drew us yet more firmly together as Cavaliers against
Cousin Ruddy's whole-hearted impersonation of a Roundhead. . . . The
war between Cavaliers and Roundheads raged furiously as long as the
Kiplings were at Rottingdean, Josephine and I leading forlorn hopes against
the Regicide and being perpetually discomfited by his superior guile.

During those long warm summers Cousin Ruddy used to try out the
Just So Stories on a nursery audience. Sometimes Josephine and I would
be invited into his study, a pleasant bow-windowed room, where Cousin
Ruddy sat at his work-table looking exactly like the profile portrait of him
that Uncle Phil painted.

The *Just So Stories* are a poor thing in print compared with the fun of hearing them told in Cousin Ruddy's deep unhesitating voice. There was a ritual about them, each phrase having its special intonation which had to be exactly the same each time and without which the stories are dried husks. There was an inimitable cadence, an emphasis of certain words, an exaggeration of certain phrases, a kind of intoning here and there which made his telling unforgettable.[1]

Whenever there were young children within call, Rudyard cultivated their society and told them stories. That was his pleasure, which did not check the regular work he had on hand. The volume called *The Day's Work,* containing his short stories written in Vermont, was passed for press and published in 1898. A dramatized version of *The Light that Failed* was also approved, and produced a little later by Forbes-Robertson. Rudyard completed a batch of 'Stalky' stories and sent them off to his agent for publication in monthly magazines. On the very next day he turned again to *Kim,* his fourth attempt to knock that picaresque romance into printable shape. He paid a visit to Tisbury to consult the 'Pater' about it, and spent some days with the Baldwins in Worcestershire. Back at Rottingdean, his evenings were spent with Aunt Georgie, or at the Boys' Social Club he had founded in the village.

The year ended in gloom with bad news from Rudyard's parents. Trix and her husband had come home from India after many years during which she had been at the hub of Simla society, as gracious as her mother and far more beautiful. A person of extreme sensibility — imaginative and nervous — she was, in the expression of those days, 'psychic', so unworldly that she seemed sometimes to move in a land of phantoms. In December her mind gave way, and it became necessary to place her under her mother's care at Tisbury; the happiness of the family square was shattered.

At rather short notice the Kiplings decided not to winter in the south that year but to pay a visit to the United States. Carrie wished to see her mother, and Rudyard had business to attend to, as a tiresome dispute over copyrights had arisen with a New York publisher.

But to take a family of young children across the North Atlantic in midwinter gave Rudyard some qualms of anxiety. His mother advised against it and was overruled by Carrie.

> When the darkened Fifties dip to the North,
>   And frost and the fog divide the air,
> And the day is dead at his breaking-forth,
>   Sirs, it is bitter beneath the Bear![2]

In frost and fog they left Liverpool for their roughest passage, meeting a full gale in mid-Atlantic. All three children and their nurse were very sick, and the two little girls developed colds which weakened them distressingly. On 2nd February when the family landed at New York they were detained for two hours at a draughty custom-house, pestered by reporters to whom they would say nothing, so that, by the time they reached the Hotel Grenoble in West 56th Street, Carrie was seriously concerned for the children. Luckily the faithful De Forests had met them at the dock, and, at the hotel, Carrie found her mother and her sister Josephine who had recently married Theo Dunham, a rising doctor. The children grew worse; their cases were now diagnosed as whooping-cough with complications, not easy complaints to care for in a city hotel, while outside in the streets there were blizzards of snow. Rudyard hardly had time to notice that the newspapers were full of quotation and comment that week, inspired or provoked by 'The White Man's Burden'. By 8th February Rudyard and Carrie were in 'great anxiety' and on that day Carrie, too, fell ill, with a high temperature. Dr. Dunham was always at hand and Rudyard was comforted when Conland arrived to stand by his friends. The news he brought from Brattleboro was less encouraging. Beatty Balestier had announced to the press that he was coming to New York to sue his brother-in-law for $50,000, on a charge of malicious prosecution three years since.[3]

Carrie's illness did not last long, or she mastered it for the sake of the children. By the 12th she was up and about and, during the following week, she and Rudyard were able to attend to the social and business matters which had brought them to New York, travelling, with delighted astonishment, in an 'electric cab'. On the 20th, as the weather was milder, they even took the children for an outing in Central Park, and visited the office of Doubleday & McClure.

There was much business to be done. There was the house, 'Naulakha', to be disposed of — or reoccupied; family affairs to be settled, and a new and very serious campaign to be fought over Rudyard's American copyrights. A. P. Watt had at last succeeded in securing the rights in Rudyard's old articles written for the Allahabad *Pioneer,* and all that he was willing to keep in print was reissued in the volume *From Sea to Sea,* fully protected by copyright at last. At the same time, friendly discussions persisted between Rudyard and the American publishing house of Scribner's, who were making slow progress with the complete edition of his works. Frank Doubleday, the moving spirit in this scheme, had issued twelve volumes of the *Outward Bound* edition in 1897. He had tried to make it inclusive, while Rudyard, as usual, had done his best to suppress his juvenile

trifles. Frank had urged him to revise the early work and Rudyard
had preferred to leave his past alone. Frank had pushed on, while
Lockwood Kipling, the true craftsman, had taken his time, ever striving
for perfection in the production of his illustrations.

When Frank left Scribner's in order to set up his own publishing
house of Doubleday & McClure, the *Outward Bound* edition hung fire.
Again as in 1890 Kipling was out-smarted by one of the classical
American publishers, who kept within the rules of trade practice while
doing what Kipling thought plain piracy. No less a firm than
Putnam's planned to put upon the market a rival to the *Outward
Bound* edition which seemed to be at a stop. There were all sorts of
Kipling pieces not covered by American copyright, and all sorts of ways
of acquiring a limited right, within the letter of the law, to print the
rest, in a limited edition. They accordingly set to work, quite openly,
to issue the *Brushwood Boy* edition, in competition with Scribner's.
The commencement of long legal proceedings against Putnam's was
the major part of Kipling's business in America in 1899, so far as the
state of his domestic affairs allowed.*

When Rudyard came back to his hotel from the Century Club on
20th February, Carrie noticed that he was dull and feverish. Next
day, when he was seriously ill, Theo Dunham diagnosed the case as
'inflammation in one lung'; called in a specialist, Dr. Janeway; and
engaged a night-nurse.

> An anxious night and more anxious day [wrote Carrie in her diary
> on the 22nd]. Rud so good and patient — sleeps much — good friends
> and helping hands, and I feel how everyone Rud has ever spoken to has
> loved him, and is glad and happy to help do for him.

On the 22nd he was conscious and quiet, while little Josephine was
in a fever, with a high temperature. Carrie decided to take her away
from the hotel to the De Forests' house on Long Island, a parting
which was 'a moment of conscious agony'.

From 23rd February until 17th April there are but two short entries
in Carrie Kipling's diary, the longest intermission since her marriage.
There she was, in an uptown New York hotel, weakened after her own
bout of fever, in charge of two children — one aged three years, the
other aged eighteen months — both with the whooping-cough, torn
with anxiety for her darling elder daughter, her doors besieged by press
reporters, her irresponsible brother Beatty threatening her with an

---

* The legal proceedings were not completed until 1901, when the United States
Court of Appeal gave judgment, with costs, for the defendant. The case, which cost
Kipling over £1000, hardened his prejudice against the publishing trade, even though
Putnam's decided not to proceed with the *Brushwood* edition.

action, her husband's affairs deeply involved in legal complications, and her husband fighting for his life — delirious for many days.

Carrie Kipling to C. E. Norton

February 22, 1899

Rud is rather ill. I trust the papers will not exaggerate it. . . . His simple life and decent habits, they say, will count in his favour, but his lifelong tendency to fever makes him rather a difficult patient. I have arranged to give the papers a daily bulletin which is all I know.

All who were near her commented on the iron resolution with which she took charge of everything. In addition to the day- and night-nurses who attended Rudyard, she engaged a third nurse for Elsie who showed signs of following her sister into pneumonia. But Elsie recovered quickly, and it was almost a relief to add to this news that Baby John had *only* a slight bronchitis. Two doctors, Dunham and Janeway, were giving almost their whole time to Rudyard while Conland took over the case of little Josephine. Business affairs fell to Frank Doubleday, a devoted friend, who neglected his own profession to become secretary and manager to Carrie. After the 21st, when the news leaked out, there were always fifteen or twenty reporters in the hotel lobbies clamouring for news. Frank took them in hand, protecting Carrie from interference and feeding them, every few hours, with news-bulletins which were flashed all over the world. He had a vast correspondence to deal with — inquiries, congratulations, and — at last — condolences.

Now began a demonstration of affection and sympathy for Kipling such as no other writer, perhaps, has ever experienced. It was headline news in all the papers of the world that the inflammation had spread from Rudyard's right lung to the left, and from the lower to the upper lobes. On Friday, 24th, the doctors admitted that his condition was 'serious'. On Saturday, respiration was 'alarmingly difficult', and the bulletin admitted the 'greatest apprehension for the outcome' of his illness. Throughout the week-end Rudyard was delirious, with his mind wandering on frustrated journeys in search of R. L. Stevenson, or endless voyages with Conland in a wooden ship, or riding with armies across the steppes of Central Asia, or he was protesting against his treatment by New York crowds when put on trial with no bail allowed. On Monday, 27th, the doctors could say no more than that they were 'not without hope'. The crisis came next day. After midnight on the 28th his temperature fell and he lapsed into a natural sleep for a few hours; on Wednesday the doctors admitted improvement; and by Saturday 4th March he was out of danger though desperately weak.

The faithful Frank Doubleday sent the good news to Rudyard's relatives in England, and then indeed the letters and telegrams poured in like a flood — too soon. While the progress of little Josephine's illness followed the pattern of her father's, a day or two behind him, she had not his reserve of strength. Always hampered in health by a delicate digestion, she was unable during this time of weakness to retain nourishment. They dared not tell her father that something like dysentery had set in, and as he passed out of the shadow, she passed into it. Carrie left Rudyard's bedside for one day to visit her child at the De Forests' house.

Sunday, March 5th.
    I saw Josephine 3 times today — morning, afternoon, and at 10 P.M. for the last time. She was conscious for a moment and sent her love to 'Daddy and all'.

Monday, March 6th.
    Josephine left us at 6.30 this morning.

The doctors forbade that Rudyard in his weakness should be told of this calamity, but it could not be long withheld. An appeal was made to the reporters not to publicize the child's death and, though it could not be kept out of the daily papers, it had little news-value beside the state of health of the world's most popular author. When Carrie went from the funeral straight to his bedside, remembering in time that she was dressed in black, she snatched up a scarlet shawl as she entered the room and threw it around her shoulders so that he would ask no question. How and when she broke the news to him was their own secret. Months passed before he recovered from his illness; from the shock of his daughter's death he never recovered; nor did Carrie. Reserved and self-contained as their family life had always been, it now became more exclusive.

Nevertheless the whole world had offered its sympathy, with demonstrations of a kind which, as a rule, only royalty knows. While Rudyard lay in delirium, unconscious of the tribute paid to him, hushed crowds gathered outside the Hotel Grenoble blocking the traffic in Seventh Avenue. Prayers were offered in the New York churches, and people were seen kneeling in prayer before the hotel door. It happened that no political crisis, no massacre or earthquake occurred in those days to divert the world's attention from the door behind which a poet lay at the point of death, no other news of moment except the illness of Pope Leo XIII. The *Pall Mall Gazette* splashed the two news-items across its posters, ' KIPLING AND POPE '.

Among the hundreds of letters and telegrams that came when he was reported past his crisis, the most valued were from the family, and on these we need not linger. To posterity interest lies in the uncounted messages from casual acquaintances and unknown admirers: from George Meredith and John Ruskin, from G. F. Watts and Holman Hunt, from Henry Irving and Beerbohm Tree, from Lord Dufferin and Lord Curzon, from Theodore Roosevelt and John Hay, from Conan Doyle and Rider Haggard, from Mark Twain and Marie Corelli, from Cecil Rhodes and the Editor of *The Times* and the German Kaiser.

Rudyard would have been more pleased, perhaps, by the letters from lesser folks: from Kay Robinson, from Stanley de Brath with whom he had once tramped the Himalaya Road, from the crew of H.M.S. *Pelorus,* and from the Sergeants of the Suffolk Regiment, from the Soldiers' Institute at Allahabad, from the Council of his old school at Westward Ho!, or from the boys of St. Edmund's, Canterbury — there were dozens of such messages — but they came when he was too ill to see them, and were not shown him until his bereavement had made them a mockery. His nearer friends has hastened to write condolences displacing their congratulations. What could they say?

Henry James was more than usually emotional and illegible:

Henry James to Rudyard Kipling

March 6, 1899

MY DEAR DAEMONIC INDESTRUCTIBLE YOUTH,

You are a good one, and your wife is, if possible, a better, and your two doctors between them are the best ones of all. . . . You have been magnificent and have made us all live with our hearts in our mouth. I fold you both in my arms. You have visited the mountains of the moon and some back on a tense wire, in the cold light of that satellite and with every opera-glass on earth fixed on you — with no balancing-pole but your own inimitable genius. What you must have got out of it! . . .

Believe me, my dear boy, your very constant and jubilant old friend.

Henry James to Carrie Kipling

March 8, 1899

I wrote last night to Rudyard — but my letter will have had the effect of a jubilation so mistimed that I now wish I could recall it. . . . Dear little delightful vanished Josephine, dear little surrendered, sacrificed soul! Forgive this incoherent expression — I am only thinking of her being worsted in the battle, and of the so happy form in which I saw her last winter at Rottingdean. But how can I even seem to allude to what you feel. . . . I believe in you [both] up to the hilt.

The consolations of religion could give little help to this free-think-ing family. Even the ‘ Pater ’, writing very tenderly, could not find it in his heart to say more than: 'I can't help fancying all this weight of love may count for some thing', but one minister of religion ventured to write to Carrie as a pastor:

The Rev. C. O. Day to Carrie Kipling

BRATTLEBORO, March 8, 1899

I know too well the profound faith of Mr. Kipling and his unfaltering courage, to doubt as to his power to accept the bereavement. He will feel that a new world is his by possession; one of his own has claimed it for him and flies his flag there. A new wonder will arise in his soul, and new sweetness and depth in his poetry. He will reveal some new, clear, indubitable vision upon which many mourners for children will look and be comforted.

It was a long and dreary convalescence, cheered only by many signs of friendship. At Easter Rudyard was able to authorize a reply to the world-wide expression of sympathy in an open letter which was issued by Reuter's to unnumbered newspapers.

Will you allow me through your columns to attempt some acknowledgment of the wonderful sympathy, affection, and kindness shown towards me in my recent illness, as well as of the unfailing courtesy that controlled its expression? I am not strong enough to answer letters in detail, so must take this means of thanking, as humbly as sincerely, the countless people of goodwill throughout the world, who have put me under a debt I can never hope to repay.[5]

The Kiplings then withdrew from the public notice for many months, so far, that is to say, as the tiresome lawsuit with Putnam's permitted. A. P. Watt came over from London, as did Lockwood Kipling, to confer with lawyers and to give what comfort they could to Rudyard, who was still under the care of nurses by night and day. On 17th April Frank Doubleday carried him off to a private hotel at Lakewood, 'standing the journey better than we hoped'. The Hotel Grenoble, which had endured much, took the opportunity to give the rest of the family notice, since two children with the whooping-cough had exhausted their patience. By 6th May Dr. Conland was able to report that Rudyard's lung was healed, but ordered him six months' rest; he also categorically forbade Rudyard to spend any more winters in England. When in June the whole family were fit to return home, their rendezvous was Frank's house, at Cold Springs, and on their last evening Rudyard was even well enough to attend a farewell dinner in a New York restaurant with Conland, Sam McClure, De Forest, Frank, and the 'Pater'. Rudyard was 'a little more cheerful', wrote the 'Pater' to Mrs. Norton. 'I find his dim time brighter than the best of many men I know.'

With that the Kiplings said their last farewells to the United States. 'Never was such kindness shown', wrote Carrie, and on Frank Doubleday's part it was not yet over. He accompanied them across the Atlantic with his wife, and did not return to his own affairs until he had seen them settled at Rottingdean, still protecting Rudyard from the hated glare of publicity. 'Many friends came to see us off,' wrote Carrie, 'but reporters do not get a look at him.' It was different on the ship where 'folks with no manners' were a great trouble to her, snapshotting with the hand-cameras which were coming into use. By 24th June they were back at 'The Elms', listlessly taking up the threads of life.

An admirer, Andrew Carnegie the steel magnate, had expressed his sympathy to Rudyard by offering him the use of a small house in the Highlands, and in accepting his invitation Carrie prudently improved the occasion by touching Carnegie for a subscription towards the boys' club at Rottingdean.[6]

In Scotland Rudyard regained physical well-being and slowly turned again to his work. At Creich he wrote the dedicatory verses to *Stalky & Co.;* 'Let us now praise famous men . . .'

> Wherefore praise we famous men
> From whose bays we borrow —
> They that put aside To-day —
> All the joys of their To-day —
> And with toil of their To-day
> Bought for us To-morrow!

The routine of life, when the Kiplings returned to Rottingdean, was changed in the one important respect that there was now a private secretary, Sarah Anderson, who became the mainstay of the household. Her story, which she never told, would have been worth reading, for she had first been secretary to John Ruskin, then to Meredith, and then had worked for George Moore; the model of discretion, she destroyed all her papers, saving nothing for posterity.

However weakened, however saddened, Rudyard did not slacken in his interests. That autumn, after Frank Doubleday had gone, Phil Burne-Jones was working at the portrait now in the National Portrait Gallery and, as soon as he had done with Rudyard, he began the portrait of Carrie which now hangs at 'Bateman's'. Rudyard was delighted with his picture and wrote to Norton: 'Phil's portrait of me is a Regular Stunner and shows specially well in the reproduction.

I resent the sleek baldness of my head, but the intellectual air and the tummy are beyond dispute.'   When not engaged on the portrait Phil and Rudyard amused themselves with a hand printing-press which they had installed at 'The Elms', and it was at this time, too, that Rudyard made his first experiments with a hired motor-car, at a very early date in motoring history.

The publication of *Stalky & Co.,* on 6th October 1899, brought Rudyard back into the headlines six months after the crisis of his illness.   Though all the morning papers gave it space, the reception was mixed, and perhaps no other Kipling book has been more variously estimated.   There was no doubt that schoolboys swallowed it with gusto, and continued to do so for generations, while their elders often found it distasteful, even nauseating.   'A more odious picture of school life can seldom have been drawn', wrote Somerset Maugham. But Aunt Georgie liked it, and Cousin Florence liked it, and 'Uncle Crom' Price, the hero of the tale, liked it, and with them were some hundreds of thousands of other adults with strong digestions.

It added much to the Kipling cult because, alone among his works of fiction, it was plainly founded upon fact.   Since all the characters, if not the events, were real, the book led to an immediate investigation for origins.   The souvenir-hunters located 'Uncle Crom', in retirement; 'Old Boys' of the College proudly identified themselves with this or that character in the book; interviewers called upon Sergeant-major Schofield and found him a little pained at the figure he was made to cut as 'Foxy'; someone found out that 'Stalky' was Captain Dunsterville of the Sikhs, serving at the very time in the expedition to Pekin.   'M'Turk' came to light as Beresford, and gave an interview about 'Stalky' to a Cambridge newspaper, with a consequence that was no fault of Beresford's.   The editor was sued for damages, soon after, on a charge of fabricating news-items, and one question asked in court was whether the 'Stalky' stories were fact or fiction.   The Judge ruled them fiction, whereupon that part of the charge collapsed, except in the sense that it stimulated publicity.[7]

Kipling had now reached the height of his fame, with the inevitable consequences that his daily letter-bag was loaded down, and his path beset by sightseers.   Social invitations, most of which he declined, came showering in when he was in England.   There was a day, in the Season of 1900, when Carrie refused two dinner-invitations for the same evening, from Mrs. Humphry Ward and the Duchess of Sutherland.   No one could fly higher than that in the literary and fashionable worlds.   Much more tiresome were the trippers from Brighton who had now discovered the colony of celebrities at Rottingdean. There were times when Carrie had to force her way through crowds of gaping tourists before she could get at her own garden-gate. Rotting-dean, so full of happy memories of the three carefree years before the calamitous visit to New York, had lost its charm.

CHAPTER XIII

THE SOUTH AFRICAN WAR (1899–1902)

THE SETTLER (1903)

Here, where my fresh-turned furrows run,
  And the deep soil glistens red,
I will repair the wrong that was done
  To the living and the dead.
Here, where the senseless bullet fell,
  And the barren shrapnel burst,
I will plant a tree, I will dig a well,
  Against the heat and the thirst.

Here, in a large and a sunlit land,
  Where no wrong bites to the bone,
I will lay my hand in my neighbour's hand,
  And together we will atone
For the set folly and the red breach
  And the black waste of it all;
Giving and taking counsel each
  Over the cattle-kraal.

                .   .   .   .

Earth, where we rode to slay or be slain,
  Our love shall redeem unto life.
We will gather and lead to her lips again
  The waters of ancient strife,
From the far and the fiercely guarded streams
  And the pools where we lay in wait,
Till the corn cover our evil dreams
  And the young corn our hate.

            .   .   .   .

Here, in the waves and the troughs of the plains,
  Where the healing stillness lies,
And the vast, benignant sky restrains
  And the long days make wise —
Bless to our use the rain and the sun
  And the blind seed in its bed,
That we may repair the wrong that was done
  To the living and the dead!

THE year 1899, which had been so disastrous for the Kiplings, ended gloomily. It was rather a doleful Christmas, with influenza running through the family, bad news from Tisbury of 'Trix's' health, annoyance from New York at the state of the Putnam lawsuit. Rudyard was ill again and, as soon as legal business allowed it, he prepared to leave the country. All he could find to say as a closing note to his wife's diary for the year was: 'I owe my life to Carrie'.

During his long illness the situation had taken a turn for the worse in South Africa, and before the year's end the expected war had broken out. Actually, it was Kruger who, on 9th October, sent an ultimatum to Lord Salisbury demanding that the Queen should ship no more troops to her African Dominions. This was followed, on 11th October, by the British declaration of war and the despatch of an Army Corps of 47,000 men to the Cape, under command of Sir Redvers Buller. Meanwhile the Boers made a brisk offensive against the supposedly overbearing empire, and on every front the British garrisons were thrown on their guard. Mafeking in the far north, and Kimberley on the western frontier, were invested, and the largest concentration of British troops was soon besieged at Ladysmith in the northern salient angle of Natal. This was the decisive point of the first campaign and it was towards Ladysmith that General Buller directed the concentration of his Army Corps from England.

The first counter-moves were made by the British early in December with conspicuous lack of success. Every new war produces its own surprises, and no army before 1899 had marched into the face of well-aimed fire from magazine rifles using smokeless powder; no one could foresee its effect. Boer tactics proved to be as effective as Boer strategy was futile and in one week three British armies were soundly defeated at three widely separated points on the vast front, the most alarming being General Buller's defeat at Colenso. These were staggering blows, far more violent than the battle of Majuba, twenty years before, which had been followed by a British withdrawal; but times had changed and there was now no suggestion of submission. The Army Reserve was called out in England and Lord Roberts, England's greatest soldier, was despatched to the Cape as Commander-in-Chief.

Was Kruger fighting for liberty? Or for domination? In his own Transvaal, his own *burghers* were a minority of the white population, while the *uitlanders* mostly of British origin, created three-quarters of the States' wealth, paid three-quarters of the taxes, and were allowed no more political rights than the Kaffir labourers whose interest no politician of those days put forward. Milner claimed for the *uitlanders,* in form, only the same political rights that Afrikaners enjoyed in British Natal. In principle, and he made no secret of it, he took a

longer view. Emancipation for *uitlanders* meant progressive government, efficient administration, the federation of all South Africa under
the British flag. This was a political objective, and it was fair to
regard the struggle between Milner and Kruger as a combat for
control of all South Africa.

There was another factor in the sum, a factor that Milner and
Rhodes each interpreted in his own way; it was the world-wide up-
surging of the generation for whom Kipling in the previous decade
had found a voice. The bridge-builders, the engineers, the road-
makers, the miners, the prospectors, the ranchers — the men of the
new age were led by a new star:

> The gull shall whistle in his wake, the blind wave break in fire.
> He shall fulfil God's utmost will, unknowing his desire.
> And he shall see old planets change and alien stars arise,
> And give the gale his seaworn sail in shadow of new skies.
> Strong lust of gear shall drive him forth and hunger arm his hand,
> To win his food from the desert rude, his pittance from the sand.
> His neighbours' smoke shall vex his eyes, their voices break his rest.
> He shall go forth till south is north, sullen and dispossessed.
> He shall desire loneliness and his desire shall bring,
> Hard on his heels, a thousand wheels, a People and a King.
> He shall come back on his own track, and by his scarce-cooled camp
> There shall he meet the roaring street, the derrick and the stamp:
> There he shall blaze a nation's ways with hatchet and with brand,
> Till on his last-won wilderness an Empire's outposts stand! [1]

'Strong lust of gear shall drive him forth and hunger arm his hand'
— indeed the motive force that peopled all the temperate regions of
the world with emigrants from Great Britain and Ireland, was set to
work by economic pressures, but not by economic pressures simply.
Rhodes was the greatest of money-spinners but love of money was a
minor element, if an element at all, in his make-up. With great
energy and longer views he typified his generation:

> We were dreamers, dreaming greatly, in the man-stifled town;
> We yearned beyond the sky-line where the strange roads go down.

When the Americans and the British embarked upon those two
campaigns, the Cuban War and the Boer War, which to the observer
to-day seem so curiously out of key, they fought with an enthusiasm
that is not easily explained away by economic catch-words. The petty
corrupt tyrannies of the Spaniards in Cuba and of the Boers in the
Transvaal were felt by enlightened men like Roosevelt and Milner to
be unworthy obstacles in the way of progress. By sweeping such
cobwebby anachronisms away, they conceived themselves to be re-

leasing the life-giving processes that would make the twentieth century and, in America as in Britain, the people supported them. With a cry of dismay, in both countries, the intellectuals of the left wing denounced this technocratic enthusiasm, these aggressive wars against weaker nations, fought, as they supposed, for the benefit of industrialists and exploiters. The Mackails at Oxford and the Nortons at Harvard alike deplored the woeful events that their friend Rudyard celebrated with such gusto, but their voices were lost in the outcry of the imperialists.

The presidential election which gave McKinley his second term, and the British General Election which retained Lord Salisbury in office — a vote of confidence for Joseph Chamberlain — demonstrated that the intellectuals were out of touch with public opinion in 1900. A far more significant symptom of real popular support for the two wars was that, in both countries, great numbers of volunteers from all classes of society offered themselves to serve overseas in campaigns that would certainly be painful and profitless for the fighting troops. Nothing like that had ever happened in either England or America before.

In his letter to C. E. Norton during the Venezuela Crisis, Kipling had taken some small comfort from the observation that a foreign war would serve to draw Britain and her colonies closer together. An outsider might have supposed that the undisciplined, democratic colonials would resent the British pressure on the two small states in South Africa, but Kipling was right. The two most advanced social democracies in the world, the colonies of New Zealand and Queensland, were the first to send 'contingents' of volunteers to fight for the Empire against the Transvaal. Australian sheep-farmers and gold-diggers certainly had no interest in the finances of Rhodes's Chartered Company. They fought for the *uitlanders,* who were 'white men' deprived of political rights by Kruger's oligarchy, and 'white men' whose manifest destiny was to unite South Africa as a free and progressive country.

In September 1899, just before the breaking-point, Rudyard was at work upon one of those pronouncements in verse which the public now expected from him, on national occasions. It was published in *The Times,* on the 29th, under the title of 'The Old Issue'. To a modern reader, steeped in the propaganda of the anti-imperialists, this poem has become almost unintelligible. A war against Kruger, Rudyard suggested, was a war for liberty, which should rally the English to their old traditions of resistance against tyranny.

> Cruel in the shadow, crafty in the sun,
> Far beyond his borders shall his teachings run.

> Sloven, sullen, savage, secret, uncontrolled,
> Laying on a new land evil of the old —
>
> Long-forgotten bondage, dwarfing heart and brain —
> All our fathers died to loose he shall bind again.

A few days later the storm broke and Rudyard immediately set himself to two tasks of war work: one was to form a volunteer company in the village at Rottingdean; the other was to raise money for the Soldiers' Families' Fund.

Henry James came over from Rye to lunch with the Kiplings at Rottingdean, on 17th October, and Carrie noted in her diary — 'nice man, much beloved'. He must have been astonished at the vitality of his 'indestructible', 'daemonic' friend, because Rudyard, that day, was hard at work on the most robust, full-blooded, verses he ever wrote. * These verses, Rudyard admitted, 'had some elements of direct appeal but lacked poetry'. He called them 'The Absent-minded Beggar' and published them in the *Daily Mail* on 31st October.

Sir Arthur Sullivan wedded the words to a tune guaranteed to pull teeth out of barrel-organs. Anybody could do what they chose with the result, recite, sing, intone or reprint, etc., on condition that they turned in all fees and profits to the main account — 'The Absent-minded Beggar Fund' which closed at about a quarter of a million [pounds sterling]. Some of this [he wrote modestly] was spent on tobacco.[2]

Having thus served their purpose, these verses were allowed to drop from sight and for many years were not admitted by the author into a 'collected' volume. Their pace and force justify their survival. It may be noted that they sound no aggressive or imperialistic note, contain no swagger or defiance, but appeal to those who stay at home to do something better than 'killing Kruger with your mouth'.

A hundred years earlier the original 'Tommy Atkins' had marched to Brighton Camp, when Napoleon's Grand Army lay at Boulogne, singing to a delicate old air the ballad of 'The Girl I left behind me'. Some soldiers even then were absent-minded beggars (the phrase is a barrack-room euphemism), and hence the theme of the new song, written to a tune that was anything but delicate.

> There are girls he married secret, asking no permission to,
>   For he knew he wouldn't get it if he did.
> There is gas and coals and vittles, and the house-rent falling due,
>   And it's more than rather likely there's a kid.
> There are girls he walked with casual. They'll be sorry now he's gone,
>   For an absent-minded beggar they will find him,

* He was also, that week, writing 'The Elephant's Child '.

But it ain't the time for sermons with the winter coming on.
  We must help the girl that Tommy's left behind him!
Cook's son — Duke's son — son of a belted Earl —
  Son of a Lambeth publican — it's all the same to-day!
Each of 'em doing his country's work
  (and who's to look after the girl?)
Pass the hat for your credit's sake,
                    and pay — pay — pay!

The public paid; and wondered what next Rudyard Kipling would produce. 'The Vampire', 'Recessional', 'The White Man's Burden', and 'The Absent-minded Beggar' made a series that dumbfounded the critics. The politicians, however, took their cue. On 14th December Lord Salisbury sent his private secretary to Rottingdean to ask whether Rudyard would accept a knighthood. Carrie noted in her diary that he declined, 'feeling he can do his work better without it. We are much pleased to be offered it however.'

Harmsworth of the *Daily Mail* (afterwards Lord Northcliffe) struck up an acquaintance with the Kiplings over 'The Absent-minded Beggar'. Naturally he wanted to give Kipling's name the utmost publicity in his campaign to raise funds, but even in this cause Kipling shrank from it. 'I should prefer my name being kept out', he wrote. 'The verses are fetching money in a wonderful way — thanks to your management — but don't make so much of their author.' [3]

On 20th January 1900 the Kiplings left England for South Africa, and on 5th February reached Cape Town to learn that the British forces in Natal had suffered another defeat, at Spion Kop.

The Mount Nelson Hotel, a huge red-brick *caravanserai* on the slope of Table Mountain, was crammed with war-reporters, sightseers, adventurers, contractors, officers' wives, and hordes of the non-combatants who crowd upon the heels of an army. All the world passed through it on the way to the Front; and there Rudyard met a group of journalists who were to become his friends: young Mr. L. S. Amery who had represented *The Times* at Kruger's capital, Percival Landon, correspondent for *The Times* with Roberts's army, Bennet Burleigh of the *Daily Telegraph,* H. A. Gwynne of Reuter's, and Julian Ralph, an American who was in Africa for the London *Daily Mail*. It was one of Lord Roberts's distinctions that he was perhaps the first general to appreciate the importance of the press in warfare and to take the journalists into his confidence. He sent for Rudyard and spent with him his last evening before leaving to take command of the army in the field.

During the next fortnight Rudyard occupied his time visiting the military hospitals, where he was doubly welcome, first as the soldiers' poet who could occasionally be persuaded to recite his ballads at a smoking-concert, secondly as the purveyor of all the comforts provided by the Absent-minded Beggar Fund. He went about loaded with the plug tobacco that the soldiers loved, and this was not all that he had to give away. As must occur at the beginning of a war, when crowds of wounded suddenly appear at the Base, shortages of all kinds were revealed in the improvised hospitals.

My note-of-hand [he said] was good for as much as I cared to take about with me. The rest followed. My telegrams were given priority by sweating R.E. sergeants from all sorts of depots. My seat in the train was kept for me by British Bayonets in their shirtsleeves. My small baggage was fought for and servilely carried by Colonial details, who are not normally meek, and I was *persona gratissima* at certain Wynberg Hospitals where the nurses found I was good for pyjamas.[4]

The first good news, after Roberts had taken hold of the campaign, reached Cape Town on 16th February. The siege of Kimberley was raised, which meant the release of Cecil Rhodes who was in the besieged town. Rudyard was one of the first to greet him, and together they set off to visit Rhodes's estates in the Western Province. When pent up in Kimberley, Rhodes had pondered over many new constructive plans, great and small, among them his plan for building a house on the Groote Schur estate which he could put at the disposal of artists or men of letters. In the first instance he would offer it to the Kiplings for as long as they cared to stay. Carrie took up this scheme with enthusiasm; on 7th March she went with Herbert Baker, the young architect to whom Rhodes gave his patronage, to select a site for the house, to be built in the Dutch Colonial style which Baker was reviving and developing. He too became a lifelong friend of the Kiplings.

Meanwhile, at the Front, Roberts followed up this success at Kimberley by striking eastwards towards Bloemfontein and, on the day after relieving Kimberley, his leading troops engaged General Cronje, the most formidable of the Boer leaders, in the long hard-fought action of Paardeberg, the decisive battle of the war — or so it seemed. Before Cronje could be forced to surrender (27th February 1900) more than 1500 British soldiers had been killed or wounded in front of his entrenchments, and a stream of wounded was passing down the railway line to Cape Town. In the middle of the battle, Rudyard went up with an ambulance train to the rail-head at Modder River, the scene of heavy fighting a few weeks earlier, and returned with a train-load of wounded, his first experience of the realities of

war. On 24th February, while on the train, he wrote a home-letter to
the dictation of a wounded soldier who had lost his right arm at
Paardeberg. This letter was sold for war charities, was reproduced in
facsimile and was widely advertised, a form of publicity that did not
please Rudyard and that he did not allow to recur.

On 12th March Lord Roberts entered Bloemfontein, the capital of
the Orange Free State, and a pause was necessary before he could
invade the Transvaal. During a halt of six weeks his army was
ravaged by typhoid and enteric fevers, against which, in those days,
there was no adequate protection.

On the day after his entry, among a hundred administrative duties,
Roberts found time to arrange for the establishment of an army newspaper, perhaps the first of its species in military history. It was set
on foot by his Press Censor, who commandeered the plant of a little
local sheet, *The Friend* of Bloemfontein, sent for four war correspondents, and told them to begin. They were Julian Ralph, Percival
Landon, H. A. Gwynne, and F. W. Buxton (of the Johannesburg
Star). Landon had the foresight to telegraph to Kipling for a contribution, and got by return some verses about the heroism of the
Irish troops, in time for publication on St. Patrick's Day. That was
not all, for on the same day, 17th March, Lord Roberts wired to
Kipling, asking him to join the staff of *The Friend*.

Rudyard spent his last day before going up the line walking with
Milner on the slopes of Table Mountain discussing policy at the Cape.
On the 21st he joined his friends at Bloemfontein, and was thus
described by Julian Ralph who was now thrown into daily intimate
contact with him:

a man of such broad build and short neck that you do not realise him to
be of the average stature, wearing a broad-brimmed, flat brown hat of
Boer pattern, and below that a brown short coat and very full trousers
to match; a vigorous figure, quick in movement as a panther, quicker
still in speech; a swinging and rolling figure with head up and hat well
back, out of the way of his sight which is ever thrown upward as if he
searched the sky while he walked. His face is quite a match for his body,
being round and broad as well as wide-eyed and alert. His eyes are its
most notable features, for they are very large and open, and each one is
arched by the bushiest black eyebrows. They are habitually reflective
and sober eyes, but, like a flash, they kindle with fun, and can equally
quickly turn dull and stony when good occasion arises.[5]

Thriving in the dry warm air, Rudyard renewed his youth; he
flung himself into the work of the office, correcting proofs, sub-editing,
and writing 'copy' with the others. 'Never again', he said, 'will

there be such a paper. Never again such a staff. Never such fine larks.'

For a fortnight he played the sub-editor with delight and energy among congenial comrades. So pleasant was their comradeship that Rudyard founded a dining-club, the 'Friendlies', with a badge and a masonic ritual which they maintained for some years, until Julian Ralph's early death. Their status was demi-official, since Lord Roberts used *The Friend* as a propaganda sheet in which to make announcements to the people of the conquered Republic. The first page was taken up with official notices; the inner pages contained campaigning news, local gossip, a few cables from overseas, and a great deal of light reading for the troops. Rudyard contributed a number of satirical pieces — 'Kopje-Book Maxims', 'Fables for the Staff', and so on, and two poems which he thought worth a place in his collected works: 'A Song of the White Men' — a still stronger version of 'The White Man's Burden' — and the generous tribute written on the death of General Joubert, the enemy's Commander-in-Chief. His hardest work was reading and editing the numerous contributions offered by soldiers, all of which he examined with care and many of which he printed. One of his best contributors was A. B. Paterson of the *Sydney Herald,* the Australian ballad-writer, whose verses, written in Kipling's own earlier manner, were as popular as Kipling's. But Rudyard had moved into a new phase and his mind was turned to something stronger than satirical light verse.

He had already made up his mind to return to England and to throw himself into the support of Milner's policy, at home. He was held in Bloemfontein a few days longer, by the duty of nursing one of his friends who had gone down with the typhoid that raged through the army. It was Julian Ralph's son and 'until we could get him into hospital', wrote Ralph, 'Mr. Kipling nursed him with consummate skill and the gentleness of a woman '.[5] But, in the last week, Rudyard allowed himself a day's holiday, to watch a battle.

Just as in Afghanistan, twenty years earlier, Lord Roberts attempted to pacify the country by detaching columns of troops to 'show the flag' in outlying districts. A small engagement ensued, the action of Karee Siding, which cost the British 180 casualties. Rudyard had long been known as the soldier's poet, the author of realistic battle-pieces, and it would have surprised many of his readers to know that this was the first time he had seen troops under fire.

Karee Siding was an inconclusive, unsatisfactory affair like many in the South African War. The general's intention was to engage the Boers frontally with a holding attack by the infantry, while mounted troops worked round both flanks to cut off their retreat. The flogged-out, ill-fed cavalry could not or would not move fast enough, and when the leading infantry — they were the East Lancashires, Mulvaney's 'Ould Regiment' — charged with fixed bayonets, they found the enemy positions abandoned and empty. The Boers had slipped away on their ponies before the trap could close behind them.

Rudyard set off with Bennet Burleigh of the *Daily Telegraph*,[6] in a Cape cart loaded with food and drink for the party from *The Friend*. Burleigh described for his paper how he and Kipling walked forward among the extended lines of riflemen, halting now and then for Kipling to distribute plugs of tobacco among the nearest soldiers. Rudyard told his own story of their approach characteristically,

the enormous pale landscape swallowed up seven thousand troops without a sign along a front of seven miles. . . . At last we came to a lone farm-house in a vale adorned with no less than five white flags. Beyond the ridge was a sputter of musketry and now and then the whoop of a field-piece. 'Here,' said my guide and guardian, 'we get out and walk.'

The farm-house (you will see in a little why I am so detailed) held two men and, I think, two women, who received us disinterestedly. We went on into a vacant world full of sunshine and distances, where now and again a single bullet sang to himself. What I most objected to was the sensation of being under aimed fire — being, as it were, required as a head. 'What are they doing this for?' I asked my friend. 'Because they think we are the Something Light Horse. They ought to be just under this slope.' I prayed that the particularly Something Light Horse would go elsewhere, which they presently did, for the aimed fire slackened and a wandering Colonial, bored to extinction, turned up with news from a far flank. 'No; nothing doing and no one to see.' Then more cracklings and a most cautious move forward to the lip of a large hollow where sheep were grazing. Some of them began to drop and kick. 'That's both sides trying sighting-shots,' said my companion. 'What range do you make it?' I asked. 'Eight hundred, at the nearest. That's close quarters nowadays. You'll never see anything closer than this. Modern rifles make it impossible. We're hung up till something cracks somewhere.' There was a decent lull for meals on both sides, interrupted now and again by sputters. Then one indubitable shell — ridiculously like a pip-squeak in that vastness but throwing up much dirt. . . . Every twenty minutes or so, one judgmatic shell pitched on our slope. We waited, seeing nothing in the emptiness, and hearing only a faint murmur as of wind along gas-jets, running in and out of the unconcerned hills.

Then pom-poms opened. These were nasty little one-pounders, ten in a belt (which usually jammed about the sixth round). On soft ground they merely thudded. On rock-face the shell breaks up and yowls like a cat. My friend for the first time seemed interested. 'If these are *their* pom-poms, it's Pretoria for us,' was his diagnosis. I looked behind me — the whole length of South Africa down to Cape Town — and it seemed very far. I felt that I could have covered it in five minutes under fair conditions, but — *not* with those aimed shots up my back. The pom-poms opened again at a bare rock-reef that gave the shells full value. For about two minutes a file of racing ponies, their tails and their riders' heads well down, showed and vanished northward. 'Our pom-poms,' said the correspondent. . . . Then to the left, almost under us, a small piece of hanging woodlands filled and fumed with our shrapnel much as a man's moustache fills with cigarette-smoke. It was most impressive and lasted for quite twenty minutes. Then silence; then a movement of men and horses from our side up the slope, and the sangar our guns had been hammering spat steady fire at them. More Boer ponies on more skylines; a last flurry of pom-poms on the right and a little frieze of far-off meek-tailed ponies, already out of rifle range.

'*Maffeesh*,' said the correspondent, and fell to writing on his knee. 'We've shifted 'em.'

Leaving our infantry to follow men on pony-back towards the Equator, we returned to the farm-house.[7]

They jogged back to Bloemfontein happily with Rudyard composing ballads in the cart: 'he was making a humming over new verses, like Robert Burns', wrote Bennet Burleigh.

The visit to the Boer farm had a sequel. Nine months later the producers of anti-British propaganda put out a story in French Switzerland which they ascribed to Rudyard himself. He was alleged to have taken part in the murder of a civilian at the farm and to have described it with gusto.[8] The continental press, just then, was flooded with lies about the British, and this tale was not more absurd than many others which were taken as true. It infuriated Rudyard who commented with asperity that what the propagandist saw was the 'reflection of his own face as he spied at our back-windows'. It gave him a notion for his own powerful but vindictive tale, 'A Sahibs' War', a hint of what the British imperialists might have done if they had behaved as they were expected to.

Throughout the war Rudyard showed admiration and even tenderness for the fighting 'burghers' on the veldt, but bitter, unrelenting hatred for the fawning non-combatants who betrayed each side in turn, for the few colonials of British origin who favoured the republican cause, for the many Afrikaners in Cape Colony who claimed protection as British subjects while openly expressing their sympathy with the rebellion which they dared not join. The point of view was common among British regular soldiers, who could hardly fail to respect the military virtues of their enemies in the field; it was quite beyond the comprehension of the average Englishman at home.

Two days after the action at Karee Siding, another British force was sharply defeated in a battle which was to alter the character of the war. Roberts had sent a column to the eastward to secure the pumping station which supplied Bloemfontein with water and, on the return march, two batteries of artillery marched into an ambush at Sanna's Post. A confused, irregular battle flared up around the waterworks and left a general impression of heroism on the part of the junior officers, but of indecision and inactivity on the part of the higher command. The British lost six guns and five hundred men.

Early on the morning of 31st March fugitives from the battle found their way back to Bloemfontein with alarming stories.

In an interval of our editorial labours [wrote Rudyard] I went out of the town and presently met the 'solitary horseman' of the novels. He was a Commissariat Sergeant — who reported that the 'flower of the British Army' had been ambushed and cut up at a place called Sanna's Post, and passed on obviously discomposed. I had imagined the flower of the Army to be busied behind me reading our paper; but a short while after, I met an officer who, in the old Indian days, was nicknamed 'the Sardine'. He was calm, but rather fuzzy as to the outline of his uniform, which was frayed and ripped by bullets. Yes, there had been trouble where he came from, but he was fuller for the movement of professional admiration. . . . 'Expert job they made of it.' And with many compliments to the foe, he too passed on.

After he'd told his tale I said to him: 'What are we going to do about it?' He said: 'Oh, I don't know. Thank Heaven we have within the land five hundred as good as they.' [9]

To restore the immediate situation at the water-works was no very difficult task, whereas the moral effect of the defeat at Sanna's Post, a classic incident in the annals of guerilla warfare, was lasting. In Bloemfontein the civilians expected the return of the Boers, and, while the water-works were out of British control, the typhoid cases in the hospitals multiplied day by day. But Rudyard could stay no longer; as soon as the panic subsided and the town was secure, he left for the south and was back in Cape Town on 3rd April.

Carrie in Cape Town had been ill and anxious, heartened only by visits from an old friend, Mary Kingsley, who had just arrived from England. Like all the world, Rudyard had been captivated by the tale of her West African travels; he used to describe her as the bravest woman he ever knew, and his admiration was increased by her unselfish desire to be useful at the Base Camp of the army. 'Being human, she must have been afraid of something,' he said, 'but one never found out what it was.' [10] She offered herself for any employment, however uncongenial. Would she nurse Boer prisoners-of-war at Simonstown in a fever hospital? She would, and with enthusiasm. Before starting work she dined with the Kiplings — 'a delightful woman', wrote Carrie in her diary — and, when they returned to England, the first call Rudyard paid was on his 'old ladies' in West Kensington, at whose house he had first met Mary Kingsley. He reached London on 28th April, and six weeks later news came that she had died of fever at Simonstown.

The pleasant way of life at Rottingdean, with its round of visits from aunts and cousins, was resumed, not without some changes. Rudyard was now drawn deeply into local and national politics. He twice dined with Joseph Chamberlain at his club, and he released several articles and stories with a strong political flavour. 'The Sin of Witchcraft', a fierce attack on disloyal elements in Cape Colony, appeared in *The Times* in April, and in May he wrote 'A Burgher of the Free State', a story with angry comments on the facing-both-ways citizens of Bloemfontein. It was his custom to read his new work aloud to Aunt Georgie at Rottingdean until, for the first time, he found her an unsympathetic listener. The 'Burgher' was 'not received well'. On politics, aunt and nephew could not agree and the rift which divided the nation could be perceived even in this devoted family circle.

When Rudyard came back from Bloemfontein, Carrie noted in her diary that he 'feels he has joined up all his ideas with the others of many years ago'. He had seen young England at war and, though no one questioned the courage and endurance of the soldiers, no one could fail to see their lack of training, their physical unfitness, their slow reaction when initiative and intelligence were needed. On the last page of *Stalky & Co.*, published just before the outbreak of war, he had written rather flippantly:

India's full of Stalkies — Cheltenham and Haileybury and Marlborough chaps — that we don't know anything about, and the surprises will begin when there's really a big row on. Who will be surprised? The other chaps! The gentlemen who go to the front in first-class carriages. Just imagine Stalky let loose on the south side of Europe with a sufficiency of Sikhs and a reasonable prospect of loot. Consider it quietly.

There were no Sikhs and no loot worth taking at Sanna's Post or Karee Siding, but there was also a conspicuous lack of those qualities which 'Stalky' was supposed to possess. Were all the best of the British overseas, in Australia, or in the Indian Army which was not allowed to fight in the Boer War? Or was the public-school product less admirable than he had supposed?

Perhaps the English nation needed reorganizing even more than did the Empire, a task to which he applied himself and, in the first instance, locally as a citizen. He had built a drill-hall in the village, had formed a volunteer company, and a branch of the Navy League, and was chairman of all their managing committees. One of the lessons from South Africa seemed to be that half the art of war was accurate long-range rifle-shooting. All over England, rifle clubs sprang up; at Rottingdean, Rudyard spent many hours on the range, many evenings at committee meetings in the village.

Meanwhile the summer of 1900 saw the completion of his last word on India, the story called *Kim,* at which he had been working inter- mittently for more than seven years. It called for many discussions with the 'Pater' at Tisbury, and even for reference to the old manu- script of *Mother Maturin* which he had started at Lahore in 1885. There came a day in August 1900 when the first draft was pronounced finished, after 'great conferences' with the 'Pater' and Sallie Norton. Even then there was much work to be done over the illustrations, and on one of his visits to Tisbury Rudyard spoke at an election meeting, on behalf of Arthur Morison, the Conservative candidate.

Rudyard Kipling to Dr. James Conland

July 24, 1900

Dear old man —

I haven't had a word out of you for goodness only knows how long — and except a little news now and again from Mrs. Balestier you might just as well be in another planet.

As you know we went down to South Africa (Cape Town) for the winter and there happened to be a bit of a war on, and I had the time of my life. Carrie and the children stayed at Cape Town and I sort of drifted up country looking at hospitals and wounded men and guns and generals and wondering as I have never wondered before at the huge size of the country, but it was all deeply interesting — specially when I met the people who had been through the Siege of Kimberley. You could always tell 'em by the way they looked round for a place to hide in when- ever they heard the *whizz-boom* of a Cape Town trolley car. It reminded 'em of the noise of an approaching shell. I was mean enough to laugh at 'em first — but I don't do so any more since I got under shell-fire myself and heard the cussed things booming over the small of my back.

War is a rummy job — it's a cross between poker and Sunday-school. Sometimes poker comes out on top and sometimes Sunday-school — but most often poker. The Boers hit us just as hard and just as often as they knew how; and we advanced against 'em as if they were street-rioters that we didn't want to hurt. They spied on us at their leisure, and when they wanted a rest they handed up any old gun and said they'd be loyal subjects. Then they went to their homes and rested for a week or two; and then they went on the warpath again with a new coat and a full stomach.

Then I've been down fishing with the Father and looking at old houses in Wiltshire but my *real* work this summer has been connected with our new rifle-range. I think I told you about it. We've started a rifle-club in the village of some 50 members and at last after months of waiting, we've got a 1,000 yards range among the downs; not ten minutes walk from the village. Now we are putting up a tin drill-shed where they can drill and practise Morris-tube shooting in the winter. An American workman would have run it up in a week. I've had to wait five — for non-delivery of materials and their slack laziness. The contractor who supplies the ironwork invited me to look round his forge the other day. Says I: ' Yes it would be all right if we lived in Queen Elizabeth's time. It's only three hundred years out of date — all your machinery.' Somehow or other he wasn't one little bit pleased.[11]

The Kiplings arrived in South Africa again on Christmas Day 1900. Rudyard spent the voyage working at a long story which was to give the key-note for his next book. It was to be called ' The Army of a Dream ', a vision of England trained and prepared for war by freely offered service. It was a dream, from which he rudely awakened his readers on the last page by reminding them that the men who might have made it a reality had thrown away their lives in such holocausts as the ambush at Sanna's Post.

Confidence and readiness were not the keynotes of the situation in South Africa. Far from being finished, the war was breaking out anew. Lord Roberts had wiped the memory of early defeats off the slate, and had solved the gigantic problems of supply and transport which were the real obstacles to the conquest of the two republics. At political warfare he had failed, since he never realized the strength of the resistance movement which sprang up wherever the main Boer armies were defeated and dispersed. It was with the agreement of the Boer Generals that he collected women and children from the disaffected districts into concentration camps — an ill-omened name. Since the armies had not learned to master the epidemic camp-fevers, what could be expected of the undisciplined civilians in the camps? They died in thousands, the true tragedy of the Boer War, which has never been forgotten in South Africa, though it is often forgotten that at the Peace Conference the Boer Generals thanked the British for organizing the camps.

Roberts had no sooner gone home than the Boer leaders had opened their new guerilla campaign, which meant that his successor Kitchener had to fight a new war and to raise a new army of mounted infantry at the same time. When Rudyard called on Milner, a few days after his arrival, it was to hear a tale of woe.

During this visit Rudyard did not again go up-country. On their arrival at the Docks, Rhodes sent a carriage to meet them with a message that their new cottage was ready and furnished. It was a low white house surrounded by a shady *stoep* and built in a modification of the Dutch Colonial style, standing low on the mountain-slope, and separated from Rhodes's Groote Schuur only by woods and gardens. The 'Woolsack'* was Carrie's ideal house, her 'dear Woolsack' which, every year from 1901 to 1908, she occupied with joy and left with regret.

There Rudyard worked in peace, avoiding the English winters, and there Elsie and John spent their doubled summers within reach of the snow-white beaches of Muizenberg. It gave the Kiplings the social setting they required, at once private and yet frequented by the friends they wished to see. In 1901 almost daily visits were exchanged with Rhodes, who kept open house for all who had work to do in making South Africa. Rudyard also met Baden-Powell, now commanding a unit at the Cape, Dr. Jameson, Gwynne of Reuters, and many officers from Australia and New Zealand.

Rudyard Kipling to Dr. J. Conland

20 Feb. 1901

We came out here, as usual, to avoid the English winter and have settled down in a Dutch-model house in a garden of figs and loquats and grapes *and* oranges.

Meantime, the war goes on — over a front of something like two thousand miles and a depth of a thousand roughly. The Boers are doing it very well. They keep in small parties looting and riding away and except where the carelessness of our infantry gives them a chance they take care not to attack. They can't take prisoners; they haven't any bases and they are very like Apaches in their movements. But they are having the time of their lives — stealing from friends & foes alike and living on the fat of the land. I never saw such a comic war in all my born days. Cape Town is full of rebels and is the only place where martial law is not proclaimed. A man gets as much as 12 months imprisonment sometimes for assisting the enemy, and six months for helping to blow up a railway culvert. And then we wonder why the war doesn't end. They make no secret of their intentions. They want to sweep the English into the sea, to lick their own nigger and to govern South Africa with a gun instead of a ballot box. It is only the little Englanders in London who say that the Transvaal is merely fighting for its independence; but out here both sides realize it is a question of which race is to run the country.[12]

* The nickname 'Woolsack' was a play upon the name of a previous owner of the land on which it stood — Mr. Wools-Sampson.

The last year of Rhodes's short life had come; his heart was failing, and he knew now that he would never live to see his vision realized of a united British Africa from the Cape to the Zambesi, with open communications through to Cairo. He, too, was content to wait for the end of the useless campaign at 'Groote Schuur' where, sooner or later, all who counted in Africa came to visit him.

Rhodes's dream, that ideal world which had sustained him through so many vicissitudes, had changed its character again, as dreams change, and had resolved itself into its final form. No longer a conspiracy of rich men to enforce peace, nor an Anglo-Saxon world-empire, the dream now shaped itself as the education of a new ruling class. The men with moral strength should rejuvenate the academies of the old world, while the learning of the academies should stimulate arts and sciences in the new frontier lands. Once he had thought that money was the source of power, but now he knew that knowledge was power. To link Oxford with his own Rhodesia was the last task he would set himself and, having spent money lavishly on material projects, he saved and economized at the end of his life to increase the endowment for his scholarships. The plans were laid in February 1901 and long were the discussions in the warm summer evenings at 'Groote Schuur'. Rhodes was not a ladies' man, but clever women, if they had something to say, were welcomed at his hospitable table, none more so than Carrie Kipling. It was she who persuaded him to increase the amount of the Rhodes Scholarships from £250 to £300 a year, which she knew was necessary for the support of a young man from overseas with no home in England.

She approved his schemes of building and planting, his encouragement of South African arts and architecture, his love of landscape and trees and animals. Wild beasts in their natural surroundings in a park enclosure pleased him deeply, and no little thing pleased him more than Carrie's decision to bring up a neglected lion-cub by hand.

When Rhodes was obliged to leave for England — his last voyage — Rudyard wrote:

> Life in your cottage has been as perfect in its peace and quiet as anything in this world could offer. It has filled me full of notions — over and above the work that I have managed to get through — so that it will take me all my time to get them in order. I've done one or two things that I'm rather pleased with but it has been horribly lonely since you left. Rather like living in a landscape with half the horizon knocked out.[18]

Their summer visit to England in 1901 was uneventful. The Catlins came over from America and bore off Carrie and Rudyard on a visit to Paris, which they had not seen for many years. She had been ill that summer and Rudyard had written tenderly to her mother in America:

You have no notion what a sweet and winning little woman your Carrie has grown into. Her face gets more beautiful, year by year, and her character deepens and broadens with every demand upon it. She is near an angel, but her Puritan conscience which she has inherited from her New England forbears still makes her take life too blame seriously.[14]

Just before he sailed again for Africa he made a pronouncement in *The Times* which provoked violent discussion, giving offence to many who had been his fervent admirers. It was a long poem called ' The Islanders', an appeal to the English to take national service as seriously as they took their organized games. An early result was a letter from Lord Roberts to Kipling on the subject of a campaign for compulsory military training.

The complaint of the critics about ' The Islanders' was that Rudyard did not so much warn the English of their peril as scold them for their inadequacy.

> No doubt but ye are the People — your throne is above the King's.
> Whoso speaks in your presence must say acceptable things:
> Bowing the head in worship, bending the knee in fear —
> Bringing the word well smoothen — such as a King should hear.

He began by repeating his old assertion that the craft of soldiering was held in contempt in England:

Ye hindered and hampered and crippled; ye thrust out of sight and away
Those that would serve you for honour and those that served you for pay.
Then were the judgments loosened; then was your shame revealed,
At the hands of a little people, few but apt in the field.
Yet ye were saved by a remnant (and your land's long-suffering star),
When your strong men cheered in their millions while your striplings went to
    the war.

      .   .   .

And ye vaunted your fathomless power, and ye flaunted your iron pride,
Ere — ye fawned on the Younger Nations for the men who could shoot and ride!
Then ye returned to your trinkets; then ye contented your souls
With the flannelled fools at the wicket or the muddied oafs at the goals.

This was indeed a shock to a generation that gave such moral consequence to cricket, and many a *pater-familias* wrote to one or other of the more solemn organs of the Press, in dismay that Rudyard Kipling, the Bard of Empire, should blaspheme the national idols, with his talk of ' flannelled fools' and ' muddied oafs'. Rudyard enlarged upon this theme. Their inherited way of life could be maintained only if the English would learn how to fight for it.

Ancient, effortless, ordered, cycle on cycle set,
Life so long untroubled, that ye who inherit forget
It was not made with the mountains, it is not one with the deep.
Men, not gods, devised it. Men, not gods, must keep.
Men, not children, servants, or kinsfolk called from afar,
But each man born in the Island broke to the matter of war.

He scorned his critics and derided their alternatives. What would they do in the event of war?

Will ye pitch some white pavilion, and lustily even the odds,
With nets and hoops and mallets, with rackets and bats and rods?
Will the rabbit war with your foemen — the red deer horn them for hire?
Your kept cock-pheasant keep you? — he is master of many a shire.

.   .   .   .   .

Will ye pray them or preach them, or print them, or ballot them back from
      your shore?
Will your workmen issue a mandate to bid them strike no more?

No earlier pronouncement of Rudyard's had touched so many victims on the raw. It flicked the old conservatives on a tender spot, hurting them more than it hurt the hostile hide-bound radicals who cared little for criticism from this quarter. The intellectuals were the last people he thought of influencing; they were 'incurious', a damning epithet which he applied to them in a single sweeping line. They were

Arid, aloof, incurious, unthinking, unthanking, gelt,

and he wasted no more words on them. So much for Jack Mackail and his friends. 'England is a stuffy little place, mentally, morally, and physically', he wrote to Rhodes.[15]

The Kiplings did not reach the 'Woolsack' again until 7th January 1902. It was to find a deputation of newspaper reporters urgent for 'copy' about 'The Islanders'. Among them was a young man named Edgar Wallace who had come out to the Cape as a private soldier and, having graduated into war-reporting, now held Julian Ralph's old place as correspondent of the London *Daily Mail*. Rudyard advised him upon starting a career which was to win him wealth and fame as a writer of thrillers, but the profession of literature, as he warned Wallace, was 'a good mistress but a bad wife'.[16] Rudyard's own work, in January, was in a lighter vein. The nursery fables which he had devised for children in past years were ready for publication. He ended the series with 'The Cat that Walked by Himself' and 'The Butterfly that Stamped', both completed at the 'Woolsack' early in 1902. The 'Cat' was perhaps inspired by the gift of a handsome Persian which Carrie had just received from her Wolcott cousins.

Thereafter Rudyard had to turn to graver matters. On 6th February he heard that Rhodes was mortally ill and, until his death, called, almost every day, either at 'Groote Schuur' or at the Muizenberg cottage where the invalid was taken, in that torrid season, for sea air. Fifty years ago, when there was no air-conditioning, even the money of a multi-millionaire could not command coolness in summer heat.

On 18th March Rhodes was reported unconscious and, on the evening of the 26th, word came to the 'Woolsack' that he had died, murmuring 'so little done — so much to do'. Next day his body was brought to lie in state at 'Groote Schuur', and Rudyard was called into council by Dr. Jameson, one of the executors, to advise about the funeral ceremonies and about putting the will into effect. At a short private service held at 'Groote Schuur' on 2nd April Rudyard recited the obituary verse, of which some lines were afterwards engraved on Rhodes's memorial:

> Dreamer devout, by vision led
>   Beyond our guess or reach,
> The travail of his spirit bred
>   Cities in place of speech.
> So huge the all-mastering thought that drove —
>   So brief the term allowed —
> Nations, not words, he linked to prove
>   His faith before the crowd.
>
>   .   .   .   .
>
> The immense and brooding Spirit still
>   Shall quicken and control.
> Living he was the land, and dead,
>   His soul shall be her soul!

On the following day, after a public ceremony, which the Kiplings attended, in the Cathedral at Cape Town, Rhodes's body was carried in procession to the railway station and thence to Bulawayo. The executors had begged Rudyard to go with them to Rhodes's North, and when he would not, in his last days before leaving Africa, Jameson and Frank Rhodes sent him special messages from Rhodesia describing the reading of his verses over the grave in the Matoppos.[17]

It seemed hardly relevant to notice that the funeral train had passed for a thousand miles through the war-zone which was still harassed by Boer guerillas. As late as 7th March, the Boer General, Delarey, had overrun a British garrison and captured a British general, the last Boer exploit in a campaign on the point of collapse.

The concentration camps were now under efficient control and the absurd situation of fighting the men while feeding their dependents could not be indefinitely maintained. 'At long last', wrote Rudyard,

' we were left apologizing to a deeply-indignant people, whom we had been nursing and doctoring for a year or two.'[20] Formal negotiations for peace were opened on 9th April, a week before the Kiplings left for England. It was a joyous voyage because the 'Pater' and Dr. Jameson were in the same ship with them. They came home to a summer of rejoicing; there was peace, and there was to be a Coronation; and best of all, Rudyard's mother came to stay at Rottingdean with Trix now restored to health.

Whit Sunday, 1st June 1902, brought the news that peace was signed in South Africa; in an announcement that was a 'scoop' for the *Daily Mail,* managed by that enterprising young journalist, Edgar Wallace. The next day, a public holiday was kept with more sober celebration than the relief of Mafeking, two years before. Public opinion had changed about the war and there were many who could not share Rudyard's complacency about the treatment of the Afrikaner nation, among them Aunt Georgie, a woman of inflexible puritan morality. Since to her the day of the Boer capitulation — and that was what the Treaty of Vereeniging amounted to — was a day of mourning, she took the remarkable step of hanging a black banner from the window of 'North End House' with a notice in large letters:

We have killed and also taken possession.

In quiet Rottingdean, on a summer holiday, no one at first was in a mood for polemics; but when the evening came and the young men of the village were in a noisy mood, a crowd gathered around 'North End House' to protest. Some attempt was made to pull the black flag down, even, according to one account, to set fire to the hedge over which it hung. This demonstration brought Rudyard hurrying across the green from 'The Elms' to the rescue of his dear Aunt Georgie. There could be no doubt of Rudyard Kipling's loyalty and, after a speech which was much interrupted, he persuaded the demonstrators to go away, a strange role for Rudyard to play, and one which could not be kept out of the newspapers.[18]

A few months earlier he had been writing, in Africa, the verses on 'Sussex' which seemed to root him there for ever.

> God gives all men all earth to love,
>   But since man's heart is small,
> Ordains for each one spot shall prove
>   Belovèd over all.
>
> .   .   .   .   .
>
> Each to his choice, and I rejoice
>   The lot has fallen to me
> In a fair ground — in a fair ground —
>   Yea, Sussex by the sea!

In fact, Rottingdean, with its painful memories, was becoming unbearable to him and Carrie, all the more because the character of the place had changed. They hated the trippers from Brighton; there were radicals in the village — a group of them with whom Rudyard used sometimes to argue in the 'Plough Inn'; and now even the loyal patriots had set his teeth on edge, so that in chagrin Rudyard closed temporarily the hall he had built for the rifle club. Luckily they had at last found a suitable house; on 10th June Rudyard's solicitor cousin, George Macdonald, negotiated the purchase of the house called 'Bateman's' at Burwash, with thirty-three acres of land, for the sum of £9300.

Carrie had been pleased to receive invitations to seats in the Abbey for the Coronation of King Edward VII. When, on 24th June, news came of the King's sudden illness which caused the postponement of the ceremony, Rudyard was deeply moved. So far, in his life, he had felt no more than a formal respect for the Monarchy. The 'Widow at Windsor' had retained his loyal submission without winning that passionate, fervent, devotion which she inspired in so many of her subjects. His great Jubilee poem contained no reference to Queen Victoria. During the last weeks of her life he had paid her a graceful tribute in his verses on the Commonwealth of Australia ('The Young Queen'), and that was all. Her death, in January 1901, produced no contemporary comment, in Rudyard's published works or in Carrie's private diary. The month of June 1902, when he was thinking and feeling so deeply, with such mixed emotions, about the state of the nation, turned his mind, perhaps for the first time with its full force, to the meaning of the English Monarchy. 'Rud greatly shocked,' wrote Carrie on the day of the King's illness, 'and more interested than ever before in the King as a man.' His verses, 'The King's Task', followed not long after. But when the deferred Coronation at last took place, on 9th August, it did not suit them to go to London, and they spent the day quietly at Rottingdean.

During the war the verses and stories that Rudyard had published had been largely political; his literary achievement had been the completion of *Kim*, which harked back to an earlier period of his life. The political pieces, from 'The Absent-minded Beggar' to 'The Islanders', were not of a kind to make a direct appeal to posterity. Those who remember the mental climate of the turn of the century are now past middle age and, for the most part, it is students of social history who will turn to 'The Old Issue', 'The Song of the White Men', or 'The Reformers'. The tone of his comment on the war, as it affected his own countrymen, is best preserved in the facetious verses called 'The Lesson', which appeared in *The Times* on 29th July 1901.

Let us admit it fairly, as a business people should,
   We have had no end of a lesson: it will do us no end of good.

       .   .   .   .   .

It was our fault, and our very great fault — and now we must turn it to use.
We have forty million reasons for failure, but not a single excuse.
So the more we work and the less we talk the better results we shall get —
We have had an Imperial lesson; it may make us an Empire yet!

As for the aftermath of the war, in South Africa, his programme was what Rhodes would have commended if he had lived to see it— magnanimity — to wipe out and to forget the cruel past, to face the future in a creative, co-operative spirit. The verses printed at the head of this chapter were his epilogue to the war.

      Here in a large and sunlit land,
        Where no wrong bites to the bone,
      I will lay my hand in my neighbour's hand,
        And together we will atone
      For the set folly and the red breach
        And the black waste of it all;
      Giving and taking counsel each
        Over the cattle-kraal.

His vision of the war, which he shared with Rhodes and Milner, was always cast forward to a future when settlement of new white men on the land would prove the key to recovered prosperity. That note recurs often in his stories and songs of the war. The popular soldier-ballads, 'Chant-pagan', 'Stellen-bosch', 'M.I.', 'Boots', 'Lichtenberg', 'Piet', mostly written in 1901, were not published until 1903 when he issued a new volume of collected verse, *The Five Nations*. Though the sales of this book were gigantic compared with those of any other contemporary poetry, they never achieved the universal popularity of *Barrack-Room Ballads* and *The Seven Seas*. This was a matter of timing, as they appeared in that season of doldrums after a war when no one but the old soldiers wants to hear it mentioned. Most are topical verses, and only in one or two instances do they approach the level of pure poetry, even as ballads. Perhaps the most remarkable of these pieces is 'Lichtenberg', a poem suggested by the casual remark of an Australian soldier. 'I smelt wattle at Lichtenberg, riding in, in the rain.' The rhythmical phrase was enough to set Rudyard's imagination at work and to produce a composition shot with light from two contrary angles, a web of two colours varying as the light catches warp or woof. The scene is magically like war in Africa, and the response is wholly Australian, told in the simplest terms, with no bright colours or startling disclosures. Even the sing-song Australian accent comes through in the rhythm without need for a word of dialect.

> There was some silly fire on the flank
>   And the small wet drizzling down —
> There were the sold-out shops and the bank
>   And the wet, wide-open town;
>
> *And* we were doing escort-duty
>   To somebody's baggage-train,
> And I smelt wattle by Lichtenberg —
>   Riding in, in the rain.
>
> It was all Australia to me —
>   All I had found or missed:
> Every face I was crazy to see,
>   And every woman I'd kissed . . .

In the collected works there are three full-length stories about the Boer War, all dealing with unusual aspects of it. 'The Comprehension of Private Copper' is a dialogue between a private soldier and a renegade British colonial fighting on the Boer side. 'A Sahibs' War', based upon Rudyard's visit to the farm near Karee Siding, is a version of the war as seen by a Sikh soldier who has found his way there by accident, Rudyard's notion of how the war might have been fought if the Indian Army had been employed. 'The Captive', of which we may suppose that the motive was suggested by an episode at Cape Town,* is one of Rudyard's most sophisticated, most thoroughly elaborate, stories packed with allusion and technicality, and making no concession to the casual reader. To throw yourself into it is like listening to another man's 'shop'. Rudyard described 'The Captive' as one of the stories which came to him subconsciously or, as he preferred to say, was offered to him by his 'daemon', and which therefore might have merit if laboriously polished.

I could not get my lighting into key with the tone of the monologue. The background insisted too much. My Daemon said at last: 'Paint the background first once for all, as hard as a public-house sign and leave it alone.' This done, the rest fell into place with the American accent and outlook of the teller.

* R. K.'s letters to Conland reveal (1) that Rudyard himself imported an experimental machine-gun for trial in the field, and (2) that he made friends at Cape Town with an American soldier of fortune, a sergeant 'who had been at San Juan, and was a Democrat — a grey, grizzled tough old bird'. This American, unlike the 'captive', had volunteered to fight on the British side.

Here is the frame, in which the tale within the tale is presented, and in which Rudyard presents his version of the topsy-turvy political situation in the last year of the war.

The guard-boat lay across the mouth of the bathing-pool, her crew idly spanking the water with the flat of their oars. A red-coated militia-man, rifle in hand, sat at the bows, and a petty officer at the stern. Between the snow-white cutter and the flat-topped honey-coloured rocks on the beach the green water was troubled with shrimp-pink prisoners-of-war bathing. Behind their orderly tin camp and the electric-light poles rose those stone-dotted spurs that throw heat on Simonstown. Beneath them the little *Barracouta* nodded to the big *Gibraltar,* and the old *Penelope,* that in ten years has been bachelor's club, natural history museum, kindergarten, and prison, rooted and dug at her fixed moorings. Far out, a three funnelled Atlantic transport with turtle bow and stern waddled in from the deep sea.

Through the mouth of his Yankee adventurer, a prisoner of the British, Rudyard speaks of two men, with the love that an author extends to his favourite characters, the Boer Commandant and the English General. In the story, all the British regular officers admit themselves 'pro-Boers' in politics; while the Boer fighting men show much more animosity against the half-hearted Cape rebels than against the British. The Boer Commandant, Van Zyl, who does not want to fight, fights well; the British General, who respects the Boers, almost dreads the end of the war for professional reasons. He wants time to put more young troops through the mill in this 'dress-parade for Armageddon'.

The General wanted to train soldiers; Van Zyl could not see how the war would ever be finished. 'If you hold an ox by the horn and hit him by the bottom he runs round and round.' The American thought he was beginning to understand the British and had evolved his own plan for South Africa. 'If you want to realize your assets, you should lease the whole proposition to America for ninety-nine years.' But it didn't work out that way.

CHAPTER XIV

KIPLING AND HIS CONTEMPORARIES

—————◆—————

'When 'Omer smote 'is bloomin' lyre,
  He'd 'eard men sing by land an' sea;
An' what he thought 'e might require,
  'E went an' took — the same as me!

'The market-girls an' fishermen,
  The shepherds an' the sailors, too,
They 'eard old songs turn up again,
  But kep' it quiet — same as you!

'They knew 'e stole; 'e knew they knowed.
  They didn't tell, nor make a fuss,
But winked at 'Omer down the road,
  An' 'e winked back — the same as us!'

W HEN the Kiplings made their home at 'Bateman's', Rudyard had been in the public eye for twelve or thirteen years and was yet no more than thirty-six years old. He was rich and famous, by far the most quoted of contemporary writers, the most talked-about, the most sought-after by snobs and sightseers. It was exasperating to critics that a man whose work could not be fitted into any of the approved categories should enjoy such sustained and growing popularity. In 1890 it had been suggested that he lacked staying-power; in 1902, whatever he was, he could not be called the 'comet of a season'.

Kipling's first success had been among persons of discrimination. When Hunter had spoken of a new star rising in the East, when Low had regarded Kipling as 'possibly greater than Dickens', when *The Times* leader-writer had compared him with Maupassant, these were tributes paid to the writer of cynical tales about the governing class in India. It was an accident of his career that the Simla stories were not the first to catch the attention of a wider public in London and New York. The soldier songs and stories of his second phase captured the market in 1890 and grew in popularity through the decade, sweeping his reputation away into a wider world where the pronouncements of the professional critics counted for little. All that generation of young men who volunteered to fight in the Spanish-American and Anglo-Boer wars derived their notion of colonial warfare and of the soldier's life largely from Kipling, particularly from his cockney ballads. He was the first writer of eminence to compose serious verses in the cockney dialect, used hitherto for comical treatment only; and perhaps his addiction to cockney, in that phrase, lowered him in the estimation of men of letters. Grotesque misspellings in such solemn verses as 'Follow me 'Ome', or 'Sestina of the Tramp-royal', discouraged some readers and dissuaded others from regarding these works as literature. Year after year, however, he produced his cockney verses, to the delight of the unacademic.

Meanwhile, in 1893 and 1894, he had embarked upon the new experiment of the *Jungle Books,* an even greater success than the *Barrack-room Ballads,* and still, after sixty years, the most popular of Kipling's works. It is in the *Jungle Books* that we must search for the principle called 'the Law' which dominated Kipling's philosophy of life. It is not new; it had been expressed a generation earlier with force and eloquence in Emerson's essay on 'Self-reliance', which, significantly, had been prefaced with the gnomic rhyme:

> Cast the Bantling on the rocks.
> Suckle him with the she-wolf's teat;
> Wintered with the hawk and fox,
> Power and speed be hands and feet.

The message given by Emerson to his child cast into the world-jungle had been: 'accept the place the divine providence has found for you, the society of your contemporaries, the connexion of events'. How, then, to reconcile a fearless independence in action with an acquiescence in the universal plan?

'Your genuine action will explain itself, and will explain all your other actions. Your conformity explains nothing. Act singly, and what you have done singly will justify you now. Power is in nature the essential measure of right. Nature suffers nothing to remain in its Kingdom which cannot help itself.'

It was Kipling's corollary to the philosophy of self-reliance to expound the relation of the man to the machine in the new industrial age. The engineer, more than most men, is a master because, in Emerson's awkward phrase, he is 'plastic and permeable to principles'.

> From coupler-flange to spindle-guide I see Thy Hand, O God —
> Predestination in the stride o' yon connectin'-rod.
> John Calvin might ha' forged the same — enormous, certain, slow —
> Ay, wrought it in the furnace-flame — *my* 'Institutio'.

So speaks M'Andrew, the Scottish engineer, of his machine, the engine of which he is at once master and servant, which conforms to the law of nature and yet is altogether dependent on his skill and courage.

> Fra' skylight-lift to furnace-bars, backed, bolted, braced an' stayed.
> An' singin' like the Mornin' Stars for joy that they are made;
> While, out o' touch o' vanity, the sweatin' thrust-block says:
> 'Not unto us the praise, or man — not unto us the praise!'
> Now, a' together, hear them lift their lesson — theirs an' mine:
> 'Law, Orrder, Duty an' Restraint, Obedience, Discipline!'
> Mill, forge an' try-pit taught them that when roarin' they arose,
> An' whiles I wonder if a soul was gied them wi' the blows.
> Oh for a man to weld it then, in one trip-hammer strain,
> Till even first-class passengers could tell the meanin' plain!

Kipling was a modest man about his own achievement — too modest, as he wrote to Charles Eliot Norton, to claim that he himself was the new Robert Burns, sent to 'sing the song of steam'. No other has appeared and no one could have done it better.[1]

From 1889 until 1908 there was no year in which he did not take a long sea voyage, and his love of sailors as types of self-reliant men of action came to surpass even his earlier love of soldiers. The relation of the seaman to his ship gave him a version of modern life more consonant with the widening world of the eighteen-nineties than his earlier image of the wolf-child in the jungle. 'The game is more than the player of the game, and the ship is more than the crew': there were times when he felt this as a sort of animism. Had the engine a soul, the ship a life of its own? There is a letter to Henley in which he allowed his fancy to run free with this conceit:

The way collisions at sea come about is this . . . the iron in the mine and under the hammer, and in the plates and engine-room, has a sort of blind lust beaten into it, for to meet and I suppose nautically to copulate with other iron and steel being linked into the frame of another ship. All the seven seas over, the ship yearns for its mate, tearing along under moon and cloud, sweating in oily tropic ports; rusting in dock; and so forth. At last comes the bridal night — wind, current and set of the sea aiding, while the eyes of men are held, and steamer meets steamer in a big kiss, and sink down to cool off in the water-beds. What I want to get at is the steamer's unconcern about the men who happen to be crawling about her innards at the time.[2]

This was fancy — and morbid fancy, not to be released in published work; yet it goes only a little further than the light-hearted animism of 'The Ship that found Herself'. That notion, of an engine acquiring a personality, by the gradual adaptation of its parts to one another, was new and strange to Kipling's contemporaries, though familiar enough in these days when everyone is used to the effect of running-in a new motor-car.

To write poetry and prose about steamships, for the men who worked in engine-rooms, was so new a practice that it left the literary critics gasping, but Kipling's own public was to be found among the makers of the world as it was at the turn of the century. They found no difficulty in his vocabulary, no unfamiliarity in his subject-matter. The generation that bridged the Forth, built the Uganda Railway, dammed the Nile, laid the Pacific Cable, irrigated the Punjab, sent radio messages across the Atlantic, crushed the ore of the Golden Mile at Kalgoorlie, served with the Mounties at the Klondyke, tunnelled through the Rockies, revealed the last secrets of the earth's surface, and learned to fly, had found its own laureate and not upon the advice of the approved literary critics. 'What an interesting illustration Kipling affords of the poetic imagination working under difficulties!' wrote Norton to a friend. 'There is little to nourish or quicken the spiritual side of his nature, but he has done a better work for his time than any other man in treating, through the poetic imagination, the material conditions which surround us all.'[3]

The image of the ship was to recur frequently in his later writings. Its origin may perhaps be traced to memories of childhood when a liner bore him away from the happy nursery-life at Bombay to misery and routine at Southsea. Whatever its origin, the image haunted Kipling's fancy for forty years. The Galley, or Galleon, or sometimes a modern ship — the ship of state — was his symbol for the material circumstances of a man's working life. In the relation between the galley and the galley-slave he pictured the antithesis between determination and free-will. The ship was an expression of the Law, of that undefined *nomos* which provided him with a sort of stoical substitute for religion. His verses on 'The Derelict' (1896) personify the deserted ship as a heartbroken creature: 'Man made me, and my will is to my maker still', he writes; but the seaman is the servant of the ship just as the ship is the prerequisite of the seaman's life. The seaman's duty to the ship is the measure of his manhood.

Life was a voyage; the profession he embraced was like a ship's routine; his farewell to India almost inevitably took the form of a ballad called 'The Galley-Slaves'. His delightful valediction to the outmoded three-volume novel was phrased as the passing of an old ship, 'The Three-Decker' (1894). His quarrel with the literary pirates of New York was transmuted into 'The Rhyme of the Three Captains' (1890), a ballad about sea-pirates. 'The Finest Story in the World' (1891), his tale about a masterpiece that could not get itself written, had for subject the adventures of a galley-slave, or rather a confusion between the adventures of two sorts of galley-slave. His Norman Knight who settled in Sussex after the Conquest (*Puck of Pook's Hill,* 1906), a story-hero described subjectively with some features of Kipling himself, made a voyage in a galley and toiled at the oar. One of the last stories he published ('The Manner of Men', 1930), thirty years later, told of the galley that carried Saint Paul to Rome. And in his posthumous autobiography he wrote of his unful-filled ambition:

> Yet I dreamed for many years of building a veritable three-decker out of chosen and long-stored timber — teak, green-heart, and ten-year-old oak knees — each curve melting deliciously into the next that the sea might nowhere meet resistance or weakness . . . a vessel ballasted on ingots of pure research and knowledge, roomy, fitted with delicate cabinet-work below-decks, painted, carved, gilt and wreathed the length of her, from her blazing stern-galleries outlined by bronzy palm-trunks, to her rampart figure-head — an East Indiaman worthy to lie alongside *The Cloister and the Hearth*.[4]

Since the true story of the British, fifty years ago, was the story of the British Overseas, in the age of Cromer, Curzon, Kitchener, Milner, Johnston, Lugard, and Rhodes, it was Kipling's task to reveal the secrets of their actual life to his contemporaries. For a whole genera-tion homesickness was reversed by Kipling's magic spell. Englishmen felt the days of England sick and cold and the skies grey and old, heard the East a-calling, fawned on the younger nations, learned to speak the jargon of the seven seas; while, in the outposts of empire, men who read no other books, recognized and approved the glimpses of their own lives in phrases from Kipling's verse: the flying-fishes and the thunder-clouds over the Bay of Bengal, the voyage outward-bound till the old lost stars wheel back, the palm-tree bowing down beneath a low African moon, the wild tide-race that whips the harbour-mouth at Melbourne, the broom flowering above the windy town of Welling-ton, the islands where the anchor-chain goes ripping down through coral-trash.

He distinguished always the self-reliant labour of the pioneer, up-country and alone, from the ponderous remote bureaucracy of White-hall and Simla. Kipling has been described as if he were the poet of orthodox conservatism. He was the very opposite of that; his admira-tion was always for the irregulars, the

> Legion that never was 'listed,
>   That carries no colours or crest,
> But, split in a thousand detachments,
>   Is breaking the road for the rest.[5]

In solitary places young Englishmen of the middle classes toiled and improvised at the task of civilizing backward countries, making wealth out of poverty and knowing very well that they would not get the profit of it.

> By the bitter road the Younger Son must tread,
>   Ere he win to hearth and saddle of his own, —
> 'Mid the riot of the shearers at the shed,
>   In the silence of the herder's hut alone —
> In the twilight, on a bucket upside down,
>   Hear me babble what the weakest won't confess — ...

'The Song of the Banjo' was not written of the governing-class, the 'Sons of Mary' who accepted power and wealth as a right, but of the 'Sons of Martha', the middle-class adventurers who shrank from no responsibility and were never too proud for any task.

Even at sea, the engineer, down below, is his hero rather than the gold-laced captain on the bridge. Though all his own voyages were in liners, and it was with the eye of imagination that he saw the breaking waves as they towered over a tramp-steamer's hull, he could project himself into the skin of the drenched deck-hand:

> Once we saw between the squalls, lyin' head to swell —
>   Mad with work and weariness, wishin' they was we —
> Some damned Liner's lights go by like a grand hotel;
>   'Cheered her from the *Bolivar* swampin' in the sea.*

Some extracts from early critical reviews of Kipling's work have been quoted in a previous chapter. It will now be proper to consider the maturer judgment of the reviewers, and the rise of hostile criticism as the eighteen-nineties drew to their close. There are times in the history of literature when the art of the approved masters is in harmony with popular sentiment, and times when it soars away into another sphere. In the eighteen-nineties, as again in the nineteen-twenties, popular art was a term of reproach, so that the painters and the poets in those two decades ignored and even despised the preferences of the great majority of their fellows, preferring to put out their work for the benefit of a small society of *illuminati,* sometimes, as it seemed, for the benefit of one another. The significant writers of the eighteen-nineties, according to the usual classification, are taken to be the group whose slogan was 'Art for Art's Sake'. There had been a change in literary fashion since the robust phase of Henley's *Scots Observer*

---

* A comparison may here be drawn between Kipling, who sang the Song of Steam, and Conrad who, though a professional seaman, always harked back to the passing age, the age of Sail. Conrad visited Kipling at 'Bateman's' and each was an admirer of the other's work.

which had led the fashion in 1889. 'Decadence' had triumphed, even in the persons of two or three writers who transferred their allegiance from Henley to the new group that surrounded Aubrey Beardsley.

It is in the numerous references of Henry James to Kipling (who remained his close family friend) that Kipling's decline from reputation with the leading critics can be traced. When in the spring of 1891 Kipling had circumvented Harper Brothers by producing a collection of stories in America, under the name of *Mine Own People,* Henry James had written a long adulatory preface.

His bloom lasts from month to month, almost surprisingly. This same freshness is such a very strange affair of its kind — so mixed and various and cynical, and, in certain lights, so contradictory of itself. At times he strikes us as shockingly precocious, at others as serenely wise. On the whole, he presents himself as a strangely clever youth who has stolen the formidable mask of maturity and rushes about making people jump with the deep sounds, the sportive exaggerations of tone, that issue from his painted lips. He has this mark of a real vocation, that different spectators may like him — must like him, I should almost say — for different things.

I hasten to add that the truly appreciative reader should surely have no quarrel with the primitive element in Mr. Kipling's subject-matter, or with what, for want of a better name, I may call his love of low life. What is this but essentially a part of his freshness? And for what part of his freshness are we exactly more thankful than for just this smart jostle that he gives to the stupid superstition that the amiability of a storyteller is the amiability of the people he represents — that their vulgarity, or depravity, or gentility, or fatuity are tantamount to the same qualities in the painter himself.

He never arranges or glosses or falsifies, but makes straight for the common and the characteristic.

In his private correspondence, James was not so flattering. The letters he exchanged with R. L. Stevenson contain several allusions to the newcomer whose genius both admired but both suspected. Was there some alloy of base metal in his composition? 'The talent enormous,' wrote James, 'but the brutality even deeper-seated.' 'He alarms me by his copiousness and haste', wrote Stevenson; and again, 'He is all smart journalism and cleverness; it is all bright and shallow and limpid. No blot of heart's blood, no harmony to the music.'[6]

Another shrewd and subtle criticism appeared about the same time from the pen of Oscar Wilde, then known only as an aesthete and a wit, whose dramatic successes and personal catastrophe still lay in the future. In September 1890 Wilde wrote an insufferably drawn-out dialogue for the *Nineteenth Century* on contemporary letters. The reader who can stomach page after page of the verbal confectionery flavoured with synthetic perfumes that, in the eighteen-nineties, passed for fine writing will come, towards the end, to this comment on the young Kipling:

he who would stir us now by fiction must either give us an entirely new background, or reveal to us the soul of man in its innermost workings. The first is, for the moment, being done for us by Mr. Rudyard Kipling. As one turns over the pages of his *Plain Tales from the Hills,* one feels as if one were seated under a palm tree reading life by superb flashes of vulgarity. The bright colours of the bazars dazzle one's eyes. The jaded, commonplace Anglo-Indians are in exquisite incongruity with their surroundings. The mere lack of style in the story-teller gives an odd journalistic realism to what he tells us. From the point of view of literature Mr. Kipling is a man of talent who drops his aspirates. From the point of view of life he is a reporter who knows vulgarity better than anyone has ever known it. Dickens knew its clothes. Mr. Kipling knows its essence. He is our best authority on the second-rate.*

Realism in subject-matter was not Oscar Wilde's forte and he could hardly be expected to admire a man who went 'straight for the common and the characteristic', but, making allowance for that, his observations are telling. To a modern reader, whether he likes Kipling's style or not, the repeated statement that in Kipling's early stories there was a 'mere lack of style' reads strangely. It must be remembered that by 'style' Wilde meant high-falutin. Kipling was not the sort of writer, as Edward Shanks has pointed out, who wrote 'drops his aspirates' when he meant 'drops his aitches'.

All these comments were made upon Kipling's Indian stories, which, with the *Barrack-room Ballads,* produced a vast volume of criticism, all at first to much the same effect. The reviewers were fascinated, startled, and shocked. 'Idle people are beginning to ask each other idle conundrums about him', said a writer in the *Saturday Review* on 14th May 1892. 'He is within measurable distance of the foundations of a Kipling Society.' Very soon, a reaction began against the undiscriminating praise given to all his work, copious and various as it was in his London years, by the less fastidious public. As early as 29th January 1891 a set of verses appeared in the *Cambridge Review,* over the signature 'J. K. S.', which the literary world knew to stand for J. K. Stephen, a brother of Kipling's early patron, Herbert Stephen. Would there never be a season, asked 'J. K. S.' —

> When the world shall cease to wonder
> At the genius of an ass,
> And a boy's eccentric blunder
> Shall not bring success to pass:

* Wilde's celebrated comment that Kipling had seen remarkable things 'through keyholes' does not appear in the essay as originally published.

When there stands a muzzled stripling,
Mute beside a muzzled bore:
When the Rudyards cease from Kipling
And the Haggards ride no more?

Kipling took no offence; he often used to chaff his friend Rider
Haggard about it. They were stanzas, he said, which he would have
given much to have written himself, which 'might survive when all
but our two queer names are forgotten'. On the other hand, it is
J. K. Stephen who is now remembered chiefly for his rhyme about
Kipling and Haggard, but, in 1891, anything written by a Stephen of
Cambridge was admired, and while the world laughed at this amusing
nonsense jingle it was hardly noticed that it was not criticism. To
say that Kipling was an ass and should be muzzled was neither liberal
nor polite; to couple him with Rider Haggard, a mere writer of
romantic thrillers, did his reputation some undeserved damage.
Though these two popular writers were contemporaries and lifelong
friends, they had little in common, professionally.

A year or two after J. K. Stephen's jibe was published, a young man,
who was to become Kipling's most malicious critic, arrived in London.
Max Beerbohm published very little, and while he protested so prettily
that his muse was no bigger than the servant-girl's baby, the literary
world learned to wait expectant for each of his tiny little pronouncements, for Max had charm and talent. No one could deny, or did
deny, that his work was polished, his wit penetrating — more penetrating with pencil than with pen. For fifty years anything spoken or
written or depicted by Max called forth a shrill chorus of delight from
the reviewers, and the present writer supposes himself almost the first
to utter an unkind word about this incomparable master of the smirk
and titter. Max was, as a rule, gentle, except when he touched upon
one topic. He hated Rudyard Kipling. He set himself to destroy
Kipling's reputation and, later, to assure the world that it had been
destroyed, with no small degree of success among the literary coteries,
but with no visible effect upon Kipling's ever-growing fame and
influence in wider circles. At least nine caricatures, two critical articles,
and a ferociously malevolent parody of Kipling's style have been
recorded as the work of Max Beerbohm, and while he discharged
these arrows, Kipling, for thirty years, remained entirely unmoved
by them. * [7]

* A sketch in the *Strand Magazine*, December 1892, seems to be Beerbohm's earliest
caricature of Kipling. The boys of Horsmonden School induced Kipling to write a
facetious article for their school magazine (*The Budget*, 14th May 1898). The following number, 28th May, contained a comment and a caricature by Beerbohm. Neither
contribution is worth much, but they were reprinted in New York, 1899.

Among the hostile critics there was one who showed, as early as 1893, a disposition to love and hate together, a phenomenon not rare in writers on Rudyard Kipling. Francis Adams was a debunker who made a name (before his early death by suicide) for exploding the inflated reputation of the great Victorians. Tennyson was no sooner dead, in October 1892, than Adams belittled him, and then turned with gusto to attack the new young man who was succeeding Tennyson in popularity. He began with the handsome admission that *Barrack-room Ballads* gave him 'the keenest pleasure had in reading a book of verse for years'; but the lapses from taste, he added, were unpardonable. 'The drop in Mr. Kipling is always from the stars straight into the puddles.' Much of Adams's criticism consisted in a shrewd selection of weak episodes from early books, and weak lines from early poems which Kipling himself would have pruned away from his maturer work. Since no one now reads the early pieces which Francis Adams condemned, the substance of this criticism is largely irrelevant, yet the general impression persisted, and many of his judgments passed into the common stock of opinion in literary circles. Kipling's picture of life at Simla was 'duty and red tape tempered by picnics and adultery'. His view of the 'goodness of God in relation to Englishmen and "niggers" seems always to consist in the opportunity and ability of the former to give the latter "hell".'

On Kipling's characters Adams had interesting observations to make. 'Description is his forte', but his characterization is weak.

He cannot escape from his own subjectivity. His *dramatis personae* melt away rapidly out of the memory, leaving us nothing but the impression of an admirably piquant and clever delineation.[8]

These notions were developed by Richard Le Gallienne, the editor of the liberal *Star* who, in 1900, wrote the first systematic study of Kipling's prose and verse. Le Gallienne was able to judge the *Barrack-room Ballads* more adequately than some earlier writers because he was an enthusiast for the London music-halls. The ballads, he said, were perfect in their kind, like the art of Albert Chevalier; and the best of them, 'though made of the very refuse of language', was 'Mandalay'. 'Like Burns when he forsakes his dialect, Kipling is cramped and dull when he forsakes his cockney.' But here Le Gallienne is not quite ingenuous; he dislikes Kipling's later verses for their politics and so decries them as verses. 'The Song of the English' is a 'mild cantata'; 'Recessional' is a 'political catchword embedded in a hymn'. As for the technical songs and stories, he can make nothing of them, beyond noting Kipling's debt to Walt Whitman:

In the labour of engines and the fields,
    to show the developments and the eternal meanings.

As for Kipling's characters, 'the more pains he takes with them the
less they live. He is deft at giving you sufficient notion of this man
or that woman to last out the story. But mainly the story is the
thing, and the characters are little more than pegs on which to hang
an anecdote.' Kipling 'loves to pretend that he has no feelings', says
Le Gallienne, and he must be blamed for a growing love of violence
in the English character. 'As a writer he is a delight, as an influence
he is a danger.' [9]

Early American criticism followed the same path as English criticism,
at first a chorus of injudicious praise, varied by warnings against the
author's 'smartness'. In America, too, the Simla stories were thought
to be shocking. A writer in the *New York Herald* (1890) remarked:
'The most forcible impression which is left on the average mind by
Mr. Kipling's works is the dismalness, insincerity, brutality and utter
worthlessness of all classes of British humanity in India'. William
Dean Howells, who had deplored Kipling's 'jaunty' 'wink-tipping'
manner in 1890, quite came round, as did, gradually, the Brahmins of
Boston. A man who was praised by Henry James and Charles Eliot
Norton must be taken seriously. The *Atlantic Monthly,* which had
resisted the new enthusiasm for some years, capitulated in January
1897, by publishing Norton's long and laudatory article on *The Seven
Seas,* the review which so delighted Rudyard and Carrie at Torquay.

It is now some six or seven years since *Plain Tales from the Hills*
gave proof that a man who saw through his eyes was studying life in
India and was able to tell us what he saw. And those who read the
scraps of verse prefixed to many of his stories, if they knew what poetry
was, learned that their writer was at least potentially a poet, not by virtue
of fantasy alone, but by his mastery of lyrical versification. . . .
    The dominant tone of his verse is indeed the patriotic . . . it is this
passionate, moral, imperial patriotism that inspires the first poem in the
book, 'The Song of the English' . . . but if this be the dominant tone,
the full scale which includes it and every other tone of Mr. Kipling's
verse is that of actual life seen by the imagination intensely and compre-
hensively, and seen by it always, in all conditions and under all forms,
as a moral experience, with the inevitable consequences resulting from
the good or evil use of it.
    'What is a poet?' asked Wordsworth, and he answers the question:
'He is a man speaking to men. . . . He binds together by passion and
knowledge the vast empire of human society.' And this vast empire of
society includes the mean and the vulgar no less than the noble and the
refined. The brutality of Tommy Atkins, the spirit of the beast in man,
all appear in the *Barrack-room Ballads,* but not less his courage, his fidelity,

his sense of duty, his obscure but deep-seated sentiment. The gist of all these Ballads is the display of the traits of human nature which make this semi-savage 'most remarkable like you'.

And so vivid are his appreciations of the poetic significance of even the most modern and practical of the conditions and aspects of sea life that in 'McAndrew's Hymn', a poem of surpassing excellence alike in conception and in execution, he has sung the song of the marine steam-engine . . . in such wise as to convert the clanging throbs and beats into a sublime symphony.

He has thus fulfilled a fine prophecy of Wordsworth's, that when the time should come, when the discoveries and applications of science shall become 'familiarised to men, and shall be ready to put on, as it were, a form of flesh and blood, the Poet will lend his divine spirit to aid the transfiguration'. The qualities which distinguished Mr. Kipling's stories were not lacking in his poems. There was the same sure touch, the same insight, the same imaginative sympathy with all varieties of life, and the same sense of the moral significance of life even in its crudest, coarsest, and most vulgar aspects.

He continues the great succession of English poets . . . such a succession of poets as no other land can boast.

Norton had come nearer to appreciation of Kipling's technical songs and stories than had Richard Le Gallienne, but here Henry James quite failed. What was the song of steam to him? An oft-quoted letter of James should be read in this context, as a light-hearted flippancy by a friend writing about a friend, whose work he had praised both publicly and privately, for its other merits. If this letter is to be taken more seriously, it is a devastating admission of the limitations of its writer.

Henry James to Miss Grace Norton

Xmas Day, 1897

His talent I think quite diabolically great; and this in spite of the misguided, the unfortunate Stalky. His ballad future may still be big. But my view of his prose future has much shrunken in the light of one's increasingly observing how little of life he can make use of. Almost nothing civilised save steam and patriotism — and the latter only in verse, where I *hate* it so, especially mixed up with God and goodness, that that half spoils my enjoyment of his great talent. Almost nothing of the complicated soul or of the female form or of any question of *shades* — which latter constitutes, to my sense, the real formative literary discipline. In his earliest time I thought he perhaps contained the seeds of an English Balzac; but I have given that up in proportion as he has come down steadily from the simple in subject to the more simple — from the Anglo-Indians to the natives, from the natives to the Tommies, from the Tommies to the quadrupeds, from the quadrupeds to the fish, and from the fish to the engines and screws.[10]

But Kipling had yet something to say about 'natives' which would reveal James's aside to Miss Norton as shallow and frivolous indeed.

A far more serious blow was struck at Kipling's standing with the New England writers by the publication of 'The White Man's Burden'. Just as his South African pieces were an offence even to such dear friends as Aunt Georgie and Margot Mackail, so 'The White Man's Burden', which Theodore Roosevelt and his millions of supporters welcomed, made an end of Kipling's reputation in the stricter circles around Boston. William James and even Norton were much hurt by the tone of these verses, and liberals who had not known Kipling in America were quite disgusted. E. L. Godkin of the *Nation* wrote in a private letter:

> Kipling has long been a most pernicious vulgar person. I only admire one thing of his, the 'Recessional'. He may have written other things as good but I don't read him. I think most of the current jingoism on both sides of the Atlantic is due to him. He is the poet of the barrack-room cads.[11]

It was only too common for critics of the left to condemn Kipling on hearsay evidence, without making Godkin's naïve admission that they hadn't read his works. Political passions then ran too high, in England and America, to allow justice to a writer who seemed to have given to party what was meant for mankind. Long afterwards a cooler view of his influence upon his generation could be taken, and a remarkable account of it was given by a man of the left wing — certainly no sympathizer with the views commonly attributed to Kipling. In his novel of Edwardian life, *The New Machiavelli*, H. G. Wells puts the following tribute into the mouth of his hero:

> The prevailing force in my undergraduate days was not Socialism but Kiplingism.
> It is a little difficult now to get back to the feelings of that period; Kipling has since been so mercilessly and exhaustively mocked, criticised and torn to shreds — never was a man so violently exalted and then, himself assisting, so relentlessly called down. But in the middle nineties this spectacled and moustached little figure with its heavy chin and its general effect of vehement gesticulation, its wild shouts of boyish enthusiasm for effective force, its lyric delight in the sounds and colours, in the very odours of empire, its wonderful discovery of machinery and cotton waste and the under officer and the engineer, and 'shop' as a poetic dialect became almost a national symbol. He got hold of us wonderfully, he filled us with tinkling and haunting quotations . . . he coloured the very idiom of our conversation. He rose to his climax with his 'Recessional'.
> He helped to broaden my geographical sense immensely, and he provided phrases for just that desire for discipline and devotion and organised

effort the Socialism of our times failed to express, that the current socialist movement still fails, I think, to express. The sort of thing that follows, for example, tore something out of my inmost nature and gave it a shape, and I took it back from him shaped and let much of the rest of him, the tumult and the bullying, the hysteria and the impatience, the incoherence and inconsistency, go uncriticised for the sake of it:

> Keep ye the Law — be swift in all obedience —
> Clear the land of evil, drive the road and bridge the ford.
>   Make ye sure to each his own
>   That he reap where he hath sown;
> By the peace among Our peoples let men know we serve the Lord!

To conclude this series of opinions we may select a still later verdict, by Desmond MacCarthy:

He made every character in his stories an artist in his lingo: the school-boy, the engineer, the soldier, the bagman — even, by a stretch of imagination, different kinds of animals in the *Jungle Books*. But the most significant thing of all about him as a story-teller was that he put these gifts at the service *not* of the love-story, not of some adventure in sensibility, not of worldly success, but for the first time at the service of a man's relation to his work.

He wrote poems about what a farmer felt watching his fat cattle go through a gate, what an ex-soldier thought while mowing the vicar's lawn, what an engineer felt about his engine. He wrote poems not only about love and death — the eternal themes — but what the average man felt to be romantic in his daily life.

There is a feeling abroad that it is time the Muse ceased to repeat her ancient divinations and that she dealt with *everyday* emotions, with common not rare experiences. Who else has made anything like so spirited, so sincere, so unselfconscious an effort to do so? [12]

(2)

VERSIFICATION

If names were to be proposed for admission to the roll of English poets, during the last fifty years, the first choice of critical readers would probably be given to Yeats and Eliot, but not to Kipling who earned a wider fame than either of them in his lifetime, and whose works, as yet, have retained the affection of their readers for a longer period. Why is Kipling not commonly ranked as a major poet? Both Yeats and Eliot have made considered pronouncements on this subject, and both, while expressing admiration for his achievement and technical proficiency, confess themselves baffled by the nature and purpose of his art. He was felt by his literary contemporaries to be out of the stream of English Literature, though the lettered, as well as the unlettered, were obliged to admit, even if they deplored the necessity of admitting it, that he was well in the stream — even for a time directing the current — of English life.

In his preface to the *Oxford Book of Modern Verse,* Yeats permits himself to write with humorous nostalgia of literary London in the 'nineties, and to place Kipling among his fellows. No one could do it better than Yeats, who was also one of Henley's young men and a contributor to the *Scots Observer.* For Yeats there was but one whom all contemporaries accepted as the master of style — Walter Pater.

We poets [he says], continued to write verse, convinced that it would be disgraceful to take part in the social and political disturbances of the age. Then in 1900 everybody got down off his stilts; henceforth nobody drank absinthe with his black coffee; nobody went mad; nobody committed suicide; nobody joined the Catholic church; or if they did I have forgotten. Victorianism had been defeated, though two writers dominated the moment who had never heard of that defeat or did not believe in it; Rudyard Kipling and William Watson. Indian residence and associations had isolated the first, he was full of opinions, of politics, of impurities — to use our word — and the word must have been right, for he interests a critical audience to-day by the grotesque tragedy of *Danny Deever,* the matter but not the form of old street ballads, and by songs traditional in matter and form like *A St. Helena Lullaby.*

Yeats's competence to write on Anglo-Irish folklore may pass without question, but he put himself out of court in writing of English folklore by his attitude to the English scene in the eighteen-nineties. With the other young writers of the 'decadent' period, he deliberately cut himself off from the English common people. He could not recognize the fact that Kipling had rejected his own Pre-Raphaelite upbringing and had renewed his strength by contact with red earth, the proof being in the very example, 'Danny Deever', that Yeats selected to disprove it. To be sure, Yeats and his young friends did not sing the living folklore of the proletariat at their literary parties. They were unaware that it existed, and when Kipling used that live idiom they supposed that he had invented it. 'Danny Deever' is instantly recognizable by anyone who has served as a soldier (a larger class today than it was sixty years ago) as actually and firmly composed in the style of the songs that the soldiers sang (and still sing) in the canteen. But what the soldier sang was not evident to Yeats. *

The theme was taken up, far more intellectually, by Mr. Eliot, in his introduction to *A Choice of Kipling's Verse.* At the end of his

---

* The 'St. Helena Lullaby', a mature work of Kipling's middle age, is traditional in quite another sense; it is a Victorian drawing-room ballad, owing little to the folklore of the old street-singers.

analysis Mr. Eliot comes to no very clear conclusion. He defines Kipling's work, with some exceptions, 'as verse and not as poetry', but as 'great verse'; and it is worth noting that Kipling himself used the same terms, always referring to his own work as his Verses not as his Poems. 'Kipling', says Mr. Eliot, 'employed rather simple rhythms with adroit variations.' The paternity of Kipling's verse eludes Mr. Eliot's search because he looks in the wrong place.

Historically, a parallel may be drawn between the position in literary history of Kipling, and that of Sir Walter Scott. We do not now rank Scott very high as a 'pure' poet though much of his verse reaches a high level of accomplishment, and a ballad, here and there in his work, seems to be rather more than 'great verse'. He was immensely prolific, and often duplicated his effects by writing a succinct comment in verse on a theme he treated at greater length in prose. He enjoyed a vast popularity and made a great fortune by his pen. Even when his name and influence dominated the British world he knew well that the unacknowledged legislators of mankind had shifted their ground. In an age when the enlightened were swinging sharply to the left, he was a Tory and not the sort of man to care much for changing fashions in the republic of letters. It was with conscious liberality that he handed on the laurels to Byron; it was beyond his comprehension to learn that he must hand them equally to Keats. For the mass of his own contemporaries Keats had no message at all; he was not of an age but for a continuing posterity. Scott was the writer of and for his age and, as the interpreter of Scotland in the eighteenth century, he is now remembered. His strength came right out of the soil of the Border dales; his style, vocabulary, metre, rhythm, lilt, and turn of phrase were effective just in the degree that they were close to that soil. The tradition in which he worked was a living tradition and the favour he won was from people who recognized his work as an indisputable aspect of real life as they knew it, as folklore. So were Rudyard Kipling's early ballads folklore not pure poetry. Whether it is in any way a derogation of his work to make this assertion I shall leave to the professional critics to determine.

Walter Scott, like Robert Burns before him, used the traditional models of Lowland popular verse, never hesitating to adapt or borrow freely from his predecessors, according to the classic usage of folklore in all countries: such characteristics as the stylized imagery, the use of incantatory repetitions, the harmonics of a verse intended to be recited against a background of simple instrumental music, the turns of sentiment marked by a change of rhythm, the violent alternations of the grotesque, the horrible, and the pathetic.

But literary London in 1895 was occupied in turning its back on most of the things for which the rest of London cared, and when a young writer — an outsider from India — began to write in the living folklore tradition of the London streets, they could truthfully declare that they had never heard of it. When they discovered that the young Anglo-Indian was indifferent to their criticisms, scornful of their views, and devoted to a political cause they disliked, he was simply written off. 'Kipling does not revolutionize', says Mr. Eliot.

He is not one of those writers of whom one can say, that the *form* of English poetry will always be different from what it would have been if they had not written. What fundamentally differentiates his 'verse' from 'poetry' is the subordination of musical interest.

If we consider him as a composer of ballads in the folklore tradition, we must examine what was the popular music of the English, in the year 1890 when Kipling abandoned his juvenile practice of writing facile imitations or parodies of Swinburne, Poe, and Browning, and began to write Ballads. Obviously he was strongly affected by the Scottish tradition, not least because his mother was a Macdonald. It is not difficult to trace a direct connexion between his narrative ballads and the similar work of Sir Walter Scott. A link between 'The Ballad of East and West' and 'Young Lochinvar' would not be hard to establish. The reader of Kipling's verse will not fail to notice a tendency to slip into Scotticisms (for example in 'Tomlinson') where there seems no need for that dialect in particular. The most impressionable of writers, Kipling seems unconsciously to have drifted into the style of the poet who gave him the momentary impetus to compose. It may be relevant to mention here an idiosyncrasy in his private conduct; he had a strange tendency, when writing an intimate letter to a dear friend, to vary his handwriting and to imitate the script of the person he was writing to.

We have seen that his early verse was largely imitative. His own account of his reading in 'Uncle Crom's' library at Westward Ho! gives the direction of his taste. The Jacobean poets (not so fashionable in the eighteen-eighties as they became forty years later) always interested him and, in his early manhood, he made a special study of Donne; Border Ballads have left their mark on his style in numerous instances; but none of these influences was half as potent in forming him as the evangelical teaching of his childhood. Both his father and his mother came of Methodist families and, though not devout church-members, they were born and bred in the evangelical tradition. They sent Rudyard, at his most impressionable age, to be brought up at Southsea in a Calvinist household, where Bible-reading and hymn-singing provided the standards for verse and prose. This was the common fare of the great bulk of the English people in the nineteenth century — of almost all of them, it may be said, except the deracinated intellectuals. It was precisely because Kipling's prose repeatedly echoes Biblical rhythms and turns of phrase that it was accepted and understood by a public that read the Bible, but did not read Walter Pater. When it came to verse, Kipling tended to write in one of two styles. His more serious effects were made in a sonorous and didactic style that directly derived from *Hymns Ancient and Modern,* by far the most popular volume of verse in nineteenth-century England. Here again the intellectuals were out of tune with the national taste, and it was left for Kipling to adapt the *genre* of the popular hymn to the purpose of contemporary ballads. On his voyage in 1891, when Kipling had 'General' Booth of the Salvation Army for a travelling-companion, they struck up an unexpected friendship. Kipling was much nearer to the 'General' in his approach to life than he was to the professional poets. The 'General's' appeal to the English people was also made through the medium of hymns treated as folklore, and he declined to let the devil have all the best tunes.

Like 'General' Booth, Rudyard Kipling went into barrooms and barrack-rooms and music-halls to find out the songs the people were really singing, and fitted new words to them. The tunes they knew best were hymn-tunes, and after that the range of popular songs, largely American in origin, that arose about the time of the Civil War and are still not forgotten — such songs as 'John Brown's Body', 'Marching through Georgia', and 'Tramp, tramp, tramp, the boys are marching', the songs that the boys had shouted in chorus at Westward Ho! Then there were the music-hall ditties, as strongly traditional as the evangelical hymns. At the end of the century, 'The Man that broke the Bank at Monte Carlo' and 'Knocked 'em in the Old Kent Road' were the direct successors of 'Vilikins and his Dinah' which dated back to the beginning of it. Since childhood Kipling had been fascinated by the London music-halls — too much fascinated his father thought — and when he returned to London in 1889 he told a friend that he found them more satisfying than the theatre. During his lonely year in London his solace was Gatti's, the same music-hall which Sickert was to 'discover' and depict in another medium a few years later. The *Barrack-Room Ballads* essentially are songs for the 'Halls' in which the 'patter' dominates the musical setting. Apart from Kipling, the greatest master in that art was W. S. Gilbert (whom Kipling several times imitated in *Departmental Ditties*); but Gilbert's method was to compose the 'patter' and then employ Sullivan, so long as he could hold him to the task, at writing tunes to it. Kipling once co-operated with Sullivan in this way, when producing 'The Absent-minded Beggar'; his usual method was just the opposite. When the substance of a poem was forming in his mind he found a tune — not a metre but a tune — and absorbed himself in its rhythm until the words arranged themselves, whereupon the poem was made.

I know of no writer of such great gifts [says Mr. Eliot] for whom poetry seems to have been more purely an instrument. . . . For Kipling the poem is something which is intended to *act* — and for the most part his poems are intended to elicit the same response from all readers, and only the response which they can make in common.

That is to say, the ballad is addressed to an audience not to an individual; it is to be sung, not read in an arm-chair; or, if not sung, it is presented in dramatic form as if it were being sung to an audience. The overtones which distinguish Kipling's verse from his prose are semantic rather than harmonic, getting their effect more from the associations of words than from the combination of sounds.

He experimented in almost every conventional verse-form, and wrote remarkably successful *vers libres* but, though the greater part of his verse is in regular rhymed stanzas, it will be found that the rules of scansion give little help in appreciating his rhythms. Take, for example, so celebrated a poem as 'Mandalay':

> By the old Moulmein Pagoda, lookin' eastward to the sea,
> There's a Burma girl a-settin', and I know she thinks o' me;
> For the wind is in the palm-trees, and the temple-bells they say:
> 'Come you back, you British soldier; come you back to Mandalay!'

It will throw no light upon this poem to say that it is written in trochaic lines of eight feet, the metre of Tennyson's 'Locksley Hall', for the timing is entirely different.

> Thro' the shadow of the globe we sweep into the younger day:
> Better fifty years of Europe than a cycle of Cathay.

We shall come a little nearer if we notice that the rhythm of 'Mandalay' is similar to that of Poe's 'Raven'. The key-phrase, repeated with such powerfully nostalgic effect, 'Come you back to Mandalay', is identical in its timing with 'quoth the Raven, "Nevermore"', and could be sung to the same tune, though it would not be appropriate. Kipling's method was to study the flow and timing of an air and to arrange his words accordingly. Instead of scanning his verses by setting them out in metrical feet with regularly recurrent accents, or stresses, it would be more significant to give them a musical notation since, actually, 'Mandalay' was written to the air of a popular waltz.

When Kipling was in America in 1889 he recorded his intention of composing a poem on the theme of the English Race, and of writing it to the tune of Handel's 'Dead March' in *Saul*. This project was not completed but, two or three years later, he wrote a *Barrack-Room Ballad* about a soldier's funeral, and used the *motif* he had intended for the other composition. 'Follow me 'Ome', which was selected by Hilaire Belloc as one of Kipling's two best poems,[13] is singularly effective in the variety of time and tone which is achieved in a few lines, and it concludes with a sudden break into the rhythm of a slow march:

> 'Take 'im away! 'E's gone where the best men go.
> Take 'im away! An' the gun-wheels turnin' slow.
> Take 'im away! There's more from the place 'e come.
> Take 'im away, with the limber an' the drum.'

This, simply, is the tune of the 'Dead March' expressed in words, and suggests, inevitably to the reader, the slow thumping music of the military band in the distance. Kipling's ballads are not, as a rule, intended to be sung; but by giving the reader a hint of an old tune they provoke an unexpected emotional response:

> And the tunes that mean so much to you alone —
> Common tunes that make you choke and blow your nose —
> Vulgar tunes that bring the laugh that brings the groan —
> I can rip your very heartstrings out with those.

Sometimes he used a tune in this way, suggestively. An example is the savagely cynical-sentimental song, which he called 'The Birds-of-Prey March', about soldiers embarking in the rain for some colonial war. In a ribald, drunken style, the cockney song, 'Knocked 'em in the Old Kent Road', drifts in and out of the rhythm of the ballad:

> Cheer! An' we'll never march to victory.
> Cheer! An' we'll never live to 'ear the cannon roar!
> The Large Birds o' Prey
> They will carry us away,
> An' you'll never see your soldiers any more!

When Mrs. Hill wrote her reminiscences of Kipling in India she claimed to have been present at the inception of the *Barrack-Room Ballads* in 1889.

We were on the British India steamer *Africa* sailing towards Singapore, standing by the rail when he suddenly began to hum 'Rum-ti-tum-tra-la' — shaking the ashes from his pipe overboard. I was used to this, knowing something was stirring in his brain. Humming in a musical tone, he exclaimed, 'I have it. I'll write some Tommy Atkins Ballads,' and this idea simmering for months, with an occasional outbreak in soldier-like language.[14]

Kay Robinson described his method of composition in similar words: ' When he had got a tune into his head, the words and rhyme came as readily as when a singer vamps his own banjo accompaniment'. Kipling's phrasing is usually remarkable for its appropriateness, and his rhymes seem inevitable. Among his notebooks there is a tell-tale draft for a piece of society verse which he never finished. It is of no importance but for the form in which it is written down, in complete stanzas but with the rhyming last syllables left blank, to be filled in when the subconscious mind should provide them.

In one of his articles sent out to India,[15] Kipling recounted his delight in composing a song for Gatti's music-hall and hearing it bandied across the footlights between the comedian and the chorus in the gallery.

> At the back of the Knightsbridge Barracks
>   When the fog's a gatherin' dim,
> The Lifeguard waits for the under-cook,
>   But she won't wait for 'im.

Perhaps truth, perhaps fiction; but, truth or fiction, this is where the inspiration for the ballads comes from, and their execution recalls the technique of the old music-hall.

The orchestra strikes up a few bars of the air in unison; the singer comes forward and throws himself into the first verse of his song with a heavily orchestrated accompaniment *con molta espressione*. The second verse is light comedy, a patter-song spoken across the footlights in conversational tones, with a little gagging here and there, inserted so as not to break the rhythmical beat of the tune which the orchestra maintains, *allegro pianissimo*. The third verse is pure melo-drama, rich with sentiment, and only bearable because it has been salted with the wit of the previous verse; and then the gallery is ripe for the conclusion, a release of emotion that has been uncomfortably stimulated. The singer gesticulates, the band crashes out in torrents of noise, the gallery sings and shouts, until even the genteel people in the stalls find their resistance broken down. The process is described by Kipling in his farcical story which turns on the promotion of publicity by means of a popular song, ' The Village that Voted the Earth was Flat'.

Imagine what its rage and pulse must have been at the incandescent hour of its birth. She only gave the chorus once. At the end of the second verse, ' Are you *with* me, boys? ' she cried, and the house tore it clean away from her — ' Earth was flat — Earth was flat — Flat as my hat

— Flatter than that' drowning all but the bassoons and the double basses that marked the word. 'Wonderful,' I said to Bat. 'And it's only " Nuts in May " with variations.' 'Yes — but *I* wrote the variations,' he replied.

Lower still in the social scale of literature were the bawdy songs that the soldiers sang in the canteen. Sailors' songs had already been collected by the literary, long before 1890, because sailors were 'romantic', but no one had thought of collecting genuine soldiers' songs, and when Kipling wrote in this traditional style it was not recognized as traditional. We must now return to 'Danny Deever', which Yeats and Eliot both selected for special notice. It is a question-and-answer ballad of a kind which has flourished in English folklore for many hundred years. Neither Yeats nor, more recently, Mr. Eliot seems to have known that a grotesque bawdy song in much the same style was sung in the Army in Kipling's day, and is still to be heard. Like most folklore it exists in many versions, and had better be called, here, 'Barnacle Bill the Sailor'. In its earlier form, the alternate couplets in contrasted tones may well have served as a model for 'Danny Deever'.

A simple example of the use of a music-hall song for a music-hall theme is the ballad, 'Shillin' a Day', which goes to the tune of 'Vilikins and his Dinah', or any other Irish jig. The lover of Kipling's verse will no doubt be able to identify other basic tunes. 'Boots' may be assigned to the tune of 'John Brown's Body', with some confidence, and the irregular punctuation seems designed to point out the variations. 'Kabul River' has at least an echo about it of 'Tramp, Tramp, Tramp'; and if these assignments are not accepted as Kipling's actual use, there is still no doubt that these ballads were written to some familiar tunes of those days. Mrs. Kipling's diary repeatedly uses the expression: 'Ruddy was singing a new poem today . . .' He would say 'Give me a hymn-tune' and, when someone suggested one, would go about for days humming it over, drumming it out with his fingers until words framed themselves to the tune, intent upon that and oblivious of the world, until he had finished his verse. It did not matter, for that purpose, that the song whose tune he borrowed was quite incongruous with the poem he intended; it was the rhythm he wanted and made his own. In an earlier chapter, the haunting verses, 'Let us now praise famous men' were quoted. They are like nothing else in the language in their strong unusual rhythm except 'Pop goes the Weasel'. The assiduous student can find stranger incongruities.

(3)

KIM

'He has come down steadily', said Henry James, 'from the less simple to the more simple.' If this was true of Kipling's middle period, the years of writing the *Jungle Books* and *Captains Courageous,* it was not to be true of the period into which he was moving. Kipling in the twentieth century was certainly not a simple writer. His verse was to acquire new harmonies and even to reveal those blots of heart's blood which R. L. Stevenson had failed to find in the early *Barrack-room Ballads*; his prose stories which Henry James had thought deficient in shades and subtleties were to become as richly polyphonic as Henry James's own. If the reader will compare 'The Finest Story in the World' (1891) with 'Wireless' (1903), or 'The Brushwood Boy' (1894) with 'They' (1904), the change will be apparent.

There was a turning-point in Kipling's life when his youthful exuberance was put behind him, with much of his youthful gaiety, when certain dreams had faded with the loss of a beloved child, when he felt himself to be launched into the bleak, unpromising sea of middle age. In the *Inclusive Verse* two poems stand side by side, dated 1902 and 1903. One of them, with the title of 'The Second Voyage', seems to allude, defiantly and rather facetiously, to the process of settling down in middle life. Youthful enthusiasm is discounted, adverse criticism is ignored, as life runs through sunless seas, like a liner on its charted course, under the serene guidance of married love.

> The sea has shorn our galleries away,
>   The salt has soiled our gliding past remede;
> Our paint is flaked and blistered by the spray,
>   Our sides are half a fathom furred in weed
>   (Foul weather!)
> And the Doves of Venus fled and the petrels came instead,
>   But Love he was our master at our need!

The other poem (of which some lines appeared as chapter-headings in *Kim*) contains obscurities which have baffled many readers.

> There walks no wind 'neath Heaven
>   Nor wave that shall restore
> The old careening riot
>   And the clamorous, crowded shore —
> The fountain in the desert,
>   The cistern in the waste,
> The bread we ate in secret,
>   The cup we spilled in haste.

Now call I to my Captains —
For council fly the sign —
Now leap their zealous galleys,
Twelve-oared, across the brine
To me the straiter prison,
To me the heavier chain —
To me Diego Valdez,
High Admiral of Spain!

It is a ballad set in the heroic age of Spain expressing the longing with which Diego Valdez the Admiral looks back to the buccaneering days of his youth, as Kipling the celebrity looks back with longing to his laborious boyhood in India. There can be no doubt about the allusions to the chain which still binds the Admiral, a galley-slave, in the servitude of duty.

The valediction to his old life was the publication of *Kim,* his last word on India, so many times laid aside, so long on the anvil. Ten years had passed since he had been an Anglo-Indian by right of service, ten years in which much had happened in India which he never appreciated. Lord Curzon invited him to Simla as a guest in 1899, but viceroys, he said, were not much in his line. India remained, in his eyes, the unchanging East, as he remembered it from childhood, and so he described it, lovingly, in *Kim.*

The new book owed something to his youthful romance, *Mother Maturin,* but how much cannot be told since no one now living has read the earlier work. Mrs. Hill gave the following account of it:

Mother Maturin I have read, which was never published because John Lockwood Kipling was not satisfied with it. It is the story of an old Irishwoman who kept an opium den in Lahore but sent her daughter to be educated in England. She married a Civilian and came to live in Lahore — hence a story how Government secrets came to be known in the Bazaar and *vice versa.*[16]

In London Rudyard had turned to *Mother Maturin* again, and then perhaps realized that his father had judged rightly in condemning it. The manuscript remained for years in the safe at A. P. Watt's office until in 1899 Rudyard brought it down to Rottingdean to ransack it for notions which he could work into *Kim.* Thereafter *Mother Maturin* vanished, probably destroyed by the author, though, many years later, Kipling prepared a draft for a film scenario which contained episodes from the old story.

The second plan for an Indian Romance took shape at 'Naulakha' in 1894. Now it was to be the life-story of *Kim O'rishti,* an Irish soldier's orphan, living foot-loose in India. Three times begun and laid aside, it was abandoned in favour of *Captains Courageous.* In the

fall of 1899, having finished with *Stalky,* he turned again to *Kim.*
Many times he took the draft down to Tisbury to be smoked over
with the 'Pater' until, in August 1900, Carrie wrote triumphantly in
her diary that it was pronounced complete by a family council, which
included the 'Pater' and Sallie Norton.

It grew like the Djinn released from the brass bottle [Rudyard wrote],
and the more we explored its possibilities the more opulence of detail did
we discover. I do not know what proportion of an iceberg is below water-
line, but *Kim* as it finally appeared was about one-tenth of what the first
lavish specification called for.

.*Kim* took care of himself. The only trouble was to keep him within
bounds. Between us we knew every step, sight, and smell on his casual
road, as well as all the persons he met. Once only, as I remember, did I
have to bother the India Office, where there are four acres of books and
documents in the basements, for a certain work on Indian magic which
I always regret that I could not steal.

At last I reported *Kim* finished. 'Did *it* stop, or you?' the Father
asked. And when I told him that it was *It,* he said: 'Then it oughtn't
to be too bad.' He would take no sort of credit for any of his suggestions,
memories or confirmations — not even for that single touch of the low-
driving sunlight which makes luminous every detail in the picture of the
Grand Trunk Road at eventide. The Himalayas I painted *all* by myself,
as the children say. So also the picture of the Lahore Museum of which
I had once been Deputy Curator for six weeks — unpaid but immensely
important. And there was a half-chapter of the *lama* sitting down in the
blue-green shadows at the foot of a glacier, telling Kim stories out of the
Jatakas, which was truly beautiful but, as my old Classics master would
have said, 'otiose', and it was removed almost with tears.[17]

Kim was published at the end of 1900 about the time of the 'Khaki
Election', when public opinion was sharply divided over the political
views with which Kipling's name was linked, and so did not at first
produce the chorus of applause which had greeted some of his earlier
work. There was some hostile, and more of cool and grudging,
criticism like that of Arnold Bennett, who said in an essay: '*Stalky*
chilled me and *Kim* killed me'.[18] Since then the book has grown in
stature and is often now selected as the Kipling book with the highest
measure of artistry. It is, however, in the author's own words, not
a novel but 'nakedly picaresque and plotless'.

Surely no other Englishman has written of India which such loving
interest! Mr. Forster's *Passage to India* is the only work which can
be laid beside it, and, in many respects, *Kim* comes well out of the
comparison. In this instance Forster, not Kipling, is the political
writer, the observer of a passing phase. With his cool, sensitive regard
Forster appraises the Indian character and the Indian scene, noting

conscious and unconscious processes, analysing with a skill that Kipling did not and could not attempt to equal. In the cold light of Forster's observation all is clear and all unlovable.

Kim is not a political romance; the reader soon loses interest in a plot which the author does not trouble to elaborate. The education of a police spy — and that is what, superficially, *Kim* seems to be about — is hardly a subject for an *epos;* nor does it much matter. The hero, 'Kim', is thrown by this path into the vagabond life of India so that we may see, and smell, the hot scented dust and the people of the land. Here is a boy roving through India, loving it and causing us to love it. Politics, the Empire, the Law, are taken for granted. It is not 'Kim's' affair; nor the reader's to question the credentials of the *Pax Britannica,* but to savour life within its borders. Nothing is explained or excused or justified.

Apart from a slight sketch of Lockwood Kipling ('the Keeper of the Wonder-house') in the opening chapter, Englishmen do not play a conspicuous part in the story. 'Bennett', the English Chaplain, is shown in an unfavourable light, and the Irish Chaplain, though less unpleasing, is merely a stock figure.* The drummer-boy who chums with 'Kim' in barracks is allowed none of the charm which, in spite of their depravity, was conceded to the 'Drums of the Fore and Aft'. 'Lurgan, the healer of sick pearls', is a nondescript, not a true *sahib*. Kim's kindly patron, 'Colonel Creighton', is kept in the background.

The interest is all concentrated upon Kim's relation with four natives of India: the Pathan horse-dealer, Mahbub Ali; the Bengali, Hurree Chunder; the old dowager *sahiba* from Saharunpore; and the Tibetan lama who steals the limelight to become hero of the book. The lean ferocious Pathan and the suave sophisticated Babu seem at first to be stock characters, until they burst into life by showing the contradictions of living persons. The faithless, cruel Mahbub is gradually revealed as true and even tender; the volatile, timid Babu as discreet and courageous when put to the test; and the interaction of

---

* Kipling's views on missionaries, when he was a young man, are expressed in a letter written from 'Naulakha' to the Rev. J. Gillespie, on 16th October 1895. The original is in the Houghton Library.

'It is my fortune to have been born and to a large extent brought up among those whom white men call "heathen"; and while I recognize the paramount duty of every white man to follow the teachings of his creed and conscience as "a debtor to the whole law", it seems to me cruel that white men, whose governments are armed with the most murderous weapons known to science, should amaze and confound their fellow creatures with a doctrine of salvation imperfectly understood by themselves and a code of ethics foreign to the climate and instincts of those races whose most cherished customs they outrage and whose gods they insult.'

these characters illumines Kim's slow adolescence. This is a display of the novelist's art which Kipling rarely achieved in his other works (unless perhaps in that juvenile *tour de force, The Story of the Gadsbys.*) There was a real Mahbub Ali, as Kay Robinson put on record; Babus looking like Hurree Chunder are plentiful in Calcutta to this day, but the *sahiba* and the lama were original inventions, new in literature. The *sahiba* was the first full-length in Kipling's gallery of elderly women, a group worth examining. The lama has no literary ancestry or progeny; he is Kipling's final comment on Buddhist Asia.

The author dwells lovingly upon some minor characters, the Jat, the Ressaldar, the 'Woman of Shamlegh' (who had made an earlier appearance as 'Lispeth' in *Plain Tales*); but all disappear from the scene before the end, leaving the stage to Kim and the lama, the two principals. The lama withdraws his mind into the world of reality, having rejected all the appearances of the world of illusion, even such symbols of infinity as his beloved Hills. Kim, too, has reached a stage of maturity and must take a decision. No longer a ragamuffin of the bazaars, but a beautiful godlike youth, he must choose between contemplation and action. Is he to follow the lama or to return to the chains which enslave the Pathan and the Babu to their material duties. Divided in loyalty, like Mowgli between the Village and the Jungle, living like the Brushwood Boy on two mental planes, he can be more conscious of the marriage of East and West than the Calcutta-trained Babu or the Pathan who has learned to outwit the English by their own devices. In the last stage of the lama's pilgrimage, Kim quite forgets his own task in the world, while absorbed in the humble duty of love and gratitude.

He begged in the dawn, set blankets for the lama's meditation, held the weary head on his lap through the noonday heats, fanning away the flies till his wrists ached, begged again in the evenings, and rubbed the lama's feet, who rewarded him with promise of Freedom — to-day, to-morrow, or, at furthest, the next day.

And when that day came, it was the lama who reminded 'Kim' that he was a *sahib* with another course of life to pursue. Again the dilemma was presented, East or West, the Jungle or the Village, the world of dreams or the world of action; and, though it is not expressly stated, the reader is left with the assurance that Kim, like Mowgli, and like the Brushwood Boy, will find reality in action, not in contemplation.

With an almost audible click, he felt the wheels of his being lock up anew on the world without. Things that rode meaningless on his eyeballs an instant before slid into proper proportion. Roads were meant to be walked upon, houses to be lived in, cattle to be driven, fields to be tilled, and men and women to be talked to. They were all real and true.

The desire to penetrate the occult exercised a strong fascination over Rudyard throughout life, an attraction which he resisted, not altogether successfully. In this respect Rudyard was a man of his day, interested in what interested his contemporaries, a reader of the numerous novels and poems that touched on these themes. His youth was passed in a circle where Madame Blavatsky and the early Theosophists had made no small impression. Later he was a friend of William James and acquainted with the speculation which, in 1902, were to be formulated in the *Varieties of Religious Experience,* the book which made a rational analysis of Eastern and Western mysticism.

The study of the irrational, the subliminal, the supernormal made great strides after the Viennese psychologists had found the key to the unconscious mind, with the consequence that many of the phenomena which the men of the eighteen-nineties regarded as supernatural were examined by the men of the nineteen-twenties in terms of the new psychology. Rudyard's later stories were to provide some evidence of his movement with this stream of thought.

CHAPTER XV

A HOME IN SUSSEX (1902–8)

SIR RICHARD'S SONG (1906)

I followed my Duke ere I was a lover,
   To take from England fief and fee;
But now this game is the other way over —
   But now England hath taken me!

     .   .   .   .

As for my Father in his tower,
   Asking news of my ship at sea,
He will remember his own hour —
   Tell him England hath taken me!

As for my Mother in her bower,
   That rules my Father so cunningly,
She will remember a maiden's power —
   Tell her England hath taken me!

As for my Brother in Rouen City,
   A nimble and naughty page is he,
But he will come to suffer and pity —
   Tell him England hath taken me!

As for my little Sister waiting
   In the pleasant orchards of Normandie,
Tell her youth is the time for mating —
   Tell her England hath taken me!

As for my comrades in camp and highway,
   That lift their eyebrows scornfully,
Tell them their way is not my way —
   Tell them England hath taken me!

     .   .   .   .

IN October 1899, Mr. Harmsworth of the *Daily Mail,* for whom
Rudyard wrote 'The Absent-minded Beggar', came down to see
the Kiplings in a motor-car of his own. They were instantly converted to the new form of transport which released them from
restraints that were beginning to bear heavily and, in December,

Rudyard hired a motor from Brighton, with an 'engineer' at three and a half guineas a week. It was a

Victoria-hooded, carriage-sprung, carriage-braked, single-cylinder, belt-driven, fixed-ignition, Embryo which, at times, could cover eight miles an hour.[1]

The next summer, when they returned from Africa, they looked for something better in a market that was rapidly expanding. Rudyard bought a steam-driven American car of a long-forgotten type, called a 'locomobile', and for two years drove it from end to end of Sussex, in a world still unprovided with petrol-pumps, spare tyres, or repair shops. Every motorist had to be his own mechanic and had to learn how to do running repairs as new problems arose. Two or three times a week, Rudyard and Carrie set off for long drives with the 'engineer', and her diary gives the impression that few outings were completed without mishap.

Motoring misadventures play a large part in his stories during the next few years, and, once or twice, dominate the scene. The 'loco-mobile' is faithfully described in 'Steam Tactics', a complex tale of sailors ashore, officious policemen, and Mr. Loder's private zoo; the machine alone draws these diverse elements together. Rudyard often exercised his mind with parodies in verse, and to this period belongs his series, *The Muse among the Motors,* which first appeared in the *Daily Mail.*

House-hunting was the ostensible reason for their drives across the country. One day when the 'locomobile' had broken down, they went by train to Etchingham, then took a 'fly' through woodland lanes to Burwash where there was talk of a house named 'Bateman's'. It was a well-built square Jacobean house of stone in a lonely valley, at the foot of a steep lane running down from an unfrequented village. 'Bateman's' took their fancy so that for three days they talked of little else, but while they hesitated, someone stepped in and rented it. That was in August 1900, and nearly two years passed before they heard that 'Bateman's' was vacant again. It happened that again the 'locomobile' was out of order so that the second visit to Burwash, like the first, was made by train and hired fly. There was no doubt in their minds: this was the dream-house, the 'very-own-house' of their private baby-talk, and they snatched it out of the market.

When all was signed and sealed, the seller said: 'Now I can ask you something. How are you going to manage about getting to and from the station? It's nearly four miles, and I've used up two pair of horses on the hill here.' A motor-car? 'Oh, those things haven't come to stay.'

By this time the Kiplings had bought their second automobile, a Lanchester, and, so primitive was the motor-trade in those days, Mr. Lanchester in person delivered the car at their door.

In three years [said Rudyard] from our purchase, the railway station had passed out of our lives. In seven, I heard my chauffeur say to an under-powered visiting sardine-tin: 'Hills? There ain't any hills on the London road.' [2]

The removal to 'Bateman's' on 3rd September 1902 — it was their last house-moving as they were sure it would be — was taken easily by Rudyard and desperately hard by Carrie. She rather thought the contractor's men were drunk, and the state of the house when she took charge was like 'chaos and black night', as she wrote in her diary. It was the end of the month before she began to enjoy the comfort of a fine mild autumn. Rudyard and the children had already taken the place to their hearts, and when the first family visitors, Stan and Cissie Baldwin and Hugh Poynter, were received, they too pronounced 'Bateman's' charming.

Rudyard then took his final decision to dispose of 'Naulakha'. He would never again now live in Vermont, never again visit the United States to stir the dreadful memory of 1899. He emptied 'Naulakha' of what they needed; invited Dr. Conland to help himself to guns, rods, and sporting gear, and sold the estate to the Cabots for $8000, much below cost price. It seems likely that Beatty Balestier had done his brother-in-law one more ill turn by hinting that he would dispute the title, and this may have been one reason why 'Naulakha' did not fetch a more adequate price.[5]

Rudyard Kipling to C. E. Norton

30 November, 1902

We left Rottingdean because Rottingdean was getting too populated, though we didn't want to part from Aunt Georgie. Then we discovered England which we had never done before . . . and went to live in it. England is a wonderful land. It is the most marvellous of all foreign countries that I have ever been in. It is made up of trees and green fields and mud and the gentry, and at last I'm one of the gentry — I'll take a new pen and explain.

Behold us lawful owners of a grey stone lichened house — A.D. 1634 over the door — beamed, panelled, with old oak staircase, and all untouched and unfaked. Heaven looked after it in the dissolute times of mid-victorian restoration and caused the vicar to send his bailff to live in it for 40 years, and he lived in peaceful filth and left everything as he found it.

It is a good and peaceable place standing in terraced lawns nigh to a walled garden of old red brick, and two fat-headed oast-houses with red brick stomachs, and an aged silver-grey dovecot on top. There is what they call a river at the bottom of the lawn. It appears on all maps and that, except after very heavy rains, is the only place where it puts in any appearance. . . . Its name is the Dudwell, and it is quite ten feet wide.[3]

He learned to know the River Dudwell better. Almost every autumn it flooded the meadows, overflowed the garden on several occasions, and at least once came into the house — not always a 'Friendly Brook'.

In 1903 *The Five Nations,* his book of South African verse, was sent to press, and with that he felt an instant sense of relief. It was the end of an epoch for him as for the Empire. A strong reaction was setting in against the sentiments of wartime patriotism, and the prospects of the imperialists in Parliament were blighted by Joseph Chamberlain's resignation in October. A day of great events was over, and Rudyard recorded the fact oracularly:

> Things never yet created things —
> 'Once on a time there was a Man.'

Political urgency, gloomy though the outlook might be, was shifting back from Africa to Westminster and, though he continued to winter at the Cape for four years longer, Rudyard put South African affairs behind him, with the publication of *The Five Nations,* as he had put India behind him, long ago and far away, with the publication of *Kim.*

Never was the width of his interest more noticeable or his power of assimilating new technical information more astonishing than in the work he began at the end of 1903. Among many celebrities who made it their business to know him about that time were the two makers of Nigeria, Sir George Goldie whom he met at the Cape, and Sir Frederick Lugard whom he met in Sussex. Though Rudyard had never been in tropical Africa, he wrote one convincing story, 'A Deal in Cotton', about the last days of the Arab slave-trade, which must have been derived from his talks with the two proconsuls. He told it as if at a reunion of his old school-friends, with 'Stalky' as one of the group; and Major Dunsterville of the 20th Sikhs had, in fact, re-entered Kipling's life. He visited 'Bateman's' in May 1904 and frequently thereafter.

This was a slight switch of interest but, as well as 'A Deal in Cotton', Rudyard wrote three other stories on widely differing themes in 1904. A settled way of life in Sussex, a home of his own with seclusion and privacy, stimulated a flow of new notions, as the first happy years in Vermont had done.

'Mrs. Bathurst' is a strange and difficult tale. Rudyard had now quite outgrown the diffuseness and exuberance which marred some of the stories of his Allahabad period. He could afford to take his time, and let nothing go to press until it had been exhaustively edited and revised. It was not uncommon for the first draft of a story to be two or three times longer than its published form, as he whimsically explained:

In an auspicious hour, read your final draft and consider faithfully every paragraph, sentence and word, blacking out where requisite. Let it lie by to drain as long as possible. At the end of that time, re-read and you should find that it will bear a second shortening. Finally, read it aloud alone and at leisure. Maybe a shade more brushwork will then indicate or impose itself. If not, praise Allah and let it go, and ' when thou hast done, repent not '. . . . I have had tales by me for three or five years which shortened themselves almost yearly.[4]

He had not acquired this technique when he wrote 'The Drums of the Fore and Aft'; he perhaps overdid it when he shortened 'Mrs. Bathurst', a complex story which would have supplied most writers with a full-length novel. It suffers from too much compression, so that in parts it is unintelligible. Nevertheless, for all its obscurity, 'Mrs. Bathurst' is a powerful story, the account of a woman who is described as not very seductive or amusing or intelligent, but who was never forgotten by any man who made her acquaintance.

' 'Tisn't beauty, so to speak, nor good talk necessarily. It's just It. Some women'll stay in a man's memory if they once walk down a street.'

The original of Mrs. Bathurst is said to have been a barmaid in Christchurch, New Zealand;[5] the setting of the tale is at Simonstown, the naval base at the Cape, but these are subsidiary matters. What the reader remembers is the glimpse of ' Mrs. Bathurst walking down towards us with that blindish look in her eyes and the reticule in her hand ', as the two sailors saw her in a cinema film. It is one of the earliest allusions to the cinematograph in fiction, as it is, perhaps, the earliest use of the word ' It ' for feminine charm.

The critics had fallen foul of Kipling's early attempts to portray women, finding them all detestable, from ' the Colonel's Lady to Judy O'Grady '. The gently smiling, faithful, mature Mrs. Bathurst was different indeed, but so elliptic is the process of her story that the reader is never plainly told what becomes of her. She is flashed on to the screen and off, with disastrous but incomprehensible consequences to the sailor who has pursued her round the world. Such a tale could never be a popular favourite and it seems hardy credible that it should have been written by the author of ' The Absent-minded Beggar '.

It was no sooner finished than he set to work at ' They ' (begun at Cape Town in February 1904), another story which some readers found obscure when it was first published. Since ' Baa, Baa, Black

Sheep', he had made no direct personal revelations in his prose work, though many of his stories, of course, were founded upon incidents or characters that had come under his observation. When Rudyard himself appeared in these stories it was behind the mask he assumed to protect himself from publicity, not Rudyard as he was but Rudyard as he wished to be seen. Three times and, I think, three times only, he dropped the mask, revealing, in one instance, his unhappy childhood, in the others the unforgotten pain of his child's death. To early critics the story called 'They' was merely psychical fiction in his new style with a theme that was in the fashionable taste, another story like Henry James's *Turn of the Screw* (1898). The setting of the story is drawn from Rudyard's memories of motoring through Sussex, with many brilliant landscapes in his Pre-Raphaelite manner. The allegory is drawn straight from his own sorrow; the years of house-hunting, at last concluded, had been darkened by a shadow that never lifted from the heart of either parent. Soon after their return from America in 1899, Lockwood had written with unwonted openness to their old friend Sarah Norton:

Rud and Carrie, I may confide to you and Mr. Norton who love them, found going back to the 'Elms' much harder and more painful than they had imagined. The house and garden are full of the lost child and poor Rud told his mother how he saw her when a door opened, when a space was vacant at table, coming out of every green dark corner of the garden, radiant — and heart breaking. They can talk of her, however, which is much, for Carrie has hitherto been stone-dumb. But to Mrs. K. she softened and broke forth and they had long discourse, mingling their tears as women may and mothers must. Over every grave, at long last, the high road must run, and nobody wishes to hasten the time of indifference — but a sore heartache, I am sure, is relieved by sympathetic — (Lord! in the blue sky! What twaddle I'm writing). Of course, it is relieved by speech and friendly hands; all I meant to say was that those poor souls have got thus far with their burden — which will grow easier to bear with time.[6]

He are Carrie often went to visit his father's friend, St. Loe Strachey, the editor of the *Spectator,* near Guildford in Surrey. They stayed a week-end with the Stracheys in June 1900 and on a Sunday morning walked together through the countryside, while their hosts went to church.

> There runs a road by Merrow Down —
> A grassy track to-day it is —
> An hour out of Guildford town,
> Above the river Wey it is.
>
> Here, when they heard the horse-bells ring, . . .

In the mind's eye, Rudyard saw the long procession of the dead who had walked the Pilgrims' Way throughout the centuries, till time lost its significance. The transience of life was its one persisting feature and a year as long to the grief-stricken as a thousand years. From Merrow Down to Brook lands in Romney Marsh, there was no landscape, now, that did not recall to Rudyard that slight figure, dancing through the fern; and when, deep in woods of stilly oak, he found his dream-house at last, it lacked one blessing only for him, the child that might have taken his hand. It was not for him to beat against the bars of space and time in so-called psychical research. So, in his story, the blind woman in the haunted house, whose second-sight reveals the presence of the dream-children, was no true guide for him, who saw with open eyes so deeply into the world of actuality. She, too, recognized his vocation as craftsman not as mystic: 'For you it would be wrong,' she said, 'you who must never come here again.' This prohibition lay upon the world of dreams, not upon real Sussex and its living people.

A day or two after finishing 'They', his resilient intelligence had fastened upon a new subject which, wrote Carrie, was 'a keen pleasure to him', a subject as far removed from the enchantments of the occult as it could well be. He set to work at an experiment in science fiction — as popular then as now — a vision of the future called 'With the Night Mail'. It is cast in the form of a journalist's account of an Atlantic crossing, by air, in the year 2000. Never before had he allowed himself such a debauch of technical writing as in this story, for which he invented thousands of words of shop-talk to be put into the mouth of his 'McAndrew' of the future, and filled up pages with answers to imaginary correspondents and advertisements for machines not yet invented.

Far more remarkable than his vision of the airship — which was paralleled by the similar picture H. G. Wells painted for *The War in the Air* — is his astonishing forecast of the contrivances, the utilities, and the safety precautions that airborne commerce would bring into being. Radio communication was new in 1904. Although a few ships were fitted with wireless telegraphy, there was no radio-telephony, no hint or suggestion of public broadcasting; but Kipling's air-liner moved through a world-wide network of radio services, supplying weather forecasts, and allotting safety-levels and landing priorities, thirty years before anyone else had dreamed of 'flying control'. His airship is engined with gas-turbines and is navigated on light-beams which pierce the clouds.

Three years later, in 1907, that is still before Wilbur Wright had come to Europe or Blériot flown the Channel, he wrote the draft of a sequel to 'With the Night Mail', calling it 'As Easy as A.B.C.', a political invention, filling out a sketch which he had lightly indicated in the first story.

It is not a Utopia: there is no suggestion that this is what Rudyard would have wished to come about; nor is it, like George Orwell's *1984*, a forecast of horror; it is a mere statement of what might occur when the technocrats should have made the progress which, to a seeing eye in 1907, they seemed likely to make. Broadcasting techniques were foreseen with uncanny accuracy and the transmission of energy by radio is carried to much greater length in his fantasy than has yet been achieved in real life, with the consequence that an international Utility Company of radio technicians, the 'Aerial Board of Control', has imperceptibly taken over the administration of the planet. The sovereign states have withered away, and political ideologies exist only as picturesque survivals or atavistic patches of superstition. The solution is 'as easy as A.B.C.'; power must pass to the organization that directs traffic through the world-wide radio network. Of its structure he has nothing to say except that it is cosmopolitan.

On the passing of politics, Kipling speaks clearly enough in his own voice. How gladly will the men of the future abandon the follies of Democracy, the slogans, the street-processions, the mob-oratory, the ancient corruptions, the corroding sentimentalities, in return for a system that secures privacy for private persons and adequate public services. 'Transportation is Civilization.', and if the 'A.B.C.' takes responsibility for the 'traffic and all that that implies', politics may be forgotten.

The point of the story, the fable, is the emergence in Chicago of a group of political sentimentalists who alarm their neighbours by assembling in crowds, making speeches, and casting votes; and the solution triumphantly propounded by the Aerial Board of Control is to let them do it as a comic turn on the light programme of the London Broadcasting Service. Strangely enough, this situation is not treated as farce but as a narrow escape from social disaster, in an age when all sane men have realized the reckless cruelty of men in the mass. The future is not, in Kipling's view, a pleasant world to live in, but beset with neuroses, and doomed to extinction by a birth rate dwindling towards zero.

Radio techniques had engaged his attention since his cruise with the Channel Fleet in 1898, when the Navy was experimenting with Marconi's new devices; and Rudyard used their attempts to communicate through a half-comprehended medium (which physicists, in those days, called the 'aether') as a foil to communications of another sort, in his brilliantly constructed story, 'Wireless'. If messages could pass through the impalpable 'aether', as if material obstructions in space were of no account, why should not time be equally penetrable?

After writing 'With the Night Mail' he had swung back to the past, and in September of that year sat down to a series of tales from English history. 'You'll have to look up your references rather carefully', said his father.

Something of the kind had been stirring in his imagination for a year or two. At Rottingdean he had consulted his 'Uncle Ned', a good mediaeval scholar, about historical reading, and had received a letter of advice couched in terms which give no hint of the mystical solemnity suggested by Burne-Jones's pictures. This reveals another side of life at 'North End House'.

Sir E. Burne-Jones to Rudyard Kipling

(Summer 1897?)

SIR,

I should like to caution you against the new-fangled bicycle you mention. I knew a gentleman most respectable on the Stock Exchange and connected by marriage with the Pocklington family who stand very high in the county as had a fatal injury in his *latissimus dorsi* in consequence of one of these bicycles. My advice would be if I might presume, Sir, stick to books.

The last volume of Mr. Mommsen, a German gentleman, History of Rome, has about the state of Britain and other countries at the time of the withdrawing of the legions. The legionary system, Sir, had broke down some time before, in Constantine's time, but though short it is a very good account and would repay your perusal.

I will send you Geoffrey of Monmouth where is a lot of names — might prove useful — rum names, Sir, as ever was. He's a author as has been down in the market but is looking up now, and though his style is pomptious, being wrote in Latin he didn't understand, scholars is beginning to depend on him a good deal, as having got his stories out of old books, and not making them up himself as was for a long time supposed.

In the same humble volume is the writings of a cross old cove as ever lived, named Gildas, who didn't approve of the way people went on. Nennius, Sir, in the same volume is very skimpy but said to be all right as far as he goes.

Glastonbury and Iona was going it pretty strong in the Christian line, a good hundred years — I dare say — before the English come, as were Pagans of the most outrageous kind, though with great aptitude for religious teaching, as our glorious reformation shows later on.

Your tale, Sir, as I think you call the Best Story in the World, shows what the public might look for in your treatment of a ancient subject, and I think it about time the matter was took out of the hand of Canon Farrar — it's worse than rot, Sir, all that.

And I'll send you a book of costumes, civil and military, and anything else as I can lay hands on, in my limited libery. But I find, Sir, in getting up a subjeck, it's no good expecting a good book about it. The sort aren't written and that's the truth; get the lumber together, I say, and set fire to it yourself, if I may make so bold.

Yours very respectful

E. BURNE-JONES.[7]

Rudyard's mediaeval studies led him to Domesday Book, and the first product of his invention after the removal to 'Bateman's' was the fable of the cat and the rat in Dudwell Mill, which he called 'Below the Mill Dam', an amusing piece of satire told to the accompaniment of the mill-wheel grinding out extracts from the Sussex Domesday.

The valley was alive with historic memories:

Just beyond the west fringe of our land stood the long, over-grown slag-heap of a most ancient forge, supposed to have been worked by the Phoenicians and Romans and, since then, uninterruptedly till the middle of the eighteenth century. The bracken and rush-patches still hid stray pigs of iron, and if one scratched a few inches through the rabbit-shaven turf, one came on the narrow mule-tracks of peacock-hued furnace-slag laid down in Elizabeth's day. The ghost of a road climbed up out of this dead arena, and crossed our fields, where it was known as 'The Gunway', and popularly connected with Armada times. Every foot of that little corner was alive with ghosts and shadows.[8]

When Rudyard, in October 1904, asked his friend Gwynne to buy a paper donkey's head for the children's play of Puck and Titania, the setting for the historical stories presented itself. Their theatre was a fairy ring beside the brook, at the foot of a grassy slope which they knew as Pook's Hill.* By January 1905 Rudyard was hard at work with the historical stories that occupied the greater part of his attention for the next five years. The first series, *Puck of Pook's Hill* (1906), came rapidly off his pen. Then came a pause in publication while he made a number of experiments. He tried and rejected a story of Dr. Johnson, a story of Defoe, a story of King Arthur, but at last elaborated and approved the eleven stories which were issued as *Rewards and Fairies* in 1910. Much of the writing was done at the 'Woolsack', and much of the research in the admirable South African Public Library at Cape Town. In the summers, the stories were often taken down to Tisbury to be 'smoked over' by Lockwood Kipling.

* It is the long spur running up from the Dudwell Brook to Burwash Common, and is visible from the western windows of 'Bateman's'. There are several Pook's Hills in Sussex, but I can find no evidence that the name was attached to this hill before 1904.

As these were primarily stories for children it is not surprising that their style changed as his own children grew older. In 1904, when John and Elsie (the 'Dan' and 'Una' of the books) acted their fairy play, they were no more than seven and eight years old. When *Puck of Pook's Hill* was published they were nine and ten, when *Rewards and Fairies* were published, thirteen and fourteen. At a glance the stories seem rather beyond the comprehension of children of these ages, but Rudyard wrote, as he wrote his other 'juvenile' works, on more than one mental level.

I worked the material in three or four overlaid tints and textures, which might or might not reveal themselves according to the shifting light of sex, youth and experience. The tales had to be read by children, before people realised that they were meant for grown-ups.[9]

Even making this allowance, the later stories are best suited to adult readers; and the tale of Rahere the Jester (')The Tree of Justice') may even be classed as one of Rudyard's obscure psychological pieces.

The plan, of introducing historical incidents into modern life, as if in another dimension, was not original; Rudyard never hesitated to borrow, and, in this instance, his model was taken from the stories of the talented lady who wrote under the name of 'E. Nesbit'. That autumn the children had been delighted with her *Phœnix and the Carpet,* and Rudyard had written to thank her for it. In 'E. Nesbit's' tales, as in most others of magical intrusion into common life, the focus of interest is contemporary. *The Phœnix and the Carpet* is a story about shabby-genteel life in Camden Town, illuminated by the odd contrast of the supernatural episodes. The author scarcely troubles to make you believe in her magic; she is content to show you with awful clarity and delightful humour what Camden Town makes of it. In Kipling's 'Puck' stories the emphasis is reversed. The mechanism by which Puck confronts the two children with characters from English history, though skilfully worked, is a mere subsidiary device; nor are the historical episodes, themselves, at the heart of the matter. The Land and the People, persisting through Time and all its revolutions, are the theme of the two 'Puck' books.

> So to the land our hearts we give
>   Till the sure magic strike,
> And Memory, Use, and Love make live
>   Us and our fields alike —
> That deeper than our speech and thought,
>   Beyond our reason's sway,
> Clay of the pit whence we were wrought
>   Yearns to its fellow-clay.[10]

RUDYARD KIPLING'S MOTHER, ALICE KIPLING, IN MIDDLE AGE

Striking his roots into Sussex, Rudyard now explored the dimension of time as, in his travelling days, he had explored the dimension of space. His old inquiry: ' What should they know of England who only England know? ' was taking a new direction. What can they know of present-day England who do not feel its continuity with England's past? So, the hero of the two books is not Puck, not Dan or Una, not Parnesius or Sir Richard Dalyngridge; the hero is old Hobden, the yeoman who understands the whole story of the valley and the brook, by instinct and tradition. Proud as he was to become a land-owner in Sussex, Rudyard's pride soon humbled itself before the historical figure of Hobden the Hedger, who is relevant to the life of the place in all its phases.

> His dead are in the churchyard — thirty generations laid.
> Their names were old in history when Domesday Book was made;
> And the passion and the piety and the prowess of his line
> Have seeded, rooted, fruited in some land the Law calls mine.

As newcomers, the Kiplings were, naturally, accepted with reserve by the village people; and with their passionate love of privacy, Rudyard and Carrie were content to keep themselves to themselves at ' Bateman's '. They nourished no romantic illusions about the peasantry.

Of the little one-street village up the hill we only knew that, according to the guide books, they came of a smuggling, sheep-stealing stock, brought more or less into civilisation within the past three generations. Those of them who worked for us, and who I presume would to-day be called ' Labour ', struck for higher pay than they had agreed on as soon as we were committed to our first serious works. My foreman and general contractor, himself of their race, and soon to become our good friend, said: ' They think they've got ye. They think there's no harm in tryin' it.' There was not. I had sense enough to feel that most of them were artists and craftsmen, either in stone or timber, or wood-cutting, or drain-laying or — which is a gift — the aesthetic disposition of dirt; persons of con-trivance who could conjure with any sort of material.

There was one among them,* close upon seventy when we first met, a poacher by heredity and instinct, a gentleman, who, when his need to drink was on him, which was not too often, absented himself and had it out alone; and he was more ' one with Nature ' than whole parlours full of poets. He became our special stay and counsellor. In his later years — he lived to be close on eighty-five — he would, as I am doing now, review his past, which held incident enough for many unpublishable volumes. He spoke of old loves, fights, intrigues, anonymous denuncia-tions ' by such folk as knew writing ', and vindictive conspiracies carried

* His real name was Isted.

out with oriental thoroughness. Of poaching he talked in all its branches, and of pitched battles (guns barred) with heavy-handed keepers in the old days in Lord Ashburnham's woods where a man might pick up a fallow-deer. His sagas were lighted with pictures of Nature as he, indeed, knew her; night-pieces and dawn-breakings; stealthy returns and the thinking out of alibis, all naked by the fire, while his clothes dried; and of the face and temper of the next twilight under which he stole forth to follow his passion. His wife, after she had known us for ten years, would range through a past that accepted magic, witchcraft and love-philtres, for which last there was a demand as late as the middle 'sixties.

Rudyard did not search out historical episodes from books but drew them from the life around him. Never was his sense of dedication more clear, that in his best writing he surrendered himself to an impulse that came from without.

The whole thing set and linked itself. I fell first upon Normans and Saxons. Parnesius came later, directly out of a little wood above the Phoenician forge; and the rest of the tales followed in order. The Father came over to see us and, hearing 'Hal o' the Draft', closed in with fore-reaching pen, presently ousted me from my table, and inlaid the description of Hal's own drawing-knife. He liked that tale, and its companion piece 'The Wrong Thing', which latter he embellished, notably in respect to an Italian fresco-worker, whose work never went 'deeper than the plaster'.
Of 'Dymchurch Flit', with which I was always unashamedly content, he asked: 'Where did you get that lighting from?' It had come of itself. *Qua* workmanship, that tale and two night-pieces in 'Cold Iron' are the best in that kind I have ever made, but somehow 'The Treasure and the Law' always struck me as too heavy for its frame.[12]

In the whole range of Rudyard Kipling's work, no pieces have been more effective in moulding the thought of a generation than the three stories of the centurions defending Hadrian's Wall during the decline of the Roman Empire. 'There is no hope for Rome', said the wise old father of the centurion. 'She has forsaken her Gods, but if the Gods forgive *us* here, we may save Britain.' The story of the centurion's task is told as a panegyric of duty and service, which press their claims all the more urgently when leaders fail to lead and statesmen study only their own careers. It strengthened the nerve of many a young soldier in the dark days of 1915 and 1941, and, if that was its intention, it mattered little that Rudyard's Roman soldiers of the fourth century too much resembled subalterns of the Indian Army.
To many readers the verses that accompany these stories mark the height of Kipling's literary achievement and here, if anywhere, he attained to the level of pure poetry, free from the cockney mannerisms,

the occasional vulgarities and brutalities that the critics had been so quick to detect and to denounce in his earlier verse. *Puck of Pook's Hill* (1906) includes 'Puck's Song', the 'Harp-song of the Dane Woman', 'Cities and Thrones and Powers', 'The Children's Song' ('Land of our Birth . . .'), 'A Smuggler's Song'. The verses for *Rewards and Fairies,* written in the autumn of 1909, are even more remarkable; they include 'A Charm' ('Take of English Earth . . .'), 'Cold Iron', 'The Looking-Glass', 'A St. Helena Lullaby', 'Brookland Road' and 'The Way through the Woods'. And the series continues with the songs written in the following year for C. R. L. Fletcher's *History of England,* among them 'The Roman Centurion's Song' and 'The Glory of the Garden'.

Much as these verses have been admired and quoted, they were far surpassed in popularity by the four stanzas of 'If —— ' which first appeared in *Rewards and Fairies.* We have Rudyard's word that it was drawn from the character of Dr. Jameson whom he had known for about ten years in Africa, and who visited 'Bateman's' in October 1909. The verses were written sometime during the next six months. As Rudyard himself put it, they were 'anthologised to weariness', and translated into twenty-seven languages. Some day, when the sneers of the silly-clever, who suppose that what has become a truism is no longer true, have died away, these verses will renew their influence; and it will be noticed that their fluid rhythm and intricate rhyme-scheme make them a technical masterpiece. *

The poem was printed as an epilogue to the story in which George Washington makes an appearance, a story beginning in Sussex but ending among the Quakers of Pennsylvania. This was his most sympathetic attempt to treat an American theme; and the introductory verses, 'If you're off to Philadelphia in the morning', recall clearly the fall of 1889 which he had spent in Pennsylvania with Mrs. Hill and her parents. He had resumed his old correspondence with her and, when she wrote to him on the publication of each new book, he replied as old friends write, with no other emotional content than is implied by common memories of youth.

Otherwise, the 'Puck' stories are home-centred, sometimes moving away from Sussex but always returning to it with affection. The children, Dan and Una, are ingeniously drawn into each episode and not long overlooked. In the second book, each child has a particular, personal, tale. John Kipling's story is of craftsmanship, 'The Wrong Thing', and is located in the village builder's workshop: Elsie Kipling's story, 'Marklake Witches', is shot through with level evening light

---

* I am obliged to Sir Maurice Bowra for pointing out to me that both the theme and the rhythm owe something to Browning's *Epilogue to Asolando.*

over the pastures where the farmer's wife is teaching her to milk a cow, as Elsie, actually, was taught. The delicacy of 'Marklake Witches', a tale told by a young girl to a young girl, in the manner of the Age of Sensibility, is so penetrating that the reader might suppose himself to be listening to a minor character from Jane Austen; and the tale is perfectly set off by the haunting lyric, 'The Way through the Woods'. Rudyard had now attained to a mastery over his own technique that he never surpassed, and to a tenderness far removed from the emotional crudity of his Anglo-Indian tales.

In his quiet, secluded English home, surrounded by his family, wealthy, honoured by the world which yet he held at a distance, blessed with many friends, sought out by the men who did the world's work, he was almost happy. At Tisbury, his parents still lived, aged and ailing, but, well as he loved them, it was not now to them that he turned for comfort. With his wife, his daughter, and his son, he had again based his life upon a 'family square', a reality which made all other social groupings seem vague and fluctuating. As the security and solidity of his life at 'Bateman's' was slowly strengthened, the pattern of the world outside was slipping into confusion. These were bad times for a Conservative in politics. Every winter, still, he went to South Africa, and his visits to the 'Woolsack', he used to say, were his political times.

The children were now old enough to make their own comments on the transition:

Every winter [wrote Elsie] the family left for South Africa just before Christmas, accompanied by large, black, dome-topped trunks, boxes of books, two faithful maids and the children's governess.

Things went according to a fixed routine. First the experienced appraisal of the ship and passengers by the two children, then the unpacking and stowing away of their travelling possessions in the tiny cabins of those days, and then their hunt to discover if any of their numerous friends among the stewards and crew were in this particular ship. A 'good trip' meant one on which several friends, from the captain downwards happened to be on board. One special crony was a certain grizzled cabin steward, who could always be counted upon for escorted visits to otherwise forbidden parts of the ship, as well as plates of dessert after the grown-ups' late dinner.

The first few days through the Bay were generally chilly and sea-sick misery. But once Madeira was passed the sun gathered strength daily, the twilights shortened as the semi-tropical nights shut down swiftly, and the first lifting of the Southern Cross above the horizon was eagerly looked for. It was all familiar, yet ever exciting.

R. K. always worked during these voyages, mostly in a tiny cabin opening on to the noisy promenade deck, but sometimes seated at a small folding table on the deck itself. He was quite oblivious to the noise and movement round him, and would pace the deck, come back to his writing pad for a few moments, and pace the deck again, just as if he had been in his own study. His fellow-passengers interested him enormously and he invariably made many friends, specially with some young soldier or mining engineer just going out to start a career, or perhaps with a ship's officer. The delights of the captain's table were always courteously offered and as courteously declined, and the family had a small table just inside the door of the dining saloon.

R. K. was always quite unconscious of the interest that his presence aroused among his fellow-passengers. One chilly evening, going below to get his overcoat, he absent-mindedly put on the first thing that came to hand in his cabin, which happened to be a brown camel-hair dressing-gown. As he came on deck a young acquaintance diffidently drew his attention to the mistake; but R. K. simply remarked that the dressing-gown kept him very warm and that was what was needed! The young man went away muttering: 'Fancy being the sort of man who can do a thing like that and not have it matter.'

Often old friends were on board, Dr. Jameson, Abe Bailey, Baden-Powell, mining engineers, and many of the big men who were shaping the destiny of South Africa at that time; endless talks and deck pacing went on in their company. Often after tea and before bed-time his children would collect various small friends, and sit in an enraptured circle round him on the sun-warmed deck in some quiet corner while he told them stories.

The end of the three-weeks' voyage to Cape Town meant the joyful arrival at the lovely, small, single-storied, white house, set under the shadow of Table Mountain, which Cecil Rhodes had given to R. K. for his life. A wide verandah or stoop ran on two sides of it, and there was an open court in the centre on to which all the rooms opened. Huge oak and pine trees sheltered the house, and the garden tumbled down the hillside, ending in a vast view across flat country to the Drakenstein mountains. Myrtle and plumbago hedges, oleander and fig trees, wild cannas and arum lilies, roses and violets grew under the lazy eye of Johnston, the Malay gardener, while a hedge of banana plants gave the children the daily fun of hunting for an unsplit banana leaf, the finding of which unknown treasure was never accomplished.

After lunch a siesta was the custom of the house, and R. K. was often read to sleep by his small daughter. Careful pronunciation of words was insisted upon, until he was too sleepy to bother about it; but when a specially long or difficult word had to be dealt with, the ruthless, wide-awake child would rouse her father to ask how it should be pronounced!

At an early age the two children were taught a proper respect for the use of words, and an appreciation of poetry. Very often in the evenings R. K. would sit in the nursery, intoning rather than reciting poetry by the hour. Wordsworth, Longfellow, the Sagas of King Olaf, the *Lays of Ancient*

Rome, Percy's Reliques, and the old Border ballads became so familiar to the two small and eager listeners that quotations from them became part of their everyday talk. Misquotations were frowned upon, and the careful learning of verse insisted upon. ' The man took trouble to find the exact word to fit into the line; the least you can do is not to change it,' was his point of view. A feeling of fury at misquotation remains with his daughter to this day, and when a certain official of the B.B.C. in quoting four lines of verse by R. K. on the air managed to make three mistakes, it was with difficulty that she refrained from angry protest.

One of Rudyard's principal occupations at the Cape was the planning of the Rhodes Memorial, for which the contract was allotted to Herbert Baker. Should they erect a statue on the Lion's Head, to be visible from ships far out at sea? No, that could not be seen from the city. Should they place it near ' Groote Schuur'? It lay too low. Should they employ the sculptor Swan to cast a colossal bronze head, or an equestrian statue?

Having considered many schemes they agreed to use G. F. Watts's bronze statue of Physical Energy and to place a memorial verse by Rudyard Kipling in the shrine.

Rudyard Kipling to Herbert Baker

9 Feb. 1905

We both enormously like your sketch. Of course, being florid in my tastes, I should like, against the dark green, a vermilion entablature; and columns sheathed at the base in bronze — after the insolent Egyptian fashion. Something that to the vulgar suggested Cape to Cairo and to others — other things. No need to make it Dutch. Make it continental.

As to the statue, you are right in that Physical Force lies ready to our hands and will not delay the job. But that statue is the work of a great man grown old and — does it altogether jibe with the idea of a greater man cut off in his strength? But I can see that it is far better than the risk of a colossal error in bronze. Of course, somewhere on God's earth exists a sculptor who could give us, gigantically, the man as he was; half hitched round on his great horse, right hand laid on the beast's rump, the bootless flannelled legs flung anyhow, and in his left hand the bit of stick that he always used. To illustrate, Let us say, these lines:

> As tho' again — yea, even once again,
>   We shall rewelcome to the stewardship
> The Rider with the loose-flung bridle-rein,
>   And chance-plucked twig for whip,
>
> The down-turned hat-brim, and the eyes beneath
>   Alert, devouring, and the imperious hand
> Ordaining matters swiftly to bequeath
>   Perfect the works he planned.

But if that statue were an hair's breadth wrong, or forced, what a sub-continental blister it would be! So it will be old Watts after all? [13]

The inscription on the monument, to which Rudyard gave much thought, spacing the letters with great care — 'it's bad enough', he said, 'having to fit fluid things like tales into spaces' — was not this new verse but the old one written for Cecil Rhodes's funeral.

> The immense and brooding Spirit still
>   Shall quicken and control.
> Living he was the land, and dead,
>   His soul shall be her soul! [14]

Long before the completion of the memorial, affairs in South Africa had taken a turn which the Kiplings thought deplorable. Lord Milner's reconstruction of South African administration, begun before the end of the war, and financed by generous grants of money from the pockets of the British taxpayer, made admirable progress until 1905, when Milner returned to England, having completed his term of service. His design, to stimulate British emigration and so to create an enlightened, progressive, white Dominion in South Africa, needed time to mature, and it required that responsible self-government should not be granted to the two conquered Afrikaner states, until land-settlement and reformed administration were well advanced. But, in England, the Conservative Government, led by Arthur Balfour since Lord Salisbury's retirement, had outlived its mandate.

Balfour resigned in December 1905, and the General Election, in January 1906, returned the Liberals in an overwhelming majority. So malicious were the new Liberal members against the outgoing Conservatives, they revenged themselves by striking at Lord Milner, who was formally censured by a vote of the House of Commons. The Under-Secretary for the Colonies, whose duty it was to lead the debate, was a young man named Winston Churchill — then a Liberal — and Rudyard never forgave him for his part in this affair.

The cause was lost. Milner retired into private life. An immediate grant of self-government was made to the Transvaal, with the result that the Afrikaner General Botha became its first Premier, and the Boer nationalists resumed their traditional policy. To Chamberlain, Milner, Rudyard Kipling, and their friends, it seemed that the Boer War had been fought and won in vain. Rudyard wrote bitterly from Cape Town to his friend, H. A. Gwynne, now editor of *The Standard*.

Rudyard Kipling to H. A. Gwynne

7 Feb. 1906

Yes it has been a big turn over. . . . To me it seems a savage protest

against the infernal and eternal slackness of the last years of the Govt. —
the years after J[oseph] C[hamberlain] left them. (For further details
kindly read over *Below the mill-dam* and note where the miller threw the
cat.) . . . The fact that Gussy, Teddy, Willy, Algy, etc., are knocked out
seems to me a very cheering point and I notice that the *Standard* doesn't
want Balfour to come back. Here I am with you altogether. What's
happened to us [the Conservatives] is what happened to the nation in the
Boer War, and we must change the quality of our recruits and demand
more work from our officers. Moreover (like the Army) we mustn't be
so dam' gentlemanly in future. Out here the Dutch naturally assume
that the return of the Liberal party means '81 over again, and that the
' two republics ' are going to be quietly put back in their old position.

Much worse news for the imperialists in South Africa was to come.
At the provincial election of 1907 the same turn-over of votes was seen
in Cape Colony, and Dr. Jameson, who had been Premier since 1903,
lost his majority.

Rudyard Kipling to H. A. Gwynne

1907?

DEAR OLD MAN,
   The cables will have told you how the elections have been a debacle for
us. J. X. M[erriman] comes in, without a policy, and all South Africa
goes voted Dutch. It aint to be wondered at. The Imperial Government
cut off the steam in the main boiler (the Transvaal) and the auxiliary
engines, of course, follow suit and cease working. One advantage is that
the ' Bond ' don't much want to be led by Merriman. They prefer Malan.
I fancy Jameson will soon resign.
   The election of course was fought on fierce racial issues, and it is generally understood that all who were in any way loyal will duly come up
for punishment. . . . When it comes to unifying South Africa, you'll see
things! I don't mind betting they'll monkey with the franchise. Remember that Rhodesia *must* be kept out of the federation and our ploy must
be to develop Rhodesia as well as we can. It's the last loyal white colony.[15]

As Premier Dr. Jameson had lived in Rhodes's house ' Groote
Schuur ' and, like Rhodes, had been on close terms of friendship with
his neighbours at the ' Woolsack '. No letters survive, and little other
evidence to show that for many years Jameson was one of Rudyard's
few intimate friends. Apart from the one dramatic moment of his
life, the ' Raid ', Jameson was a quiet confident man who had emerged
from tumults of abuse and flattery quite unmoved — treating those
two impostors just the same. In his day there was a circle of friends,
Fitzpatricks, Baileys, Strubens, all politically-minded people, among
whom he and Rudyard lived sociably. His leaving office, which
Rudyard thought a disaster for South Africa, was at least a sore blow
to the Kiplings' comfort. With ' Groote Schuur ' occupied by an

unsympathetic Afrikaner of the opposition party, the life had faded from their society. There was no more company in that hospitable house, he wrote gloomily to Milner, no trade, no activity in Cape Town. Inefficiency and corruption would soon prevail and the English would be *uitlanders* in South Africa again. To Gwynne he wrote, 'the handing over of a higher civilisation to a lower is a heart-breaking job'.

It was time to be done with South Africa. The divided year, eight months in Sussex and three at the Cape, was becoming difficult to adjust as the children grew older. John was now ready to go to boarding-school, the destiny of his class, and, with great unwillingness, the Kiplings bade farewell to their dear 'Woolsack' for the last time, in April 1908. Jameson, though out of office, was able to assure them that the house remained at their disposal, under provision made by the trustees of the Rhodes Estate. They never came back but, even twenty years later, at the end of his life, Rudyard rather tetchily refused to surrender his rights to the exclusive use of it.

Perhaps the children had the best of it. Among their visitors one sharp-eyed observer was a young girl who gratified a secret passion by meeting her favourite author.[15] She was between ages, and sometimes sat with the grown-ups, sometimes played with the children on the beach at Muizenberg; she thus saw two different Rudyard Kiplings. When he was with the children, as he loved to be, the author of *Just So Stories,* she said, far surpassed her expectations, and his conversation excelled his printed books in its fascination for her. Indoors among the grown-ups she was not so sure, she felt that he was acting a part. It was only when a lady happened to mention that she had bought a new cooking-stove that his genius awoke. He would hear of nothing but technicalities about cooking-stoves, to the annoyance of the other guests who hoped for something higher.[16]

CHAPTER XVI

AT 'BATEMAN'S' (1908–14)

THE FABULISTS (1917)

When all the world would keep a matter hid,
   Since Truth is seldom friend to any crowd,
Men write in fable, as old Aesop did,
   Jesting at that which none will name aloud.
And this they needs must do, or it will fall
Unless they please they are not heard at all.

When desperate Folly daily laboureth
   To work confusion upon all we have,
When diligent Sloth demandeth Freedom's death,
   And banded Fear commandeth Honour's grave —
Even in that certain hour before the fall
Unless men please they are not heard at all.

Needs must all please, yet some not all for need,
   Needs must all toil, yet some not all for gain,
But that men taking pleasure may take heed,
   Whom present toil shall snatch from later pain.
Thus some have toiled but their reward was small
Since, though they pleased, they were not heard at all.

This was the lock that lay upon our lips,
   This was the yoke that we have undergone,
Denying us all pleasant fellowships
   As in our time and generation.
Our pleasures unpursued age past recall.
And for our pains — we are not heard at all.

    ·   ·   ·   ·

THERE is, among the Kipling papers, a thick file of letters recording his systematic refusal, throughout his whole career, of the titles and offices that were sometimes thrust upon him. He could not and he would not write to order, and he would not accept any public honour which might be construed as limiting his freedom to say what, as he thought, should be said. But he did not extend this rigidity of principle to his colleagues in the republic of letters, and often expressed his pleasure when they were rewarded with public honours. The knighthood given to his friend Rider Haggard gave Rudyard sincere pleasure, perhaps the more because it was a tribute to Haggard's services as an agricultural reformer rather than to his eminence as a novelist. As for himself, Rudyard had been offered a knighthood (K.C.B.) by Salisbury in 1899 and had refused it. Balfour repeated the offer (this time a K.C.M.G.) in 1903 and again it was refused. On this occasion Rudyard made the sardonic comment to Carrie that ‘title-conferring is as slack as other Government business. Evidently they knew nothing of the K.C.B. of 1899.’[1]

On the same ground — that he must be free — Rudyard refused many proposals to take part in public life. In 1904 he was pressed by the Conservative Party in Edinburgh to stand as their candidate for Parliament. He replied that he could serve them better outside Parliament as an independent writer. Later, two or three other constituencies offered to adopt him as their candidate, with the same result. Nor would he serve in official posts; he repeatedly refused to return to India in any public capacity. He declined an invitation to join the royal party when the Prince of Wales (afterwards King George V) went to India in 1903, and again when he went, in 1911, after his accession to the throne. There were several occasions when Rudyard considered revisiting India as a private person, and might have gone if family affairs had allowed it; as a public personage he would not go.

The story of the Poet-Laureateship, after Tennyson's death, has been told in an earlier chapter. When Alfred Austin died, in 1913, there could be no doubt who ought to be the Crown's first choice as his successor. For many years it had been Kipling, not Austin, who had spoken for the nation on great occasions. Asquith, the Prime Minister, after considering Kipling's name, decided that it would be useless to approach him. I am permitted to repeat the following account given by Asquith's daughter, Lady Violet Bonham Carter, in a letter to Lord Baldwin:

The vacancy occurred when we were on the Admiralty yacht in the Mediterranean as Winston's guests, and I remember very well my Father discussing the problem with me. The obvious choice was Rudyard Kipling. Bridges was the alternative choice in my father's mind. What weighed with him was the very reason you give — that Kipling was inspired and could not write to order. Bridges, with his classic chiselled gift would be more likely to be able to do so. He wrote, offering it to Bridges, I think, during our cruise or directly he came back.[1]

Nevertheless it was still Rudyard's occasional verses in *The Times* that made him the laureate of the people. His standing as a national figure was recognized in 1911 at the Coronation of King George V when places were reserved in the Abbey for Rudyard and his wife.*

He was somewhat less exclusive in respect of academic than of public honours, though, here too, he refused any that might commit him to any class, or party, or coterie. When Gosse, and some others of Kipling's friends, laid the foundations of the British Academy, in 1910, and pressed him to become one of the original members, he applauded their intention, he gave them helpful advice, but he would not be one of their number. He had made it a rule never to criticize any of his fellow-authors, and he could not join a society that was to sit in judgment on them. There were others, like Henry James, he suggested, who were better qualified as critics. Having refused to join the British Academy, he made that a precedent for (twice) refusing nomination to the American Academy of Arts and Sciences. Later in life, however, he showed gratification when elected to the Institut de France.

His early talents had not been of a kind to attract the notice of the universities. McGill University at Montreal was the first to offer him an honorary degree, as early as 1899. His later decision to revisit Canada and to accept a doctorate may perhaps be connected with the visit to 'Bateman's', in May 1907, of the distinguished McGill professor, Stephen Leacock. In June Rudyard accepted the offer of a doctorate from the University of Durham, and immediately afterwards a similar offer from Oxford. Lord Curzon had just been elected Chancellor of Oxford and, according to custom, it was his privilege to nominate some eminent persons for admission to honorary degrees. Among the other names he chose were those of Mark Twain and 'General' Booth, both of them old friends of Rudyard. By chance, the University of Cambridge also elected a new Chancellor, Lord Rayleigh, a few months later, and he, too, brought forward Rudyard Kipling's name for a Cambridge doctorate. Thus the following twelve months, 1907–8, were largely taken up for Rudyard with visits of ceremony to universities.

Carrie and Rudyard spent two or three days sight-seeing at York and Durham, in dark rainy weather, his first visit to the north of England since boyhood. At Durham, crowds of students met him at the station and drew his carriage up the steep narrow street which leads to the hilltop on which stand the University and Cathedral.

---

* We have it on the authority of Sir Harold Nicolson that, when Bridges died in 1930, King George V desired to offer the laureateship to Kipling. No evidence survives that an offer was made. If made, it would certainly have been refused.

There was barely time to complete the ceremonies before it was necessary to turn southward, for Oxford. In unaccustomed gowns of grey and scarlet which, said Rudyard, made him look like a West African parrot, the visitors were kept waiting in the cloisters until, one by one, they were led into the Sheldonian Theatre, to be greeted by the Chancellor in ceremonious state, by the Public Orator who made a Latin speech in honour of each of them, and by the undergraduates in the gallery who received them with cheers and ribald comments. As 'General' Booth, Mark Twain, and Kipling awaited their turn, the 'General', magnificent as a Hebrew patriarch in his scarlet gown, took note of his fellow-traveller of seventeen years ago. 'Young man,' he said striding across the quadrangle to meet him, 'how's your soul?' Mark Twain was a friend on a more material level; he had given evidence for Rudyard Kipling in the Putnam copyright case, and Carrie, who had met him in those days, had said he reminded her of Whistler. It was with Mark Twain that Rudyard slipped away to smoke under an archway, with guilty apprehension, until they were summoned to the theatre, Rudyard last of the batch. The Public Orator, no doubt fluent in Latin, was deficient in eloquence, and mumbled an inaudible address. 'Never mind, Rudyard!' shouted an undergraduate from the gallery. 'You'll tell us all about it afterwards.' But he didn't. It was said by spectators that the ovation given him was more lively than any since Cecil Rhodes had been given a doctorate.[2]

Political interests, joined with the invitation from McGill, also induced him to look at Canada again. The Colonial Conference of 1907 had been a deep disappointment to the Conservative imperialists, and especially to Rudyard, though he met all the Premiers from the overseas Dominions at a private party. At this conference a new concept came into prominence, to which the name of Dominion Status was afterwards given; it was sponsored by Sir Wilfred Laurier, of whom Dr. Jameson said bitterly to Kipling: 'that damned dancing-master bitched the whole show'.[3] The Commonwealth of free nations was in Jameson's view a poor substitute for a strong and federated Empire. South Africa seemed to be lost and the other Dominions discouraged, as Rudyard wrote in a letter to Deakin, the Prime Minister of Australia, who thus replied:

Alfred Deakin to Rudyard Kipling

21 March 1908

Your wish that I could realise what it means to 'live in a land without hope' awakens no response. After all one must not measure nations by the life span of individuals, and despite our endless blunders we cannot avoid being caught in the wider sweeps of the Empire's growth. Hold

South Africa for another half century and people it with sufficient men and women of British blood and they will drag up the primitives in spite of themselves.

Melbourne in '90 looked stricken and was worse than any other part of Australia has ever been. But that crisis was almost confined to Melbourne and Sydney, and was simply a reaction against over-speculation at the moment. Since then, every institution and every individual that kept hold has emerged unscathed, without loss and in most cases with large profits. . . . Australia today was never more prosperous. Our [trade] figures surpass those of Canada, although she is a million ahead of us and there is no boom here. Laurier is charming but he is not British in anything, and cares nothing for British interests outside the Dominion. Jameson is worth a hundred Lauriers, and will yet come to his own in a federated South Africa, if his health and patience endure. Very few statesmen in the Empire are better gifted for carrying on in a Dominion Parliament, or more capable of managing a small majority to advantage.[4]

But Jameson was out of office, and Rudyard turned for comfort to a Canada that prospered even under Laurier.

In the autumn of 1907 Rudyard and Carrie crossed the Atlantic again, she to visit her mother whom she had not seen for eight years, and he to receive his honorary degree from McGill. He made a rare concession to Canadian enthusiasm by giving a series of lectures to the chain of Canadian clubs, the only occasion in his life when he submitted to the compulsions of a lecture-tour. Canada as seen from the railway renewed Rudyard's faith.

Above all, I saw what had actually been achieved in the fifteen years since I had last come that way. One advantage of a new land is that it makes you feel older than Time. I met cities where there had been nothing — literally, absolutely nothing, except, as the fairy tales say, 'the birds crying, and the grass waving in the wind'. Villages and hamlets had grown to great towns, and the great towns themselves had trebled and quadrupled. And the railways rubbed their hands and cried, like the Afrites of old, 'Shall we make a city where no city is; or render flourishing a city that is desolate?' They do it too, while, across the water, gentlemen, never forced to suffer one day's physical discomfort in all their lives, pipe up and say, 'How grossly materialistic!'[5]

His speeches were all appeals to young Canadians to realize and to accept their responsibilities:

Your own labour, your own sacrifice have given you material prosperity in overwhelming abundance. . . . There is no man, and here I must quote again, 'that can foresee or set limits to your destiny'. But any man, even I, have the right to remind you, that to whom much has been given, from them much — much — shall be required.[6]

The rancour which Rudyard sometimes showed against the United States was strangely bitter at this time. He did not cross the border but drew comparisons, perhaps overstated, between the disorderly 'Wild West' in the Republic and the King's Peace in the Dominion:

Always the marvel — to which the Canadians seemed insensible — was that on one side of an imaginary line should be Safety, Law, Honour, and Obedience, and on the other frank, brutal decivilisation; and that, despite this, Canada should be impressed by any aspect whatever of the United States.[7]

Though more than twenty years passed before Rudyard set foot in Canada again, he maintained a copious correspondence with many Canadian friends. Andrew Bonar Law and Max Aitken (Lord Beaverbrook) were shortly to introduce a Canadian flavour into English Conservative politics, and both became close friends of the Kiplings. Canada was a land of friendship and of hope when South Africa was written off, and Rudyard's enthusiasm increased, three years later, when he and Aitken together heard of the overthrow of Laurier and the return to office of an imperialist government at Ottawa. After his return to England, at the end of 1907, Rudyard wrote a long letter to Milner giving a more personal and candid account than is to be found in his *Letters of Travel.*

Rudyard Kipling to Lord Milner

[1908]

You will have to face the impact of young, callous, curious, and godlessly egotistical crowds who will take everything out of you and put nothing back. Their redeeming point is a certain crude material faith in the Empire, of which they naturally conceive themselves to be the belly-button.

Tell your bottle-holder to disconnect your bedroom telephone, so soon as ever you get to a hotel. Otherwise you will continue to enjoy the horrors of publicity in your bath and in your bed. Allah knows I have long since ceased to be a virgin, but I cannot help blushing when I am rung-up by women — with nothing on but spectacles and a bath-towel. Moreover I find it interferes with the peristaltic process, and Canada is a constipating land.

Sir William Van Horne's house at Montreal — it is a palace — is efficiently guarded against the world by an English butler of the gypsy name of Pharaoh. Outside that house there is very little peace except at Rideau Hall [the Governor's residence].

I am bringing out my Canadian *Letters to the Family* in a pamphlet for use in Canada where they are displeased with them. But I write them with a single loving wish to annoy the Radicals in England, and because I loved greatly I managed to irritate a little. I have just come out of a trough of blank bloody pessimism — a cold reasoned despair of the Republic — which has oppressed me for months. So I realise yet again the pits and gulfs you have been through.[8]

A horror of publicity and a dislike of making patriotic orations on public platforms were shared by Milner and Kipling, those two notable imperialists. They always spent Empire Day together, not, as might be supposed, in order to indulge in imperial rejoicings, but in order that each might be able to quote a prior engagement in the highly probable event of being asked to address a public meeting.

Soon after his return from Canada, Rudyard received a letter from the Secretary to the Swedish Academy offering him the Nobel Prize * for literature, the first time it had been awarded to an English writer. In this instance he accepted the honour, and crossed with Carrie to the Continent in severe wintry weather. Both were very seasick.

Even while we were on the sea, the old King of Sweden died. We reached the city, snow-white under sun, to find all the world in evening dress, the official mourning, which is curiously impressive. Next afternoon, the prize-winners were taken to be presented to the new King. Winter darkness in those latitudes falls at three o'clock, and it was snowing. One half of the vast acreage of the Palace sat in darkness, for there lay the dead King's body. We were conveyed along interminable corridors looking out into black quadrangles, where snow whitened the cloaks of the sentries, the breaches of old-time cannon, and the shot-piles alongside of them. Presently, we reached a living world of more corridors and suites all lighted up, but wrapped in that Court hush which is like no other silence on earth. Then, in a great lit room, the weary-eyed, over-worked, new King, saying to each the words appropriate to the occasion.

Morning did not come till ten o'clock; and one lay abed in thick dark, listening to the blunted grind of the trams speeding the people to their work-day's work. But the ordering of their lives was reasonable, thought out, and most comfortable for all classes in the matter of food, housing, the lesser but more desirable decencies, and the consideration given to the Arts.[9]

After the last visit to South Africa, in 1908, Rudyard and Carrie decided to send John to a boarding-school at Rottingdean, with the knowledge that Aunt Georgie could be kind to the homesick little boy as, thirty years earlier, she had been kind to his father. She was growing old and sometimes forgetfully called the boy 'Ruddy'.

During Rudyard's years in Sussex, his parents had aged rapidly. In particular, his mother, a little older than her husband, had become an invalid, worn out partly by care for her unfortunate daughter, 'Trix'

* A gold medal, a diploma, and a sum of money estimated at £7700.

Fleming. After the first breakdown, 'Trix' had recovered and had again joined her husband in India, until his retirement from the service. She was childless, and the charm and talent of her youth had wasted away with little to show in achievement, except a novel of Anglo-Indian life. Apart from this she was so other-worldly as to be hardly able to live a normal life, and her husband, John Fleming, a plain blunt man, was unable to give her understanding sympathy, though his patience was endless. The Flemings were, however, at hand when Alice Kipling's health collapsed. Rudyard, too, was summoned to Tisbury and Lockwood wrote bravely to a friend to say that the presence of his two children was a comfort to him. But 'Trix' was too overwrought to give the least assistance and all the painful toil of supervising his mother's death-bed and funeral fell upon Rudyard. She died on 22nd November 1910 and was buried at Tisbury.

Lockwood, old and tired, lingered a few weeks longer in a world which had lost interest for him. We have a last glimpse of him, paying a visit to Wilfrid Blunt at Crabbet and talking of the new political reforms in India, the Morley-Minto constitution, in terms of deep dejection.[11] His last satisfaction in life was to see the appearance of *Rewards and Fairies* which he had watched over with loving care. In January 1911 Rudyard was recalled from his family holiday in Switzerland by bad news of his father. The old man had been taken ill while on a visit to the Wyndhams at Clouds and there died of a heart attack before Rudyard's arrival. Again all the arrangements for the funeral and for disposing of his little property were left to Rudyard.

It was not only Rudyard that mourned the death of Lockwood Kipling. His granddaughter wrote this of him:

Lockwood Kipling was a short, rather square figure; bald even early in life and with a beard. His wonderful blue eyes beamed upon the world, with endless interest and kindly tolerance, and his voice was mellow and enchanting. People who met him only once, never forgot him. His knowledge of every art and craft, even the most unusual, was amazing, while his skill with his hands was a joy to watch. In his old age, he wrote long and charming letters to his ten-year-old granddaughter, instructing her in the best method of making and gilding gesso work. To further illustrate his meaning he decorated several delightful boxes for her in this way.

His knowledge of many things was profound, his kindness and interest unending.

There comes a time in every man's middle age when his relatives and friends of the older generation seem to die in quick succession, leaving him naked against the cold blast of the passing years, when he feels himself alone, no longer protected by the comfortable guardians of his childhood. Rudyard's aunts and uncles, who had once meant so much to him, were slipping away: 'Ned' Burne-Jones long since, 'Aunt Aggie' Poynter in 1906, Alfred Baldwin in 1908; his old teachers, the beloved 'Crom' Price in 1910, William Crofts ('Mr. King') in 1911; Dr. Conland and Charles Eliot Norton dead in America, Henley dead in England. The death of his parents marked an epoch, but did not crush Rudyard as it would have done fifteen years earlier. His father, his dearest, most helpful, critic, had inspired his best work, and, still more, had restrained his exuberance, but the lesson was now learned, the style matured. Well as he loved his parents, he had cut loose from their control, and was devoted to his own new family square. Stan Baldwin's family renewed in the next generation the friendship of their parents; and Rudyard's debt to 'Crom' Price was repaid by his affection for 'Crom' Price's son and daughter, Ted and Dorothy. 'Crom' had left them ill-provided and among the friends who helped them it was Rudyard and Carrie who saw to their education, and frequently invited them to spend their holidays at 'Bateman's'.

Rudyard was still a newspaper-man at heart. The printer's ink of the *Civil and Military Gazette* had left so permanent a stain that he was rarely as happy as when talking Fleet Street shop with others of the craft. Of his old associates, the 'Friends' of Bloemfontein, Julian Ralph was dead but two of the others were still near him. Percival Landon, when not away on some assignment in Tibet or Turkey, saw much of Rudyard who built for him a cottage at Keylands on the 'Bateman's' estate. Landon was Rudyard's most intimate friend in middle life. There was also H. A. Gwynne who first managed Reuter's in London, then became editor of the *Standard,* a London daily that struggled to make headway against the new men who were converting journalism into a branch of high finance.

Rudyard Kipling to H. A. Gwynne

November 1904

There isn't in our minds the least doubt as to where you could best serve the Empire — i.e. in charge of a new, reconstructed, enthusiastic and wealthy paper. . . . You have an unrivalled chance of preaching your Imperial Labour Party views; army and navy reform; protection and all the rest that is vital. You will be toadied to by all classes of men — and women — but that you won't mind — and you will be lied to a good deal. But that also is usual. Your strong pull should be knowledge of affairs. The business of an editor is not to write but to get the men who can, brigade them, and edit them.

18 October, 1905

I am having the *Army of a Dream* reprinted in pamphlet form, as there have been numerous requests from adjutants of volunteers etc. to get it to give to their companies. Hope to get it out for 6d. shortly. If you can make any use of it as a peg to hang more debate on, for goodness sake use it.[10]

To the *Standard* (29th April 1907) Rudyard gave the set of verses which best summarize his social philosophy. He called them 'The Sons of Martha'.

It is their care in all the ages to take the buffet and cushion the shock.
It is their care that the gear engages; it is their care that the switches lock.
It is their care that the wheels run truly; it is their care to embark and entrain,
Tally, transport, and deliver duly the Sons of Mary by land and main.

.   .   .   .   .

They do not preach that their God will rouse them a little before the nuts
    work loose.
They do not teach that His Pity allows them to leave their job when they
    dam'-well choose.
As in the thronged and the lighted ways, so in the dark and the desert they
    stand,
Wary and watchful all their days that their brethren's days may be long in
    the land.

And the Sons of Mary smile and are blessèd — they know the Angels are on
    their side.
They know in them is the Grace confessèd, and for them are the Mercies
    multiplied.
They sit at the Feet — they hear the Word — they see how truly the Promise
    runs.
They have cast their burden upon the Lord, and — the Lord He lays it on
    Martha's Sons!

Ten years earlier he would have given these verses to *The Times,* under the reign of Moberly Bell, but *The Times* was about to change its ownership and policy, and Rudyard transferred his influence to a grouping in politics and journalism that was sounder in allegiance to a traditional morality. In 1911 Gwynne became editor of the *Morning Post,* the organ of the right-wing Conservatives. Under his control, as even its political opponents admitted, the *Post* was the best edited and the best printed among the London dailies. Rudyard maintained a regular correspondence with Gwynne, not only on political questions but on the technicalities of journalism, often suggesting subjects for 'feature' articles, and lines of action in matters of public interest.

In May 1909, at 'Bateman's', Rudyard was at work upon 'Marklake Witches' when Lloyd George opened his campaign to expropriate the rich and to destroy the power of the House of Lords. Many wealthy households as well as the household at 'Bateman's' took alarm. Rudyard usually left financial affairs to Carrie, who had 'golden fingers', and she usually took advice about their investments from Sir George Allen, Rudyard's former employer in India, who had now retired and was living in Sussex. They insured against death-duties, bought some shares in America, and watched the progress of politics with anxiety. From 1909 until 1914 he threw himself into party activity on the extreme right wing, attending party meetings in London and even speaking for Max Aitken, at an election meeting. Rudyard Kipling lost some of his popularity in those years; no longer the spokesman of the forgotten men, the soldiers and sailors, the British overseas, he seemed to have become the propagandist of the Tory Party. This was not his intention, and when a politician in Canada so described him he at once threatened to bring an action for libel.

Rudyard Kipling to H. A. Gwynne

25 January, 1913

The *Morning Post* of the 24th has a quotation from M——'s speech at Ottawa in which he alludes to the 'hired versifier and Poet Laureate of the Unionist Party'. This is not pretty but I think it may be useful. As I wired to you today I want you to watch if any of the Rad. papers quote it. . . . If they do it seems to me that it would be sound business to jump on 'em for libel as that kind of lie is apt to grow. . . . I don't think the Unionist party ought to be saddled with me as their 'hired versifier and poet laureate' and my position is that I don't in the least intend to have it said of me.[11]

His considered opinion on the routine of politics is to be found in 'The Village that Voted', a story completed and published in 1913. Politics, he said, was 'a dog's life without a dog's decencies'.

Kipling's method of accumulating material can be closely studied in the preliminaries of 'The Village that Voted'. The characters, though not drawn from the life, are reminiscent of the sort of men he knew. One of them was a specialist in bringing moribund newspapers to life, like Gwynne. Kipling advised him, and occasionally spent evenings with him in his office. In the late summer of 1909 Kipling saw much of two friends in Parliament, his cousin Stanley Baldwin and Andrew Bonar Law, and attended one of the violent debates over the Budget, when Bonar Law, that calm unimpassioned man, displayed his skill at goading the Opposition into fury with violent and telling blows, delivered quite without emotion. In the following year, some political capital was made out of a police-court case at Croydon in which Bonar Law was fined for a motoring offence, under circumstances which suggested a vexatious prejudice against him on the Bench. Finally, in the summer of 1913, Landon and Kipling enjoyed themselves renewing their old acquaintance with the London music-halls. Here were all the ingredients which Kipling combined in his gigantic farce about 'the village that voted the earth was flat'. The subject is crowd-hysteria and the key-note is the anguished cry of the vulgar impresario: 'Curse Nature! She gets ahead of you every time.' Nothing could exaggerate the political hysteria of those days, and, many years later, Kipling had to confess the insufficiency of his own invention. In a letter to Frank Doubleday in 1920 he admitted that even his 'Village that Voted' had not made itself as ridiculous as Dayton, Tennessee, at the time of the Evolution controversy.

Any estimate of Kipling's work must take account of the series of elaborate farces which he produced at intervals throughout his career. Four, at least ('Brugglesmith', 1891; 'My Sunday at Home', 1895; 'The Vortex', 1914; 'The Village that Voted', 1917), must be classed among his greater achievements and, like almost everything else he wrote, they have been described in flatly contradictory terms by various critics. Certainly, they are not meat for delicate stomachs. Kipling admitted to his friends, more than once, that comical outbursts gave relief to his own feelings, and these tales reveal a common pattern. They are all told in the first person, but the part he casts for himself is whimsical, puckish, malicious, not dignified or dominating. He is there to make sport and laugh at it. In each case an enormous practical joke is not so much induced as released, to develop by some law of its own, involving all sorts of innocent people but recoiling upon the head of the victim, a pretentious intruder. The punishment seems too heavy for the offence and, like many of the world's comic masterpieces, like the tale of Malvolio and the tale of Don Quixote, these stories reveal a strange streak of cruelty that almost spoils the fun, until all ends with a shout of gargantuan laughter that seems to purge away the hatred and resolve the tangle of emotion.

All Kipling's comic tales are strongly localized, and among his best landscapes are the backgrounds against which these farces are staged. In 'The Vortex', for example, when those portentous members of the Round Table bored him with their ideals, it was Kipling the lover of England who saw the reality of the scene on which they mouthed their irrelevant parts.

Well settled on the back seat, he did not once lift his eyes to the mellow landscape around him, or throw a word at the life of the English road which to me is one renewed and unreasoned orgy of delight. The mustard-coloured scouts of the Automobile Association; their natural enemies, the unjust police; our natural enemies, the deliberate market-day cattle, broadside-on at all corners, the bicycling butcher-boy a furlong behind; road-engines that pulled giddy-go-rounds, rifle galleries, and swings, and sucked snortingly from wayside ponds in defiance of the notice-board; traction-engines, their trailers piled high with road-metal; uniformed village-nurses, one per seven statute miles, flitting by on their wheels; governess-carts full of pink children jogging unconcernedly past roaring, brazen touring-cars; the wayside rector with virgins in attendance, their faces screwed up against our dust; motor-bicycles of every shape charging down at every angle; red flags of rifle-ranges; detachments of dusty-putteed Territorials; coveys of flagrant children playing in mid-street; and the wise, educated English dog safe and quite silent on the pavement if his fool-mistress would but cease from trying to save him, passed and repassed us in sunlight or shaded settings. But Mr. Lingnam only talked. He talked — we all sat together behind so that we could not escape him — and he talked against the worn gears and a certain maddening swish of the badly patched tire — *and* he talked of the Federation of the Empire against all conceivable dangers except himself.

It will be remembered that ' Mr. Lingnam ' was at last silenced by a swarm of bees. Rudyard had become an enthusiastic bee-keeper at 'Bateman's', and more than once made symbolic use of the social life of the bee in his comments on the contemporary human scene. His fable, 'The Mother-Hive', presaging the possible regeneration of society after a national disaster, was a story which pleased its author. He quoted it in his letters to Gwynne as typical of his philosophy. Kipling was a technocrat, believing that the world of the future would be ruled by technicians, not by demagogues. Loose talk about liberty led only to disaster; what the age needed was economic organization by competent, and preferably silent, professionals.

His thousands of readers, themselves largely young technicians, found this a practicable philosophy, but there was a rival attitude to life, most competently thought out, to which Kipling was almost blind. He had no appreciation of the practical administrative schemes of national organization which had been produced during his lifetime by the Fabian Society, the social gospel preached, in their respective styles, by his rivals for public attention, Wells and Shaw. The lunatic fringe of radical pacifists on the left wing disgusted him, and he saw nothing more in the Liberal schemes of social betterment than: ' Robbing selected Peter to pay for collective Paul '.

In the crisis of 1910 when Parliament was twice dissolved and the Liberals were maintained in power only by favour of the Irish Nationalist vote, and when the prerogative of the Crown was invoked to overrule the House of Lords, Kipling was among the group called the 'die-hards' who wanted the House of Lords to protest to the last. However, the majority of the Tory peers preferred to submit gracefully.

Rudyard wrote to Milner during the December Election to say that he had been 'slushing about in the wet with a car, taking voters to the poll'. 'I have a horrible fear', he went on, 'that the Lords will now compromise — like "gentlemen" — out of some vague idea of saving the country, playing the game, pleasing the King, or some other devil's excuse for selling the pass.'[12]

Nineteen-eleven, Coronation year, with the hottest summer in living memory, was a year of strikes. The new doctrine of syndicalism — to force general reforms by 'direct action' expressed in nationally organized strikes of key industries — then first appeared in England. If the Lords could threaten to sabotage the constitution, why not the railwaymen?

Rudyard Kipling to H. A. Gwynne

21 April, 1912

How much foreign influence was there behind the coal-strike and how much foreign influence will there be behind the transport worker's strike? I want a temperate and lucid article . . . on the benefits which an average working-man actually gets from joining a union. At present, it seems to me that he is confiding his cash to the only bank in the world whose cashiers may embezzle without punishment.

Rudyard Kipling maintained a long correspondence with Duckworth Ford, an American friend serving in the Philippines, and pressed him repeatedly for technical details about the country: hygiene and sanitary measures, plague and cholera control, statistics of venereal disease, etc. In December 1911 he wrote:

Things in England are as mad as usual. If there were any logic in the English we should be steering straight for at least three revolutions at the same time, so I presume that they will neutralize each other. Meantime the Teuton has his large cold eye on us and prepares to give us toko when he feels good and ready. Our chances are not so slim as they look for the reason that the Teuton knows all about war as it should be waged scientifically, and my experience has been that when a man knows exactly how everything ought to be done under every conceivable contingency he is apt to be tied up by his own knowledge. But we ought to see in a few years now.[13]

The failure of the Tories to mobilize public opinion and to make their opposition effective provoked a revolution in the Party, engineered by the young Canadian, Max Aitken. In November 1911 Balfour was deposed, and Bonar Law, also a Canadian by origin, succeeded him.

A cool, uncompromising politician, with none of the arts that bewitch the masses, Bonar Law concentrated, ruthlessly, upon a policy of maintaining the union and consolidating the Empire by Tariff Reform. He and Aitken and Kipling were close friends in those years.

Rudyard Kipling to H. A. Gwynne

27 February, 1906

I can't tell you how highly I think of the work of the *Standard* during the past grave months: but I am glad you have seen the politicians at close quarters. They are a macaroni-backed crew, even the best of them, and they will follow only winning causes. You must wake up some of the young men on our side. Our great weakness, of course, is that we have no understudy to Chamberlain, and I think that is due to the way in which the inner caste of Conservatives has stifled and hampered the young blood. Can't you find a young 'un and enthuse him?

2 November, 1910

I very much like Aitken and I'm glad of what you told me about him. I wish I could manage something about Canada and U.S. reciprocity.

I got your betting list (most immoral). I say that Bonar Law will be leader. He's dead sound on Tariff Reform and it's a feather in Canada's cap! And mark my word, from now on, A. J. Balfour will give us no end of fireworks just to show that he can do it. His resignation speech was very fine.[14]

In the years when the strikers and the Ulstermen were resorting to ' direct action ', another outburst of sabotage occurred in a form so irrational as to be rather ludicrous than tragic. In a declared democracy there seemed to be no logical answer to the claim that men and women should have equal political rights, and the steady opposition of a Liberal reforming government against the concession of the franchise to women was indefensible. Kipling, with his lifelong devotion to two women, his mother and his wife, was no scorner of female intelligence, and his comment on the suffragettes was the set of satiric verses containing the well-known line:

The female of the species is more deadly than the male.

They appeared in the *Morning Post,* and stung a little. One lady who expressed her disapproval was his daughter Elsie, seventeen years old and endowed with a will of her own. He warned Gwynne that he would have to excuse himself to Elsie for publishing these verses, when next he came to ' Bateman's '. But she was to form her own opinion of the suffragettes, a few months later, when she was presented at Court. The débutante in front of Elsie was a suffragette, and repaid the royal hospitality by a display of ill-mannered exhibitionism before the King and Queen.

Rudyard Kipling to H. A. Gwynne

30 January, 1913

Doesn't all this suffragette racket remind you rather of Ladies' Sports on ship just before a heavy gale? When the men ought to be furling awnings or lashing boats they're told off to slice the potatoes, get out buckets, chalks and string for chalking the pig's eye and the officers who ought to be on the bridge are hanging around advising their respective females how to pick up eggs and spoons — specially spoons.[15]

At one moment the Liberal Government made a false step by condoning what looked perilously like political corruption. Kipling was quick to strike at them and with such force that future generations are likely to remember the name of Rufus Isaacs chiefly because he was Kipling's Gehazi, as they remember Hervey because he was Pope's Sporus and Buckingham because he was Dryden's Zimri.

> Well done, well done, Gehazi!
>   Stretch forth thy ready hand.
> Thou barely 'scaped from judgment,
>   Take oath to judge the land
> Unswayed by gift of money
>   Or privy bribe, more base,
> Of knowledge which is profit
>   In any market-place.

Though it was as a politician that Rudyard came before the public in the years before the First World War, he cared much less for politics than for his family and for the land. The process of setting root in a congenial soil is described, from alternative points of view, in two stories written in these years, 'A Habitation Enforced' which presents the return to England of an Anglo-American family, and 'My Son's Wife' which presents the return to the country of an urban intellectual. There would be no justification for describing either as an aspect of autobiography, but both are realized in terms of the Sussex landscape and society. The 'county' was more rapid than the 'village', and perhaps more whole-hearted, in accepting the Kiplings, whose love of seclusion and dislike of intruders prevented them from mixing freely with their neighbours; yet the protective barrier which Carrie always built around Rudyard was not as insurmountable as some accounts have made it. The flow of visitors to 'Bateman's' was controlled by her determination that the merely inquisitive, the mere lion-hunters, the mere snobs should not waste his time. She was a captious, rather niggling housekeeper, who made a great to-do over her hospitality, but hospitable she was to those she wanted Rudyard to see, and a good friend to her friends. On the other hand, everyone wanted to meet the Kiplings.

Among the neighbours her closest friend was Lady Edward Cecil who had been at the Cape with them during the Boer War and shared their memories of Rhodes and his circle. While her husband was serving in Egypt, Lady Edward took a house, 'Great Wigsell' not far from Burwash. Her son, a little older than Elsie, and her daughter, a little younger than John Kipling, were among the neighbours that the children knew best, and Lady Edward was Carrie's closest friend in England. With the Baileys, the Bonar Laws, the Baldwins, the Cecils, Ted and Dorothy Price, and one or two of John's school-friends, John and Elsie began to make a social circle of their own.

Not far away were Sir George Allen at Free Chase, Percival Landon at Keylands, and nearer still was Colonel H. W. Feilden, an old soldier who had retired after an adventurous life into a Queen Anne house in Burwash village street. His wife, an American from the Old South, makes a brief appearance in the story called 'The Edge of the Evening'. The Colonel played a larger part in the domestic life of 'Bateman's' than any other of the neighbours. He was Rudyard's regular confidant and adviser on village politics, on developing the estate, on stocking the brook with trout. He fished with Rudyard on the summer evenings and rented the shooting in the winters when the Kiplings were away. It was to the Colonel that the Kiplings turned in each domestic emergency and Rudyard's letters to him, from South Africa or Switzerland, reveal his trust in the Colonel's tact and judgment.

When the children were younger they had been brought up by governesses, notably by Miss Blaikie who remained a dear friend. Later when more expert teaching was required Miss Dorothy Ponton took charge since she could coach John in mathematics as well as Elsie in Latin and German. A memoir written by Miss Ponton gives a pleasant account of life at 'Bateman's'. It was in the autumn of 1911 that she arrived and went to live, with the private secretary and a maid, at Park Mill Cottage beside the Dudwell Brook.[16]

At this time Rudyard Kipling was forty-six years of age, short, but well-proportioned. He had a pronounced cleft in his chin and very dark, bushy eyebrows, beneath which his blue eyes glowed through his spectacles. In the country he usually dressed in 'plus-fours' with a remarkably shabby cap, or a Trilby hat. After working in his study most of the morning, he often did a little gardening before lunch. He was also fond of fishing and, in wet weather, usually donned leather gaiters and tramped across the fields with Mrs. Kipling to inspect the farms on the estate. Mrs. Kipling, in spite of a rather hard face, had a kindly smile. She was between forty and fifty years of age, short and stout and had very small feet. Her hair was almost white, and her eyes were greyish and shrewd. Elsie, the daughter, was a well-developed girl of sixteen years with nut-brown hair fastened loosely at the back with a black bow. Her dark hazel eyes were bright and intelligent. She had been brought up simply and, except for three months' holiday during the winter when her parents took her abroad, saw little of society. John, a typical schoolboy of thirteen [actually fourteen], was dark and thin and wore glasses.

During the school holidays there were usually young visitors at 'Bateman's'. Mr. Kipling was fond of children and was adored by them, so they had great times together. But there were moments when Mrs. Kipling found them rather too boisterous and exacting. As soon as Elsie had settled down to her term's work, Mrs. Kipling asked me to give one hour's 'holiday work' to the other children [Oliver Baldwin and his sister], so that they might be kept quiet. The day when these lessons were to commence, Mr. Kipling took his young relatives mushrooming, and I met them hilariously carrying back the harvest in his hat.

Elsie also wrote an account of life at 'Bateman's' in those days:

An average day at Bateman's was always a busy one. Breakfast was at 8 A.M. summer and winter, and the large morning post was dealt with immediately afterwards. Anything from sixty to a hundred letters came into the house daily, and were opened mostly by C. K. and her secretary — sorted out, discussed, torn up or answered as the case might be. The whole family developed an uncanny sense for knowing more or less what a letter might contain by its envelope, and R. K. would seize anything he thought promised to be interesting to open himself.

These letters, which always constituted a real task and which followed R. K. everywhere, were incredibly varied, came from every corner of the world, dealt with every subject, and contained every possible request and suggestion; Dr. Marie Stopes asking that *If* should be re-written to deal with women; H. G. Wells urging R. K. not to review a book of his (a thing R. K. never did) as their points of view were so different; or perhaps an unknown spinster wanting new words written for *The Red Flag*, though the Socialists were not to know who had done it! There were numbers of lunatics, and above all endless people wanting help and advice about writing. The latter were generally dealt with at length and with great sympathy, specially if the enquirers were young.

R. K. usually worked in the morning, if he had anything in hand, either doing the actual writing, or pacing up and down his study humming to himself. Much of his best known verse was written to a tune, the 'Recessional' to *Melita,* the tune usually sung to 'Eternal Father, strong to save '; 'Mandalay' to an old waltz tune: and so on; this was curious as R. K. was quite unmusical.

A walk or more work followed lunch, the second post was dealt with, and there would probably be visitors for tea. His interest in his garden was only mild, but on occasion he would take a swop hook or spud, and deal furiously with nettles and other weeds. In the early days at Bateman's he would sometimes fish for trout in the Dudwell, but his eyesight prevented him from doing much shooting. 'Farm walks' were often taken and while C. K. discussed with the foreman ditches to be cleaned out, barns to be repaired or crops to be sown, he stood by listening and only sometimes making a suggestion.

If he was really busy with a piece of work he was utterly absorbed in it and quite oblivious to anything else. Thus his children learned very early to keep any requests or plans until he had safely finished whatever was engaging him, until he 'came back' as they called it, and was again ready to enter their daily life.

It was for Carrie's sake that they went on to Vernet-les-Bains in the eastern Pyrenees after the usual family holiday in Switzerland in 1910. The cure here gave her some relief, and for several years the visit was repeated. Rudyard made friends among the numerous English visitors, and contributed *Why the Snow falls at Vernet* to a magazine which was run by them. It was one year when Lord Roberts and his daughter were also at Vernet that Rudyard acted as interpreter at a formal meeting between the aged Field Marshal (very worried because he was in plain clothes), the commander of the area garrison (very much in uniform), and the local Archbishop. This somewhat incongruous party, was recorded in a stiff photo group, done by the excited hotel photographer.

Every January, from 1909 until the outbreak of war, they travelled by steamer and train to Engelberg or St. Moritz. For a month or six weeks the children gave themselves up to ski-ing and skating and then, when John had returned to school, the other three toured the continent, sometimes visiting the Château d'Annel near Compiègne, the home of Chauncey Depew, who had married their old friend, Julia Catlin.

Rudyard was by nature a lover of France, and of the French, who now read his books as avidly as the English. The childhood holiday which he had spent with his father in Paris, in 1878, had started a tendency which motoring enabled him to cultivate in middle age, but his family used to say that he could never stay more than three days anywhere without being found out. When he visited a church the priest would recognize him and make an occasion of the visit; or some soldier in the street would accost him, challenge him, and carry him off in triumph to the officers' mess. By the third day there would be a call from the mayor with threats of a civic reception. All doors were open to Rudyard Kipling. No matter if it were closing-day, the management of any gallery or the owner of any historic house was willing —anxious — to show him round.

In the 'nineties, when rival imperialisms had forced a breach between France and England, Rudyard had passed through a short anti-French phase and, in 1900, had written a story, 'The Bonds of Discipline', ridiculing the conduct of a French spy who introduced himself into a ship of the Royal Navy. There had also been an anti-Kipling outburst in France. Soon after the Boer War, a remarkable novel by Jean and Jerome Tharaud was published under the title of *Dingley,* and was awarded the Goncourt Prize. It was plainly a hostile criticism of Rudyard Kipling presented in the form of a romance about his experiences in South Africa, written by someone who knew something about his domestic life and rather less about his writings. 'Dingley', the hero of the tale, was an English imperialist author who glorified war and was disillusioned when his own son was killed by the Boers. The treatment was topical and the book has now been forgotten.

After the Entente Cordiale of 1904, as England and France drew closer together, this short phase of antipathy vanished. Some of Rudyard's early works had long been issued in French translations (as in all the principal languages of the world). His vogue, in France, especially, was much increased when his sympathy with French ideals became known. A link with French politics was Georges Clemenceau, an anti-imperialist but a man after Rudyard's heart, and a friend of Lady Edward Cecil who brought him over to 'Bateman's' more than once. Rudyard declared his devotion to the Anglo-French *entente,* a firm foundation of his political ideals for the rest of his life, by publishing his poem, 'France', in the *Morning Post,* on the occasion of the French President's state visit to London, 24th June 1913.

It was a tribute to the French national character in terms far different from the conventional English view:

> Furious in luxury, merciless in toil,
> Terrible with strength that draws from her tireless soil;
> Strictest judge of her own worth, gentlest of man's mind,
> First to follow Truth and last to leave old Truths behind —
> France, beloved of every soul that loves its fellow-kind!

A by-product of the Boer War, which men of goodwill approved, was the extension of new and manly principles into popular education, in accordance with the active philosophy which Roosevelt called the Strenuous Life. All these and many other desirable qualities were fostered by the Boy Scout movement which Baden-Powell, the 'Hero of Mafeking', gradually brought into existence in 1907 and 1908. Rudyard was an early and enthusiastic supporter, proud to style himself 'Commissioner of Boy Scouts'. Just what is the debt of the Scout Law to Rudyard's concept 'The Law', which the *Jungle Books* had made familiar to a whole generation of boys, cannot be calculated; but Rudyard Kipling and Baden-Powell were friends and had discussed these questions. The debt is evident in *Scouting for Boys,* and when the 'wolf-cub' organization was provided for little boys, its origin in the 'Mowgli' stories was obvious. In the summer of 1909, Rudyard wrote his Boy Scouts' 'Patrol Song' (to the tune of 'A Life on the Ocean Wave') for Baden-Powell and, a few weeks later, visited one of the early Scout camps in the New Forest. Thereafter he appeared more than once at Scout rallies.

Furthermore, he was an active supporter of the National Service League to which old Lord Roberts devoted his declining years, but conscription in any form, even compulsory registration and training, was not regarded by any political party in those days as a policy for winning elections. In Rudyard's soldier-stories of this period there is always a note of bitterness against the military reforms of the Liberal Government, even against Haldane's Territorial Army which so nearly resembled his own 'Army of a Dream'.

Rudyard was more at home with the Navy than with the Army in those years. He had become a serious student of naval records, and he maintained his interest in naval techniques. From time to time he tried his hand at stories of life as seen from the lower deck, which might have been comparable with his earlier stories of life in the barrack-room. They are grouped round the character of his talkative petty-officer ashore, Pyecroft, who acts, like Mulvaney, as the author's mouthpiece. Though the virtuosity is immense, the stories themselves lack vigour and, while they have their admirers, there is not one of the Pyecroft stories which is likely to find its way into a selection of Rudyard Kipling's best six, or best twelve. Obviously they gave their author great pleasure, but this enthusiasm is rarely conveyed to readers who are not already familiar with naval jargon. The best of the series, perhaps, is the set of light verses, 'Poseidon's Law', which accompanies 'The Bonds of Discipline'.

Rudyard's devotion to the Navy was bound up with his hope that his only son should have a naval career. John Kipling had been dedicated to this service from birth, and his way was smoothed before him by the patronage of England's greatest living sailor. Sir John Fisher wrote to Rudyard offering to nominate John for a naval cadetship, thus giving him a historic line of succession because he, himself, had been nominated to a cadetship, fifty years earlier, by the last survivor among Nelson's captains. This offer was in vain, for when little John grew up into boyhood, his eyesight revealed a fault, and, like his father, he was obliged to wear spectacles. It became certain that he would never reach the rigorous standard of eyesight required for naval service, and hardly even the lower standard required by the army. For a career as a regular soldier, or indeed for any professional career in those days, he must next be sent to a Public School. Westward Ho!, which Rudyard still regarded as superior to all others, was a memory of the past, a school no longer, and he decided to send John to Wellington

College, another school with a strong military tradition. During the three years that John spent at Wellington (1911–13), Rudyard used frequently to drive over to Farnborough, not far away, where he stayed at the Queen's Hotel. He could visit his son and could meet many friends in the services, for the Queen's Hotel was much frequented by army officers from Aldershot. He and Gwynne made it their head-quarters while watching the Army Manœuvres in the blazing heat of August 1913. Still more interesting was the rapid growth of something new, at Farnborough, the Royal Aircraft Establishment. Rudyard and John had first seen aeroplanes in France, in 1910, and during John's schooldays at Wellington grew familiar with them around Aldershot and Farnborough.

Rudyard Kipling to Colonel L. C. Dunsterville

10 December, 1912

I've been down at Aldershot exploring a new world — the Royal Flying Corps. It's a rummy sensation to stand at the very beginning of things, as it might be with Primitive Man when he first launched his canoe. They don't know a dam thing but they are finding it out by experience — such of 'em as live. It's exactly like a kid rolling down a flight of steps and discovering the laws of gravity at the age of two. But they seemed to me to have already developed a typical eye and face. I noticed also that there is a New Smell in the Service — not Infantry (hot or cold) — not Artillery (which is horse-sweat and leather) — not motor transport which is petrol and oil, but a fourth and indescribable stink — a rather shrill stink if you understand, like chlorine gas on top of petrol fumes plus gummy calico in a shop. That's the stink of the aeroplane.[18]

John was a straightforward, popular and good-natured boy, with quick wit, a great sense of fun and much charm, but with no marked talents. At school he worked with moderation but played with spirit and energy, being a keen footballer. Rudyard was delighted when John brought home 'a piece of poetry that he had found in a book'; he had taken a fancy to it without knowing that his father had written it. When John joined a literary society at school, he easily prevailed on his father to read a paper to them, a privilege asked by much more distinguished societies in vain.

But John proved backward in his school-work, even with coaching from Elsie's governess in the holidays, and it seemed doubtful whether he could pass the examination for Sandhurst. In 1913 he left Welling-ton and went to a private coaching establishment at Bournemouth — one of those 'Army crammers' whom Stalky and Co. had so despised at Westward Ho!, and spent his last year there before the crisis of 1914 changed all their lives.

While at Bournemouth an event occurred which suggests that John

Kipling was maturing. Though nominally members of the Church of England, neither Rudyard nor Carrie had made a practice of attending church services, except occasionally on ceremonial occasions. The children had been taught the elements of religion by governesses and had been taken to church but, it appears, John had never been baptized. There are signs that Rudyard, who had been rather strongly anti-clerical as a young man, was growing more disposed to accept the Christian revelation in middle age. Some of the stories in *Rewards and Fairies,* though far from orthodoxy, show a reverent religious sense which can hardly be paralleled in Kipling's earlier work, with its stoic cosmology, its impersonal deism, and its puzzling over mortality and immortality. The author of the verses headed 'Cold Iron' was in another mood. Whatever Rudyard's religious progress, his son John now made a decided step and, early in 1914, was baptized into the Church of England at the age of sixteen, with the approval of both parents who acted as sponsors.

In the spring of 1913 the Kiplings extended their usual tour as far as Egypt, their first visit to the East for twenty years. It was a renewal for Rudyard of the sights, smells, and sounds of Asia, which he faithfully recorded in a series of letters for the *Morning Post* (reprinted in *Letters of Travel*). It is strange to reflect how slight had been his earlier acquaintance with Egypt — that the author of *The Light that Failed* and of 'Little Foxes' set eyes on the Nile Valley for the first time at this late date. In Cairo they called on Lord Kitchener who made a bad impression on Rudyard. He was a 'fatted pharaoh in spurs'; he had 'gone to seed physically'; he was 'garrulously intoxicated with power'. Rudyard tackled the great man about Egyptian finances and supplied Gwynne with columns of statistics for use in denouncing Kitchener's agricultural policy.

When they returned home it was to find Ireland on the brink of civil war. The Ulster volunteers were equipping themselves with rifles obtained from Germany, and now the Catholic Irish of the south were forming a rival army. Rudyard and Carrie had visited Ireland in 1911 when they had found the 'dirt and slop and general shiftlessness of Dublin past belief' and had returned convinced that a firm stand by the Ulstermen could and should force the Liberal Government to abandon the Home Rule Bill.

Rudyard Kipling to H. A. Gwynne

2 December, 1913

You talk of the German danger. Does it occur to you that a betrayed Ulster will repeat 1688 in the shape of a direct appeal to Germany? And that in doing this she will have the sullen sympathy of a great many people

THE YOUNG FAMILY, 1898:
CAROLINE KIPLING WITH JOHN, ELSIE, AND JOSEPHINE

in England who are suffering under intolerable misgovernment? Ulster is nearer than South Africa; and a betrayed Ulster is more dangerous than twenty southern Irelands in open revolt. The South Irish have no passion for Home Rule as such. They realize it would be against their business interests; their leaders know that the money to finance a new revolt could not come from Ireland but must come from the U.S. Which is the more dangerous enemy? The South playing a game it has not got its heart in, or the North in a blind rage, led by *its own leaders not by politicians*! [19]

'Sullen sympathy' was not a strong enough term for the support already given to the Ulster cause by the Conservative Opposition in England. The Ulster Covenant, pledging resistance against any attempt to subject Protestant Ulster to the Catholic south, had been signed by thousands of English Protestants. Among the leaders of the Covenanting movement were Rudyard's close associates — Bonar Law, Milner, Gwynne — and none went further than he did in defiance. Throughout the early months of 1914 the Irish crisis grew more intense, blinding Rudyard's eyes, or so it seemed, to the imminent threat of a greater disaster, the European War against which he had, for so long, been warning his fellow-countrymen.

When the Government fumbled, in March, over the 'Curragh Incident', allowing their hands to be forced by a group of Army officers who sympathized with the Ulstermen and said so, it was clear that Ulster could not be coerced. The Government had lost control, and Rudyard had no doubt that the time was come to call their bluff. One day in April he sat down and wrote, for the journal of the Ulster party, his inflammatory verses:

> We know the wars prepared
> On every peaceful home,
> We know the hells declared
> For such as serve not Rome —
> The terror, threats, and dread
> In market, hearth, and field —
> We know, when all is said,
> We perish if we yield. [21]

A few days later, 16th May 1914, he made one of his rare public speeches, to ten thousand cheering Unionists on the common at Tunbridge Wells, a bitter personal attack upon the Liberal leaders, in terms that were virulent even by the standard of those ill-tempered days. The Government, he said, were like 'a firm of fraudulent solicitors who had got an unlimited power of attorney from a client by false pretences and could dispose of their client's estate how they pleased'. He taunted them as common rogues for the Marconi scandals, saying flatly that, though they did not stick at murder, money-getting was their strongest motive. They were now reduced to the necessity of handing Ulster over to a gang of criminals 'for no other reason than that they might continue in enjoyment of their salaries'.

This 'wild outburst', as the *Manchester Guardian* described it in a headline, was reported at length in the newspapers. So crude an overstatement was an embarrassment to Rudyard's own party and a self-inflicted wound to his own reputation. Never, perhaps, had his reputation been so low with all those good people of temperate opinions who were sorely puzzled by the intricacy of the Irish problem. This was the Kipling of the Beerbohm caricatures, a figure far removed from the author of 'Recessional'.

Luckily, he had two sides still to his head. While the Radical press took advantage of the joint in his armour which he had exposed to their blows, another Rudyard was corresponding in another vein with a friend at Oxford. Sir William Osler, the Regius Professor of Medicine, was a man of rare social accomplishment and wide reading — far beyond his professional studies. Kiplings and Oslers were connected on the distaff side, for Lady Osler was a Revere of Boston and so related to the Balestiers. It was from Osler that Rudyard acquired an interest in the history of medicine. To Osler he owed the story of René de Laennec, the inventor of the stethoscope ('Marklake Witches'), and to Osler's judgment he submitted the story of Nicholas Culpeper ('A Doctor of Medicine'). In the second case Rudyard was on his own ground, since botany had long been one of his hobbies and old English herbals were his delight.

Sir W. Osler to Rudyard Kipling

9 May, 1914

Dear Kipling,
The Roger Bacon celebration is on June 10th. . . . Bridges has promised to write a brief ode, in which he says he will deal only with philosophy and that he might not mention Roger Bacon at all. . . . The Committee empowers me to ask you to write and recite something for us at the luncheon, dealing particularly with the personality and tragedy of Roger Bacon. Do please accept, and come to us, and bring Mrs. Kipling.

Rudyard Kipling to Sir W. Osler

10 May, 1914

Dear Osler,
I can't tell you how shocked I am to find the practice of medicine at Oxford (Roger's own university) so grossly behind the age. It was Galen who laid down that 'anger at meat' (by which he meant all mental emotion save of the mildest) is the mother of evil; and here are *you* —

Regius Professor — counselling me to recite my own verses 'at' not before or after, but *at* a bountiful meal. May I refer you to *Libellus R.B. etc. etc. de retardandis senectutis accidentibus et de sensibus conservandis* (Oxford 1590). But seriously, much as I should love to be of use to you I fear I am no good in the matter. I don't know Bacon except from the popular legend; I have no 'Brewer' and I can't get up to Oxford on the 10th and I am up to my eyes in work and arrears of work of all sorts.

Forgive me, and send me, as soon as you can, your paper on R. B. to file with my old doctors. Nicholas Culpepper, who could write even if he couldn't cure for nuts — says at the beginning of his Herbal, 'I knew well enough the whole world and everything in it was formed of a composition of contrary elements, and in such a harmony as must needs show the wisdom and power of a great God.' That seems to me to cover Roger Bacon's outlook and I present it to you for a quotation.[21]

The prospect of civil war in Ireland seems not to have imposed any change in the routine of the English upper classes. Rudyard attended meetings of political groups in London; Carrie was a prominent member of a ladies' committee which was to provide relief for loyal refugees from Ulster; and these occupations did not prevent them from taking their summer holiday, at Kessingland Grange, a lonely house near Lowestoft, lent them by their friend Rider Haggard.

While their eyes were set upon Ulster they paid small heed to affairs in the Balkans which were of greater moment. Carrie's diary contains no mention of the Archduke's murder at Serajevo or of any event in south-eastern Europe until 31st July when Helen Cecil who had joined them at Kessingland was sent for. Her father, Lord Edward, had been recalled from leave 'because of the war'. For a few days more the young people bathed, Carrie was 'possessed by' a bad cold and on 4th August Rudyard noted in her diary: 'Incidentally armageddon begins'.

It has been recorded in many novels and memoirs how swiftly the world was changed in those few days of August 1914, yet no account is adequate to recall the alteration in the magnitude of events, as if western civilization had gone into another gear. Ulster, the Strikes, the Suffragettes, shrank to insignificance. The tiresome jaded political struggle with which the people, though they might not admit as much, were bored; the sham fights; the empty threats in which no one quite believed, because no living Englishman had seen war or revolution on English soil; all this vanished like a nightmare, leaving a clean issue, to resist German aggression. Even the pacifists felt this relief from the trivial, the second-rate. At least Mrs. Pankhurst and Sir Edward Carson could be forgotten. It was this sense of relief that inspired those words of Rupert Brooke, a Liberal, which have sometimes since seemed so hard to justify:

> Now God be thanked who has matched us with His hour,
>   And caught our youth, and wakened us from sleeping,
> With hand made sure, clear eye, and sharpened power,
>   To turn, as swimmers into cleanness leaping,
> Glad from a world grown old and cold and weary,
>   Leave the sick hearts that honour could not move. . . .

But that indeed was how it seemed in August 1914, and Rudyard's words for *The Times,* though more sombre than Rupert Brooke's, were in the appropriate key.

> Comfort, content, delight,
> The ages' slow-bought gain,
> They shrivelled in a night.
> Only ourselves remain
> To face the naked days
> In silent fortitude, . . .[22]

CHAPTER XVII

THE FIRST WORLD WAR (1914–18)

MY BOY JACK (1916)

'Have you news of my boy Jack?'
   Not this tide.
'When d'you think that he'll come back?'
   Not with this wind blowing, and this tide.

'Has any one else had word of him?'
   Not this tide.
For what is sunk will hardly swim,
   Not with this wind blowing, and this tide.

'Oh, dear, what comfort can I find?'
   None this tide,
   Nor any tide,
Except he did not shame his kind —
   Not even with that wind blowing, and that tide.

Then hold your head up all the more,
   This tide,
   And every tide;
Because he was the son you bore,
   And gave to that wind blowing and that tide!

AT Kessingland, where the traffic route ran in deep water past the eastward promontory of Norfolk, some movement of warships could be seen, which stirred Rudyard's imagination, partly because he was better informed than most men about military and naval affairs, and had friends in Fleet Street who could tell him more. On 4th August, before the declaration of war, he wrote to R. D. Blumenfeld of the *Daily Express*.

Rudyard Kipling to R. D. Blumenfeld

Kessingland Grange, 4 August, 1914

Many thanks for your wire *re* ultimatum. I somehow fancy that these sons of Belial will wriggle out of the mess after all — or it may be worth Germany's while to avoid Belgium if we stay neutral. *How* the Teutons must despise us — and how justly! Meantime we look as if we were losing time. I'd be greatly your debtor if you could tell someone in the office to send me a wire, of evenings, when they have time, giving me the day's news.

The place we have taken here is for practical purposes the side of a ship. The garden runs about fifteen yards to a cliff — then the sea and all the drama of the skirts of war laid out before us. Destroyers going up and coming down in twos and fours — then a gunboat or so — then a N.Y.K. (Jap. boat) all white and disinterested going to London; then a Nelson liner with a sort of 'Mike, you're wanted', look on her; then steam trawlers and the usual procession of tows and barges.

The strain on *you* must be awful but there is the ancient text of the Rabbi (I think it was Hillel) to console one with. It says substantially that the worst that men and women meet in this world is just men and women and their notions. The old boy was a bit of a freethinker like so many of the Rabbis were at heart. My father used to quote it to me as:— 'Nothing worse in the world than yourself — and nothing better.' [1]

Three days later, on the 7th, Kitchener made his first public appeal to the nation for voluntary recruitment in the New Army which was to bear his name and, on the 10th, John went up to London alone to offer himself for a commission, just before his seventeenth birthday. Forty years ago, when education beyond the primary stage was enjoyed only by a small minority, any reputable young man with a good education and a good character was eligible for appointment as 'Temporary Second Lieutenant', and might get a commission as soon as a regimental commander applied for his services. John had some training in his school Officers' Training Corps, but his poor sight would still prejudice commanding officers against him. He was rejected on his first application, and proposed to try his luck at enlisting as a private soldier, a more heroic decision in those class-conscious days than it would seem today, but Rudyard had another card to play. He asked their old friend Lord Roberts for a nomination to his own regiment, the Irish Guards, which was arranged in time for John to report for duty at Warley Barracks on 14th September. This was the last evidence of friendship between the Kiplings and Lord Roberts, who died a few weeks later while visiting the armies in France.

Meanwhile the other three had returned from Kessingland. In mid-August they were at Brown's Hotel among crowds of stranded American tourists whom Carrie described as 'noisy, restless and excited'. Then, at 'Bateman's' again, they busied themselves with aid to the Belgian Refugees and with work for the Red Cross, sending piles of linen to the London Hospital, and using for a greater purpose the organization they had formed in preparation for civil war in Ireland. They were avid for news and could get none or little, though Landon, Aitken, and Stanley Baldwin came to tell what they knew.

While the French and British drew back from Flanders into France, Rudyard set himself to write his poem, 'For all we have and are'. Landon, who had offered some amendments which Rudyard accepted, took it to town on the last day of August for publication in the next day's *Times*. It was promptly pirated in America by the syndicated Press.

The war news, as it came in, revealed a situation that grew more disquieting. One day in September Julia Depew arrived from Compiègne as a refugee, with a tale of German atrocities in France and Belgium, and the first gap in their own circle of friends came when Lady Edward had news that her son, George Cecil, was missing in the retreat from Mons. The strain of John's departure was increased for Rudyard by the renewed illness of his sister 'Trix' for whom he had to make himself responsible, and his own health showed signs of giving way to these anxieties. As several times in his earlier life, nervous exhaustion showed itself in a partial paralysis of the facial muscles, which kept him at home for some days. Then in October he began a round of visits to hospitals and training-camps, so as to form his own impressions of the New Armies in training, of the veteran troops from Flanders, and especially of the Indian troops who had been brought to France. It was a peculiar pleasure to visit the hospital for Indian soldiers at Brighton.

Again and again, he was invited to write official propaganda for the Government, and refused to do so, but when his friend Aitken (after 1916 Sir Max Aitken) was appointed official correspondent with the Canadian Army in Europe, Rudyard saw him frequently and gave him much help with his work. John had leave at Christmas which they all spent together with the Bonar Laws, at the Aitkens' house near Leatherhead.

Meanwhile the ferocity of the German war-machine grew more apparent. In January 1915 the first air-raids were made on undefended English towns; and in February the German Admiralty announced its policy of unrestricted submarine warfare. Rudyard's reaction took the form of three short stories written that winter, 'Swept and Garnished', written in October, 'Sea-Constables' in February, 'Mary Postgate' in March.*

'Swept and Garnished' is a rather horrid little story about the delusions of a German woman, lying in bed with a high fever, who sees the victims of the policy of 'frightfulness', dream-children who make a shocking contrast with the happy child-ghosts in 'They'. In the development of Kipling's art, the story is worth noticing as another

---

* Since there has been controversy on this point, it will be worth while to mention that Carrie Kipling's Diary describes Rudyard as working at 'Mary Postgate' on 8th March 1915.

example of his growing interest in the mental processes of elderly women.

The second story, 'Sea-Constables', like most of his sea-stories, is so technical as to be almost unintelligible to a landsman. Furthermore, its construction is so complex as to require the closest attention from the reader. Four men, all temporary naval officers, talking together over a good dinner enjoyed ashore, reconstruct, in snatches of dialogue, their relentless pursuit of a neutral skipper whom they know to be supplying German submarines. With good consciences and good digestions they recount their parts in hounding him to death.

Ethically, 'Sea-Constables' is a deplorable tale, but war is a deplorable business, and Kipling was never the man to paint it in pretty colours. Perhaps because of its obscurity the detractors of Kipling have never condemned this story as roundly as they have condemned 'Mary Postgate', which somebody has described as 'the wickedest story ever written'. It is the tale of a plain, unloved, elderly governess and her secret maternal passion for her pupil who is killed in the war. While she is engaged in disposing of the boyish possessions he has left behind, destroying them on a bonfire as a sacrifice to her vain and unrequited love, she has the opportunity of saving the life of a wounded German airman, after a bombing raid on the village. She deliberately, exultingly, lets him die, which she says, 'no man would ever have done'. This is entirely personal, a tale about frustrated passion and vicarious revenge, not about any particular campaign. It is concerned with the quality of ruthlessness, an extension of the sardonic verse, 'the female of the species is more deadly than the male'.

One task that Rudyard willingly undertook in 1914 was to find a place for 'Stalky' in the New Armies. Times had changed since Dunsterville had been the leader in their enterprises and Kipling his admirer and lieutenant. Dunsterville had not achieved the career that Kipling had forecast for him. By some mischance he had missed, not only the campaigns in Burma, Egypt, and South Africa in which the successful generals had made their names, but also the more spectacular events in campaigns on the Indian frontier. He had seen much hard service with his Sikhs but not in affairs which caught the public eye. Perhaps, too, the peculiar talents which impressed the other boys in Number Five Study at Westward Ho! were not so much esteemed by the bureaucrats in Simla and Whitehall. At any rate Dunsterville's career seemed to have come to an end after his term in command of a Sikh battalion and, in 1914, he found himself in England, an unused, retired, Anglo-Indian colonel on a very small pension, while Kipling was rich and famous. Rudyard was kind to 'Stalky's' son — as to all children — and helped 'Stalky' from time to time with loans of money which were scrupulously noted and repaid. At forty-nine 'Stalky' was unlikely to get command of a battalion in the field and, having no friends in high places, he found no easy billet.

Among their contemporaries from the College, Aleck Godley was commanding the New Zealanders, Maclagan had a brigade of Australians, 'Potiphar' Rimington was Chief Engineer in Mesopotamia, Cunliffe was fighting a campaign of his own in the Cameroons, while 'Stalky' found no better job than conducting trainloads of soldiers up and down the line in France, one of the humblest tasks a staff officer could be called upon to do, while his special qualifications as a Russian interperter were overlooked. Rudyard, who had many friends at the War Office, attempted to get 'Stalky' a brigade in Kitchener's Army, but the War Office preferred to send him back to India as a brigadier on the North-West Frontier, where, in due course, his long-awaited opportunity appeared.

In the spring of 1915 it was still possible for Englishmen to be optimistic about the war. They had survived the first shock of the German onslaught and had made some progress in building up the resources which eventually must bring victory. The war had settled down into its second phase, the period of trench warfare, and in Sussex the life of the countryside was adjusting itself to new ways. A party of New Army officers (of the 'Loyals') were billeted for a time at 'Bateman's'. Then came a day when the Kiplings offered the house to the War Office for use as a hospital, and, though this offer was not accepted, they spent less time there. Rudyard was very busy with visits to camps and hospitals and seaports, and with writing descriptive articles about them for the *Daily Telegraph*. On Salisbury Plain there were Canadian troops, among whom several of his friends were serving, and Carrie was an active member of the committee of the 'Maple Leaf', the club for Canadian soldiers on leave in London. The Rolls-Royce was laid up, and, since there were now numerous occasions for visiting London, they tended to save the awkward train journeys by staying longer at Brown's Hotel, where John, from Warley Barracks, could sometimes join them in the evenings.

At seventeen John was a slim, good-looking boy, the tallest of the family, with quick dark eyes behind his glasses, with a great sense of fun and a passion for motor-bicycles. He found his life in barracks interesting though hard, and made many friends. A natural quickness and imaginative sympathy enabled him to get on well with the men of his company, mainly Irishmen in those early days; and it is said that his handling of a new draft of very drunken recruits from Dublin was masterly.

Scanty hours of leave in London were all his family saw of him that winter. John would arrive in his own car from Warley Barracks, sometimes alone but often with friends who would eat large meals and go to the theatre, or sit talking till late in the Kiplings' sitting-room at Brown's Hotel (always their London headquarters). Then, their few hours of leave over, they would pack into John's little car and rattle back to Warley.

His close friendship with his sister continued unshaken; they wrote often to each other and, when they met, discussed life with gusto and animation. He would criticise her frocks and give her errands to do for him at Fortnum and Mason's, while there was always a demand for the socks she knitted for him and his friends.[2]

But when May 1915 came, a month that brought news of heavy British losses in men on two battle-fronts, with small gains in ground, the shadow of John's departure overseas loomed nearer. Draft after draft went out from Warley Barracks to fill the gaps in the Regiment and, for his part, John was deeply humiliated at being left behind, though his name was put back only until he should reach his eighteenth birthday. In July his friend Oscar Hornung, who had often stayed at 'Bateman's', was killed in France, a shock that merely served to sharpen his impatience. Then plans were changed, the Brigade of Guards was expanded into a Guards Division and John was assured that he would be sent abroad with the newly formed Second Battalion, if his father should give permission.

On 10th August the Second Irish Guards were put under orders for France and on the following day Rudyard met his son in London to say goodbye, for he, too, was going abroad. Rudyard and Percival Landon had been invited to pay a visit to the French Armies in the field. Father and son lunched together at the Bath Club, and then John had still three days of leave, which he spent with his mother and sister at 'Bateman's'. On the 17th, his birthday, he left them, looking, as his mother said, 'very smart and straight and young and brave' as he turned at the top of the stairs to say goodbye.

Rudyard was first of the two to see the realities of war.

Rudyard to Carrie Kipling

August, 1915
12 Aug. in the train between Abbeville and Amiens

I was buttonholed by the Duchess of Rutland . . . about a hospital that she wants to start. . . . Right in the midst of this clack a man with tinted spectacles passes. She says to me:— 'Ain't that Munthe — doctor to the Queen of Sweden?' As he passes she hails him — and Munthe it was. . . . I fell into talk with him at once and he tells me of all his grief and sorrow to find that Sweden is so — not pro-German but afraid of Russia — and how he has got himself into trouble in Sweden for his English and French leanings; and how he has dismissed himself from his Queen's service and how, but for the sad fact that our naturalization laws now insist that a man must put in twelve months' continuous residence in England, he would have 'already, my dear Mr. Kipling, have been a British subject '. Of all of which you may believe as much as I did. He was immensely curious to know where I was going.

We left the pier with a quick stealthy turn and two destroyers came up out of the warm grey sea (or that was the effect of it) and fell in alongside us on either side, sort of lounging along to keep pace with our modest 22 knots.

13 Aug. HOTEL RITZ, PARIS

Back from that amazing human explosive, Clemenceau, who, on the instant of my coming held forth without break and so continued for forty coruscating minutes. All truth too, backed with very real power and the widest knowledge. I should say from what he said that *their* Government is the twin of ours, mentally and spiritually — same incompetence, same lawyer's explanations, same complete inability for anyone to admit that they were wrong in any particular, and the same furious intrigues. . . .

He had no earthly doubt of the issue but — munitions, munitions was his cry throughout. I talked French. And talking of talking French, Mons. Ponsot at lunch said to me: 'If I had known you talked French so well, Mr. Kipling . . .'

14 Aug. HOTEL BRIGHTON, PARIS

I sent in my card to Briand, Minister of Justice, whom you remember we met at the Princess's Now C[lemenceau]'s view of Briand is absolutely unprintable. He would endure, he says, a thousand Millerands sooner than one B. On that I can pronounce no opinion. He reminded me more of Lloyd-George than ever. It's a born demagogue with his mouth crammed with smooth things — but I can't help liking it . . . the same L-G like shrug and lean forward of the shoulders at critical points, a sort of political bedside manner. A windbag, yes, but of the most unscrupulous.

15 Aug. A VILLA (!) IN JONCHÉRY

We were received on the château steps. It overlooked a heavenly valley and was surrounded on two sides by a platform of stone rather reminding me of Ewhurst. . . . The General, who was called Nivelle, told me that his mother was English but he didn't talk good English for all that. He was a charming man of gentle manners. Lunch wouldn't be till one. Would I come out and see somthing? So we came . . . to a tree — to a huge tree — an acacia, Landon says, about 60 feet high, with a ladder going up to a platform in the top branches. At last we came to a crow's nest in the tree, with a map under a little roofed table, a telephone and a man or two. . . . Then, looking through the leaves and the branches, I saw the whole countryside falling away for miles in a long yellow slope. (The Boches had used gas weeks ago and the grass had perished for three or four miles). Twas like a stretch of lonely African veldt. . . . Regularly all along the line of the horizon, three miles away, the shells from our guns in the discreet park raised clouds of white smoke precisely like the spouts of water up a breakwater in a storm.

Then we climbed down the ladder (which I loathed but I didn't bungle) and were taken to a set of enormous limestone caves or quarries where troops were resting. The General said to me with a wave of the hand: '*All* these men know your books.' I smiled politely. He turned on the nearest group and asked 'em. 'Yes, Yes,' said they, 'specially the Jungle Books.' . . . The fuss about this tour is there's too much dam R. K. in it. I have to lead all the processions.

20 Aug. TROYES

Yesterday was a somewhat full day. It began at 6 A.M. . . . among the wooded hills of Alsace. . . . We stopped to look at a battery of mountain guns; got out and walked under the gloom of many trees . . . thence we got into communication trenches and walked and walked and walked, till we met a fatherly and motherly Colonel who took us into the first line trenches which are 7, or to be exact $7\frac{1}{2}$ metres — say the length of a cricket pitch, from the Germans. They were Bavarians and had been carefully attended to the night before, with the result that they were *quite* tame, and I had peeps at 'em through loopholes blocked with plugs. The Colonel pulled the plugs and bade me look. I saw green sandbags in a wilderness of tree trunks and stones and no Bavarians saw me. . . . The trenches were beautifully clean and kept like a museum. There was no smell save the smell of cookery. There was no noise because we were so close and — nothing whatever happened.

22 Aug. PARIS

I got here at 7.30 from Troyes — after a rather ludicrous time about the passport, when we tried to buy our tickets to Paris. The Commissary of Police . . . knew nothing about us. . . . Then up rose a very dirty little corporal with a restless face and haled us out. Once away from the presence of the officer his visage changed. 'I knew,' said he. 'You are that Rutyar Kiplen of whom we read. Our officers are all asses. Come along with me.' . . . When I owned to being 'Rutyar', he launched a long, friendly and enthusiastic 'Ah God-dam!' which was the first I'd ever heard of that much-described word.

Rudyard to John Kipling

HOTEL BRIGHTON, PARIS. 22 Aug. 1915

DEAR OLD MAN,

I hope you'll never get nearer to the Boche than I did. The quaintest thing was to watch the N.C.O. gesticulating to his Colonel and me to keep quiet — and to hear a hopefully expectant machine gun putting in five or six shots on the chance and then, as it were, stopping to listen. I don't mind trenches half as much as going in a motor along ten or twelve miles of road which the Boches may or may not shell — said road casually protected at the worst corners with thin hurdles of dried pine-trees.

Also, I hate to be in a town with stone pavements when same is being bombarded. It's a grand life though and does not give you a dull minute. I found boric acid in my socks a great comfort. I walked 2 hours in the dam' trenches.

Don't forget the beauty of rabbit netting overhead against hand-grenades. Even tennis netting is better than nothing.[3]

After his return from France, strong pressure was brought on Rudyard by the Admiralty to write something about the Royal Navy. So firm were the traditions of the silent service that no one knew what the Navy was doing, and our allies supposed it was doing nothing. Here was a task that Rudyard could undertake and he spent September visiting ships of the Dover Patrol and the Harwich Flotilla. Having done this task, he arrived home, out of sorts, on 27th September. News had come through of a great attack in France, the Battle of Loos, which at first seemed likely to be a British victory; but Rudyard was ill with gastritis, unable to pay much attention to the news. The doctor saw him and put him on a strict diet.

The Battle of Loos was no triumph. Although the British had captured a section of the German front at great cost on 25th September, reserves were badly placed so that the first success was not exploited. An attempt by two fresh divisions to force their way through a narrow gap in the German front failed on the 26th. The Germans rallied and were regaining ground to right and left of the gap when the last reserve, the Guards Division, was thrown in, on the 27th, to save a situation that was crumbling. The attack of the Guards was unsuccessful also; they made ground, lost it, recovered part of what they had lost, and then consolidated an unfavourable line, while the battle flickered out with little to show for all the valour expended, except 20,000 British dead. The picture of this fruitless struggle was beginning to take shape in the newspapers when, on the morning of 2nd October, a telegram from the War Office announced that John Kipling was wounded and missing.

Elsie's friend Isabel Bonar Law (who was later to lose two of her brothers) was spending the day with her, and Carrie at once decided not to break the news until Isabel had gone. Somehow Carrie forced herself to go through with the day's routine. The next day it was fine after the rain — a 'beautiful, perfect day' she wrote in her diary — and action must be taken. She drove to Wigsell in the morning to share her sorrow with Lady Edward, who had lived through the same experience twelve months earlier, and before she had entered the house Lady Edward knew from her calm, set features what was the message Carrie had come to bring.

That afternoon Aitken arrived from France with such slight news as

he had been able to gather, more than was known at the War Office.
On the 5th Rudyard was well enough to work at his correspondence
while Carrie and Elsie went to London to seek for news at the Guards
Depot. They got very little beyond a word from the Colonel to say
that John had been wounded while leading a small party of his men
against the Germans. Only one of the party had returned wounded,
to a hospital at Hythe where at last they found him, 'very sorrowful
to hear the news about Mr. Kipling who was good to us men and
never downhearted'. The staff at Brown's Hotel, old friends of the
family, were equally distressed.

Rudyard resolutely returned to work at *Sea Warfare* while awaiting
further information. The routine went on as before except that
Christmas, and Rudyard's fiftieth birthday four days later, passed without celebration. The War Office had urged him to write an account
of the epic Battle of Ypres, 'M.I.5', to help them with propaganda;
but such tasks as these he was unwilling to do. He was busy at writing
accounts of his own visits to camps and ships, in his own time.

Meanwhile there was a faint chance that inquiry through neutral
channels might discover John as a prisoner in Germany. Gwynee set
up an inquiry through the British Minister to the Vatican. Walter
Page, the American Minister, formerly a partner of Frank Doubleday,
did his best, and Rudyard himself consulted the American Minister at
the Hague, and a friend in the Swiss Red Cross, without much hope.
All clues which seemed to offer a spark of promise were eagerly followed — to end in disappointment. The Kiplings continued to track
down wounded men of John's battalion, seeking some hint of what
had really happened that day, and for more than two years did not
quite abandon hope. Carrie, at least, nourished a faint ray long after
Rudyard, with his greater knowledge of war, had accepted his loss.

Rudyard Kipling to Brigadier L. C. Dunsterville

12 November, 1915

Our boy was reported 'wounded & missing' since Sep. 27 — the Battle
of Loos and we've heard nothing official since that date. But all we can
pick up from the men points to the fact that he is dead and probably
wiped out by shell fire. However, he had his heart's desire and he didn't
have a long time in trenches. The Guards advanced on a front of two
platoons for each battalion. He led the right platoon over a mile of open
ground in face of shell and machine-gun fire and was dropped at the
further limit of the advance, after having emptied his pistol into a house
full of German m.g's. His C.O. and his Company Commander told me
how he led 'em and the wounded have confirmed it. He was senior
ensign tho' only 18 yrs and 6 weeks, and worked like the devil for a year
at Warley and knew his Irish to the ground. He was reported on as one

of the best of the subalterns and was gym instructor and signaller. It was a short life. I'm sorry that all the years' work ended in that one afternoon but — lots of people are in our position — and it's something to have bred a man. The wife is standing it wonderfully tho' she, of course, clings to the bare hope of his being a prisoner. I've seen what shells can do, and I don't.[4]

More than two years passed from the day of John's disappearance before a full account of his last hours came to light. Oliver Baldwin at last discovered Sergeant Farrell of the Irish Guards who had been with John when the leading companies had forced their way into the gap between Hill Seventy and Hulluch, the deepest penetration made by any British troops in the Battle of Loos. They had fought their way through Chalk-pit Wood, a copse of straggled undergrowth, and had then encountered strong resistance among some houses beyond the wood. John was using his revolver when he was shot through the head and was laid under cover in a shell-hole, by the Sergeant. Soon afterwards the leading troops were driven back and years passed before the further edge of Chalk-pit Wood again passed into British hands. In this confused and bitter fighting among the slag-heaps and miners' cottages, more than ten thousand British soldiers were reported missing and not seen again. There was little doubt that John was one of the unlocated dead.

The time of uncertainty had been all the more agonizing for the Kiplings because of their unspoken resolution to maintain the ordinary routine of life unchanged. As the fact of John's death became inevitable, the family — a square no longer — became more withdrawn and self-sufficient. Neither Rudyard nor Carrie ever talked much about their son, but their life without him was never the same; it had lost a motive force. Elsie now stood as the one barrier between her ageing parents and their numbing sorrow, bearing a burden of which they were hardly aware.

In those gloomy days, with the shadow never off his mind — a son lying among thousands of other men's sons in an unmarked grave — it was perhaps a slight consolation to Rudyard to receive scores of letters bringing sympathy from every part of the world. He had unknown enemies as well as unknown friends, and among his letters were some which reviled him with the brutal assumption that he deserved his loss because, in some way, he had provoked the war. One such letter that came through a neutral country from Germany was openly exultant. Letters that he found peculiarly trying came from psychic mediums who offered to 'get in touch' with John by occult methods, and it was to this suggestion that he replied in the verses

called 'The Road to En-Dor', written in the wet summer of 1917
when the mutter of gunfire from the bloodstained swamps of Pass-
chendaele, a hundred miles away, could be heard distinctly at Burwash.
For a few months then he had the partial comfort of his sister's company; she stayed in the cottage at Dudwell Mill and every day they
took long walks together. Dear as she was to him, since she shared
his earliest memories, he could not share her flight from reality into
the world of the psychic.

The Kiplings pressed on with their work, still going to London frequently. They took their place at more than one Memorial Ceremony,
always a heartbreaking experience, even to iron-nerved Carrie, since
'Recessional' was always sung. Twice, at least, they were in London
on air-raid nights, but no authentic account survives of any incident
they did not share with millions of Londoners. Rudyard used to lunch
regularly at the Athenæum where he met many of the political leaders.
A social honour he had particularly appreciated was his election, in
December 1914, to one of the most exclusive societies in London, the
dining-club that since Dr. Johnson's day has been known simply as
'The Club'. On another social level, it was an equal delight to him
to be made an honorary member of 'The Goat', the rendezvous of
naval officers on leave in London.

Apart from two visits to quiet sectors of the war-front, in France
and Italy, his closest contacts with fighting men were made in ships
of the Royal Navy. He visited the Grand Fleet in Scottish waters and
went more than once to Dover and Harwich. The ship's company of
H.M.S. *Maidstone,* the depot-ship for submarines, were his special
friends and for them he wrote several songs and epigrams.* One day
at Harwich he went down in a submarine, and hated it since he was
inclined to claustrophobia. His naval songs and ballads are perhaps
the most firmly realized of his studies of active service, especially the
sharply-etched seascapes in the poem 'Mine-sweepers' with its charming word-pattern of the ships' names:

> Sweepers — *Unity, Claribel, Assyrian, Stormcock* and *Golden Gain.*

Rudyard could hardly fail to be gratified when, in January 1917, a
Coalition Government was formed to include all the resolute men who
were determined to fight the war to a finish. If the hated Lloyd
George was Prime Minister, it was some consolation that Milner was
Secretary of State for War, while Bonar Law was Chancellor of the
Exchequer and Stanley Baldwin his Financial Secretary.

On all questions of moulding public opinion, Rudyard was now

---

* At the request of some naval friends Kipling designed crests and badges for several
ships and naval units.

consulted, since his friends were in office, and when Sir Max Aitken (raised to the peerage as Lord Beaverbrook in 1917) formed the Ministry of Information he tried hard to draw Rudyard in.

Though Rudyard would never submit to any routine of writing sponsored propaganda, he undertook three tasks arising out of the war and gave the best of his time to them for about five years. The first was to write the History of the Irish Guards, his son's regiment. An approach was made to him in January 1917, and by March he was immersed in the task. It obliged him to hold frequent conferences with officers and to consult scores of wounded men in hospitals. The last hope that John might miraculously have survived as a prisoner did not flicker out until the end of the year, and by then the Kiplings had admitted, almost into their family circle, a group of John's young brother-officers who could tell him about their own battles and so enrich the History with the visual details that he loved. Rupert Grayson, John de Salis, Lord Castlerosse, Harold Maxwell, and other young ensigns, came to 'Bateman's' to tell their story. These and other visitors continued to come to 'Bateman's' after the war, among them many soldiers and sailors from overseas, who became Elsie's friends as well as admirers of her father. A series of convalescent officers brought their families to stay as guests in one of the estate farmhouses which was refurnished for their use and, besides, there were the Irish rank and file who had fought under John to be consulted. Rudyard diligently sought them out and his Regimental History is full of their sayings, as vivid and pungent as those of the Irish he had known long ago in India.

'Private Mulvaney', that once celebrated Irish soldier, had been out of mind for twenty years, while Rudyard, in his Ulster Covenanting days, had spoken with contempt of the Southern Catholic Irish. This was an attitude he could not maintain when writing of the men who had followed his own son to battle, and had suffered with him. He made amends, in the poem, 'The Irish Guards', written as a prologue to the History and as a tribute to those Irishmen who had fought in the old wars, for or against the English.

> Old Days! The wild geese are ranging,
>   Head to the storm as they faced it before!
> For where there are Irish their hearts are unchanging,
>   And when they are changed, it is Ireland no more!
> > > > Ireland no more!

The war dead presented their own problem: never in Europe's wars had so many thousands died, in campaign after campaign, crowded in so constricted a battlefield that war-cemeteries on a gigantic scale had to be constructed. It was this that suggested his whimsical fantasy, ' On the Gate ', about the queue of flocking souls from Europe's battle-fields and St. Peter's improvisations to deal with the emergency. Herbert Baker and Rudyard had been considering it for some months — as had many others — when, in September 1917, Sir Fabian Ware came down to ' Bateman's ' to invite Rudyard to become one of the Imperial War Graves Commissioners. The scope of this undertaking ever widened, as a million British dead were found, exhumed, identi-fied and reburied in permanent cemeteries with headstones, inscriptions, gardens, and memorial crosses, by agreement with the authorities of many allied or formerly hostile countries. Rudyard used to say it was ' the biggest single bit of work since the Pharaohs — and they only worked in their own country '.[5] For the remaining eighteen years of his life Rudyard was a diligent member of the War Graves Commis-sion, active in all its practical decisions. At one of the earliest meet-ings, with Lord Milner in the chair, he proposed the standard inscription — ' Their name liveth for evermore ' — which was inscribed on the Stone of Sacrifice in each cemetery. The inscriptions for the British memorials in French cathedrals — in short, every inscription and almost every form of words used by the Commission was of Rud-yard's drafting. He inspected many cemeteries and appeared at many functions on behalf of the committee. He was one of the originators of the plan to bury an unknown British soldier in Westminster Abbey, a ceremony adopted by the other belligerent nations, and was responsi-ble for the nightly ceremony of ' The Last Post ' at the Menin Gate. Thus responsible for marking the graves of so many thousands, for providing a visible shrine at which so many bereaved parents could lay their grief, he identified no shrine of his own. John Kipling's fate was never surely known, his body never found.[6]

About the same time as the formation of the War Graves Commis-sion, Dr. Jameson came down to ' Bateman's ' to ask Rudyard to become one of the Rhodes Trustees, thus involving him in the admin-istration of millions of money for a purpose to which he was devoted. Rudyard and Carrie had been in Rhodes's counsels when the Rhodes Scholarships were initiated and, after Jameson himself, no one knew better than Rudyard what had been in Rhodes's mind. No public cause could lift up his heart more buoyantly than the provision of scholarships at Oxford for young men from the Dominions and the United States, and no task of reconstruction was more important than to revive the scheme after the war. The Graves Commission and the History of the Irish Guards turned his mind back upon old unhappy things, the Rhodes Trustees were guardians of the future.

He had no more than made up his mind to become one of the Trustees when, in October 1917, Jameson died, leaving Rudyard to maintain the tradition that Rhodes had passed on to them. Their friends, the group of survivors from South African days, urged Rudyard to write Jameson's Life, which he might have done if the *Irish Guards* had not engrossed his time. Instead, he suggested to Milner that the Life should be written by Ian Colvin, a young journalist who had worked for Gwynne. This proved an unsatisfactory arrangement and Rudyard found himself obliged to edit the book.[7] In so doing he took pains to suppress allusions to himself, and no reader of the *Life of Jameson* would suppose that he and Kipling had been intimate friends who shared political confidences for fifteen years. That tale is now lost.

In 1917 Rudyard went off to Italy with Landon to write an account of the Italian campaign (*The War in the Mountains*). He attended the beatification of a saint in St. Peter's, saw the Pope — who looked, he said, like Woodrow Wilson, and then had lunch in the palace of a cardinal in

a little wonder of a study full of priceless old prints and a genuine Holbein. . . . There was only Landon and I and the Cardinal and his domestic chaplain who was also general secretary. The latter was of quite a new type to me. I never knew before that domestic chaplains contradicted Cardinals. Well, we talked and we talked (the domestic Chaplain talked most) for about two hours. I am a low-minded beast and I suspected from the first that we had not been asked for nothing. We hadn't; but that is a matter I must tell you *viva voce* when we meet. This land, rightly or wrongly, gives me the idea of being more full of eyes and ears than a peacock's tail. . . .

And so we got away — much — oh much interested. This is the d—dest queerest trap-doorest world I've ever got into. . . . I shall be main glad to meet real plain soldier men again.[8]

He met the soldiers a few days later where the Italian Army was fighting the Austrians on the mountain front.

Rudyard to Elsie Kipling

11 May, 1917

Oh Bird! I've just received your note of the 4th on my return from war among the Alps. An inconceivable trip at the height of 4000 feet, in a country to which the Engelberg Valley is tame and of no account. . . . And all the time guns were booming one against another, lazily as they tried trial shots. They were 8″ and 11″ howitzers on our side; and when we climbed (or our car did) up to the very bare tops of mountains behold the grass was all pitted with shell-holes. It's a war of giants among mountains. I looked into Tolmino and along 30 mile of Austrian front — wholly different from all I saw yesterday. The immensity of the landscape and the work dwarf all comparison. I don't know how on earth or in the clouds I can describe it.[9]

During the years of American neutrality, exasperation against President Wilson's policy was widely spread in England. In his letters to American friends, Rudyard wrote on this with bitterness, and his low opinion of Woodrow Wilson was shared by at least one old friend in America, Theodore Roosevelt, whom the vagaries of Republican party policy had thrust into the obscurity that ex-Presidents often experience. Roosevelt told Kipling that Wilson was a hereditary shirker, he came of an old Virginian family of which no member had fought on either side in the Civil War. What could one expect from such a breed?[10]

On his part, Woodrow Wilson had no such prejudice against Kipling. He wrote, through a mutual friend, to ask Rudyard for an autographed copy of 'If——', which, he said, had been a constant inspiration to him.[11]

When, at last, Wilson felt able to bring the United States into the war, the decision resolved in Rudyard's mind the dilemma which had so long embittered him. A grand alliance of England, France, and America (that doubtful partner, Russia, had just fallen away into chaos) united all that he thought worthiest in the civilized world. But this was an alliance of men as colleagues in action, not a politician's compromise, and his contempt for the political leaders, in England and America alike, was unmitigated.

The arrival of American ships in European waters, of American soldiers in British training-camps, aroused his enthusiasm. He went at once to Winchester to visit them — was even persuaded to make a speech of welcome to a parade of 7000 men; and when a correspondent [12] wrote from America asking for leave to reprint some of his verses, he gave it only on condition that all profits should be given to American Army charities. Later, he collected some news of the American Navy for Roosevelt.

I have been seeing one of our Naval Officers . . . and he brings me first hand news . . . of the almost comically good relations between the two Navies. Your destroyers shine especially in convoy and anti-submarine work. Both sides groan together over the enormous amount of unnecessary paper-work. The American reports are held up to our people as models of what concise and accurate reports should be. . . . All our young men speak very highly indeed of the U.S.N. and are getting on as sociable as a 'basket of kittens', to quote Uncle Remus. I've heard a good deal about your airmen — their competence, modesty, and insatiable zeal.[13]

Rudyard transferred to Roosevelt some of the confidence and devotion that he had formerly given to Rhodes, and for the same reasons. He approved the things that Roosevelt did, and had not the least objection to his hero's occasional roughness and violence in speech. They met only once in twenty years, in 1910 when Roosevelt was honoured at Oxford, but, through those years, exchanged many letters which are now in the Library of Congress.

War-work and war-journalism left little time for imaginative writing in prose. *A Diversity of Creatures,* Rudyard's volume of stories including all that was outstanding since 1912, was published in 1917. Two or three more stories which he had in draft were laid aside, for five years, while he concentrated on the tasks he had set himself. In verse he was more productive, and these years saw the publication of many finely imaginative pieces, often barbed with some political message. The epitaphs of the war belong to this period.

Even more forceful were his diatribes in verse against those whom he held responsible for the errors of the war, notably his poem on 'Mesopotamia'. It was the Government of India that so mismanaged the first Mesopotamian campaign, especially the medical services, and in denouncing this incompetence Rudyard returned to the criticisms he had passed upon Simla thirty years before.

> They shall not return to us, the resolute, the young,
> The eager and whole-hearted whom we gave:
> But the men who left them thriftily to die in their own dung,
> Shall they come with years and honour to the grave?
>
> .   .   .   .   .
>
> Shall we only threaten and be angry for an hour?
> When the storm is ended shall we find
> How softly but now swiftly they have sidled back to power
> By the favour and contrivance of their kind?

A reading public, that was learning to expect from Rudyard Kipling these harsh and uncompromising sentiments, opened *The Times,* one day in May 1918, to find a new poem printed over his name at the foot of the middle page, in that place where 'Recessional' and 'For all we have and are' had once appeared. It was called 'The Old Volunteer' and quite lacked the least spark of fire or spot of venom; it was mild and silly. Though no critical reader could doubt that this was some kind of hoax, *The Times* plunged itself into deeper confusion by an unwillingness to laugh it off. They almost refused to accept Rudyard's indignant repudiation, and Scotland Yard failed to discover who was responsible. This was the most absurd and the most annoying of the many occasions in Rudyard's literary life when sentiments he had not uttered, or verses he had not written, or ephemeral work which he had tried to suppress, were published over his name without his permission. He could never free himself for long from the hateful publicity that these episodes brought him.[14]

When the war news was at last favourable, Rudyard was slow in turning to optimism. As late as 13th October 1918 he and Landon ruefully agreed that they had 'no conviction of the prospect of peace', but rather some anxiety lest there should be a compromise without exemplary victory. This was the theme of the poem 'Justice', which was syndicated in 200 newspapers during October, a plea for the disarmament of Germany and the punishment of war-criminals. It was with no exultation that the Kiplings faced the end of the war. There was as yet no radio-broadcasting and at 'Bateman's', they had not even installed a telephone.* Quietly, they spent 11th November at home and learned only by the ringing of the church bells that the armistice was signed.

The activities of President Wilson still filled Rudyard with alarm. He wrote to Roosevelt (7th November 1918) in the hope of mobilizing Republican opinion against the President. 'The guts of Europe are sliding into our laps, day by day, but at the one moment when we allies ought to have our hands free to deal with a continent *in extremis* we are tied up by Wilson's idiotic Fourteen Points. They open the door to every form of evasion and quibble. . . . England takes her victories very grimly.' Roosevelt replied amicably. But, revealing the mistrust of Kipling's judgment that can often be observed in their correspondence he warned him not to overstate the case. Roosevelt also was bitterly opposed to Wilson, 'a mere doctrinaire with no ideals'. He hoped for an Anglo-American alliance but did not hold with the American anglophiles and English americanophiles 'who do more harm than good'.[15] Rudyard took this correspondence to Milner, the Secretary for War, but there was little to be done. Though Republican gains in the elections might weaken Wilson, they would not tend to an American alliance with France and England. In any case the President had come to Europe to solve its problems, by a mere announcement of some liberal sentiments. On 27th December 1918 Rudyard was commanded to Buckingham Palace to meet the President, who 'impressed him not at all'. He was 'arid — first, last, and all the time a schoolmaster'.

The President's moment of triumph was followed by a blow that struck Rudyard to the heart. In January 1919 Theodore Roosevelt died. Rudyard, who had lately been reading his *Pilgrim's Progress* and applying it to the times, wrote of him as Great-Heart:

---

* It was not installed in Kipling's lifetime. He rarely used a telephone, disliked it, and much more disliked intrusive calls.

Oh, our world is none the safer
Now Great-Heart hath died!

The outlook for the family at 'Bateman's' was no brighter: 'and now a world to be re-made', wrote Carrie bleakly in her diary, 'without a son'.

CHAPTER XVIII

AFTER THE WAR (1919–24)

———◆———

A CHARM (1910)

Take of English earth as much
As either hand may rightly clutch.
In the taking of it breathe
Prayer for all who lie beneath.
Not the great nor well-bespoke,
But the mere uncounted folk
Of whose life and death is none
Report or lamentation.
    Lay that earth upon thy heart,
    And thy sickness shall depart!

It shall sweeten and make whole
Fevered breath and festered soul.
It shall mightily restrain
Over-busied hand and brain.
It shall ease thy mortal strife
'Gainst the immortal woe of life,
Till thyself, restored, shall prove
By what grace the Heavens do move.

Take of English flowers these —
Spring's full-facèd primroses,
Summer's wild wide-hearted rose,
Autumn's wall-flower of the close,
And, thy darkness to illume,
Winter's bee-thronged ivy-bloom.
Seek and serve them where they bide
From Candlemas to Christmas-tide,
    For these simples, used aright,
    Can restore a failing sight.

These shall cleanse and purify
Webbed and inward-turning eye;
These shall show thee treasure hid,
Thy familiar fields amid;
And reveal (which is thy need)
Every man a King indeed!

WHEN Dorothy Ponton, who had once been Elsie's governess, returned to 'Bateman's' in 1919 as Rudyard's secretary, she noticed some small but ominous changes in the family routine. 'Mr. Kipling had lost his buoyant step, though his genius and courage remained unabated.' His physical health had deteriorated, after recurrent attacks of gastric trouble, which Miss Ponton attributed to suppressed anxiety rather than to any physical cause.[1] Carrie relaxed none of her diligent watchfulness over his well-being. Visitors noticed that she habitually followed him about the room with her eye. Not only did she guard his health; she opened his letters, dictated replies to the secretary, corresponded with the literary agent, managed the household, and eventually farmed the land, watching all expenditure with a prudent eye; and it was commonly said in the neighbourhood that she would have got more out of the estate if she had put more into it. She paid the bills. There had been a time when Rudyard found his accounts disordered because his cheques were often retained as souvenirs instead of being presented for payment. His autograph was now so strictly guarded that no unauthorized scrap of his handwriting was allowed to leave the house; even his personal letters were checked in and out by the secretary, a precaution which has enabled the students of his work to detect several forgeries.* So dependent was he upon Carrie in money matters, there came a day when his own bank denied knowledge of its most celebrated client. He had run short of cash and dropped in casually to draw a cheque, but, not having been seen there before, he was treated as a stranger until the manager came to identify him.

Carrie's life was devoted to guarding and cherishing the husband whom she had married when he was a young man with precocious talents and bohemian habits, and the protective crust she formed around his life grew harder as she grew older. Even more than Rudyard she hated prying eyes.

When Carrie's mother died, in 1919, her last personal link with America was snapped. Though she had seen her mother only once in twenty years, at Montreal in 1907, Carrie had written her long weekly letters (now, it seems, no longer extant), and had never quite thrown off her mother's guidance. Rudyard, too, judging by a few surviving letters, respected and liked his mother-in-law. It was unpleasant to discover, when Mrs. Balestier's estate was valued, that Beatty had been sponging on her for years, so that she had been obliged to use up her capital in gifts to her scapegrace son. The same charming, drunken, good-for-nothing, he was still the scandal of the strait-

---

* The 'Dorian' correspondence, now in the Houghton Library, which Mrs. Livingston pronounced a forgery, is condemned on these grounds (and on other internal evidence).

laced, the admiration of the wilder set in Brattleboro, still disposed to boast in his cups of his victory over the Kiplings. It was quite in character that when he came to die, in 1936, he expressed regret for the harm he had done them, and a wish that they could have met again in friendship. His name had been mentioned so rarely in the Kipling household that Elsie hardly knew she had an uncle in Vermont.[2]

The sister, Josephine Dunham, was never intimate with Carrie, though the two were on terms of civil acquaintance. When the Dunhams visited England, their young family found a key to Rudyard's affection, especially since the eldest boy so much resembled his uncle Wolcott Balestier, the long-lost friend.

Rudyard's own relatives often visited him at Burwash and, for a man who was reputed to be an inaccessible recluse, he lived a sociable life. The Visitors' Book contains the names of half the people in England who were eminent in the world of action, not merely the fashionable or the literary. A stream of visitors came, averaging in the nineteen-twenties a hundred and fifty a year, of whom many were invited to stay the night; and many more would have come if they had got past Carrie's scrutiny. As time passed, the numbers tended to increase, especially the number of children. The descendants of 'Aunt Louie' Baldwin, through three generations, came regularly and the book sometimes records an exclamation of delight when a new youngster appears for the first time. Names of relatives and family friends, Sussex neighbours, and young men who had known John in the Brigade of Guards, recur frequently, as do certain old-faithfuls, bound to the Kiplings by some personal tie: Aleck Watt and Frank Doubleday, Ted and Dorothy Price, Miss Anderson who had once been Rudyard's secretary, Miss Blaikie who had once been Elsie's governess, 'Ellen' a beloved and retired housemaid.

To take as an example the casual visitors in a single year, they included for 1921 — as well as Percival Landon back from the Far East and Oliver Baldwin back from Armenia — William Nicholson the painter and Siccard the sculptor, Burton Hendricks who was writing the life of Walter Page, Fabian Ware of the War Graves Commission, Sir Hugh Clifford the Governor of Nigeria, Eveleigh Nash the publisher and Randolph Lewis the script-writer, the Princess Christian, Admiral 'Blinker' Hall, Charles Scribner from New York and Sallie Norton from Boston, the Rector of Strasbourg University, Mr. Tompsett the porter from Brown's Hotel, and Dr. Frank Buchman with a team of young men who gate-crashed and sang hymns on the lawn. This is a group picked at random, and another year might show 'Stalky' back from the Caspian, Sir William Willcocks who dammed the Nile, Cameron Forbes from the Philippines, Kermit Roosevelt, Bishop Gwynne from the Sudan, or Jarvis Bey the Governor of Sinai.[3]

The flying men in this new generation turned to Rudyard as their fathers had done in the 'nineties when he was known as the poet of *The Seven Seas*. One great airman, Sir John Salmond, traced on the globe in his study at 'Bateman's' the air-routes which, twenty years later, were to encircle the earth; which, twenty years earlier, Rudyard had already foreseen. When the first Atlantic flight was achieved, by the British airship 'R.34' in 1919, the crew took with them a single book, 'Traffics and Discoveries', so that they could refer to his story, 'With the Night Mail'. Then, autographed by each member of the crew, the book was presented to the author.

The daily correspondence at 'Bateman's' included many letters from would-be authors asking the Master's advice, which he often gave, if they seemed young and modest. In later life, when his contemporaries had done their work and made their names, he urged them sometimes to write their reminiscences. Sir John Bland-Sutton's entertaining book, Sir Walter Lawrence's *The India We Knew,* and 'Stalky's' *Dunsterforce* owe much to his advice. As in the case of the *Life of Jameson* and the *Milner Papers,* the price of Rudyard's help was the suppression of his own name. We are the poorer for not knowing what Lawrence might have written about the young Kipling at Simla.

Rudyard's fame, and the public work in which he was engaged, brought an inevitable result. The admission to the Cabinet of his friends, Bonar Law and Baldwin, during the last years of the war had meant that he would again be pressed to accept some public honour. Stanley Baldwin brought a message from the Prime Minister, in May 1917, to say that Rudyard might have 'any honour he will accept'. His reply was that he would accept none. Even after this private communication, he heard a rumour that he was to be one of the first knights in the new Order of the British Empire, and hastily warned Bonar Law that 'it must not be'. And again, in spite of that, he received an official notification, a few days later, that without his knowledge he had been appointed a Companion of Honour. This third time his temper was ruffled and he wrote to Bonar Law: 'how would you like it if you woke up and found they had made you Archbishop of Canterbury?'

The Order of Merit, which had no political significance, seemed the appropriate mark of distinction to offer to Kipling the poet and story-teller, and his name had more than once been canvassed when vacancies occurred in earlier years. The strongest recommendation came from the Poet Laureate, Robert Bridges,* in a letter written to the Palace in 1916.

It is plain that he is the greatest living genius that we have in literature; and it is generally thought that he has been passed over on account of his politics. The only other reason I could think of would be that he has written so much in slang and low dialect. But much of his later work is altogether above any such reproach and some of it is extremely beautiful on any standard.

In December 1921 the new offer was made. One morning at ' Bateman's ', Rudyard, looking through his letters, passed one of them over to Carrie ' with characteristic lack of interest '. It was a proposal from the King's Private Secretary, Lord Stamfordham, that he should accept the Order of Merit: ' in recognition of the eminent services you have rendered to the Science of Literature and of the almost unique estimation in which your works are regarded throughout the British Empire '.

It was a grand letter, noted Carrie in her diary, adding that she felt sure he would decline it even though it seemed to come direct from the King. ' The fact that the King has been pleased to signify his approval of my services to Literature ', he wrote, ' will be, to me, the great honour of my life. But I would ask you, while presenting my humble and loyal duty . . . to pray that His Majesty may hold me excused.'

It was felt due to the King, in whose personal gift the Order of Merit lay, to make a discreet announcement to the press of this rejected offer. As Rudyard was not consulted and as he had shown the correspondence to no one but his wife, he was deeply distressed at the publication of his decision which seemed to imply a discourtesy to the King. He was mollified only when further explanations had been made by Lord Stamfordham, and when he had again been able to assure the King that he could do better service, without a title or award, than with one. From this time, Lord Stamfordham, whom Rudyard met occasionally dining at ' The Club ', was one of his friends, and his association with the Royal Family and Household became closer. Yet even this friendship did not save Rudyard from further pressure to accept some honour. In 1924 the Order of Merit was again offered to him, since it was believed that he had changed his mind; and again he was obliged to refuse while assuring the King of his loyalty and gratitude.[4]

Academic honours he did not refuse. In 1920 the University of Edinburgh awarded him a doctorate.

* See also the footnote on p. 394.

Rudyard Kipling to Colonel H. W. Fielden

9 July 1920

In the evening I went to my dinner. . . . I strictly remembered your injunction about my speech, eschewed prolixity and the Scotch accent and got a good reception. . . . The Moderator (*such* a Scot) in replying to my speech for the University expatiated on Edinburgh having annexed an Englishman! I said nought but watched him deliver himself deeply into my hands. Next morn he comes to me and says: 'Am I rightly informed that your grandmother was a MacDonald?' 'No,' I said. 'It was my mother but — how should you lowlanders know these things?' He was out of Midlothian, and in a temperate way I danced on his carcase Selah!

The Degree giving began at 9.30 and endured without a break till 11.45, when we went to St Giles and were prayed over for an hour by the clock; and then to lunch at the Union. . . . What I admired most were the faces of the boys and girls as they came up to be capped. It was a cross-section of the Scottish race. They made rather a row when my turn came.[5]

In the autumn of 1920 the Kiplings were at last able to resume the motoring-tours in France which had given them such delight in the happy years before 1914. But every visit to France, after the war, had the character of a pilgrimage, because Rudyard's duty as a War Graves' Commissioner obliged him to visit and report upon the cemeteries where the million dead of the British Armies were reburied. To drive or wander across the waste ground, bought with dear blood in five long campaigns, was an enterprise that touched his own heart-strings. As well as his stories of the battlefields, he left other fragments:

'I plough deep' said the car,
'I plough old wounds afresh —
'What you thought was a scar,
'I will show you is stricken flesh. . . .'[6]

He made careful inspections of more than thirty cemeteries in northern France and, on his first tour, turned aside to see the battlefield of Loos and to identify the shattered stumps and brambly undergrowth of Chalk-pit Wood.

The next visit to France was very different in character — a personal triumph. A message was brought to him by André Chevrillon that the University of Paris wished to give him a doctorate, and this was followed by a similar message from Strasbourg. In Paris and in Alsace, during November 1921, he was welcomed with the acclamation due to a national hero, fêted by the Chamber of Deputies, received by the President of the Republic, and overwhelmed with invitations. From this time, his frequent visits to Paris brought him often into contact with the leaders of French political and social life, especially in the circles where he was introduced by his old friend, Clemenceau.

Rudyard had a gift for penetrating the undertones of conversation. His own French was fluent though inaccurate, and powerfully helped out by gestures; his skill at extracting the sense of what was said to him seemed uncanny. Not only could he fall into casual talk with some patois-speaking peasant in France, and come away after five minutes, equipped with minute technical knowledge of his farming methods and family history; there were occasions when he achieved the same result in Spain and even Czecho-Slovakia by signs and gestures, without pretence of knowing the language at all. In Parisian society, the language was no barrier to him and, at a pinch, he could make a short speech in French. In his addresses to the Sorbonne and to the University of Strasbourg, however, he spoke in English, after careful preparation. Each of these deliberate speeches was a variation on a theme that was the foundation of his politics for the rest of his life, the necessity for Anglo-French co-operation. 'The whole weight of the world at the present moment lies again, as it used to lie in the time of our fathers, on the necks of two nations, England and France.' [7]

By the spring of 1922 the construction of cemeteries in France was so far advanced that the King and Queen decided to make a solemn pilgrimage to them on behalf of the whole nation. This was a State occasion, in which Rudyard took part, not as a national poet but as a Commissioner for War Graves.

The Kiplings were already touring the battlefields when, on 11th May 1922, they were instructed to meet the King at Vlamertinghe near Ypres. Rudyard arranged to change into clothes of ceremony in a peasant's cottage, then waited in the lee of a wall — it was bitterly cold — for the arrival of the King with Field-Marshal Haig, an incident that suggested to him the charming little tale which he wrote some years later and called 'The Debt'. This was a preliminary meeting and, on the 13th, he and Carrie were present at the great ceremony at Terlincthun, near Boulogne, under the shadow of Napoleon's Colonne de la Grande Armée. There were many graves of Indian soldiers in this vast cemetery and, while waiting for the King's arrival, Rudyard happened upon a memorial to 'Gunga Din, Stretcher-bearer'.

The King spoke his words, as Rudyard noted, 'with splendid delivery and dignified bearing'. 'In the course of my pilgrimage', he said, 'I have many times asked myself whether there can be more potent advocates of peace upon earth than this massed multitude of witnesses to the desolation of war.' It was his hope, he concluded, that these visible memorials would 'serve to draw all peoples together in sanity and self-control' as it had already set the relations between 'our Empire and our Allies on the deep-rooted basis of a common heroism and a common agony'.[1]

After the Queen had laid a wreath on the memorial, the Commissioners were presented to the King who had a short private conversation with Rudyard and Carrie, the first occasion, it appears, on which they spoke freely together. Since fanciful accounts of this meeting have been put about, it may be as well to set down the only authentic record, Rudyard's own. The King spoke to Carrie Kipling about her son John, and Rudyard took proud notice of her graceful curtsey. Rudyard was then presented 'and the King said what was seemly'. 'I praised his delivery,' said Rudyard, 'which was also seemly.' They then spoke a little 'about the politicians' and Rudyard noticed that the look in the King's eye was that of 'a decent man who suspects he is being carted'. There was no talk of honours or awards. A few days later, when both had returned to England, Rudyard was asked to meet the King again, at a private party, the first evidence that a link of personal affection was growing up between these two elderly men.

The summer of 1922, even after a happy trip to Spain in the spring, had been exhausting to Rudyard's vitality. His work for the War Graves Commission had reached a climax, and *The Irish Guards in the Great War,* the most sustained of all his literary efforts, was at last finished. As always, mental fatigue reacted on his physical condition which now began to give Carrie much anxiety. She watched his weight with solicitude, noting that it had fallen below 130 pounds. He looked old, yellow, and shrunken. Since the gastric trouble of 1915, he had long suffered from intermittent pain which the local doctor treated with purging and dieting but could not diagnose. The great surgeon, Sir John Bland-Sutton, who had been a friend of the family for many years, was frequently consulted — to no effect, and by August there was no doubt that Rudyard was seriously ill. He withdrew to London, into a nursing home in Fitzroy Square, for a prolonged course of X-ray examination by several specialists. No conclusion was reached except that there was no sign of the cancer he had always dreaded.

Carrie, much exasperated by servant troubles, the common complaint of the post-war world, brought him home to 'Bateman's', an invalid, on a strict diet and strangely listless in manner. He was bed-ridden, did no work, and took little interest in the political crisis of that autumn. A few weeks earlier he had drafted a political manifesto for the Conservative Party. Now he hardly noticed the progress of the intrigue which overthrew Lloyd George's Coalition and made Bonar Law Prime Minister, with Stanley Baldwin as his Chancellor of the Exchequer.

Carrie suddenly found herself in the middle of a storm of hostile publicity which she had to weather alone, since Rudyard was too ill to bear his part. On 11th September 1922 the *New York World* published an account of a supposed interview with Rudyard Kipling which was at once repeated, as front-page news, by the press of England, France, and America. It purported to be a statement made by Rudyard to Clare Sheridan, on Anglo-American relations which, at that time, were in a delicate state. Rudyard, like many well-informed Europeans, was indeed distressed by the triumph of the isolationists. The callous withdrawal of President Harding from Europe seemed as irresponsible in one way as the pontifical meddling of President Wilson had seemed in the other; and it is not unlikely that Rudyard had let slip some casual remarks to that effect, in private conversation.

Clare Sheridan was the married daughter of a family who were near neighbours of the Kiplings — the Frewens of Brede Place. When she invited herself to tea at 'Bateman's', with her two young children, she was welcomed, and it had never occurred to Rudyard that an old friend, for he had known her almost since her childhood, could sink to the vulgarity of selling his tea-table conversation to the American press. His distaste of interviewers, and his unwillingness to make general statements to reporters, were notorious and, if he had talked freely, she must have known his words were not for publication. He was alleged to have said that America had come into the war too late and had pulled out of it too soon with the satisfaction of cornering all the gold in the world, and that the American nation was corrupted by low-class immigrants since her best blood had been spilt and wasted in the Civil War. The isolationists made so much capital out of this tirade that official disclaimers were made both by the French and the British Governments. While they took pains to explain that the point of view expressed was not their own, it was left for Rudyard to make his own explanations. Rather late and grudgingly, he issued a notice to the press, which gave it no priority: 'I did not give Mrs. Sheridan an interview. I did not say the things which I see she ascribes to me, and have not discontinued the habit of saying what I wish to say over my own signature.' [9] Though Clare could hardly repeat her allegations after this disclaimer, she consoled herself by sneering at the Kiplings' domestic life, in her next book.*

* 'R. K.', she said, 'a jolly little man with a school-boy humour, would not have seemed anything much if his eyebrows had been shaved and one had not known his name.' He was 'wrung dry by domesticity. When he had a good story to tell, Mrs. K. always intervened to tell it better.' (*Nuda Veritas.*)

In October Rudyard was well enough for a visit to London where Stan Baldwin came to see him at his hotel immediately before going to Buckingham Palace to receive the seals of office. A few days later the gastric pains returned, more violently than before, and the specialist Sir Humphrey Rolleston was sent for. He recommended an operation which was performed by Bland-Sutton on 15th November.

Again, as in New York in 1899, Carrie took charge of everything, and again Frank Doubleday — on a visit from America — stood by his friends. But this time, publicity was kept under control, and by mighty efforts on the part of Carrie, the reporters were held at bay. No crowds waited at the Kiplings' door; and only the well-informed, among them the King and the Queen, sent their sympathy. Rudyard, though very ill indeed, survived the operation and was able to return to 'Bateman's' for Christmas, 'very low and depressed' but, as Carrie thought, 'improving'. In February 1923 there was a relapse, but when the spring returned he rapidly grew stronger.

In April Rudyard and Carrie went by sea to Cannes. As they bucketed through the Bay, they saw a ship called the *Bolivar,* behaving just as Rudyard's *Bolivar* did in the ballad, to his great delight and to that of all the other passengers. They stayed on the Riviera and there a new access of strength came to him. He wrote 'The Janeites' and a 'Stalky' story, the beginning of his last great burst of literary activity.

In October 1923 Rudyard's election as Lord Rector of the University of St. Andrews gave him the opportunity to speak to the rising generation, in an address which was afterwards published under the title of *Independence*. The author of 'If——' and 'The Sons of Martha', here, succinctly expressed his social philosophy, which attracted much notice and some hostile criticism in a world that had grown unaccustomed to that message. He began with a quotation from Burns:

> To catch Dame Fortune's golden smile
> Assiduous wait upon her,
> And gather gold by every wile
> That's justified by honour —
> Not for to hide it in a hedge
> Nor for the train attendant,
> But for the glorious privilege
> Of being independent.

He made a side-glance at thrift, which, he supposed, needed little encouragement at a Scottish university. 'You, for the most part, come, as I did, from households conversant with a certain strictness', he said, ' which has taught us to look at both sides of the family shilling — we belong to stock where present sacrifice for future ends was accepted, in principle and practice, as part of life.' To people of such an up-bringing the desire for Independence, 'the singular privilege of a man owning himself' comes naturally, and, though the world of 1923 was unstable, there were hard facts that the young should remember. 'Except for the appliances we make, the rates at which we move our-selves and our possessions through space, and the words we use, nothing in life changes.' 'The utmost any generation can do is to rebaptize each spiritual or emotional rebirth in its own tongue . . . and . . . no shortcomings on the part of others can save us from the consequence of our own shortcomings.'

'Yet in all ages the younger generation, beside its own burden, must bear the burden imposed upon it by the past and the present. The past few years have so immensely quickened and emphasized all means of communication, visible and invisible, in every direction, that our world . . . is not merely " too much with us ", but moves, shouts, and moralizes about our path and our bed through every hour of our days and nights.' 'Partly through a recent necessity for thinking and acting in large masses, partly through the instinct of mankind to draw together and cry out when calamity hits them, and very largely through the quickening of communications . . . the power of the Tribe over the individual has become more extended, particular, pontifical, and, using the word in both its senses, impertinent, than it has been for many generations. Some men accept this omnipresence of crowds; some may resent it. To the latter, I am speaking.

'Nowadays, to own oneself in any decent measure, one has to run counter to a gospel, and to fight against its atmosphere; and an atmosphere, so long as it can be kept up, is rather cloying. Thanks to the continuity of self-denial on the part of your own forbears, the bulk of you will enter professions and callings in which you will be free men — free to be paid what your work is worth in the open market, irrespective of your alleged merits or your needs. Free, more-over, to work without physical molestation of yourself and your family as long and as closely as you please; free to exploit your own powers and your own health to the uttermost for your own ends.

'At any price that I can pay, let me own myself. And the price is worth paying if you keep what you have bought. . . . A man may apply his independence to what is called worldly advantage, and dis-cover too late that he laboriously has made himself dependent on a mass of external conditions for the maintenance of which he sacrificed himself. So he may be festooned with the whole haberdashery of success, and go to his grave a castaway. Some men hold that the risk is worth taking. Others do not. It is to these that I have spoken.'[10]

CHAPTER XIX

THE LAST PHASE OF HIS WORK

THE STORM CONE (1932)

This is the midnight — let no star
Delude us — dawn is very far.
This is the tempest long foretold —
Slow to make head but sure to hold.

Stand by! the lull 'twixt blast and blast
Signals the storm is near, not past;
And worse than present jeopardy
May our forlorn to-morrow be.

If we have cleared the expectant reef,
Let no man look for his relief,
Only the darkness hides the shape
Of further peril to escape.

It is decreed that we abide
The weight of gale against the tide
And those huge waves the outer main
Sends in to set us back again.

They fall and whelm. We strain to hear
The pulses of her labouring gear,
Till the deep throb beneath us proves,
After each shudder and check, she moves!

She moves, with all save purpose lost,
To make her offing from the coast;
But, till she fetches open sea,
Let no man deem that he is free!

THE publication, in 1923, of *The Irish Guards in the Great War* released Rudyard from an obligation; he had paid a debt, but he had also snapped a link with his past days of happiness. While his house was frequented by the young men who had been John's friends, who came and talked in the language of soldiers about the Regiment and its experiences, John's world was still alive in his imagination. It was never Rudyard's habit to hanker back toward the past, and, having put the *Irish Guards* behind him, he moved with characteristic resilience into a new creative phase, as he slowly recovered health after his illness. In this respect he was more fortunate than Carrie who had no such secret resources and never quite reconstituted her life after the loss of her only son.

In 1924 he sent 'The Janeites' to press and followed it up by a succession of effective tales, several of which were psychological studies of the war. They were collected in 1926, with a variety of other pieces, under the general title, *Debits and Credits*. Nine years had passed since the appearance of *A Diversity of Creatures*, which had included 'Mary Postgate' and the other early war-stories. Meanwhile the literary fashion had changed and Kipling, if he was remembered at all in literary circles, was remembered as a political writer whose politics were sadly out of date. This estimate took no account of one important factor in judging his status in the world. The sale of his books, in England, in America, and in those many countries where they were sold in translation, never flagged but increased year by year, even though they were never issued in cheap editions.*

The new book, *Debits and Credits,* was at first received coolly by the critics, though rapturously by the Kipling fans. It has had the experience, rare in the chronicle of his career, of steadily rising in favour with students of literature. I would venture the assertion that if Kipling had published nothing but 'The Bull that Thought', 'The Eye of Allah', 'The Janeites', 'The Wish House', 'A Madonna of the Trenches', and 'The Gardener', his name would stand high among the world's story-tellers. It would be hard to find such variety of subject, such richness of treatment, in the work of any contemporary, and, when compared with his own earlier work, these stories will be found to express a more delicate sensibility and a deeper penetration of motive. The other stories in the book, and even these six, display also Kipling's characteristic faults; some passages which gave offence to the thin-skinned, some almost incomprehensible jargon, and some lapses into obscurity. 'A Madonna of the Trenches' must be grouped among his 'difficult' stories. It was typical of his indifference to public opinion that he began the book with an allegorical tale ('The Enemies to Each Other') that seemed to be a kind of private joke. In form it is a version of the legend of Adam and Eve expanded at great length in a pseudo-oriental style like a stilted version of the *Koran*. It is remarkable that he published it, not that he wrote it.

---

* During Kipling's lifetime Macmillan's, who held the English rights of his collected volumes of stories, sold about seven million copies, Doubleday's, who held the American rights, nearly eight million.

Kipling's stories are sometimes cryptic, sometimes obscure, sometimes allegorical. Quite early in his career he developed a technique of leaving the story half-told and so maintaining the suspense. This is the traditional method of the ghost-story, which is spoiled if an explanation is offered, a method used by Poe in *Tales of Mystery and Imagination* which Kipling imitated as a young man.

He was not, strictly speaking, a writer of adventure-stories except in his books for children. The form of his stories for adults is usually a descriptive comment on a group of characters in a dramatic situation. For example, even so romantic a tale as 'The Man who Was' tells next to nothing of the hero's adventures, which are left to the reader's imagination; but presents, almost visually, the effect of his sudden reappearance. In this instance enough is revealed, though in some others the narrative never emerges. 'At the End of the Passage', for example, is a problem-story in the same mode as the problem-pictures which were so popular at the Academy in Kipling's younger days. This is all I am going to tell you, says the author. Make what you can of it. His 'knowingness' which infuriated some critics, his hints that he could say a great deal more if he chose to, were marks of juvenility which he grew out of. In later life, the hints were of what he did not know, the esoteric, the subliminal, the occult. There are cryptic elements in 'They', in 'The House Surgeon', in 'A Madonna of the Trenches', in 'The Gardener', but here they are dictated by humility in presence of the uncomprehended.

Other stories are found difficult for the reason that they seem to be wilfully obscure, through strangeness of vocabulary or complexity of construction. His love of jargon for its own sake (delightfully exhibited in *Just So Stories*) sometimes betrayed him, as it betrayed Rabelais, into mere avalanches of words. Sometimes the composition of his narrative, partially and gradually revealed in dialogue, is confusing. 'The Devil and the Deep Sea' appears to have been written out of sheer delight in the terminology of marine engineering. Those parts of the narrative which concentrate upon this main theme are, in their way, a triumph of virtuosity, while the rest of it is so compressed, so pruned and cut, chopped off so short, that I, for one, have never been able to discover what happens at the end. The sea stories in general are the most technical, and 'Sea-Constables', a dialogue between four characters, all of them talking naval 'shop', is, if not the most obscure, perhaps the most difficult story Kipling ever wrote. By contrast, 'The Bonds of Discipline', also told in dialogue by two characters alternately speaking different jargons, is quite clear.

The cryptic and the obscure styles are combined in several stories and are carried to their greatest length in 'The Dog Hervey', which presents more puzzles the more it is examined; it abounds in literary, masonic, psychological, and canine clues which lead nowhere. Like 'Mrs. Bathurst', 'The Dog Hervey' seems to have been made incomprehensible by ruthless cutting. Perhaps the themes of both are too complex for treatment within the limits of a short story.

Yet another group of difficult stories are the allegories or fables. In November 1891 he had published 'The Children of the Zodiac', a long fable of which no satisfactory explanation has been offered by any commentator. All that can be said about it with conviction is that it deals with the marriage of a young poet who dreads death by cancer of the throat, and that in 1891 Kipling was a young poet contemplating marriage, and ill with an affliction of the throat. We have his word for it elsewhere that he regarded cancer of the throat as the 'family complaint'.[1] The fable, then, is personal — something between himself and the woman he was about to marry.

A problem piece in which the obscurity is gradually and skilfully made plain, is 'The Gardener', his story of the unmarried mother and the war-graves in Flanders. It is told with such tenderness as to efface the memory of the parallel tale of 'Mary Postgate'. This is quite another view of the soul of a hard, efficient, loveless woman. All these war-stories — as the name *Debits and Credits* implies — turn upon loyalties, the part played in love or friendship by the one who gives and the one who takes, a relation often seen in reverse when seen with intimate understanding. In war who bears the greater burden, the one who lives or the one who dies? Kipling's obsession with the war-dead dwelt upon his understanding that the soldiers were initiates, admitted to a higher degree of the suffering which is the law of life, and so separated from their lovers at home.

The strongest continuing motive in his work throughout his whole career was the sense of comradeship among men who share a common allegiance because committed to a common duty. His love of technical jargon, though partly a mere delight in the richness of language, was strengthened by a conviction that the best talk is 'talking shop', the kind of conversation which lives and is genuine because it is based upon a secret shared between those who know how something is done, a secret conveying that kind of knowledge which is power. Freemasonry, with its cult of common action, its masculine self-sufficiency, its language of symbols, and its hierarchy of secret grades, provided him with a natural setting for his social ideals. In India, when very young, he had been a keen and loyal mason, and the ritual of masonry had first revealed to him the underlying unity of Indian life in the one context where race, religion, and caste were overlooked. Even a non-mason can point out scores of allusions to masonic ritual, dispersed through the whole of Kipling's verse and prose, proving how deeply the cult affected his mode of thought. Yet it does not appear that the circumstances of his later life allowed him to attend lodge-meetings frequently, or to pass through the course of office that leads to the higher degrees of the craft. He is said to have been a member of the Authors' Lodge and to have occasionally attended its meetings, but no evidence has been brought forward that there is any foundation in fact for the irregular war-time lodge which he used as the background for several of his later stories.* Perhaps some single occurrence at a lodge-meeting was enough to set his mind at work.

His avowedly masonic episode, 'In the Interests of the Brethren' (written in 1917), was a demonstration to his brother-masons of what they might do to help soldiers on leave from the front, if they would take some liberties with masonic rules; and whether they accepted this advice his fellow-masons will know best. To the general reader 'Lodge Faith and Works, 5837' is merely the scene set for the narration of some powerful stories in his later manner, notably 'The Janeites' (begun in 1922) and 'A Madonna of the Trenches' (1924).[2]

'The Janeites' is a cunningly contrived story written with as many skins as an onion. It is told in the first person by Kipling himself, who begins with a description of the masonic lodge, in elaborate and loving detail. Within this frame the hero is introduced by another mason, Anthony, whose comments, interjected from another point of view, serve as a foil to those of Kipling the narrator. Humberstall, the hero of the tale, a gentle bewildered giant unaware of his own strength and reduced by shell-shock almost to witlessness, is persuaded by Anthony to talk of his experiences in France. Between these three men there is a sympathetic bond, the comradeship of Freemasonry which, says Humberstall, is all the religion he has got, the faith to which he clings, and which, as it seems to the reader, preserves his sanity.

But Kipling the narrator knows that Anthony and Humberstall have another bond of sympathy which they can never fully reveal to him, the secret sympathy that unites soldiers who have been on active service in the war. The comradeship of the trenches constitutes, as it were, a second degree with its own passwords and ritual, a degree to which no mere civilian can be admitted.

Then the mild and puzzled Humberstall modestly reveals that he has graduated, almost unconsciously, to a still higher degree. Though he understands imperfectly what are its implications, he has become a 'Janeite'. Now it is Kipling's turn to give the password and talk the secret language, because he too is a 'Janeite', while Anthony, quite

---

* Kipling was a founder-member of two lodges connected with the War Graves Commission, 'Silent Cities' No. 4948 in England and No. 12 in France.

unaware of this ritual, limps forlornly behind a conversation he cannot keep up with.

What is the subject of this curiously involved story? In a sense, of course, it is Kipling's tribute to the genius of Jane Austen (he would never pass through Winchester without reflecting that, after Stratford, it was the holiest place in England, for the sake of Jane Austen and Isaac Walton). But the story would have the same point if it had been called 'The Trollopians' and if the password had been 'Hiram's Hospital' instead of 'Tilneys and trap-doors'. Where the action strikes home is revealed in the character of Humberstall the innocent, who can fulfil himself only in loyalty to a dedicated group of friends.

Unless 'Jane' herself is to be counted one of the characters, 'The Janeites' is a masculine story. Let us turn to another written entirely about women. 'The Wish House' demands of the reader a willing suspension of disbelief. Two old villagers, each of them aware that one of the two is stricken with cancer and condemned to death, sit and gossip about their past. How far Kipling had advanced in his craft, since the slick stories of his boyhood with their condescending attitude to women, is nowhere seen more clearly than in his study of 'Mrs. Ashcroft', the dying woman. Not the least effective feature of her conversation is the mixture of suburban smartness with traditional peasant cunning. She knows her way about London, she listens to the wireless; but she remains at heart a country-woman and a believer in the ancient lore. It was typical of Kipling's method that he borrowed several of her features (and admitted doing so) from Chaucer's 'Wife of Bath'.

Gradually 'The Wish House' takes the shape of a ghost-story about a curse which is lifted from the back of one who is beloved but unworthy, and is faithfully borne by one who loves and forgives. A generation had passed since 'Tomlinson' at Hell-gate had received the Devil's warning:

> The sin that ye do by two and two ye must pay for one by one!

which had then seemed audaciously original. At sixty years old Kipling had acquired a deeper understanding of life's retributive processes, and knew that 'Mrs. Ashcroft' might well pay the reckoning for her lover's sin as well as for her own, and do it gladly; nor was it necessary to call in a supernatural mechanism for transferring the burden. Yet 'Mrs. Ashcroft' believed, and the reader finds himself also believing, that she deliberately took up the burden of her man's troubles by a magical device, by trafficking with an evil spirit, potent with curses though not with blessings. The effect is gained by Kipling's careful rejection of all the trappings of romance. The 'Wish House' is no picturesque haunted grange but a dingy villa in a surburban street, infested by a shabby, wheezing, down-at-heel, fumbling elemental, the dregs of ghosthood. It serves, and the story-teller makes his point.

> . . . she builded an Altar and served by the light of her Vision —
> Alone, without hope of regard or reward, but uncowed,
> Resolute, selfless, divine.
> These things she did in Love's honour . . .
> What is a God beside Woman? Dust and Derision.[3]

The impulse to write was not exhausted when *Debits and Credits* was published in 1926. Hugh Walpole has preserved in his diary a pleasant word-picture of 'a wonderful morning with old Kipling in the Athenæum. He was sitting surrounded by the reviews of his new book, beaming like a baby.'[4] He was already hard at work upon a new set of stories to succeed it. The last volume, however, *Limits and Renewals*, mostly written in 1927 and 1928 though not 'collected' until 1932, shows some falling away in the author's skill; it is the book of a tired and ageing invalid. Professor Dobree, in his penetrating study of Kipling's later style,[4] has pointed out his obsession with the problem of pain, natural enough in a man who was never free from pain, for more than a few weeks at a time, during the last twenty years of his life. A theme in all the war-stories was the 'breaking-strain', the amount of pressure human beings can stand from physical tortures and mental terrors without a psychological collapse; and his favourite treatment of this problem is the salvation of a personality by devotion to another personality, by loving rather than by being loved. Yet love may seem too strong a word for a mere clinging to life at whatever point an emotional attachment can be secured. It may be simply gratitude as in 'A Friend of the Family', or love of animals as in the story significantly named 'The Woman in His Life'. The fear of fear, the knowledge that mental hells are more racking than physical hells, the unwillingness of even the bravest to face ultimate and hideous realities, may even reduce wretched mortals to a state where physical pain brings relief by numbing the mind.

> Dread mother of Forgetfulness
> Who, when Thy reign begins,
> Wipest away the Soul's distress,
> And memory of her sins.[5]

That last shrinking from the ultimate and the inevitable is the subject of the war-poem 'Gethsemane' which many readers have found difficult.*

* R. K. gave this explanation to F. N. Doubleday (Doubleday Papers). The verses, he said, referred to 'the horror that overtakes a man when he first ships his gasmask. What makes war most poignant is the presence of women with whom he can talk and make love, only an hour or so behind the line.'

> The Garden called Gethsemane,
>> It held a pretty lass,
> But all the time she talked to me
>> I prayed my cup might pass.
> The officer sat on the chair,
>> The men lay on the grass,
> And all the time we halted there
>> I prayed my cup might pass.

His 'Epitaphs of the Great War', 'naked cribs of the Greek Anthology' he called them, include much comment on this theme; one that Rudyard Kipling thought good of its kind was 'The Coward':

> I could not look on Death, which being known,
>> Men led me to him, blindfold and alone.

These were his final comments on the First World War: to every man his own private terror, his own vein of courage, his own breaking-strain, his own salvation by a loving attachment to life; and the other aspect of the picture may be seen in the strange, elaborate — not quite successful — allegories of the after-life, 'On the Gate' and 'Uncovenanted Mercies'. The reader is not expected to believe in them unreservedly.

Limits and Renewals includes one *comédie humaine* in Rudyard's happier style, the study of the village *curé* and the village atheist which he called 'The Miracle of Saint Jubanus', based upon an incident he had once seen when visiting a Spanish Cathedral. The book also includes an ill-natured anecdote, 'The Tie', written long since and dredged up from the bottom of his notebooks where it might better have been allowed to stay. But the strength of the book lies in the stories about doctors and disease, topics which now meant more to him than the life of soldiers and sailors that he had written about in his youth.

On any count, 'Dayspring Mishandled' is an astonishing performance, a profound, obscure, and singularly unpleasant story about a vindictive feud between two expert bibliophiles, or rather the vindictive persecution of a sham expert by a genuine expert. Revenge goes so far that the victim is not spared further taunts and triumphings when dying of a painful disease. But more engaging than the revenge-motive is the virtuosity with which a spurious poem by Chaucer is composed, a fifteenth-century manuscript faked, and the specious scholar is deceived.* As if this involution were not enough, the progress of the plot is contrasted with the degeneration of the victim, as

---

* It was just like R. K. to go through the whole process of faking a mediaeval manuscript with his own hands before writing the story.

disease wears him down, until the combined assaults of pain and disillusion reveal his breaking-strain.

The progress of an incurable disease is also the subject of 'Unprofessional', a story that repays study. Sir John Bland-Sutton said Kipling had here foretold the course of medical research, as far ahead as his 'Easy as A B C' had foretold the progress of aviation. An early draft had borne the name 'Stars in their Courses', which suggested its theme, the revival of an old notion that had stimulated the astrologers in antiquity but had led them astray. When reconsidered in a modern laboratory, this notion might reveal, or so the author's fancy suggests, recurrent and rhythmical changes in the cells of the body — 'tides' in the tissues produced by influences from without, 'the main tide in all matter'.

Rudyard's later writing, even more involved, compressed, and elaborate, had lost nothing in force or in range. While he reached out continually to master new technologies and to bring them within the scope of his art, he seemed less able to visualize a scene in a few unforgettable words. We are given situations rather than scenes, conversations rather than characters. The faking of the manuscript in 'Dayspring Mishandled' is not likely to be forgotten, but one cares little about the two bibliophiles, and less about the victim's wife who is given an illicit love affair, by way of underplot.

It was an old joke in the book trade that two classes of books will always find a market in England, books about doctors and books about dogs. After his medical stories Rudyard indeed turned to the other category and enjoyed his last success with dog stories, in a new mode. He had always been a dog-lover and, from his earliest days as a writer, had introduced some favourite dogs into his stories about people. In 'Garm, a Hostage' and 'The Dog Hervey', the dogs had been among the leading characters, but dogs seen through the human eye. His beasts, in the *Jungle Books* and elsewhere, had been treated allegorically, in another traditional style, as characters personified appropriately, like Circe's swine, in some animal garb that suited them. *Thy Servant a Dog*, published in 1930, was not a beast fable in the conventional form, but a genuine attempt to present a dog's point of view, in a simplified vocabulary which seemed adequate to a dog's intelligence, an experiment in the rudiments of language.

Since the marriage of their daughter had left Rudyard and Carrie alone in their house, he had submitted to a dynasty of Aberdeen terriers, the companions of his solitary hours, giving 'his heart to a dog to tear'. His dogs were the last creatures on whom he turned his exact and penetrating gaze, to the renewed delight of his readers who bought 100,000 copies of *Thy Servant* in six months. The author of

that book was a student of life on a familiar level; the author of 'Dayspring Mishandled' was no mean scholar. Not much information
survives of Rudyard's reading habits and some of the critical remarks
ascribed to him are spurious. There was, however, one friend with
whom Rudyard habitually discussed literary matters, the American
novelist, Edward Lucas White. They had first met as fellow-masons
and for more than thirty years they corresponded, using masonic
phrases, and commenting on one another's books. Rudyard told him
much about the origin of his own stories and in so doing revealed
something of his literary technique. 'How far is a man justified', he
had once asked White, 'in using onoma — (I can't spell it) — topoeic
metres reproducing the beat of engines and so on? Where does
legitimate art end and trick-work begin?' And again: 'I have been
experimenting with divers metres and various rhymes. The results
serve excellently to light fires with.' It was to White that he first
confided his interest in the poems of Donne, many years before they
became a literary fashion. Donne, he said, was 'Browning's great-
grandfather' and no small singer, 'a haughty proud-stomached
individual in his life, with Browning's temperament for turning his
mind upside-down as if it were a full bottle and letting the ideas get
out as best they could'. Another Jacobean they discussed was Phineas
Fletcher, 'who sat down before the human carcase and hammered out
God knows how many lines of high and disposed allegory'. Not of
the first rank, Rudyard admitted, but, like Drayton and Drummond,
he 'worked largely' and gave all he had to his verses.

Rudyard confided to White a number of facts about the origin of
the 'Puck' stories, particularly an account of the song sung by 'Philadelphia' in 'Marklake Witches'.

Shenstone has somewhere or other, about the end, I think, of a long and
dreary ode, four lines of pure tears thus:

> Yet time may diminish the pain.
> The flower and the bud and the tree
> That I reared for her pleasure in vain
> In time may bring comfort to me.

— or words to that effect. I quote without the book but my heart knows
it too well. Well! of course they were the words for my Philadelphia only
they wouldn't have been set to music. So I had to invent a new sort
of parallel passage of about the same age and appearance; and if you look
closely you'll see that they in turn owe something to the meditation of
Alexander Selkirk, 'I am Monarch, etc.' The actual effect comes out of
'desolate', 'rare', and 'change'. I'm rejoiced that you spotted it.[6]

In his letters to another literary friend, George Saintsbury, he could
assume that his correspondent needed no prompting. From 1916

onwards Carrie Kipling went at intervals to Bath to be treated for her rheumatism, while to Rudyard these visits meant renewing his friendship with Saintsbury who lived at Bath in retirement. Sending him a set of his collected verse, Rudyard wrote: 'Look at some of the smaller ones in the third volume. *You'll* know the heifers I've ploughed with, from Herrick to Donne.'[3]

In his later life Rudyard accepted Saintsbury as a sort of literary patron to fill the place once held by Charles Eliot Norton. He treated the old critic with deep respect and was inordinately proud when Saintsbury dedicated to him his *Notes from a Cellar-Book*. He consulted Saintsbury about Frank Doubleday's plan for a *de luxe* edition of Lesser English Classics (Skelton, Christopher Smart, Crashaw, Tourneur, Raleigh, Tusser, Coryat), for which Stanley Morison was to lay out the typography; he ventured to question Saintsbury's comments on the English Novelists. 'Thackeray', said Rudyard, 'had the bit of Victorian convention uneasy in his mouth and champed on it.' Hence the restlessness of his 'interjected moralities'.

Their discussions turned mostly on French literature, and when Saintsbury produced his standard work on the French Novel, Rudyard wrote:

I've had a superior sort of Whitsuntide holiday. My cousin who is Financial Secretary [Stanley Baldwin] came down very tired for a rest. *He* bagged the 2nd Volume first because he wanted to know your faith about Balzac and I got the first (not without heat) to see about Rabelais. Then he curled up in the house and garden, and I browsed in my room and we didn't do anything else at all on Saturday and Sunday except read and compare notes. . . . I haven't had as good a time for years . . . till I almost felt that I'd made my own researches. (Well, I *did* once bite pieces out of the *Grand Cyrus*.)

Then I got on to the second, specially Maupassant . . . and the result . . . an earnest resolve, which I shall never have time to fulfill, to renew my old French readings.

Later he made a separate comment on a French contemporary. 'I've been reading the Anatole France estimate at the end of the volume. Ages ago, my Dad introduced me to Anatole in the *Reine Pédauque,* etc. No, he ain't a serious thinker. (Hell's too full of that class of fraud.)' But Rudyard added with pride that, when they met, Anatole France had embraced him.[7]

Rudyard's interest in French novels has been recorded from another aspect by a French writer with whom he sometimes corresponded. When they first met, wrote M. Joseph-Renaud, at a dinner of the Authors' Club, 'this little dark man with the blinding gold spectacles and the enormous eyebrows, came up and shot a rapid fire of questions at me, without any sort of introduction. 'Are the duels in Dumas correct in detail? Are there any such Bretons as those described by Pierre Loti? Is it true that Madame Bovary was a real person? Tell me about this Colette whose animal stories are so much better than mine! And so on, and so on.' The questions followed one another so fast that I had hardly time to answer.

As he listened to me, he stroked his bald head with a hand so brown that you might have thought him a Hindu (he was so dark that some people put about a rumour — quite false — that he was a half-caste), and when he was sure he had drained me dry he turned abruptly away with a quick 'good night'. I had never met so tenacious an interviewer. A few minutes later, I told my story to Frank Harris who replied: 'Ruddy is a journalist still; he always wants to know a little more.' [8]

Comments on his contemporaries are rare in Rudyard's private letters and almost unknown in his published works. He wrote with freedom to C. R. L. Fletcher, the Oxford historian with whom he had collaborated in a *History of England* for schools, and in these letters one or two critical comments may be found, for example, some early contempt for that overrated author, Lytton Strachey. 'I've been reading *Eminent Victorians*. . . . It seems to me downright wicked in its heart.' Or on R. G. Collingwood's autobiography: 'I've read Collingwood. It's the old finale to most things in this world — the *dénouement* is that there isn't any *dénouement* — only deliquescence. But Collingwood's tremendously interesting.' [9]

Rudyard was a rapid reader who skimmed through whole parcels of newly published books, sent him by A. P. Watt, and then returned to his English Classics. While he was writing dog stories he wrote to a friend: 'I haven't been doing much outside reading of late. Beaumont and Fletcher mostly, and some Dekker, and Evelyn's Tree-book and John Milton.'

John Evelyn's 'Tree-book' (*Sylva*) was evidence of Rudyard's long interest in systematic botany. He travelled always with a well-used copy of that old classic, *Flowers of the Field* by C. A. Johns, and noted observations in its margins. He arranged the ninety-three orders of British plants in a mnemonic rhyme for easy mental reference and, as might be expected of a writer who so much enjoyed 'bating his hook with gaudy words', he was avid to acquire new rustic names for flowers and herbs.* In France he made a point of collecting French varieties of English wild flowers and recording their French rural names.

---

*
> 'Eyebright, Orris, and Elecampane,
> Basil, Rocket, Valerian, Rue,
> (Almost singing themselves they run) . . .'
>   'Our Fathers of Old.'

The other book that accompanied him wherever he went was one of his many editions of Horace, in his later years the handsome vellum-bound volume which he 'grangerized' with glosses, translations, parodies, and comments beautifully written in the margins. If space permitted, a critical essay might be written on Kipling's devotion to this Master. It would begin with his schooldays when his teachers at Westward Ho! laid the foundation of his studies, making him 'loathe Horace for two years, forget him for twenty, then love him for the rest of his days'. His version of *Donec gratus eram tibi* suggests that, even as a schoolboy, he did not hate it as much as he supposed. Horatian allusiveness and compression, Horatian overtones, are to be found in all Kipling's national hymns, and it is clear that his interest had been completely recaptured by 1917, when he wrote 'Regulus', the story of the boys who wrestled with the fifth ode of the Third Book and understood it better than they knew. When the volume, *A Diversity of Creatures,* containing 'Regulus', was published it also included a parody, or perhaps we should say an imitation, of one of Horace's slighter, wittier poems. It was put out as a translation of the 'third ode of the Fifth Book' with a catch-title from the Latin, *Ubi Lollius, etc.* Some reviewers in the less-academic organs of the press fought a little shy of this ascription. Might it be genuine? And Kipling began to build up an elaborate joke, with his friends at the Universities, based upon this 'translation'.

Rudyard Kipling to C. R. L. Fletcher

21 April 1917

Kindly supply me with the original of that Horatian Ode which I have so inadequately translated. As a matter of fact I only came across the second (Urbino's) copy of the missing Fifth Book in the Library of the Vatican a few years ago quite by chance, and transcribed the Third Ode in haste, by very indifferent light, in the Crypt of the Dogale. There is another copy of the Fifth Book at Upsala — as you of course know — but it is in a bad condition and the marginal notes of Clavesius add nothing to its value. The third copy — if Sir James Urquhart's statement to the Spanish Ambassador can be trusted — should be in the Bodleian. . . . My excuse for troubling you is that I have already been attacked in a private letter, by a so-called scholar, who asserts that no such book as the Fifth ever existed.[9]

The letters to Fletcher and Saintsbury thereafter contain many allusions to this imaginary work which actually appeared in print in 1922: '*Q. Horati Flacci Carminum Librum Quintum a Rudyardo Kipling et Carolo Graves Anglice Redditum . . .*' The Latin versions, by A. D. Godley who, as Public Orator at Oxford, was skilled in such learned witticisms, were much admired by scholars. It was a true collaboration and, while Kipling wrote most of the English versions, he had his say in the Latin versions also.

Some readers may think that his best versions of Horace are the marginal glosses — hitherto unpublished — in his favourite copy. Yet they are not versions, but commentaries, sometimes facetious commentaries, on the poet's character and method. He translates a line or two as the starting-point for an epigram of his own or, as if Horace were not already the most concise of authors, he adds a version of his own which is still more concise.

Beneath the beautiful

> *Vides ut alta stet nive candidum Soracte . . .*

he writes:

> 'Tis cold! Heap on the logs — and let's get tight!
> The Gods can turn this world for just one night.
> I will enjoy myself and be no scorner
> Of any nice girl giggling in a corner.

Integer vitae scelerisque purus moved him to no such enthusiasm as the Regulus Ode aroused in the breast of Mr. King, but to this flippancy:

> The Pure and Perfect Bore
> Goes scatheless evermore,
> Arrows and Poison never yet destroyed him.
> Such is the Mantle thrown
> By Dulness on Her own
> That when he sings the very Beasts avoid him.

> So he pervades the Earth
> Absorbed in His own Worth
> No Tact restrains — no Grace — no Humour move Him,
> And yet — Oh Womankind!
> This God's Own Ass can find
> Some long-enduring Lalage to love Him!

He was not always so flippant; here is an epigram based upon: *Quis desiderio sit pudor aut modus . . .*

> They pass, O God, and all
>   Our grief, our tears,
> Achieve not their recall
>   Nor reach their ears.
> Our lamentations leave
>   But one thing sure.
> They perish and we grieve
>   But we endure.

There are signs that these Horatian fragments were but sketches and studies for something Rudyard did not live to complete.

CHAPTER XX

THE LAST YEARS OF HIS LIFE (1925-36)

'NON NOBIS DOMINE!'

(Written for 'The Pageant of Parliament', 1934)

Non nobis Domine! —
  Not unto us, O Lord!
The Praise or Glory be
  Of any deed or word;
For in Thy Judgment lies
  To crown or bring to nought
All knowledge or device
  That Man has reached or wrought.

And we confess our blame —
  How all too high we hold
That noise which men call Fame,
  That dross which men call Gold.
For these we undergo
  Our hot and godless days,
But in our hearts we know
  Not unto us the Praise.

O Power by Whom we live —
  Creator, Judge, and Friend,
Upholdingly forgive
  Nor fail us at the end:
But grant us well to see
  In all our piteous ways —
Non nobis Domine! —
  Not unto us the Praise!

IN October 1924 Elsie Kipling was married to Captain George Bambridge, who had served in the Irish Guards. She was to live abroad, since he was in the diplomatic service, and, without her, Rudyard found the grey old house at Burwash 'resonant, silent, and enormously empty'. Still, as Rudyard and Carrie grew older — both in poor health, he clung to his young friends and, until the end of his life, continued to make new ones among the youngest present in any company. Carrie's diary never fails to record his pleasure in the visits of the children of his old acquaintances. Rudyard would have no party manners and, when inviting his friends to bring their children, always insisted they should come in their oldest clothes, fully prepared to fall into the pond.

Those of his own contemporaries who still survived were as dear as ever, but Colonel Fielden died in 1922, Rider Haggard in 1925, Percival Landon in 1927, and these he never replaced in his affections. Rider Haggard, the only professional novelist in the small circle of his intimates, was endeared to Rudyard, as Henley had been, by a common sorrow; each of the three had lost a beloved young child. To Haggard he extended the signal honour of allowing him to work at his own table when he came to stay at 'Bateman's'. Rudyard would make suggestions to him for names and picturesque episodes, and one of Rider Haggard's later romances (Red Eve) owes much of its fantastic quality to suggestions from Rudyard Kipling. He was prolific of notions for stories which he did not write, this one, for example, which he offered to Lord Dunsany:

30 May 1935

DEAR DUNSANY,

Here is a thing which has come up in my head, which I can't handle because I don't know present-day Irish (Mick) language and backgrounds. So I send it for you to consider. Substantially, I have made it boil down to three of four young I.R.A. — Rebels — Mountainy Men, or cattle of that kidney who, for their own purposes — revenge, politics, a row about a girl or what you please — have fired into — set light to — bombed — or otherwise terrorized a neighbor's house. Or, alternatively, they have way-laid and hammered a man in the dark, or cut off a girl's hair (you have large choice in the matter, I believe). Anyway, they find themselves landed with a dead or dying person who must be disposed of before the dawn breaks.

They discuss the situation among themselves, and finally, pick up the corpse and bear it off with intent to dispose of it in a kindly bog. En route, they find that there has attached himself to their little procession, an odd-looking person in some sort of clerical garb that they can't identify. He seems to have taken on himself charge of the whole situation — even to the extent of turning round and furiously (*sic*) bidding them, in dumb show, (*sic*) go on when they (Irish fashion) begin to waver in their precise objective.

It is his amazing eyes that they notice first of all. Then it dawns on them that he is not of this earth, and, further, that he is mad — a mad ghost.

In great fear they follow his signals, to the lip of the bog where he takes charge of the committal, and delivers a sermon on the dead, on them, on Ireland at large. It is rather a notable sermon — as you will find when you try to write it; he being, or, rather, having once been, Dean of St. Patrick's in whose crypt his body, he tells them, lies. Cut it off at that point, or, if you like, add frills and grace-notes at discretion — such as one of the lads telling his priest the tale at Confession, or something of that kind.

You are the only man who can do it with comprehension and venom.[1]

Another surviving friend was Sir John Bland-Sutton, not only a celebrated surgeon but an original investigator into pathology, and a diligent collector of odd scraps of learning. His hobby was comparative biology, and, expert as he was in human anatomy, he did not disdain to draw parallels from the digestive organs of birds. It was remarked in Burwash that Rudyard and his distinguished visitor spent a Sunday afternoon catching domestic fowls and listening to the digestive noises in their gizzards. Bland-Sutton gave Rudyard much delight in the way of friendship but failed altogether to master his illness. Watching over Rudyard for twenty years, he could never relieve his abdominal pain.

After the war, Rudyard used often to motor to Oxford on business for the Rhodes Trust. He would call on Dr. Parkin, the first Warden of Rhodes House, and would arrange to receive parties of Rhodes Scholars at his hotel. As an honorary doctor of both Oxford and Cambridge, as Lord Rector of St. Andrews, Rudyard had shaken off a certain uneasiness he had once shown in academic society, and now had many friends in the Universities. It was Oxford that he knew first and best, as a Rhodes Trustee, but it was Cambridge that admitted him to full membership as Honorary Fellow of Magdalene College. For each of the old English Universities he wrote a ballad — two variations on one theme, the almost unnatural regression from manhood to boyhood of the post-war students.

> The merry clerks of Oxenford they stretch themselves at ease
> Unhelmeted on unbleached sward beneath unshrivelled trees. . . .

It was his perpetual theme in the nineteen-twenties when the return of peace seemed an incredible fantasy after the reality of war.

There was one man in Oxford in 1919 who, more than all his generation, was aware of these contrasting atmospheres. Rudyard met T. E. Lawrence in London before the Armistice and later at Oxford. He was able to do Lawrence a slight service by introducing him to his own American publisher Frank Doubleday, and in the correspondence between Frank and Rudyard there are some remarks upon the inscrutable 'T. E.', a greater puzzle to his friends in 1919 than he became later after the publication of the *Seven Pillars*. Lawrence 'fusses about himself too much', wrote Rudyard and gave Frank his opinion that there 'must be a woman at the back of it'.[2]

There came a day, after Lord Milner's death in 1925, when Rudyard refused to adapt himself to new modes of thought at Oxford. As internationalism prevailed he stuck grimly to the lost cause of sheer conservatism. The times had passed him by and it was a crucial point in political progress as he saw it, when Philip Kerr (afterwards Marquess of Lothian) was appointed to the vacant place in the Rhodes Trust; for Kerr was a Liberal and an internationalist. When the British Empire itself was changing its shape to become a liberal commonwealth, Rudyard found the new concept mightily different from Rhodes's Dream. He accordingly resigned from the Rhodes Trust and dismayed his colleagues by insisting that his resignation should be publicly announced, as made on principle.[3]

The following year, 1926, saw the General Strike which revealed at once the leftward swing of English opinion and the weak irresponsibility of the Socialist leaders. In this crisis Rudyard played no part and contributed no message for the hour, since his health had collapsed again. In December 1925 he had again been struck down with pneumonia and, at the time of the Strike, was convalescing in France. There followed another long period of ill-health, for the abdominal pains returned as soon as he left the regimen of the sick-room.

His cousin Stanley, leader of the Tory Party for most of Rudyard's later life, was Prime Minister in this critical year but, fond as Rudyard was of his cousin as a man, he progressively thought less of him as a politician. It was Stanley Baldwin's destiny, perhaps his strength, that for a large part of his career he acted in concert with men of very different views and principles. He served in Lloyd George's Coalition Government (1917-22) as a junior minister, and in Ramsay MacDonald's Coalition Government (1931-5) as a senior minister; and in his own three terms as Prime Minister (1923-4, 1925-9, 1935-7) his policy was easy and accommodating. In Ireland and in India he loosened imperial ties with a willingness that was shocking to Rudyard, who used to say: 'Stanley is a Socialist at heart'. Carrie Kipling mistrusted him and thought him spoiled by power. Nevertheless, the close family friendship was maintained; the Kiplings often stayed at Astley, the Baldwins' home in Worcestershire; were regularly invited to Chequers, the Prime Minister's official country house; often dined in Downing Street. Rudyard's remarks upon the allies with whom Cousin Stanley worked in political coalitions were often unprintable. He was not alone in noticing that Baldwin was born rich and gave away much of his fortune anonymously to the nation, whereas Lloyd

George was born in poverty and grew rich on politics. When an old friend, Philip Gosse, sent Rudyard a copy of his book on *Pirates,* it elicited the comment: 'on the whole, as you almost hint in your opening remarks, I don't suppose that the pirate did much more harm than the politician. And no pirate that I ever heard of came out of his business with a couple of millions "personal fund" for which he absolutely refused to account! Nothing like modern science after all!'[3] A little later he was using the same analogy of a Socialist Chancellor of the Exchequer. 'If you re-read *Treasure Island',* he wrote jocularly to a friend at Oxford, 'substituting Viscount Snowden for Long John Silver, you'll be amazed.'[4]

An event which saddened Rudyard and Carrie was the breach with Stanley Baldwin's son, Oliver, who had meant much to them when they lost their own son. Carrie had regarded him almost as one of the family and had spoken more affectionately of him than of any of her other nephews or nieces; and Rudyard had been proud of Oliver's enthusiasm as a young soldier. That he should change sides in politics was his own affair, but conduct which they thought unfilial they could not forgive.

Another friendship that began to cool was that with Lord Beaverbrook, as Rudyard came to realize that there were many things which they no longer saw in common, and after Beaverbrook's admission of certain of his political ambitions, they never met again.

Like many another elderly Conservative in the nineteen-twenties Rudyard reacted at the news of events in Ireland, Egypt, India, by moving further to the right in politics. The *Morning Post,* superbly edited by H. A. Gwynne, continued to fight its rearguard action, and Rudyard continued to urge Gwynne to take stronger stands. He was for years closely associated with the editorial policy of the *Post* and on terms of friendship with Lady Bathurst, the proprietor. The Kiplings spent many week-ends at Cirencester with the Bathursts; and in other country houses frequented by the High Tories: at Chevening with the Stanhopes, and at Whiteladies with Sir W. Joynson-Hicks. At these houses they met, for the most part, political and 'service' friends, such men as Sir Roger Keyes, Sir Archibald Montgomery-Massingberd (an old friend from the South African War, who became the Chief of the General Staff), and Lord Lloyd the last hope of the stern unbending Tories. When Lloyd was Governor of Bombay he again urged Rudyard to revisit India, but Rudyard replied that Carrie's health would never stand it, and to go without her was out of the question.

House-parties at the Cazalets' in Sussex were drawn from a wider section of society and always included some celebrities from the world of art and letters. Here Rudyard met P. G. Wodehouse and challenged him: 'Tell me, Wodehouse, how do you finish your stories? I can never think how to end mine.' On this occasion Hugh Walpole was one of the guests, and thus described the party:

> Kipling at Fairlawne is like a little gnome. All sorts of people about. The Athlones — she with her funny old German governess who says not a word but suddenly breaks out once with 'Ach, Thomas Mann — he's a splendid writer' and looks across the table scornfully at Kipling as though she'd like to tell him how inferior she thinks *he* is. And J. H. Thomas suddenly putting his arm confidentially through mine after lunch, although he scarcely knows me, and chuckling: 'You're a novelist. Well, keep your eye on me, my boy, for I'm your next P.M. 'Ow's that for a prophecy?' And then catching Kipling's arm and chuckling in *his* ear some rather dirty joke about Labour Gentlemen of the Bedchamber. Not that Kipling cares in the least about any of them. He is kindly, genial, ready apparently to be friends with anyone but keeping all the time his own guard.
>
> I asked him at luncheon whether he approved of censorship (apropos of this tiresome stupid *Well of Loneliness*). No, he doesn't approve of the book. Too much of the abnormal in all of us to play about with it. Hates opening up reserves. All the same he'd had friends once and again he'd done more for than for any woman. Luckily Ma Kipling doesn't hear this. . . . She's a good strong-minded woman, who has played watch-dog to him so long that she knows now just how to save him any kind of disturbance, mental, physical, or spiritual. That's *her* job and she does it superbly. . . .
>
> He really, I think, has no vanity. He's a zealous propagandist who, having discovered that the things for which he must propagand are now all out of fashion, guards them jealously and lovingly in his heart, but won't any more trail them about in public.
>
> He walks about the garden, his eyebrows all that are really visible of him. His body is nothing but his eyes terrific, lambent, kindly, gentle and exceedingly proud. Good to us all and we are all shadows to him.
>
> 'Carrie,' he says turning to Mrs. K., and at once you see that she is the only real person here to him — so she takes him, wraps him up in her bosom and conveys him back to their uncomfortable hard-chaired home. He is quite content.[6]

General Dunsterville ('Stalky'), with whom Rudyard remained on terms of affection throughout life, was in a special position. It was a powerful comfort to Rudyard that his early faith in his friend was, at last, justified, when Dunsterville leaped at one of the few opportunities for brilliant initiative offered in the dreary routine of slaughter that constituted the First World War. His audacious expedition to save North Persia from the Bolsheviks was an exploit surpassing anything the young 'Stalky' could have imagined. Rudyard had been right and 'Stalky' only needed scope. But, after the war, as a retired major-general on a small pension, with no private means and no employment, what could Dunsterville do but exploit his own publicity? First, of course, he could write an account of his campaign and go for a lecture tour; and then, since all the world knew he was 'Stalky', there was nothing for it but to cash-in on his reminiscences of Rudyard Kipling. This was not so popular at 'Bateman's' where 'Stalky' became, perhaps, suspect. Furthermore, he was an early worker for the formation of a Kipling Society, which the object of attention regarded with gloomy distaste, disliking these monumental tributes while he was still alive — none more than the books by Sir George MacMunn who, as a British officer, should, he thought, have known better. There was no stopping the formation of the Society.

Since 1919 at least, Mr. J. H. C. Brooking had been trying to bring enthusiasts for Kipling's works together. In 1922 he persuaded 'Stalky' to lend a hand, though 'Stalky' expected opposition from the Kiplings. A convening committee, Brooking, 'Stalky', and 'Ian Hay' (Major J. H. Beith) met in 1923, but it was not till 1927 that the Society was formally constituted, with about a hundred members, and 'Stalky' as their first president. The difficulty had been that the keen members expected some leading 'Kipling-ites' to lend their names, and the obvious leaders were deterred by Kipling's dislike of the whole affair. 'Stalky' was persuaded to become president, and the first committee included Brooking, Beresford ('M'Turk'), and MacMunn. There are now (1954) more than 700 members in the United Kingdom and active branches in the United States and other countries, and the quarterly *Kipling Journal* has passed its 100th number.[7]

Even more than the flatteries of the Kipling Society, he disliked the activities of bibliophiles who trafficked in his private letters, draft manuscripts, rejected trifles, and unauthorized editions. All this was what he called the 'Higher Cannibalism'. When his old friend, Mrs. Hill, offered some of his early manuscript fragments for sale he wrote a letter of remonstrance; and when an American devotee formed a classified study of all his works, authorized and unauthorized, he disliked the intention. The devotee, Admiral L. H. Chandler, made several approaches to Rudyard, and was repulsed more than once, with letters in the coldest terms from Rudyard's secretary, before his persistence was rewarded with an interview. The Kiplings liked him, and the Chandler Index (now in the Library of Congress) is the completest analysis that exists of Kipling's writings. When a *Summary* of its conclusions was published Rudyard annotated a copy in his own hand.

After Admiral Chandler came Mrs. Flora Livingston, the Houghton Librarian from Harvard. She forced the defences of 'Bateman's', with recommendations on the ground of sheer scholarship, was received with civility, and became a friend. Her Bibliography, based upon the immense collection of Kipling-iana now in the Houghton Library, is a model of its kind.

In London, his clubs provided him with the variety of talk that he loved. He lunched usually at the Athenæum until, upon the proposal of his publisher, Sir Frederick Macmillan, he was elected to the smaller and more private Beefsteak Club. A man who was always on a diet of more or less strictness could take little pleasure in the luxuries of the table. He rarely dined out, never ate more than a little of the plainest food, and always left early so that he attended dining-clubs, Grillion's or 'The Club', for the conversation rather than the food and drink. Sir William Osler has preserved an account of a dinner at 'The Club', in 1919, with the Archbishop of York in the Chair and John Buchan, Henry Newbolt, Charles Oman, H. A. L. Fisher, and Kipling among the company. 'Kipling was in very good form, and told many good war-stories. He said he would not be sur-prised if in a few years the monastic life was revived — as men were seeking relief from the burdens of a hard world and turning more and more to spiritual matters.' [8]

From time to time Sir Abe Bailey gave vast dinner-parties to forty or more guests, all men at the head of their professions, and to these parties Rudyard was usually invited. But the circle of his intimates was small and the functions he attended were few. So long as his Uncle Edward Poynter was alive, he was regularly invited to the Royal Academy Banquets. He enjoyed the London theatres and — in the old silent days — occasionally visited the cinema. To get Kipling to speak at a public function was no small achievement, and when he undertook to speak, his address was always prepared, many days in advance, with as much care as if it were a poem or short story. As his academic connexions were strengthened he was frequently asked to give more formal addresses, and there can be few other men who have declined to deliver the Gifford Lectures at Edinburgh, the Romanes Lectures at Oxford, the Leslie Stephen Lecture at Cambridge, and the Reith Lectures of the B.B.C. He was proud to be a member of the Stationers' Company and a freeman of the City of London, but refused to be president of the Authors' Society. In 1926 a signal honour, which he accepted, was conferred upon him by the Royal Society of Literature — the gold medal which had been awarded only three times before, to Walter Scott, George Meredith, and Thomas Hardy. At this point in his life, perhaps, Rudyard Kipling came nearest to the frigid altitude of being an accepted classic, and, in consequence, was all the more out of fashion with the *avant-garde*.

In February 1928 the death of Thomas Hardy at a great age marked a turning-point in English literature, which was recognized by the solemnity of his funeral in Westminster Abbey, on a wet dark day. Among the pall-bearers were a group of Hardy's younger contemporaries, all of them revered in the republic of letters, and all doomed to pass, before many years, into the temporary eclipse that marks a change of fashion. The coffin was escorted by the Prime Minister and the Leader of the Opposition, by the Heads of the Oxford and Cambridge Colleges which had given honorary fellowship to Hardy, by Gosse and Barrie, Galsworthy and Housman, Kipling and Shaw. This was the first and only occasion when those two 'essentially good-hearted men', Rudyard Kipling and Bernard Shaw, came together. They were introduced at the Abbey door by Edmund Gosse but genial as both could be, they found nothing to say to one another. Gossips noted with malicious glee that in the procession Rudyard tried to pair himself with Galsworthy, and Shaw remarked afterwards that it was ludicrous to marshal so little a man as Kipling with so tall a man as himself.[9]

A few months after Hardy's funeral the King and Queen were guests at a private party in a London house. King George had no sooner made his entry than he caught sight of Rudyard, sent for him, remained all the evening in conversation with him in a corner of the room, and when it was time to go, felt obliged to apologize to his hostess for neglecting her other guests. A few weeks later Rudyard was invited to Balmoral for a week-end. The friendship was now ripening so that Rudyard felt more than a loyal dismay when, at the end of the year, the King was struck down with pneumonia. The Kiplings were staying at Chequers with the Prime Minister, who was supplied with bulletins sent directly from the Palace; and when the crisis was past Rudyard still got private reports from Lord Stamfordham. When the spring returned the King went down to recuperate by the sea at Bognor, in quiet seclusion. Rudyard was one of the few who were invited to visit him there — it was no more than fifty miles from 'Bateman's'. What Rudyard could then do for his sovereign was to prescribe him a course of light reading. He sent the King parcels of novels by Edgar Wallace, which were read and carefully returned, marked 'R. K.' in the King's hand. He said it was his rule to return borrowed books, most scrupulously, which was more than others did when they borrowed books from him.

King George V was the first sovereign of England to travel widely throughout the British Dominions, as Kipling was the first English poet to do so. Their experience had endowed both men with a devoted love for India and the Indian peoples; and both retained a marked distrust for those professional politicians, in England and in India, whose projects for solving India's problems seemed to be guided by other motives than love.*

All who personally knew the two men remarked upon their fundamental humility. King George's strength was that he knew himself to be just an ordinary man; and it was a feature of Kipling's greatness, too, that he would never allow admirers to pay him compliments. He was a craftsman who sometimes felt that words were put into his mouth, by a daemon or genius that came from without, not from within. In this way only was he distinguished from other men, and by this sense of inspiration was dedicated to a duty. The King, also, was a dedicated man and each of them recognized this quality in the other.

Even before his cousin became Prime Minister, Kipling had often been consulted about an epitaph, an inscription, or the phrasing of a formal statement, by the discreet organizers of public ceremonies. It was no new thing when Baldwin appealed to him for help in such matters, and it is no secret that several of Baldwin's most eloquent addresses, notably those delivered at functions where party politics would have been out of place, were revised and polished, if not actually composed, by Kipling. When called upon to advise the sovereign, in his constitutional capacity, about forms of words, Baldwin made a practice of taking his cousin's advice.

Since there was so great a natural sympathy between King George V and Rudyard Kipling, who had so many likes and dislikes, so many virtues and prejudices, in common, it was not surprising that the King's celebrated Christmas broadcasts, which so widely extended the influence of the Crown and drew the nations of the Commonwealth so close together, echoed Kipling's message.

Twenty years back, he had foreshadowed the technical broadcasting services which were to encircle the earth; and it was with quiet satisfaction that he listened, on the afternoon of Christmas Day 1932, to King George's words. He never thereafter alluded to his part in this achievement. It was a personal triumph for the King, whose honesty, simplicity, and kind-heartedness instantly impressed themselves upon a world of listeners, not less because his rich, low, unaffected voice — the voice of a sailor — revealed his natural talent for broadcasting. It was something of a triumph for Rudyard Kipling, too.

Life at 'Bateman's' was diversified by many motor tours. Whether they turned north for the road to Scotland, or southward from Calais

* For an appreciation of Kipling by a talented Indian nationalist see the *Memoirs of the Aga Khan* (p. 226), on Mrs. Sarojini Naidu.

for the Latin lands, the adventure was always new and uplifting. Rudyard kept careful records of his journeys, with notes on mileage, the state of the roads, and the comfort of hotels, and duly reported defects to the Automobile Association.[10] Often his motoring journals provide comments on scenery, and architecture, with word-pictures of landscapes or wayside happenings which might reappear one day in a story. Such notes as these were the raw material he packed away in his memory for future use, sketches which happen to have survived from thousands.

> For me this land, that sea, these airs, those folk and fields suffice.
> What purple Southern pomp can match our changeful Northern skies,
> Black with December snows unshed or pearled with August haze —
> The clanging arch of steel-grey March, or June's long-lighted days?

Yet in the dark days of January and February the south called him, not only into the sunshine but into a land of warmer temperaments where he need not record, as often in England: 'the waitress scornful and abstracted'. The contrast of north or south was never put more lovingly than by his own centurion:

> You'll take the old Aurelian Road through shore-descending pines
> Where, blue as any peacock's neck, The Tyrrhene Ocean shines.
> You'll go where laurel crowns are won, but — will you e'er forget
> The scent of hawthorn in the sun, or bracken in the wet?

One tour of France may be described from a long letter written by Rudyard to Rider Haggard:[12]

14 March 1925. All the landscape round Havre looked like a new (& rather cheap) bridecake with its light powdering of snow. Just enough not to hold up the car, and the Seine looking like pewter between the glittering banks. Too cold for comfort as we ran into Rouen. Went off at once to Rouen Cemetery (11,000 graves) and collogued with the Head Gardener and the contractors. One never gets over the shock of this Dead Sea of arrested corps.

That evening in his hotel he began to write what he describes as 'the story of Helen Turrell and her nephew and the gardener in the great 20,000 cemetery'. He worked at it every evening and finished it at Lourdes on 22nd March.

We crashed into Evreux whose Cathedral is a wonder — but not *the* wonder; and thence to Dreux — more gothic and sparser; and at last, in the tail of a dripping day to Chartres — the great blue-grey bulk of the Cathedral dominating, it seemed, half France. Our old hotel had been modernized, to our immense wrath, and was full of *ouvriers,* paint, petrol, and noises. Got into the Cathedral on the very last fading of the twilight and it was as though one moved within the heart of a jewel. . . .

At Perigueux, you strike the real, overbearing, brute, Byzantine of the 10th century; and one realises what a toss-up it was that our creed hadn't taken a dominantly oriental twist (might have been better if it had, p'haps). I liked the naked convention of strength and rigidity which doesn't lend itself to internal haberdashery. . . .

I like the Spaniards for not worrying about the rest of the world, but I can't love 'em. . . .

Consider now a day that gives you a couple of hours in the morning above the caves of the Dordogne — incised and painted Cro-magnon piccys of bison, horse, wolf, and rhino traced on the irregularly dimpled roofings and sides of those limstone grottoes, as smooth as candle-drippings. All you hear is now and then the one wee drop of water from the tip of a stalactite. The rest is all warm, stone-walled stillness and these inexplicable figures. Well, one steps outside and beyond one's own notions of time in such places.

Then a couple of hours later you are at Lourdes — same sort of smooth bluish-white rock grottoes in a hillside but instead of incised totems, a lavender and white presentation of Our Lady just in the spot where Bernadette, the peasant girl, had the visions. And all the smooth nodular scarped rock below smeared and covered and runnelled with the gutterings of countless candles — lighting up and going out like the children of man. . . . Huge gardens and public spaces round the church, flanked by huger hospices where the many sick of the summer can wait and lie up when they come to be healed. Miracles do not occur in the winter.

On a later holiday he crossed the Channel with a shipload of pilgrims returning from Lourdes and noticed with pity the many for whom there had been no miracle. ' It was like watching the return of the damned to Hell after a few breaths of hope.' [13]

In the winters, as they grew older, they went farther afield to avoid the cold, often for a short sea-voyage which revived and rested Rudyard but weakened and exhausted Carrie. Their later travels usually ended in illness for one of the two, since the changes of diet — on motor tours which he so much enjoyed — usually upset his digestion. The search for sunshine took them to Algiers, Sicily, and Spain to find that these countries had no certainty of warmth in early spring, and even Egypt proved chilly. Twice they went up the Nile as far as the First Cataract, to seek at Assouan the comforting heat they both needed. In Egypt Rudyard could pursue his tasks for the War Graves Commission, the more pleasantly since he had made a friend of the Australian soldier, Colonel C. E. Hughes, who was in charge of war graves in the Middle East. Together they visited the cemeteries and battlefields of the Palestine campaign, and made an expedition into Sinai with Major Jarvis the Governor.

An unpublished poem, written to the tune of a bawdy old song, expressed Rudyard's views on the imbroglio of Jews and Arabs under the British mandate:

> In ancient days and deserts wild
> There was a feud — still unsubdued —
> Twixt Sarah's son and Hagar's child,
> That centred round Jerusalem.

Tracing the progress of the feud down the ages, he discovered it still smouldering in the land of Israel:

> For 'neath the Rabbi's curls and fur,
> (Or scents and rings of movie-kings)
> The aloof, unleavened blood of Ur
> Broods steadfast at Jerusalem.[14]

The most rewarding winters were spent on the Riviera, where they could be sure of the regular, simple diet they both needed, and could enjoy sunshine and scenery in the company of their friends, without losing access to good doctors in case of illness. Elsie, too, would often join them, coming from Madrid or Paris. Carrie had always been, and Rudyard became as he grew older, a creature of habit so that, having found the landscapes and the lodgings that suited them, the two were inclined to return to them again.

Most of their journeys began or ended in Paris where they stayed at least once in every year after the war. A friend of very long standing, who as Julia Catlin had met them first in Bermuda, and then as Mrs. Depew had entertained them at Compiègne in the old happy days, was often their hostess, and made for them what was almost a second home, in Paris. She was now married to General Taufflieb, one of Rudyard's many friends in the French Army, and when Julia's daughter married Peter Stanley, an English surgeon practising in France, the friendship was extended to the younger generation.

After Rudyard's illness in 1926 Bland-Sutton recommended a long sea voyage which enabled him to realize an old dream. He had written in *Just So Stories*: 'I'd love to roll to Rio, some day before I'm old' and, after nearly twenty years of absence from the tropics, he crossed the line again in 1927 on a voyage to Brazil, taking the deepest interest in his fellow-passengers, mostly Spaniards and Portuguese. With some firmness he detached himself from publicity, declining to become a guest of the nation; and revelled in the prospect of a race of Europeans, at home in a tropical climate, and busily engaged in pioneering a new country. *Brazilian Sketches*,[15] written for the *Morning Post,* had the gusto of his early *Letters of Marque,* and were lightened with verses in his simplest, sincerest style.[15]

In 1929 it was Carrie who was ordered abroad for her health. That indomitable woman, never relaxing her care for her husband, now had no daughter at home, no one to nurse and tend her own ailments.

> If you can force your heart and nerve and sinew
>   To serve your turn long after they are gone,
> And still hold on when there is nothing in you
>   Except the Will that says to them: Hold on!

The verse might have been written for her when, her eyesight failing, racked with rheumatism, and now diagnosed as a diabetic, she pursued her unaltering routine. In February 1930 the two of them again broke new ground, sailing for the West Indies and taking with them Helen Hardinge, Lady Milner's daughter. It was an uneventful voyage which Rudyard spent restfully, working only a little at the dog story called 'The Woman in his Life'. In Jamaica, after refusing an invitation to be the guests of the Governor, they started a tour of the islands, which was spoiled by Carrie's sudden collapse with appendicitis. At first they pressed on hopefully and had reached Bermuda when she was obliged to go into the hospital, seriously ill. Helen Hardinge could stay no longer and Rudyard was left in solitary lodgings from March to June, his longest separation from Carrie in forty years of married life.

He had his own resources, and was witness of a scene (the sailor and the parrot that misbehaved) which he worked up into the story, 'A Naval Mutiny'; and, harking back to observations made, years previously, into the background of Shakespeare's *Tempest,* he made a ballad of them. Otherwise it was a blank period with little to do beyond watching the cruising liners put ashore their crowds of American tourists, who had come to Bermuda, in those days of Prohibition, solely to get drunk as soon as possible.

With a wife seriously ill, and no medical care he could rely on, Rudyard's anxiety was when and how to escape from Bermuda, since the regular shipping lines ran only to the United States. He wrote anxiously to Frank Doubleday for advice, with the proviso that even if an operation was necessary Carrie could not face a visit to New York, which would bring back dreadful memories to her, The mental strain would kill her. In any case, Rudyard went on, the United States was 'not a civilized country for the sick'. They must arrange to return by way of Canada.[16] Carrie grew worse, and it was only on 1st June that he got her aboard a ship for Halifax, Nova Scotia, and so to England. This was their last experience of the New World, and left him less in sympathy with America of the nineteen-thirties than before. In Canada they still had good friends but, apart from

Frank Doubleday — and he, like Rudyard, was elderly and ailing — there were few left of their acquaintances from the old days. Thirty-five years had passed since they had left Vermont.

Rudyard's last serious work was done in the early months of 1932, the charming conversation-piece called *Proof of Holy Writ*,[17] in which Ben Jonson and Shakespeare are shown discussing the Authorized Version of the Bible. It appeared just too late for inclusion in *Limits and Renewals,* and has not been reissued in any popular collection of his stories. Thereafter, as if he knew his life-work was over, he turned to collection and recollection. He took pains over arranging a new volume of *Collected Verse,* concluding it with an appeal to biographical writers to respect his private life.

> And for the little little span
> The dead are borne in mind,
> Seek not to question other than
> The books I leave behind.

It was in vain; a man who endears himself to a whole generation by his art cannot reject their natural desire to know more of his life. He had made himself their friend and had to accept the demands of friendship.

He prepared for the American market a select volume of verse and prose with the title, *A Pageant of Kipling,* and supervised the preparation of the gigantic *Sussex* Edition, luxuriously bound in thirty-five red leather volumes. Then he began to write a book which, said Carrie, was to ' deal with his life from the point of view of his work '. As its title, *Something of Myself,* suggested, it was hardly an autobiography but a reluctant release of what little he wished his readers to know; it contains no mention of Flo Garrard or of Mrs. Hill, of Wolcott or Beatty Balestier, no allusion to the deaths of Josephine and John Kipling. There are few dates and those not always accurate. But, as a picture of the mood in which he approached his work at each period of his life and as a record of self-criticism it is worth much, and without it this book would have been poorer.

Meanwhile his growing distrust in the social tendency of the nineteen-thirties was expressed in his address to the Royal Society of St. George. It was the time of King George's Silver Jubilee, and Rudyard spoke on the ' immemorial continuity of the nation's life under its own sovereigns '. The burden of his speech, as of so many of his later utterances, was the weak and negative policy of the lesser men who were left in charge of the nation's affairs, since their worthier contemporaries had sacrificed themselves in the First World War. Not these men's half-hearted self-delusions but enduring springs of vitality drawn from the nation's past would save us in the new perils that frowned upon the world. These men

were not happy. There was a necessity laid upon man to justify himself. . . . It was in accord with human nature that a theory should have sprung up that the War had been due to a sort of cosmic hallucination. . . . The theory absolved those who had not interested themselves in the War and, by inference, condemned those who had. . . . It was what men said and did to prove to themselves that their errors were really laborious virtues that built up the whole-time hells of life.[18]

The summer of 1935, which had begun with a visit to the Stanleys in Paris, passed pleasantly for Rudyard though poorly for his wife. He contributed a belated Just So Story, 'Ham and the Porcupine' to the gift-book for the little Princess Elizabeth, and wrote a poem, 'The King and the Sea', which was published in all the newspapers. A friend of whom he saw much was Sir Percy Bates, the shipowner, with whom he went to the Naval Review, and with whom he corresponded in a welter of technicalities about the launching of the giant Cunarder, the *Queen Mary*. He went to the Academy (and thought it 'rotten'); he dined at 'The Club'; he attended the annual reunion of the Old Boys of his school. Carrie's ill-health dictated their movements, and for her sake they went to Marienbad for the cure. To pass through Germany was an unpleasant ordeal, by their way of thinking, but at Marienbad Rudyard was supremely happy. He had not seen such woods and hills, he wrote to Frank Doubleday, since leaving Vermont. He made good progress with his autobiography, but Carrie made no progress in health; she had 'hoped so much of the visit and nothing came of it'.

In the autumn they were home again and Rudyard frequently in London, busy with Hollywood agents. A film of *Thy Servant a Dog* was projected, shown to the Trade, and dropped, but at last two Kipling films went into production, *The Light that Failed,* and *Elephant Boy* which the genius of Sabu, the Indian boy actor, made into a work of art as well as a commercial success. *

The Kiplings voted at the General Election of 1935, which established Stan Baldwin in office with a sure majority, though Rudyard had never been more out of sympathy with his cousin. The liberal policy of the Cabinet towards India was not of a kind to enlist Rud-

---

* Neither film was released before R. K.'s death. Many experiments were made at filming his early stories in the 1920's, but rarely with success. A script for a silent film of 'Without Benefit of Clergy', in which 'Mother Maturin' appears as a character, is in the Kipling Papers. It has little merit. *The Light that Failed* has been filmed at least three times.

yard's support, and the policy of sanctions against Italy during the Abyssinian War seemed to him sheer lunacy. We were making the Italians our enemies for three generations by threats which we could implement, he said, with no weapon ' more formidable than a surplice '. In December he wrote one of his political poems for *The Times* on the subject of Sanctions. It was in the post on the day, 20th December 1935, when the story of the Hoare-Laval negotiations came to light. Whatever it was that Rudyard had written, it was vitiated by the ensuing political crisis so that he had some difficulty in suppressing and destroying his poem before publication. About the same day, he worked for the last time at *Something of Myself*.

Rudyard was now nearing his 70th birthday, an event he said, that ' somehow seems to lack charm '. To another friend he wrote, ' You have my acutest sympathy over what you delicately call the " nuisance " of growing old. A train has to stop at some station or other. I only wish it wasn't such an ugly and lonesome place, don't you? '[19] He was engaged in redrafting his will and when his birthday came, 30th December, in a dark wet winter at ' Bateman's ', with the Brook in high flood, neither he nor Carrie was in a mood for jubilation. Rather to their surprise, the event made a stir in the world, and critics who had ignored Rudyard's existence for years paid him unwonted tributes. Carrie noted grimly that she celebrated her birthday (her 73rd) on the following day ' by dealing with Rud's mail. So far 108 telegrams and 90 letters.' It gratified her, in spite of illness and fatigue, that there was a personal letter from the King as well as the pile of congratulations from the unknown — ' all very nice and cordial and affectionate, and many from quite simple folk telling of what he has meant to them '.

One letter that Rudyard wrote on his 70th birthday was to an American friend, Mrs. Jackson Stoddard, who had charged him with misunderstanding her country. His last word on that theme may be worth recording. ' Remember ', he wrote, ' that I lived in the land for four years just as a householder. . . .' ' As the nigger said in Court: " If Ah didnt like de woman, how come I'd take de trouble to hit her on de haid? " '[20]

In a very different mood he wrote to Edith Macdonald, the last survivor among his aunts, to whom since childhood he had given confidence and affection.[21]

2nd Jan. 1936

DEAREST AUNT EDIE,
 Bless you for your note which has just come in. He who put us into this life does not abandon His work for *any* reason or default at the end of it. That is all I have come to learn out of my life. So there is *no* fear.

I was hoping for your letter, my dear; and it makes me feel better to have got it.

Ever your loving

RUDDY.

The Kiplings had planned to go to Cannes early in January 1936 and came up to Brown's Hotel for a few days before leaving.

On 12th January they both went to Hampstead to visit George Bambridge who was ill in bed with bronchitis. Rudyard was in good health and spirits and looking forward to going to France, but Carrie seemed far from well, as indeed she had been for some time. The last phase is told in the words of her daughter:

Early on 13th Elsie was rung up from the Middlesex Hospital and told that her father had had a sudden and violent haemorrhage in the night, and had been rushed to hospital, where a dangerous operation had been performed.

She went at once to the Middlesex, where she met her distracted mother and the surgeons, and learnt how serious things were. Anxious as she was for her own husband, ill at home, and yet feeling that she should be with her mother, Elsie finally decided to join her at Brown's Hotel, making visits to the Hospital and dashes home to see how George was progressing.

Carrie was very brave, and after the first shock, calm, but the strain of the anxiety and publicity were very great. Varying bulletins as Rudyard fought for his life, grew worse and then rallied, were reflected on the posters in the streets, while press photographers haunted the entrance to the Middlesex and Brown's, and letters, telegrams and telephone calls poured in. The see-saw of hope and anxiety went on but — on 16th he grew rapidly worse and Carrie and Elsie were warned to be ready to return to the Hospital at a moment's notice. When they left after their last visit to him in the evening of the 16th they lay down, fully dressed and tried to rest, but at 2 A.M. on 17th the urgent call came, and they left the hotel in falling snow and chilly darkness for their final vigil.

All that day they never left the Hospital, where the thoughtful kindness they received made these dreadful hours as bearable as possible. When night came they were given rooms in which to rest. Soon after midnight Rudyard died, having been unconscious for some hours, and his body was placed in the beautiful little chapel of the Hospital. It was 18th January, 1936, the 44th anniversary of his marriage. Now, for the first time Carrie broke down utterly, but not for long; her usual courage soon reasserting itself. She and her daughter left the Hospital, to face a barrage of cameras on the doorstep, and a nightmare day of telephones, telegrams, letters and callers at their hotel. Stanley Baldwin spoke most movingly on the wireless about his cousin.

Weak and ill as he still was, George Bambridge came to the hotel to help deal with the flood of correspondence from all over the world, and with arrangements for the cremation at Golder's Green. Just as his coffin arrived, covered with the Union Jack, the followers of Saklatvala, the Indian Communist who had been cremated just before Rudyard Kipling, were singing the Red Flag.

In the falling dusk of January 22nd, Elsie and George went to the Middlesex Hospital chapel, to go with the urn to Westminster Abbey. From Dean's Yard the little procession of Clergy and the two mourners, moved through the dimly lit cloisters and Abbey to the Warrior's Chapel, where, after a short service, the urn was left to await the funeral next day.

The newspapers, which so recently had celebrated Kipling's 70th birthday, were cramped for space on 18th and 19th January by news of the King's illness. It was generally known that he, too, was dying and, before preparations could be made for Kipling's funeral, the King's death plunged the whole nation into mourning. Nevertheless, before the Abbey was put in order for the royal ceremony, the writer whose devotion had been rewarded by the King's friendship was buried in Poets' Corner. The last occasion of that kind had been the burial of Hardy who was borne to the grave by an escort of poets and dramatists. Not so was Kipling; his pall-bearers were the Prime Minister, an admiral, a general, the Master of a Cambridge College, Professor Mackail from Oxford, Sir Fabian Ware, and two old friends, H. A. Gwynne and A. P. Watt; and the congregation consisted of men of action, the men with whom he had spent his life, rather than men of letters.

The funeral service in Westminster Abbey was thus described in George Bambridge's diary:

When Carrie, Elsie, and I followed the ashes into Poets' Corner and stood on the edge of the grave above the urn I feared C. K. would fall, as she was swaying to and fro. Elsie and I had her arms and she recovered gradually to some extent. The service was long and the ordeal great, but music was good and arrangements quite flawless. Every seat in choir and lantern and both transepts was filled and the general public was admitted as well; thousands could not obtain entry. The scene was wonderful, the mourners represented every branch of the Services, every art and craft, a more distinguished gathering could not be imagined.

My sorrow at losing R. K. is great. He was wonderfully kind to me and I shall miss him much. He was far away the greatest living Englishman to-day, wonderfully far-seeing and great-hearted, and his work will live. I like to think he will lie all Tuesday so near his late King to whom he was devoted and who was devoted to him. After the service a procession past the grave of all those present took place and the singing of the 'Recessional' and 'Abide With Me' (he chose this hymn) was most affecting.

Never was any man buried in Poets' Corner with more clear a title as master in the craft of letters, never any man more worthy to lie beside Charles Dickens and Thomas Hardy. His impact upon the age he lived in had been greater than that of any writer since Dickens, and, like Dickens, Rudyard Kipling had always been a man of the people. Neither had forfeited even a fraction of a vast publicity by reason of the strictures of the fastidious. There had always been critics who said that Dickens was 'vulgar' because sentimental, and Kipling 'vulgar' because brutal, but the people knew better. Kipling, except in one or two immature pieces written in youth, had never lapsed into the sentimental optimism with which Dickens deceived himself; the puritan strain in his ancestry preserved him from that error, placing him rather in the same company with Thomas Hardy, the Hardy — that is — who wrote the final choruses of *The Dynasts*. From early middle age Kipling had been a pessimist, if to face unpleasant truths with candour and resolution is pessimism. His greatest poem looked to the end of an epoch not to a Utopian future, and was rightly called 'Recessional'; his firmest message to his generation — to take up 'The White Man's Burden' — offered them no hope of easy triumph.

The impulse and the circumstance of his own life were important only in relation to the Law, that temple built to the design of the Great Overseer.

> If there be good in that I wrought
> Thy Hand compelled it, Master, Thine —
> Where I have failed to meet Thy Thought
> I know, through Thee, the blame was mine.
>
> The depth and dream of my desire,
> The bitter paths wherein I stray —
> Thou knowest Who hast made the Fire,
> Thou knowest Who hast made the Clay.[22]

Though compounded, like all men, of two elements, one akin to clay and one to fire, it is not in this mingling of opposites that we can account for his two soul-sides, the 'separate sides to his head' of which he had once written so buoyantly. There was one side which the world knew well, for he was one of the few in his generation whose name and face and message were universally familiar. Streets and terraces and frontier townships were named after him, branches of the Kipling Society flourished in five countries, the sale of his books, in many languages as well as in English, maintained his rank as a best-seller throughout his life and for twenty years after. His admirers in every land were numbered by scores of thousands; he was by far the most frequently quoted of contemporary authors, as the Dictionaries of Quotations demonstrate. To this day, in allusion, quotation — and misquotation — the Kipling Tradition is revived almost daily in the newspapers. Whether liked or disliked, he was the only poet of his day whose verse was known by men and women of all classes, all creeds, all walks of life.

His message was addressed to his generation in its active mood, and was accepted. The sailors and the soldiers, the engineers and artificers, the administrators and pioneers — all who knew the Secret of the Machines, all the 'Sons of Martha' were on Kipling's side, all those, that is to say, who were concerned with what was being done, rather than what was being said — or thought — in the modern world. But, before his death, the word-spinners, for the most part, had passed him by, despising his adherence to the old Law and to the Gods of the Copy-book Headings.

So much for that side of his soul which he exposed to the world, but what has been revealed of his soul on its other side? 'Seek not to question other than the works I left behind', he pleaded to posterity: Question, then, the last story in the *Jungle Books,* where Mowgli is torn between the jungle and the village, that is to say between the world of fancy and the world of fact. Or question Kim who overcame his inclination to follow the higher path with his beloved Lama and returned to the service of the *raj.* Or question 'The Children of the Zodiac', his allegory of a poet who rejects the life of an immortal in order to work among men with the certainty of pain and death, the probability of loneliness and disrepute.

His solution of these problems was found by intuition, not by reason. His genius — or, as he preferred to say, his *daemon* — showed him the heart of the matter by a sort of second-sighted faculty, that he himself mistrusted. By preference he aligned himself with his hard-headed Anglo-Saxon father, called himself a Yorkshireman, and sometimes spoke slightingly of the Celtic blood derived from his Macdonald mother; all the more because his mother and his mother's family meant so much to him. An other-worldly Celtic seer he would not consent to be. The dreams and delusions that afflict and stimulate the adolescent had sometimes rapt him away, out of himself, into occult imaginings, which he repelled, while his sister, lacking his earthly fibre, surrendered to them. Though he never doubted the actuality of the unseen world, from which there came to him the words he was bound to speak, he could never accept the rationalized formulas of any church or sect. His contacts were immediate, and best stated in his own words:[23] 'I expect that every man has to work out his creed according to his own wave-length, and the hope is that the Great Receiving Station is tuned to take *all* wave-lengths'.

EPILOGUE

MEMOIR BY MRS. GEORGE BAMBRIDGE

THE sunlit months we spent every winter in South Africa seem to dominate the memory of my early childhood rather than our English summers. The hot, pine-scented days and cool nights were delightful, and I know that, in later years, my father was often homesick for that lovely country.

The *Just So Stories* were first told to my brother and myself during those Cape winters, and when written, were read aloud to us for such suggestions as could be expected from small children. The illustrating of the stories gave their author immense pleasure, and he worked at them (mostly in Indian ink) with meticulous care and was delighted when we approved of the results.

The 'Woolsack' seemed constantly full of grown-up visitors, one of whom (we only knew him as 'Dr. Jim') was especially delightful, while a rather ponderous and silent man, we were later to realize, was Cecil Rhodes.

About this time a lunatic took it into his head that my father was the reincarnation of someone he did not like and that it was his duty to shoot him. To this end he followed us from England to the Cape, arriving at the 'Woolsack' late one hot night. Hearing a banging on the heavy teak side-door, my father went to investigate and was confronted with the business end of a revolver held in the shaking hand of an excited and voluble man, obviously with a grievance. Talking to this madman gently but without pause, my father enticed him into the house, where they sat talking for hours, until many strong whiskies and the endless drone of his unwilling host's voice at last sent the man to sleep. At intervals during several years, and in various places the same lunatic (whose family announced that he was not mad enough to certify) reappeared, and finally he fired a revolver at my father one day as he came out of the Athenæum. This was too much even for the most patient of men, and the reluctant relatives were at last induced to have their kinsman shut up. When he died some time later, my father himself ordered, and sent to his funeral, a large wreath, with his card attached.

From our earliest years my father's relations with us children were close and intimate, and his patience in answering our questions was immense. Because I knew that I should always receive a careful answer, my stream of queries was endless and earned me the nickname of 'Elsie Why'. The verses 'I keep six honest serving-men' are a memory of those ceaseless questions.

One summer in the early 1900's we children and my father acted scenes from *A Midsummer-Night's Dream*. Our stage was an old grass-grown quarry, and there my brother as Puck, myself as Titania, and my father as Bottom, rehearsed and acted happily. A most realistic cardboard donkey's head had been donned by Bottom for his part, and the village policeman, passing along the lane, was amazed to see the familiar tweed-clad figure of my father topped by this extraordinary headgear.

This was the first beginning of the stories that afterwards became *Puck of Pook's Hill*.

The affectionate, but firm, discipline of our lives was in my mother's hands and we were brought up with a strict sense of obedience to parental authority, and a simplicity which verged on the austere. There was no question of regarding my father as an aloof genius, or of having any special reverence for his writings; indeed, for many years most of his books remained unread by his children, and it was only after his death that I first read *Kim*. From an early age his bookshelves were open to us, and the only attempt to restrict our reading was the advice that certain books might interest us more when we were older. He read aloud to us for hours in his expressive and flexible voice, and it was in this way that, as we grew older, we came to know Scott, Jane Austen, much of Thackeray and endless poetry: Dickens we none of us much cared for. His great knowledge of both English and French literature made him a wonderful guide to reading, and he would draw up elaborate lists of the classics in both languages for me to read. An elderly and long-suffering French governess had given both us children a firm and fluent grounding in French, so that we became almost bilingual at an early age.

Switzerland for winter sports replaced our Cape voyage after 1908, when my brother had gone to school. There my father cautiously took to ski-ing, a sport at which his cousin, Stanley Baldwin, was more ambitious and successful. Some weeks in France or Italy usually followed, and then back to Sussex in the early spring.

Visitors were frequent at 'Bateman's', often total strangers who came from all the corners of the world to discuss their work and problems, to ask advice or help, or merely to tell of their adventures and experiences. The visitors' book, kept in my father's small handwriting, is a strange medley of names, which sometimes had notes against them, such as 'cold rice pudding' or the initials 'F.I.P.' The former note was a reminder that a certain Colonial Administrator liked cold rice pudding instead of early tea, while the latter meant 'Fell in pond'. These letters come after a surprising number of distinguished names, as boating on the square, shallow pool in the garden was a favourite summer amusement which often ended in an overturned boat and dripping figures on the lawn.

'Bateman's' lies in a steep valley, its formal yew-hedged and flag-pathed garden going down to the little River Dudwell, with oak and chestnut woods rising on the slope to the south. Inside the house is darkly panelled and with small latticed windows, the effect (except on a bright day) being of a certain sadness. The stiff furniture is very much of the period of the house — about 1630 — with a resulting lack of comfort which my parents never seemed to notice. Many of the things were beautiful in themselves, but the whole effect was rather sparse and, in the winter, chilly, in spite of the huge wood fire in the hall. The study, a large square room on the first floor, facing south and east, is lined on two sides with ceiling-high book shelves. The desk, a large birch-wood table, with a wooden-seated chair and an enormous waste-paper basket, faces the eastern window looking down the valley. He wrote on large-pale-blue pads that were specially made for him, and for many years used a thin, silver penholder, Waverley nibs, and a large pewter inkpot. During the last few years of his life he took to using a typewriter, though he was never very expert with it. During my father's life a large canvas-covered case labelled 'Notions' lay on the desk, containing unfinished stories and poems, notes and ideas, collected through the years. After his death my mother burnt this, though the interest of its contents would have been immense. A hard sofa is at right angles to the small fireplace. Lying on his side, his head propped on his right hand, my father spent many hours on this sofa while he brooded over the work he was busy with at the moment. From time to time he would jump up and go to the desk, write a line or two, make a note or correction, then resume his place on the sofa. When writing verse, he usually paced up and down the study humming to himself. He was never disturbed while at work, but at intervals he would call over the stairs for either my mother or myself, to 'come and listen' while he read part of a story or poem, and to discuss it with him. When something was too obscure, I would protest that it was impossible to understand and we would argue the best way of rewriting it to make it clearer. When deep in some piece of work he was so utterly absorbed as to be quite absent-minded, even when away from his desk. As children, we learned to recognize these periods as ones in which he must not be bothered with the things of everyday life. When he 'came back', as we put it to each other, he would quickly again enter into our lives and interests.

His only attempt at play-writing was in 1913, when he and I together wrote a one-act play called *The Harbour Watch,* of which Pyecroft was the hero. Vedrenne and Eadie produced it in a series of matinées at the Royalty Theatre, but it was not a great success.

When in 1914 I duly 'came out' and went to the stately London balls of that last summer of the old world, my father would often come with me, talking to chaperones and eating late suppers with other parents of his generation. Invitations to the large week-end parties of those days would be accepted by my parents if I wanted to go. There was an evening at one of these gatherings at Cliveden when my father, acting in charades with convincing horror, made his fellow-guests' flesh creep.

The strain of the first war (the coming of which he had so long predicted) and my brother's death, left both my parents in poor health in 1918, and my father subject to severe attacks of internal pain. Numbers of doctors tried to cure him, but with little success, though endless treatments were prescribed. The courage and patience with which he bore the recurring pain and the cures that were tried were truly heroic. His self-control was superb and the sweetness of his temper unfailing; he would only ask to be left alone until the pain was over. It was not till 1933, when he was terribly ill while in Paris, that a French doctor found that for some fifteen years he had been suffering from duodenal ulcers. What endless pain and suffering he could have been saved had this conclusion been arrived at earlier; now he was too exhausted to undergo an operation.

During the years following my brother's death in 1915 until my marriage in 1924, I was hardly ever away from my parents, and my father and I were close and constant companions; the three of us went everywhere together. Visits to France, Algiers and Spain he always enjoyed, though the inevitable publicity which accompanied his travels abroad sometimes made it difficult for him to have a quiet holiday. But, though his recognition by strangers in every country ranged from the eager request for an autograph from the customs official who had opened his luggage in Czechoslovakia to the Mayor of some smart Riviera resort asking us to a Gala banquet at the Casino, the kindness and interest were always the same. He was always happy in France and knew much of the country well from our many long motor trips there.

The honorary degrees given him in Paris and Strasbourg pleased him very much, though the speeches, banquets, and parties that went with them were rather an effort. He gave so much of himself while meeting people that he was often exhausted after a big dinner or reception, though a short rest quite restored him.

One evening in Paris, while staying at the Meurice, he was asked by the leader of the hotel orchestra if there was any piece he would like played. Without any hesitation he asked for 'Sambre et Meuse', to the delight of the band and the amazement of the other guests. The rococo hall of the hotel was so splendidly unsuitable a place to hear the swinging strains of this most stirring of marches.

After the 1914-18 war his work with the War Graves Commission took him often to the devastated regions. This work was very close to his heart, and I think the feeling that his own son had no known grave made him take an intense interest in the laying out of the cemeteries.

My mother introduced into everything she did, and even permeated the life of her family with, a sense of strain and worry amounting sometimes to hysteria. Her possessive and rather jealous nature, both with regard to my father and to us children, made our lives very difficult, while her uncertain moods kept us apprehensively on the alert for possible storms. There is no doubt that her difficult temperament sometimes reacted adversely on my father and exhausted him, but his kindly nature, patience, and utter loyalty to her prevented his ever questioning this bondage, and they were seldom apart. She had great qualities; a keen, quick mind and ready wit, a business ability above the average and loyalty and kindness to old friends; but above all, an immense and never-failing courage in pain and sorrow, both of which she bore unflinchingly. My father's much exaggerated reputation as a recluse sprang, to a certain extent, from her domination of his life and the way in which she tried to shelter him from the world. To a certain degree this was a good thing and enabled him to work without too much interruption, but he needed also the stimulus of good talk and mixing with people, and as the years went on and his life became more restricted, he missed these keenly.

My father inherited a great deal of his own father's artistic ability and was often busy with pencil and paint-brush illuminating, for instance, his various copies of Horace's Odes with designs and pictures. His knowledge of lettering of all ages and his skill in reproducing it was great, and he took infinite pleasure in the drawing of the delicate and fantastic letters for 'How the Alphabet was made' in the *Just So Stories*. Sometimes to amuse himself he would fake old documents, and the results, having been 'aged' by careful rubbing with soot and dust, were marvels of convincing antiquity. If painted masks or gilded paper crowns with splendidly real-looking jewels were wanted for theatricals or fancy-dress parties, he made them with the greatest skill and endless trouble. The writing of limericks delighted him, and there exists an old copy of Lear's Nonsense Book on the blank sheets of which appear many verses, illustrated with spirited little drawings of the Old Maid of Zug, the Young Lady of Brie, the Three Young Ladies of Nice and many more.

Deftness and certainty of movement were characteristics of his. The way he handled things, lit a cigarette, made a gesture or movement, was compact of neatness and energy. He never fumbled, and his gestures were always expressive. Up to the time of his death at seventy his slim and upright figure moved surely and lightly.

The gift of being able to talk to anyone about the things that interested them was peculiarly his, and the shyest person would respond quickly to the quite genuine interest he always took in people. On one of the rare occasions when he was being interviewed, the young reporter chatted happily about his own life and ambitions at some length and only realized after he had left that my father had said nothing about himself.

He was interested in food and wine to a certain extent, and enjoyed reading old cookery books, such as Mrs. Glass's. I remember a time in France when we made a long detour in a day's motoring to sample the pigs' trotters in a town noted for this delicacy, and which a French general had said should not be missed. At home he mostly drank cider out of a pewter tankard. The strict diets of his later years made his meals very dull, and his smoking was much curtailed. At one time he had smoked some 30-40 cigarettes a day, but this was firmly rationed by his doctors, to his great annoyance, though he was still allowed his pipe.

He was quite uninterested in his clothes, and his collection of aged and battered hats was large. When my mother thought he needed another suit, he went obediently to his tailor, who provided him with a new one of the same cut and much the same material as the previous one. He never grumbled, however, when he had to wear formal clothes for a special occasion, and always changed for dinner at home.

Card games were a mystery to him, though there was a legend that he had played poker in his youth. Cribbage and Patience were the only games I ever saw him play, except Mah-Jong, which fascinated him for a time.

Though great honours were offered to him, he refused to accept any but literary or academic ones, holding that accepted honours would mean the loss of that complete independence to say, in prose or verse, what he thought should be said. An instance was his speech to the Society of St. George in 1935, with its urgent warning that Germany was again preparing for war. This was resented as being 'unsuitable for Jubilee Year', and was hardly reported in the press. The poem, giving the same warning in 1932 and called 'The Storm Cone', was criticized as being 'exaggerated and gloomy'.

The two great sorrows of their lives, my parents bore bravely and silently, perhaps too silently for their own good. My mother hardly ever spoke of her two lost children, but sometimes my father would talk of them to me. There is no doubt the little Josephine had been his greatest joy during her short life. He always adored children, and she was endowed with a charm and personality (as well as enchanting prettiness) that those who knew her still remember. She belonged to his early, happy days, and his life was never the same after her death; a light had gone out that could never be rekindled. My brother, John, took after his American forbears in looks, with brilliant hazel eyes, dark eyebrows and hair, and a slim figure. A quick and vivid personality of much charm was evident, even before he was eighteen. My father was devoted to him, and his pride and interest in his son's short time as a soldier were intense. The long drawn-out agony of the years during which his fate was uncertain left its mark on both my parents, though outwardly they remained calm.

Among the young officers who had given my father their account of many episodes in France for the regimental history of the Irish Guards in the first war was Captain George Bambridge. His exploits (he was several times wounded, won the M.C., and was mentioned in despatches) are duly noted in the history. His friendship with us continued when peace came in 1918, and he often visited 'Bateman's'. After leaving the Army he became Honorary Attaché at the Embassy in Madrid, and during a visit we made there in the spring of 1924, he and I became engaged.

Though my father was delighted by my obvious happiness and was fond of George, something like despair filled him as he looked forward to life at 'Bateman's' without his only remaining child. The years since John's death had brought us very close together, and he had come to depend on my constant companionship. Now, not only was I to marry, but to live abroad. My mother, who was always more reserved, filled the time before my wedding with busy plans for clothes, furniture, and house linen. But I think that she, too, was sad at my leaving home, besides having grave doubts of my housekeeping abilities!

We were married at St. Margaret's, Westminster, in October 1924 and left at once for Brussels, where George had now been appointed. That winter was a dreary one at 'Bateman's'; the house seemed 'very large and quiet' my father wrote me. His abiding interest was now to be everything that concerned my new life. The house, furniture, domestic arrangements, friends, social doings, and above all my health, everything interested him. He wrote me long letters, demanding details of every kind, from the description of a court ball to our plans for improvements in the kitchen. My parents visited us in Brussels, afterwards in Madrid (where we returned in 1926) and later in Paris. They enjoyed, I think, the parties we gave for them, as well as the more formal entertainments at the Embassies, and our various homes were a constant source of interest to them. When I was asked (by a not-to-be-ignored personage) to urge my father to make a speech at a big dinner in Paris, he undertook the task to please me without question.

In 1933 we returned to England, and our life in the delightful old house and garden which we rented in Hampstead was a source of happiness to him to the end of his life.

After his death, a destroyer was named after him, which I launched at Greenock just before the war. There is an epic story of the *Kipling's* heroic rescue of the survivors of the *Kelly* during the battle off Crete, of her terrible four-hundred-mile journey, crowded with wounded, listing heavily and ceaselessly attacked by German bombers, of her arrival at Alexandria with the rescued men, wounded, dirty, and exhausted, lined up on deck, to be greeted by a great roar of cheers echoing across the harbour. All this might have been one of my father's own stories.

All my life I have been surrounded by the kindness and interest of people, from many countries and in many walks of life, who knew my father personally, or felt they did so through his writings. In out-of-the-way corners of the world his name has brought me new friendships. Often still, I have letters from complete strangers saying how a poem or story has helped and encouraged them, or remembering some quiet kindness he had done them, long ago.

THE END

SOURCES

(*a*) Bibliography of Printed Sources. (*b*) Unprinted Sources

References to Rudyard Kipling's works in the Notes are given (in *italic*) by their titles as in the *Bibliography* by F. V. Livingston. *Something of Myself* is abbreviated as *S of M*. References to printed works, if listed in (*a*) are given under their authors' names and, if not listed, in full. References to unprinted sources are given under the abbreviations listed in (*b*), or in full.

(*a*) printed sources

F. Adams: *Essays in Modernity.*
L. S. Amery: *My Political Life.*
The Athenaeum, November–December 1890.
Sir H. Baker: *Cecil Rhodes.*
G. C. Beresford: *Schooldays with Kipling.*
Wilfrid Blunt: *Memoirs.*
The Bookman, May 1901.
E. J. Buck: *Simla Past and Present.*
G. B.-J. [Burne-Jones] — *Memorials of Sir Edward Burne-Jones.*
D. Chapman-Huston: *The Lost Historian* (Memoir of Sir Sidney Low).
A. Chevrillon: *Rudyard Kipling.*
H. Cushing: *Life of Sir William Osler.*
John Connell: *Life of W. E. Henley.*
Daily Mail, London, October 1899 to March 1900.
Daily Telegraph, London, April 1900.
Bonamy Dobrée: *Rudyard Kipling.*
Dufferin and Ava, Marchioness of, *Our Viceregal Life.*
L. C. Dunsterville: *Stalky's Reminiscences.*
T. S. Eliot: *Introduction to A Choice of Kipling's Verse.*
The Friend, Bloemfontein (complete set in the Carpenter Collection).
E. Gosse, article in *Century Magazine,* April 1892.
Ian Hamilton: *Listening for the Drum.*
R. Hart-Davis: *Hugh Walpole.*
(Mrs.) Edmonia Hill: article in *Atlantic Monthly,* April 1936.
R. Thurston Hopkins: *Rudyard Kipling.*
G. Ireland: *The Balestiers of Beechwood* (unpublished).
H. James, article in the *Cosmopolitan,* May 1892.
I. Kaplan: *Rudyard Kipling in America,* 1889 (unpublished).
The Kipling Journals, Nos. 1–112.
Margaret Lane: *Life of Edgar Wallace.*
B. Lee-Booker: *Yesterday's Child.*
Richard le Gallienne: *Rudyard Kipling.*
W. R. Lawrence: *The India we Served.*

F. V. LIVINGSTON: *Bibliography of the Works of Rudyard Kipling*, & *Supplement*.
D. MACCARTHY: *Memories*.
J. H. MCCARTHY: *Reminiscences*, vol. ii.
EDITH MACDONALD: *Annals of the Macdonald Family*.
F. W. MACDONALD: *As a Tale that is Told*.
    Letters of James Macdonald.
J. W. MACKAIL: *Life of William Morris*.
Sir G. F. MACMUNN: *Rudyard Kipling, Craftsman; Kipling's Women*.
GUY PAGET: *Letters from Rudyard Kipling* (privately printed).
B. PATCH: *Thirty Years with G. B. S.*
The Pioneer, Allahabad.   75th anniversary number, 1940.
DOROTHY PONTON: *Rudyard Kipling at Home and at Work*.
JULIAN RALPH: *War's Lighter Side*.
H. C. RICE: *Rudyard Kipling in New England*.
E. K. ROBINSON: article in *McClure's Magazine*, July 1896.
The Scots Observer, 1889–90.
G. SEAVER: *Francis Younghusband*.
R. L. STEVENSON: *Complete Works*, vol. xxv.
H. A. TAPP: *The United Services College, 1874–1911.*
ANGELA THIRKELL: *Three Houses*.
The Times: History of the War in South Africa.
The United Services College Chronicle (complete set in Houghton Library).
F. F. VAN DE WATER: *Rudyard Kipling's Vermont Feud* (an amusing account
    from Beatty Balestier's point of view).
Sir F. WARE: *The Immortal Heritage*.
ARTHUR WAUGH: *One Man's Road*.
H. G. WELLS: *The New Machiavelli*.
W. B. YEATS: *Introduction to The Oxford Book of Modern Verse*.

(*b*) UNPRINTED SOURCES

(1) The Kipling Papers, the property of Mrs. George Bambridge (KP).   They
    include his press-cutting books, Mrs. Kipling's diaries, and many port-
    folios of correspondence.
(2) The Kipling and other collections founded by Mrs. F. V. Livingston at the
    Houghton Library, Harvard (Houghton).   Notably the Henry James and
    C. E. Norton letters.
(3) The Berg collection in the New York Public Library (Berg).   They include
    several early drafts of Kipling MSS.
(4) The Carpenter collection in the Library of Congress (Carpenter), including
    the Conland letters and many documents formerly belonging to Mrs.
    S. A. Hill.
(5) The Theodore Roosevelt Papers in the Library of Congress (Roosevelt).
(6) Private papers of Mr. F. Cabot Holbrook, Brattleboro, Vermont (Holbrook).
(7) Private papers of Mrs. Nelson Doubleday, Oyster Bay, Long Island
    (Doubleday).
(8) The Kipling–Henley correspondence, the property of Mr. 'John Connell'
    (Henley).

(9) Letters of Kipling to Rhodes and Herbert Baker at Rhodes House, Oxford (Rhodes).
(10) The Milner Papers at New College, Oxford (Milner).
(11) The Kipling–Barry correspondence in the Toronto Public Library (Barry).
(12) Papers in the possession of Mr. Howard Rice, Junior, Columbia University (Rice).

Other sources are acknowledged in full.

NOTES

THE Quotation on the title-page is from a letter to Sir H. Baker (Rhodes).

Chapter I

(1) KP. (2) This is conjectural. The date and place of J. L. Kipling's birth
are uncertain. (3) KP.

Chapter II

(1) *Daily Gazette,* Karachi, 19 Jan. 1936. (2) Dates identified by the P. & O.
Company. (3) *S of M.* (4) Capt. H. Holloway, R. N., 4 Campbell Rd.,
Southsea. (5) *Letters to Guy Paget.* (6) & (7) *S of M.* (8) 'Baa, Baa, Black
Sheep'.

Chapter III

(1) G. C. Beresford. (2) L. C. Dunsterville. (3) *Souvenirs of France.* (4)
Land and Sea Tales. (5) *S of M.* (6) *Stalky & Co.* (7) *Sussex Edition,* vol.
xxxv. (8) Memorandum by A. M. ('Trix') Fleming (KP). (9) Berg.

Chapter IV

(1) *The Light that Failed.* (2) *Letters of Travel.* (3) KP. (4) *From Sea
to Sea.* (5) KP. (6) *Plain Tales from the Hills.* (7) *Sussex Edition,* vol. xxxv.
(8) KP. (9) *S of M.* (10) KP. (11) and (12) R. K.'s diary for 1885
(Houghton). (13) *S of M.* (14), (15), and (16) KP. (17) *Kim.* (18)
S of M. (19) and (20) KP. (21) *McClure's Magazine,* July 1896. (22) KP.
(23) *From Sea to Sea.* (24) KP. (25) *McClure's Magazine,* July 1896. (26)
'My First Book', *The Idler,* 1892. (27) *S of M.* (28) 'A Song in Storm'.

Chapter V

(1) Photograph in Carpenter Collection. (2) *Atlantic Monthly,* April 1936.
(3) Carpenter. (4) 'Three and an Extra' (*Plain Tales*). (5) 'Miss Youghal's
Sais' (*Plain Tales*). (6) KP. (7) *S of M.* (8) G. F. MacMunn; also N. W.
Bancroft, *From Recruit to Staff-Sergeant* (reviewed by R. K. in *Civil and Military
Gazette,* 5 Feb. 1886); G. F. Younghusband, *Story of the Guides; Civil and
Military Gazette,* 1 Jan. 1887 (for 'Taking of Lung-tung-pen'); *Glasgow Herald,*
14 Aug. 1889 (for 'Namgay Doola'). (9) 'The 'Eathen'. (10) 'Drums of
the Fore and Aft'. (11) 'Rikki-tikki-tavi'. (12) KP. (13) *The Pioneer,* 75th
anniversary number; *The Bookman,* May 1901. (14) KP.

Chapter VI

(1) Authorities for the voyage: *From Sea to Sea; Atlantic Monthly,* April
1936; papers and photographs in Carpenter Collection. (2) For travels in
Western America the published version in *From Sea to Sea* is not wholly reliable.
Corrected from letters to Mrs. Hill (KP). (3) *From Sea to Sea,* corrected from

Hill letters; also I. Kaplan. (4) Reviews from press-cutting book (KP). (5) Letter from L. de Forest (Houghton). (6) KP. (7) *Kipling Journal*, Dec. 1950; Livingston. (8) *S of M.* (9) D. Chapman-Huston. (10) Tennyson to C. V. Stanford (KP). (11) *Kim.* (12) Kipling Journal, Dec. 1950. (13) 'In Partibus', Sussex Edition, vol. xxxv. (14) *S of M;* 'One View of the Question'. (15) *Letters to A. P. Watt.*

Chapter VII

(1) Henley correspondence; F. Harris, *Contemporary Portraits; Time and Tide,* 20 Feb. 1937; *Kipling Journal,* Dec. 1939; *S of M.* (2) Memorandum by A. M. ('Trix') Fleming (KP). (3) Hill letters (KP). (4) *S of M* is inaccurate here. Corrected by press-cutting book (KP) and Lyall, Sir A., *Life of Lord Dufferin.* (5) Henley correspondence. (6) R. le Gallienne. (7) *Saturday Review,* 14 Feb. 1903. (8) C. P. Trevelyan, *Life of Mrs. Humphrey Ward.*

Chapter VIII

(1) For the Balestier family: G. Ireland; Howard C. Rice; Holbrook Papers; Registers of St. Luke's Church, Rochester, N.Y.; personal information. (2) E. Gosse; J. H. McCarthy; H. James (in *Cosmopolitan,* May 1892); Arthur Waugh; Holbrook Papers; 'The Book of Gosse' (Camb. Univ. Library); personal information. (3) *S of M.* (4) 'The Three-Decker'. (5) Personal information. (6) Press-cutting book (KP). (7) F. W. Macdonald. (8) *S of M.* (9) KP. (10) Letters of Henry James (Houghton); R. L. Stevenson, *Complete Works,* vol. xxv. (11) *S of M,* corrected by courtesy of the editor, the *New Zealand Herald; Kipling Journal,* Nos. 47, 52, 56, 57, 85. (12) R. H. Croll in *Australian National Review,* Nov. 1937. (13) 'William the Conqueror'; correspondence with George Allen (KP); personal information from Mr. F. H. Andrews. (14) Letters of Henry James (Houghton). (15) C. K.'s diary. (16) Personal information. (17) An early draft of 'The Long Trail' (Berg Collection); Lawrence Hutton, *Talks in a Library.* (18) Henley Correspondence; C. K.'s diary; D. Chapman-Huston.

Chapter IX

(1) *Letters of Travel.* (2) R. W. Emerson, Monadnoc. (3) Reprinted in *Letters of Travel.* (4) 'Rhyme of the Three Sealers'. (5) *S of M.* (6) C. K.'s diary. (7) *S of M.* (8) C. K.'s diary. (9) R. K. to Rider Haggard, 20 Oct. 1895 (Houghton). (10) C. K.'s diary, 11 Nov. 1893. (11) Henley Correspondence. (12) 'The Coiner'. (13) U.S. College *Chronicle,* Dec. 1894. (14) KP. (15) R. K. to Mrs. Twiss, 24 Aug. 1896 (Berg Collection). (16) Personal information. (17) *S of M.* (18) 'An American'. (19) Houghton. (20) *S of M.* (21) *Letters of C. E. Norton,* vol. ii, p. 236. (22) Houghton. (23) *S of M.* (24) S. S. McClure, *Autobiography;* C. K.'s diary. (25) The trial from a transcript in the Holbrook Papers; files of the *Vermont Phœnix;* personal information. (26) KP. (27) Houghton.

Chapter X

(1) Carpenter. (2) Holbrook. (3), (4) and (5) Carpenter. (6) Houghton.

(7) R. K. to Stephen Wheeler, 1 Feb. 1897 (KP). (8) R. K. to Mr. Rockhill, 1 Mar. 1897 (Houghton). (9) Personal information. (10) Many authorized and unauthorized editions of 'The Vampire' in Houghton and Carpenter Collections. (11) Carpenter.

Chapter XI

(1) Houghton. (2) KP. (3) A collection of letters to Earl Baldwin on Kipling and the laureateship is in KP. (4) R. T. Hopkins. (5) 'What the People Said'. (6) *The Times,* 20 Dec. 1937, confirmed by C. K.'s diary. (7) Letters to R. K. about 'Recessional' in KP. (8) KP. (9) and (10) Personal information. (11) 'Song of the Wise Children', 1899(?). (12) 'The Fairies' Siege'. (13) *S of M.* (14) 'The Elephant's Child'. (15) *Kipling Journal,* Dec. 1947. (16) 'Kitchener's School', and letter in KP. (17) *S of M.* (18) 'The Truce of the Bear'. (19) Roosevelt. (20) *Stalky & Co.* (21) Roosevelt.

Chapter XII

(1) A. Thirkell. (2) 'Song of the Wise Children'. (3) *Evening Sun,* New York, 2 Feb. and 12 Feb. 1899. (4) Papers relating to the Putnam lawsuit in the Carpenter Collection. (5) *The Times,* 4 April 1899, and many other newspapers. All letters and other papers relating to R. K.'s illness in 1899 were preserved by C. K. in KP; F. N. Doubleday's letters and other papers are in the Doubleday Collection; also letters of A. Woollcott (Library of Congress). (6) Carpenter. (7) L. C. Dunsterville; *Kipling Journal,* No. 23; *Cambridge Gazette,* 18–19 Jan. 1900.

Chapter XIII

(1) 'The Voortrekker'. (2) *S of M.* (3) KP. (4) *S of M.* (5) Julian Ralph. (6) *Daily Telegraph,* 13 April 1900. (7) *S of M.* (8) *Tribunal de Genève,* 18 Jan. 1901. (9) *S of M; A Book of Words.* (10) *Journal of the African Society,* Oct. 1932. (11) and (12) Carpenter. (13) Rhodes Papers. (14) KP. (15) Rhodes. (16) Margaret Lane. (17) H. Baker and Rhodes Papers. (18) *The Echo,* Brighton, Sussex, 17 June 1902.

Chapter XIV

(1) Houghton. (2) R. K. to Henley, 31 Dec. 1896. (3) *Letters of C. E. Norton,* vol. ii; to S. Weir Mitchell, 31 Jan. 1907. (4) *S of M.* (5) 'The Lost Legion', 1895. (6) H. James to E. Gosse, 6 Aug. 1891 (Houghton); and letters of R. L. Stevenson (*Complete Works,* vol. xxv, p. 213). (7) Max Beerbohm; *Poet's Corner, Christmas Garland, Things Old and New, Around Theatres, Fifty Caricatures,* etc. (8) Francis Adams. (9) R. le Gallienne. (10) Houghton. (11) R. Ogden, *Life of E. L. Godkin,* letter dated 23 Dec. 1899. (12) D. MacCarthy. (13) Personal information. (14) *Atlantic Monthly,* April 1936. (15) 'My Great and Only' (*Civil and Military Gazette,* 11 Jan. 1890). (16) *Catalogue of English and American Authors,* issued by the American Art Assn., 30 April 1921. (17) *S of M.* (18) A. Bennett; *Books and Poems,* 1917.

Chapter XV

(1) and (2) S of M. (3) Houghton. (4) S of M. (5) Kipling Journal
No. 85. (6) Houghton. (7) KP. (8) and (9) S of M. (10) Sussex. (11)
'The Land'. (12) S of M. (13) Rhodes. (14) 'The Burial'. (15) KP.
(16) Personal information.

Chapter XVI

(1) and (2) KP. (3) S of M. (4) KP. (5) Letters of Travel. (6) A Book
of Words. (7) S of M. (8) Milner Papers. (9) S of M. (10) and (11)
KP. (12) Milner. (13), (14) and (15) KP. (16) D. Ponton. (17) Un-
fortunately no documentary evidence has come to light on this point. (18) and
(19) KP. (20) 'Ulster', wrongly dated in Inclusive Edition. (21) H. Cushing.
(22) 'For All We Have and Are'.

Chapter XVII

(1) Daily Express, 18 Jan. 1936. (2) Personal information. (3) and (4)
KP. (5) and (6) Sir F. Ware. (7), (8), (9) and (10) KP. (11) R. K.,
letter to E. Bok, 15 Nov. 1920 (KP). (12) KP. (13) Roosevelt. (14) S of M;
The Times, 27 May 1918. (15) Roosevelt.

Chapter XVIII

(1) D. Ponton. (2) Personal information. (3) The 'Bateman's' Visitors'
Book, written and annotated in R. K.'s hand, is in KP. (4) R. K.'s correspondence with members of the Royal household, and other relevant letters, are
quoted by gracious permission of H.M. the Queen. (5) and (6) KP. (7) A
Book of Words. (8) Sir F. Ware. (9) The Times, 11, 13 and 14 Sept. 1922.
(10) A Book of Words.

Chapter XIX

(1) R. K. to Mrs. Hill, 29 June 1906 (KP). (2) Masonic certificates in KP;
Freemason's Magazine, No. 678; Kipling Journal, passim; personal information.
(3) 'Late came the God'. (4) R. Hart-Davis. (5) 'Hymn to Physical Pain'.
(6) and (7) KP. (8) Le Figaro Littéraire, 19 Sept. 1953. (9) and (10) KP.

Chapter XX

(1) KP. (2) Doubleday. (3) Rhodes. (4) R. K. to Dr. Philip Gosse,
21 Dec. 1927. (5) R. K. to C. R. L. Fletcher, 24 June 1932 (KP). (6)
R. Hart-Davis. (7) Kipling Journal, No. 8; personal information. (8)
H. Cushing. (9) B. Patch: Thirty Years with G. B. S.; personal information.
(10) KP. (11) 'The Roman Centurion's Song'. (12) KP. (13) R. K. to
J. W. Barry, 14 Sept. 1935 (Toronto). (14) British Museum, MSS. Add.
45680W (15) Brazilian Sketches were reissued as a book in America but not
in England. They are in the Sussex Edition. (16) Doubleday. (17) Strand
Magazine, April 1934, and Sussex Edition (18) The Times, 7 May 1935. (19)
R. K. to Ernest Snow, Dec. 1935 (Houghton). (20) R. K. to Mrs. Jackson
Stoddard, Dec. 1935 (Carpenter). (21) KP. (22) 'My New-cut Ashlar'.
(23) R. K. to Henry Arthur Jones (Houghton).

GENERAL INDEX

Characters in R. K.'s works are collected together under the general entry Characters. R. K.'s works are separately indexed under their titles, beginning on page 429.

Abbey, Edwin, 90, 102
Abdurrahman, Amir, 46, 47
Aberdeen, Lady, 173
Absent-minded Beggar Fund, 235–37
Abyssinian War, 391
Academic honours conferred on R. K., 306–8, 354–56, 377, 399
Academy, The, 101
Adams, Francis, criticism of R. K., 265
Adams, Henry, 153–54
Adventures of Tom Sawyer (Mark Twain), 22
Ahmed Khel, battle of, 78 n., 83
Airship, R. K.'s vision of, 290, 353
Aitken, Max. *See* Beaverbrook, Lord
Alcott, Louisa, 100
Aldershot, 325
Algiers, 386
Allahabad, 67–68, 74, 86, 89, 147
Allen, Sir George, 37, 40 n., 67–68, 90, 147; R. K.'s neighbour at Burwash, 314, 320
All in a Garden Fair (W. Besant), 64–65
Amber (the 'Cold Lairs'), 74
American Academy of Arts and Sciences, 306
American isolationists, R. K. on, 358
American troops, R. K. on, 346
Amery, L. S., 236
Anderson, Sarah, R. K.'s private secretary, 228, 352
Arabi Pasha, 35
Armistice (1918), 348
Art for Art's sake, xviii, xx, 261
Arundell of Wardour, Lord, 167
Asquith, Lord, 394
Astley, Worcestershire, 378
Athenæum, 78, 126–27, 367
Athenæum Club, 193, 195, 342, 382
Athlone, Countess of, 380
Atlantic flight by 'R. 34', 353
Atlantic Monthly, 193, 266

August 1914, 330
'Aunty Rosa', 10–14, 20, 32
Aurora Leigh (E. B. Browning), 30
Austen, Jane, 366
Austin, Alfred, 178, 179 *and* n., 196, 203 *and* n., 204
Authors' Lodge, 365
Authors' Society, 114, 371, 382
Autour du Mariage (Gyp), 75

Bacon, Roger, 328–29
Baden-Powell, Sir R. S., 246, 299, 323–24
Bailey, Sir Abe, 299, 382
Baker, Herbert, 237, 300, 344, 406
Baldwin, Alfred, xxiii, 5, 46, 312
Baldwin, Mrs. Alfred (Louisa Macdonald), xxiii, 5, 6, 46, 352
Baldwin, Oliver (2nd Earl Baldwin), xxiii, 305, 321, 341; breach with the Kiplings, 379
Baldwin, Stanley (1st Earl Baldwin, R. K.'s cousin), xxiii, 5, 46, 203 n., 314, 353, 371, 397; boyhood holidays with R. K., 15; at R. K.'s wedding, 149; at Rottingdean, 199–200, 220; at 'Bateman's', 286; Financial Secretary to the Treasury, 342; Chancellor of the Exchequer, 358, 359; Prime Minister, 378–79, 383; speeches polished by R. K., 384; R. K. out of sympathy with, 390–91; on R. K.'s death, 392.
Baldwin, Lady (Lucy Ridsdale), xxiii, 199–200, 286
Balestier family, 134–36, 328
Balestier, Beatty, 135–36, 138, 148–49, 154, 157, 286; conveys land to R. K., 155; acts as R. K.'s general agent, 158–59, 166, 169–71; quarrel with the Kiplings, 176, 181–82; bankrupt, 181; summoned for assault by R. K., 183–186; threatens to sue R. K., 222, 223–24; 'sponges' on his mother, 351–52

INDEX OF KIPLING'S WORKS

Readers who despair of finding the story .007 in an alphabetical list are hereby informed that there are references to it on pages 165 and 192.